PARK LEARNING CENTRE
The Park Cheltenham
Gloucestershire GL50 2RH
Telephone: 01242 714333

UNIVERSITY OF
GLOUCESTERSHIRE
at Cheltenham and Gloucester

NORMAL LOAN

DESIGN AND DEVELOPMENT OF KNOWLEDGE-BASED SYSTEMS

From Life Cycle to Methodology

Giovanni Guida
Department of Electronics for Automation,
University of Brescia, Italy

Carlo Tasso
Department of Mathematics and Computer Science,
University of Udine, Italy

JOHN WILEY & SONS
Chichester · New York · Brisbane · Toronto · Singapore

Copyright © 1994 by John Wiley & Sons Ltd.
Baffins Lane, Chichester
West Sussex PO19 1UD, England
National Chichester (0243) 779777
International (+44) 243 779777

Other Wiley Editorial Offices

John Wiley & Sons, Inc., 605 Third Avenue,
New York, NY 10158-0012, USA

Jacaranda Wiley Ltd, 33 Park Road, Milton,
Queensland 4064, Australia

John Wiley & Sons (Canada) Ltd, 22 Worcester Road,
Rexdale, Ontario M9W 1L1, Canada

John Wiley & Sons (SEA) Pte Ltd, 37 Jalan Pemimpin #05-04,
Block B, Union Industrial Building, Singapore 2057

Library of Congress Cataloging-in-Publication Data

Guida, Giovanni, 1951–
   Design and development of knowledge-based systems : from life
cycle to methodology / Giovanni Guida, Carlo Tasso.
      p. cm.
   Includes bibliographical references and index.
   ISBN 0 471 92808 9
   1. Expert systems (Computer science) 2. System design.
   I. Tasso, Carlo. II. Title.
   QA76.76.E95G85   1994
   006.3'3'0684—dc20
                                              94-6715
                                              CIP

British Library Cataloguing in Publication Data

A catalogue record for this book is available from the British Library

ISBN 0 471 92808 9

Produced from camera-ready copy supplied by the authors
Printed and bound in Great Britain by Redwood Books, Trowbridge, Wilts.

to our daughters

Diana and Marta

CONTENTS

III   THE PRIMARY PROCESSES: DEVELOPMENT

6   DEVELOPMENT OF THE PROTOTYPE

IV   THE PRIMARY PROCESSES: OPERATION

PREFACE

Knowledge-based systems (KBSs) have been rapidly growing over the last decade and are now considered a crucial factor for innovation and competition. Their impact on industry and business applications has been impressive and convincing. However, the number of real operative applications is still limited. Knowledge-based technology still largely relies on empirical methods and is not supported by sound and general design and development methodologies. It is more like handicraft than engineering, and it lacks several of the desirable features of an industrial process, such as reliability, repeatability, work-sharing, controllability, cost estimation, and quality assurance.

The development of a new technological field depends on two factors: the scientific and technical progress which provides the basic components of the technology, and the methodological progress which prescribes how to use such components effectively for the construction of useful applications. In the KBSs field these two dimensions have not developed in an organic and balanced way. While a very rich and sound collection of basic techniques is available, the methods for applying them in a systematic way to solve real problems is still in an early stage of development. A primary need today is to devise robust and effective methodologies for the design and development of KBSs. This way, the bottleneck which presently hampers the large-scale application of knowledge-based technology can be overcome, thus boosting the diffusion of KBS applications.

Purpose of the book

This book focuses on the methodological aspects of design and development of KBSs. The analysis of specific techniques for building KBSs is outside its scope. This choice is motivated by the perception that what is primarily needed today to develop successful KBS applications is not a larger and deeper technical know-how, but a more disciplined and structured development methodology. In fact, KBS projects usually do not fail due to scarce or wrong technical know-how, but for a lack of technical management. To manage a KBS project successfully within an acceptable time span and a reasonable budget, it is necessary to face several issues, including: the definition of a suitable approach to technology transfer, the assessment of potential application domains, the adoption of correct and effective methods for KBS design and development, the selection of appropriate development tools, the integration of the KBS in the target application environment, the management of maintenance and extension.

There is a large and rapidly growing number of very good books that focus on the technical aspects of knowledge-based technology, but only a few try to illustrate the practical engineering principles which should guide the design and development of a KBS and the relevant project management techniques to be adopted. This knowledge, a precious know-how that designers and project leaders acquire through practical experience, is usually conveyed only partially in the literature and has never been presented in a well-organized and structured way.

Therefore, this book aims to illustrate how to exploit knowledge-based technology in the most effective and appropriate way. It does not focus on the transfer of technical knowledge, but rather on the methods that make it possible to apply this technical knowledge in a correct and goal-oriented way. This book does not deal with the specific technical mechanisms used to build a KBS. It does not face issues such as knowledge representation, search techniques, user interfaces, justification, qualitative reasoning, distributed architectures, etc., but it concentrates on how to use such elements in the design of a real system and on how to manage the development process. The above topics which are purposely left outside the scope of the volume are well-covered by several text-books and technical publications.

Teaching how to manage a KBS project to success is a challenging issue, which cannot be achieved only through a book. A book can help transfer professional know-how in a disciplined and effective way, but cannot transform an apprentice into an expert KBS project leader.

Organization and structure

The book is organized around the central concept of KBS life cycle, understood as a reference framework for defining and organizing the tasks and activities that must be carried out to design, to produce, and to maintain a KBS, independently of the various methodologies that may be adopted to put them into practice. Therefore, the life cycle specifies "what" to do and "when", while a development methodology focuses on "how" to actually execute the tasks and activities prescribed in the life cycle. While we believe that it is possible to identify a concept of life cycle which is abstract and general enough to be assumed as a reference for a very large class of application contexts, the same is not possible for the concept of development methodology. This is much more concrete and specific, and therefore it basically depends on the objectives and characteristics of the application environment where it is expected to be applied. Thus, while the book proposes a specific life cycle concept, called KLIC (KBS Life Cycle), it does not develop a full methodology. Instead, it provides the fundamental ideas which can enable an organization to build its own.

Three standpoints have inspired the concept of KLIC:
- anticipating potential problems in KBS development, in such a way as to reduce risks and to ensure a smooth project management;
- controlling the explorative attitude and the iterative approach typical of KBS development, so as to reduce time and costs;

- gradually establishing clear and transparent design principles in order to ensure a more sound and controllable development process and, at the same time, a higher quality of the delivered KBSs.

The book includes twelve chapters and is structured in five parts:

Part I - Process Model, Life Cycle, and Methodology, after a brief account on knowledge-based technology, introduces the concepts of KBS process model, life cycle, and methodology. The main concepts of the KLIC life cycle are then illustrated, and an original approach to the design and construction of a KBS methodology is proposed.

Part II - The Primary Processes: Analysis illustrates the first steps of the process of KBS design and construction. More precisely, it focuses on phase 0 'Opportunity analysis', phase 1 'Plausibility study', and phase 2 'Construction of the demonstrator' of the KBS life cycle. Such phases are supposed to explore, from different perspectives, the opportunity, feasibility, and appropriateness of candidate KBS projects, before starting the development effort.

Part III - The Primary Processes: Development focuses on phase 'Development of the prototype' and phase 4 'Implementation, installation, and delivery of the target system' of the KBS life cycle, which constitute the central part of a project. Phase 3 includes the three fundamental design steps of conceptual modeling, design of the logical model, and detailed system design. It encompasses the choice of the software tools to be adopted for the development of the prototype. It includes the set of activities specifically dedicated to the construction of the knowledge base, which constitute the most peculiar activity of knowledge-based technology. Phase 4 concludes the design and construction process and ends with the delivery of the KBS for operational use.

Part IV - The Primary Processes: Operation focuses on phase 5 'Maintenance and extension' of KBS life cycle. It encompasses the whole duration of the operational life of a KBS and deals with those activities which can make the exploitation of the benefits of a KBS more effective and of longer extent.

Part V - The Supporting Processes focuses on the three main processes that support the KBS life cycle, namely: quality assurance, verification and validation, and documentation development.

Part VI - The Management Processes discusses the principles which should be applied to guide a KBS initiative to success, be it a specific KBS project or the global effort of introducing and exploiting knowledge-based technology within an organization. Such principles are derived from practice, and are illustrated through a collection of exemplary cases reporting successful projects and failed initiatives.

Audience

This book is primarily intended as a text-book for an advanced course in KBS project management. Therefore, it is designed to be used as teaching material for advanced courses, continuing education, and management seminars. However, it may also be profitably used as a reference hand-book by anyone involved in KBS design and construction. Finally, it can be also a useful tool for individual reading and study.

The book is particularly addressed to:
- graduate (and undergraduate) students developing KBS projects as term assignments or thesis work;
- KBS designers and knowledge engineers who aim to expand their competence in the critical domain of technical project management;
- project managers, technical advisors, and technical decision makers in any field of science, technology or business who want to have a concrete insight into knowledge-based technology, its application and its use.

The book does not provide an introduction to knowledge-based technology. Its use requires a prerequisite knowledge of the basic artificial intelligence techniques.

Giovanni Guida and Carlo Tasso

SHORT BIOGRAPHIES

Giovanni Guida is full professor of computer science at the University of Brescia, Faculty of Engineering, and leader of the Knowledge-Based Systems Laboratory at the Department of Electronics for Automation. He taught at the Politecnico di Milano and at the University of Udine, where he founded a new research group in the area of artificial intelligence in 1980 and directed it until 1990.

He is a principal investigator in the area of Factory Automation at CEFRIEL, Milano, where he coordinates a research program in the field of industrial applications of knowledge-based systems and teaches a post-doctoral course on knowledge-based system design and development.

His research interests include: problem solving and search, distributed artificial intelligence, modeling of physical systems and model-based reasoning, applications of knowledge-based systems (industrial diagnosis, planning and scheduling, supervision and control, design), knowledge-based system life cycle and design methodologies, evaluation of knowledge-based systems, man-machine interfaces, natural language processing, dialogue, and user modeling. He has also carried out research activity in the fields of formal languages and programming.

He is a co-editor of *Computational Models of Natural Language Processing* (North-Holland, 1984 - with B.G. Bara), *Expert System Design: Methodologies and Tools*, (North-Holland, 1989 - with C. Tasso), and *Industrial Applications of Knowledge-Based Diagnosis* (Elsevier, 1992 - with A. Stefanini), and author of more than one hundred scientific publications.

Since 1979, he has been active as a scientific and technical consultant in the area of artificial intelligence technologies and, in particular, knowledge-based system applications. He frequently teaches advanced courses and conducts executive seminars.

Address: Università degli Studi di Brescia, Dipartimento di Elettronica per l'Automazione, Via Branze 38, 25123 Brescia, Italy.

Carlo Tasso is associate professor of computer science at the University of Udine, Faculty of Sciences. In 1984, he founded the Artificial Intelligence Laboratory of the Department of Mathematics and Computer Science of the same University, where he is currently responsible for several research projects. He has taught graduate courses for a Master in Computer Science jointly organized by the University of Houston and the University of Udine.

His major research interests are in the areas of knowledge-based systems. More specifically, his research projects have included intelligent interfaces for information retrieval, natural language interfaces, knowledge representation methods for natural language texts, user modeling, multiple modeling of physical systems, diagnostic knowledge-based systems, and intelligent tutoring systems.

He is the author of more than 60 scientific papers in international journals, conference proceedings, and contributed volumes. He is co-editor of the volume *Expert System Design: Methodologies and Tools* (North-Holland, 1989 - with G. Guida).

He has been involved in several research and development projects in the area of artificial intelligence and expert systems in industrial environment, where he is active as scientific and technical consultant He has organized international schools in the area of expert systems.

He is member of AAAI and ACL, and one of the founders of the Italian Association of Artificial Intelligence.

Address: Univeristà degli Studi di Udine, Dipartimento di Matematica e Informatica, Via Zanon 6, 33100 Udine, Italy.

PART I

PROCESS MODEL, LIFE CYCLE, AND METHODOLOGY

1

THE TECHNOLOGY OF
KNOWLEDGE-BASED SYSTEMS

1.1 BASIC CONCEPTS

1.1.1 Knowledge-based systems: a definition

A knowledge-based system (KBS) is a software system capable of supporting the explicit representation of knowledge in some specific competence domain and of exploiting it through appropriate reasoning mechanisms in order to provide high-level problem-solving performance. Therefore, a KBS is a specific, dedicated, computer-based problem-solver, able to face complex problems, which, if solved by man, would require advanced reasoning capabilities, such as deduction, abduction, hypothetical reasoning, model-based reasoning, analogical reasoning, learning, etc. For example, a KBS may be devoted to process supervision and control, production scheduling, diagnosis of complex machinery, tax advising, financial decision making, troubleshooting of electronic circuits, configuration of computer systems, cooperative and user friendly human-computer interaction - and a variety of other challenging tasks [Reitman 84], [Winston and Prendergast 84], [Buchanan, 86], [Harris and Davis 86], [Lawler and Yazdani 87], [Feigenbaum et al. 88], [Richardson and DeFries 90], [SEAI 90], [Narayannan and Bennun 91], [Partridge 91], [Yazdani and Lawler 91], [Partridge 92-a], [Watkins and Elliot 93].

From an abstract point of view, a KBS is composed of two parts:

- a central part which implements the basic problem-solving capabilities of the KBS;
- a peripheral part which is aimed at providing additional functions necessary for a practical and effective use of the KBS, such as a user interface, an explanation system, etc.

In the following we focus on the central part of a KBS, called *kernel*. The peripheral part is discussed in section 1.1.3.

A KBS kernel is a system including three main components, as shown in Figure 1.1.

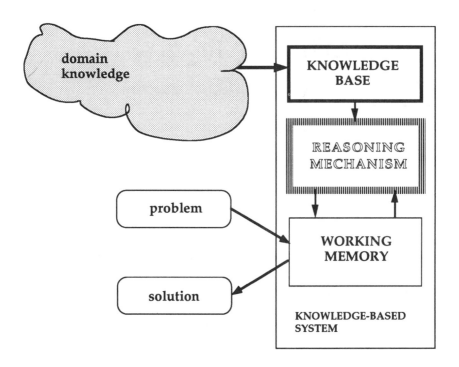

Figure 1.1 Schema of a KBS kernel.

The *knowledge base* stores available knowledge concerning the problem domain at hand, represented in an appropriate explicit form and ready to be used by the reasoning mechanism. It may contain knowledge about domain objects, their structure and properties, the relations existing among them, the operations which may be executed on objects and relations, the structure of typical problems, and the problem-solving strategies. The knowledge base is a highly structured, long-term memory, which can store knowledge permanently during the whole life-time of the KBS. The *reasoning mechanism* is constituted by a complex set of programs capable of performing high-level reasoning processes in order to solve problems in the considered domain by exploiting the knowledge stored in the knowledge base. The *working memory* is used to store all information relevant to a problem solving session of the KBS, that is: a description of the problem at hand, the intermediate solution steps, and eventually the solution found. The working memory is thus a short-term memory which is updated each time a new problem is considered. Its content lasts as long as the problem-solving session does.

The specific mode of operation of a KBS strictly depends on two facts: (i) the techniques used to represent and structure knowledge, and (ii) the problem-solving methods on which the reasoning mechanism is based upon. At a high level of abstraction the operation of a KBS kernel may be schematically described through the procedure shown in Figure 1.2.

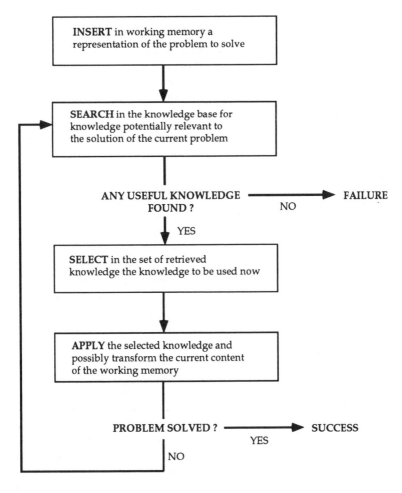

Figure 1.2 Mode of operation of a KBS kernel.

Using these definitions as a basis, we can now easily note that, if the reasoning mechanism of a KBS is complete and correct, then the class of problems it can actually solve only depends on the content of its knowledge base. It is the extent, correctness, and quality of the knowledge base which determines the problem-solving power of a KBS.

Note that, although the conceptual structure of the procedure shown in Figure 1.2. seems very simple, it hides several critical problems, including:

- How can the knowledge relevant to the solution of the problem at hand be retrieved from the knowledge base? How can the search be carried out efficiently, especially for very large knowledge bases?
- What criteria should be used to select from the knowledge retrieved, the knowledge to apply in solving the problem at hand? What should be done with the knowledge retrieved but not used?
- How can it be guaranteed that all available knowledge relevant to the solution of the problem at hand is actually considered?
- How is it possible to ensure that knowledge is used correctly, according to logically valid and cognitively plausible rules?
- How can the exploration of alternative solution paths be carried out effectively and efficiently? How can it be guaranteed that all possible solution paths are actually tried?

The specific methods and techniques used to construct a KBS are globally indicated by the term *knowledge-based technology*. Knowledge-based technology is a composite technology, which includes several specific topics with complementary roles, such as: knowledge representation, problem solving and automatic reasoning, machine learning, explanation, knowledge acquisition, man-machine interaction, etc. Moreover, each one of these topics encompasses many different methods and techniques which can be used either in isolation or in an integrated way in the design of a specific KBS.

Most of the methods, techniques, and tools of knowledge-based technology are derived from the field of computer science known as *artificial intelligence*. This book is not intended to provide an introduction to artificial intelligence and knowledge-based technology, since it is assumed that the reader has a good technical background in these fields. The following list suggests basic references for people lacking an adequate background in this area:

- general reference: [Barr et al. 81-89], [Shapiro 87];
- artificial intelligence: [Charniak and McDermott 85], [Boden 87], [Ford 87-b], [Banerji 90], [Schalkoff 90], [Rich and Knight 91], [Winston 92];
- knowledge-based systems: [Hayes-Roth et al. 83], [Addis 85], [Waterman 86], [Martin and Oxman 88], [Rolston 88], [Guida and Tasso 89-a], [Chorafas 90], [Harmon and Sawyer 90], [Jackson 90], [Prerau 90], [Edwards 91];
- knowledge representation: [Ringland and Duce 84], [Sowa 84], [Brachman and Levesque 85], [Bench-Capon 90]; [Davis et al 93];
- problem solving and reasoning: [Nilsson 80], [Pearl 84], [Genesereth and Nilsson 87];

- artificial intelligence programming [Laubsch 84], [Charniak et al. 87], [Tanimoto 87], [Schalkoff 90].

From another perspective, we may consider a KBS kernel as having two parts:

1. a container, called the *empty system kernel*, which holds the complex set of programs defining the structure and organization of the knowledge base and of the working memory of a KBS and implementing its reasoning mechanism;

2. a content, made up by the actual, specific knowledge stored in the knowledge base.

The first part is general and mainly application independent, while the second part strictly depends on the specific application considered. The term empty kernel system derives from the fact that the content of the knowledge base has been removed from the KBS, thus leaving the KBS empty. The empty system can be viewed as an abstract, general problem-solver which can be used to solve problems in a specific application domain through the insertion of appropriate knowledge in the initially empty knowledge base. Figure 1.3 illustrates the concept of empty system kernel.

Let us note that, although the very nature of the empty system kernel is that of being general and application independent, this does not mean that it is universally applicable and actually suitable to any application context. In fact, the design of the empty system kernel largely depends on the specific features of the application domain considered, as it is illustrated in chapters 6 and 7.

As a last remark, let us note that the concept of KBS presented here does not take into consideration the possibility of autonomous learning. In fact, no long-term record is kept of past problem-solving sessions, and the reasoning mechanism is not allowed to change the content of the knowledge base. So, the behavior of the KBS is not supposed to autonomously change during the operational life of the system. Only an external maintenance or extension intervention can change the content of the knowledge base or even the structure of the KBS. Of course, one might easily extend the concept of KBS presented above to also include the issue of autonomous learning. With reference to Figure 1.1, an arrow directed from the reasoning mechanism back to the knowledge base satisfies this purpose. However, machine learning is presently a challenging research issue, and only a few results are really mature for concrete applications in industry and business. The reader interested in machine learning can refer to: [Michalski et al. 83], [Michalski et al. 86], [Forsyth 89], [Kodraftoff and Michalski 90], [Shavlik and Dietterich 90], [Natarajan 91]. In any case, most of the topics dealt in this book are largely independent of the specific issue of machine learning, being valid both for KBSs which do not include learning and for KBSs which do include it.

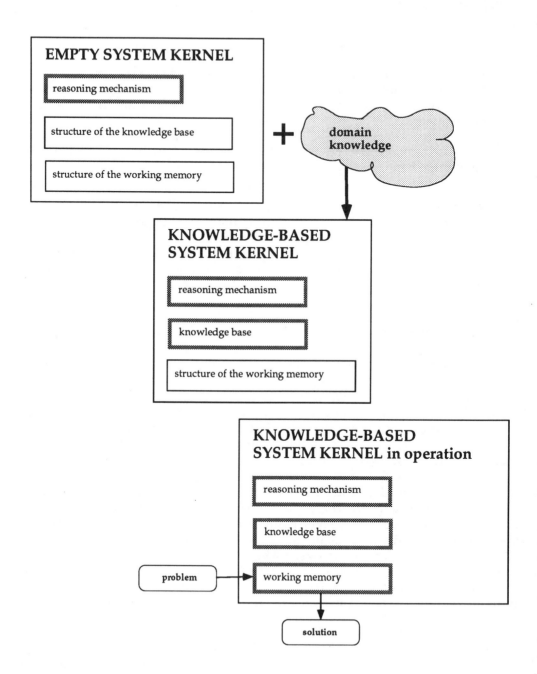

Figure 1.3 The concept of empty system kernel.

1.1.2   Knowledge-based systems and traditional software systems: distinctive features and complementary roles

Software systems which are not knowledge-based, i.e. whose development relies upon classical information processing methods, will be indicated here as traditional software systems and the technology they rely upon as traditional software technology. For example, a program for numerical analysis, an application for information storage and retrieval, a business administration package, an operating system, a system for linear programming are all traditional software systems. Clearly, the distinction between knowledge-based and traditional software technology is very clear in several cases (consider, for example, a rule-based system and a Fortran program), but is less defined in others (consider, for example, a frame-based system and an object-oriented program, or a logic inference system and a deductive data base). There are several important points where the two technologies meet, such as, for example, rapid prototyping or object oriented programming. Moreover, both technologies rapidly converge towards a closer integration [Simon 86], [Alonso et al. 90], [Partridge 91].

With respect to traditional software technology, knowledge-based technology offers a new approach to problem solving. The traditional, well-known approach to problem solving with the computer is schematically shown in Figure 1.4.

As we can note, this approach is centered around two issues, that is: invention of a solution method and construction of the program. More specifically, it can be described in three steps:

1.   initially, a domain expert analyzes the problem of the user and designs an appropriate solution method;
2.   then, a software designer, an analyst, and a programmer construct a suitable program which correctly and effectively codifies the solution method proposed by the expert;
3.   eventually, the program is loaded in the computer and can be executed each time the user needs to solve a specific instance of the problem considered.

The new approach proposed by knowledge-based technology is very different. The focus of attention is no longer on algorithm design, but on the representation of knowledge which is considered relevant and useful to the solution of a class of problems in the application domain of the user. The responsibility of deciding which knowledge to use and how to use it to solve a specific problem, is left now to the computer, appropriately equipped with special problem-solving software, namely the empty system kernel of the KBS. This approach is illustrated in Figure 1.5.

It can be described in three steps:
1.   initially, the knowledge engineer analyzes the application domain of the user, and both a KBS designer and a programmer develop a suitable empty system kernel;
2.   then, the knowledge engineer, together with domain experts, acquires knowledge and represents it, thus constructing the knowledge base of the KBS;

3.   finally, the KBS is available to solve user problems in the considered
      application domain.

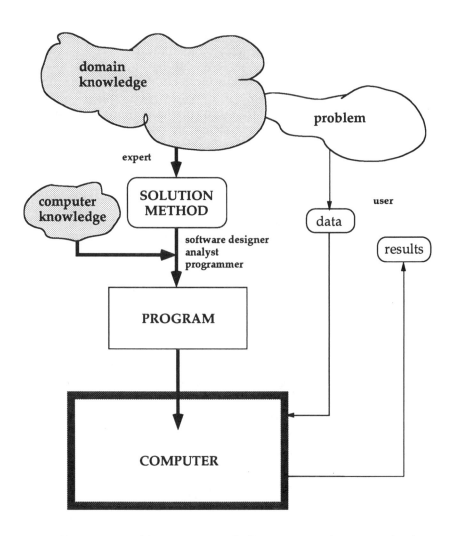

Figure 1.4 Problem solving with the computer: the approach of
traditional software technology.

To sum it up, the main conceptual difference between a KBS and a traditional
software system is the fact that a KBS can solve problems in a given application
domain by means of explicit representation of knowledge and by exploiting
general reasoning mechanisms, while a traditional software system can produce
the solution to a given problem by applying a fixed solution algorithm designed
by man.

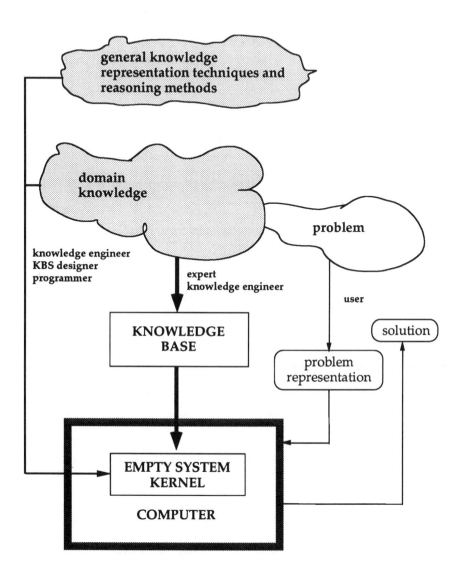

Figure 1.5 Problem solving with the computer: the approach of
knowledge-based technology.

Knowledge-based and traditional software technologies, in addition to proposing different approaches to computer problem solving, also feature quite different technical and functional characteristics, appropriate for facing different kinds of problems. Generally, traditional software technology is very useful in all those cases where a solution method for the user problem is known and can be easily and carefully described and coded in a computer program. Knowledge-based technology, on the other hand, can help in those cases where knowledge concerning the problem domain is available, however it is difficult - or even impossible - to envisage an algorithmic solution method.

The distinctive features of knowledge-based technology with respect to traditional software technology are summarized in the table of Figure 1.6 (a and b) - see also [Alonso, Maté, and Pazos 90].

This table focuses on three main points:
- knowledge representation - what knowledge is represented and how;
- mode of operation - how the system operates and how knowledge is used in problem solving;
- performance - what kind of performance is supported.

It is worth emphasizing two points, considered as the key characteristics of KBS technology:
1. the explicit representation of domain knowledge;
2. the separation between the representation of the general problem-solving algorithm, coded in the procedures of the reasoning mechanism, and the representation of domain-specific knowledge, stored, in a mainly declarative form, in the knowledge base.

The former point entails such important performance features as robustness, transparency, naturalness, and flexibility. The latter enables the system developer to focus separately on the design of the problem-solving strategy to be implemented in the reasoning mechanism and on the representation of the knowledge that goes into the knowledge base. This, in turn, makes it possible to create more complex systems in comparison to those which could be built if the system developer had not only to acquire and represent domain knowledge, but also to assemble it into an algorithmic solution.

The above discussion shows how knowledge-based technology offers a definitely new approach in exploiting the power of a computer system for problem-solving tasks. However, it should be noted that, from a theoretical point of view, knowledge-based technology implements an abstract machine whose computational power is exactly the same as the one offered by the traditional software technology (i.e., that of a Turing Machines or general recursive functions [Cutland 80]). If a problem can be solved using a traditional program it can also be solved through the knowledge-based approach and vice versa. What makes the difference between the two approaches is the complexity of the design process and the type and quality of the solutions which can be implemented. Some problems can be more conveniently faced with the traditional software technology, while others are better and more easily tackled through a knowledge-based technology approach. Moreover, when solving complex, real-size problems, it is often appropriate to use both technologies in an integrated way to cope with different technical and functional requirements which coexist in the same application.

Therefore, knowledge-based technology is in general a complement - not an alternative - to traditional software. Three main points substantiate this statement. Firstly, knowledge-based technology allows solving complex and very large problems which are practically intractable with traditional software technology. In fact, the solution of several problems of high practical interest seems to escape an algorithmic treatment. Although easily solvable in principle, their solution method cannot be described in algorithmic terms. Such problems involve extensive knowledge, for example, large collections of cases or practical rules. They require a typically non-deterministic approach based on tentative reasoning, such as hill-climbing, generate-and-test, trial-and-error, means-ends analysis, heuristic search, etc. - see [Nilsson 80], [Hayes 81]. They use knowledge which is intrinsically fragmentary, incomplete, approximate, or uncertain, and their data are time-varying or noisy [Stefik et al. 83-a]. Consider, for example, diagnosis of an industrial plant or machinery, design of a digital circuit, space mission planning, monitoring of a continuous production process, financial advice giving, simulation of macro-economic scenarios, integrated building design, etc. In such cases, knowledge-based technology can be of great value and can help face complex tasks which otherwise would remain beyond the limits of computer problem solving. Secondly, knowledge-based technology supports the solution of sophisticated problems which are unsatisfactorily faced with traditional software technology. In fact, several problems can be solved with traditional software technology only after they have been heavily simplified and transformed so as to fit the power and peculiarities of a traditional software technology. However, such a solution does not always turn out to be fully satisfactory for the users. Quite often, a more accurate and thorough approach would be preferred. Consider, for example, an application concerning tax advising, more specifically filling out an income tax form. A traditional software system can interactively support the user in the task of filling out a tax form correctly and completely through queries, reminders, and checks. It can guarantee the formal correctness and, as much as possible, the completeness of the form-filling task, but it can hardly go beyond the level of a novice bookkeeper. It cannot suggest skilled solutions to critical problems, nor can it discuss the interpretation of specific tax laws, take into account particular user goals or constraints, reason about specific user problems, devise and evaluate alternatives, provide explanations and tutoring, or justify the advice given. In most such cases, knowledge-based technology can be of great help either by complementing an existing traditional software system with a new knowledge-based module or by facing the problem from scratch and designing a new and more suitable application. Thirdly, knowledge-based technology allows identification of new problems to be tackled. In fact, a new technology - like knowledge-based technology - opens up new frontiers; new tasks can be faced and new applications developed. The more we realize the potentials of the new technology and experience its power, the more we can identify new issues which might be achievable and useful. Quite often reality goes far beyond our expectations; a tool (a method or a technology) originally designed for some purpose, may turn out to be useful for other tasks well beyond the intentions of the designer as well. So,

KNOWLEDGE-BASED SYSTEMS	TRADITIONAL SOFTWARE SYSTEMS
knowledge representation	
domain knowledge is represented explicitly in the knowledge base	domain knowledge is not explicit in the program code; it is only in the mind of experts, software designers, and analysts
domain knowledge is represented in a natural, structured and organic way	domain knowledge is fragmented, deeply transformed, and hidden in the program code
general problem-solving and control knowledge is separate from domain knowledge	general problem-solving and control knowledge is hidden in the program code
computer knowledge is separate from domain knowledge	computer knowledge is intermixed with problem-solving and control knowledge in the program code
knowledge is mainly represented in a declarative form	knowledge is mainly represented in a procedural form
fragmentary, unstructured qualitative, uncertain, approximate, non-algorithmic, association-based, case-based, classification-based, model-based knowledge can be easily represented	only structured and algorithmic knowledge can be represented

mode of operation	
operation is basically non-deterministic	operation is strictly deterministic
knowledge is dynamically used by the inference engine to construct a solution to the problem considered	knowledge is used by experts, software designers and analysts at the moment of program design and construction

Figure 1.6 Knowledge-based and traditional software technology: distinctive features - a.

performance	
robust: KBSs can operate with incomplete knowledge or data, their performance depending on the amount and quality of knowledge locally available	fragile: traditional software systems can operate only with complete information
transparent: KBSs can explain and justify their mode of operation	opaque: traditional software systems can hardly explain and justify their mode of operation
natural: KBSs can account for human mental models and processes	unnatural: traditional software systems hardly correspond to human mental models and processes
wide coverage: KBSs can deal with a large variety of problems in a given application domain	narrow coverage: traditional software systems can only deal with the problems for which they have been explicitly designed
flexible: KBSs are developed in an incremental way and are open to easy refinement, maintenance, and extension during their operational life: their level of performance depends on the amount and quality of knowledge available	rigid: traditional software systems are developed in a modular way and it is generally hard to refine, modify and extend them after they have been released for operational use: their level of performance is fixed, being determined at the moment of system design

Figure 1.6 Knowledge-based and traditional software technology: distinctive features - b.

experience with knowledge-based technology can enormously broaden our view on possible computer applications, and may enable us to identify and solve new problems, which had not been considered previously [Edwards 91].

Figure 1.7 shows how the set of all problems potentially interesting for computer problem-solving can be divided into four parts:
- the part on the left represents those problems which man cannot solve and, therefore, are also unsolvable even by using the computer;
- the bottom part represents the problems appropriate for a solution through traditional software technology;
- the middle part represents the problems appropriate for knowledge-based technology;

- the top part represents frontier problems which, at present, are object of basic research and for which no viable computer-based solutions exist.

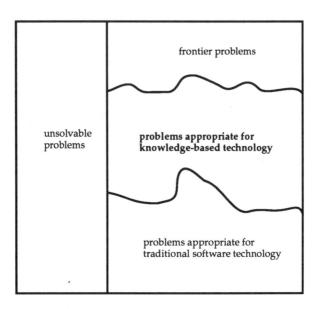

Figure 1.7 Knowledge-based and traditional software technologies: appropriate problems.

Even though the borderlines between the three central parts are obviously not clear-cut, the limitations of knowledge-based technology are clearly identified and can be summarized in the following three statements:
- It does not make sense to resort to knowledge-based technology to tackle problems that even the most experienced specialists cannot solve. KBSs cannot do anything that man cannot do himself.
- It is generally inappropriate to adopt knowledge-based technology if the application problem considered can be appropriately solved using a traditional software approach. The traditional solution, if possible and appropriate, always compares favorably over the knowledge-based approach on cost, time, and technical complexity. Therefore, traditional solutions should be tried first and, if applicable, always preferred. However, if the traditional solution turns out to be very complex or definitely impossible from a practical point of view, the knowledge-based solution should be considered [Greenwell 88]. The diagram in Figure 1.8 gives a qualitative idea of the relationship existing between the complexity of the problem to be faced and the cost of the solution for the two cases of traditional software and knowledge-based technologies. Problem complexity refers here to the difficulty of describing the solution method in algorithmic terms through an appropriate information processing procedure, while solution cost denotes the global effort (resources, time, etc.) required to

design and construct the computer-based system for solving the problem considered. As it can be noted, for low problem complexity the traditional approach has always to be preferred, while for high problem complexity only the knowledge-based approach is applicable in practice. Moreover, in the range of problem complexity between the point where the two curves intersect and the limit of traditional software systems, both technologies may be applicable but the knowledge-based approach is generally more appropriate and convenient. On the right of the limit of KBSs, there is the frontier of unsolvable problems already mentioned in Figure 1.7.

- It may be unwise to resort to the knowledge-based approach for borderline problems whose solution is beyond the current state-of-the-art of the available technology. It should not be forgotten that knowledge-based technology is still evolving. New results are continuously being produced by scientific research, and some of them are rapidly becoming accepted design and production tools.

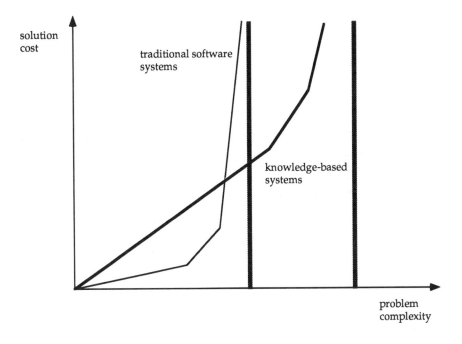

Figure 1.8 Knowledge-based and traditional software systems: complexity and cost.

1.1.3   The architecture of knowledge-based systems

A software system designed to serve some specific application-oriented purpose is generally called an *application*, no matter what technologies are used for its construction. As we have outlined in section 1.1.2., knowledge-based technology and traditional software technology offer complementary specific contributions to the construction of complex applications. Therefore, an application based only on traditional software technology is called a *traditional application*, while an application system which relies on knowledge-based technology (but not necessarily only on it) is called a *knowledge-based application* or simply a *KBS application*.

Note that what distinguishes knowledge-based from traditional applications is not the type of problems they solve, but the technology they are based upon. So, it would be meaningless to say, for example, that a system for structural analysis is a traditional application, and a system for financial decision making is a knowledge-based application. Their nature depends on the technology used for their construction; both of them may well be traditional applications as well as knowledge-based applications.

Let us outline that the recent development of knowledge-based technology has been featured by a progressive integration with the traditional areas of software engineering, data bases, and information system [Nomura and Lunn 87]. Stand-alone KBSs are still prevailing, but most KBSs are designed today to be connected or integrated with existing traditional software packages and data bases [Ketonen 89] or to be embedded into new advanced applications. KBSs are also being integrated with the most recent outcomes of information processing technology, such as multimedia and hypermedia [Bielawski and Lewand 91], neural nets [Hillman 90], object-oriented and deductive data bases [Martin and Oxman 88], [Schur 88], [Bielawski and Lewand 91], information retrieval systems [Ingwersen 92], etc. Moreover, several KBSs are explicitly designed to extend and enhance traditional applications for decision support, information management and retrieval, industrial control and supervision, simulation, numerical computing, computer-aided design, etc.

A large class of KBS applications are the well-known *expert systems*. These are special-purpose software systems which support, or perform automatically, cognitive tasks which are usually carried out by human experts. They provide high-level problem-solving performance in specific application fields, such as financial decision making, medical diagnosis, process supervision and control, industrial diagnosis, tax advising, planning and scheduling, etc. The aim of emulating the behavior of human experts in some application field, making their competence and experience available in a computer software, characterizes expert systems. Note, however, that KBSs are not only the central part of expert systems - which, incidentally, may also incorporate traditional software components - but are also important components of a variety of innovative computer-based applications, such as intelligent human-computer interfaces, advanced decision support systems, intelligent robot-control systems, diagnostic systems, intelligent tutoring systems, etc. These systems do not really belong to the class of expert systems, as they do not necessarily aim at reproducing the competence and experience of a human expert, although they are true KBSs.

On the basis of the above discussion, the concept of KBS introduced in section 1.1.1 can now be defined in more specific terms. A KBS is made up of two parts:
• a central part which implements the basic problem-solving capabilities of the KBS and comprises a collection of dedicated *problem-solvers*;

- a peripheral part which is aimed at providing additional functions necessary for a practical and effective use of the KBS, and comprises a collection of *special-purpose modules.*

The components of a KBS, either problem-solvers or special-purpose modules, may be developed using either traditional software or knowledge-based technology (or both), with the only constraint that at least one problem-solver is knowledge-based. Problem-solvers that are not knowledge-based (for example, procedural programs, routines for numerical computation, neural networks, data bases, spread-sheets, etc.) are called heterogeneous problem-solvers. The special-purpose modules of a KBS are:

- A *software interface* which connects the KBS to the external software systems with which it must interact, such as operating systems, data bases, specific utilities, application packages, etc.
- An *external interface* which connects the KBS to the external environment in which it operates, such as sensors, data acquisition systems, actuators, etc.
- A *user interface* which is aimed at making the interaction between the user and the KBS friendly and effective. It may include advanced man-machine interaction facilities, multimedia systems, and dialogue capabilities. The user interface often includes also user modeling capabilities, which can make user-system interaction more attuned to the various classes of users who are expected to utilize the KBS. A smart help system and a problem-solving support system may be an appropriate addition to the user interface.
- An *explanation system* which is directly connected to the knowledge-based components of the KBS and explains and justifies the behavior of the KBS to the user. The explanation system can show the knowledge utilized, demonstrate the problem-solving strategies used, justify the choices made, and illustrate the main reasoning steps. It can answer user queries or take an active initiative providing explanations and justifications when it deems necessary. The explanation system often includes user modeling capabilities, which tailor the behavior of the system and the types of explanations generated to the various classes of users who are expected to utilize the KBS.

The generic architecture of a KBS is illustrated in Figure 1.9. If we empty the knowledge bases of the various knowledge-based components of a KBS, we obtain the so-called *empty system.*

1.1.4   Knowledge-based systems: some classifications

As a conclusion of this introductory section, let us introduce here four useful practical classifications of KBSs.

A first classification concerns the intended role of a KBS in the target operational environment, with particular reference to user-system interaction in terms of sharing tasks and responsibilities [Rasmussen 86]. Under this perspective three types of systems can be identified:

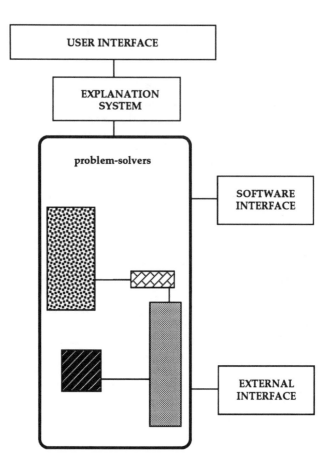

Figure 1.9 Generic architecture of a KBS.

- *Support systems* can provide expert support to a human operator or to a professional in the execution of specific, complex tasks. A support system may act in a number of different roles, as assistant, colleague, critic, second opinion, advisor, consultant, tutor, etc. [Edwards 91]. It offers knowledge and competence to interested users but does not prescribe solutions or decisions; it acts as a job aid for a human user, without the intention of replacing him [Prerau 90].
- *Prescriptive systems* can guide, constrain, and control the activity of a human operator or professional in the execution of specific, complex tasks. Prescriptive systems improve the quality and the response-time of human performance without replacing the users which still maintain a certain degree of intellectual and operational autonomy; prescriptive systems have the authority of imposing goals, constraints, solutions or decisions.

- *Autonomous systems* do not interact with any human user since they are aimed at replacing human operators or professionals in specific jobs.

A second distinction concerns how the KBS is connected to external traditional software systems. Three types of systems are possible [Edwards 91]:

- *Stand-alone systems* do not interact with external traditional software systems.
- *Integrated systems* interact with external traditional software systems (like data bases, spreadsheets, management information systems, application systems, operating systems, specific utilities, communication systems, etc.). The global operation of an integrated system is controlled by the KBS, which manages the interaction with the user and utilizes the connected traditional software systems as providers of specific services or information which are necessary for its operation.
- *Embedded systems* are encapsulated in an external traditional software system which is in charge of controlling the overall operation of the system and of handling the interaction with the user.

A third distinction concerns the type of connection existing between the KBS and the external environment in which it operates. In this respect, a KBS can be:

- *On-line*, if it is directly connected with the external physical world through sensors, data acquisition systems, and actuators. Typical examples of on-line systems are applications for continuous process supervision, in-field fault diagnosis, environment pollution control, monitoring of patients under intensive therapy, etc.
- *Off-line*, if it is not connected with the external physical world. Of course, physical world data may be provided manually to the KBS by the user. Typical examples of off-line systems are applications in financial advice, mechanical design, production scheduling, field testing of simple devices, etc.

A fourth and last distinction concerns the purpose for which the KBS is developed. In this respect, a KBS can be [Edwards 91]:

- *application-oriented*, if it is aimed at solving some concrete problem in a real application context;
- *exploration-oriented*, if it is devoted to support the first steps of technology transfer with tangible evidence, without having, however, any concrete application goals;
- *research*-oriented, if its only purpose is to support basic research, applied research, and innovative experimentation, by offering a suitable test-bed for experimenting new concepts, methods, and techniques;
- *training-oriented*, if it is developed in the frame of a training initiative to support a more concrete and practical acquisition of the main concepts and techniques of knowledge-based technology.

1.2   KNOWLEDGE-BASED SYSTEM PROCESSES

1.2.1   Process model, life cycle, and methodology

KBS development is a complex issue, and there are often many alternative ways to organize and perform the various tasks involved in the design, production, maintenance, and extension of a knowledge-based product. A defined *KBS process model* can help through these choices in an orderly way and can provide an organization with a consistent working framework [Humphrey 90], [ISO/IEC CD 12207.2 93]. A general and abstract definition of the KBS process model is shown in Figure 1.10.

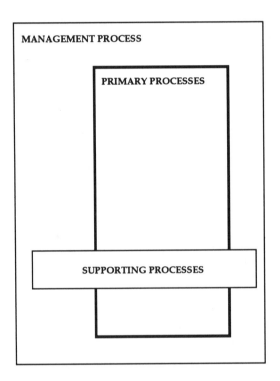

Figure 1.10 KBS process model.

The proposed KBS process model includes three main processes:
- the *primary processes*, which include the specific activities necessary to design, produce, maintain, and extend a KBS;
- the *supporting processes*, which cross through the primary processes and support them by contributing to the success and the quality of a KBS project;
- the *management processes*, which includes the basic activities of project management.

At a lower level of abstraction, the primary processes can be implemented through the concept of KBS life cycle. The term *KBS life cycle* refers to how the various tasks involved in the design, production, maintenance, and extension of a KBS are defined and organized. More precisely, the life cycle is a reference schema which specifies [Boehm 88] [Hilal and Soltan 93]:

- what to do, i.e. which specific tasks should be performed, and
- when to do it, i.e. in which contexts, under what conditions, and in which temporal and logical order.

The concept of the life cycle features two distinctive points:

- it is abstract, i.e. low-level details of real design, production, maintenance, and extension processes are omitted; attention is focused on a simple, schematic representation of those features which are assumed to capture the specific and individual aspects of the knowledge-based technology;
- it is general, i.e. it aims at capturing the common features shared by a large class of real design, production, maintenance, and extension processes, discarding all aspects which are found only in specific production organizations or application contexts, and focusing on the characteristics necessary to characterize the involved production technology.

In order not to lose generality, a life-cycle concept must not be too detailed, nor must it deal with specific implementation aspects. Clearly, various definitions of KBS life cycle, based on different standpoints and different conceptions of the specific features of knowledge-based technology, may be proposed.

At a still lower level of abstraction, the implementation of the concepts of primary processes (i.e., the KBS life cycle), supporting processes, and management processes must deal with the specific methods and practices used to design, produce, maintain, and extend a KBS. These cannot be general since they are closely bound to the individual choices of a specific production or application environment. The term *KBS methodology* indicates an integrated set of methods and practices to effectively perform all the individual tasks involved in the design, production, maintenance, and extension of an artifact. More precisely, it specifies, in detail, how the tasks defined in the KBS life cycle should be carried out [Boehm 88]. Therefore, the concept of methodology requires a pre-existing definition of life cycle, which constitutes the corner stone supporting its definition [Allard 93]. The concept of methodology is, therefore, characterized by two points:

- it is concrete, i.e. it takes care of all low-level details needed to specify the execution of a task in an effective and unique way for the operator in charge;
- it is specific, i.e. it takes into account - and therefore depends on - a large set of environmental conditions and technical choices, including:
  - management and organizational characteristics of the organization (company, institution, government department, etc.) where the KBS is developed;
  - technical standards and preferences of the organization and of the KBS project team;

- particular features of the end-user community;
- type of KBS project: explorative, production-oriented, training-oriented, etc.;
- type of application area and domain: factory automation, professional activities, information systems, office automation, decision support, etc.;

Of course, the level of detail of a KBS methodology may vary greatly according to the specific needs of the organization where it is supposed to be applied. The more a methodology is detailed and fine-grained, the more it becomes specific and particular. The choice of the most appropriate level of detail and granularity is strictly dependent on features and requirements of the organization, and there is no general-purpose solution.

There is an important consequence due to the points discussed above. While it is possible to propose an abstract and general concept of life cycle which can fit the needs of a large variety of organizations, the concept of a universal, largely applicable methodology turns out to be meaningless. Therefore, we should use the term "KBS methodologies", rather than "KBS methodology". Each organization should have its own, designed to fit its specific and individual requirements and constraints.

1.2.2   Knowledge-based systems and traditional software systems development

As a KBS is a very special kind of software product, the first step towards developing a life cycle and methodology has been to explore whether or not the results obtained for traditional software systems in the field of *software engineering* could be appropriately transferred to the new area of knowledge-based technology. For an introduction to software engineering the interested reader may refer to: [Wirth 71], [Metzger 73], [Yourdon 75 and 89], [Dijkstra 76], [Boehm 76], [Freeman and Wasserman, 77], [Yourdon and Constantine 79], [Boehm 81], [Davis 84-a], [Shooman 83], [Fairley 85], [Sommerville 89], [Humphrey 90], [Ould 90], [Pressman 92], [van Vliet 93]; for the specific issue of software engineering standards: [IEEE 91], [ESA PSS-05-0 91], [ISO/IEC CD 12207.2 93].

In the last decade, a widely discussed question has been "Do software engineering principles and techniques fit knowledge-based technology?"; and more particularly, "Can the approaches to system development originally proposed in the field of software engineering be easily and effectively carried over to the new field of KBSs?" Extensive literature exists on these points; the most representative works are mentioned below for the readers interested in exploring this aspect further: [Freiling et al. 85], [Bobrow et al. 86], [Gudes et al. 86], [De Salvo et al. 87], [Ebrahimi 87], [Ford 87-a], [Heng 87], [Maguire 88], [Greenwell 88], [Rolston 88], [Guida and Tasso, 89-b], [Alonso, Maté, and Pazos 90]. Some of these proposals support an affirmative answer to the above questions, claiming that with minor modifications and extensions traditional software engineering principles and techniques can be effectively applied to the design and production of KBSs, while others tend to be less optimistic and show several reasons which make software engineering techniques not completely appropriate for KBS development.

Before discussing this issue more closely, let us remember that the starting points for this investigation are the two main classical models of software life cycle, namely the waterfall model and the spiral model of software development. These are briefly surveyed below.

Waterfall model

The *waterfall model* [Royce 70], [Boehm 76], [Agresti 86] assumes that software development is organized into phases which are executed sequentially. Requirements analysis is executed first, being followed by the definition of specification. Then design is carried out which proceeds coding and testing. Clearly defined criteria are used in order to assess the completion of each phase. These criteria are basically document-driven or code-driven, since they generally specify that a given document or piece of software must be produced in order to successfully complete the phase. Feedback loops are confined to successive phases. This organization relies on the assumption that it is possible to produce complete and correct requirements and specifications before design and implementation begin. Such linear approach may sometimes be appropriate for traditional software systems, but it is certainly not adequate for KBS development, which typically features an explorative and highly iterative nature that needs to be closely reflected in the life cycle adopted [Kiss 89].

Spiral model

The spiral model [Boehm 88] proposes a different approach which is characterized by a risk-driven process. The development is organized around several cycles, each one devoted to progress in the development of a portion of the software system. Each cycle includes the same sequence of the following four steps:
1.   determine objectives, alternatives, and constraints;
2.   evaluate alternatives, identify and resolve risks;
3.   develop and verify products;
4.   plan next phases and review all results of the current cycle.

The specific approach exploited for software development in step 3. depends on the risk analysis performed in the previous step. It may happen that the risk resolution strategy for a specific portion of the system is based on prototyping [Alavi 84], [Boar 84], whereas for another portion it is based on a more traditional specification-driven approach. Risk-management considerations are also important for decision making about the time and effort to be spent on activities such as planning, quality control, testing, and so on.

The spiral model provides a very flexible framework for organizing the software development process, which can accommodate various development approaches in an iterative risk-driven fashion. This development strategy where the system evolves through multiple stages, represents indeed a very general approach, applicable - at least in principle - to any kind of software system. It may even be adequate for describing the development process of a KBS [Agarwal and Tanniru 90], [Hull and Kay 91]. However, to define a life cycle and a methodology which can concretely organize and guide the design and production of KBSs, the spiral model is not sufficient, since it lacks an adequate level of specificity. It does not take into account the particular features of knowledge-based technology and it underestimates such fundamental issues as domain selection, technical feasibility, conceptual modeling, design criteria, knowledge acquisition, project management - to name just e few [Kiss 89].

As shown in sections 1.1.1 and 1.1.2, KBSs and traditional software systems are essentially different artifacts, and they definitely entail different approaches to computer problem solving. Moreover, their development is based on essentially different processes [Alonso, Maté, and Pazos 90]. The schemes reported in Figures 1.11 and 1.12 illustrate the main steps of the development processes of traditional software systems and KBSs, respectively. Design and construction steps are written in lower-case letters in the rounded boxes, while inputs, outputs and major intermediate products are written in upper-case letters.

The overall structure of the development process of traditional software systems and of KBSs is straightforward. The only point deserving specific attention are the cycles. The production process of traditional software systems is essentially linear, without iterations (see Figure 1.11). The dashed lines show unwanted returns to previous design and production steps, which may however be necessary to fix possible design or coding errors. On the contrary, the production process of KBSs is essentially iterative and includes three fundamental cycles (see Figure 1.12):

- an iteration around the 'knowledge acquisition and knowledge base construction' step, which characterizes the intrinsically incremental nature of this task;
- a return to the 'knowledge analysis and empty system development' step, which denotes the progressive refinement of the technical design of the prototype through experimentation;
- a return to the 'requirement analysis and definition of specifications' step, which shows how the definition of the specification may be refined during the development of the prototype.

According to the above illustration of the development processes of traditional software systems and KBSs, the following points stress some important differences between the two technologies:

- The design of a traditional software system is primarily directed towards what the user wants, its main purpose being the solution of a user problem. The development of a KBS, on the other hand, is directed towards acquisition and representation within a computer of knowledge of a specific application domain to be used in a variety of problem-solving tasks.

• In the development of traditional software systems it is assumed that it is possible to define a complete and correct system specification before design and construction begins. This is not true for KBSs; requirements cannot all be elicited at the beginning of a project, and it is difficult - if not impossible - to define a complete and correct system specification before the implementation starts [Prerau 90].

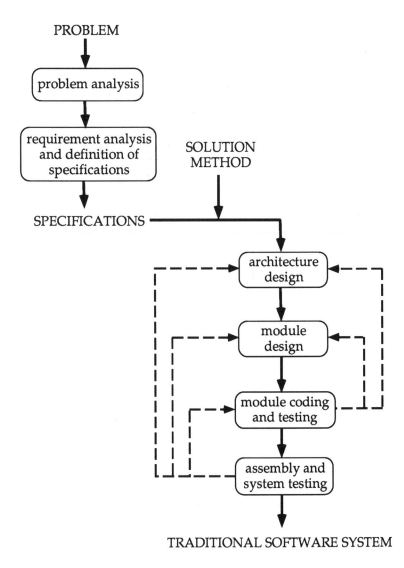

Figure 1.11 The development process of traditional software systems.

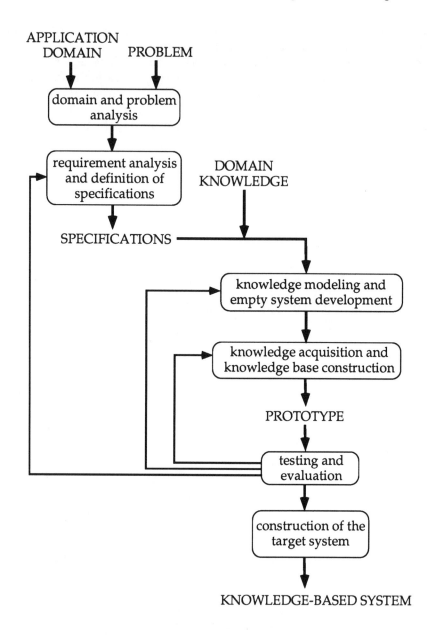

Figure 1.12 The development process of KBSs.

- In traditional software technology a basic point of the development process is to proceed sequentially through the design and construction steps. Backtracking and iteration are accepted, but minimized as much as possible. In knowledge-based technology, instead, the development process is characterized by explorative programming, iterative design, repeated prototyping, and extensive experimentation. This is a fundamental aspect of KBS development, which cannot be completely discarded without neglecting the most peculiar characteristic of knowledge-based technology. Note that prototyping in knowledge-based technology does not share the same concept of prototyping proposed in traditional software engineering. The latter focuses primarily on user requirements and aims at validating specification definition and ensuring quality and usability, while the former is devoted to experimenting, refining and validating the solution methods identified and the technical decisions made [Irgon et al. 90].

- The concepts of modularization, abstraction, and top-down refinement, typical of traditional software technology, are still appropriate for KBS design and construction, but their practical application is different.
- KBSs are developed incrementally. The empty system can operate with an incomplete knowledge base; as more knowledge is added, system coverage and quality of reasoning improve. Consequently, a KBS can also be debugged, tested, and validated incrementally while it is being developed. Such features can hardly be recognized in the design and construction of traditional software systems; development is not incremental in the sense mentioned above, and program construction and testing are separate phases of the production process.

The above discussion shows that KBSs are built in a substantially different way from traditional software systems. Also practical experience confirms that there are several important differences between the traditional software development cycle as experienced in a typical data processing environment and the process of developing a KBS [Sagalowicz 84], [Waterman 86], [Irgon et al. 90]. So, even though some basic concepts can be inherited from software engineering through the new field of KBSs, significant extensions and modification are needed in the definition of life cycle and methodology.

Undoubtedly, general principles of software engineering constitute a significant background for the new knowledge-based technology. Due to recent evolution, software engineering and knowledge-based technology have had more and more converging trends which will possibly merge in the end [Zualkernan et al. 86], [Jacob and Froscher 90], [Lowry 92]. However, software engineering techniques do not completely fit the features of KBSs and cannot be directly applied to KBS development. Methods and intuitions learned in the development of traditional software do not carry over well to the production of KBSs [Freiling et al. 85]. This raises new challenges. A novel concept of life cycle and methodology explicitly directed towards knowledge-based technology is needed [Guida and Tasso 89-b], [Park et al. 91]. Note, in fact, that the development of KBSs, although featured by such concepts as explorative programming, experimentation, and prototyping, should not be fully free and undisciplined. The stage-wise approach of the waterfall model should be inherited in the KBS production process, which can then be naturally divided into separate steps, each one characterized by precise starting points and goals. Moreover, this organization should be further refined through the definition of a suitable concept of methodology, capable of imposing precise constraints and guidelines for experimentation and creativity [Sol 83]. Finally, in order to cope with the peculiarities of the new emergent and still evolving knowledge-based technology, a general risk-driven approach should be adopted to guide the development and the transition from one stage to the next [Perot 91].

2

LIFE CYCLE AND METHODOLOGY

2.1   OBJECTIVES AND REQUIREMENTS

The main objectives which motivate the introduction of a KBS life cycle and methodology into an organization are:
- having a clear and explicit reference framework for organizing the KBS development process;
- supporting a correct and effective planning and control of KBS projects;
- improving the productivity of the personnel involved in KBS development;
- improving the quality of the delivered KBS applications;
- promoting the standardization of design, production, maintenance, and extension methods and practices, so as to allow personnel mobility through different project teams, as well as easy transfer of intermediate products.

To fulfill these objectives, the definition of a life cycle and methodology for KBSs should satisfy a set of specific requirements [Wasserman et al. 83], [Freiling 85], [Guida and Tasso 89-b], [Edwards 91], [Allard 93]. The most significant ones are listed below:

Life cycle
- it should be complete, covering all aspects of the KBS development process, from initial analysis to operational use;
- it should feature a clear structure, based on a hierarchical decomposition of the KBS development process;
- it should be simple, based on few key concepts and featuring a transparent organization.

Methodology
- it should offer effective support to all major technical and managerial activities related to the design, production, maintenance, and extension of a KBS;
- it should be efficiently applicable without a sensible overhead for the design, production, and maintenance tasks;
- it should be concrete, supporting the use of existing methods, techniques, and tools, while encouraging the development of new ones;
- it should be easy to teach and to learn;
- it should especially focus on those activities which are typical of the KBS development process, such as domain and problem analysis, knowledge modeling and acquisition, knowledge base construction and refinement, verification and validation, and maintenance and extension;
- it should be exploration-oriented, supporting disciplined evaluation of several design alternatives, their experimentation, and their step-wise refinement, being open to the discovery of new problems and to the exploration of new solutions; exploration should, however, be organized in a planned and structured "propose-analyze-evaluate" cycle, aimed at controlling and reducing uncertainty, non-determinism, incoherence, and inefficiency;
- it should be modular, allowing for an incremental construction, through the production of independent and immediately usable methodology modules;
- it should be open, easily modifiable and extensible in order to take into account the new results of the continuous evolution of knowledge-based technology.

The topics of KBS life cycle and methodology have received a great attention in the past years and a several proposals can be found in the literature. A list of selected references concerning the most interesting and concrete proposals is reported below:
- Tektronix methodology: [Freiling et al. 85];
- DEC methodology: [Wilkerson 85];
- RUDE methodology: [Partridge 86], [Partridge and Wilks 87], [Bader et al. 88];
- Greenwell's methodology: [Greenwell 88];
- DOD methodology: [DOD 88], [Rock et al. 90];
- KADS methodology: [Breuker et al. 86], [Anjewierden et al. 90], [Breuker and Wielinga 87], [Hayward et al. 88], [Breuker and Wielinga 89], [Hickman et al. 89], [Hayball and Barlow 90], [Kingston 92], [Tansley and Hayball 93], [Schreiber et al. 93];
- POLITE methodology: [Bader et al. 88], [Edwards 91];
- ESDM methodology: [Goddard 89-a], [Goddard 89-b], [Goddard 89-c], [Hull and Kay 91];
- ESA methodology: [Allard 93];
- other proposals: [Waterman 86], [De Salvo et al. 87], [Ebrahimi 87], [Freeman 87], [Badiru 88], [Rolston 88], [Vesoul 88], [Liebowitz and De Salvo 89], [Montgomery 89], [Weitzel and Kershberg 89], [Harmon and Sawyer 90], [Prerau

90], [Hilal and Soltan 91], [Partridge 92-b], [Watson et al. 92-a], [Hilal and Soltan 93].

2.2   KNOWLEDGE-BASED SYSTEM LIFE CYCLE

2.2.1   Life cycle organization

Taking into account the objectives and requirements stated in section 2.1, we propose a concept of *KBS life cycle* based on a two-levels structure. At the highest level of abstraction, a life cycle is made up of *phases* corresponding to the major stages of the design, production, and maintenance process. At a lower level, each phase is decomposed into a reasonably limited number of *tasks*. The execution of the life-cycle phases is supposed to be strictly sequential. The execution of tasks within a phase may be guided by several control regimes, including conditional execution (if ... then), case analysis (case... end-case), loops (loop... until), parallel execution (parallel... end-parallel), and jumps (go-to). Moreover, in order to make the organization of the life cycle more transparent and explicit, phases are grouped into *macro-phases*, and tasks are grouped into *steps*. Macro-phases outline the high-level organization of the life cycle, while steps bring together set of tasks which share a common goal and, therefore, represent a unitary effort in the execution of a phase.

Our concept of KBS life cycle, called *KLIC (KBS Life Cycle)* is organized in three macro-phases and six phases as shown in Figure 2.1. Each phase is defined in terms of tasks and steps, as illustrated in chapters 3, 4, 5, 6, 7, and 8.

The definition of the KLIC life cycle is the result of extensive professional experience and of critical analysis of various alternatives reported in the literature. It makes the phases well-defined and independent while maximizing their internal strength [Parnas 72], [Yourdon and Constantine 75].

2.2.2   Phases outline

In this section we briefly outline the phases of KLIC. A more detailed illustration is presented in the subsequent chapters 3, 4, 5, 6, 7, and 8.

Phase 0: Opportunity analysis

Before starting any specific KBS project in a given organization, it is generally appropriate to develop a broad-spectrum investigation to locate, evaluate, and rank opportunities for KBS applications in the organization. This is the subject of *opportunity analysis*. More specifically, this phase identifies within a given organization (company, institution, government department, etc.) the application areas which could benefit from the development of KBS projects, and ranks them according to their strategic value, tactic importance, expected benefits, technical complexity, suitability and readiness for KBS application, involved risk, logical and temporal precedences, etc. This phase does not strictly belong to the life cycle of a specific KBS, but it constitutes a sort of background study which precedes the development of several specific KBS projects.

The product of opportunity analysis is a document called *opportunity analysis report*, which includes the master plan, a coarse-grained plan used as a long-term reference to guide an organization in the most appropriate application and exploitation of knowledge-based technology. When a specific KBS project is then initiated, the master plan can suggest the most appropriate application area to focus on, thus providing a useful input to phase 1. The results of opportunity analysis are reported to top managers.

Opportunity analysis is usually carried out by an independent consultant (or consulting company) in close cooperation with personnel and managers of the client organization. The duration of this phase may vary between 3 to 9 months (elapsed time) for organizations having medium dimensions and complexity (small and medium size companies, small government departments, etc.) and 10 to 15 months for organizations having large dimensions and high complexity (large companies, groups, large government departments, large institutions, etc.).

Opportunity analysis is not a mandatory phase of the life cycle, even if it is highly recommended, except for organizations of small dimensions and complexity.

Phase 1: Plausibility study

The *plausibility study* encompasses the following main goals:
- analyzing a given application domain - possibly suggested by the master plan, and identifying a specific problem to face;
- analyzing the requirements and defining the overall project goals;
- identifying the main functional, operational, and technical specifications of the KBS, and the acceptance criteria;
- developing a draft technical design, a draft organizational design, and a draft project plan;
- assessing the global plausibility of the KBS application.

The concept of plausibility includes five aspects, namely: technical feasibility, organizational impact, economic suitability, practical realizability, and opportunities and risks. A positive evaluation of plausibility requires that all such aspects receive a positive independent evaluation.

The product of the plausibility study is the *plausibility study report*. It is a technical document for the management which illustrates the activities done and the results obtained, it suggests choices and decisions about the KBS project, and it proposes a draft system design and a draft project plan.

A plausibility study is usually carried out by an independent consultant (or consulting company) in close cooperation with personnel and managers of the client organization. Less frequently, it is directly carried out internally by the most

experienced people available in the field of knowledge-based technology. The duration of this phase may largely vary:
• 1 to 2 months (elapsed time) for applications of low complexity (restricted domain, known solution approach, simple organizational aspects);

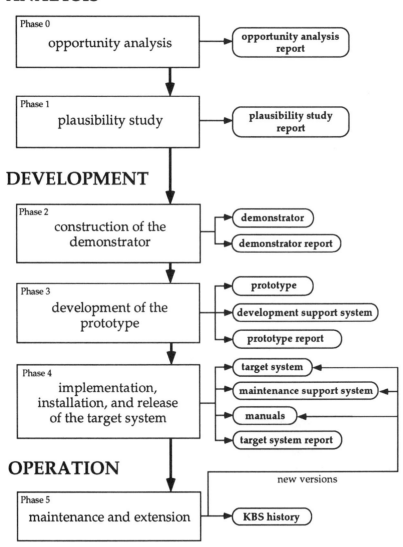

Figure 2.1 The KLIC life cycle: macro-phases, phases, and main products.

- 3 to 6 months for applications of medium complexity (large domain, known solution approach, difficult organizational aspects);
- 7 to 9 months for applications of high complexity (large and multifaceted domain, solution approach to be identified, difficult organizational aspects).

Plausibility study is a mandatory phase of the life cycle; no justification for its omission is acceptable.

Phase 2: Construction of the demonstrator

The main goal of the *construction of the demonstrator* is to develop and demonstrate a first, limited version of the KBS in order to meet one or more of the following issues:
- obtaining a concrete insight in the complexity of the problem considered, and validating, refining, and, if necessary, revising technical decisions outlined in the plausibility report;
- validating, refining, and, if necessary, revising the draft project plan developed in phase 1;
- collecting useful feedback from the users, and refining the identification of requirements and the definition of KBS specifications stated in phase 1;
- gaining involvement and commitment from the management or from the potential client;
- securing the interest and cooperation of experts and users, that will be crucial in later phases of the project.

The products of this phase are:
- a running KBS, called *demonstrator*, which anticipates the KBS performance on a limited part of the considered problem;
- the *demonstrator report*, which contains a synthesis of the activities carried out and a detailed illustration of the results achieved.

Note that, according to the goals actually considered, several types of demonstrators may be possible, including promotional, commercial, involvement, exploratory, experimentation, organizational, and planning.

The construction of the demonstrator is usually carried out by a project team internal to the user organization, or - less frequently - it is assigned to an external supplier. The duration of this phase is generally between two to six months (elapsed time), depending on the complexity of the application and the goals of the demonstrator. Due to the limited objectives of this phase, greater commitment is not encouraged.

Construction of the demonstrator, although common in several KBS projects, is not a mandatory phase of the life cycle. In fact, if the goals of a demonstrator are considered of little importance or already achieved at the beginning of the project, phase 2 may be skipped. It is one of the objectives of a plausibility study to suggest whether a demonstrator should be developed or not.

Phase 3: Development of the prototype

The *development of the prototype* is the main endeavor of a KBS project. Its main objective is to find the most suitable technical solutions for the application considered, and to implement these in a running system.

The products of this phase are:
- a full KBS, called *prototype*, which can adequately meet all functional specifications stated;
- an integrated set of software tools, called *development support system*, which supports the construction of the knowledge base of the prototype;
- the *prototype report*, which contains a synthesis of the activities carried out and a detailed illustration of the results achieved.

The prototype, although satisfying the functional specifications stated, is not the final output of the production process, since:
- it is not yet installed in the real operational environment, but it is running only in the development environment (if necessary, connections with the external world are simulated);
- it has only been tested with sample data prepared by the system designer with the support of experts and users;
- it is still embedded in the development environment and it is neither engineered nor optimized.

Let us point out that the prototype is generally a completely different system from the demonstrator. Only very seldom can the prototype be obtained from the demonstrator through appropriate extension and refinement. In fact, the objectives, the design principles, and the development tools used for the two systems are so different that an incremental development of the prototype from the demonstrator is generally neither appropriate nor convenient.

The development of the prototype is usually carried out by a project team internal to the user organization, or - less effectively - it is assigned to an external supplier. In the latter case, a close cooperation between the supplier and the user organization is needed. The duration of this phase may greatly vary between 6 to 24 months (elapsed time), depending on the complexity of the application.

Development of the prototype is, of course, a mandatory phase of the KBS life cycle.

Phase 4: Implementation, installation, and delivery of the target system

The goal of *implementation, installation, and delivery of the target system* is to develop a complete KBS. It must have the same behavior of the prototype, but in addition it must be:
- installed in the real operational environment;
- filed tested with real data;
- engineered and optimized;
- eventually delivered to the end-users for routine operation.

The products of this phase are:
- the *target system*, that is, the final output of the whole KBS production process;
- the *maintenance support system*, that is the specific system devoted to support effective and efficient maintenance;
- the complete set of manuals, including user, maintenance, and technical manuals, necessary for correct and effective system operation;
- the *target system report*, which contains a synthesis of the activities carried out and a detailed illustration of the results achieved.

Let us note, that the implementation of the target system may require very different approaches, depending on the requirements and constraints imposed by the operational environment, ranging from the automatic generation of the delivery version through specific support tools, to the incremental refinement and engineering of the prototype, to complete re-implementation - in the most unfortunate cases. Of course, each approach entails different production plans, costs, time, and technical features of the obtained target system.

Implementation, installation, and delivery of the target system may be carried out by a project team internal to the user organization or may be assigned to an external supplier. The duration of this phase may greatly vary between 4 to 24 months (elapsed time), depending on the approach taken for the implementation of the target system.

Implementation, installation, and delivery of the target system is a mandatory phase of the life cycle.

Phase 5: Maintenance and extension

Maintenance and extension starts after the delivery of the target system to the users for operational use and lasts for the entire life of the KBS. This phase is of primary importance to ensure a long and effective operational life of the KBS and to exploit all potential benefits of the project. It comprises the following main goals:
- monitoring the operational life of the KBS and collecting feedback, remarks, and requests from the users;
- correcting errors in KBS behavior (corrective interventions);
- updating the delivered KBS in order to meet the changes in the hardware and software environment in which KBS must operate (adaptive interventions);
- progressively updating the delivered KBS in order to meet the evolving or expanding needs of the users (perfective and evolutionary maintenance);
- periodically assessing the global state of the KBS and to planning its future development.

Maintenance only involves modifications to the knowledge base of the KBS, while extension requires changes to be made even to the fundamental structures of the empty system.

The products of this phase are:

- new versions of the knowledge base of the target system and updated manuals, concerning maintenance;
- new versions of the target system and of the maintenance support system, and updated manuals, concerning extension;
- the *KBS history*, which includes the collection of *operation reports* collected form the users, containing their feedback, remarks, and requests, and a record of all activities carried out during maintenance and extension.

Maintenance and extension are usually carried out by different project teams. The former is often assigned to a specific maintenance team, the latter is always carried out by a regular KBS project team (either internal to the user organization or provided by an external supplier). Maintenance and extension intervention are carried out when needed and appropriate. Each maintenance intervention usually does not require more than three to ten days (elapsed time). Extension, being much similar to a limited and focused KBS development project, may require one to eight months (elapsed time).

Maintenance and extension is a mandatory phase of the life cycle.

2.2.3   Variations on the reference life cyle

KLIC is intended to be a reference standard for KBS development and a general framework for methodology design. An extensive experimentation in a significant sample of KBS projects has shown that a large majority of concrete situations are covered. However, some deviations may be possible and appropriate in particular cases. Typical variations are mentioned below.

Postponing opportunity analysis
In several cases, the execution of phase 0 may be appropriately carried out not just as the first action of a KBS initiative, but after one or two KBS projects have been developed (see section 3.1.1). This may be useful to support awareness of the management and to give a more concrete basis to the opportunity analysis.

Replacing the plausibility study by the preliminary analysis
In projects of very limited dimensions and complexity - to be judged carefully by an experienced KBS project leader - or in some cases where there is insufficient commitment of the management for a full execution of phase 1, it may be appropriate to propose the development of a limited version of the plausibility study, called *preliminary analysis* (see section 4.1.1).

Replacing the demonstrator by the early prototype
For projects with strong management support, carried out by an experienced project team, and involving users already acquainted with the technology, phase 2 may be skipped. In this case, phase 3 may be appropriately organized so that, after a reasonably short period of time from the beginning (for example, 4-8 months), a preliminary running version of the prototype, called *early prototype,*

can be demonstrated to the management and the users to show the concrete progress of the project (see section 5.1.1).

Anticipating the construction of the demonstrator
For projects not particularly endorsed by the management, it may be appropriate to invert the execution of phases 1 and 2, developing a demonstrator first, to gain management involvement, and postponing the execution of the plausibility study (see section 5.1.1).

Staged development
For complex and long projects concerning the development of large KBS applications, it may be appropriate to organize phases 3 and 4 stage-wise. If the functional specifications of the KBS can be broken down into groups (for example: basic, full, and advanced specifications), incremental versions of the KBS can be defined (for example, version 1 concerning basic specifications, version 2 concerning basic and full specifications, and version 3 concerning basic, full, and advanced specifications). In this case, phases 3 and 4 can be divided into stages, each one producing a new version of the KBS (*staged development*). Thus, the prototype of version 1 is developed first and then the corresponding target system produced and released. Later the prototype and then the target system of versions 2 and 3 are developed. Staged development is appropriate in KBS projects of large dimensions (see sections 6.1.1 and 7.1.1).

Technology transfer projects
Projects with the main purpose of technology transfer in the field of knowledge-based technology (see section 11.1) can focus just on phases 3 and 4 (adopting, if possible, an incremental enhancement approach - see section 7.3.4). Note that discarding phase 4 and developing just phase 3, would not be appropriate for technology transfer. In fact, this can not be limited to the technical aspects of knowledge-based technology, but must consider as well its operative impact and its effective exploitation within an organization.

Research and development projects
Applied research or innovative experimentation projects usually focus only on phase 3 (see section 11.6).

Training projects
Training projects can focus on phases 1 and 3 only (see sections 11.5.2 and 11.5.3).

Note that, while the above listed variations on the reference life cycle may be appropriate in specific situations, arbitrary modifications without any plausible, technical justification cannot be accepted and should be considered as serious project management errors. For example, the elimination of phase 1 (in order to meet cost constraints) is always unjustified and, in most cases, it irremediably damages project results. Similarly, an attempt to merge phases 3 and 4, or, in other words, to skip phase 4 (in order to meet time constraints) may be harmful to the project and ruin the correct and effective delivery of the KBS.

2.3   KNOWLEDGE-BASED SYSTEM METHODOLOGIES

2.3.1   Methodology organization

Taking into account the objectives and requirements stated in section 2.1, a concept of *KBS methodology* is proposed. It extends and completes the definition of life cycle introduced in section 2.2.1. This is done in three steps [Wasserman et al. 83]:
- first the tasks of the life cycle are decomposed into a limited number of *activities* which provide a detailed and concrete definition of what to do, specifying the elementary actions of the design, production, maintenance, and extension processes;
- later, appropriate *technical methods* are defined which:
  - support the execution of the primary processes, stating how activities should be actually carried out in a technically sound, effective, and disciplined way;
  - provide the necessary technical indications for the execution of the supporting processes;
- finally, *management methods* are provided which support the execution of the management processes.

The reason why it is useful to organize methods in the two classes defined above is that they depend on different facts, namely: management methods mainly depend on standards and procedures typical of the organization for which the methodology is developed, while technical methods primarily depend on the specific features of knowledge-based technology.

Note that, as already mentioned in section 1.2.1, the identification of activities and the design of methods imply making technical and organizational choices, which contribute to the development of a specific and concrete methodology.

Finally, let us stress that the correspondence between life-cycle activities and supporting processes on one hand and technical methods on the other is not always necessarily supposed to be one-to-one. In a fully developed and rich methodology it can be one-to-many, while in partial, still developing methodologies some activities may not yet have any related method.

Figure 2.2 summarizes the concepts of KLIC life cycle and methodology.

2.3.2   Launching and managing a methodological project

The design of a KBS methodology is a long, complex, and costly process. The development of a complete KBS methodology may involve hundreds of methods. may last several years, and may require a substantial project team.

Moreover, the design of a KBS methodology may often go along with the development of a proprietary KBS development tool, as illustrated in section 6.4.4.

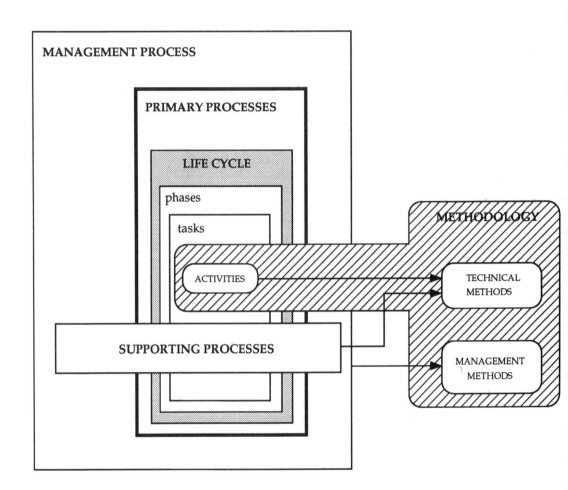

Figure 2.2 KLIC life cycle and methodology.

Therefore, the design of a methodology, called here a methodological project, cannot be initiated without precise motivations and objectives, and without appropriate management. A guide to determine whether a methodological project is appropriate and how it can be managed to success follows.

First of all, before starting a methodological project it may be appropriate to give some attention to the analysis and evaluation of existing methodologies. This task is not easy since methodologies are generally not of public domain. However, it can be very useful to gain a concrete and practical insight into problems and solutions, thus providing a useful background of ideas for the following activities. To this purpose, a descriptive framework to support an effective and structured analysis and evaluation of KBS methodologies is needed. A proposal, derived from [Hilal and Soltan 91], is shown in Figure 2.3.

A suggested work-plan for the preparation and start-up of a methodological project is shown in Figure 2.4. It is organized in three stages, as illustrated in detail below.

The first stage includes three steps, and is directed towards verifying whether all the preconditions for launching a methodological project are met. First of all, let us note that launching a methodological project cannot be one of the initial steps of the acquisition of knowledge-based technology (see chapter 10 for a detailed account on technology transfer). The *basic prerequisite* for a methodological project is a rich and long experience in the design, development, and maintenance of real, concrete KBS applications (step 1). Without such a solid and practical background people in a KBS department cannot be fully aware of the needs of a methodology and can hardly appreciate its potential benefits. So, without this prerequisite a methodological project should not be initiated.

If the basic prerequisite mentioned above is satisfied, a specific analysis of the current state of the KBS department should be carried out in order to verify whether there are *specific indications* for a methodological project or not (step 2). This analysis can be developed by taking into account the following two paradigmatic situations.

Problems with time, cost, and quality

The manager of the KBS department, the company management, the customers, or the users are not fully satisfied with time, cost, and quality of the delivered KBSs. In this case, a check-up of the KBS department by an independent consultant (or consulting company) is appropriate. Quite often, a precise diagnosis of the situation is possible, the causes of the observed symptoms are identified, and appropriate actions can be taken. If such actions are successful, there is no evidence that a methodological project should be initiated. Otherwise, if a precise diagnosis cannot be formulated or the faults identified cannot be fixed, there is generally evidence that a methodological project could be appropriate.

Issues of growth

Even if the company management, the customers, and the users are quite satisfied with time, cost, and quality of the delivered KBSs, the manager of the KBS department realizes that his team does not work at its highest possible level, both from a quantitative and qualitative point of view. Productivity could be increased, development time and cost could be reduced, personnel turn-over could be limited, technical skills could be extended, the quality of delivered KBSs could be improved, more challenging applications could be faced. In other words, the manager of the KBS department is fully aware that the work and the products of his team can be improved. However, he cannot articulate how the improvements can be effected. In this case, there are sufficient indications for launching a methodological project.

origin

In which environment was the methodology developed? With which objectives? When?

coverage

Which is the intended coverage of the methodology? Does it cover the whole life cycle or does it focus on specific issues only (conceptual design, knowledge modeling, knowledge acquisition, quality assurance, validation and verification, etc.)? Does it support some specific point of view (project management, documentation, technical activities, etc.)?

generality

Is the methodology oriented towards specific domains or problems? Is it limited to specific classes of KBSs (on-line, off-line, support systems, prescriptive systems, autonomous systems, real-time systems, etc.)? Is it constrained by particular background choices (knowledge representation techniques, reasoning methods, development tools, etc.)?

background approach

On which approach is the methodology based (rapid prototyping, incremental prototyping, evolutionary prototyping, structured development, etc.)

structure

How is the methodology structured? Which are the main components and the organization of the reference life cycle adopted?

presentation

How is the methodology presented (manuals, graphical models, computer-based tools, etc.)?

development stage

Which is the present stage of development of the methodology? Is it completed? Was it practically tested? Was it delivered to the users?

feedback

Was the methodology used in practice? What reactions did the users have? Was it accepted? Was it used successfully? Which are the main benefits reported? Was it rejected? Did it reveal to be useless? Which are the main problems reported?

Figure 2.3 Descriptive framework for the analysis and evaluation of KBS methodologies.

VERIFICATION OF PRECONDITIONS
1. verification of basic prerequisite
2. identification of specific indications for a methodological project
3. analysis of motivations

PREPARATION
4. definition of specific requirements for the KBS development methodology
5. development of a project plan
6. cost/benefit analysis
7. preparation of a formal project proposal
8. presentation to the management and revision of the project plan

START-UP
9. final approval and project start

Figure 2.4 Main steps of the preparation and start-up of a methodological project.

At this point, if there is evidence for starting a methodological project, a specific analysis of *motivations* is needed. Usually, several motivations can be informally listed, however, practical experience shows that most of such motivations do not constitute a good reason for initiating a methodological project. Our proposal for a simple and effective analysis of motivations (step 3) is to proceed in two stages:
1. First, compile a list of motivations in a spontaneous, unbiased, and extensive way.
2. Then, cross out from the list any motivation which refers to needs which could be satisfied through some specific action not necessarily implying a methodological project. If not all motivations are eliminated, then the methodological project can be considered as definitely appropriate, otherwise it should not be started. A sample list of relevant motivations, useful for a preliminary analysis, is reported below:
   - KBS development and delivery is generally too long;
   - technical personnel is so strictly bound to the project it is assigned to, that it becomes a necessary, irreplaceable component of the project team: in other words, mobility of technical personnel among project teams in the KBS department is scarce;

- inserting newly hired technical people in the project teams is time-consuming and ineffective;
- personnel turn-over is a critical aspect of the KBS department;
- the quality of released KBSs is highly variable, depending on the specific capabilities and skills of the team in charge of the project;
- each KBS project is a new challenge: re-use of previously developed KBS components is not easy and in any case very infrequent.

Of course, all items listed above may be strong or weak points, depending on the context; therefore, a careful, specific analysis is necessary.

If the verification of preconditions is concluded positively, then the preparation of the methodological project can be started. This stage includes four steps. First, specific *requirements* have to be identified for the methodology (step 4). This task is especially critical and should be carried out with the highest attention. Requirement definition should be accurate, detailed, correct, and complete. This step determines to a large extent the adequacy and benefits of the methodology for the KBS department. A superficial or incomplete requirement definition can seriously damage the whole endeavor. Definition of requirements should focus on three aspects, namely:

- scope of the methodology: type of projects usually carried out in the KBS department, type of application areas and domains considered, type of clients or users, etc.;
- basic technical choices concerning basic development environments, specific tools or techniques to be adopted, etc.
- basic organizational choices concerning company standards, accepted management practices, current organization of the KBS department, etc.

Later, a project plan is developed (step 5). This should include the definition of:
- main activities and time schedule;
- deliverable documents and due dates;
- human resources required for the whole project and for each specific activity in particular;
- other resources required for the project: hardware, software, documentation, etc.

The above points deserve some comments. First of all, let us stress that since the global effort needed to design and construct a full methodology may be very long (several years), it is of primary importance that partial results be deliverable and usable in a short time. In fact, it is often not appropriate to develop a complete methodology, where (i) all tasks are decomposed into activities, (ii) for any activity at least one technical method is provided, and (iii) management methods are defined for all phases, tasks and activities. This is generally extremely time-consuming and costly, and the return of investment may turn out to be too slow. In general, it is better to analyze the real deficiencies and needs of a KBS department in detail, to identify the main critical points, and to focus on the bottlenecks only, postponing the possible treatment of the less critical aspects to later phases of the project. This strategy can ensure high benefits in a short time.

Therefore, after defining a reference life cycle (phases and tasks) and the overall structure of the methodology, the project can develop incrementally focusing on one task (or on a small set of interrelated tasks) at a time according to the priorities established, such as, for example: "most needed first" or "highest return first". Each task is decomposed into activities, and the relevant technical and management methods are then developed. This type of incremental development through progressive design and integration of methodological islands relevant to a single task ensures the possibly best compromise between the immediate use of partial results and the effective and balanced global growth of the methodology. Figure 2.5 illustrates the above practice, which could be assumed as a guideline for planning a methodological project.

BASIC DEFINITIONS
    define a reference life cycle
    define the general structure of the methodology

INCREMENTAL DEVELOPMENT
LOOP
    identify a set of priority tasks (one task or a small set of interrelated ones)
    LOOP FOR EACH task IN set of priority tasks
        decompose the task into a set of activities
        LOOP FOR EACH activity IN set of activities
            design appropriate technical methods (one or more)
        END-LOOP
    END-LOOP

    release methods for experimental use
    collect user feedback
    revise methods
    release methods for routine use

    IF   management methods are needed
    THEN   design the needed management methods

UNTIL   all the necessary components of the methodology
         are fully developed

Figure 2.5 Guideline for planning a methodological project.

After a project plan has been developed, a *cost/benefit analysis* is appropriate (step 6). This should include:

- the estimate of project costs - divided into appropriate categories - and of their distribution over time for the whole duration of the project;
- the identification of the benefits - both direct and indirect - which are expected from the application of the methodology, with particular attention to their distribution over time according to the incremental release of partial results scheduled in the project plan;
- the estimate of the value of the expected benefits.

Later, a *formal project proposal* is prepared, which summarizes the activities carried out so far and presents the results achieved (step 7). The methodological project is then presented to the management, and, according to the feedback received, the project plan may be eventually revised (step 8).

In the last stage, the projct receives the final approval, and then it is started (step 9).

Let us point out that a methodology cannot be assigned to an external supplier. Each organization should design and construct its own methodology internally, importing, however, from outside possibly available components, such as the life-cycle concept, the definition of phases and tasks, specific technical methods, etc. These can then be used as such or tailored to the specific individual needs.

We also stress that for a methodological project the best available technical personnel should be employed. This, however, is not always possible since a methodological project generally runs in parallel to several other specific KBS projects which must also be well-staffed. A satisfactory solution is to organize a project team which includes:

- one or two persons allocated to the methodological project full-time for its entire duration, with the background of a knowledge engineer, if possible;
- other technical staff who, although assigned to specific KBS projects, are available to contribute to the methodological project on a part-time basis.

Clearly, in different steps of the project, different people may be involved, according to the specific needs of the project and to the competence and experience of the technical people available. In most cases the team can be supplemented with an external consultant, who can bring its own experience in similar projects, contribute to the most critical technical choices, support the overall project management, and carry out appropriate project reviews. This type of organization turns out to be very convenient from several perspectives:

- it allows accumulation of many, diverse experiences and competencies;
- it allows the involvement of a larger number of people in the KBS department;
- it supports a faster distribution and a higher acceptability of the results of the methodological project in the various project teams;
- it guarantees a correct and effective management of the whole effort and a high technical quality of the results.

Finally, we stress that a suitable computer-based environment for managing texts, graphics, and documentation is a useful tool for supporting an effective development of a methodology.

In the following sections we will explore in more detail two key issues in the construction of a KBS methodology, namely identification of activities and design of methods.

2.3.3   Identifying activities and designing methods

In the design and construction of a methodology the identification of activities is a key point. In fact, their role is that of providing a bridge between life-cycle tasks and technical methods, i.e. connecting together the two main components of the methodology. Their identification is, therefore, constrained on one hand by the structure of the life cycle, and on the other, by the technical methods, which still have to be designed at the time the activities are identified.

Since activities actually foresee technical methods, activity identification and method design are not independent. When defining activities, we must have at least an initial idea of which technical methods we are going to design and what they are expected to accomplish.

Activity identification can be guided by the following criteria:
- the decomposition of tasks into activities should not aim at the finest possible refinement: the best activity identification is not necessarily the finest-grained;
- technical methods should generally not cover a whole task, thus, making the identification of activities useless;
- the set of activities identified for a given task should be, if possible, of a uniform grain-size.

Method design is based on very different approaches, depending on which methods are considered. The design of technical methods is generally a rather complex and demanding task. It can be based on the following criteria (to be used in the suggested order), intended to minimize the effort needed and to guarantee the best possible match between the technical methods being designed, on one hand, and the specific requirements of the methodology and peculiarities of the considered KBS department, on the other:
1.   identifying, formalizing, generalizing, and completing technical methods already used within the KBS department, even if not often stated in a formal way and not exploited in their full generality;
2.   importing available technical methods from outside (literature, experience with other methodological projects, etc.), and revising and tailoring them according to the specific requirements of the methodology being constructed;
3.   deriving technical methods from literature proposals, through appropriate investigation, tailoring, formalization, and experimental testing;
4.   designing new and original technical methods only if strictly necessary and feasible with a reasonable effort.

In designing technical methods, priority should be given to the following classes of methods, which generally correspond to critical points in the development of a KBS:
- knowledge analysis and modeling;
- conceptual design;
- logical design;
- selection of the basic development environment;
- knowledge elicitation and protocol analysis;
- KBS maintenance;
- quality assurance;
- verification and validation;
- documentation development.

The design of management methods is generally simple, however long and boring. It can be based on the following two principles:
- first of all, importing - and, if necessary, tailoring - those management methods which are mostly independent of knowledge-based technology; these are often imposed as a standard by the target organization, and may concern, for example, project planning and control, financial planning, accounting, and management report;
- later, designing the remaining methods which are more closely related to knowledge-based technology, deriving them as far as possible from existing methods for related fields of the target organization, such as software development, data bases, and information systems.

Note that, in the rather exceptional case where the target organization has not a set of established management methods, the design of such methods should be very limited and anyway confined to the methods which are specifically related to KBS development. The design of an organization-wide set of management methods is far beyond the scope and objective of a methodological project in the KBS field.

In designing management methods, priority should be given to the following classes of methods, which may be more concretely affected by knowledge-based technology:
- project team organization and management;
- personnel selection;
- personnel evaluation, continuing education, and career management;
- productivity evaluation;
- project planning;
- project control and review;
- management of contracts with external suppliers and consultants.

PART II

THE PRIMARY PROCESSES: ANALYSIS

3

OPPORTUNITY ANALYSIS

3.1   PHASE OVERVIEW

3.1.1   Motivations and objectives

The purpose of the 'opportunity analysis' phase is to define a strategic, long-term plan for the correct and effective introduction of knowledge-based technology into an organization. Therefore, opportunity analysis does not strictly belong to the life cycle of a specific KBS application, but it constitutes a broad-spectrum background study for the development of several KBS projects.

Several motivations make this phase useful in a variety of situations, and necessary in the most complex cases. First of all, let us stress that when an organization undertakes a KBS initiative, it is very important to choose and manage the first project very carefully. In fact, the global evaluation of the technology and the assessment of its potential impact on applications will largely depend on the success - or failure - of the first steps which, therefore, represent a very special challenge. If the first project fails, there will most often be no second chance; the technology will be totally rejected. Therefore, a possible fault in a single project can entail the definitive loss of a great opportunity for the whole organization.

Moreover, if the first project is successfully concluded and the continuation of the KBS initiative is decided, it is obviously necessary to figure out how to proceed. Sometimes, the group promoting the first project is not able to propose a second meaningful step, and thus the KBS initiative comes to a dead-end. In other cases, the success of the first project stimulates a number of new projects, which may, however, cause overheads which a growing project team is not yet ready to handle, thus causing problems that can turn out to be detrimental.

Finally, let us mention that without a long-term reference plan it is difficult to assess the progress of a KBS initiative, which indeed is a vital step for a correct and effective management.

The potentially critical situations outlined above could have b n avoided if a broad-spectrum, company-wide plan would have been defined bei ie the start of any specific KBS initiative. Such a plan would have suggested the first project, provided criteria for choosing the subsequent ones, given a precise direction to the whole application development effort, supported a disciplined exploitation and growth of the project team, offered a precise reference for evaluation. The construction of this type of broad-spectrum, company-wide plan is the main purpose of opportunity analysis [Harmon and Sawyer 90].

The goals of the 'opportunity analysis' phase are:
- identifying opportunities for using knowledge-based technology within an organization, i.e. potential KBS applications which are considered technically appropriate and useful for the organization;
- characterizing opportunities in terms of their technical appropriateness and usefulness for the organization and verifying that the applications considered are appropriate for knowledge-based technology;
- ranking opportunities on the basis of their intrinsic characteristics and on the objectives the organization has in starting a KBS initiative;
- defining an organization-wide master plan, to guide, in the long-term, the global effort devoted to introducing knowledge-based technology and to exploit its potential benefits in the most appropriate and profitable way.

Opportunity analysis is not a mandatory phase of the life cycle. It is, however, strongly recommended for nearly all organizations of medium-large size and medium-high complexity. For small-size and low-complexity organizations, it is generally difficult to motivate the real need for a full opportunity analysis. Moreover, it is inappropriate to propose, or even encourage, an opportunity analysis in such cases where the prerequisites cannot be fully satisfied. The effort would either fail to produce the expected results, or turn out to produce a valid result that would not be appropriately understood and utilized.

Let us note that in several cases opportunity analysis may be appropriately carried out not just as the first action of a KBS initiative, but after one or two KBS projects have been developed. This may be useful to support awareness of the management and to give a more concrete basis to a study that, otherwise, could appear to be very abstract and academic.

3.1.2   Inputs and products

Like any initiative concerning strategic planning, the opportunity analysis is usually requested by the top management of an organization. The 'opportunity analysis' phase takes in input a document called *management indications*, which includes requirements, objectives, and constraints provided by the management, to be taken into account in the execution of the analysis.

The product of the 'opportunity analysis' phase is the *opportunity analysis report*, which contains a synthesis of the activities carried out, and a detailed illustration of the results achieved. In particular, it includes the *master plan*, an action plan which serves as a reference document to guide the application of knowledge-based technology throughout the organization in the long-term.

Finally, the 'opportunity analysis' phase may produce a specific *management report* in the case the prerequisites for its execution are not satisfied and the phase is stopped (see task 0.1). The products of the opportunity analysis are directed to the top management. They will also constitute an important input of phase 1.

3.1.3   Phase structure and task outline

Figure 3.1 presents an outline of the KLIC tasks of the 'opportunity' analysis phase.

START-UP		
	0.1	verification of prerequisites
IF		prerequisites are not satisfied
THEN	0.2	writing of management report
		stop phase
	0.3	planning of opportunity analysis
ANALYSIS OF THE EXISTING ORGANIZATION		
	0.4	analysis of objectives
	0.5	process and structure analysis
PARALLEL		
	0.6	analysis of the level of automation
	0.7	identification of areas and domains
END-PARALLEL		
ANALYSIS OF OPPORTUNITIES		
	0.8	characterization of domains
	0.9	identification of knowledge problems and definition of potential KBS applications
	0.10	definition and characterization of opportunities
SYNTHESIS AND RELEASE		
	0.11	construction of the master plan
	0.12	writing of draft opportunity analysis report
	0.13	presentation and acceptance of results
IF		revision is needed
THEN	0.14	revision of opportunity analysis
	0.15	writing of final opportunity analysis report

Figure 3.1 Opportunity analysis: KLIC tasks outline.

Here, steps are represented in upper-case letters, while tasks are lower-case and numbered. Tasks are supposed to be executed sequentially, unless otherwise specified through appropriate control commands: IF ... THEN, CASE ... END-CASE, LOOP ... UNTIL, PARALLEL ... END-PARALLEL, GO TO.

The overall logical structure of the 'opportunity analysis' phase is organized into four steps:

• the 'start-up' step verifies that the prerequisites are satisfied and plans the whole phase;

• the 'analysis of the existing organization' step goes through four tasks, namely: the analysis of the objectives of the KBS initiative, the process and structure analysis of the organization, the analysis of the current level of automation, and the identification of areas and domains; this provides the necessary background for the following steps;

• the 'analysis of opportunities' identifies opportunities for KBS application within the organization; this is the most important step of opportunity analysis and includes three specific tasks: characterization of domains, identification of knowledge problems and definition of potential KBS applications, and definition and characterization of opportunities;

• finally, in the 'synthesis and release' step the opportunities identified are appropriately ranked, and the master plan is constructed; the results of opportunity analysis are then presented to the top management for acceptance; if necessary, the work done is revised and eventually the final opportunity analysis report is prepared and delivered.

As shown in Figure 3.1, some tasks in the 'analysis of the existing organization step' may be executed in parallel.

As we have already mentioned in section 2.1.3, the time it takes for the 'opportunity analysis' phase may vary between three to nine months (elapsed time) for organizations with medium dimensions and complexity (small and medium size companies, small government departments, etc.) and between 10 to 15 months for organizations with large dimensions and high complexity (large companies, groups, large government departments, large institutions, etc.).

It may be useful to split the complete duration of the entire phase into the individual duration of its component tasks. The table of Figure 3.2 shows in percentages the duration of each task with respect to the duration of the whole phase. The data reported are, of course, only indicative; they refer to an average situation, and may vary from case to case. Percentages shown in parentheses refer to tasks which are carried out only subject to specific conditions, and, therefore, count over 100.

3.1.4   Project team composition

The opportunity analysis is usually carried out by an independent consultant (or consulting firm) in close cooperation with personnel and managers of the client organization.

TASKS	time %
START-UP	
0.1 verification of prerequisites	2
0.2 writing of management report	(5)
0.3 planning of opportunity analysis	5
ANALYSIS OF THE EXISTING ORGANIZATION	
0.4 analysis of objectives	8
0.5 process and structure analysis	25
0.6 analysis of the level of automation	5
0.7 identification of areas and domains	5
ANALYSIS OF OPPORTUNITIES	
0.8 characterization of domains	5
0.9 identification of knowledge problems and definition of potential knowledge-based system applications	5
0.10 definition and characterization of opportunities	10
SYNTHESIS AND RELEASE	
0.11 construction of the master plan	10
0.12 writing of draft opportunity analysis report	5
0.13 presentation and acceptance of results	5
0.14 revision of opportunity analysis	(20)
0.15 writing of final opportunity analysis report	10

Figure 3.2 Opportunity analysis: task duration in percentage.

In particular, for the opportunity analysis the project team is typically made up of:

- 1 project manager, usually a senior manager, in charge of formally representing the target organization from the contractual and administrative point of view;
- 1 project leader, usually a senior professional, responsible for the results of the opportunity analysis and in charge of the technical and organizational management of the project team;
- 1 to 3 knowledge engineers, at least one of them being in a senior position, in charge of the execution of most of the tasks of opportunity analysis;
- 0 to 1 system analysts, in charge of supporting or substituting the knowledge engineers for some specific tasks not strictly bound to knowledge-based technology (task 0.5, 0.6, and 0.7);
- 2 to 3 representatives of the top management;

- intermediate managers of all departments involved in opportunity analysis;
- domain experts of all departments involved in opportunity analysis;
- representatives of the potential users of KBS applications.

In particularly complex and large cases an advisor can be consulted to support the project leader in the most important technical decisions and in the most critical steps of project management.

The table shown in Figure 3.3 summarizes the composition of the project team for opportunity analysis.

	REGULAR MEMBERS	SUPPORTING MEMBERS	CONSULTING MEMBERS
project manager		1	
project leader	1		
knowledge engineers	1-3		
system analysts	0-1		
top managers		2-3	
intermediate managers		as appropriate	
domain experts		as appropriate	
potential users		as appropriate	
advisor			if needed

Figure 3.3 Opportunity analysis: project team composition.

As it can be noted, the composition of the project team is nearly the same in all possible situations. In complex and large cases the only possibility to speed-up the execution of the phase is to employ two or three knowledge engineers, rather than just one. This implies that complex cases will usually take much more time (elapsed time) than simple ones.

Note that non-trivial problems in complex cases may arise when all the intermediate managers from the different departments involved in the opportunity analysis participate in the project team. In fact:

- intermediate managers are often very numerous; working with all of them individually may cause problems of time;
- intermediate managers are usually very busy; scheduling meetings may be difficult;
- it is often difficult - and sometimes inopportune - to bring intermediate managers together;
- several meetings with the same persons at different stages of opportunity analysis may be necessary for the purpose of familiarization, knowledge acquisition, examination of important issues, verification, etc.;
- intermediate managers may be requested to read and analyze documents prepared by the project team between meetings.

Finally, let us stress that top management must be involved as little as possible. Too many meetings may cause a loss of interest or an exaggerated involvement in the activities of the project team. Moreover, it is the specific duty of the project leader to keep contacts with the top management.

3.2   START-UP

3.2.1   Step execution

Figure 3.4 presents a detailed view of KLIC tasks and products of the 'start-up' step.

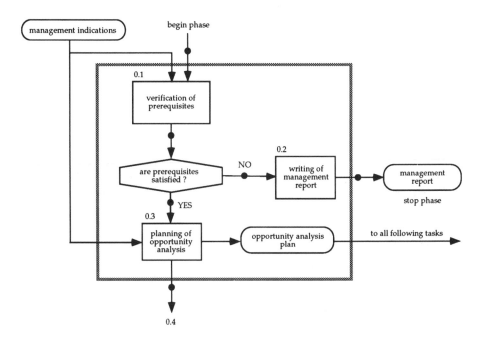

Figure 3.4 Star-up: KLIC tasks and products.

Here - and in all similar figures illustrating KLIC steps - tasks are represented by rectangular boxes, and task products by rounded ones (more precisely, documents are denoted by normal rounded boxes and software systems by bold rounded boxes). Arrows that directly connect a pair of tasks represent transfer of control. Arrows that connect a task to a product or a product to a task may represent either transfer of information (documents and software systems) or transfer of both information and control. In order to avoid possible ambiguities, control flow is explicitly represented by marking the relevant arrows with a dot.

Conditions are represented by hexagonal boxes. Inputs to a step (documents and software systems) are represented by rounded boxes outside the step boundaries, and they explicitly indicate the tasks they come from. All products of a step are represented inside the step, while phase products are represented outside the step boundaries. Transfer of information or control between tasks belonging to different steps are indicated by arrows numbered according to the tasks they are directed to or they come form.

3.2.2   Task 0.1: Verification of prerequisites

Task 0.1 takes in input the management indications. Several prerequisites should be satisfied before starting an opportunity analysis. The most important and critical ones are listed below:
- the management should be familiarized with knowledge-based technology;
- the top management must be fully aware of the need, scope, and objectives of opportunity analysis;
- the top management should make a firm decision about execution of the opportunity analysis;
- the intermediate management should be available to cooperate with the project team in charge of opportunity analysis;
- the top management should authorize and support the project team in charge of opportunity analysis to explore any aspect of interest in the organization (strategic, management, organization, business, production, technical, etc.);
- the project team in charge of opportunity analysis must be free from any type of possible biases or constraints which could alter the results of the analysis in any way;
- the requirements, objectives, and constraints proposed by the management must be consistent with the purpose and nature of the opportunity analysis;
- the needed resources for the execution of the phase must be available.

Verifying prerequisites is an essential preliminary task of opportunity analysis. If prerequisites are not satisfied, the opportunity analysis should not continue. If such a case occurs, a report should be prepared for the top management (task 0.2) and the opportunity analysis should be stopped. Otherwise, the execution of the phase continues with task 0.3.

3.2.3   Task 0.2: Writing of management report

In the case where prerequisites are not satisfied, the project leader in charge of opportunity analysis should prepare a report for the management and stop the execution of the phase. The product of task 0.2 is a document called *management report*. It should explain in detail why an opportunity analysis is not convenient or even impossible to execute. It should be appropriately motivated and personally discussed by the project leader with the top management of the organization.

If appropriate actions are then undertaken to satisfy the prerequisites, the execution of the phase can continue.

3.2.4   Task 0.3: Planning of opportunity analysis

Task 0.3 takes in input the management indications. The product of task 0.3 is a document called *opportunity analysis plan*.

The opportunity analysis plan should be discussed with all members of the project team, who should be aware of their role and of their engagements. It should also be formally approved by the management of the end-user organization. Note that, as shown in Figure 3.4, the opportunity analysis plan is not an input to any specific step. It will be used by the project leader for management and control issues throughout the whole phase (see section 10.3.2).

The opportunity analysis plan should be refined when, during the development of phase 0, new information is made available for a more precise and realistic definition and scheduling of the activities to carry out. Actually, a revision of the plan is probably appropriate after task 0.7.

3.3   ANALYSIS OF THE EXISTING ORGANIZATION

3.3.1   Step execution

Figure 3.5 presents a detailed view of KLIC tasks and products of the 'analysis of the existing organization' step.

3.3.2   Task 0.4: Analysis of objectives

Generally, an organization may have a variety of reasons for starting an initiative in the field of knowledge-based technology. Only seldom is there a global and unitary view of the organization on such points; different people at different levels (top management, intermediate management, technical management, operative personnel, etc.) may have very different ideas about objectives. Objectives are seldom explicit and stated officially and are generally not fixed. They evolve over time and if no record of their expression is kept, changes can hardly be appreciated and taken into account.

The above illustrated situations may entail harmful consequences which can be easily imagined. First of all, without a clear identification of objectives, it is quite impossible to analyze opportunities for KBS applications, the concept of opportunity itself becoming meaningless. Without an overall unitary concept of objectives, anyone can assume that his own point of view is the one of the organization; this constitutes a dangerous background for the rise of false expectations that, later, can be misleading. Moreover, the lack of officially stated objectives implies that newly perceived objectives tend to supersede the initial ones, and later the results of a KBS initiative are incorrectly evaluated.

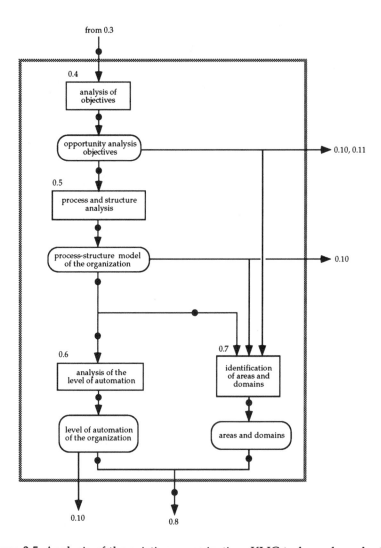

Figure 3.5 Analysis of the existing organization: KLIC tasks and products.

Therefore, it is of primary importance that the motivations and the goals which lead an organization start a KBS initiative be clearly analyzed and stated at the very beginning of opportunity analysis. This is the purpose of task 0.4.

A usual way to start-up this task is through a few meetings involving the project leader and top managers, representatives of the potential users of KBS applications, as well as intermediate managers. Figure 3.6 shows a realistic proposal for a meeting plan involving four phases and seven steps.

INITIAL MEETING WITH TOP MANAGERS

    1. initial definition of objectives

MEETINGS WITH REPRESENTATIVES OF POTENTIAL USERS OF KBS APPLICATIONS

    2. collection of the point of view of the users
    3. analysis of user expectations and requirements
    4. user feedback to the initial definition of objectives

MEETINGS WITH INTERMEDIATE MANAGERS

    5. refinement and merging of the various points of view
    6. formulation of a tentative statement of objectives

FINAL MEETING WITH TOP MANAGERS
    7. final definition of objectives and official statement

Figure 3.6 Analysis of objectives: a meeting plan.

Let us stress that it is of primary importance that the analysis and statement of objectives starts and ends at the level of top management. This task has a great strategic impact and should be highly supported by the organization.

The objectives an organization may have in starting a KBS initiative are always related to the achievement of some classes of benefits more or less specific. Therefore, the identification, analysis, and statement of objectives may be facilitated by considering a list of possible benefits that may derive from a KBS project. One such list is reported in section 4.6.7 (identification and assessment of benefits). This list is by no means complete, it may serve as a useful starting point for discussion in the initial meeting with top managers.

Note that the purpose of analyzing objectives is only to make opportunity analysis attuned to the global objectives of the organization as much as possible. Therefore, it is not important that objectives are characterized in great detail; a specification of the relevant time frame (for example: short-term, mid-term, long-term), and a ranking according to their importance for the organization (for example: low, medium, high, very high) are generally enough.

The product of task 0.4 is a document called *opportunity analysis objectives*, which contains a precise statement of the objectives of the organization in approaching knowledge-based technology.

Let us note that, even if the task of analyzing objectives has been placed at the very beginning of opportunity analysis, it is sometimes appropriate to resume and complete it after the steps devoted to the analysis of the existing organization has been completed (tasks 0.4, 0.5, and 0.6). In fact, analyzing objectives, although easy in principle, is often very critical in reality. Eliciting the true objectives of an organization is difficult. In fact objectives are often controversial, confused, vague, contradictory, or simply not explicitly stated until the analysis is started. So, after the project team has gained a deeper and more concrete insight into the structure of the organization a final check and possibly a revision of objectives definition may be useful, at least in the most complex cases.

3.3.3   Task 0.5: Process and structure analysis

The goal of this task is to develop an abstract, coarse-grained model of the organization that can serve as a reference schema for identifying, locating, and analyzing opportunities for KBS applications. In fact, opportunities can be defined and characterized only in relation to a specific organization; thus, before looking for opportunities, we must establish a precise context.

Let us recall that a *model* is a partial representation of reality, constructed to serve some purpose. It should include all those aspects which are considered relevant to the considered objectives, abstracting from all the rest. So the concept of the model cannot be fully independent of the subjective judgment of the person in charge of constructing it; the choice of what is relevant to the purpose and what is not, cannot be fully objective. Moroever, a good model should guarantee three basic properties:
- *correctness*, i.e. the model should provide a faithful representation of reality, allowing derivation of all the properties of interest of the system in question;
- *consistency*, i.e. the model should be free from logical conflicts;
- *completeness*, i.e. the model should include, at the selected level of detail, all the elements of interest, represented in the appropriate way.

A variety of techniques for modeling organizations has been proposed in the literature, each one characterized by different goals. For example, models for studying the economical aspects of a company, models for investigating the productivity of a manufacturing process, models for simulating the evolution of a process over time, models for supporting the analysis design of information systems, models for planning processes, etc.

To the purpose of task 0.5, we can assume a simplified definition of an *organization*, intended as a system devoted to the production of a set of products (both material and immaterial, i.e. goods and services) through the execution of specific processes, made possible by dedicated organizational structures (including production tools, human resources, etc.). According to this concept, the model of an organization can focus on the following points:
- the *processes* which characterize the activity of the organization;
- the *structures* which support the realization of the processes.

- the relationship between structures and processes, called the *support relation*, which defines which structures contribute to the realization of which processes.

We call this type of model a *process-structure model*. The construction of the process-structure model of an organization goes through the following three steps.

1. Construction of the process model

The *process model* of an organization describes the processes that characterize the activity of the organization. By the term *process* we mean a series of actions carried out to achieve a given goal. From an abstract point of view, a process can be defined through the following:
- the set of possible *inputs*;
- the set of possible *outputs*;
- the *function* which maps inputs into outputs, thus implementing the goal of the process;
- the *preconditions* that must be satisfied before the process can be actually executed;
- the *post-conditions* that will be satisfied after the process has been executed;
- the set of *resources* (for example, a device, a tool, an algorithm, etc.) exploited for the execution of the process.

Process analysis is carried out through iterative decomposition. Initially, the organization as a whole is considered to be dedicated to the execution of a unique global process. Later, this process is decomposed into sub-processes. Each sub-process fulfills a sub-part of the original process and the conjunction of all the sub-processes identified must completely replace the original process. Each one of the sub-processes thus obtained (called level-1 sub-processes) can then be further decomposed into finer grained sub-processes (level-2 sub-processes), and so forth, until the model obtained shows the desired level of detail. Of course, there is no general rule for stopping the decomposition. Depending on the nature of the organization and on the goals of the analysis, a finer or coarser process model may be appropriate. Attention should be paid, however, to keep the process model sufficiently abstract and coarse-grained, to avoid irrelevant details. In practice, in the opportunity analysis, two to three levels of decomposition are enough in most cases, and five levels can be considered as an upper bound.

Clearly, the result of this decomposition can be organized into a hierarchical representation. The sub-processes defined at a given level of the decomposition (the level-n processes) are generally not isolated but are connected through several types of *relationships* which may concern, for example, inputs and outputs, logical or temporal precedences, resources exploited, etc. In the construction of the process model, at least one of these relationships must be made explicit, namely the *input/output relation* which allows the inputs and outputs of the various sub-processes to be appropriately connected so that their interaction can truly reproduce the original inputs and outputs of the process from which they have been derived through decomposition.

Note that the process model of an organization is not unique. In fact, it depends on the goals considered, on the aspects of the organization focused in the modeling activity, and on the viewpoint taken. For example, the process model may concern the production processes, the logistic processes, the secondary processes, the decision-making processes, the management processes, etc. - or combinations thereof.

2. Construction of the structure model

The *structure model* of an organization describes the structures which constitute the body of the organization and are in charge of supporting the execution of the processes. It represents all the *structures* of the organization, from the top-level ones (chairman of the board, board of directors, etc.), down to the intermediate (departments, offices, etc.), and to the operative ones (plants, production lines, machines, working teams, etc.). The structure model concerns all kinds of systems which constitute the physical structure of an organization, including human resources, production tools, infrastructures, etc. It is obtained through top-down analysis and step-wise decomposition. It allows identification of the structures of an organization and of the *relationships* among them.

Similarly to the process model, the structure model of an organization is not unique. In fact, it depends on the goals considered, on the aspects of the organization focused in the modeling activity, and on the viewpoint taken. For example, the structure model may concern the functional structure, the responsibility structure, hierarchical structure, the physical structure, etc. - or combinations thereof.

3. Identification of the support relation between structures and processes

The *support relation* defines which structures contribute to the execution of which processes. Clearly, such a relation is generally many-to-many, since a single structure can support several processes, and one process may require more than one structure for its execution.

Note that generally the construction of the process model is a complex task which requires a specific analytical skill. Quite often processes are not easily identified; the more evident processes are not always the most important ones, and some crucial processes may be hidden in a first analysis. On the other hand, the construction of the structure model, is much easier; organizations usually have clear and well-defined structures, which can be simply recognized through careful analysis. Identifying the support relation is often not an easy task. In fact, it is generally not enough to analyze the formal assignments of the various structures, since these may actually support processes which do not coincide with those they were originally designed to perform. Specific attention should be paid that no process or structure remains isolated after the support relation has been fully identified. Note also that the identification of the support relation, in addition to the primary goal of completing the process-structure model, has also the important function of compelling the knowledge engineer to a critical verification of both the process and structure models for correctness, consistency, and completeness.

Experience has shown that for each individual case a different practical implementation of the abstract concept of process-structure model may be appropriate. For each specific case, the following key questions have to be considered and answered:

• Which is the most appropriate abstraction level for the process model?
• Which aspects of a process have to be considered and which ones omitted? (for example: temporal aspects, use of resources, human factors, etc.)
• Which is the correct level of detail of the process model and how much process decomposition must be iterated?
• Which language should be adopted for a clear and effective representation of process-structure model?
• How can an appropriate vocabulary of controlled terms about processes, structures, and the support relation be defined and maintained?

Note also that, since the modeling activity requires a deep interaction with the organization, any pre-existing background document should be carefully taken into account. For example, in some cases a draft structure model already exists in the organization outline, or parts of the process model have already been developed for some components of the organization for some specific purpose such as standardization of the operative procedures, automation projects, quality assurance, cost accounting, etc. In all such cases, pre-existing materials can offer a useful starting point for the new modeling activity. Of course, particular attention should be paid when distinguishing what should be inherited and what revised or definitely redefined.

Let us stress that the development of the process-structure model of an organization should be based - in any case - on a well-defined representation language, even if not formal. We do not propose any standard form for the process-structure model. In fact, as already discussed above, different formalisms may be appropriate for the different concepts of process-structure model suitable for different organizations. Quite often, the representation of the process-structure model is based on some graphic language, purposely designed for this task. This is often inspired to well-known modeling languages available in the literature; for example: HIPO [IBM 75], entity-relationships models [Chen 76], SADT (Structured Analysis Design Technique) [Dickover et al. 77], [Ross 77], [Ross and Schoman 77], PSL/PSA (Problem Statement Language / Problem Statement Analyzer) [Teichroew and Herschey 77], data flow diagrams [Yourdon and Constantine 75], [De Marco 79], [Gane and Sarson 79], Petri nets [Peterson 81], conceptual graphs [Sowa 84], flowcharts [Tripp 88], SSADM (Structured System

Analysis and Design Method) [Downs et al. 88], finite-state transition diagrams and state-charts [Harel 88].

Task 0.5 takes in input the opportunity analysis objectives (from task 0.4). The product of task 0.5 is a document called *process-structure model of the organization*, which illustrates the model designed and comments on its main features.

3.3.4   Task 0.6: Analysis of the level of automation

The purpose of this task is to enrich the process-structure model of an organization with information concerning the current level of automation. In particular, two aspects are analyzed:
- the processes supported by computer-based procedures;
- the computer installations used in the organization to implement the existing computer-based procedures.

This information will be of primary importance later in task 0.8, which focuses on the definition and characterization of opportunities.

It is important to stress that this task does not evaluate existing computer-based applications in order to possibly suggest revisions or improvements. Its purpose is much more limited; it just analyzes the two aspects relevant to the development of KBS applications mentioned above.

Task 0.6 takes in input the process-structure model of the organization (from task 0.5). The information needed to carry out this task can usually be gathered through a small number of interviews to electronic data processing (EDP), software engineering (SE), and management information system (MIS) department managers. Only seldom are interviews with the intermediate managers of the departments using computer-based procedures needed.

The information collected should concern the following main points:

Software applications
with identification, for each major application, of the following:
- process supported, with reference to the process model;
- name of the application, supplier, and main functional and technical data;
- computer system installation where the application is located;
- users, current frequency of use (regularly, rarely, not used), estimated frequency of use in the short/medium-term;
- links to other applications.

Data bases
with identification, for each major data base, of the following:
- process or structure supported, with reference to the process-structure model;
- name of the data base, type of data base management system, supplier, and main functional and technical data;
- computer system installation where the data base is located;

- current level of updating (regular, rare, not updated), expected modifications in the short/medium-term;
- links to other data bases;
- connected applications.

Computer system installations
with identification, for each major installation, of the following:
- name of the installation, type (mainframe, mini-computer, workstation, personal computer, etc.), supplier, and main functional and technical data
- installation site, with reference to the structure model
- network connections (if any)
- current level of maintenance (regular, rare, not maintained), expected modifications in the short/medium-term
- supported applications and data bases.

The product of task 0.6 is a document called *level of automation of the organization*, which presents in a structured and organic way the information mentioned above. This task is executed in parallel to task 0.7.

EDP, MIS, and SE department managers may sometimes be skeptical when confronted with the new knowledge-based technology. So, they are not always willing to cooperate with opportunity analysis or are not fully objective in their evaluations. This can cause major problems to the project team in charge of opportunity analysis. Such an uncooperative attitude is usually due to a natural skepticism in view of a new and poorly known technology. Managers who are used to dominating situations are faced with something they cannot master and which, they believe, could be detrimental to their personal power and position. In such cases, correct and early information for the management can greatly contribute to their cooperation, or at least reduce any hostility that might exist. In any case, even in the most critical cases, the project team in charge of opportunity analysis should never forget the objectives set, and should always try to reach them directly with the minimum possible disturbance for the working environment. Opportunity analysis, as stated in section 3.1.3, is requested by the top management, that is why the project team in charge of its execution should have the highest degree of authorization. The project leader and the knowledge engineers should also be authoritative professionals, accepted for their competence and experience, and trusted for their correctness and absolute independence of any possible external or internal influence.

3.3.5   The concepts of area and domain

The concepts of area and domain are a focal point of opportunity analysis (as well as of plausibility study, as discussed in sections 4.4.4 and 4.4.5).

An *application area*, or simply an *area*, within a given organization is a sub-part of the organization, including one or more structures, which has a specific role for the execution of a set of processes. For example, in a manufacturing company, examples of application areas are a mechanical assembly line, a design department, a quality control unit, a production planning department.

An *application domain*, or simply a *domain*, within a given organization is a set of strictly interrelated processes which pursue a common goal. For example, in the mechanical assembly line of a manufacturing company, examples of application domains are on-line diagnosis, job-shop scheduling, quality control, process supervision, preventive maintenance. A domain is characterized by a specific and well-identified set of knowledge, called the *knowledge set* of the domain, which constitutes the background on which the processes of the domain are based. Generally, the knowledge set of a domain is neither homogeneous nor unitary, and may include several, different *knowledge classes*. For example, the knowledge set relevant to on-line diagnosis of an assembly line might include the following knowledge classes:

- knowledge of the physical structure of the plant;
- knowledge of the basic physical and engineering principles on which plant behavior is based;
- knowledge of the function and purpose of the plant, as well as of it sub-system and components;
- a concept of fault and a concept of diagnosis; for example, given a set of fault symptoms identifying a (minimal) set of faults that can explain the symptoms observed (i.e., may be considered as their causes);
- causal knowledge connecting malfunction and fault symptoms to their causes;
- fault models, which can account for how a component or a sub-system behaves under given fault conditions;
- empirical knowledge of diagnostic experts, including associations between fault symptoms and possible faults that may be considered as acceptable diagnoses.

Often, domains are identified as sub-parts of a given application area. However, areas and domains are generally independent of each other, each being of an essentially different nature. The main distinction between areas and domains is the fact that the concept of area is static, being a part of the structure model of an organization, while that of domain is essentially dynamic, being a set of interrelated processes. Clearly, the appropriate grain-size of both the concepts of area and domain is not defined a priori, but depends on the specific nature of the organization and on the goals considered. In particularly complex cases, areas and domains of different grain-size may be identified and organized hierarchically.

The main reason for introducing the concepts of area and domain is that different instances of the same area or domain in different organizations usually share a large number of common features. So, these concepts turn out to be useful abstractions for analyzing an organization.

3.3.6   Task 0.7: Identification of areas and domains

The goal of this task is to identify areas and domains and, in particular, to define their boundaries. This task largely relies on subjective evaluation. There are no precise rules to decide how wide an area or a domain should be, which structures should be included in an area, what processes should be considered as belonging to a domain. Execution of this task is based on personal experience of the knowledge engineers and project leader in charge of it. Clearly, identification of areas and domains depends on the features of the specific organization at hand, such as the type of products supplied, the production technologies employed, the organizational principles adopted, etc.

Task 0.7 takes in input the opportunity analysis objectives (from task 0.4) and the process-structure model of the organization (from task 0.5). The product of task 0.7 is a document called *areas and domains*. It contains the following information:

- the list of the identified areas, each one described by (i) a name, (ii) the list of the structures of the organization it includes, and (iii) the involved processes;
- for each area, the list of all relevant domains, each one specified by (i) a name, and (ii) a short informal description of the main processes belonging to the domain.

This task is executed in parallel to task 0.6.

3.4   ANALYSIS OF OPPORTUNITIES

3.4.1   Step execution

Figure 3.7 presents a detailed view of KLIC tasks and products of the 'analysis of opportunities' step.

3.4.2   Task 0.8: Characterization of domains

After the analysis of the existing organization has been concluded, the domains identified are further analyzed focusing on the involved knowledge. Task 0.8 takes in input the level of automation of the organization (from task 0.6) and the areas and domains (from task 0.7).

Domain analysis is carried out in two stages. First of all, for each domain identified in the previous task, the relevant knowledge set is defined and the main knowledge classes are identified. Later, each domain is considered in turn again and carefully checked in order to determine whether it knowledge-intensive or not. A *knowledge-intensive domain* is an application domain such that:

1.   the knowledge set of the domain is extensive (i.e., it involves a large amount of knowledge) and possibly highly structured (i.e., it includes several interrelated knowledge classes);
2.   it involves a significant part of non-procedural knowledge, i.e. knowledge which cannot easily be organized in algorithmic, procedural-oriented form;
3.   it contains knowledge relevant to a large class of problems in the domain;
4.   domain problems generally do not feature explicitly stated solution algorithms, but their solution requires complex knowledge-processing activities, basically involving search, and the exploitation of both general problem-solving methods and specific heuristic strategies.

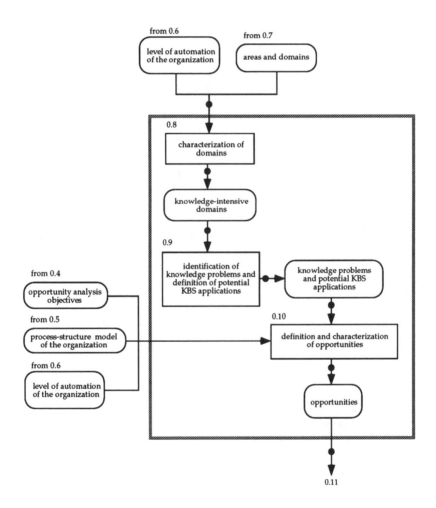

Figure 3.7 Analysis of opportunities: KLIC tasks and products.

Note that a domain is generally considered knowledge-intensive only if all four conditions mentioned are satisfied. However, if only some conditions are satisfied while others are not, it is always necessary to push the analysis further - for example with different domain experts - before reaching a negative conclusion. Moreover, there might be exceptions to this rule; for example, a small, but highly structured and heterogeneous knowledge set, or a mainly procedural, but very extensive knowledge set.

One key-point for an effective and efficient execution of this task is the identification of the right domain experts. The analysis needed to identify knowledge-intensive domains is usually not too detailed, so a single domain expert can often cover several domains. Sampling knowledge acquisition techniques may be used for performing this task (see section 6.5.2).

The product of task 0.8 is a document called *knowledge-intensive domains*. It is obtained from the areas and domains document produced in task 0.7, by discarding all the domains which turn out to be not knowledge-intensive and by completing the remaining ones with indication of the following:

- the relevant knowledge set, together with the main knowledge classes identified;
- a list of the reasons that make the domain knowledge-intensive.

3.4.3   Task 0.9: Identification of knowledge problems and definition of potential KBS applications

After knowledge-intensive domains have been identified and characterized, it is necessary (i) to check whether such domain encompasses unsolved problems that may be suitable for knowledge-based technology, and (ii) to define potential KBS applications appropriate to face the problems identified.

To this purpose, we first introduce the concept of knowledge problem. A *knowledge problem* is an information-processing problem which concerns the availability, the quality, or the processing of knowledge. Knowledge problems are generally appropriate for a knowledge-based solution. There are three main types of knowledge problems:

- problems in knowledge elicitation, organization, and storage, which impede disciplined and effective accumulation of knowledge (*knowledge loss*);
- problems in knowledge collection and distribution, which negatively affect the availability of knowledge in the appropriate places, at the right time, and in the most effective form (*knowledge bottleneck*);
- problems in knowledge use, which hinder the effective and efficient exploitation of available knowledge for specific problem-solving tasks (*knowledge waste*).

Here are some examples of the above defined knowledge problems:

- A common case of knowledge loss is the situation where a critical expert (for example, a senior designer, an experienced process operator, etc.) retires or resigns. His knowledge and know-how, poorly organized or dispersed in informal documents, is often a definitive loss for the organization.

- A typical and very frequent case of knowledge bottleneck is the situation where knowledge crucial to the success of an organization is possessed only by one or a few individuals [Freiling et al. 85]. Some critical steps of a process (for example, tuning of a continuous chemical process, maintenance of a complex device, proper intervention in case of accident, etc.) depend on human experts which are not available 24 hours a day or which cannot always intervene in the location where they are needed. Another case of knowledge bottleneck is the knowledge transfer needed to train newly hired people; quite often experienced personnel is unwilling to waste time on the job to teach and support novices, thus training becomes problematic and long. A case of knowledge bottleneck is also the very frequent situation where knowledge relevant to some specific task (for example, design of a device, operating procedures for critical situations, etc.) is virtually available in detailed and extensive manuals, but it is not effectively usable in practice.

- A typical example of knowledge waste is apparent in the case where a great extent of knowledge relevant to a specific application domain exists (for example, technology assessment from the industrial, economical, social, environmental, and political perspectives). This may cause practical difficulty in effectively exploiting all the available knowledge, thus often implying that part of it is lost.

Application domains that do not include (unsolved) knowledge problems are not of interest for our analysis. Task 0.9 initially looks for possible knowledge problems. Each identified knowledge problem is given a name, a type, according to the above classification, and a description in informal terms. Let us note that in a knowledge-intensive domain more than one knowledge problem may be present. It is very important that the analysis of a domain is carried out until every possible knowledge problem has been identified. In fact, the completeness of this part of the analysis is crucial for the correct and effective execution of the following tasks.

After knowledge problems have been identified, task 0.9 proceeds through the definition of *potential KBS applications*, that might be appropriate for solving the knowledge problems identified (clearly, each potential KBS application may deal with several knowledge problems in a domain). Potential KBS applications are characterized by a name, the set of knowledge problems addressed, and an informal specification of the main functions expected.

Task 0.9 takes in input the knowledge-intensive domains (from task 0.8). The product of task 0.9 is a document called *knowledge problems and potential KBS applications*. It is obtained by discarding from the knowledge-intensive domains document produced in task 0.8 those domains for which no knowledge problems have been identified, and then by completing the description of the remaining domains with the list of all relevant knowledge problems identified, each one specified through:

- a name;

- the type, according to the above classification;
- a brief informal description;

and with the list of the potential KBS applications defined, each one specified through:
- a name;
- the set of knowledge problems addressed;
- an informal specification of the main functions expected.

3.4.4   Task 0.10: Definition and characterization of opportunities

An *opportunity* is a potential KBS application in a given domain, for which concrete evidence exists of its appropriateness from the technical point of view and of its usefulness for the organization.

Task 0.10 takes in input the opportunity analysis objectives (from task 0.4), the process-structure model of the organization (from task 0.5), the level of automation of the organization (from task 0.6), and the knowledge problems and potential KBS applications (from task 0.9). It is devoted to further refine the analysis so far developed in order to evaluate whether any of the potential KBS applications previously defined constitute concrete opportunities.

This task is organized in two stages, namely an analytical assessment and a task-based analysis. These are illustrated below.

Analytical assessment

Initially, the technical appropriateness and the usefulness for the organization are assessed through the analysis of a limited set of characteristics which are supposed to represent the main aspects of interest for the evaluation. For example, the following characteristics might be considered [Wilkerson 85], [Freiling et al. 85], [Irgon et al. 90]:

technical appropriateness
- *availability of knowledge sources*: Are domain experts available? Are written documents available? Is naturalistic observation likely to be possible?
- *evidence for technology need*: Are the knowledge problems considered difficult to solve if other approaches, different from the construction of a KBS are used - for example, changing the existing organization, developing a new traditional software system, enhancing or rebuilding an existing computer-based system, purchasing a new vendor package, etc.?
- *technical complexity and risk*: Is the project expected to be complex from the technical point of view? Is the domain of a very large size? Are advanced knowledge-based techniques needed?

- *integration*: Are there systems (traditional software, KBSs, data acquisition systems, etc.) which should closely interact with the KBS or be integrated with it?
- *preconditions*: Are there problems that should be solved, or events that should occur, or systems that should be built in advance in order to allow the KBS to be developed and exploited correctly and effectively?
- *support*: Is the project likely to have an internal sponsor with sufficient power in the organization?

usefulness for the organization
- *strategic fit*: Does the KBS fit into the strategic plans of the organization? Is the KBS considered of interest by the top management?
- *necessity*: Is the KBS expected to solve existing and persistent knowledge problems, which are not only temporary or might find natural solutions due to external events?
- *subjective importance*: Are the knowledge problems that the KBS is expected to solve considered really important by the people who would benefit from their solution?
- *urgency*: What is the urgency in solving the knowledge problems that the KBS is expected to solve?
- *purpose*: Will the KBS enhance current operations by integrating with existing systems, such as management information systems, data base management systems, decision support systems, hypertext, multimedia and hypermedia, and virtual reality (*integration-type*)? Or will it constitute a completely new application (*innovation-type*)?
- *role*: Will the KBS replace human operators, performing in a nearly autonomous way in place of current methods or on tasks which cannot be done by current methods (*replacement-type*)? Or will it support and enhance human performance, assisting users in performing their jobs (*assistant-type*)?
- *expected benefits*: What benefits are expected from the KBS? Which is its expected return and potential payoff?
- *KBS re-use*: In addition to the primary target environment for which the KBS is intended, are there other potential sites where other versions of the KBS could be used?
- *technology re-use*: Will the KBS project provide technologies or system components which are likely to be re-usable in other KBS projects?

This is clearly only a sample list. In some cases it may be too extensive and can be simplified; in other cases, it may be too generic, and therefore more specific characteristics must be considered. Whichever might be the list of considered characteristics, they should be evaluated in a precise and detailed way. The ranges of values that each characteristic may assume should be appropriately defined according to the desired level of accuracy of the analysis. In some situations quantitative values may be appropriate, while in others qualitative values may be more suitable.

Task-based analysis

By the term *KBS task* we mean a class of problem-solving activities appropriate for knowledge-based technology which, abstracting from those specific elements characterizing a particular application domain, share a set of common features that can be expressed in abstract and general terms. Design, diagnosis, planning, control, etc., are examples of possible KBS tasks, independent of any specific application domain and applicable in a variety of different contexts (for example, considering the diagnosis task, the diagnosis of a mechanical artifact, of the state of chemical process, of a disease, of water pollution in a lake, etc.).

A first, very abstract and general classification of KBS task includes [Clancey 85]:
- *analytical tasks*, aimed at identifying unknown properties of a system described through an given set of knowledge concerning its structure, behavior, function, and purpose;
- *synthetic tasks*, aimed at finding out a structured description of a system at the desired level of abstraction and granularity, starting from a given set of basic constitutive elements and from a set of desired properties.

This first classification may be refined by considering finer-grained domain-independent tasks which provide a general characterization of a variety of specific tasks which may be appropriate for a KBS. These elementary and general tasks are called *generic tasks* [Chandrasekaran 86]. Several lists of typical generic tasks have been proposed in the literature [Chandrasekaran 83-b], [Stefik et al. 83-b], [Chandrasekaran 86], [Breuker and Wielinga 89], [Steels 90], [Chandrasekaran and Johnson 93], [Yen and Lee 93]. We consider here the following six generic tasks:
- *data interpretation*, aimed at transforming sensory data (signals) into a symbolic representation which meaningfully describes a system;
- *decision making*, aimed at assessing a set of possible alternatives, according to given goals and constraints;
- *diagnosis*, aimed at identifying abnormal behaviors (symptoms) in a system and at tracing their possible causes (faults);
- *configuration*, aimed at defining the structure of a system that can satisfy a prescribed specification, given a set of resources and constraints;
- *simulation*, aimed at generating predictions about the behavior of a system, given an initial state and a set of inputs;
- *planning*, aimed at defining a temporally structured set of actions (a plan) that can achieve a prescribed goal, given a set of resources and constraints;
- *action compilation*, aimed at transforming a symbolic representation into command data (signals) directly influencing a system.

This list has been put together by taking into account the fundamental requirement that generic tasks should be usable as elementary building blocks to describe a large variety of situations a KBS can deal with. Therefore, their definitions should be independent from each other, with no overlapping. Moreover, they should be of a reasonably small grain-size. Of course, this proposal is not intended to be the ultimate list of generic tasks. It includes the most common generic tasks considered in the KBSs developed so far, and proved appropriate to cover most of the situations encountered in practice. However, in specific application domains other or additional generic tasks might be considered.

Generic tasks offer a very useful aid to evaluating the appropriateness of a potential KBS application. Task-based analysis is founded on the following empirical assumption: if the global function a potential KBS it is requested to perform may be recognized to be an instance either of one of the generic tasks listed above or of an appropriate composition of such tasks, then there is a sufficient evidence that the application considered may be appropriate for knowledge-based technology. The validity of this standpoint is mainly based on experience, but is made more transparent and robust by the definition of the concept of generic tasks presented above. Therefore task-based analysis requires two capabilities, namely: (i) being able to recognize specific instances of generic tasks abstracting from the specific features of the various application domain considered, and (ii) being able to decompose the global function of a potential KBS in such a way to recognize whether its domain-independent aspects can be expressed through an appropriate composition of generic tasks. These abilities must be acquired through practice. In fact, the concepts of task-based analysis are fairly easy to understand but really difficult to apply.

The results of analytical assessment and task-based analysis illustrated above should be used together to evaluate technical appropriateness and the usefulness for the organization of a potential KBS application. In particular, task-based analysis should corroborate the results of the analytical assessment as far as the technical appropriateness is concerned.

The product of task 0.10 is a document called *opportunities*. It is obtained by:

1.   discarding from the knowledge problems and potential KBS applications document produced in task 0.9 those potential KBS applications that turned out not to be opportunities;

2.   refining the description of the remaining potential KBS applications (name, set of knowledge problems addressed, informal specification of the main functions expected) and completing it with a list of all characteristics considered for assessing the technical appropriateness and usefulness for the organization, together with the outcome of the analysis performed.

The opportunities document will be the basis for the conclusive step of opportunity analysis.

3.5   SYNTHESIS AND RELEASE

3.5.1   Step execution

Figure 3.8 presents a detailed view of KLIC tasks and products of the 'synthesis and release' step.

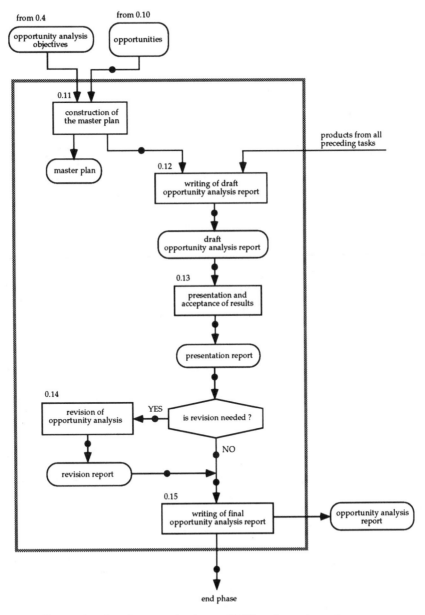

Figure 3.8 Synthesis and release: KLIC tasks and products.

3.5.2   Task 0.11: Construction of the master plan

The opportunities document produced in task 0.10 provides a full list of all potential KBSs which have been identified and have received a positive assessment as far as technical appropriateness and usefulness for the organization is concerned. The main purpose of this task is to propose a schedule for the execution of such KBS projects over a multi-annual time frame.

For this purpose opportunities must be ranked on the basis of their intrinsic characteristics and on the objectives an organization has in starting a KBS initiative. Task 0.11 takes in input the opportunity analysis objectives (from task 0.4) and the opportunities (from task 0.10).

The result of the ranking activity will generally provide only a partial order, since opportunities may exist for which no precedence relation can be defined. This partial order can be represented, for example, through a global *ranking factor* (a positive integer) attached to each opportunity. In particularly complex or critical cases, a set of ranking factor may be used instead of just one, denoting, for example, strategic importance, expected impact, level of expected benefits, etc.

The product of task 0.11 is a document called *master plan*. It is obtained by enriching the opportunities document produced in task 0.10 with the appropriate ranking factors. Therefore, the master plan will include the list of all opportunities defined, divided into groups corresponding to the areas they belong to, and described through all the relevant information produced so far.

As already mentioned in section 3.1.3, the master plan is intended to constitute a long-term reference for choosing specific KBS projects to carry out in an organization. So, it must be synthetic and easy to use, but it must also provide the main motivations behind the suggested opportunities and their ranking. Note that the master plan, even if intended as a long-term reference (for example, 10 years), is a dynamic document. It should be periodically revised (for example, every 4-5 years), so as to ensure its coherence with the changing features of the organization.

3.5.3   Task 0.12: Writing of draft opportunity analysis report

The goal of this task is to produce the draft version of a document which contains a synthesis of the activities done, a detailed illustration of the results achieved, and, in particular, the master plan. Task 0.12 takes in input the products from all preceding tasks. The product of task 0.12 is a document called *draft opportunity analysis report*. It is directed to the top management, who will use it as a decision support aid when starting specific KBS projects. It also contains useful information for the project leaders who will be in charge of organizing, starting-up, and managing future KBS projects. A possible table of content for the opportunity analysis report is shown in Figure 3.9.

Needless to say, the draft opportunity analysis report, being an important document directed to the top management, should be well-written in a concise and clear style. A good, but poorly written document might not be understood in the right way and definitely spoil even a well-done opportunity analysis.

3.5.4   Task 0.13: Presentation and acceptance of results

Once the draft opportunity analysis report is compiled, it should be presented to the top management for evaluation and eventually acceptance. Let us stress that, since the opportunity analysis report is specifically directed to the top management, presenting or discussing it in advance with intermediate managers to gain their support, may often turn out to be inappropriate, in addition to being formally incorrect. The results of opportunity analysis should be delivered directly to the top management.

Generally, presentation of the draft opportunity analysis report, evaluation, and acceptance are carried out during a specific meeting involving the project leader and the top managers. Sometimes, these activities are carried out in a larger meeting, which includes intermediate managers as well.

Task 0.13 takes in input the draft opportunity analysis report (from task 0.12). The product of task 0.13 is a document called *presentation report*, which reports and discusses the result of the presentation.

At the end of this task, it must be verified whether the opportunity analysis can be accepted as it is or if it needs corrections, refinements, or extensions. If this is the case, opportunity analysis must be revised (task 0.14). Otherwise, the execution of the step continues with task 0.15.

---

1. Introduction
 - short introduction to the *opportunity analysis* phase
 - specific management indications considered
 - difficulties encountered and solutions adopted
 - synthesis of the activities carried out and of the main results
   obtained

2. Analysis of the existing organization
 - the process-structure model
 - map of the level of automation of the organization
 - areas and domains table

3. The master plan
 - presentation of the master plan
 - motivations, comments, and remarks

Figure 3.9 Opportunity analysis report: suggested table of content.

3.5.5   Task 0.14: Revision of opportunity analysis

Top management quite often feel the need to comment on the draft opportunity analysis report and make requests for revisions. In such cases, the relevant tasks are resumed and the necessary revisions are carried out.

Task 0.14 takes in input the presentation report (from task 0.13). The product of task 0.14 is a document called *revision report*, which contains the detailed illustration of all points of the study that have been revised and the corrections, refinements, or extensions done. Note from the table shown in Figure 3.2 it is apparent that this task should not exceed 20% of the whole work.

3.5.6   Task 0.15: Writing of final opportunity analysis report

After the needed revisions have been carried out, the opportunity analysis report is compiled and then released. Task 0.15 takes in input the draft opportunity analysis report (from task 0.12), the presentation report (from task 0.13), and the revision report (from task 0.14) - if any. The product of task 0.15 is a document called *opportunity analysis report*, which represents the final, updated and corrected version of the previously produced draft.

The opportunity analysis report, and more specifically the master plan, once approved and released, will become an official document and will constitute the basis for any future action in the area of knowledge-based applications. Each time a specific need to initiate a concrete KBS project is reported, the master plan will be used to check whether it is appropriate and timely, and the information it contains will constitute the background for starting the plausibility study.

Sometimes, the final, official release of the opportunity analysis report takes place during a specific technical meeting where the results of opportunity analysis are presented to a wide management audience.

4

PLAUSIBILITY STUDY

4.1   PHASE OVERVIEW

4.1.1   Motivations and objectives

The purpose of the 'plausibility study' phase is to evaluate whether the conditions exist to make a potential KBS project possible, and to help to make the first set of basic technical and organizational choices. The plausibility study is a mandatory phase of the life cycle. It is essential to set up and organize the development effort correctly, thus ensuring the success of a KBS project. The need for this phase is motivated by the following considerations:

- The novelty of knowledge-based technology may lead to wrong, unrealistic, and exaggerated expectations about the potentials of the knowledge-based technology. Such an attitude can easily cause one to select the wrong problems to face in a KBS project. Knowledge-based technology may not be really necessary for the problems in question, or they may be too difficult to be solved with the presently available technology [Casey 89]. Incorrect expectations should be avoided as much as possible by helping the management and the potential users set up realistic goals.
- KBSs can provide interesting advantages to an organization, such as economic benefits and organizational improvements. However, developing a KBS is a demanding task from the technical, organizational, and economic viewpoints. Therefore, at the beginning of a new KBS project, the conditions that make it feasible and appropriate have to be analyzed in details in order to make the right decisions.
- Introducing a KBS as a routine working tool into an organization may have a strong impact on operative, tactic, and strategic levels. This should be carefully evaluated before the start-up of the project.

- Finally, the development of a KBS application usually involves risk. Therefore, the decision to start a KBS project must be based on a thorough assessment of all the critical factors of the project. The failure of a KBS project always entails a tremendous waste of effort and money, and, more importantly, it may give the management the wrong idea of the potentials of the technology. Every possible care should be taken to ensure success.

The execution of a good plausibility study is a challenging task since its scope, accuracy, and depth must guarantee the highest degree of credibile results. Moreover, the plausibility study has to take into consideration the peculiarities of the specific organization where it is carried out. It cannot be a generic, situation-independent analysis. It should be carried out by highly competent and experienced people (if necessary hired outside of the organization), and involvement on the part of management, domain experts, and potential users should be guaranteed.

The importance of the plausibility study should not be underestimated. The cost of this phase should not frighten decision makers. A good plausibility study helps avoid errors, wastes, and delays, with consequent considerable savings for the budget of the project. A plausibility study carried out with insufficient resources will produce only partial results, thus failing to ensure the KBS project a sound foundation.

The goals of the 'plausibility study' phase are:
- analyzing an application domain and a potential KBS application - possibly suggested by the master plan produced during opportunity analysis - to assess whether they are globally appropriate from the technical point of view and useful for the organization;
- analyzing the requirements and defining the overall goals of the project;
- defining the specifications of the KBS and the acceptance criteria;
- evaluating the individual components of plausibility - namely: technical feasibility, organizational impact, practical realizability, economic suitability, opportunities and risks - and, then, assessing the global plausibility of the KBS application;
- developing a draft technical design, a draft organizational design, and a global project plan.

It is worth mentioning that sometimes the plausibility study may be performed simultaneously on several candidate application domains and potential KBS applications in order to select the most adequate one. This type of plausibility study, referred to here as *multiple plausibility study*, is especially appropriate when no opportunity analysis has been carried out in advance. In this case, the study serves two simultaneous purposes: (i) to evaluate the plausibility (and opportunity) of each candidate application, and (ii) to use the results of the evaluation to compare and rank the candidates, to screen them, and to identify the most appropriate one. The general methodology used to carry out a multiple plausibility study is the same one as usual. Clearly, if during a multiple plausibility study, some early results indicate that a candidate should be eliminated, the study will continue only with the remaining ones. Generally, the candidates considered in a multiple plausibility study are not more than 4 or 5, often reduced to 1 or 2 after the initial analysis step.

In projects of very limited dimensions and complexity - to be judged carefully by an experienced KBS project leader - or in some cases where there is insufficient commitment of the management for the execution of a full plausibility study (due to length, cost, complexity, etc.), it may be worthwhile proposing the development of a limited version, called *preliminary analysis*. For example, a preliminary analysis might be organized as follows (see Figure 4.1 for a list of the tasks of phase 1):

- tasks 1.1 to 1.3:
  should be carried out very quickly, but never totally skipped; verification of prerequisites and planning are crucial issues for the success of a preliminary analysis;
- tasks 1.4 to 1.9:
  should be limited to a restricted level of detail and depth, as the one suggested for the corresponding tasks 0.5 to 0.10 of opportunity analysis;
- tasks 1.11 to 1.16:
  should be thoroughly and carefully carried out; requirement analysis, definition of KBS specifications, and definition of acceptance criteria are a crucial aspect of a preliminary analysis
- task 1.17 to 1.24:
  should be carried out very quickly, excluding the development of an extended and detailed analysis, but without skipping any of the five components of the plausibility; in particular, tasks 1.18 and 1.20 do not have to produce complete draft designs, but only preliminary indications;
- tasks 1.25 to 1.29:
  should be thoroughly and carefully carried out; however, the preliminary analysis report may be very brief, focusing only on the main results obtained.

Of course, the preliminary analysis is technically very different from the plausibility study. It is typically a compromise between the need for a plausibility study and the lack of a sufficient management support. Thus, the preliminary analysis has generally far less information than a full plausibility study, but it is nevertheless useful and often enough to start-up a KBS project. Moreover, it has the great advantage of being less costly and time consuming. For example, one to two months (elapsed time) may be enough in the major part of the cases of practical interest - preliminary analysis is not recommended for applications of high complexity. A reduced project team, may be enough, including just the project leader and one knowledge engineer as regular members. However, let us note that the execution of a preliminary analysis is generally more difficult than that of a regular plausibility study. Doing things well and fast requires much experience and skill, thus only top-level personnel should be employed.

4.1.2   Inputs and products

The plausibility study is usually requested by the top management of an organization or - less frequently - by the middle management specifically interested in the KBS application considered. The 'plausibility study' phase takes in input:

- a document called *management indications*, which defines one or more application domains and potential KBS applications proposed by the

management, and includes requirements, objectives, and constraints to be taken into account in the execution of the study;
• the opportunity analysis report produced in phase 0, if available.

The product of the 'plausibility study' phase is the *plausibility study report*, which contains a synthesis of the activities done, and a detailed illustration of the results achieved. In particular, it includes:
• the definition of the *functional, operational,* and *technical specifications* of the KBS to be developed;
• the *draft technical design* and the *draft organizational design*, giving a technical account on how the KBS should be structured and a proposal for the actions to undertake in order to effectively put it into use;
• the *global project plan*, presenting a breakdown of the major steps and tasks of the subsequent phases of the development process (namely, phases 2, 3, and 4).

Finally, the 'plausibility study' phase may produce a specific *management report* in the case the prerequisites for its execution are not satisfied and the phase is stopped (see task 1.1) or in the case the initial analysis concludes with a negative evaluation (see task 1.10). The products of the plausibility study are directed to the management. They will also constitute an important input of phases 2, 3, and 4.

4.1.3   Phase structure and task outline

Figure 4.1 (a and b) presents an outline of the KLIC tasks of the 'plausibility study' phase.
    The overall logical structure of the 'plausibility study' phase is organized into five steps:
• the 'start-up' step verifies that the prerequisites are satisfied and plans the whole phase;
• the 'initial analysis' step analyzes the application domain and the potential KBS considered, and assesses whether it is globally appropriate from the technical point of view and useful for the organization; the results of opportunity analysis can constitute, if available, a very useful background for this step, whose execution can turn out to be quite simplified;
• the 'basic definitions' step, focuses on the analysis of requirements, and provides an explicit formulation of the functional, operational, and technical specifications of the KBS and of the acceptance criteria;
• the 'analytical assessment of plausibility' step is the core of plausibility study; it focuses on the different aspects of plausibility, and it develops a draft technical design, a draft organizational design, and a global project plan;
• finally, the 'synthesis and release' step provides a global evaluation of the plausibility of the KBS project; the results of the plausibility study are then presented to the management for acceptance; if necessary, the work done is revised and eventually the final plausibility study report is prepared and delivered.

As shown in Figure 4.1, several tasks (or group of tasks) in the 'basic definitions' and in the 'analytical assessment of plausibility' step may be executed in parallel.

As we have already mentioned in section 2.1.3, the time it takes for the 'plausibility study' phase may vary between one to two months (elapsed time) for applications of low complexity (restricted domain, known solution approach, simple organizational aspects), between three to six months for applications of medium complexity (large domain, known solution approach, difficult organizational aspects), and between seven to nine months for applications of high complexity (large and multifaceted domain, solution approach to be identified, difficult organizational aspects). Note that the duration of this phase basically depends on whether or not it may rely on the results of opportunity analysis. If this has been carried out carefully and recently, the whole 'initial analysis' step can be carried out very quickly, otherwise it may require a substantial amount of time.

It may be useful to split the complete duration of the entire phase into the individual duration of its component tasks. The table of Figure 4.2 shows in percentages the duration of each task with respect to the duration of the whole phase, for the case where opportunity analysis has not been carried out.

START-UP		
	1.1	verification of prerequisites
IF		prerequisites are not satisfied
THEN	1.2	writing of management report
		stop phase
	1.3	planning of plausibility study
INITIAL ANALYSIS		
	1.4	process and structure analysis
PARALLEL		
	1.5	analysis of the level of automation
	1.6	verification of domain
END-PARALLEL		
	1.7	characterization of domain
	1.8	identification of knowledge problems and verification of potential KBS application
	1.9	characterization of potential KBS application
IF		initial analysis does not conclude with a positive evaluation
THEN	1.10	writing of management report
		stop phase
BASIC DEFINITIONS		
	1.11	analysis of requirements
	1.12	definition of project goals
PARALLEL		
	1.13	definition of functional specifications
	1.14	definition of operational specifications
	1.15	definition of technical specifications
END-PARALLEL		
	1.16	definition of acceptance criteria

Figure 4.1 Plausibility study: KLIC tasks outline - a.

ANALYTICAL ASSESSMENT OF PLAUSIBILITY		
PARALLEL		
	BEGIN	
	1.17	assessment of technical feasibility
	1.18	development of draft technical design
	END	
	BEGIN	
	1.19	assessment of organizational impact
	1.20	development of draft organizational design
	END	
END-PARALLEL		
	1.21	development of draft project plan
PARALLEL		
	1.22	assessment of economic suitability
	1.23	assessment of practical realizability
	1.24	assessment of opportunities and risks
END-PARALLEL		
SYNTHESIS AND RELEASE		
	1.25	global evaluation of plausibility
	1.26	writing of draft plausibility study report
	1.27	presentation and acceptance of results
IF		revision is needed
THEN	1.28	revision of plausibility study
	1.29	writing of final plausibility study report

Figure 4.1 Plausibility study: KLIC tasks outline - b.

The data reported are, of course, only indicative; they refer to an average situation, and may vary from case to case. Percentages shown in parentheses refer to tasks which are carried out only subject to specific conditions, and, therefore, count over 100.

4.1.4   Project team composition

The plausibility study is usually carried out by an independent consultant (or consulting company) in close cooperation with personnel and managers of the client organization. Less frequently, when there is a good experience in the field of KBS development, it is directly carried out internally by the most experienced people available in the field of knowledge-based technology. Resorting to an external consultant is the only possible choice when the organization is just starting with the knowledge-based technology, and may be appropriate in all cases where the organization wants to obtain a highly independent and competent plausibility study.

In particular, for the plausibility study the project team is typically made up of:
• 1 project manager, usually a senior manager, in charge of formally representing the target organization from the administrative point of view;

TASKS	time %
START-UP	
1.1 verification of prerequisites	2
1.2 writing of management report	(5)
1.3 planning of plausibility study	3
INITIAL ANALYSIS	
1.4 process and structure analysis	6
1.5 analysis of the level of automation	2
1.6 verification of domain	1
1.7 characterization of domain	3
1.8 identification of knowledge problems and verification of potential KBS application	3
1.9 characterization of potential KBS application	5
1.10 writing of management report	(2)
BASIC DEFINITIONS	
1.11 analysis of requirements	7
1.12 definition of functional specifications	7
1.13 definition of operational specifications	2
1.14 definition of technical specifications	2
1.15 definition of acceptance criteria	2
ANALYTICAL ASSESSMENT OF PLAUSIBILITY	
1.16 assessment of technical feasibility	9
1.17 development of draft technical design	5
1.18 assessment of organizational impact	3
1.19 development of draft organizational design	2
1.20 development of draft project plan	4
1.21 assessment of economic suitability	7
1.22 assessment of practical realizability	2
1.23 assessment of opportunities and risks	3
SYNTHESIS AND RELEASE	
1.24 global evaluation of plausibility	4
1.25 writing of draft plausibility study report	6
1.26 presentation and acceptance of results	2
1.27 revision of plausibility study	(20)
1.28 writing of final plausibility study report	8

Figure 4.2 Plausibility study: task duration in percentage.

- 1 project leader, usually a senior professional, responsible for the results of the plausibility study and in charge of the technical and organizational management of the project team; the project leader also provides specific support to all critical tasks of the study;
- 1 designer, in charge of the most technical tasks of plausibility study (tasks 1.17 and 1.18), in particular in complex and large cases;
- 1 to 3 knowledge engineers, one of them being in a senior position, in charge of the execution of most of the tasks of plausibility study;
- 0 to 1 system analysts, in charge of supporting or substituting the knowledge engineers for some specific tasks not strictly bound to knowledge-based technology (tasks 1.4, 1.5, and 1.11);
- 1 or more representatives of the top management;
- intermediate managers of all departments concerned with the application domain considered;
- domain experts of the application domain considered;
- representatives of the potential users of the KBS.

In particularly complex cases, the need may arise to support the project team with external consulting members. If some specific in-depth analyses are necessary in technical areas where the project team is not particularly competent, specialists can be temporarily hired. In addition, an organization analyst can be consulted to assess the impact of the KBS on the organization and to develop the draft organizational design (tasks 1.19 and 1.20). Finally, for complex and large cases an advisor may be consulted to support the project leader in the most important technical decisions and in the most critical steps of project management.

The table shown in Figure 4.3 summarizes the composition of the project team for opportunity analysis.

	REGULAR MEMBERS	SUPPORTING MEMBERS	CONSULTING MEMBERS
project manager		1	
project leader	1		
designer	1		
knowledge engineers	1-3		
system analyst	0-1		
top managers		1 or more	
intermediate managers		as appropriate	
domain experts		as appropriate	
potential users		as appropriate	
specialists			if needed
organization analyst			if needed
advisor			if needed

Figure 4.3 Plausibility study: project team composition.

As it can be noted, the composition of the project team is nearly the same in all possible situations; in complex and large cases the only possibility to speed-up the execution of the phase is to employ two or three knowledge engineers, rather than just one. This implies that complex cases will usually take longer (elapsed time) than simple ones.

4.2   THE CONCEPT OF PLAUSIBILITY

4.2.1   Defining plausibility

The concept of plausibility has a broad and multifaceted meaning. In order to provide a clear definition of plausibility it is useful to decompose it into its components.

We assume that a KBS project is *plausible* if it satisfies all the conditions that guarantee that development of a KBS application appropriate from the technical point of view and potentially useful for the target organization. Plausibility is assumed to include the following five components:

- *technical feasibility*, which assesses whether the knowledge-based technology is appropriate to deal with the application domain considered and to solve the problems in question;
- *organizational impact*, which deals with the conditions that make the KBS actually acceptable and usable by the end-users;
- *practical realizability*, which focuses on the availability or acquirability of the resources needed to carry out the project (personnel, hardware, software, knowledge sources, services, etc.);
- *economic suitability*, which comprises an analysis of the costs to be incurred for the project, an estimate of the expected benefits, as well as their quantification and distribution over time;
- opportunities and risks, which concerns the evaluation of possible favorable conditions to launch the project (such as, for example, funding opportunities, technology transfer programs, commercial and competition issues, corporate strategies, etc.), and the analysis of possible risks.

Plausibility, is quite often confused and mistaken for the more traditional concept of feasibility. Plausibility, however, represents a wider concept. In fact, the feasibility of a traditional software system is generally restricted to the estimate of the effort needed to build the system and, consequently, of the time and costs required. The technical possibility of actually building a traditional software system is usually not a main concern of a feasibility study, as well as other strategic and organizational issues and possible technology transfer problems.

4.2.2   Evaluating plausibility

The process of assessing the plausibility of a KBS project is inherently very complex. It is a typical multi-perspective analysis, which has to focus on several facets which have to be simultaneously analyzed from different perspectives (technical, organizational, economic, etc.). This may cause two problems:

- Mutual influence among perspectives. It is quite common that the results obtained by considering one perspective implicitly or explicitly influence the

evaluation of other perspectives, thus producing poorly objective and credible results.
- Improper switching of perspectives. It sometimes happens that while analyzing a specific perspective and being unable to come up with clear results, one groundlessly shifts to another perspective, thus trying to overcome the problems encountered. This generally causes the analysis to fluctuate among various perspectives, failing to produce a transparent result.

To cope with these potential problems, the assessment process is organized into different stages, each one corresponding to one of the five components of plausibility and carried out separately. A global evaluation of plausibility is then achieved by combining the individual results obtained for each component, after all of them have been analytically assessed. This clear separation allows - and compels - the evaluator to focus one component at a time, thus avoiding the two problems mentioned above, namely mutual influence and improper shifting. Moreover, this makes the evaluation task easier and ensures the production of more accurate, transparent, and objective results.

As already illustrated in section 4.1.3, the 'analytical assessment of plausibility' is preceded by the 'initial analysis' step, which provides the necessary background, and allows stopping the study if the domain and the potential KBS application considered turn out to be inappropriate. Moreover, before plausibility can be analytically assessed, requirements must be analyzed, project goals defined, and detailed KBS specifications stated. In addition, note that the assessment of some components of plausibility also requires that preliminary decisions about the KBS have to be already made. In particular:
- technical feasibility and organizational impact can be assessed only in relation to a specific proposal of technical and organizational design, respectively;
- economic suitability, practical realizability, and opportunities and risks can be assessed only after a specific proposal of technical and organizational design and a detailed project plan have been devised.

Therefore, as illustrated in the following sections, the tasks dedicated to the assessment of the individual components of plausibility must be appropriately intermixed with tasks which provide a precise definition of the aspect of the KBS (technical and organizational design) and of the KBS project (project plan) necessary to proceed in the analysis.

4.3   START-UP

4.3.1   Step execution

Figure 4.4 presents a detailed view of KLIC tasks and products of the 'start-up' step.

4.3.2   Task 1.1: Verification of prerequisites

Task 1.1 takes in input the management indications and the opportunity analysis report (from task 0.15), if available. Several prerequisites should be satisfied

before starting a plausibility study. The most important and critical ones are listed below:
- the management must be fully aware of the need, scope, and objectives of plausibility study;
- the management's decision about starting a specific KBS project should be clear and resolute;
- the intermediate managers, domain experts, and potential users should be available to cooperate with the project team in charge of the plausibility study;
- the top management should authorize the project team in charge of opportunity analysis to explore any aspects of interest in the organization (strategic, management, organization, business, production, technical, etc.);
- the requirements, objectives, and constraints proposed by the management must be consistent with the purpose and nature of the plausibility study;
- the needed resources for the execution of the phase must be available.

Verifying prerequisites is an essential preliminary task of plausibility study. If prerequisites are not satisfied, the plausibility study should not continue. If such a case occurs, a report should be prepared for the top management (task 1.2) and the plausibility study should be stopped. Otherwise, the execution of the phase continues with task 1.3.

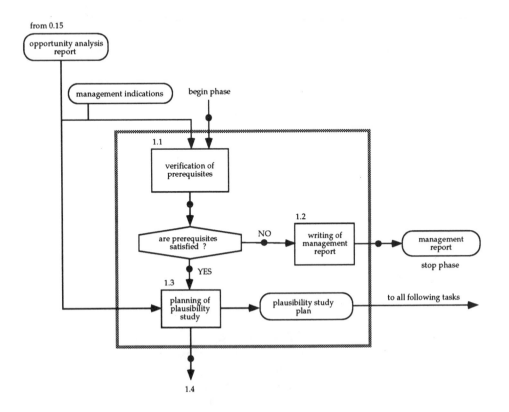

Figure 4.4 Start-up: KLIC tasks and products.

4.3.3   Task 1.2: Writing of management report

In the case where prerequisites are not satisfied, the project leader in charge of plausibility study should prepare a report for the management and stop the execution of the phase. The product of task 1.2 is a document called *management report*. It should explain in detail why a plausibility study is not convenient or even impossible to execute. The report should be personally discussed by the project leader with the management of the organization when appropriate.

4.3.4   Task 1.3: Planning of plausibility study

Task 1.3 takes in input the management indications and the opportunity analysis report (from task 0.15), if available. The product of task 1.3 is a document called *plausibility study plan*.

The organization of the plausibility study plan substantially depends on whether the results of a preceding opportunity analysis are available or not. In the former case, the execution of the 'initial analysis' step is greatly simplified and shortened, since it can focus on refining and updating the analysis already developed during opportunity analysis. In the latter case, instead, it has to start from scratch, involving a substantial engagement of resources and a long period of time.

The plausibility study plan should be discussed with all members of the project team, who should be aware of their role and of their engagements. It should also be formally approved by the management of the end-user organization. Note that, as shown in Figure 4.4, the plausibility study plan is not an input to any specific step. It will be used by the project leader for management and control issues throughout the whole phase (see section 10.3.2).

The plausibility study plan should be refined when, during the development of phase 1, new information is made available for a more precise and realistic definition and scheduling of the activities to carry out. Actually, a revision of the plan is probably appropriate after tasks 1.9 and 1.16.

4.4   INITIAL ANALYSIS

4.4.1   Step execution

Figure 4.5 presents a detailed view of KLIC tasks and products of the 'initial analysis' step.

This step has two objectives: (i) establishing a sound background necessary for the correct and effective performance of the following tasks of plausibility study, and (ii) carrying out a preliminary assessment of the domain and of the potential KBS application proposed by the management, before entering the core parts of the study, which are more costly and time consuming.

To a large extent, this step resumes, refines, and updates the steps dedicated to the analysis of the existing organization and to the analysis of opportunities developed during opportunity analysis (phase 0). The tasks of this step are, therefore, only briefly illustrated; a more detailed analysis can be found in the description of corresponding tasks of phase 3.

4.4.2   Task 1.4: Process and structure analysis

The goal of this task is to develop an abstract, coarse-grained model of the application domain suggested in the management indications. Task 1.4 takes in input the opportunity analysis report (from task 0.15), if available. The product of task 1.4 is a document called *process-structure model of the domain*, which illustrates the domain model designed and comments on its main features.

   The execution of this task is very similar to task 0.5, even if more limited in scope and generally of a higher level of detail. A thorough account can be found in section 3.3.3. Clearly, if task 0.5 has been carried out, this task only refines and updates the analysis developed during opportunity analysis.

4.4.3   Task 1.5: Analysis of the level of automation

The purpose of this task is to enrich the process-structure model of the domain with information concerning the current level of automation. Task 1.5 takes in input the opportunity analysis report (from task 0.15), if available, and the process-structure model of the domain (from task 1.4). The product of task 1.5 is a document called *level of automation of the domain*. It presents in a structured and organic way the information concerning software applications, data bases, and computer system installations relevant to the domain in question. This task is executed in parallel to task 1.6.

   The execution of this task is very similar to task 0.6, even if more limited in scope. A thorough account can be found in section 3.3.4. Clearly, if task 0.5 has been carried out, this task only resumes and updates the analysis developed during opportunity analysis.

4.4.4   Task 1.6: Verification of domain

The goal of this task is to verify, if the application domain which is the subject of plausibility study is correctly identified and, especially if their boundaries are appropriately defined. Task 1.6 takes in input the opportunity analysis report (from task 0.15), if available, and the process-structure model of the domain (from task 1.4). The product of task 1.6 is a document called *domain definition*. It defines the domain which is the subject of plausibility study, specified through (i) a name, and (ii) a short informal description of the main processes belonging to the domain. This task is executed in parallel to
task 1.5.

   The execution of this task is very similar to task 0.7, even if more limited in scope. A thorough account can be found in section 3.3.6. Clearly, if task 0.7 has been carried out, this task only resumes and updates the analysis developed during opportunity analysis.

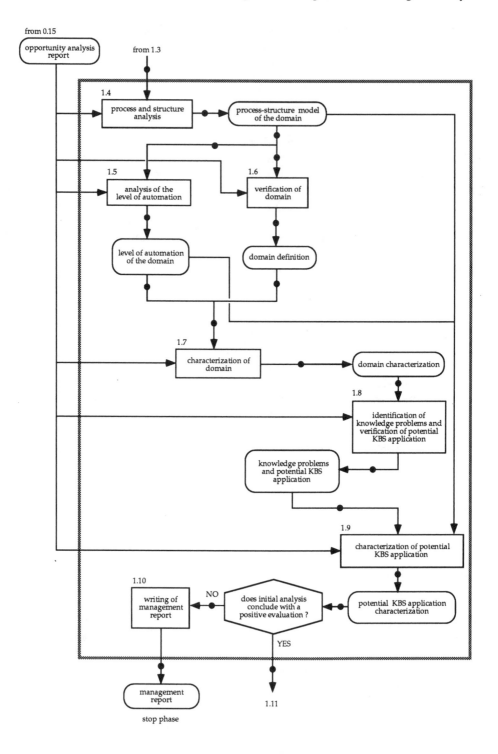

Figure 4.5 Initial analysis: KLIC tasks and products.

4.4.5   Task 1.7: Characterization of domain

The goal of this task is to further analyze the domain which is the subject of the plausibility study, and to focus on the involved knowledge. Domain analysis is carried out in two stages. First of all, the knowledge set of the domain is defined and the main knowledge classes are identified. Later, the domain is carefully checked in order to determine whether or not it is knowledge-intensive. Task 1.7 takes in input the opportunity analysis report (from task 0.15), if available, the level of automation of the domain (from task 1.5), and the domain definition (from task 1.6). The product of task 1.7 is a document called *domain characterization*. It is obtained by completing the information already provided in the domain definition, indicating the following:
- the relevant knowledge set together with the main knowledge classes identified;
- a list of the reasons that make the domain knowledge-intensive.

The execution of this task is very similar to task 0.8, even if more limited in scope and generally of a higher level of detail. A thorough account can be found in section 3.4.2. Clearly, if task 0.8 has been carried out, this task only refines and updates the analysis developed during opportunity analysis.

4.4.6   Task 1.8: Identification of knowledge problems and verification of potential KBS application

The goal of this task is (i) to check whether the domain which is the subject of plausibility study encompasses unsolved problems possibly suitable for knowledge-based technology, and (ii) to verify whether the potential KBS application suggested in the management indications is correctly defined. Task 1.8 takes in input the opportunity analysis report (from task 0.15), if available, and the domain characterization (from task 1.7). The product of task 1.8 is a document called *knowledge problems and potential KBS application*. It is obtained by completing the information already provided in the domain characterization with the list of all relevant knowledge problems identified, each one specified by:
- a name;
- the type, according to the classification defined in section 3.4.3;
- a brief informal description;

and with the definition of the potential KBS application which is the subject of plausibility study, specified by:
- a name;
- the set of knowledge problems addressed;
- an informal specification of the main functions expected.

The execution of this task is very similar to task 0.9, even if more limited in scope. A thorough account can be found in section 3.4.3. Clearly, if task 0.9 has been carried out, this task only resumes and updates the analysis developed during opportunity analysis.

4.4.7   Task 1.9: Characterization of potential KBS application

The goal of this task is to refine the analysis developed so far in order to evaluate
if the potential KBS application previously defined is appropriate from the
technical point of view and useful for the organization. This task is organized in
two stages: an analytical assessment and a task-based analysis. Task 1.9 takes in
input the opportunity analysis report (from task 0.15), if available, the process-
structure model of the domain (from task 1.4), the level of automation of the
domain (from task 1.5), and the knowledge problems and potential KBS
application (from task 1.8). The product of task 1.9 is a document called *potential
KBS application characterization*. It is obtained by refining the description of the
potential KBS application already provided in the knowledge problems and of
potential KBS application document produced in task 1.8 (name, set of
knowledge problems addressed, informal specification of the main functions
expected) and by completing it with a list of all characteristics considered to assess
the technical appropriateness and usefulness for the organization, together with
the outcome of the analysis performed.

The execution of this task is very similar to task 0.10, even if more limited in
scope and generally of a higher level of detail. A thorough account can be found
in section 3.4.4. Clearly, if task 0.10 has been carried out, this task only refines and
updates the analysis developed during opportunity analysis.

At the end of this task, it must be verified whether or not the initial analysis
carried out through tasks 1.4 to 1.9 concludes with a positive evaluation of the
application domain and of the potential KBS application suggested in the
management indications. If there is any evidence that the potential KBS
application might not be globally appropriate from the technical point of view
nor useful for the organization, the plausibility study should not continue. If
such a case occurs, the plausibility study should be stopped and a report made for
the management (task 1.10). Otherwise, the execution of the phase continues
with task 1.11.

4.4.8   Task 1.10: Writing of management report

In the case where the initial analysis does not conclude with a positive
evaluation, the project leader in charge of plausibility study should prepare a
report for the management and stop the execution of the phase. The product of
task 1.10 is a document called *management report*. It should present a detailed
account of the following:
* characteristics of the application domain that, eventually, make it
  inappropriate for a KBS application;
* evidence supporting the conclusion that the potential KBS application
  considered might not be appropriate from the technical point of view nor
  useful for the organization;
* reasons that make the execution of plausibility study not convenient or
  impossible.

The report should be appropriately motivated and personally discussed by the
project leader with the management of the organization.

If appropriate actions are then undertaken to choose a more appropriate domain or potential KBS application, the execution of the phase can continue.

4.5   BASIC DEFINITIONS

4.5.1   Step execution

Figure 4.6 presents a detailed view of KLIC tasks and products of the 'basic definitions' step.

4.5.2   Task 1.11: Analysis of requirements

This task analyzes the requirements to consider for the KBS being developed. By the term requirements we refer to the description of functional, operational, and technical characteristics of the KBS that are perceived as a need by the different participants of the project, in particular by the users, managers, and domain experts. The requirements constitute the background for the definition of the specifications.

Defining requirements cannot be completely carried out at the beginning of a KBS project. The iterative approach to the development of a KBS also entails an iterative definition of requirements. Task 1.11 is the first stage of this iterative process. In the subsequent phases of KBS life cycle the requirements identified will be refined and updated each time the KBS specifications will be refined (see tasks 2.6, 3.6, 4.5, and 5.6).

Task 1.11 takes in input the potential KBS application characterization (from task 1.9). The product of task 1.11 is a document, called *requirements*, which contains an accurate, detailed, and well-structured statement of the requirements to be considered in the KBS project.

Requirements may be obtained from potential users, managers, domain experts, designer and project leader. Therefore, requirements may be appropriately classified according to their source, thus reflecting the different perspectives from which they are perceived [Walters and Nilsen 88]. The following classes of requirements can be distinguished:
- *user requirements*, originating from the potential users of the KBS; these may concern:
  - the functions users expect from or consider appropriate for the KBS;
  - the desired interaction modes, including the quality, quantity, and format of the information exchanged with the KBS;
  - the desired operational modes and response time;
  - the extent to which the users can tolerate KBS failures (providing wrong answers, not being capable of solving specific problems, etc.);
  - the need for explanation and justification facilities;
  - the need for specialized or advanced interfaces;
- *management requirements*, originating from the management interested in the project; these usually concern general functional aspects of the system, operational conditions and target environment, organizational constraints, resources, and costs;

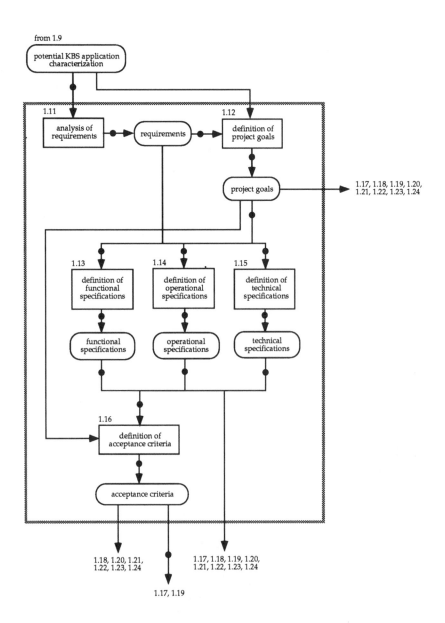

Figure 4.6 Basic definitions: KLIC tasks and products.

- *domain expert requirements*, originating from domain experts; these mostly concern the functions of the system, the explanation and justification capabilities, the features of domain knowledge to use for the development of the knowledge base, and the knowledge sources available;

- *design and development requirements*, originating from the designer and the project leader; these may affect the high-level approach to KBS design and development, concerning the basic technical choices, the selection of the basic development environment, the connection or integration needs with other software systems, etc.

Requirement analysis may rely on a variety of techniques [Moll 86], [van Vliet 93]. Asking interested people through interviews, brainstorming or questionnaires is certainly the most natural way to start, but it can hardly provide all the information needed to set precise requirements. Users, managers, and domain experts cannot always state precisely what they actually want nor what can help them overcome a poor situation. Moreover, in order to build a sound background, it is necessary that requirements not only describe current needs, but also anticipate future changes. Therefore, in addition to asking, it is necessary that the people involved in requirement analysis are given a variety of possible concrete solutions to the problems, for example, through simulated scenarios or demonstrations of existing systems in related fields. This allows one focus the right problems and to identify the real needs.

Requirements should be clearly stated, explicitly, concretely, and in detail. Moreover, it is important that the requirements identified are precisely characterized by the following information [ESA PSS-05-0 91], [ESA PSS-05-02 91]:
- *need*: essential requirements which are not negotiable should be distinguished from optional requirements that only express preferences or desired properties;
- *priority*: the urgency to satisfy a requirement should be defined, in order to devise an appropriate production and delivery plan (possibly including staged dvelompent, see section 2.2.3);
- *stability*, requirements that are known to be stable over the expected operational life of the KBS should be distinguished from other requirements that are unstable, being more dependent on external events and therefore subject to change;
- *source*: the source of each requirement should be stated.

4.5.3   Task 1.12: Definition of project goals

The goal of this task is to provide a clear statement of the objectives which motivate the KBS project considered in the plausibility study. Task 1.12 takes in input the potential KBS application characterization (from task 1.9) and the requirements (from task 1.11). The product of task 1.12 is a document, called *project goals*. It contains a detailed and well-structured statement of the goals to be considered in the KBS project.

Project goals may concern several aspects, and fall into two classes:
- *strategic goals*, related to the KBS initiative, independently from the specific domain and problems tackled; for example, technology transfer, technological exploration, training, innovation, and image improvement;
- *functional and operational goals*, related to the specific problems the KBS is supposed to solve and to the solution expected.

Project goals should be stated explicitly, concretely, and in detail. However, project goals should not anticipate topics that will be the subject of later tasks of the plausibility study, such as specifications or technical choices. Moreover, it is important that the goals identified are precisely characterized by a *temporal specification* stating when the achievement of a goal is considered useful and appropriate, and by an *importance factor*, which allows one to rank goals according their importance for the organization.

Specific attention should be given to ensure that the goals identified are concrete and realistic; goals considered out of reach should be discarded or down scaled. Moreover, goals should focus on just one main objective (exceptionally two), to avoid overloading the KBS project with many, different issues.

4.5.4   Defining specifications

The goal of tasks 1.12 through 1.14 is to define KBS specifications on the basis of the requirements document produced in task 1.11. Specifications provide a detailed and univocal statement of the main characteristics of the KBS to develop. The definition of specifications is a complex task [Cohen et al. 86], [Yost and Newell 89], [Slagle et al. 90]. It can be based on the general approach illustrated in Figure 4.7.

DEFINITION OF REFERENCE REQUIREMENTS
1. evaluation of collected requirements
2. identification and solution of possible inconsistencies among requirements
3. definition of priorities and criteria for requirement ranking
4. ranking of requirements
5. production of reference requirements

IDENTIFICATION OF A FIRST SET OF SPECIFICATIONS
6. statement of a first set of specifications for the KBS being developed

VERIFICATION, EVALUATION AND REFINEMENT
LOOP
7. presentation of the proposed set of specifications to all persons concerned
8. collection of feedback and suggestions
9. refinement of KBS specifications
UNTIL a consistent, well-structured, and agreed-upon set of specifications is identified

---

Figure 4.7 An approach to specifications definition.

This approach includes three stages and nine steps. Initially, in the first stage, the requirements collected during task 1.11 are evaluated (step 1). Since these requirements originate from different sources, which usually do not share the same view on the potential KBS application, they can sometimes be incompatible and cannot be taken into account in system specifications. A compromise must often be found (step 2). Moreover, requirements are generally not all equally important. While some of them may be mandatory, others may only be suggested or optional (step 3). Therefore, the requirements collected must be ranked (step 4). Finally, a collection of *reference requirements* that can be used to form a sound background for the definition of specifications is produced (step 5). Reference requirements are consistent, ranked according to their importance, and include only those needs that must be really considered for the definition of specifications. Based on reference requirements, in the second stage, a first set of specifications for the KBS is then developed (step 6). In the third stage, the specifications are evaluated with all people concerned, namely: representatives of top management, intermediate managers, domain experts, potential users, designer, and project leader (step 7). Their feedback and suggestions are collected (step 8), and the specifications are then refined accordingly (step 9). This stage is repeated until a consistent, well-structured, and agreed-upon set of specifications is identified.

The results produced by tasks 1.12 through 1.14 must not be considered as definitive. Quite often, they are revised during the 'analytical assessment of plausibility' step. For example, it may happen that a requirement deemed important at the beginning, reveals to be critical from the technical perspectives and, therefore, it is discarded or assigned a lower priority. It may also occur that new requirements are discovered and, consequently, appropriate specifications identified. In fact, as end-users and domain experts participating to the project acquire a better understanding of the potentials of KBSs, they may change their attitude toward the application, formulate new needs, and refine or update old ones. This happens in particular if they approach the knowledge-based technology for the first time. Analogously, as the technical members of the project team progressively improve their understanding of the domain and of the problem at hand, they can better evaluate requirements and, if appropriate, formulate specifications.

Moreover, defining specifications cannot be confined to phase 1. The essential iterative approach to the development of a KBS also entails an iterative definition of specifications. Tasks 1.12 through 1.14 are the first stage of this iterative process. In the subsequent phases of the KBS life cycle (namely: tasks 2.6, 3.6, 4.5, and 5.6), the specifications here identified will be refined and updated.

Defining specifications implies making several decisions about the KBS being developed. This is indeed one of the most important efforts of the plausibility study, since it requires an in depth understanding of the domain, sound technical knowledge, and creativity. The knowledge engineers and the designer involved in the definition of specifications are engaged in a twofold activity aimed at understanding and interpreting the requirements correctly and at proposing a clear formulation for the specifications. This is indeed a difficult task, which can easily be ruined by a misunderstanding or by an exaggerated or reductive interpretation of requirements.

The importance of the definition of the overall KBS specifications can also be appreciated from another perspective. A typical pitfall of several KBSs is that they are capable of dealing only with a poorly significant sub-set of the application domain and can solve only some aspects of the problem of interest. The cause of this failure is having too much reliance on an iterative, exploration-oriented approach, which, starting from a limited sample of selected cases and without any formally stated specifications, can progressively cover all aspects of interest. This can be avoided by means of a thorough analysis of requirements and a subsequent detailed and accurate definition of specifications, including an illustration of all kinds of problems to be dealt with by the KBS [Roth and Woods 89]. Having precisely stated specifications is also of primary importance for later design and evaluation activities, which can hardly be based on an informal and unsystematic identification of user needs [O'Keefe and Lee 90].

Before releasing the final list of KBS specifications, it is necessary to verify that they be [van Vliet 93]:

- *correct*: specifications should faithfully interpret the requirements they derive from;
- *consistent*: conflicting specifications should be carefully avoided, if inconsistencies or contradictions are detected they must be removed by reformulating the relevant specifications;
- *complete*: specifications should concern all functional, operational, and technical aspects necessary to precisely define the KBS;
- *fair*, specifications should not over-specify the KBS, i.e. consider aspects of a possible solution rather than aspects of the problem to be solved;
- *realistic*, specifications should not consider characteristics of the KBS that cannot be realistically achieved;
- *self-contained*, specifications should not refer to aspects of the problem that are not defined;
- *univocal*: specifications should be univocally interpretable;
- *concise*, specifications should not contain elements that do not have relevant information.

KBS specifications generally concern three aspects, namely: functional, operational, and technical. A different emphasis should be generally put in the definition of functional, operational, and technical specifications. Functional specifications should explore every aspect concerning the expected KBS performance. They should be defined in great detail and later refined during the KBS life cycle; however, it is desirable that they do not change too much. Operational specifications should be analyzed in depth and defined in detail; however, one might expect that they will be largely revised in later phases of the life cycle. Technical specifications should be strictly limited to avoid anticipating decisions that pertain to later phases of the life cycle.

An account of the issue of software requirement specification from the point of view of standards may be found in [IEEE 830 84]; although it specifically concerns the production of traditional software, some of the concepts presented in this document may apply to KBSs as well.

Functional, operational, and technical specifications are each considered separately in specific tasks, as illustrated in the following sections.

4.5.5   Task 1.13: Definition of functional specifications

Functional specifications concern the primary problem-solving functions the KBS should perform. Functional specifications are related to the external behavior of the KBS, apart from the technical solutions that will be adopted to implement them in later stages of the project. More precisely, they may concern:

- the type of KBS considered, specified in terms of role of the system (support, prescription, autonomous system), the type of connection with traditional software systems (stand-alone, integrated, embedded), and the type of connection with the external environment (on-line, off-line) (see section 1.1.3);
- the inputs to the KBS;
- the expected outputs;
- the expected behaviors, i.e. the functions necessary to produce specific (categories of) outputs in response to specific (categories of) inputs;
- the coverage and scope of the KBS (see section 9.3.2);
- the robustness of the KBS (see section 9.3.2);
- the friendliness and usability of the KBS, with specific attention to the user interface (see section 9.3.2);
- the effectiveness and efficiency of the KBS, concerning the functional aspects;
- the user interface;
- the software and external interfaces, concerning the functional aspects;
- the explanation system and the expected transparency of the KBS (see section 9.3.2). .

Task 1.13 takes in input the requirements (from task 1.11) and the project goals (from task 1.12). The product of task 1.13 is a document, called *functional specifications*, which includes a detailed and structured statement of the functional specifications to be considered in the KBS project. This task is executed in parallel to tasks 1.14 and 1.15.

4.5.6   Task 1.14: Definition of operational specifications

Operational specifications concern the target environment where the target KBS will be inserted and utilized and the way the system will be used, maintained, and extended [Vesoul 88]. More precisely, they may concern:

- the identification and characterization of end-users, including: classes, numerosity, characteristics (skill and computer literacy level, domain knowledge, psychological profile, linguistic level, attitude towards the use of the system, etc.), expected frequency of use, etc.;
- the acceptable approaches to user-KBS interaction (textual, menu-based, icon-based, graphical, animation, direct manipulation, etc.) and the suggested communication media (video-terminal, keyboard, mouse, touch screen, voice recognition system, pen-system, etc.);
- the software and external interfaces, concerning the operational aspects;
- the number, kind, and location of the expected installations of the target KBS;
- the characterization of the operational environments where the target KBS will be installed;

- preliminary organizational indications and constraints about the insertion of the target KBS in the operational environment;
- preliminary indications and constraints about system maintenance and extension, including extensibility and maintainability (see section 9.3.2).

Task 1.14 takes in input the requirements (from task 1.11) and the project goals (from task 1.12). The product of task 1.14 is a document, called *operational specifications*, which includes a detailed and structured statement of the operational specifications to be considered in the KBS project. This task is executed in parallel to tasks 1.13 and 1.15.

4.5.7   Task 1.15: Definition of technical specifications

Technical specifications concern specific aspects of the technical solutions to adopt in the design and construction of the KBS. They may be considered as preliminary suggestions or constraints imposed on the development activity. More precisely, they may concern:
- hardware platform and related system software;
- special devices for input/output, user interaction, information storage, etc.;
- specific software tools to use in the development of the prototype or in the implementation of the target system;
- technical standards concerning, for example, the graphical user interface, the communication protocols, the data and file formats, etc.;
- the software and external interfaces, concerning the technical aspects;
- the technical performance expected, such as real-time requirements;
- the expected reliability (see section 9.3.2);
- the expected maintainability, modifiability, portability, re-usability, and interoperability of the software components of the KBS (see section 9.3.2).

Task 1.15 takes in input the requirements (from task 1.11) and the project goals (from task 1.12). The product of task 1.15 is a document, called *technical specifications*, which includes a detailed and structured statement of the technical specifications to be considered in the KBS project. This task is executed in parallel to tasks 1.13 and 1.14.

4.5.8   Task 1.16: Definition of acceptance criteria

Acceptance criteria concern the feature that the target KBS has to show to be accepted as a finished product by the organization for which it has been developed. Acceptance criteria are different from specifications [Vesoul 88]. Whereas specifications prescribe how the KBS should behave, acceptance criteria define what has to be checked in the target KBS for acceptance, and how these checks have to be carried out. Acceptance criteria are generally derived from specifications, but are narrower in scope and more formal. They also concern quality aspects of the target KBS (see sections 9.2 and 9.3). It is very important that the acceptance criteria and the evaluation methods proposed are agreed upon by the project leader, the project manager, and the management of the end-user organization.

Formulation of acceptance criteria may be hard at this initial stage of the project; nevertheless, it is very important not to overlook this task in order to have a firm point of reference.

Task 1.16 takes in input the requirements (from task 1.11), the project goals (from task 1.12), the functional specifications (from task 1.13), the operational specifications list (from task 1.14), and the technical specifications (from task 1.15). The product of task 1.16 is a document, called *acceptance criteria*, which includes an ordered list of all the acceptance criteria stated and the relevant evaluation methods.

4.6   ANALYTICAL ASSESSMENT OF PLAUSIBILITY

4.6.1   Step execution

Figure 4.8 presents a detailed view of KLIC tasks and products of the 'analytical assessment of plausibility' step.

Let us outline that the analytical assessment of plausibility produces five distinct analyses - one for each component of plausibility. Each analysis should conclude with an assessment of the relevant component, expressed either in qualitative or in quantitative terms. Quantitative scores may be particularly useful for the final task of global evaluation of plausibility (see section 4.7.2), while quantitative scores may be more significant for some specific components, such as economic suitability.

If the assessment of some components provides a negative result, its causes should be traced and the decisions responsible for the failure identified. These may depend on decisions made in the same task that concluded with a negative result or in some previous task of the same step or in some tasks of the previous one. For example, a failure in the assessment of practical realizability (task 1.23) may be due to the fact that the technical complexity of the project is too high with respect to the competence and experience of the available project team; this, in turn, may be a consequence of decisions made during the assessment of technical feasibility (task 1.17) and the development of draft technical design (task 1.18); these, finally, may depend on advanced functional or technical specifications (tasks 1.13 and 1.14), that can only be achieved through the complex technical solution proposed. After the first causes of a failure have been identified, they must be removed and the relevant tasks revised. This kind of backtracking, even if not explicitly shown in Figure 4.1, is essential to ensure that all possibilities for the success of the plausibility study are actually explored. In fact, it would be meaningless to conclude a plausibility study with a global negative assessment, without examining whether with some different but still correct and acceptable choices it could have brought to positive results.

Finally, let us note that several aspects of the analytical assessment of plausibility allow for a variety of different technical or organizational solutions. For example, there may be different technical designs appropriate for the KBS considered (task 1.18), or different organizational solutions may be suitable (task 1.20), or alternative project plans may be proposed (task 1.21). In such cases, the plausibility study should not focus on just one possibility, but should take into account the main alternatives. These should be explored one by one, and then be assessed in parallel throughout the study, postponing as much as possible a comparative evaluation. This way, all available alternatives can be considered and the most appropriate choice can be made on the basis of the information produced during the various stages of the analytical assessment.

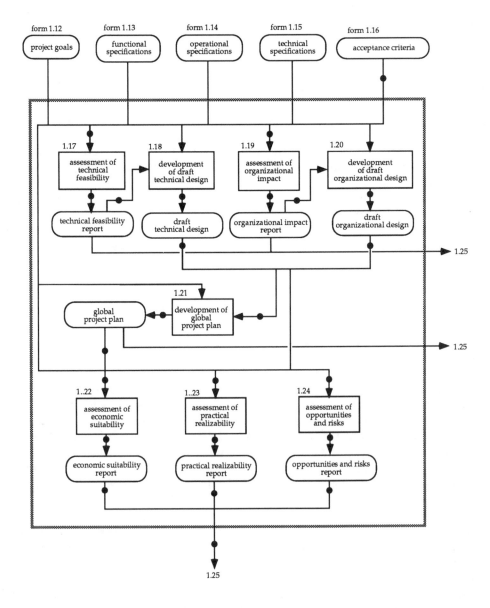

Figure 4.8 Analytical assessment of plausibility: KLIC tasks and products.

4.6.2   Task 1.17: Assessment of technical feasibility

The goal of this task is to assess the technical feasibility of the potential KBS specified in the previous tasks 1.13 to 1.15.

Task 1.17 takes in input the project goals (from task 1.12), the functional specifications (from task 1.13), the operational specifications list (from task 1.14), the technical specifications (from task 1.15), and the acceptance criteria (from task 1.16). This task (together with task 1.18) is executed in parallel to tasks 1.19 and 1.20.

This task focuses on the technical perspective, and focuses on the following three dimensions:

- technology appropriateness;
- technology justification;
- domain stability.

Each one is illustrated in detail below.

Technology appropriateness

The basic concern of technology appropriateness is to determine whether knowledge-based technology is suitable and powerful enough for the project at hand. Here we specifically refer to the available knowledge-based technology (see section 11.6.1), taking a purely application-oriented perspective (see section 1.1.4).

The assessment of technology appropriateness is based on the *conceptual analysis* of the KBS domain and task at hand [Roth and Woods 89], which is aimed at investigating the following aspects:

- what knowledge characterizes the domain and is actually used in facing the KBS task considered;
- what basic reasoning functions are utilized to process knowledge in the domain;
- what specific problem-solving strategies are adopted to face the various types of problems considered.

The conceptual analysis of the KBS task therefore includes:

- the identification of the different *knowledge classes* (see section 3.3.5) that characterize the domain and are actually used in facing the KBS task; each class is defined by: a name, a short informal description of its content and organization, an estimate of its size, an indication of the corresponding knowledge sources, a characterization of the relevant *knowledge type* according to a given set of attributes; for example, the following may be used:
  - declarative/procedural
  - symbolic/numeric
  - qualitative/quantitative
  - fragmentary/organic
  - incomplete/complete
  - uncertain/certain
  - imprecise/exact
  - subjective/objective
  - empirical/fundamental

- the identification of the *reasoning functions* utilized to process knowledge; each reasoning mode and problem-solving strategy is defined according to a given set of attributes (for example, the following may be used: procedural, data-driven deduction, goal-driven deduction, abduction, non-monotonic reasoning, analogical reasoning, model-based reasoning, generalization, specialization, hypothetical reasoning, reasoning by refutation, temporal reasoning, spatial reasoning) and carries the indication of the classes and types of knowledge it applies to;
- the identification of the main *problem-solving strategies* exploited to face the various types of problems considered, each one defined in terms of a procedural combination of elementary reasoning modes, which describe which knowledge classes are used and how the relevant basic reasoning modes are applied.

Taking into account the information collected through conceptual analysis, technology appropriateness is then evaluated. The list reported below may serve as a guide in carrying out this evaluation in an orderly way [Stefik et al. 83-b], [Prerau 85], [Slow et al. 86], [Laufmann et al. 90], [Beckman 91], [Baron-Vartian and Baron-Vartian 91]:

- Are the types of domain knowledge involved in the domain appropriate for knowledge-based processing? That is, are the knowledge types mainly declarative, symbolic, qualitative, fragmentary, incomplete, uncertain, approximate, or judgmental?
- Are the basic reasoning modes involved in the domain appropriate for knowledge-based processing? That is, are the basic reasoning modes mainly non-procedural?
- Is domain knowledge well-defined, precisely confined, and self contained?
- Are the problem-solving strategies utilized by the experts clearly identifiable and explainable?
- Do the problem-solving strategies involve a large search space? Do they involve multiple lines or reasoning?
- Do domain experts agree on the problem-solving strategies they use? Do they agree in evaluating the correctness and the quality of the solutions?
- Is the KBS task sufficiently narrow and self-contained?
- Is the KBS task judged by practitioners as not too easy, nor too difficult? Does it take more than a few minutes but not more than a few days to be executed by an expert?
- Is the KBS expected to be useful even if partial or non-optimal solutions are produced or are only complete and optimal solutions acceptable? Can the minimum acceptable performance of the KBS be clearly defined and measured?
- Does the task require capabilities within the current possibilities of knowledge-based technology or does it involve frontier technologies or research?
- Is incremental development possible? Is it possible to decompose the KBS task into (independent) sub-tasks which can be solved independently?

The conceptual analysis carried out in this rask will be refined and completed in subsequent phases of the KBS life cycle (namely: tasks 2.7, 3.4, 3.5, 5.8, and 5.10).

Technology justification

Technology justification is concerned with determining whether knowledge-based technology is really the only viable solution to the problem at hand or other simpler and less costly approaches are applicable. The questions of interest are:
- Can the KBS task be faced by means of other approaches, for example: changing the existing organization, streamlining the manual flow, upgrading an existent software package, purchasing or developing a new software package, resorting to other advanced information technologies, etc.?
- Have all other possible approaches - if any - been investigated and discarded?

Domain stability

Domain stability is concerned with determining whether the KBS domain is sufficiently stable, thus ensuring that the KBS will have a long operational life without the need of a too frequent and complex maintenance activity. Appropriate questions to be answered include:
- Is the present domain knowledge likely go become obsolete soon? In which time frame and to which extent?
- Should obsolete knowledge be immediately replaced in order to keep KBS performance above the minimum acceptable level?
- Will substantial new knowledge on the application domain be available in the future? In which time frame and to which rate?
- Should new knowledge should be taken into account soon?
- Are sophisticated maintenance procedures likely to be necessary, requiring, for example, direct interaction with domain experts or users?

The analysis of the technical feasibility can often be supported through a specific state-of-the-art investigation of other known KBS applications in similar domains. This can provide useful suggestions to direct the analysis and enhance the confidence in the obtained results.

The various analysis activities carried out in task 1.17 and, in particular, the conceptual analysis, may be based on the techniques utilized in phase 3 for knowledge analysis and modeling (task 3.4) and for the design of the conceptual model (task 3.5). A detailed illustration can be found in sections 6.5.2 and 6.5.3.

The product of task 1.17 is a document, called *technical feasibility report*, which includes the results of the analysis performed and draws a final conclusion.

4.6.3   Task 1.18: Development of draft technical design

This goal of this task is to produce a draft technical design of the KBS. Task 1.18 takes in input the project goals (from task 1.12), the functional specifications (from task 1.13), the operational specifications list (from task 1.14), the technical specifications (from task 1.15), the acceptance criteria (from task 1.16), and the technical feasibility report (from task 1.17). The product of task 1.18 is a document, called *draft technical design*, which contains a first outline of the main technical features of the KBS. Producing more than one design may be very useful in providing the decision makers with a set of alternatives. The draft technical design will be refined and completed in subsequent phases of the KBS life cycle (namely: tasks 2.8, 2.9, 3.7, 3.10, 3.11, 3.12, 4.7, and 5.10). This task (together with task 1.17) is executed in parallel to tasks 1.19 and 1.20.

The draft technical design should provide a preliminary technical definition of the KBS to be developed, including:

- the overall architecture of the KBS (for example: centralized, client-server, hierarchical, modular, blackboard, distributed, etc.), comprising the knowledge bases, the reasoning mechanisms, the working memories, the heterogeneous problem-solvers, and the special-purpose modules; the architecture specifies as well the main high-level data and control flows;
- the specification of the knowledge representation techniques (for example: production rules, semantic nets, frames, scripts, logic, etc.) to exploit for the implementation of the knowledge bases, with reference to the knowledge classes identified in the conceptual analysis (task 1.17);
- the specification of the reasoning methods (for example: search with or without backtracking, forward or backward chaining, simple or multiple inheritance, specialization, generalization, procedural attachment, constraint propagation, truth maintenance, etc.) to be used for implementing the reasoning functions identified in the conceptual analysis (task 1.17);
- the specification of the main characteristics of the knowledge bases, including their internal organization and their estimated size;
- the specification of the intended representation and use of strategic knowledge;
- the specification of the traditional software systems to be connected to the KBS, and of the external devices (sensors, data acquisition systems, actuators, etc.) to be interfaced;
- a preliminary description of the technical aspects of the software and external interfaces;
- a preliminary description of the technical aspects of the user interface;
- a preliminary description of the technical aspects of the explanation system including: operation modes, links to specific inference mechanisms and knowledge bases, and design principles;
- the identification of the hardware platforms for KBS development and delivery;
- the identification of the appropriate basic development environment and of the necessary development support system (see section 6.4.2);
- the illustration of the overall operation of the KBS - possibly in different modes - with reference to the general problem-solving strategies identified in the conceptual analysis (task 1.17).

The various design activities carried out in task 1.18 may be based on the techniques utilized in phase 3 for the design of the logical model (task 3.7) and for the selection of the basic development environment (task 3.10). A detailed illustration can be found in sections 6.3, 6.4, 6.6.2, and 6.6.5.

4.6.4   Task 1.19: Assessment of organizational impact

This task analyzes the organizational impact the KBS may have on the organization, focusing on its positive and negative effects when it is installed in the target operational environment and is routinely used. Task 1.19 takes in input the project goals (from task 1.12), the functional specifications (from task 1.13), the operational specifications list (from task 1.14), the technical specifications (from task 1.15), and the acceptance criteria (from task 1.16). This task (together with task 1.20) is executed in parallel to tasks 1.17 and 1.18.

A KBS generally causes great changes in assessed organizational procedures and even in the basic structure of an organization [Harmon and Sawyer 90]. The outcome of such modifications has to be carefully foreseen and evaluated in advance: the KBS project should be targeted towards a system which is acceptable not only from the technical point of view, but also - and perhaps more importantly - from the organizational perspective.

These aspects are very important. If a project does not emphasize this point, it is very likely to become a failure. The KBS can well be very sophisticated from the functional point of view, technically well-constructed, and economically rewarding, but it may never be effectively and successfully used if it is not correctly inserted in the organization [Zack 87].

The organizational effects of a KBS may belong to three categories [Kelly 88] respectively related to: changing the role and responsibility of individuals working in the organization, changing the structure of the organization, changing the relationships of the organization with the external environment. These are analyzed in detail below.

At the *individual level*, three classes of people are affected:

- Domain experts. The primary positive effect of a KBS on domain experts is that they may be allowed to spend less time on routine work, to better exploit their skills, and to increase their professional competencies. In fact, the KBS can deal with the more usual and less difficult cases, thus allowing domain experts to focus on the uncommon and more challenging ones. This might help domain experts to overcome possible fears about a KBS project, like that of being replaced by the KBS or of losing status.

- Users. Since most frequently a KBS is developed to support the users in the execution of some activity which required the intervention of a specific human expert before, the dependence on experts decreases, and the autonomy increases. As a consequence, there is generally an increase in effectiveness and efficiency of job execution. Time is no longer wasted for interaction with the expert, there is more flexibility in work organization, more direct involvement in the problem-solving process, and better performance. Such factors contribute to a better job satisfaction. These positive effects are not, however, at zero cost. Using a KBS requires the capability to effectively interact with a sophisticated computer system. The user must be prepared for this, and must become familiar with using a computer system not only to process and manage numerical information, but also to support complex reasoning processes. Moreover, the user may be required to provide information which is new with respect to the current practice, or may be required to consider more information coming from the system. This may increase his cognitive load. In addition, using a KBS instead of relying on the assistance of a human expert changes the distribution of responsibilities; the user gains autonomy but also has more responsibility. Finally, using a KBS may require changing the physical environment the user is accustomed to. He may have to move to another desk or another room, use new devices, a new interface, or a different operating system, etc.

- Managers. The managers responsible for the departments where the KBS is installed have better opportunities of controlling specific activities which are more uniformly and consistently executed. Better planning, resource allocation, and standardization is generally possible. However, in order to exploit such opportunities, more sophisticated and focused management techniques may be required.

At the *organizational level*, the major effects of using a KBS derive from the changes in the way the organization performs some of the working processes within the relevant application domain. These effects may concern:

- the new personnel roles;
- the new sharing of responsibilities among the personnel;
- the new structure of the decision-making processes;
- the modifications in the number and type of personnel required;
- the modification of the processes and structures of the application domain considered;
- the need for new activities strictly connected to the existence of the KBS, such as KBS maintenance;
- the flow of communication among personnel; the presence of a KBS usually decreases the contacts between users and domain experts and, consequently, it may also reduce the level of socialization among personnel.

Finally, at the *external level*, the impact of a KBS may concern the specific relationships of the organization with its customers, suppliers, partners, and competitors. A KBS may support improved response times to changes in external conditions, finer tuning to customer needs, more detailed assessment of supplier offers, closer and more focused cooperation with partners, more effective interaction with competitors.

The assessment of the organizational impact should be carried out at the three levels mentioned above. Assuming that the KBS is completed and fully operational, its impact on the current organizational situation (or more precisely, on the organizational situation that is likely to exist at the moment the KBS is put into operation) is first identified. It is then analyzed and its various aspects are classified according to the following attributes:

- *safety*, if it does not bring substantial disturbance to the existing organization;
- *criticality*, if it tends to tangibly - or even strongly - change the existing organization;
- *harm*, if it is likely to jeopardize the existing organization, generating new problems or making the existing ones more serious.

The product of task 1.19 is a document, called *organizational impact report*, which provides a detailed account of the results of the analysis developed.

4.6.5   Task 1.20: Development of draft organizational design

The goal of this task is to produce a draft organizational design, which specifies a set of actions appropriate for:
* avoiding harmful effects, if they are still foreseen after a possible revision of previous decisions that may be responsible for their occurrence (for example, functional or operational specifications);
* controlling critical effects, in such a way as to ensure that the modifications to the existing organization are coherent and effective;
* supporting the correct and smooth implementation of safe effects.

Task 1.20 takes in input the project goals (from task 1.12), the functional specifications (from task 1.13), the operational specifications (from task 1.14), the technical specifications (from task 1.15), and the acceptance criteria (from task 1.16), and the organizational impact report (from task 1.19). The product of task 1.20 is a document, called *draft organizational design*. It contains a detailed specification of the actions to be carried out in order to prepare the organization for the effective insertion of the target KBS. The draft organizational design will be refined and completed in subsequent phases of the KBS life cycle (namely: tasks 4.8 and 5.10). This task (together with task 1.19) is executed in parallel to tasks 1.17 and 1.18.

The task is very critical, since it may directly influence the final success of the project. If the organization - or the departments where the KBS will be installed - has little experience in using KBSs, then the preparation of the draft organizational design should be very careful. In the cases where the organizational impact is expected to be particularly critical, the support of an organization analyst may be appropriate.

The actions stated in the draft organizational design may differ greatly from case to case. They may involve personnel training and promotional initiatives with the purpose of gaining user acceptance. The roles, the responsibilities, and the structure of the working environment may undergo substantial changes.

4.6.6   Task 1.21: Development of global project plan

The goal of this task is to produce a global project plan which structures the KBS development process into stages, identifies the major milestones and deliverables, estimates the time needed, and defines the necessary resources. Task 1.21 takes in input the project goals (from task 1.12), the functional specifications (from task 1.13), the operational specifications (from task 1.14), the technical specifications (from task 1.15), the acceptance criteria (from task 1.16), the draft technical design (from task 1.18), and the draft organizational design (from task 1.20).

Planning is a crucial activity within the plausibility study, since it influences several important aspects and decisions necessary to organize the development effort. However, it should be understood that, at this early stage of the project, planning may be only coarse and preliminary. The global project plan should cover the entire KBS life cycle; however, one might not expect that the plan is as detailed for all phases. The horizon of detailed planning usually extends over phase 2 (construction of a demonstrator) and phase 3 (development of the prototype), while phases 4 (implementation, installation, and delivery of the target system) and 5 (maintenance and extension) are planned at a lower level of detail. The product of task 1.21 is a document, called *global project plan*, which contains one or more proposals of possible project plans.

The first activity towards the development of the plan concerns the identification of basic information about goals, objectives, priorities, and constraints. More specifically it is necessary to identify:

- the priorities among the different parts or functions of the KBS, with respect to project goals and estimated technical complexity;
- the development life cycle deemed adequate for the project, taking into consideration both technical and organizational aspects of the project; for example, at this point of the development, it should be decided whether the project should include the construction of a demonstrator, or whether a staged development (see section 2.2.3) will be appropriate;
- the need for specific training of the personnel to employ for KBS development;
- the resources necessary for the various life-cycle phases, including the relevant time requirements.

The global project plan should include the following information [Waterman 86], [Brayant 88], [Greenwell 88], [Walters and Nielsen 88], [Chorafas 90], [Sacerdoti, 91]:

- the explicit identification of the goals, priorities, and constraints which have tobe be considered in the planning activity;
- the definition of the *project structure*, i.e. the actual phases and tasks through which the plan will develop; the design of the project structure can be based on the consideration of a reference life cycle (for example, KLIC), but must be more concrete and detailed in taking into account the specific features of the KBS project and of the organization at hand;
- the definition of the *project schedule*, i.e. the temporal organization of phases and tasks, together with a specific indication of the estimated time requirements (start and finish dates);
- the definition of the main *deliverables* to be produced (documents, software systems, etc.) and of the milestones of the project (demonstrations, presentations, evaluations, reviews, etc.), together with the indication of their distribution over time;
- the definition of the *resource* needed for the project, including:
  - personnel, with indication of: number of people, professional role, seniority, and an estimate of the type and number of professional roles (see section 10.2.1), time allocation for each project phase;
  - equipment, including hardware, software, and any other necessary tool or system.

4.6.7   Task 1.22: Assessment of economic suitability

The goal of this task is to analyze the costs needed for a KBS project and the benefits which are expected from it. High investments are typically involved in innovative projects, like the development of a KBS. Therefore, an important component of plausibility is the balance between costs and benefits of the project to be carefully evaluated.

Task 1.22 takes in input the project goals (from task 1.12), the functional specifications (from task 1.13), the operational specifications (from task 1.14), the technical specifications (from task 1.15), the acceptance criteria (from task 1.16), the draft technical design (from task 1.18), the draft organizational design (from task 1.20), and the draft project plan (from task 1.21). This task is executed in parallel to tasks 1.23 and 1.24.

The task includes three stages, namely the identification and assessment of benefits, the identification and assessment of costs, and the global economic assessment. These are illustrated below. Since both costs and benefits are distributed over time, their evaluation requires a reference time frame. Generally, this includes the complete 'analysis' and 'development' macro-phases, and an 'operation' macro-phase, which is supposed to last 2 to 4 times the sum of the durations of the preceding ones.

Identification and assessment of benefits

A KBS project affects the organization where it is carried out in a variety of ways, including the changes it causes on the target environment where the KBS is applied. The *benefits* of a KBS project are results considered beneficial with respect to the achievement of project goals. The identification of benefits is made through a detailed analysis of the likely consequences of the project and of their impact on the target organization. Of course, at this stage of the project, the expected benefits are only a forecast, based on the assumption that the project will continue as planned and that the target KBS will be fully operational as described in the specifications. Moreover, the assessment of benefits can only be a more or less precise estimation, since it largely relies on extrapolations, which in the long run are only partially correct.

It is difficult to identify and assess benefits because the future evolution of events related to the effects expected from the KBS project and from operational exploitation of the KBS cannot always be predicted. No specific techniques are available for this activity. Relying on experience and on comparison with other similar situations is the only methodology to follow. Performing structured comparisons and conservative extrapolations is a must in order to attain sufficiently reliable and objective results. Another important factor to take into account and to clarify in the plausibility study is constituted by the assumptions made in order to define the scenarios on which the identification of the potential benefits is based. These assumptions are important to verify and possibly revise over time the identification of benefits, especially in the cases where predicted benefits largely depend on events which are only probable but not definitely certain.

The identification of benefits usually goes through a propose-and-refine process. Initially, a list of potential benefits is compiled, possibly by means of a few working meetings with domain experts and potential users. Later, it is verified and refined with intermediate managers. Iterations of the propose-and-refine process may be possible in the most complex cases in order to achieve stable and valid results, shared by the people concerned. Eventually, a final list of expected benefits is produced.

Some classes of common benefits that may serve as a guideline for the process of benefits identification are listed below [Freiling et al. 85], [Wilkerson 85], [Philip and Schultz 90], [Prerau 90], [Weitz 90], [Liebowitz 91]:

Benefits related to the production processes
- improving the level of automation of the production proce.. ‑hus reducing their dependency on the availability, skills, and experience of t.   ‑rsonnel;
- supporting the correct and effective use of production equipment and increasing its reliability, availability, and lifetime;
- improving the quality of process supervision and control;
- improving diagnosis and maintenance services to assure continuity and quality of the production processes;
- supporting production management and logistic tasks;
- supporting production planning and scheduling;
- improving the effectiveness of the production processes in terms of productivity (products delivered within a time unit), quality (products discarded in a given batch), economy (resources used for a product unit);
- improving safety of the production environment and ensuring better working conditions;
- solving or assisting in solving specific production problems that have eluded previous solutions by other computer-based technologies.

Benefits related to the products
- improving existing products by offering new features and functions;
- developing innovative products;
- bettering the design and development of new products and services, thus enhancing flexibility and reducing time-to-market performance;
- improving product quality, both in terms of mean value and of deviations from the mean value;
- upgrading customer support, maintenance, and field service, ensuring timely, competent, effective, and low-cost assistance.

Benefits related to the work processes
- enhancing the professional level of the personnel, establishing a more comfortable and stimulating working environment for the potential users of the KBS;
- exempting experts from having to deal with the usual routine tasks, giving them the opportunity to concentrate on areas of professional interest that they otherwise would not have had the time to pursue;
- enhancing standard and consistency in work practice.

Benefits related to the management processes
- enhancing financial and marketing activities;
- supporting control tasks;
- improving decision-making procedures both at operative, tactical, and strategic levels;
- providing tools for training and re-training activities.

Benefits related to the value of knowledge
- eliciting, collecting, organizing, and preserving basic competence, specific know-how, and individual experience (for example before an expert leaves the company or retires), thus providing a standard, structured, lasting, safe, and accessible storage of valuable knowledge;
- making knowledge explicit, thereby promoting the enhancement and increase of knowledge;
- supporting distribution and effective exploitation of knowledge through the organization, where, when and how needed, thus enabling proliferation of a consistently high level of expertise at a number of sites.

Strategic benefits
- acquiring a new competitive advantage through advanced technological innovation;
- improving the image of the organization, both internally and externally;
- joining external advanced research and development programs thus having access to specific funding opportunities.

In identifying the potential benefits of a KBS project, care should be taken that the stated benefits are independent as much as possible. For example, a benefit list including the "formalization and standardization of design know-how" and the "improvement of the quality of the design process" is not well-organized, since the latter clearly depends of the former. In order to solve problems concerning inter-dependencies among benefits, a more detailed analysis is generally necessary. For example, a better statement of the benefits mentioned above might be: "reduction of the time needed for the transfer of design know-how from experts to novices", "improvement of the average quality of the designs produced", "higher uniformity of the quality of the designs produced", "shorter design time". The reason why only mutually independent benefits should be considered is to guarantee the possibility to add their values; this is requested in order to facilitate the economic assessment of benefits as well as the global process of assessment of economic suitability.

One last point to be mentioned concerns the fact that in identifying benefits only those effects that can be directly, exclusively, and unquestionably ascribed to the KBS project should be considered. Other effects that are only indirectly and partially related to the KBS project or to the KBS should be taken into account with the maximum care and analyzed in detail, in order to differentiate between those which can be considered as potential benefits from those which should be discarded.

Once a list of potential benefits has been produced, it is necessary to analyze in detail their expected evolution over time. For each benefit identified, it should be specified when it will start to be concretely visible, when it will cease its effects, and how it will evolve in between. A variety of different patterns may be observed in practice; some common ones are:
- *early benefits* start fast and well before the KBS is released for operational use (often just after the start of phase 2), then are usually constant over time, but tend to vanish early (for example, little after the KBS is released for operational use);

- *primary benefits*: these are typically obtained only after the KBS is put into use, increase slowly, reach a maximum effect in the short-term, keep more or less constant for a long period (unexpected events may, however, cause their sudden increase or decrease), and then start to decrease rapidly;
- *late benefits* are usually obtained as a consequence of some major maintenance or extension intervention, they become visible immediately after the new KBS is put into use, reach a maximum effect in the short-term, keep more or less constant for a short period, and then start to decrease gradually;
- *end benefits* are obtained when the KBS is withdrawn from operational use and possibly resold out or employed in other application contexts; end benefits are mostly monetary in nature and may be actually interesting if the end of the operational life of the KBS is appropriately planned and carefully managed (see section 8.8.3).

Finally, the benefits identified must be analyzed in order to assess their economic value. From this perspective, it is appropriate to distinguish two categories of benefits:
- *measurable benefits*, whose economic value can be effectively measured or estimated in quantitative terms (quite often easily expressed monetarily);
- non-measurable benefits, whose economic value can be appreciated only in qualitative terms.

For example, measurable benefits may concern the productivity and the quality in discrete manufacturing, the savings due to early or more accurate diagnosis of a production plant, the rate of human errors in process control, the improvement of a decision making process, the ease in know-how transfer from experts to novices, etc. Non-measurable benefits may concern the work quality, the marketing impact, the image of the company, the formalization and standardization of valuable know-how, etc. Clearly, the possibility to measure a benefit mostly depends on how it is defined. It is important to define benefits so that appropriate procedures may be identified to measure or estimate them [Walters and Nielsen 88].

The process of benefit identification and assessment ends with a document, called *benefit evaluation report*. It includes a structured list of the benefits identified, each one being described through:
- a short informal definition;
- a procedure for measuring it, if applicable;
- an indication of its expected evolution over time;
- a measure or an estimation of its economic value, with an indication of its distribution over time.

Identification and assessment of costs

Costs to sustain during a KBS life cycle may be classified into two categories:
- *production costs*, concerning the phases 1, 2, 3, and 4;
- *operation costs*, concerning phase 5.

Identifying the costs of a KBS project is generally easy on the basis of the information provided in the draft technical design, in the draft organizational design, and in the global project plan. The following list may help to remind the most common and important cost items:

production costs
- hardware and software tools necessary for the construction of a demonstrator, the development of the prototype, the implementation of the target system, and the delivery (with specific attention to the case where multiple installations of the target KBS are foreseen);
- background know-how and systems: concerning the acquisition of specific know-how and systems to be used as a background for the project (for example, a prototype developed by another organization);
- personnel: regular and supporting members of the project team;
- training: specific training necessary for the project (for example, training for a specific development tool);
- advice: external consultants for supporting KBS design and construction, specialists in some specific domain of knowledge-based technology, scientific advisors, KBS experts for project management support, organization analysts, etc.
- infrastructures and services not specifically related to KBS project considered, but necessary for its effective execution (for example: office and office systems, secretarial services, communication systems, etc.);
- any other production costs: 10-15% of the total production costs, to cover expenses and risks not anticipated.

operation costs
- maintenance, including hardware and software maintenance and upgrades, and regular and supporting members of the maintenance team;
- extension, including the cost of a reasonable number of extension interventions (see the above list for production costs);
- any other operation costs: 10-15% of the total operation costs, to cover expenses and risks not anticipated.

Clearly, the identification of operation costs is highly hypothetical, since it is based on assumptions about the expected behavior of the target KBS and the likely evolution of requirements. Generally, the identification of maintenance costs is based on experience and on the analysis of similar cases. As far as extension costs are concerned, generally no extensions are expected in the reference time frame defined for economic suitability; if a wider time frame is considered, extension costs may be estimated on the basis of a conservative forecast of two minor extensions and a major one in the operational life of a KBS.

Once the cost items relevant to a KBS project have been identified, they must be precisely quantified in monetary terms. In doing this, one should carefully distinguish between:
- cost items that pertain only to the project at hand and concern goods or services which are completely used in the frame of the project (specific costs);
- cost items that pertain to several projects at the same time and concern goods or services which are completely used in the frame of the relevant projects; the

costs of these items should be carefully divided among the relevant projects (shared costs);
- cost items that concern goods (material, like a computing equipment - or non-material, like know-how) which exhaust their value in a long time frame and, therefore, are used by several projects in different periods of time; the costs of these items should be carefully divided among the relevant periods and projects (proportional costs).

In assessing project costs, attention should be paid to analyze in detail their expected distribution over time in order to obtain a clear view of the global cash-flow of the project.

The process of cost identification and assessment ends with a document, called *cost evaluation report*. It includes a structured list of the cost items identified, each one described through:
- a short informal definition;
- a monetary quantification;
- an indication of its distribution over time.

Global economic assessment

KBS projects do not provide an immediate payoff. In other words, they require high initial investment and become profitable only in the mid-term.

Once benefits and costs have been separately evaluated, it is then possible to assess the overall economic suitability of a KBS project. This is obtained by estimating the global *benefits/costs ratio*, that is, the total value of the benefits over the total costs, in the reference time frame. If benefits do not exceed costs by at least a factor of 2 to 4 (to be carefully chosen taking into account the extent of the reference time frame), the economic suitability of the project is considered critical. Moreover, since any KBS project entails risks, the benefits/costs ratio should be in a sense proportional to the total costs met. For example, while for a small project requiring limited total costs, a lower benefits/costs ratio may be acceptable (for example, 1.7), for a large project entailing substantial total costs, a higher benefits/costs ratio is generally expected (for example, 2.5).

If the benefits/costs ratio proves to be unsatisfactory, some of the basic decisions made in the previous tasks of opportunity analysis should be revised. The benefits/costs ratio may be improved in several ways. Generally, it is preferable to revise decisions that influence benefits or both benefits and costs, rather than trying to directly cut the costs. Some common and effective interventions are:
- reducing both benefits and costs by affecting costs more than benefits - for example, by cutting down on specifications that entail high costs, but give only limited benefits;
- increasing both benefits and costs, affecting benefits more than costs - for example, by adding specifications that can ensure high benefits, and that entail only limited costs.

Note that the calculation of benefits/costs ratio should be based on a conservative evaluation of benefits. Only benefits that are certain or are likely to be obtained, and that can be precisely measured or estimated with a narrow confidence margin should be considered.

After having assessed the benefits/costs ratio, it is appropriate to represent the *cumulated benefits* and *cumulated costs* of the project - as well as the cumulated benefits/costs ratio - as a function of time (with a defined time step; for example, a quarter). This makes it possible to identify two important events:

- the *non-zero point*, i.e. the point where cumulated benefits start to exist;
- the *break-even point*, i.e. the point where cumulated benefits start to exceed cumulated costs (the two curves intersect).

The definition of the non-zero and parity points allows two other concepts to emerge; the *initial investment* of the project which corresponds to the cumulated costs met up to the non-zero point, and the *basic investment* which corresponds to the cumulated costs met up to the parity point.

The identification of the non-zero and parity points is very important since it allows to determine when the organization starts obtaining a *return* from the investment and when the return starts to exceeds the investment undertaken. Clearly, the non-zero and parity points should be found as early as possible in the KBS life cycle. The non-zero point should not exceed by much the time when the KBS is released for use, and the parity point should not be too close to the end of the reference time frame. If the placing of these points does not seem suitable for the project, appropriate revisions should be undertaken. Generally, to move the non-zero and parity points in an advantageous way a substantial re-formulation of the project plan is necessary. For example, the non-zero point may be anticipated by adopting a staged development strategy (see section 2.2.3).

The product of task 1.22 is a document called *economic suitability report*, which summarizes the main aspects of the benefit evaluation report and of the cost evaluation report, and presents the results of the final global assessment.

4.6.8   Task 1.23: Assessment of practical realizability

The goal of this task is to evaluate the practical realizability of the KBS project as it is described in the global project plan. More specifically, the proposed project plan is analyzed in order to verify whether the required resources are likely to be available when needed. Task 1.23 takes in input the characterization of domain (from task 1.7), the project goals (from task 1.12), the functional specifications (from task 1.13), the operational specifications (from task 1.14), the technical specifications (from task 1.15), the acceptance criteria (from task 1.16), the draft technical design (from task 1.18), the draft organizational design (from task 1.20), and the global project plan (from task 1.21). This task is executed in parallel to tasks 1.22 and 1.24.

The task includes two stages concerning the availability and appropriateness of the basic resources (hardware, software and technical personnel) and of the knowledge sources, respectively. These are illustrated below.

Availability and appropriateness of basic resources

Basic resources include the hardware and software equipment and the technical personnel necessary for phases 2, 3, 4, and 5 of the life cycle.

The availability of hardware and software equipment is easy to check. If some equipment has to be specifically purchased for the project at hand, it is sufficient to verify that an adequate budget is available and that the purchasing procedure is initiated in time.

As far as the technical personnel is concerned, it is necessary to guarantee that the required professional roles are covered and that the desired levels of seniority are ensured. Should these requirements be not satisfied, appropriate actions (such as hiring, training, and re-training) are to be undertaken (see section 11.5). Great attention should be paid to making sure that a concrete guarantee exists about the availability of the right technical personnel for the entire length of time required. Allocation of personnel to more than one project has to be carefully evaluated, since it may cause severe problems of availability. Moreover, personnel should not only be technically competent, but also cooperative and interested in the project.

If a reasonable guarantee about the availability of technical personnel cannot be obtained, a KBS project should be discouraged. Any compromise on this matter would substantially increase the risks of the project.

Availability and appropriateness of knowledge sources

Verifying the existence of the necessary knowledge sources is a crucial point to ensure the practical realizability of a KBS. Three classes of possible knowledge sources are considered, namely domain experts, written materials, and naturalistic observation (see section 6.8.2 for their detailed definition).

As far as domain experts are concerned, it is not possible to start a KBS project without making sure that at least the following three requirements are verified:
• existence of sufficient domain experts, with the appropriate competence to cover all aspects of interest in the application domain, i.e. all knowledge classes identified;
• suitability of domain experts for the knowledge acquisition process;
• concrete availability of domain experts, when needed and for the length of time requested.

Figure 4.9 presents a list of items to consider in evaluating the appropriateness of domain experts [Prerau 89], [Slagle and Wick 88].

As far as written documents are concerned, it should first of all be checked whether any materials exists. Later a verification of their appropriateness for the knowledge acquisition process should be performed.

Finally, as far as naturalistic observation is concerned, it should be checked whether concrete possibilities to perform it exist in the context at hand. If this is the case, the availability of the necessary conditions for appropriately carrying out naturalistic observation sessions should be analyzed in detail (authorization, infrastructures, working conditions, etc.).

The product of task 1.23 is a document called *practical realizability report*. It provides an overall evaluation of the practical realizability of the project and an indication of the most critical aspects.

APPROPRIATENESS OF COMPETENCE
- Are domain experts genuine experts? Are they outstanding experts?
  Do they significantly outperform novices?
- Do domain experts have a long experience in the KBS task?
  How and why did they become experts?
- Is the reputation of domain experts such that the KBS outputs
  will have credibility and authority?

SUITABILITY FOR THE KNOWLEDGE ACQUISITION PROCESS
- Do domain expert usually teach novices? Are they good teachers?
- Do domain experts have good communication skills?
- Are domain experts introspective and articulated?
  Are they ready to think about their problem solving strategies?
- Are domain experts easy to work with?
- Do domain experts correctly understand their role within the KBS
  development process?
  Are they able to become intellectually involved in the KBS project?
  Do they believe in the project?
- Are domain experts sufficiently motivated to contribute to the KBS project?

AVAILABILITY
- Are domain experts actually available for the KBS project?
- Are domain experts available for the entire duration of the project?
- Are domain expert cooperative and willing to invest all the necessary
  time and effort needed for the project?
- Are domain experts supported by their management in their participation
  to the KBS project? Are they formally authorized? Are they concretely allowed
  to dedicate to the KBS project all the needed time?

Figure 4.9 Evaluating the appropriateness of domain experts.

4.6.9   Task 1.24: Assessment of opportunities and risks

So far, the analytical assessment of plausibility has been centered on the specific KBS to develop and the related design and production processes. This task comprises a wider perspective and evaluates the KBS project in the context where it is going to take place. More specifically, it verifies whether inside or outside the end-user organization any condition or situation may exist or arise in the near future which could constitute an important factor either in favor or against the project. Such factors are not necessarily directly related to the KBS itself, however, they may constitute important ingredients for the success or the failure of the project.

Task 1.24 takes in input the project goals (from task 1.12), the functional specifications (from task 1.13), the operational specifications (from task 1.14), the technical specifications (from task 1.15), the acceptance criteria (from task 1.16), the draft technical design (from task 1.18), the draft organizational design (from task 1.20), and the global project plan (from task 1.21). This task is executed in parallel with tasks 1.22 and 1.23.

The task includes two stages, namely, the identification of opportunities and the identification of risks. These are illustrated below.

Identification of opportunities

By that term *opportunity* (not to be confused with the same term used in chapter 3 with a different meaning) we mean any event or situation that may positively influence the success of a project. Opportunities may constitute a major reason for a positive attitude of decision makers towards the acceptance of a KBS project. Examples of typical opportunities may include:
- the existence of a corporate strategy towards technological innovation;
- the positive attitude of some member of the top-management towards high-technology projects;
- the existence of external funding opportunities;
- the opportunity to join an external initiative in the field of interest in cooperation with third parties;
- the information that an important competitor has started a similar project.

Of course, opportunities may greatly vary from case to case.

Identification of risks

A careful and detailed consideration of risks is a fundamental component of a KBS project. By the term *risk* we mean any event or situation that might constitute a cause of failure for a project. An early identification of risks during the KBS life cycle provides a basic support for the management activity [Boehm 89], [Ould 90], [Boehm 91]. Potential sources of risk in a KBS project are:
- personnel shortage or lack of competence;
- temporal constraints placed on the project which are too tight or very severe;
- unrealistic budget;
- specifications which are too ambitious or exaggerated;
- critical dependencies on other projects or events, concerning, for example, externally supplied KBS components, or externally performed tasks;
- the nature of the tasks dealt with by the KBS, which could concern issues and aspects of the organization which are politically critical, confidential, or secret;
- lack of commitment and support from managers;
- possible changes to the organization which might invalidate some of the fundamental assumptions on which the KBS project is founded;
- external events that might cause a sudden lack of some critical resources (financial support, domain experts, etc.).

The issue of risk identification is considered so important for the evaluation of the plausibility of a KBS project, that specific methodologies and tools are available for this task [Charette 89], [Hillmer et al. 91].

The product of task 1.24 is a document called *opportunities and risks report*. It provides an overall evaluation of the positive and negative factors identified, together with an appreciation of their likely occurrence, and an indication of appropriate preventive actions to enhance opportunities and reduce possible risks.

4.7   SYNTHESIS AND RELEASE

4.7.1   Step execution

Figure 4.10 presents a detailed view of KLIC tasks and products of the 'synthesis and release' step.

4.7.2   Task 1.25: Global evaluation of plausibility

A KBS project is *plausible* if all the five components considered in the analytical assessment receive a positive independent evaluation. If one or more of the components of the plausibility do not receive a positive evaluation, the project is not plausible. Compromises are not opportune. Of course, this case occurs only seldom and in really exceptional cases. In fact, as discussed in section 4.6.1, backtracking to critical aspects of the study and revision of earlier decisions may provide a way to reach a satisfactory evaluation of plausibility. Any possibility to reach a positive evaluation should not be left unexplored.

Task 1.25 takes in input the technical feasibility report (from task 1.17), the organizational impact report (from task 1.19), the global project plan (from task 1.21), the economic suitability report (from task 1.22), the practical realizability report (from task 1.23), and the opportunities and risks report (from task 1.24).

The global evaluation of plausibility goes through two stages. First, the various alternatives generated during the analytical assessment are resumed and represented in a visual form, for example, in a graphic or table. Later, a global comparative assessment is developed and expressed in short, clear statements.

Figure 4.11 illustrates the global evaluation of plausibility by means of a diamond diagram. Each component of plausibility has been assigned five qualitative values (VP: very positive, P: positive, S: sufficient, L: low, VL: very low). Plausibility and non-plausibility areas are indicated. The diamond diagram can help visualize comparisons of different alternatives, providing an immediate idea of their differences, and helping identify ways for improving their quality. The diamond diagram supports visual reasoning and provides a useful tool for exploring alternative decisions and their effects.

The global evaluation of plausibility is not expected to conclude with a unique and definitive choice. The experts in charge of the plausibility study are not requested to make decisions, but - instead - to support the decision makers through a competent and reliable analysis and a detailed indication of the possible directions to take.

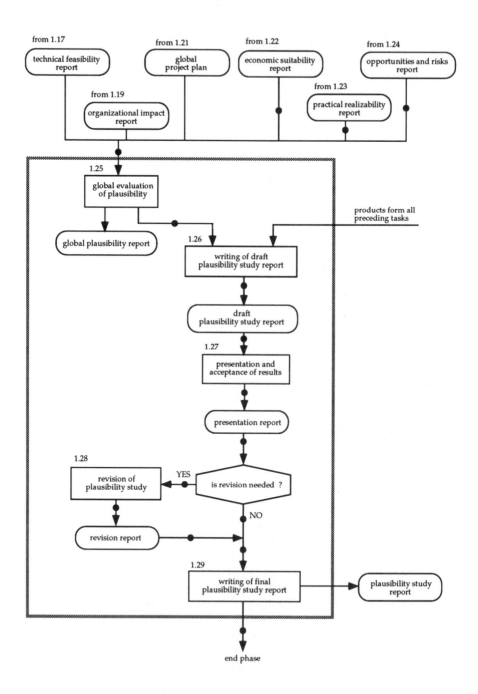

Figure 4.10 Synthesis and release: KLIC tasks and products.

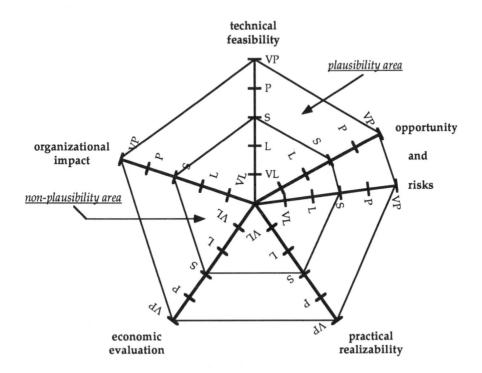

Figure 4.11 Global evaluation of plausibility.

The product of task 1.25 is a document called *global plausibility report*. It includes a summary of the assessment of the individual components of plausibility - for all alternatives developed, formulated either in qualitative or in quantitative terms, and the illustration of the results of the global evaluation of plausibility.

4.7.3   Task 1.26: Writing of draft plausibility study report

The goal of this task is to produce the draft version of a document which contains a summary of the activities done, a detailed illustration of the results achieved, and, in particular, the global plausibility report. Task 1.26 takes in input the products from all preceding tasks. The product of task 1.26 is a document called *draft plausibility study report*. It is addressed to the management, who will use it as a decision support aid to assess the appropriateness of the KBS project. It also contains useful information for the project leaders who will be in charge of organizing, setting-up, and managing the future KBS project. A possible table of contents for the plausibility study report is shown in Figure 4.12.

Needless to say, that the draft plausibility study report, being an important document directed to the top management, should be well-written in a concise and clear style. A good, but poorly written document might not be well-understood and will definitely spoil even a well-done plausibility study.

4.7.4   Task 1.27: Presentation and acceptance of results

Once the draft plausibility study report is compiled, it should be presented to the management for evaluation and eventually acceptance.

Generally, presentation of the draft plausibility study report, evaluation, and acceptance are carried out during a specific meeting involving the project leader and the managers in question. The presentation should outline the main features of the KBS proposed, focusing on potential benefits, organizational impact, and opportunities. Costs and possible risks should be highlighted and motivated as well. The most significant alternatives examined during the plausibility study should be reviewed. The global evaluation of plausibility must be presented and discussed in detail. Needless to say, the presentation of the results of plausibility study is very important, since the continuation of the project greatly depends on its success.

Task 1.27 takes in input the plausibility study report (from task 1.26). The product of task 1.27 is a document called *presentation report*, where the result of the presentation is reported and discussed.

At the end of this task, it must be verified whether the plausibility study can be accepted as it is or if it needs corrections, refinements, or extensions. If this is the case, the plausibility study must be revised (task 1.28). Otherwise, the execution of the step continues with task 1.29.

It should be stressed that task 1.27 only approves the plausibility study, possibly with a request for revision. The final choice concerning the approval of the project, including the decision whether to actually start the KBS project or not and the selection of the alternative to consider among those examined, does not pertain to the plausibility study. Generally, upon completion of the plausibility study, the management will choose whether to proceed further with the KBS development, or to abandon the project. Sometimes, it may also happen that the management is not yet convinced about the opportunity to continue, or about the right direction to take, and so it postpones these decisions to the end of the development of a demonstrator (phase 2).

4.7.5   Task 1.28: Revision of plausibility study

Top management quite often feel the need to comment on the draft plausibility study report and make requests for revisions. In such cases, the relevant tasks are resumed and the necessary revisions are carried out.

Task 1.28 takes in input the presentation report (from task 1.27). The product of task 1.28 is a document called *revision report*, which contains a detailed illustration of all revised points of the study and the corrections, refinements, or extensions applied. From the table shown in Figure 4.2 it is apparent that this task should not exceed 20% of the entire duration of this phase.

1. **Introduction**
   - short introduction to the *plausibility study* phase
   - specific management indications considered
   - difficulties encountered and solutions adopted
   - synthesis of the activities carried out and of the main results obtained

2. **Analysis of the application domain and of the potential KBS application**
   - the process-structure model
   - map of the level of automation
   - characterization of the domain
   - characterization of the potential KBS application

3. **Requirements, specifications, and acceptance criteria**
   - requirements
   - functional, operational, and technical specifications
   - acceptance criteria

4. **Draft technical design**
   - presentation of the draft technical design
   - motivations and discussion of main alternatives

5. **Draft organizational design**
   - presentation of the draft organizational design
   - motivations and discussion of main alternatives

6. **Global project plan**
   - presentation of the global project plan
   - motivations and discussion of main alternatives

7. **Summary of analytical assessment**
   - technical feasibility
   - organizational impact
   - economic suitability
   - practical realizability
   - opportunities and risks

8. **Global evaluation**
   - summary of alternatives
   - discussion of alternatives and guidelines for final decision making

Figure 4.12 Plausibility study report: suggested table of contents.

4.7.6   Task 1.29: Writing of final plausibility study report

After the needed revisions have been carried out, the plausibility study report is compiled and then released. Task 1.29 takes in input the draft plausibility study report (from task 1.26), the presentation report (from task 1.27), and the revision report (from task 1.28) - if any. The product of task 1.29 is a document called *plausibility study report*, which represents the final, updated and corrected version of the draft previously produced.

The plausibility study report, once approved and released, will constitute the basis for organizing the subsequent phases of the KBS life cycle.

Sometimes, the final, official release of the plausibility study report takes place during a specific technical meeting where the results of plausibility study are presented to a wide audience.

5

CONSTRUCTION OF THE DEMONSTRATOR

5.1   PHASE OVERVIEW

5.1.1   Motivations and objectives

The purpose of the 'construction of the demonstrator' phase is to develop a running system, namely the demonstrator, which can anticipate a sub-set of the functions of the final KBS.

There are several reasons to justify the choice of developing a demonstrator. First of all, some aspects of the problem to be tackled by the KBS may not be well-understood or not specified enough after the preliminary analyses performed during the plausibility study. In addition, some technical, organizational, or management choices made during the plausibility study may appear critical or not sufficiently justified. There may be a specific need to promote the KBS project, to gain management approval and support, and to get domain experts and potential users concretely involved and committed in the initiative.

In all the above cases, more concrete, practical evidence, based on experimentation with a demonstrator, may be useful and at the same time effectively contribute to the reduction of risks [Maude and Willis 91]. The need for the construction of the demonstrator - often called by different names: pilot system, feasibility prototype, first-cut phase prototype, initial prototype, or simply prototype - is supported by several authors [Wilkerson 85], [Oliver 86], [Oliver 87], [Greenwell 88], [Prerau 90], [Harmon and Sawyer 90].

The goals of the 'construction of the demonstrator' phase are:
- improving management awareness of the potentials of knowledge-based technology and gaining management approval and support for a KBS project;

- getting the management, domain experts, and users concretely involved and committed to the initiative, thus securing their cooperation;
- developing a better understanding of user requirements and identifying more detailed and precise specifications of the KBS [Gladden 82], [Carey and Mason 83];
- addressing some critical technical aspects of the KBS which have not been fully explored in the plausibility study, and possibly revising and improving the draft technical design;
- improving the understanding of the organizational impact of the KBS and possibly refining the draft organizational design;
- refining the draft project plan.

The construction of the demonstrator, although quite common in KBS projects, is an optional life-cycle phase. In fact, in some cases the motivations illustrated above do not always hold and, therefore, phase 2 may be skipped, by proceeding directly to the development of the prototype. This takes place when the technical complexity of the project is limited, or other projects have already been carried out within the same context, or when the people involved in the project are already well-acquainted with knowledge-based technology and have a good and positive attitude towards the initiative. By skipping phase 2 there is a significant reduction of project duration and costs. Therefore, the demonstrator should be constructed only if strictly necessary.

An interesting alternative to the execution of phase 2 consists in organizing phase 3 in such a way that, after a limited period of time (for example, 4 to 8 months), a first version of the prototype, called *early prototype*, is produced and demonstrated. Of course, the early prototype is technically very different from a demonstrator; while the former represents the first stage of development of a full KBS, the latter is a complete implementation of a KBS with limited scope and functions. The demonstrator is usually abandoned after the end of the phase 2, while the early prototype is further extended and developed during phase 3. Moreover, the early prototype has different goals from the ones of the demonstrator, being primarily aimed at showing the concrete progress of the project.

Note also that for projects not particularly endorsed by the management, it may be appropriate to invert the execution of phases 1 and 2, developing a demonstrator first, to gain management involvement, and postponing the execution of the plausibility study.

5.1.2   Inputs and products

The construction of the demonstrator may be requested by the managers specifically interested in the KBS application considered or it may be proposed by an external supplier. The 'construction of the demonstrator' phase takes in input:
- a document called *management indications*, which includes requirements, objectives, and constraints provided by the management, to be taken into account in the construction of the demonstrator;
- the plausibility study report produced in phase 1.

The products of the 'construction of the demonstrator' phase are:

- the *demonstrator*, a running KBS solving a limited and well-specified part of the entire problem that will be approached by the final system and featuring a sub-set of its expected functions;
- the *demonstrator report*, which contains a synthesis of the activities carried out and a detailed illustration of the results achieved.

Finally, the 'construction of the demonstrator' phase may produce a specific *management report* in the case the prerequisites for its execution are not satisfied and the phase is stopped (see task 2.1). The products of the construction of the demonstrator are directed to the management. They will also constitute an important input for the project team in charge of the development of the prototype (phase 3).

5.1.3   Phase structure and task outline

Figure 5.1 presents an outline of the KLIC tasks of the 'construction of the demonstrator' phase.
    The overall logical structure of the 'construction of the demonstrator' phase is organized into five steps:
- the 'start-up' step verifies that the prerequisites are satisfied and plans the whole phase;
- the 'basic choices and definitions' step, after the definition of the goals of the demonstrator, identifies the specific problems and sample cases to be addressed, and defines the demonstrator specifications;
- the 'analysis and design' step goes through three tasks: the development of the demonstrator conceptual model, the selection and acquisition of the basic development environment, the development of the demonstrator technical design;
- the 'development' step, is meant to implement the demonstrator empty system and the development support system, and then focuses on the construction of the knowledge base of the demonstrator through the iterative process of knowledge elicitation, coding, integration, checking, and validation;
- the 'demonstration, evaluation, and synthesis' step is concerned with the final demonstration, the evaluation of results, and the writing of the final demonstrator report.

As shown in Figure 5.1, some tasks in the 'development' step may be executed in parallel. Phase 2 also includes a loop; in the 'development' step, the construction of the knowledge base is organized through a cycle aimed at repeatedly performing knowledge elicitation, coding, and verification until the demonstrator specifications are fully met.
    As we have already mentioned in section 2.1.3, the time it takes for the 'construction of the demonstrator' phase is generally between 2 to 6 months (elapsed time), depending on the complexity of the application and the goals of the demonstrator.
    It may be useful to split the complete duration of the entire phase into the individual duration of its component tasks. The table of Figure 5.2 shows in percentages the duration of each task with respect to the duration of the whole phase. The data reported are, of course, only indicative; they refer to an average

situation, and may vary from case to case. Percentages shown in parentheses refer to tasks which are carried out only subject to specific conditions, and, therefore, count over 100.

START-UP			
	2.1	verification of prerequisites	
IF		prerequisites are not satisfied	
THEN	2.2	writing of management report	
		stop phase	
	2.3	planning of construction of the demonstrator	
BASIC CHOICES AND DEFINITIONS			
	2.4	identification of demonstrator goals	
	2.5	identification of sub-problems and sample cases	
	2.6	definition of demonstrator specifications	
ANALYSIS AND DESIGN			
	2.7	conceptual modeling	
	2.8	selection and acquisition of the basic development environment	
	2.9	technical design	
DEVELOPMENT			
	2.10	implementation of the empty system	
	2.11	implementation of the development support system	
LOOP			
	2.12	knowledge acquisition planning	
	2.13	knowledge elicitation and protocol analysis	
	2.14	knowledge coding	
	2.15	knowledge integration and verification	
UNTIL		demonstrator specifications are fully met	
DEMONSTRATION, EVALUATION, AND SYNTHESIS			
	2.16	demonstration	
	2.17	evaluation	
	2.18	writing of demonstrator report	

Figure 5.1 Construction of the demonstrator: KLIC tasks outline.

5.1.4   Project team composition

The construction of the demonstrator is usually carried out by a project team internal to the user organization. Less frequently, it may be assigned to an external supplier. This is especially appropriate in the case where the end-user organization intends to assign the development of the prototype to an external supplier. In such a case, the construction of the demonstrator may serve to test the validity and appropriateness of the supplier chosen, before involving him in the more complex and substantial tasks of phase 3.

In particular, for the construction of the demonstrator the project team is typically made up of:

- 1 project manager, usually a senior manager, in charge of formally representing the target organization from the administrative point of view;
- 1 project leader, usually a senior professional, responsible for the results of the entire phase and in charge of the technical and organizational management of the project team; the project leader also provides specific support to all critical tasks of the phase;
- 1 designer, in charge of the most technical tasks of construction of the demonstrator (tasks 2.8 and 2.9);
- 1 to 2 knowledge engineers, at least one of them being in a senior position, in charge of all tasks related to knowledge analysis and modeling (tasks 2.5 and 2.7), and of the development of the knowledge base (tasks 2.12, 2.13, 2.14, and 2.15);
- 1 to 2 developers, in charge of developing the software components of the demonstrator (tasks 2.10 and 2.11);
- 1 or more representatives of the top management;

TASKS	time %
START-UP	
2.1 verification of prerequisites	2
2.2 writing of management report	(5)
2.3 planning of construction of the demonstrator	3
BASIC CHOICES AND DEFINITIONS	
2.4 identification of demonstrator goals	5
2.5 identification of sub-problems and sample cases	3
2.6 definition of specifications	2
ANALYSIS AND DESIGN	
2.7 conceptual modeling	5
2.8 selection and acquisition of the basic development environment	3
2.9 technical design	2
DEVELOPMENT	
2.10 implementation of the empty system	15
2.11 implementation of the development support system	5
2.12 knowledge acquisition planning	5
2.13 knowledge elicitation and protocol analysis	20
2.14 knowledge coding	15
2.15 knowledge integration and verification	5
DEMONSTRATION, EVALUATION, AND SYNTHESIS	
2.16 demonstration	5
2.17 evaluation	3
2.18 writing of demonstrator report	2

Figure 5.2 Construction of the demonstrator: task duration in percentage.

- intermediate managers of all departments concerned with the application domain considered;
- domain experts of the application domain considered;
- representatives of the potential users of the KBS.

If possible, it is advisable that the project manager, the project leader, the knowledge engineers, and at least some of the domain experts be the same ones involved in the previous phase 1 (plausibility study).

The table shown in Figure 5.3 summarizes the composition of the project team for development of a demonstrator.

	REGULAR MEMBERS	SUPPORTING MEMBERS	CONSULTING MEMBERS
project manager		1	
project leader	1		
designer	0-1		
knowledge engineers	1-2		
developers	1-2		
top managers		1 or more	
intermediate managers		as appropriate	
domain experts		as appropriate	
potential users		as appropriate	

Figure 5.3 Construction of the demonstrator: project team composition.

As it can be noted, the composition of the project team is nearly the same in all possible situations; in the case of complex and demanding demonstrators, the only possibility to speed-up the execution of the phase is to employ 2 knowledge engineers and developers, rather than just one. This implies that complex cases will usually take much more time (elapsed time) than simple ones.

5.2   START-UP

5.2.1   Step execution

Figure 5.4 presents a detailed view of KLIC tasks and products of the 'start-up' step.

5.2.2   Task 2.1: Verification of prerequisites

Task 2.1 takes in input the management indications and the plausibility study report (from task 1.29). Before starting the construction of the demonstrator several prerequisites must be fulfilled, in particular, proof of the need must be shown. Too often in past years the construction of the demonstrator has taken place with no specific goals set, but simply as a first step preceding more considerable engagements. All these demonstrators turned out to be useless, if not detrimental to a correct management of a KBS initiative. This life cycle phase is not mandatory, and should be skipped whenever not strictly necessary. In light of this, it is important that there be specific goals that motivate the construction of the demonstrator (see section 5.1.2).

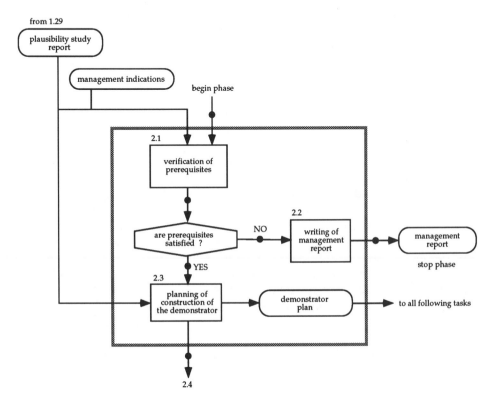

Figure 5.4 Start-up: KLIC tasks and products.

Specific prerequisites that should be satisfied before starting the construction of the demonstrator are listed below:
- a plausibility study to indicate if a demonstrator is needed should have been carried out; however, as already mentioned in section 5.1.1, the plausibility study may sometimes be postponed to the construction of the demonstrator;
- when the management requests a demonstrator, it must be fully aware of needs, scope, and objectives;
- the requirements, objectives, and constraints proposed by the management - if any - must be consistent with the purpose and nature of the construction of the demonstrator;
- the needed resources for the execution of the phase must be available.

If prerequisites are not satisfied, the construction of the demonstrator should not continue. If such a case occurs, a report should be prepared for the management (task 2.2) and the construction of the demonstrator should be stopped. Otherwise, the execution of the phase continues with task 2.3.

5.2.3   Task 2.2: Writing of management report

In the case where prerequisites are not satisfied, the project leader in charge of the construction of the demonstrator should prepare a report for the management and stop the execution of the phase. The product of task 2.2 is a document called *management report*. It should present a detailed account of why the construction of the demonstrator is worthless or impossible to accomplish. It should be appropriately motivated. If appropriate, the report can be personally discussed by the project leader with the management of the organization.

5.2.4   Task 2.3: Planning of construction of the demonstrator

Task 2.3 takes in input the management indications - if any - and the plausibility study report (from task 1.29). The product of task 2.3 is a document called *demonstrator plan*.

The demonstrator plan should be discussed with all members of the project team, who should understand the importance of their role and of their engagements. It should also be formally approved by the management of the end-user organization. Note that, as shown in Figure 5.4, the demonstrator plan is not an input to any specific task. It will be used by the project leader for management and control issues throughout the whole phase (see section 9.3.2).

The demonstrator plan should be refined when, during the development of phase 2, new information is made available for a more precise and realistic definition and scheduling of the activities to carry out. Actually, a revision of the plan is probably appropriate after tasks 2.8 and 2.12, and before task 2.16.

5.3   BASIC CHOICES AND DEFINITIONS

5.3.1   Step execution

Figure 5.5 presents a detailed view of KLIC tasks and products of the 'basic choices and definitions' step.

5.3.2   Demonstrator types

Depending on the goals considered (see section 5.1.2), several types of demonstrators may be identified [Floyd 84], [Gudes et al. 86], [Morris 90], [Maude and Willis 91]. The following list illustrates some of the most typical cases:
- *promotional demonstrator*, promotes the acceptance of knowledge-based technology by the end-user organization by concretely showing some of its potentials, and obtaining management approval and support for a KBS project;
- *commercial demonstrator*, supports the acceptance of a proposal for a KBS project by the management of the end-user organization by anticipating a sample of the performance expected from the target system;
- *involvement demonstrator*, encourages involvement of management, domain experts, and users in the project, by convincing them of the

appropriateness and power of knowledge-based technology, of the opportunity of the specific KBS project, of its potentials and benefits;

- *exploratory demonstrator*, aims at analyzing, verifying, and possibly refining or extending the KBS specifications defined in the plausibility study;
- *experimentation demonstrator*, helps experiment, validate, and possibly refine some specific aspects of the draft technical design developed in the plausibility study;
- *organizational demonstrator*, improves the understanding of the organizational impact of the KBS and possibly refines the draft organizational design developed in the plausibility study;
- *planning demonstrator*, aims at validating or correcting some critical aspects of the draft project plan developed in the plausibility study, such as scheduling, resources, domain experts to involve in the project, etc.

In order to better appreciate the differences among the various types of demonstrators defined above, each category may be described in terms of a set of attributes concerning specific aspects of the demonstrator or of its development process. The table reported in Figure 5.6 shows a comparative analysis of the various demonstrator types.

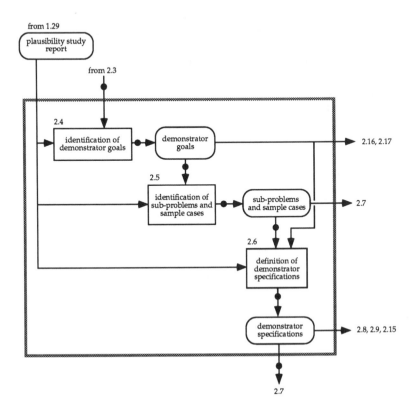

Figure 5.5 Basic choices and definitions: KLIC tasks and products.

	promo-tional	commer-cial	involve-ment	explora-tion	planning	organiza-tional	experim-entation
through-away	yes	yes	yes	yes	no		no
near-to-product					yes	yes	possible
software re-use	no	no	no	no	possible		yes
knowledge re-use	possible	possible			yes	possible	possible
time constraints	rapid	very rapid					
cost constraints	low	low					
technical complexity	low	low	medium		medium	medium	high
development time	short	short	long			long	long

Figure 5.6 Typical features of various demonstrator types.

The rows denote the features considered; the columns denote the various demonstrator types. The cells of the table contain qualitative values referred to typical situations; empty cells indicate that no reference value may be given for the relevant feature for the corresponding type of demonstrator. The features considered are defined below:

- *throw-away*: Is the demonstrator going to be developed just for the purpose of the demonstration and then abandoned [Edwards 91]?
- *near-to-product*: Is the demonstrator developed in such a way that, even if featuring only very limited functions in comparison with the full KBS, it can be inserted in the final application context anyway and be field tested or even regularly used?
- *software re-use*: Is any part of the software included in the demonstrator possibly re-usable in the development of the prototype?
- *knowledge re-use*: Is the knowledge base developed for the demonstrator re-usable in the development of the knowledge base of the prototype?
- *time constraints*: How fast should the development of the demonstrator be in order to effectively meet its goals?
- *cost constraints*: Which budget is assigned to the construction of the demonstrator?
- *technical complexity*: What is the expected technical complexity of the demonstrator?
- *development time*: What is the average development time of the demonstrator?

5.3.3   Task 2.4: Identification of demonstration goals

This task identifies the goals and the type of demonstrator to develop. Task 2.4 takes in input the plausibility study report (from task 1.29).

Initially, the real, specific goals that motivate the construction of the demonstrator in the situation at hand must be identified. To this purpose, information provided by the plausibility study report should be integrated with new indications collected through direct analysis and interviews to the management, the domain experts, and the users.

Once the demonstrator goals have been identified, the appropriate type of demonstrator for the situation at hand must be defined (see section 5.3.2). The comparative analysis of various demonstrator types reported in Figure 5.6 may help in this task. Since a variety of different goals may support the construction of the demonstrator, the appropriate demonstrator type may result being a combination of two (or three) of the types suggested in section 5.3.2. In such cases, it is important not to mix many different kinds of demonstrators, in order to keep the complexity (and, therefore, time and cost) of this phase within the usual limits. For example, it would be very difficult to develop a demonstrator for both commercial or promotional purposes as well as for technical experimentation.

The product of task 2.4 is a document called *demonstrator goals*, which presents a detailed account of the goals and the type of demonstrator to build.

5.3.4   Task 2.5: Identification of sub-problems and sample cases

The goals of this task is to precisely identify the boundaries of the demonstrator, i.e. the specific sub-problems it should focus on, as well as a certain number of sample cases the KBS should be capable of dealing with. Task 2.5 takes in input the plausibility study report (from task 1.29) and the demonstrator goals (from task 2.4).

The criteria to use to identify the sub-problems clearly depend on the goals of the demonstrator. For example, for a technical experimentation demonstrator, the chosen sub-problems will concern a part of the KBS which is considered critical from the technical point of view, while, in the case of a promotional or commercial demonstrator, the focus will be on some problem areas which can show some basic advantage or impressive benefits. The choice of the sub-problems should balance between two contrasting exigencies. They should be neither too easy or marginal so as to make the demonstrator weak, nor too complex to be satisfactorily tackled within the time and cost constraints established for this phase.

The description of the selected sub-problems may refer to the functional specifications produced in the plausibility study and must clearly indicate which classes of inputs should be accepted, and which classes of outputs and behavior should be produced. Inputs, outputs, and expected behavior are usually specified by means of sample cases. The description of sample cases is, of course, purely functional, with no commitment to specific implementation choices. In the definition of sample cases it is important to focus on the user interface, generally an important part of any demonstrator.

The product of task 2.5 is a document called *sub-problems and sample cases*, which defines the sub-problems to be faced and the sample cases to be handled by the demonstrator.

5.3.5   Task 2.6: Definition of demonstrator specifications

The goal of this task is to identify the specifications of the demonstrator. Task 2.6 takes in input the plausibility study report (from task 1.29), the demonstrator goals (from task 2.4), and the sub-problems and sample cases (from task 2.5).

The demonstrator specifications may be either a sub-set of the KBS specifications identified during the plausibility study, or they may be designed specifically for the demonstrator from scratch. This task is mainly executed by the knowledge engineer.

Similar to the prototyping techniques used for the development of traditional software systems, the functions of the demonstrator, compared to that of the full KBS, may range between two extremes [Floyd 84]:

• the demonstrator may cover only a limited set of selected functions implemented in a rather complete way (*vertical demonstrator*);
• the demonstrator may be constituted by a partial implementation of most functions of the full system (*horizontal demonstrator*).

In practice, a demonstrator may share to some extent the features of both a vertical and a horizontal demonstrator, since it is usually difficult to adhere to one of the two approaches in a very strict way. However, different types of demonstrators are usually most likely to profit more from one of the two styles. Typically, promotional or commercial demonstrators are often vertical demonstrators, while involvement of exploration demonstrators are generally horizontal demonstrators.

Another important aspect to address in this task concerns the emphasis to place on the external appearance of the demonstrator, i.e. on the level of sophistication of the human-computer interaction. This is a crucial aspect in any type of demonstrator, and any effort made for a better user interface is not wasted.

The product of task 2.6 is a document called *demonstrator specifications*, which provides a detailed definition of functional, technical, and operational specifications. As far as defining and organizing specifications is concerned, the reader may refer to section 4.5.4, where the issue is discussed in detail in the frame of phase 1.

5.4   ANALYSIS AND DESIGN

5.4.1   Step execution

Figure 5.7 presents a detailed view of KLIC tasks and products of the 'analysis and design' step.

This step is very similar to those dedicated to the conceptual design and technical design for the KBS prototype (phase 3), even if carried out in a reduced and limited way. The tasks of this step are, therefore, only briefly illustrated; a more detailed analysis can be found in the description of corresponding tasks of phase 3.

5.4.2   Task 2.7: Conceptual modeling

This task includes the analysis and modeling of domain knowledge and is dedicated to the development of the conceptual model of the demonstrator. This is clearly limited to the sub-problems identified in task 2.5. Task 2.7 takes in input the sub-problems and sample cases (from task 2.5) and the demonstrator specifications (from task 2.6). The product of task 2.7 is a document called the *demonstrator conceptual model*.

The execution of this task is very similar to tasks 3.4 and 3.5, even if more limited in scope and generally not as detailed. A thorough account can be found in section 6.5.2 and 6.5.3.

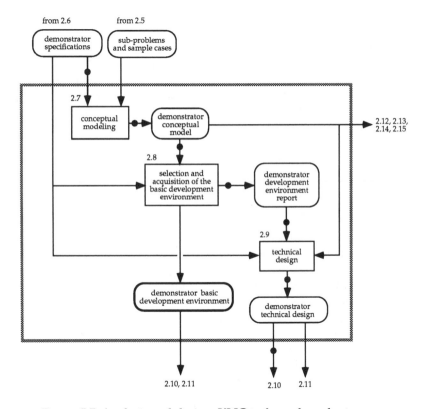

Figure 5.7 Analysis and design: KLIC tasks and products.

5.4.3   Task 2.8: Selection and acquisition of the basic development environment

The goal of this task is to select and acquire the basic development environment which is going to be utilized for the construction of the demonstrator. Task 2.8

takes in input the demonstrator specifications (from task 2.6) and the demonstrator conceptual model (from task 2.7).

Demonstrators usually do not require a sophisticated, general, or specially flexible basic development environment (a general illustration of KBS development tools can be found in section 6.4). However, different types of demonstrators (see section 5.3.2) may call for different development environments. The two extreme situations are constituted by:

- Promotional or commercial demonstrators, which can be developed using small-size tools with a limited number of knowledge representation and reasoning mechanisms, possibly not very flexible, and KBS-specific. These types of demonstrators usually need a basic development environment allowing fast development at low cost, and including effective tools for user interface development.
- Experimentation demonstrators, which are much more demanding from the technical point of view and require medium size tools, covering several knowledge representation and reasoning mechanisms, and possibly with high generality and flexibility levels. For these types of demonstrators exploration is generally very important, and should be appropriately supported by the basic development environment selected.

Once the most appropriate basic development environment has been defined, the selected tools should be actually acquired. This usually implies a careful selection of the vendor and an accurate analysis of the selling conditions.

The products of task 2.8 are:

- a document called *demonstrator development environment report*, which illustrates the comparative analysis carried out to select the basic development environment and the main reasons of the choice made;
- a set of software systems, namely the selected *demonstrator basic development environment*, to be used for the construction of the demonstrator.

5.4.4   Task 2.9: Technical design

The goal of this task is to develop the technical design of the demonstrator, including both the empty system and the development support system (a definition of the development support system can be found in section 6.4). Task 2.9 takes in input the demonstrator specifications (from task 2.6), the demonstrator conceptual model (from task 2.7), and the demonstrator development environment report (from task 2.8). The product of task 2.9 is a document called *demonstrator technical design*, which includes both the logical model of the demonstrator and the detailed design of the empty system and the development support system.

The execution of this task is very similar to tasks 3.7, 3.8, 3.9, 3.11, and 3.12, even if more limited in scope and generally not as detailed. A thorough account can be found in sections 6.6.2, 6.6.3, 6.6.4, 6.6.6, and 6.6.7.

5.5   DEVELOPMENT

5.5.1   Step execution

Figure 5.8 presents a detailed view of KLIC tasks and products of the 'development' step.
This step is very similar to those dedicated to the construction of the empty system and of the development support system, and to the development of the knowledge base for a KBS prototype (phase 3), even if carried out in a reduced and limited way. The tasks of this step are, therefore, only briefly illustrated; a more detailed analysis can be found in the description of corresponding tasks of phase 3.

5.5.2   Task 2.10: Implementation of the empty system

This task is dedicated to the implementation of the empty system of the demonstrator. Task 2.10 takes in input the demonstrator basic development environment (from task 2.8) and the demonstrator technical design (from task 2.9). The product of task 2.10 is a software system, namely the *demonstrator empty system*.
The execution of this task is very similar to task 3.13, even if more limited in scope and of a far more limited extension. A thorough account can be found in section 6.7.2.

5.5.3   Task 2.11: Implementation of the development support system

This task is dedicated to the implementation of the development support system of the demonstrator. Task 2.11 takes in input the demonstrator basic development environment (from task 2.8) and the demonstrator technical design (from task 2.9). The product of task 2.11 is a software system, namely the *demonstrator development support system*.
The execution of this task is very similar to task 3.14, even if more limited in scope and of a far more limited extension. A thorough account can be found in section 6.7.3.

5.5.4   Task 2.12: Knowledge acquisition planning

This task is the first in a loop of four (namely: 2.12, 2.13, 2.14, and 2.15), globally dedicated to the development of the knowledge base of the demonstrator. This task is devoted to the selection of knowledge sources, the overall planning of knowledge base construction, and the planning of knowledge acquisition. Task 2.12 takes in input the demonstrator conceptual model (from task 2.7). The product of task 2.12 is a document called *demonstrator knowledge acquisition plan*.

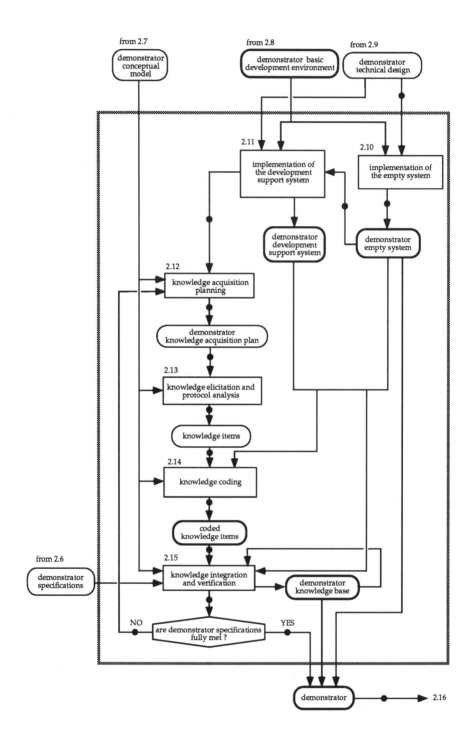

Figure 5.8 Development: KLIC tasks and products.

The execution of this task is very similar to tasks 3.15 and 3.16, even if more limited in scope and of a far more limited extension. A thorough account can be found in sections 6.8.2 and 6.8.3.

5.5.5   Task 2.13: Knowledge elicitation and protocol analysis

The goal of thsi task is to elicit domain knowledge. Task 2.13 takes in input the demonstrator conceptual model (from task 2.7) and the demonstrator knowledge acquisition plan (from task 2.12). The product of task 2.13 is a set of documented fragments of domain knowledge, called *knowledge items.*

The execution of this task is very similar to task 3.17, even if more limited in scope and of a far more limited extension. A thorough account can be found in section 6.8.5.

5.5.6   Task 2.14: Knowledge coding

This task is dedicated to the coding of the elicited knowledge. Task 2.14 takes in input the demonstrator conceptual model (from task 2.7), the demonstrator empty system (from task 2.10), the demonstrator development support system (from task 2.11), and the knowledge items (from task 2.13). The product of task 2.14, called *coded knowledge items,* is a new piece of the knowledge base of the demonstrator containing the fragments of knowledge just elicited in the previous task, appropriately represented by means of the available knowledge representation language.

The execution of this task is very similar to task 3.18, even if more limited in scope and of a far more limited extension. A thorough account can be found in section 6.8.6.

5.5.7   Task 2.15: Knowledge integration and verification

The goal of this task is to integrate the coded knowledge items produced in task 2.14 with the previous version of the demonstrator knowledge base, and to test, examine, check, and probe the knowledge base being developed (see section 9.3.2). Task 2.15 takes in input the demonstrator specifications (from task 2.6), the demonstrator conceptual model (from task 2.7), the demonstrator empty system (from task 2.10), the demonstrator development support system (from task 2.11), the coded knowledge items (from task 2.14), and the demonstartor knowledge base (from the previous execution of task 2.15). The product of task 2.15 is a new extended, improved, and verified version of the knowledge base of the demonstrator, called *demonstrator knowledge base.*

The execution of this task is very similar to task 3.19, even if more limited in scope and of a far more limited extension. A thorough account can be found in section 6.8.7.

At the end of this task, it must be verified whether the demonstrator specifications are fully met or not. If this is the case, the loop started with task 2.12 is terminated, the *demonstrator* is produced, and the execution proceeds with the next step. Otherwise, the execution of the step continues with a new iteration of the loop (starting again from task 2.12).

5.6   DEMONSTRATION, EVALUATION, AND SYNTHESIS

5.6.1   Step execution

Figure 5.9 presents a detailed view of KLIC tasks and products of the 'demonstration, evaluation, and synthesis' step.

5.6.2   Task 2.16: Demonstration

This task shows the demonstrator developed in the previous tasks to the managers, domain experts, and intended users. Task 2.16 takes in input the demonstrator goals (from task 2.4) and the demonstrator (from task 2.15). The results of the demonstration are directly related to the achievement of the goals of the demonstrator, making this task essential for the success of the whole phase.

There are two approaches to perform the *demonstration*. In fact, the demonstration may be systematic, well-structured, and formally organized (*formal demonstration*), or it can look much more like an informal meeting where the system developed is shown without following a strict experimental procedure (*informal demonstration*). The choice between formal or informal demonstration is usually strictly related to the type of demonstrator to be shown. In fact, some types of demonstrators basically communicate information to the participants in the demonstration or they increase their level of involvement, while other types of demonstrators acquire specific information for later tasks. The former type of demonstrator usually calls for informal demonstrations, whereas the latter requires a more formal approach. For example, formal demonstrations are very useful in exploration demonstrators which are focused on user interface issues. In such cases, the demonstration can be viewed very much like a psychological experiment [McBurney 83], where several knowledge elicitation techniques can be exploited, including: focused and structured interviews, thinking aloud, commentary, inquisitive observation, and brainstorming (see section 6.8.4). Formal demonstrations constitute a very useful tool for experimentation demonstrators, when the solutions proposed to some critical technical aspects have to be confronted with the opinion of other KBS experts.

The choice between a formal approach and an informal one, influences the typical number of demonstration sessions to be carried out. Formal demonstrations typically require a higher number of sessions.

The design of an adequate demonstration plan is the first activity to carry out in this task. A schedule of the demonstrations specifying the following information should be included:

- type of demonstration (formal or informal) and goals to achieve;
- participants in the demonstration, such as the users, domain experts, managers, customers, etc.;

- procedure to be followed and content of the demonstration:
  - the procedure could prescribe, for example, that the user be specifically trained to use the KBS and then asked to perform a given task for a given amount of time under the supervision of a tutor (for example, one of the knowledge engineers), which is also responsible for collecting specific information during the session;
  - the content may generally range from purely functional and operational, where attention is on the external behavior of the KBS and its performance, to strictly technical, where the focus is on the knowledge used and the reasoning steps performed;

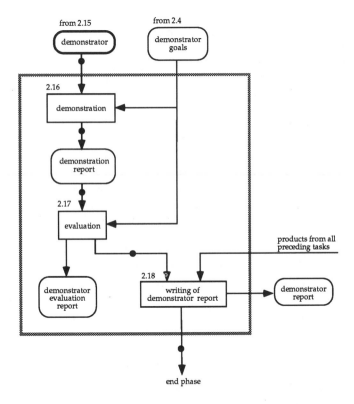

Figure 5.9 Demonstration, evaluation, and synthesis: KLIC tasks and products.

- specification of the information to acquire during the demonstration; this may include:
  - generic informal comments and reactions;
  - feedback of some specific functional, operational, or technical aspect of the KBS;
  - formal, usually quantitative measurements of user behavior, concerning, for example, learning effort, problem-solving success-rate, interaction overhead, interaction failures, etc.;
  - informal, usually qualitative observations on KBS behavior (see section 9.3.2 and Figure 9.1 for a detailed account);

- specification of the knowledge acquisition techniques to employ - if any - for gathering the specific information.

Once the demonstration plan is ready, the preparation of the demonstrations should be started. This also includes writing demonstrator documentation to be distributed to the participants in the demonstration, which includes:
- goals and scope of the demonstrator (what parts of the application domain it deals with, what it can and what it cannot do);
- illustration of the main features of the demonstration and of the demonstration plan;
- if appropriate, a simple user manual with some interaction examples, in the case of demonstrations where the user is asked to interact directly with the KBS.

During the preparation activity, the project team should carefully try out the demonstrations scheduled and discuss their content in order to find out all the potential problems and to solve them in advance.

When the preparation is completed, the execution of the demonstration plan starts. The execution modalities greatly differ from informal to formal demonstrations. In the case of formal demonstrations, the execution strictly follows the procedure specified in the plan (very much like in psychological experimentation). For this reason, we do not provide here further details since they depend on the specific technique used in the demonstration. On the other hand, we can shortly describe the typical procedure for informal demonstrations. Usually two persons carry out the demonstration. One is the operator - usually a developer, who demonstrates the KBS (operating on the computer, answering specific technical questions, showing details, etc.); the other is the conductor - usually the project leader, who presents and discusses the sequence of events.

The demonstration starts with a short presentation, an informal speech of 5 to 15 minutes, which is intended to avoid incorrect, unrealistic, or misleading expectations. In particular, it must be clear to everybody that the demonstrator is not the full KBS. Then the demonstration proceeds on the computer. A precise script is generally used to specify the course of events. The control of the interaction is in the hands of the operator who may decide to use appropriate shortcuts in order to avoid those aspects of the demonstration which appear to be less interesting for the participants. The conductor stresses the more significant points, answers general questions, and solicits reactions and comments from the participants. The typical duration of this phase is from 20 to 45 minutes. It is useful to record (on a tape or video-tape) the full demonstration. At the end, a short discussion between the conductor and the participants in the demonstration usually takes place. This makes it possible to gather further feedback and comments useful for the subsequent task 2.17.

In order to speed up operations during the demonstration on the computer and also to avoid mistakes, it is appropriate to organize the interaction so that very little keyboard input is required during the demonstration. This may be accomplished by the use of pre-stored files containing the cases under inspection, to be loaded automatically during the demonstration, or by means of pop-up menus containing the required input, or by other methods.

After the execution of each demonstration of the plan, a short review is performed to take into consideration any useful hint that may allow the plan and the subsequent demonstration sessions to be refined.

The product of task 2.16 is a document called *demonstration report*. It is prepared at the end of the execution of the whole demonstration plan, and includes all information gathered during the demonstration.

5.6.3 Task 2.17: Evaluation

The goal of this task is to evaluate the results of the demonstration performed in the previous task 2.16. Task 2.17 takes in input the demonstrator goals (from task 2.4) and the demonstration report (from task 2.16).

The evaluation process may be guided by a series of questions which help focus on important points. For example:

- Was the demonstration effective in comparison with its goals?
- Did the demonstration make it possible to gather the needed information (especially for formal demonstrations)?
- Did the demonstration allow the analysis of specific technical aspects of the project? Does any technical decision need to be changed, and how?
- Did the management become aware and convinced of the potentials of knowledge-based technology and of the advantages of the proposed KBS project?
- Did the users (and domain experts) appreciate the usefulness of the KBS? Is any modification to the KBS concept or to the user training needed in order to overcome end-users problems emerged during the demonstration?
- Did the users and domain experts agree upon the stated KBS specifications? Can the KBS specifications be refined or improved by taking into account the comments of the users and domain experts?

The importance and the difficulty of evaluation depends on the amount information collected during the demonstration, which is usually very large in case of formal demonstrations. Moreover, the demonstration evaluation is critical, because later choices may rely directly on it.

The results of demonstrator evaluation will be considered successful if they provide a confirmation - or even a refinement or an improvement - of the proposals developed during the plausibility study. If the evaluation concludes with a negative result, the project is in serious danger. There may exist substantial problems - possibly overlooked during the opportunity analysis - that might prevent the project to continue.

The product of task 2.17 is a document called *demonstrator evaluation report*, which includes the results obtained in the demonstrator evaluation.

Finally, let us note that sometimes - especially in the case of formal demonstrations - demonstration (task 2.16) and evaluation (task 2.17) may be carried out in parallel, thus contributing to a higher effectiveness and efficiency.

5.6.4   Task 2.18: Writing of demonstrator report

This task is meant to produce a document summarizing the activities carried out, the software system developed, the demonstrations performed, and the results obtained. Task 2.18 takes in input the products of all preceding tasks. The product of task 2.18 is a document called *demonstrator report*.

The demonstrator report may feature various levels of detail depending on the type of demonstrator. A possible table of contents for the demonstrator report is shown in Figure 5.10.

---

1. **Introduction**
   - short introduction to the *construction of a demonstrator* phase
   - specific management indications considered
   - difficulties encountered and solutions adopted
   - synthesis of the activities carried out and of the main results obtained

2. **Demonstrator goals, scope, and specification**
   - goals of the demonstrator and demonstrator type
   - sub-problems addressed and sample cases considered
   - demonstrator specifications

3. **Design and implementation**
   - demonstrator conceptual model
   - basic development environment
   - demonstrator technical design
   - implementation notes
   - knowledge base development notes

4. **Demonstration and evaluation**
   - demonstration plan and demonstrations
   - feedback
   - evaluation

7. **Main results**
   - results obtained
   - functional, operational, and technical indications to be considered in the following phases of the life cycle
   - indications concerning project continuation

Figure 5.10 Demonstrator report: suggested table of contents.

The demonstrator report is primarily directed to the management, who uses the information produced within this phase in order to make the final decision concerning the continuation of the project - if this was not already made at the end of the plausibility study. It also contains useful technical information for the project team in charge of phase 3.

PART IV

THE PRIMARY PROCESSES: DEVELOPMENT

6

DEVELOPMENT OF THE PROTOTYPE

6.1 PHASE OVERVIEW

6.1.1 Motivations and objectives

The 'development of the prototype' is the core phase of a KBS project. The main motivation for this phase derives from one of the most peculiar characteristics of knowledge-based technology: the impossibility to proceed sequentially from specification to implementation and the necessity to allow for experimentation during the design and development steps. In fact, the consideration of the stated specifications and the analysis of domain knowledge carried out at the beginning of a KBS project generally do not provide enough information to make all the needed technical choices. As a consequence, it is impossible to obtain a correct and complete system design top-down. The design process usually goes through some steps of experimentation and refinement before the right choices are made and a detailed design is produced. Experimentation, therefore, cannot be eliminated from the KBS life cycle, being a fundamental component of knowledge modeling and of system design. Moreover, in order to effectively support experimentation, it is often appropriate to utilize specialized tools to develop the prototype which may greatly differ from those required by the target environment. Thus, the prototype is generally a fully separate system, different from the final target system. Finally, while the methods and techniques used for developing the prototype are highly typical of knowledge-based technology, the implementation of the target system generally follows a more traditional software engineering path.

The goals of the *development of the prototype* phase are:
- facing and solving all main technical problems involved in the design and production of the KBS;
- refining, if appropriate, the functional, operational, and technical specifications initially stated, through extensive experimentation with the domain experts and users;
- building a KBS which is:
  - functionally complete, i.e. satisfying all functional specifications initially stated in the plausibility study and revised at the beginning of this phase (task 3.6);
  - equipped only with preliminary interfaces, not yet installed in the target environment, and not yet connected to the external world;
  - tested only with simulated cases.

It is worth noting that the prototype is completely different from the demonstrator. The prototype is a system that merely cannot be obtained from the demonstrator through incremental extension. The objectives are different, therefore, so are the specifications, the design principles, and the development tools.

For complex and long projects concerning the development of large KBS applications, it may be appropriate to organize phases 3 and 4 stage-wise. The functional specifications of the KBS are broken down into groups (for example: basic, full, and advanced specifications), and incremental versions of the KBS are defined (for example, version 1 concerning basic specifications, version 2 concerning basic and full specifications, and version 3 concerning basic, full, and advanced specifications). Thus, phases 3 can be divided into stages, each one producing a new version of the KBS (*staged development*). After a prototype version has been developed, one generally proceeds with phase 4, in such a way that the corresponding version of the target system is produced while a new version of the prototype is being developed. In this way the prototype version 1 is developed first and then the corresponding target system produced and released. Later the prototype and then the target system of versions 2 and 3 are developed. Staged development is appropriate in KBS projects of large dimensions. It may help reduce risk, simplify project organization and management, ensure a more acceptable distribution of costs, and anticipate the return of investment. Moreover, the development of the more advanced versions of the KBS can largely benefit from the feedback collected from the operational use of the preceding ones. Usually, staged development does not involve more than 4 versions of the KBS.

6.1.2   Inputs and products

The development of the prototype is generally requested by the managers specifically interested in the KBS application considered. The *development of the prototype* phase takes in input:

- a document called *management indications*, which includes requirements, objectives, and constraints provided by the management, to be taken into account in the development of the prototype;
- the plausibility study report produced in phase 1;
- the demonstrator report produced in phase 3, if available.

The products of the *development of the prototype* phase are:

- the *prototype*;
- the*development support system*, a set of software tools supporting the construction of the knowledge base;
- the *prototype report*, which contains a synthesis of the activities carried out, and a detailed illustration of the results achieved.

Finally, the *development of the prototype* phase may produce a specific *management report* in case the prerequisites for its execution are not satisfied and the phase is stopped (see task 3.1).

The products of the development of the prototype are directed to the project team which will be in charge of the implementation, installation and delivery of the target system (phase 3).

6.1.3   Phase structure and tasks outline

Figure 6.1 presents an outline of the KLIC tasks of the 'development of the prototype' phase.

The overall logical structure of the *development of the prototype* phase is organized into six steps:

- the 'start-up' step verifies that the prerequisites are satisfied and plans the whole phase;
- the 'conceptual design' step analyzes domain knowledge and develops the design of the conceptual model; this is the first intermediate product of KBS design and should provide a natural, significant, and accurate model of the application domain considered, representing all relevant features and discarding immaterial details; as a result of the analysis of domain knowledge, possible refinements to the specifications are also produced;
- the 'technical design' step focuses on the technical choices which have to be made to develop the logical model of the prototype; precise specifications of the empty system and the development support system are also produced; moreover, the selection and acquisition of the prototype basic development environment takes place;
- the 'construction of the empty system and of the development support system' step produces a detailed design of the two major software systems constituting the prototype and then it proceeds to their development and testing;

START-UP		
	3.1	verification of prerequisites
IF		prerequisites are not satisfied
THEN	3.2	writing of management report
		stop phase
	3.3	planning of development of the prototype
CONCEPTUAL DESIGN		
	3.4	knowledge analysis and modeling
	3.5	design of the conceptual model
	3.6	definition of prototype specifications
TECHNICAL DESIGN		
	3.7	design of the logical model
IF		shortcomings in knowledge analysis and modeling are identified
THEN		**GO TO** 3.4
	3.8	definition of the specifications of the empty system
	3.9	definition of the specifications of the development support system
	3.10	selection and acquisition of the basic development environment
	3.11	detailed design of the empty system
	3.12	detailed design of the development support system
CONSTRUCTION OF THE EMPTY SYSTEM AND OF THE DEVELOPMENT SUPPORT SYSTEM		
	3.13	implementation of the empty system
	3.14	implementation of the development support system
DEVELOPMENT OF THE KNOWLEDGE BASE		
	3.15	selection of knowledge sources
LOOP		
	3.16	knowledge acquisition planning
	3.17	knowledge elicitation and protocol analysis
	3.18	knowledge coding
	3.19	knowledge integration and verification
IF		revision of empty system is necessary
THEN		**GO TO** 3.7
IF		revision of prototype specifications is necessary
THEN		**GO TO** 3.6
UNTIL		prototype specifications are fully met
TESTING AND EVALUATION		
	3.20	prototype testing and refinement
	3.21	prototype evaluation
	3.22	writing of prototype report

Figure 6.1 Development of the prototype: KLIC tasks outline.

- the 'development of the knowledge base' step includes all the activities concerned with the acquisition of domain knowledge and the construction of the knowledge base of the prototype; this is a crucial step for the *development of the prototype* phase and, perhaps, the most characteristic of knowledge-based technology;
- finally, the 'testing and evaluation' step is dedicated to a thorough testing and evaluation of the prototype, as well as to the preparation of the prototype report.

As shown in Figure 6.1, phase 3 includes three back-jumps. During the 'technical design' steps, if the design of the logical model highlights shortcomings in knowledge analysis and modeling, a return to the 'conceptual design' step may be necessary. Moreover, the 'development of the knowledge base' step may point out the need of revising the empty system or the prototype specifications; in such cases, it is necessary to return to the 'technical design' or the 'conceptual design' steps, respectively. Phase 3 also includes a loop; in the 'development of the knowledge base' step the construction of the knowledge base is organized through a cycle aimed at repeatedly performing knowledge elicitation, coding, and verification until the prototype specifications are fully met.

As we have already mentioned in section 2.1.3, the time it takes for the *development of the prototype* phase is generally between 6 to 24 months (elapsed time), depending on the complexity of the application considered. In particular, the development of the prototype may require:

- 6 to 9 months for simple cases with narrow domains, known technical choices, and low organizational complexity;
- 12 to 21 months for cases of middle complexity with broad domains, known technical choices, and medium organizational complexity;
- 18 to 24 months for complex cases with broad and intricate domains, unknown technical choices, or high organizational complexity.

It may be useful to split the complete duration of the entire phase into the individual duration of its component tasks. The table of Figure 6.2 shows in percentages the duration of each task with respect to the duration of the whole phase. The data reported are, of course, only indicative; they refer to an average situation, and may vary from case to case. Percentages shown in parentheses refer to tasks which are carried out only subject to specific conditions, and, therefore, count over 100.

The data reported in Figure 6.2 refer to an average case where a substantial effort is required to design and implement the empty system and the development support system, namely 20% of the total duration of phase 3. As illustrated in detail in section 6.4.5, the choice of the prototype basic development environment may largely influence this percentage. It may be lowered to almost 0% when a ready-to-use commercial shell is adopted, whereas it may go up to 25% - or even more - when general-purpose programming languages or toolkits are used to developing the empty system and the development support system from scratch.

TASKS	time %
START-UP	
3.1 verification of prerequisites	1
3.2 writing of management report	(5)
3.3 planning of development of the prototype	2
CONCEPTUAL DESIGN	
3.4 knowledge analysis and modeling	4
3.5 design of the conceptual model	6
3.6 definition of prototype specifications	1
TECHNICAL DESIGN	
3.7 design of the logical model	2
3.8 definition of the specifications of the empty system	6
3.9 definition of the specifications of the development support system	2
3.10 selection and acquisition of the basic development environment	2
3.11 detailed design of the empty system	5
3.12 detailed design of the development support system	3
CONSTRUCTION OF THE EMPTY SYSTEM AND OF THE DEVELOPMENT SUPPORT SYSTEM	
3.13 implementation of the empty system	7
3.14 implementation of the development support system	5
DEVELOPMENT OF THE KNOWLEDGE BASE	
3.15 selection of knowledge sources	4
3.16 knowledge acquisition planning	3
3.17 knowledge elicitation and protocol analysis	2
3.18 knowledge coding	18
3.19 knowledge integration and checking	11
3.20 prototype testing and refinement	8
TESTING AND EVALUATION	
3.21 prototype evaluation	5
3.22 writing of prototype report	3

Figure 6.2 Development of the prototype: task duration in percentage.

6.1.4   Project team composition

The development of the prototype is usually carried out by a project team internal to the user organization. Less frequently, it may be assigned to an external supplier.

In particular, for the development of the prototype the project team is typically made up of:

- 1 project manager, usually a senior manager, in charge of formally representing the target organization from the administrative point of view;
- 1 project leader, usually a senior professional, responsible for the results of the entire phase and in charge of the technical and organizational management of the project team; the project leader also provides specific support to all critical tasks of the phase;
- 1 to 2 designers, in charge of the most technical tasks of construction of the demonstrator (tasks 3.7, 3.8, 3.9, 3.10, 3.11, and 3.12);
- 1 to 3 knowledge engineers, at least one of them being in a senior position, in charge of all tasks related to knowledge analysis and modeling (tasks 3.4 and 3.5), to the development of the knowledge base (tasks 3.15, 3.16, 3.17, 3.18, and 3.19) and to prototype testing and refinement (task 3.20);
- 1 to 4 developers, in charge of developing the software components of the prototype (tasks 3.11, 3.12, 3.13 and 3.14);
- 0 to 3 software designers and programmers, in charge of developing the parts of the empty system and of the development support system which are constituted by traditional software systems (like the software interface, the external interface, the user interfaces, specific problem-solvers, dedicated tools of the development support system, etc.) (tasks 3.11, 3.12, 3.13 and 3.14);
- 1 or more representatives of the top management;
- intermediate managers of all departments concerned with the application domain considered
- domain experts of the application domain considered;
- representatives of the potential users of the KBS.

In particular complex and large cases, the need may arise to support the project team with external consulting members. If some specific in-depth analyses are necessary in technical areas where the project team is not especially competent, specialists can be temporarily hired. An advisor can also be consulted to support the project leader in the most important technical decisions and in the most critical steps of project management.

The table shown in Figure 6.3 summarizes the composition of the project team for the development of the prototype.

As it can be noted, the composition of the project team can be tailored to the complexity and extent of the KBS application considered by employing a higher or lower number of designers, knowledge engineers, and developers.

	REGULAR MEMBERS	SUPPORTING MEMBERS	CONSULTING MEMBERS
project manager		1	
project leader	1		
designers	1-2		
knowledge engineers	1-3		
developers	1-4		
software designers and programmers	0-3		
top managers		1 or more	
intermediate managers		as appropriate	
domain experts		as appropriate	
potential users		as appropriate	
specialists			if needed
advisor			if needed

Figure 6.3 Development of the prototype: project team composition.

6.2   START-UP

6.2.1   Step execution

Figure 6.4 presents a detailed view of KLIC tasks and products of the 'start-up' step.

6.2.2   Task 3.1: Verification of prerequisites

Task 3.1 takes in input the management indications - if any, the plausibility study report (from task 1.29), and the demonstrator report (from task 2.18), if available.
   Specific prerequisites that should be satisfied before starting the development of the prototype are listed below:
• a high-level authorization to access all the sources of knowledge which are considered necessary or appropriate must be ensured by the top management;
• the intermediate managers, domain experts, and potential users should be available to cooperate with the project team in charge of the development of the prototype;
• the project team must be ready to accept a hard challenge and to start with a great effort; it must be technically well-prepared as well as free from other engagements;

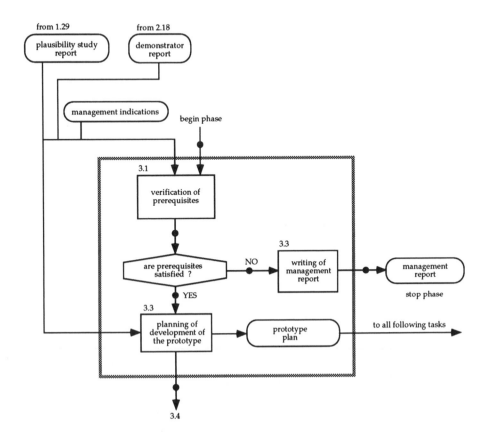

Figure 6.4 Start-up: KLIC tasks and products.

- the requirements, objectives, and constraints proposed by the management - if any - must be consistent with the purpose and nature of the development of the prototype;
- the needed resources for the execution of the phase must be available.

If prerequisites are not satisfied, the development of the prototype should not continue. If such a case occurs, a report should be prepared for the management (task 3.2) and the development of the prototype should be stopped. Otherwise, the execution of the phase continues with task 3.3.

6.2.3   Task 3.2: Writing of management report

In the case where prerequisites are not satisfied, the project leader in charge of the development of the prototype should prepare a report for the management and stop the execution of the phase. The product of task 3.2 is a document called *management report*. It should present a detailed account of why the development of the prototype is unfeasible. If appropriate, the report can be personally discussed by the project leader with the management of the organization.

6.2.4   Task 3.3: Planning of development of the prototype

Task 3.3 takes in input the management indications - if any, the plausibility study report (from task 1.29), and the demonstrator report (from task 2.18), if available. The product of task 3.3 is a document called *prototype plan*.

The prototype plan should be discussed with all members of the project team, who should understand the importance of their role and the nature of their engagements. It should also be formally approved by the management of the end-user organization. Note that, as shown in Figure 6.4, the prototype plan is not an input to any specific task. It will be used by the project leader for management and control issues throughout the whole phase (see section 9.3.2).

In the case where phase 2 has been skipped and it has been decided to have an early prototype (see section 5.1.1), this should be carefully taken into account in designing the prototype plan. In fact, developing a preliminary running version of the prototype to be demonstrated to the management and the users early (for example, 4 to 8 months from the start of phase 3), is not always an easy task and may entail complex technical and organizational problems. The best solution - often based on a compromise between contrasting exigencies - must be found case by case.

The prototype plan should be refined when, during the development of phase 3, new information is made available for a more precise and realistic definition and scheduling of the activities to carry out. Actually, a revision of the plan is probably appropriate after tasks 3.10 and 3.16, and before task 3.20.

6.3   DESIGN PRINCIPLES

6.3.1   Knowledge-based system design: concepts and goals

The design of a KBS is the process which defines the technical features of the software systems constituting the KBS, i.e. which software modules are necessary and how they have to be built and connected together. The design process starts from the specifications stated in the plausibility study report and produces a set of written documents describing the results of the design activity, namely: the conceptual model of the domain, the logical model of the KBS, and the detailed design of the KBS. Such documents are later considered by the developers and knowledge engineers in order to actually build the KBS - both its software modules and its knowledge bases.

In several engineering disciplines the design process can be accomplished by starting from the specifications of the desired behavior of the artifact to be developed, first by identifying its overall structure and internal functions, secondly by selecting the adequate components to implement the functions defined, and eventually by verifying if the resulting system actually performs according to the specifications initially stated. Components are pre-existing and they just need to be appropriately chosen and assembled together. The situation is quite different in the KBS case. Ready to use components are generally not available, and, therefore, the design process has to go deeper into the analysis of internal system functions, into the identification of the parts of the system in charge of implementing such functions, into the exact description of how such parts should be built to cooperate in order to perform the expected functions and to produce, in the end, the desired KBS behavior.

The technique currently employed for developing a KBS design can be viewed as a *model generation and transformation* procedure [Wielinga et al. 92]. Initially, an analysis of the application domain considered is carried out and a model of the involved knowledge and reasoning processes, called *conceptual model*, is developed. The conceptual model is then used to incrementally build, through successive transformations, a model of the KBS, called *logical model*. This provides a high-level coarse design of the system. On the basis of the logical model, the development tools, namely the basic development environment, to be utilized for the implementation of the prototype are then identified. Finally, a *detailed design* of the KBS is produced, which specifies exactly how the software programs and the knowledge bases have to be implemented by means of the specific development tools chosen.

Figure 6.5 illustrates the overall organization of the KBS design process. The chain of models starting with the conceptual model and terminating with the logical one is the core part of this process and is worth particular attention. Each model shows (in qualitative terms) to what extent it is an abstract representation of the application domain considered (the white area) and to what extent it represents the KBS to be constructed (dark area). At each subsequent transformation the white area decreases, and the dark one increases. Initially, the conceptual model provides a representation of just the application domain; at each step during the design process some domain features are transformed into appropriate features of the KBS; finally, the logical model provides a representation of the KBS to be produced.

Figure 6.5 also shows the various activities involved in KBS design. The design process is structured into two main parts, namely the conceptual design and the technical design, which includes in turn the logical design and the detailed design. The design process also includes some additional activities concerning the specification of the KBS prototype, the specification of the empty system and of the development support system, and the selection of the basic development environment.

In the following, we analyze in detail the concepts of conceptual and logical model.

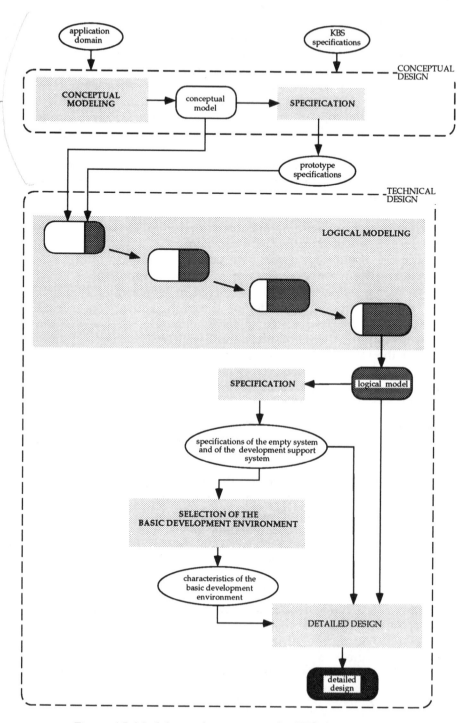

Figure 6.5 Model transformation in the KBS design process.

The conceptual model

The *conceptual model* is a formal abstract representation of the static and dynamic features of an application domain, relevant to a class of problem solving tasks. A conceptual model describes both the types and organization of knowledge in the domain (concepts, attributes, relations, constraints, operations, events, etc.) and the ways it is used to solve problems (problem types considered, reasoning mechanisms used, strategies followed, etc.). The conceptual model is a typical knowledge-level representation [Newell 82], [Wielinga et al. 92], [Van de Velde 93]: it plays a fundamental role in design, knowledge-base development, maintenance, extension, explanation, and KBS-user interaction. The conceptual model is obtained as a result of the analysis and modeling of domain knowledge.

The general goal of the conceptual model is to represent an abstraction of the application domain, which includes only those elements which are relevant to the identification of the components of the KBS capable of automatically performing the desired problem-solving tasks. It is important to understand that the conceptual model should not be thought of as the paper version of a knowledge base nor as an intermediate representation to be later converted to code. The conceptual model serves two specific purposes:
- it is the starting point used by the designers for the construction of the logical model of the KBS;
- it is the basic tool used by the knowledge engineers during the construction of the knowledge bases, for interpreting domain knowledge.

The conceptual model includes three *layers*:
1. The *entity layer*, which provides a representation of the domain knowledge supporting the problem-solving activities relevant to the KBS in terms of factual, relational, and operational knowledge. It encompasses two parts:
   a. A *static part*, providing a description of the *entities* of the domain, each one denoting, in very general terms, physical or abstract objects or events that it is appropriate to represent as single units of knowledge. The description of entities is given in terms of entity *properties* (unary relations) and in terms of *relationships* among entities (binary or higher-order relations). Typical relationships include the is-a and the part-of relations. The static part also includes the description of *constraints* concerning the definition of entities or the relationships among them. Typical constraints are integrity constraints, temporal constraints, spatial constraints, etc.
   b. A *dynamic part*, providing a description of the *procedures* that characterize an entity and of the *operations* involving entities.
   The entity layer constitutes the basic layer of the conceptual model; it describes the objects taking part in the problem-solving processes, without providing, however, any information about how they are used in the reasoning activities.
2. The *reasoning layer*, which provides a description of the *reasoning functions* utilized within problem-solving activities carried out in the

domain. Each reasoning function is described in terms of the entities it works upon and of the entities which can be obtained as a result. The reasoning functions to be considered in this layer are generic and elementary, such as: data-driven deduction, goal-driven deduction, generalization, specialization, hypothetical reasoning, analogical reasoning, reasoning by refutation, temporal reasoning, spatial reasoning, model-based reasoning, etc.

3.   The *problem-solving layer*, which describes the *problem-solving strategies* used for solving the problems of interest in the domain. Each problem-solving strategy is defined in terms of a procedural combination of elementary reasoning functions, applied to specific inputs. A problem-solving strategy may also involve the exploitation of *strategic knowledge*, utilized for supporting decision making steps eventually present in it.

The construction of the conceptual model requires availability of a suitable language to be used for the representation of the various elements of the model [Wielinga et al. 93]. The choice or the definition of an appropriate representation language is a key-point for the success of the modeling activity. A conceptual language must guarantee enough expressive power and be rather formal, but, at the same time, it must be easy to use by the knowledge engineer and easy to understand by the domain experts, flexible to adapt to a variety of different exigencies, not too formal, possibly allowing for a graphical representation. Some specific proposal can be found in the literature (for example, [Carlsen and Stokke 87], [Held and Carlis 89], [Yost and Newell 89], [Slagle et al. 90], [Yen and Lee 93]), however they do not adequately cover all the layers of a conceptual model mentioned above and all the situations which may be found in practice. It can certainly be stated that no assessed and general solution exists; for each organization, for each type of production environment, or even for each KBS project a different solution may be appropriate. A practical method is to develop a standard language within a KBS department to use as a basis for conceptual modeling, to adapt and extend when specific needs arise. More specifically, the static part of the entity layer may be represented through formalisms inspired to well-known modeling languages available in the literature; for example: entity-relationships models [Chen 76], SADT (Structured Analysis Design Technique) [Dickover et al. 77], [Ross 77], [Ross and Schoman 77], data flow diagrams [Yourdon and Constantine 75], [De Marco 79], [Gane and Sarson 79], Petri nets [Peterson 81], conceptual graphs [Sowa 84], KL-ONE [Brachman and Schmolze 85], flowcharts [Tripp 88], finite-state transition diagrams and state-charts [Harel 88], first-order logic or other logical representations [Genesereth and Nilsson 87]. The dynamic part of the entity layer can be represented by means of a high-level procedural programming language or a pseudo-code. The reasoning layer is easily represented by means of structured descriptions or specific languages based on taxonomies of reasoning functions [Chandrasekaran 83-b], [McDermott 88]. The fourth layer can be represented through a procedural programming language, a pseudo-code, dataflow diagrams, flowcharts, finite-state transition diagrams and state-charts, specific languages based on taxonomies of problem-solving strategies, eventually enriched by a declarative representation of strategic knowledge.

As it is already clear from the above discussion, the conceptual model constitutes the basic source of information for all the parts of the design process following it; the logical model, in fact, depends solely on its content. In other terms, the conceptual model acts as a filter: it represents only those parts of the application domain which are deemed relevant to the subsequent design steps, discarding the immaterial ones. For this reason, if the conceptual model contains errors, these will propagate and affect all the following stages of the development. Therefore, it is fundamental to check the quality of the conceptual model. First of all, a good conceptual model should guarantee the following three basic properties:

- *correctness*, i.e. the conceptual model should provide a faithful representation of the domain;
- *consistency*, i.e. the conceptual model should be free from logical conflicts;
- *completeness*, i.e. the conceptual model should include, at the selected level of detail, all the elements of interest, represented appropriately.

Moreover, other quality criteria should be considered:

- *objectiveness*: the conceptual model should provide a representation of the domain which is really independent from any subsequent step and decision of the design process;
- *granularity*: the aggregation level of the objects represented in the conceptual model (how much of the domain is represented in each object) should be adequate for the specific goals of the problem-solving activity considered; they should neither be too generic nor too detailed;
- *cognitive coupling*: the conceptual model should provide a natural and transparent view of the knowledge and of the problem-solving activities of the domain; in other terms, it should be a good approximation of the mental models of domain experts, so they can easily understand the model and naturally recognize a representation of their reasoning.

The logical model

The *logical model* is a representation of the architecture, knowledge representation techniques, and reasoning methods adopted to implement the conceptual model of an application domain in a real KBS. The distinction between conceptual model and logical model closely mirrors the well-known distinction in artificial intelligence between knowledge level and symbol level [Newell 82]; the conceptual model (at knowledge level) provides a specification of what the logical model (at symbol level) should represent.

The logical model provides a comprehensive and precise view of the structure of the KBS and of the main technical choices considered for its design. However, it is not detailed enough for implementation, since it is still independent from the characteristics of the basic development environment.

The logical model serves two specific purposes:
- it provides the basic technical information to identify the characteristics of the development tools;
- it is the starting point for the production of the detailed design of the KBS.

The logical model includes four layers:
1. the *architectural layer*, which defines the overall (software) *architecture* of the KBS, by specifying: the *knowledge bases* (both at domain level and meta level), the *reasoning mechanisms*, the *working memories*, the *heterogeneous problem-solvers* (realized with non-knowledge-based techonolgies, such as: procedural programs, neural networks, data-base systems, spread-sheets, etc.), and the *special-purpose modules* of the KBS; the architecture specifies the main high-level data and control flows as well;
2. the *knowledge representation layer*, which specifies for each knowledge base the *knowledge representation techniques* to adopt;
3. the *reasoning layer*, which specifies for each reasoning mechanism the kind of *reasoning methods* to use for its implementation;
4. the *special-purpose modules layer*, which specifies for each special-purpose module the main technical choices to adopt for its design (main technical approaches, overall architecture, logical representation of data structures, communication standards, etc.).

The representation of the logical model may rely on well-known design languages derived from traditional software engineering , eventually enriched or tailored as appropriate, such as: HIPO [IBM 75], data flow diagrams [Yourdon and Constantine 75], [De Marco 79], [Gane and Sarson 79], SSADM (Structured System Analysis and Design Method) [Downs et al. 88], etc.

The quality of the logical model should be carefully controlled. First of all, a good logical model should guarantee - like the conceptual model - the following three basic properties:
- *correctness*, i.e. the logical model should provide a faithful interpretation of the conceptual model;
- *consistency*, i.e. the logical model should be free from logical conflicts;
- *completeness*, i.e. the logical model should include, at the selected level of detail, all the elements of interest, represented appropriately.

Moreover, other quality criteria should be considered:
- *technical coherence*: the logical model should be internally coherent from the technical point of view, i.e. the technical choices made should guarantee coherence between architecture, knowledge representation techniques, and reasoning methods;
- *technical economy*: the logical model should guarantee that the technical solutions adopted are powerful enough to deal with the case at hand, but are not over-sized;
- *technical flexibility*, the logical model should be based on technical choices that ensure modifiability and extensibility;

- *technical transparency*, the logical model should allow easy understanding of the reasons behind the technical choices made, and clear identification of the functions of its components and of the connections among them;
- *technical efficiency* of the logical model, in terms of expected memory requirements and response time of the KBS;
- *conceptual coupling*: the logical model should provide a natural and transparent interpretation of the various elements of the conceptual model.

6.3.2   The dimensions of design

Logical modeling is the central part of design, since it provides the specific guidelines to be adopted for constructing the final KBS. It bridges conceptual-level modeling to detailed technical design. The process of logical design relies on the analysis and interpretation of the conceptual model and goes through a series of technical choices that incrementally identify and specify the various components of the logical model. Focusing on the first three layers of the logical model (the fourth layer - less critical for the design process, being dealt with separately), logical modeling can be viewed - in abstract terms - as the selection of a specific point (or region) in a *design space* which includes all possible KBS designs. The *dimensions* of the design space, corresponding to the first three layers of logical modeling, are: knowledge representation techniques (KR), reasoning methods (RE), and architecture (ARCH). Thus, the logical design consists in identifying a point in the design space (corresponding to specific choices concerning knowledge representation techniques, reasoning methods, and architecture) which satisfies the quality criteria defined above for the logical model.

The identification of an appropriate design point in the design space is not carried out in one single step, but, on the contrary, it goes through a step-wise iterative process, which involves the exploration of several alternatives, with possible backtracking and revision of previous choices. In fact, the first three layers of the logical model depend on each other, and a specific choice on a dimension may constrain the remaining choices on the other dimensions. Figure 6.6 shows a very general and abstract procedure to guide the incremental construction of the logical model.

This procedure is based on a hypothetical reasoning strategy. It involves four main operations:

- make a technical choice taking into account the stated quality criteria, and recording its justification, i.e. the set of assumptions under which the choice done is considered appropriate;
- evaluate the technical choices made, to check whether they globally satisfy the stated quality criteria;
- if a choice is responsible for violations of the stated quality criteria, revise it and its justifications;

<u>LOOP</u>
1. focus on a meaningful portion of the entity layer of the conceptual model and on the relevant part of the reasoning layer
2. make a choice on the KR dimension, taking into account the stated quality criteria, and record its justification
3. make a choice on the RE dimension, taking into account the stated quality criteria, and record its justification

<u>LOOP</u>
4. evaluate the choices made along the KR and RE dimensions, to check whether they globally satisfy the stated quality criteria
5. <u>IF</u> violations of the stated quality criteria are identified
    <u>THEN</u>
    a. revise all choices responsible for the violations and their justifications
    b. check all choices whose justifications involve the choices revised and, if needed, revise them and their justifications
<u>UNTIL</u>   the stated quality criteria are fully met

<u>UNTIL</u>   the entity and reasoning layers of the conceptual model have been fully processed

6. focus on the problem-solving layer of the conceptual model
7. make a choice on the ARCH dimension, taking into account the stated quality criteria, and record its justification

<u>LOOP</u>
8. evaluate all the choices made along the KR, RE, and ARCH dimensions to check whether they globally satisfy the stated quality criteria
9. <u>IF</u> violations of the stated quality criteria are identified
    <u>THEN</u>
    a. revise all choices responsible for the violations and their justifications
    b. check all choices whose justifications involve the choices revised and, if needed, revise them and their justifications
<u>UNTIL</u>   the stated quality criteria are fully met

Figure 6.6 Development of the logical model along the three design dimensions.

- every time a choice is revised, check all choices whose justifications involve the choice that has been revised, and, if needed, revise them and their justifications.

In order to carry out logical design in a correct and effective way, the designer should master a large variety of knowledge, including:
- knowledge about available knowledge representation techniques, reasoning methods, and architecture, i.e. knowledge about the possible technical choices on each design dimension;
- knowledge about the conditions that suggest or discourage their use in specific application contexts, i.e. knowledge about how to make the most appropriate technical choice on each design dimension individually;
- knowledge about the interactions among knowledge representation techniques, reasoning methods, and architecture, in other terms, knowledge about possible or impossible, strong or weak regions of the design space;
- knowledge about how to manage the design process effectively (collections of frequently used good-quality solutions, strategies for diagnosing possible problems, strategies for revising technical choices, technical choices to explore first or to delay, etc.).

This makes the design of the logical model a complex task - perhaps the most demanding one of the entire KBS life cycle from the technical point of view.

6.3.3   Paradigm-driven, task-driven, and model-driven design

The design approach presented in the previous sections is known as *model-driven design*, since it heavily relies on models and on model transformations. However, other alternative approaches to design exist, which are briefly described and compared in the following.

Tool-driven design consists in starting from the characteristics of a development tool and in identifying how, given the tool, it is possible to build a KBS which satisfies the given specifications. No explicit conceptual or logical modeling is performed in this approach, whose success heavily depends on the characteristics of the considered tool and on the extent to which it matches the features of the domain. The success of such an approach is often mere chance, since it is based only on scarce and surface information about the specific domain and problem at hand. It is definitely impossible to choose the right development tool if the domain has not been appropriately modeled at conceptual and logical levels first. A wrong or inappropriate tool leads to a poor design. Moreover, tool-driven design always results in a shallow and brittle design, failing to meet even minimal quality standards. This incorrect approach, that should be discouraged, is unfortunately frequently used in practice.

Paradigm-driven design consists in starting from a collection of generic logical models available from the literature or from experience, called *design paradigms*, and in looking for a design that seems to meet or at least to approach the requirements of the case at hand, which is usually modeled at the conceptual level only in a preliminary and partial way. If a good paradigm is found, a tailoring process is then undertaken, which is aimed at modifying some technical choices of the paradigm in order to adapt it to the current case. This approach is easy to carry out, but requires the availability of a rich library of design paradigms, which may not be easy to collect. Moreover, it is never guaranteed that the available library contains the right paradigm for the current KBS project. If this is not the case, either this design approach is abandoned or, if the designer tries to force-fit an inappropriate paradigm to the KBS project at hand, the resulting design will turn out to be largely inaccurate and quite often definitely wrong. Paradigm-driven design is often adopted in KBS departments where a sufficiently high number of projects have already been successfully developed in the past and the scenario of possible future projects can be precisely outlined. This approach can be effectively used for transferring design know-how to newly hired employees or to train junior designers.

Task-driven design consists in producing the overall design of a KBS by combining elementary, re-usable building blocks chosen on the basis of an accurate conceptual model of the application domain. The approach has received a lot of attention from the research community (see, for example, [Clancey 85], [Chandrasekaran 86], [Bylander and Chandrasekaran 87], [Chandrasekaran 88], [McDermott 88], [Breuker and Wielinga 89], [Chandrasekaran 90], [Steels 90], [Aben 93], [Chandrasekaran and Johnson 93], [Steels 93]). Several proposals of the basic building blocks to be used for KBS design have been made, but no general agreement on the characteristics the building blocks should feature, of their level of abstraction, and on the way they should be chosen and composed together has been found. Moreover, it is not always easy to construct a solution by combining pre-defined building blocks. The approach, however, is very attractive because the idea of re-use of primitive generic components guarantees high productivity and standardization of the design practice. Task-driven design is often adopted in KBS departments which operate in specific and sufficiently stable domains and which are mostly involved with routine design. In this case, in fact, design know-how can be easily structured in terms of a library of generic building blocks and a collection of practical rules for block selection and composition.

The choice of the most appropriate approach for a KBS project can be guided by the consideration of three main aspects: (i) the characteristics of the application domain and the requirements about the KBS, (ii) the level of competence and experience of the available designers, and (iii) the general design policy of the KBS department and the availability of the necessary background for paradigm- or task-driven design. In general, if a sound, experimented, and well-documented paradigm exists which satisfactorily matches the case at hand, then it should be taken into consideration and a paradigm-driven approach should be adopted. Since a good paradigm is generally not derived from the literature but from the internal experience of a KBS department, the paradigm-driven approach is more likely to be applicable in a sound and robust KBS development. Task-driven design may be utilized for producing re-usable generic components to be efficiently included in larger systems. Model-driven design, though, remains the main approach to adopt, especially when new complex cases are faced.

6.3.4   Design for maintainability and extensibility

The possibility to effectively and easily maintain and extend a KBS has an important role in the operational life of an application. Clearly, maintainability and extensibility of a target KBS can only be obtained if they are explicitly and carefully taken into account since the design of the prototype. In fact, these features depend on several points, namely:
- The basic technical choices made at the moment of the design of the logical model.
- The programming style adopted for the construction of the empty system.
- The coding style adopted for the development of the knowledge base, which largely influences the modularity, structuredness, understandability, and accessibility of the resulting product. In particular, for ease of maintenance of a knowledge base the following should be taken into account:
  - Divide the knowledge base into modules [Parnas 72], [Davis 90-b] which correspond to the modularity of the domain knowledge; modules should be functionally cohesive, that is, each module should perform a well-defined function. Coincidental cohesion (a set of actions or processes not related by any common function is grouped together to form a module) should be avoided. Modules should be independent of each other, and low coupling should be ensured;
  - In a rule-based system, a useful approach to make the KBS easier to maintain is to divide the information in the knowledge base and attempt to reduce both the amount of information that a single knowledge engineer must understand before he can make a change to the knowledge base and the effect of such a change. Two principles may be used to decide how to group rules: either (i) rules are grouped in such a way that a change to one rule in the group only affects one or more rules in the same group (control knowledge is segregated from other rules and handled separately) [Jacob and Froscher 90] or (ii) facts are first divided into groups and then rules are characterized and grouped according to which groups of facts they operate on [Baroff et al. 88].
  - In a rule-based system, rules should be self-standing, the clauses within the premise of a rule should be part of a single piece of domain knowledge, multiple clauses in the conclusion of a rule should be avoided if the clauses are independently true of each other, conclusions should be kept simple, the procedural content in rules should be minimized, similar rules should be grouped together, rules should be organized hierarchically.
  - Apart from the modularization techniques mentioned above, a crucial point is that knowledge bases should be maintained at the knowledge level [Newell 82] since it is the knowledge in the system that is evolving. Updates to the code are merely a consequence of changes in domain knowledge and may be supported by using *intermediate representations* to model the knowledge in the system [Watson et al. 92-b]. Maintenance can be carried out on the intermediate representation, verified, and then transferred to the code of the knowledge base; an isomorphism can be established between the

knowledge base and the knowledge sources, with the intermediate representation mediating between the two [Young 87] [Johnson 89].

- The level to which the motivations for the technical, implementation, and coding choices done are made transparent and easy to understand; the links between the conceptual model, the logical model, the detailed design and the KBS code (including both programs and knowledge) should be made explicit and provide appropriate justifications for all design and construction steps;
- The quality of the maintenance support system (see sections 6.4.1, 7.3.3, 7.3.6, 7.4.2, 7.4.5, 7.6.2, 8.6.2, and 8.7.2), which is aimed at providing specific support tools for carrying out the maintenance task in an easy, effective, and efficient way.

If maintenance and extension issues are not considered from the very beginning of a project and appropriate design decisions are made, they may become a real trouble and hamper the correct and effective exploitation of the KBS. In fact, the scope of maintenance and extension, i.e. the class of modifications that can be actually implemented in the target KBS with reasonable time and cost, is largely determined by the basic technical decisions made at the time of design. It is therefore of primary importance to have a clear idea about how domain knowledge, target environment, and KBS requirements are supposed to change in the long-range.

Note also that the boundary between maintenance (which only involves modifications to the content of the knowledge base) and extension (which concerns modifications to the structure of the empty system or of the maintenance support system) is a consequence of how the KBS is designed. A general and flexible design can make maintenance more powerful and far-reaching, but tends to contrast efficiency and to increase technical complexity. On the contrary, a more focused and specific design can ensure higher efficiency and allow for simpler solutions, but tends to restrict the scope of maintenance and cause extension to be more frequently needed. An appropriate compromise must be identified case by case.

Several approaches have been proposed to make KBSs easy to maintain and extend; however, experience in applying them for practical problems is limited. The main proposals can be found in [Jacob and Froscher 85], Explainable Expert System (EES) [Neches et al. 85], [Jacob and Froscher 90], [Prerau et al. 90], [Swafield and Knight 90], client centered approach (CCA) [Watson et al. 92-a] and [Watson et al. 92-b], [David et al. 93-a], [Philip 93], [Vargas and Raj 93].

6.4   KNOWLEDGE-BASED SYSTEM DEVELOPMENT TOOLS

6.4.1   Software systems and tools for KBS development

The KLIC life cycle includes three phases devoted to development activities: phase 2 aimed at building the demonstrator, phase 3 devoted to the development of the prototype, and phase 4 dedicated to the production of the target system.

Furthermore, phase 5 also requires the development of software extensions and refinements for the operational KBS. The different systems developed during the KBS life cycle have very different purposes and, therefore, the tools utilized for supporting their development in the various life cycle phases may be very diverse, to the point that it is very common to use different tools in the different phases. In this situation, the selection of the most appropriate development tools is not a straightforward activity. It has to be performed more than once during the life cycle. Moreover, tool selection plays an important role for the final success of the project. It is, in fact, worthwhile noticing that failure to clearly identify the appropriate tool requirements and then to select the best tool suitable for a specific task will undoubtedly damage the development effort. This will result in added costs, longer development times and lower quality of the outcomes. Money spent on the right tool - and in accurate tool selection - is money well-spent [Sagalowicz 84].

The overall scenario concerning the development of software systems through phases 3, 4, and 5 of a KBS project - namely, the core phases of the life cycle - is shown in Figure 6.7. Phase 2 is not considered here since the construction of the demonstrator is only loosely linked to the following phases of the life cycle. The demonstrator is generally not re-used in later stages of the project and is developed by means of specific tools. Of course, the construction of the demonstrator requires a development support system, similarly to phase 3. Figure 6.7 refers to the case where phase 4 does not require complete re-implementation (see section 7.3.4); in this case, in fact, a different development support system for the target system would be required, similarly to phase 3.

As it can be noted, in addition to the empty system, two more software systems are present and have an important role in the development process and, later, in the operational life of the KBS, namely the development support system and the maintenance support system.

The *development support system* is an integrated set of tools which support the construction of the knowledge base. It is produced and used during the development of the prototype (Phase 3). The primary user of the development support system is the knowledge engineer, who progressively fills up the empty knowledge base with the appropriate domain knowledge using the specific tools offered by the development support system. It constitutes, therefore, the interface between the knowledge engineer and the KBS [Gevarter 87]. It may include several classes of tools:

- *Knowledge analysis and modeling tools*, constituted by specialized systems capable of supporting the knowledge engineer in the analysis and modeling of domain knowledge by means, for example, of graphical editors or other interactive tools [Motta et al. 89], [Anjewierden et al. 90].

- *Design support tools*, supporting the transformation of the conceptual model into the logical model. Such tools have started to be developed just recently, usually within context-specific proprietary tools.

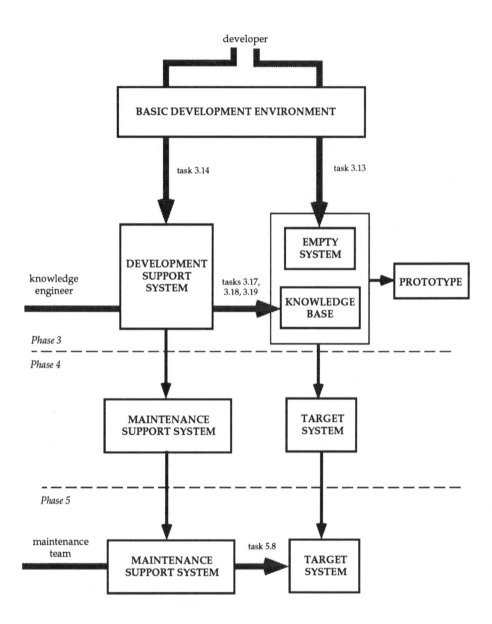

Figure 6.7 The scenario of software systems development through phases
3, 4, and 5 of a KBS project.

- *Automatic knowledge acquisition tools,* allowing a (semi)automatic generation of the knowledge bases, starting from information directly provided by domain experts and (partially) automatically processed in order to derive general knowledge on the domain [Boose 89], [Motta et al. 89], [Diederich and Linster 89]. Common examples of these tools are rule induction systems [Quinlan 79], [Quinlan 86], [Quinlan 88], verbal protocols management systems [Sanderson et al. 89], and tools based on automated repertory grids [Boose 90]. While very promising, this field is still growing and a huge amount of research work is still under development [Wielinga et al. 90].
- *Knowledge base construction tools,* aimed at supporting the knowledge base construction activity, i.e. to code the domain knowledge elicited, to access the knowledge bases already developed, to update their content, etc. [Abrett and Burstein 87]. These tools are very important and, if effective, they can greatly speed up the knowledge base construction tasks and the quality of the results. If such tools are not available, the knowledge engineer must rely on standard text editors. Specific tools of this class include:
  - *knowledge base editors,* i.e. specialized editors (menu-based, window-based, direct manipulation-based, etc.), which support the knowledge engineer in knowledge coding operations;
  - *browsers,* capable of interactively accessing and displaying portions of the knowledge base.
- *Knowledge base testing tools,* supporting knowledge base verification and validation activities. These may include:
  - *knowledge base syntactical checkers,* used to verify the presence of syntactic errors in the knowledge base, concerning format errors, type mismatches, etc.;
  - *knowledge base checkers,* capable of detecting more subtle errors, such as duplications, ambiguities, simple clashes, incompleteness, circularities, etc.; these programs are generally very complex and usually available only as research tools;
  - *debuggers,* capable of monitoring and updating the content of the working memory during KBS operation;
  - *tracers,* capable of displaying information describing the evolution of KBS operation (which data or hypotheses are considered in a given moment, which rules and methods are executed, etc.), allowing the knowledge engineer to follow the internal functioning of the KBS, possibly at various levels of details;
  - *execution control systems,* capable of controlling the operation of the reasoning mechanisms, allowing the knowledge engineer to run the KBS step-by-step, to proceed until a spy-point or a check-point is found, to proceed backward, to halt/resume execution, to monitor control-level mechanisms (for example, conflict resolution or multiple inheritance), etc.;
  - *case library managers,* constituted by specialized data base systems with the aim of storing and selectively retrieving the test cases to be used in knowledge base testing;

- *Documentation tools*, constituted by specialized systems (for example hypertext or hypermedia tools) capable of supporting the production of knowledge base documentation [Vesoul 88].

The effectiveness of all the above mentioned tools highly depends on their level of integration, both internal among the various components of the development support system, and external with the empty system.

The *maintenance support system* is an integrated set of tools which support the maintenance of the knowledge base. It is produced during the implementation, installation and delivery of the target system (phase 4) and used later in KBS maintenance activities (phase 5). The primary user of the maintenance support system is the maintenance team, in charge of maintaining the knowledge base of the KBS during its operational life. The maintenance support system includes several classes of tools, that are generally a sub-set of those present in the development support system, appropriately tailored and adapted to be easily and safely used by the maintenance team (see section 8.2.2).

Turning now to the tools used for building a KBS, by the term *KBS development tool* we refer generically to any hardware or software tool which supports the development activities performed during the KBS life cycle. More precisely, the software tools utilized for the production of the empty system and the development support system (in phases 2, 3, and 4) are globally called *basic development environment*. These are examined in the following section.

6.4.2   The basic development environment

The basic development environment may include three classes of tools:
- *General-purpose programming languages*, including high-level languages supporting all programming paradigms (imperative, functional, logical, object-oriented, and rule-based).
- *Specific KBS development tools*, i.e. software development tools which have been purposely designed in order to support and facilitate the development of KBSs. Specific KBS development tools incorporate specialized components to be used (directly or through simple tailoring, extension or integration) as part of the empty system and of the development support system. With respect to general-purpose programming languages, these tools can make the development process easier and faster, thanks to the substantial amount of pre-written code that would otherwise need to be designed, written, tested, debugged, and maintained. In fortunate cases, a well-chosen specific KBS development tool can match exactly the requirements of the empty system and of the development support system and, therefore, no development activity is necessary (tasks 3.12 through 3.15 can be skipped). If this is not the case, some parts of the empty system and of the development support system must be developed by means of the tool itself or of a general-purpose programming language. Generally, the technical background and the training needed to work

with a specific KBS development tool is lower than the one needed to use a general-purpose programming language.

- *General purpose development tools*, i.e. software development tools used to develop special-purpose modules (software interface, external interface, user interface, and explanation system) or heterogeneous problem-solvers (spread-sheets, data-base systems, neural networks tools, etc.). General purpose development tools are usually the same ones used in traditional software system development.

The basic development environment used in a KBS project generally includes a set of tools, usually not more than four to five. In a typical situation, it may include a specific KBS development tool interfaced to a general-purpose programming language and some general-purpose development tools, such as a user interface development tool and a spread-sheet.

The tools included in the basic development environment may have different origins. They may be available on the market as *commercial tools* or they may be *proprietary tools* developed internally by a specific organization.

6.4.3   Commercial tools

General-purpose programming languages

General-purpose programming languages currently used for building KBSs belong to one (or more) of the five well-known common programming paradigms, namely: imperative, functional, logic, object-oriented, and rule-based [Ambler et al. 92]. A list of such languages is provided below. For the less common ones, specific product and supplier names are reported as well. Such commercial information is, however, only indicative; it does not aim to be complete and, moreover, it is subject to change very rapidly. A survey of suppliers of general-purpose programming languages for KBS development can be found in [Shaw 93].

- Imperative languages basically include C and Fortran.
- Functional languages [McCarthy 60], [Henderson 80], [Reade 89] include:
  - Common Lisp [Steele 84], [Winston and Horn 89], available in a variety of implementations;
  - parallel Lisp, like TopCL (by Top Level Inc., Amherst, MA);
  - Scheme [Abelson and Sussman 85], [Eisenberg et al. 90], like, for example, Scheme Express and Mac Scheme (by Academic Computing Specialists, Salt Lake City, UT), Chez Scheme (by Cadence Research Systems, Bloomington, IN), and EdScheme (by Schemers Inc., Fort Lauderdale, FL);
  - functional extensions to C, that add the symbolic and functional programming capabilities of Lisp to the C programming language, like Clisp (by Drash Computer Software, Ashford, CT) and LispC (by Klondike Software Inc., Ottawa, Canada);

One should also mention the Lisp to C translators, that allow realizing the benefits of Lisp highly productive development environment and still deliver end-products in a widely accepted commercial standard, like C. This class of tool include, for example, Lisp-to-C-Translator" (by Chestnut Software Inc., Boston, MA).

- Logic languages [Apt et al. 93], [Hogger 84], include:
  - Prolog [Clocksin and Mellish 87], [Bratko 90], [Sterling and Shapiro 86], available in a variety of implementations;
  - parallel Prolog, like n(parallel PROLOG) (by Paralogic Inc., Bethlehem, PA)
  - Poplog, an hybrid language that mixes Common Lisp, Prolog and Pop-11, like POPLOG (by PSP Associates Ltd., Reading, UK), Poplog Common Lisp (by Computable Functions Inc., Amherst, MA), and Poplog/Common Lisp (by Integral Solutions Ltd., Basingstoke, UK);
  - constraint logic programming languages [Benhamou and Colmerauer 93], like Charme (by Bull/Cediag, Louveciennes, F), CHIP (by COSYTEC, Berkhamsted, UK), Pecos (by ILOG Inc., Mountain View, CA), Prolog III (by PROLOGIA, Marseilles, F), VS Trilogy (by Vertical Software Ltd., West Vancouver, Canada).
- Object-oriented languages [Stefik and Bobrow 86], [Meyer 88] include:
  - Smalltalk [Goldberg and Robson 89], [Hopkins and Horan 93], like, for example, Objectwork\Smalltalk (by ParcPlace Systems Inc., Sunnyvale, CA);
  - CLOS (Common Lisp Object System), the object-oriented extension of Common Lisp [Keene 89], [Lawless and Miller 91], [Paepcke 93], available in a variety of implementations;
  - object-oriented extension of C [Stroustrup 86], [Stroustrup and Ellis 90], like C++, available in a variety of implementations;
  - object-oriented extensions of Prolog, like Prolog++ (by Logic Programming Associates Ltd., London, U).
- Rule-based languages [Waterman and Hayes-Roth 78] include:
  - the OPS family of languages [Brownston et al. 85], [Cooper and Wogrin 88], like OPS5 (by Digital Equipment Corp., Marlboro, MA), OPS83 (by Production Systems Technologies Inc., Pittsburgh, PA), and OPS-2000 (by Intellipro, Morristown, NJ);
  - Eclipse (by The Haley Enterprise, Sewickley, PA);
  - RuleTalk (by Interdata Development Corp. Belmont, CA);
  - YAPS (by College Park Software, Altadena, CA);
  - rule-based extensions of C, like CLIPS (C Language Integrated Production System - by Cosmic/University of Georgia, Athens, GA) and RAL (by Production System Technologies Inc., Pittsburgh, PA), and rule-based extensions of C++, like Rete++ (by The Haley Enterprise Inc., Sewickley, PA).

General-purpose programming languages guarantee the highest level of generality, but require that the KBS be designed and programmed from scratch.

General-purpose programming languages are typically not utilized in phase 2, since they do not support rapid prototyping. They may be used in phase 3, but often only to build those modules of the target system and of the development support system which are not directly available or cannot be built more easily with other more specific KBS development tools. In phase 4, general-purpose programming languages have a more significant role since they may support the achievement of specific goals, such as efficiency, portability, standardization, etc.

Specific KBS development tools

Specific KBS development tools have their ancestors in spin-off tools, mentioned here only for historical reasons, which are constituted by specific KBS with the knowledge base emptied through a process known as *shellification* [Breuker and Wielinga 89]. Well-known examples of spin-off tools are EMYCIN derived from the MYCIN system for medical diagnosis, HERSAY III and AGE obtained from HERSAY-I, EXPERT from CASNET, and KAS from PROSPECTOR [Harmon and King 85].

Specific KBS development tools firstly appeared on the market in the early eighties and went through a very rapid and significant evolution [Price 91]. Presently, this class of tools includes a huge amount of commercially available systems. A survey of tools and suppliers can be found in [Shaw and Zeichick 92], [Heath 94].

We divide this class of tools into two main categories, namely: *horizontal tools* or *shells*, which feature a high generality and can be applied - at least in principle - in any type of application domain, and *vertical tools*, oriented towards specific tasks or applications. Both categories include a wide range of systems, featuring different technical and functional characteristics and running on different hardware platforms. To give a concrete idea of commercially available systems, a list of tools is reported below. The rapid evolution of these products makes any attempt to provide a complete and up-dated list meaningless; the interested reader should refer to technical and commercial literature. This list reported below is, therefore, only indicative.

- Horizontal tools or shells offer integrated collections of general-purpose utilities for KBS development.
  Generally speaking, in order to develop a KBS through a shell, it is merely necessary to provide the specific and pertinent domain knowledge. Filled up in this way, the shell is capable of providing the requested problem-solving capabilities, since it already includes most of the typical components found in an empty system. A shell usually includes a more or less sophisticated development support system. Thus, KBS development through a shell is usually much faster than by means of general-purpose programming languages, since a lot of technical decisions and implementation activities have been already incorporated into them.
  There is a wide range of commercially available shells that cover a continuum from small, simple, stand-alone, ready-to-use systems to large, powerful, open, and sophisticated development environments. While some shells feature lower flexibility and generality with respect to programming languages since

their fundamental characteristics cannot be changed by their users, others are flexible and general and include an underlying programming language (like Lisp or C or C++), that can be used to tailor and expand the basic shell functions. Some shells are very specific and include just one design paradigm, others, instead, implement a full set of knowledge representation techniques and reasoning methods. Moreover, while some shells offer very limited KBS development facilities, others include a rich collection of development support tools. Therefore, important issues like the background and the effort needed to learn a shell, the skill required to use it correctly and effectively, and the level of productivity reached greatly vary from case to case.

There is indeed a great variety of shells available on the market. Some of the most well-known are: Acquire (by Acquired Intelligence Inc., Victoria, Canada), Adept (by SoftSell, Redmond, WA), AIM (Abductive Information Modeler - by Abtech Corporation, Charlottesville, VA), Aion Development System (by Aion Corp., Palo Alto, CA), ArityExpert Development package (by Arity Corp., Concord, MA), ART*Enterprise (Automated Reasoning Tool) and CBR Express (by Inference Corp. El Segundo, CA), CA-DB Expert (by Computer Associates International Inc., Islandia, NY), Crystal (by Intelligent Environments Europe Ltd., Sunbury-on-Thames, UK), CxPert (by Software Plus Ltd., Crofton, MD), DXpress and PC-DX (by Knowledge Industries, Palo Alto, CA), Eclipse and Easy Reasoner (by The Haley Enterprise Inc., Sewickley, PA), Entrypaq Professional (by Albatheon Software Inc., San Francisco, CA), EXSYS Professional (by Exsys Inc., Albuquerque, NM), FLEX (by Logic Programming Associates Ltd., London, UK), GBB (Generic Blackboard Framework - by Blackboard Technology Group, Amherst, MA), GoldWorks (by Gold Hill Inc., Cambridge, MA), GURU (by Micro Data Base Systems Inc., Lafayette, IN), Hugin (Hugin Software, Aalborg, Denmark), Intelligence Service II (by GSI-ERLI, Charenton-le-Pont, France), IBIS (by Intelligence Mfg. Co., West Sacramento, CA), Icarus Mentor (by Icarus, Rockville, MD), IDIS (by IntelligenceWare Inc., Los Angeles, CA), KBMS (by AICorp, Waltham, MA), KDS (by KDS Corp., Wilmette, IL), KEE (Knowledge Engineering Environment), ProKappa, and Kappa-PC (by IntelliCorp Inc., Mountain View, CA), KES (by Software Architecture and Engineering Inc., Arlington, MA), Knowledge Craft (by The Carnegie Group, Pittsburgh, PA), Knowledge Works (Harlequin Inc., Cambridge, MA), LASER (by Bell Atlantic, Princeton, NJ), Level-5 Object (by Information Builders Inc., Indialantic, FL), Mahogany Professional (by Emeral Intelligence, Ann Arbor, MI), Mercury Knowledge Base Environment (by Artificial Intelligence Technologies Inc., Elmsford, NY), M.4 (by Cimflex Teknowledge Corp., Palo Alto, CA), Nexpert Object (by Neuron Data, Palo Alto, CA), PECCOS, SMECI, AIDA, and MASAI (by ILOG, Paris, France), ReMind (by Cognitive Systems Inc., Boston, MA), RuleMaster (by Radian Corporation, Austin, TX), Statute Expert (Statute Technologies Inc., Dickson, Australia), TIRS (The Integrated Reasoning Tool - by IBM Corp., San Jose, CA), VP-Expert (by Wordtech Systems Inc., Orinda, CA), Xi Plus (by Inference Corp., El Segundo, CA), XpertRule (Cincom Systems Inc., Cincinnati, OH), 1st-CLASS (by 1st-CLASS AICorp Inc., Waltham, MA).

- Vertical tools are oriented towards specific classes of application domains, such as diagnosis, scheduling, design, etc. If they match the requirements of the particular situation at hand, they allow a very fast development. Examples of vertical tools are:
  - tools for troubleshooting and diagnosis: Diagnostic Advisor (by Emerald Intelligence, Ann Arbor, MI), DXpress, WIN-DX, and API-DX (by Knowledge Industries, Palo Alto, CA), EDEN (Expert Diagnostic Environment - by Bull/Cediag, Louveciennes, France), G2 Diagnostic Assistant (by Gensym Corp., Cambridge, MA), Idea (by AI Squared Inc., Merrimack, NH), TestBench (by The Carnegie Group, Pittsburgh, PA) [Bodin 92];
  - tools for scheduling applications: DSP (Dynamic Scheduling Package - by Gensym Corp., Cambridge, MA), Intelligent Scheduling System (by Sira Ltd., Chislehurst, UK), Rhythm (by Intellection Inc., Dallas, TX), Sigma-GTBS and Operations Planner (by Itanis International Inc., Pittsburgh, PA);
  - tools for real time applications: Activation Framework (by The Real-Time Intelligent Systems Corp., Worcester, MA), Comdale/C Real-Time Expert System (by Comdale Technologies Inc., Toronto, Canada), G2 Real-Time Expert System (by Gensym Corp., Cambridge, MA) [Moore 91], [Finch et al. 92], NEMO (by S2O DEVELOPMENT, Paris, France), RT/Expert (by Integrated Systems Inc., Santa Clara, CA), RTS (by Real Time Systems Inc., Don Mills, Canada), RTworks (by Talarian Corp., Mountain View, CA);
  - tools for supervision of continuous and batch processes: COGSYS (by COGSYS, Salford, UK) [Davison 92], Comdale/X Expert System Tool (by Comdale Technologies Inc., Toronto, Canada);
  - tools for industrial and manufacturing applications: DClass (by CAM Software Inc., Provo, UT), M/Power (by Mitech Corp., Acton, MA), Rocky (by Expert Edge Corp., Palo Alto, CA);
  - tools for decision support, information systems, business, finance, and legal domains: Business Insight (by Business Resource Software Inc., Austin, TX), CAIS (Computer Aided Intelligent Service - by ROSH Intelligent Systems Inc., Needham, MA), Crystal Ball (by Decisoneering, Denver, CO), Demos (by Lumina Decision Systems Inc., Palo Alto, CA), Esteem (by Esteem software Inc., Cambridge City, IN), Expert Advisor (Software Artistry Inc., Indianapolis, IN), Extend, Extend+BPR, and Extend+Manufacturing (by Imagine That Inc., San Jose, CA), Exsys (by Jordan-Webb Information Systems Ltd., Lincolnwood, IL), Methodologist's Toolchest Professional (by The Idea Works Inc., Columbia, MO), NNConsult (by Itanis International Inc., Pittsburgh, PA), Performance Now!, Descriptions Now!, and Policies Now! (by Knowledge Point, Petaluma, CA), Ronstadt's Financial (by Lord Publishing, Dana Pointe, CA), SELECTOR II (by Chartered Electronics Inc., South San Francisco, CA), STATUTE CORPORATE (by Statute Technologies Inc., Dickon Act, Australia), SynCore (by Syntelligence, Sunnyvale, CA).

Some of the above mentioned KBS development tools may include a *delivery system generator*, capable of transforming the KBS (or a part of it) into a software module, often called *delivery* or *run-time system*, capable of running autonomously, separated from the development support system. Delivery system generators are used for a (semi)automatic production of the final target system, starting from the prototype. They generally include compilers which can convert knowledge bases into an internal form which can be efficiently exploited during KBS operation. Sometimes, they can also directly produce a high-level language code (like Fortran or C), which can be compiled and embedded in other programs, thus providing higher performance [Highland and Iwaskiw 89].

General-purpose development tools

Among general-purpose development tools, *user interface development tools*, devoted to the development of the interfaces towards the end-user and the knowledge engineer are particularly important. In fact, such modules play a critical and fundamental role for the success of a KBS. These tools include:
- *window systems* and *screen management systems*, such as Microsoft Windows (by Microsoft, Redmond, WA), Open Look (by SUN Microsystems, Mountain View, CA), and X-Window (developed jointly by the Massachusetts Institute of Technology, Cambridge, MA, and Digital Equipment Corporation, Hudson, MA);
- *user interface development systems*, including program libraries and interactive utilities to create and manage windows, menus, scroll bars, icons, buttons, graphics, etc., such as EASE+ (by Expert-EASE Systems Inc., Belmont, CA), Garnet (by Carnegie Mellon University, Pittsburgh, PA), MacApp (by Apple Computer, Cuppertino, CA), Object/1 (by Micro Data Base Systems Inc., Lafayette, IN), Open Interface Elements (by Neuron Data, Palo Alto, CA), Motif (by the Open Software Foundation, Cambridge, MA), CASE:PM (by CASEWORKS Inc., Atlanta, GA), and NexTstep (by NEXT Inc., Redwood City, CA).

Other general purpose development tools include *interconnection and interoperability tools*, including:
- network process intercommunication systems, such as IPC and RPC routines in the Unix operating systems, and OPNET (by MIL 3 Inc., Washington, DC);
- data base and spread-sheet connection systems, such as EXCHANGE (by California Intelligence, San Francisco, CA), and dBLISP (by Chestnut Software Inc., Boston, MA), which provides an effective interface between Lisp, dBASE III, and C/S Elements (by Neuron Data, Palo Alto, CA);
- interoperability systems, such as NET-Link+ (by NORRAD, Nashua, NH), which provides a link among Nexpert Object (by Neuron Data, Palo Alto, CA), a rule- and object-based KBS shell, and a neural nets tool, an abductive reasoning tool, an object-oriented fuzzy logic development tool, and a genetic algorithms package.

6.4.4   Proprietary tools

Whenever an organization has to identify the most appropriate tools to be exploited for the development of a specific KBS, a basic alternative arises; resorting on tools commercially available on the market or using internally developed tools, i.e. *proprietary tools*. The issue becomes even more important when a KBS department (or a KBS producer) is expected to face several KBS projects over time and desires to maximize productivity and improve standard, while minimizing the training effort requested to learn new development tools. Both alternatives offer various advantages and drawbacks.

An obvious benefit of proprietary tools is the possibility to optimize the match with the specific exigencies of the organization. If we consider that the very huge amount of different tools acquirable today on the market addresses only a small percentage of the possible specific problems tackled in KBS projects, the high specificity of proprietary tools becomes very attractive. A proprietary tool ensures high productivity, both in terms of reduced development times and costs. Moreover, by using proprietary tools it is possible to obtain an higher level of software and knowledge re-use. Proprietary tools may guarantee as well the best match with the internal delivery environments and an optimal coupling with internal standards; however, they may be less portable towards the outside of the native organization.

Several of the above considerations support the choice of proprietary tools for KBS development, especially in large-size organizations where a specific group is devoted to KBS development (the KBS department) on a permanent basis. However, it must be clear that developing proprietary tools is a long and economically demanding enterprise, which can be justified only in very specific circumstances. The specific reasons which may lead to the decision of developing proprietary tools are:
- the aim to improve productivity by reducing development time and cost;
- the need to standardize the KBS design and production processes;
- the need to increase the re-usability of KBS components over projects;
- the goal to become independent of suppliers of KBS development tools;
- the intent to assure a long life time for the technology and tools used, independently of the rapid evolution taking place in the market of KBS development tools, causing continuous new versions of the tools, with consequently high maintenance costs - not always justified by the improvements actually included in the new versions;
- the aim to reduce the time and cost of the training activities needed to provide technical personnel with the suitable competence to use new KBS development tools;
- the exigency to support a development methodology developed internally with specific design and development tools (see section 2.3.2).

The development of proprietary tools should be started only after several KBS projects have been successfully completed and a robust experience gathered. The development of a proprietary tool requires technical personnel with very specialized competence and sound experience. Moreover, after the tool is developed and released for routine use, a support group has to be set up in order to maintain and extend it over time as appropriate.

One of the basic problems that has to be addressed in developing proprietary tools is constituted by the identification of appropriate requirements. Failing to correctly identify requirements would cause a poor tool to be produced (not appropriately engineered, not general enough, not really modular and re-usable, functionally inadequate, etc.) and, therefore, a tremendous waste of resources. Quite frequently, a proprietary tool originates (by shellification) from a successful KBS which is gradually refined, extended, and generalized into an autonomous tool. In other cases, a proprietary tool is built starting from KBS development tools bought from the market and then tailored and extended according to the specific requirements of the target organization.

6.4.5   Selecting the right KBS development tool

Trends in KBS development tools

Development tools, both hardware and software, have evolved tremendously in the last decade and it is hard to forecast the direction of future developments. The trend of the early and mid-eighties towards specialized systems has been superseded by the preference for more general and standard tools. Most probably, the huge variety of specific products available today on the market will evolve towards a simpler scenario, where the number of products will be lower and some de facto standard will emerge. Some current trends are briefly mentioned below:

- shells and toolkits are used less than a few years ago primarily because their exploitation is not trivial; the use of such tools is then concentrated mainly to demonstrator and prototype development;
- there is a trend towards basic development environments based on standard platforms running C or C++, allowing higher portability, efficiency, extendibility, interoperability, and standardization;
- it is becoming more and more common to develop proprietary tools, based on standard commercial components, such as C, C++, X-Window, Unix libraries, etc.
- Lisp is losing impact on the application site, whereas it is still one of the most popular tools within research environments;
- Prolog is emerging more and more as a prototyping tool, both in academic and application contexts;
- Smalltalk is gaining attention, also in industrial applications;
- object-oriented programming is becoming a well-accepted standard;
- C++ is becoming a major tool for target system development, providing portability and efficiency;

- more automatic knowledge acquisition tools, and more generally computer-aided knowledge engineering tools, are going to be available for supporting knowledge elicitation and modeling, design and development activities;
- more vertical tools will appear on the market, as new application areas are approached and new solutions are developed and experimented with;
- traditional knowledge representation approaches are going to be integrated with sub-symbolic mechanisms (neural networks are the most popular and significant example);
- KBS development tools are becoming more suitable for integration with standard software development environments and CASE systems.

A methodology for tool selection

The selection of the right development tool to use in a KBS project is an important aspect of success. In this section, we present a methodology for tool selection which can be applied for the execution of all the tasks of the KBS life cycle devoted to the choice of KBS development tools (namely: 1.18, 2.8, 3.10, and 4.6) [Rothenberg 89], [Prerau 90], [Le Blanc and Tawfik Jelassi 91]. The methodology is structured in two parts: the first one defines an appropriate project-specific evaluation framework, and the second one performs the actual evaluation of candidate tools and the final selection. It includes six steps, as illustrated in detail below.

1. Identifying requirements
The goal of this step is to produce a list of *requirements* for the basic development environment. The input to this step is constituted by:
- information about the specific type of KBS to be developed, namely, demonstrator, prototype, or target system;
- the technical specifications of the system to be developed (from task 2.6 or 3.6 or 4.5);
- the logical model of the system to be developed (from task 3.7);
- the specifications of the empty system (from task 3.8);
- the specifications of the development support system (from task 3.9);
- possible constraints concerning development time and costs
- possible constraints concerning hardware and software environment;
- information about background, skill, and competence level of the project team members, and possibly of the domain experts.

The requirements for the basic development environment generally include:
- the list of the components of the empty system to be produced by means of the basic development environment and an illustration of their main technical characteristics;
- the list of the components of the development support system which are considered necessary, together with an illustration of their main technical characteristics;

- the technical constraints to be considered for the development tools, such as: hardware platforms, operating systems, proprietary tools, etc.;
- the project-specific constraints to be considered for the development tools, such as: costs, level of technical sophistication, learnability, available support and training, etc.

2. Defining the evaluation framework

By evaluation framework we understand the metrics considered for assessing candidate tools and the techniques used to measure the tools according to the metrics. Therefore, the goal of this step is twofold:

- identifying the *evaluation metrics*, i.e. the characteristics of the candidate tools to measure;
- defining the *evaluation techniques* to use for measuring the characteristics specified in the previous point.

The input to this step is constituted by the requirements for the basic development environment defined in the previous step.

The evaluation metrics may be more or less analytic; it may concern only a few coarse-grained characteristic of a tool, or it may involve a large number of highly detailed characteristics. Typical items to be included in evaluation metrics are illustrated in the following [Richer 86], [van Koppen 86], [Citrenbaum et al. 87], [Grigoriou and Willey 87], [Gevarter 87], [Harmon et al. 88], [Mettrey 87], [Alty 89], [Rothenberg 89], [Vedder 89], [Le Blanc and Tawfik Jelassi 91].

Context-dependent characteristics concern those aspects of a development tool which have to be measured with respect to the specific features of the project at hand. These include:

- *Coverage*, i.e. how much a tool matches the technical requirements concerning the components of the empty system and of the development support system. Coverage constitutes a fundamental element to evaluate since it provides a precise indication of how well a tool (or a set of tools) is directly usable in the KBS development process. Limited coverage implies an additional effort to build the missing components.
- *Adequacy*, i.e. how well the specific functions of the components of the empty system and of the development support system available in a tool (or which can be developed with the tool) correspond to the requirements. While tool coverage prescribes a quantitative evaluation (i.e., which components are available), tool adequacy implies a qualitative evaluation (i.e., how well the available components provide the functions required). The evaluation of adequacy is more demanding than that of coverage, since it requires a deep analysis of several aspects of a tool. Tool adequacy is a fundamental context-dependent item to consider. High tool adequacy implies a narrowing of the representation gap between the domain level and the implementation level, with several benefits in terms of increased productivity and better quality.

Context-independent characteristics concern intrinsic aspects of a development tool, both technical and functional. For these characteristics an absolute optimal evaluation is generally desired, independently of the specific features of the project at hand. However, in some cases, the peculiarities of the project may call for a context-dependent evaluation. These include:

- *Flexibility*, i.e. the capability to adapt to different application domains, tasks, and environments. Flexibility plays a fundamental role especially when coverage and adequacy are low. This characteristic can be further decomposed into:
  - *modularity*, i.e. how much a tool is structured into functional units, which may be used or acquired separately;
  - *extendibility*, i.e. how much a tool can be extended by adding new components;
  - *modifiability*, i.e. how much the components of a tool can be re-parameterized, modified, or tailored to different exigencies;
  - *interoperability*, i.e. how much and how easily a tool can be integrated with external software (for example, through procedure call or embedding);
  - *interconnectivity*, i.e. how much and how easily a tool can exchange data with external software packages such as data bases, spreadsheets, I/O drivers, etc.
  - *portability*, i.e. how easily an application developed with a tool on a specific hardware/software platform can be transferred to a different platform;
- *Generality*, i.e. how much a tool is general-purpose or KBS specific. On the two extremes of generality there are general-purpose programming languages on one side and vertical KBS tools on the other side.
- *Richness*, i.e. the variety of available knowledge representation techniques, reasoning methods, architectures, and development support tools.
- *Integration level*, i.e. how much the various components of a tool offer a uniform, coherent, and integrated set of facilities.
- *Size*, with reference to the size of knowledge bases that can be produced and efficiently managed.
- *Efficiency* , i.e. the capability of providing good performance. This characteristic can be further decomposed into:
  - *time efficiency*, concerning response time, both during development and in the final KBS;
  - *space efficiency*, concerning memory requirements;
  - *compilation efficiency*, concerning time and memory requirements of the compilation process, if any.
- *Robustness*, i.e. how much a tool is capable of behaving in an acceptable and cooperative way in front of improper or incorrect use.
- *Security*, i.e. how a tool is protected against erroneous or non-authorized access.
- *Reliability*, i.e. how much a tool is expected to behave correctly according to specifications.
- *Learnability*, i.e. the ease of learning about a tool and of acquiring the operative skills needed to effectively use it.
- *Usability*, i.e. the ease of using a tool during KBS development.
- *Productivity*, i.e. the property of a tool to support effective and efficient KBS development.

- *Maintenance and extension support*, i.e. the property of a tool to support the maintenance and extension interventions taking place during the operational use of a KBS.
- *Technical level*, i.e. availability of training, expected availability of updates and new versions, hotline support and on-site assistance (usual crisis reaction times), availability of the tool on other platforms, level of diffusion and standardization, availability of knowledge bases, third party add-on market, etc.
- *Vendor reputation*, including technical background, experience, marketing and sale strategies, the financial stability, etc.
- *Cost*, including royalties (for the development system and the run-time modules), contract conditions, availability of special discounts (like site licence, number discount, educational conditions, etc.), updates and new versions, support, training, consulting, and indirect costs (cost of required hardware platforms, hidden costs, etc.).

Once a suitable evaluation metrics has been identified, it is necessary to rank the characteristics to consider according to their importance within the specific KBS application at hand, taking into account project goals and constraints.

Later, appropriate evaluation techniques to be used for measuring the identified characteristics in the candidate tools have to be defined. For some characteristics simple and informal techniques, such as interviews to sales representatives or reading of technical documentation, may be appropriate. Other characteristics are much more difficult to measure, and more complex and formal techniques have to be used. Analytical comparisons among the various candidates, benchmarking, questionnaires, trial use, personal advice, analysis of previous experiences, are valuable and suitable techniques which enable a greater degree of confidence in the results of the evaluation to be reached. Note that the choice of the most appropriate evaluation technique also depends on the ranking assigned to a characteristic; in general, higher ranking requires more precise, detailed, and in-depth evaluation techniques.

3. Identifying candidate tools
The goal of this step is the identification of *candidate tools*. It is carried out by examining what is available either on the market or internally and by selecting the tools which seem compatible with the stated requirements. This process usually requires preliminary contacts with vendors and may take some time to be carefully performed.

4. Refining the evaluation framework
The goal of this step is the refinement of the evaluation framework on the basis of the preliminary information so far collected on candidate tools. An improved version of evaluation metrics may be produced by adding, deleting or refining some of the specific characteristics considered and by updating their ranking. So, for example, if most of the candidate tools appear to be approximately equivalent as far as one specific characteristic is concerned, it may be appropriate to analyze

this characteristic in more detail (for example, by decomposing it into finer-grained items) to clearly identify any possible difference among candidate tools. The evaluation techniques may also be updated according to the new version of the evaluation metrics.

5. Evaluating the tools

This is the central step of the methodology. The person (or team) in charge of the evaluation analyzes the candidate tools in detail by means of the evaluation techniques prescribed and assigned appropriate values (either qualitative or quantitative) to the evaluation metrics. A check-list method may be used for this task; of course, others scoring models and ranking techniques may be used as well, if preferred - see, for example: [Saaty 80], [Naumann and Palvia 82], [Forman and Nagy 87], [Klein and Beck 87]). If any candidate tools fail to meet minimal requirements, they can be directly excluded from the analysis.

If necessary, limited refinements to the evaluation framework may be performed again.

6. Selecting the tools

The final step considers the analytical information collected in the previous step in order to select one of the alternatives evaluated. This step is generally under the direct responsibility of the project leader. The output of this step is constituted by the precise specification of the tools that have to be used for the subsequent development effort.

It is important to note that the evaluation and selection process described above does not concern, in general, single tools in isolation, but a combination of tools which are evaluated as a whole, in order to understand how well they match the requirements for the basic development environment necessary for the KBS project at hand.

Carrying out the tool selection methodology proposed above involves the contribution of several members of the project team: the project leader, who supervises the whole procedure and is responsible for the final choice, the knowledge engineers, the designers, and the programmers, who prepare the evaluation framework and actually carry out the evaluation of candidate tools. The time it takes for carrying out the selection process usually goes from some weeks to a few months in the most complex cases. For very large KBS projects or for critical cases (for example, the selection of tools to be adopted as a standard in a KBS department), the evaluation techniques utilized may include a concrete and extended experimentation with candidate tools, requiring, in such a way, a significant amount of time.

As a final remark, let us note that, although the methodology for tool selection presented here is aimed at optimizing the matching between the requirements of a specific project and the tools adopted, it is obvious that a KBS department cannot change the development tools every time it starts up a new project. In fact, this would imply a re-training period which is too costly and time consuming, new investment for the acquisition of the new tool would be required, and re-using software would be impossible. As a consequence, it typically happens that tool selection is performed not only by taking into account the next project to develop, but by trying to foresee the possible classes of systems the KBS department will be requested to build over a sufficiently long time period. One should try to find an appropriate compromise between two contrasting exigencies, namely "tool to problem fit" that may lead to the choice of a new tool for each new KBS project, and "standard" that suggests adopting a unique development environment for all projects in a KBS department. This situation may then evolve towards the development of proprietary tools, which specifically match the exigencies of the KBS department (see section 6.4.4).

6.5   CONCEPTUAL DESIGN

6.5.1   Step execution

Figure 6.8 presents a detailed view of KLIC tasks and products of the 'conceptual design' step.

6.5.2   Task 3.4: Knowledge analysis and modeling

The goal of this task is to analyze the application domain considered in order to collect enough knowledge to support the design of the conceptual model. Task 3.4 takes in input the plausibility study report (from task 1.29) and the demonstrator report (from task 2.18), if available.

At this stage, the knowledge engineer performs *sampling knowledge acquisition*, aimed at acquiring the information relevant to the construction of the conceptual model. More specifically, as far as the entity layer is concerned, sampling knowledge acquisition is aimed at identifying the different classes of entities, properties, relationships, constraints, procedures, and operations that characterize the domain, not at developing a thorough analysis of each class of knowledge and at eliciting all the knowledge of that class. For example, in a diagnostic application, if it is discovered that the domain expert associates observed symptoms to possible malfunction causes, it is important to identify the existence of this association and to clarify its nature, but it is not necessary in this task to elicit all the possible instances of the symptoms-causes association (which will be the goal of extensive knowledge acquisition - see section 6.8). As far as the reasoning layer is concerned, sampling knowledge acquisition is aimed at identifying the reasoning functions exploited in the domain, and the classes of entity-layer objects they apply to. Finally, at the problem-solving layer, the overall organization of the problem-solving strategies is defined and the different classes of strategic knowledge exploited are identified.

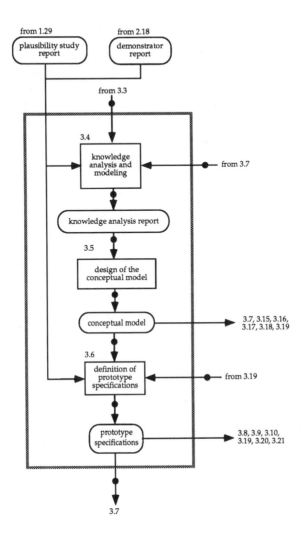

from 1.29
plausibility study report

from 2.18
demonstrator report

from 3.3

3.4
knowledge analysis and modeling

from 3.7

knowledge analysis report

3.5
design of the conceptual model

conceptual model

3.7, 3.15, 3.16, 3.17, 3.18, 3.19

3.6
definition of prototype specifications

from 3.19

prototype specifications

3.8, 3.9, 3.10, 3.19, 3.20, 3.21

3.7

Figure 6.8 Conceptual design: KLIC tasks and products.

This task is performed by means of repeated knowledge acquisition sessions and exploits verbal data, textual data, and descriptive data (see section 6.8.2). The indication of the most appropriate knowledge elicitation techniques to use can be found in section 6.8.4 (Figures 6.12, 6.13, 6.14, and 6.15). Section 6.8.2 also provides useful suggestions about the selection of the knowledge sources.

The product of task 3.4 is a document called *knowledge analysis report*. It includes all the materials collected during the knowledge acquisition sessions, together with an account of the activities carried out (sessions calendar, knowledge sources utilized, techniques applied, etc.).

6.5.3   Task 3.5: Design of the conceptual model

The goal of this task is to develop a detailed and coherent model of domain knowledge. Task 3.5 takes in input the knowledge analysis report (from task 3.4). The product of task 3.5 is a document called *conceptual model*.

This task is executed by the knowledge engineer. The modeling process is generally structured bottom-up, from the entity layer, to the reasoning layer, and, eventually, to the problem-solving layer. This way, the conceptual model is incrementally developed through a progressive synthesis of the knowledge acquired in the previous task. Of course, the modeling process is often not purely bottom-up and may require backtracking and iteration before a satisfactory result is obtained. A top-down approach to conceptual modeling is also possible, at least in principle, even if it often turns out to be less natural and less effective. Moreover, the button-up approach is more open towards an objective and innovative analysis of the domain, being especially appropriate for new application contexts, never faced before. In both approaches, an important aspect of the first stages of the modeling process is the definition of *knowledge dictionaries*, that provide a univocal linguistic reference for all domain objects. Knowledge dictionaries are glossaries where all the terms relevant to an application domain are listed in a structured and orderly way, precisely defined, and linked together through suitable pointers, whenever appropriate. Even if they merely concern the basic linguistic aspects of a domain, knowledge dictionaries should not be underestimated. They play a fundamental role in conceptual modeling and constitute a corner-stone of a good conceptual model.

6.5.4   Task 3.6: Definition of prototype specifications

The goal of this task is to update and refine the KBS specifications stated at the moment of plausibility study producing detailed specifications of the KBS prototype. Task 3.6 takes in input the plausibility study report (from task 1.29), the demonstrator report (from task 2.18), if available, and the conceptual model (from task 3.5). This task mostly focuses on functional specifications, since operational and technical specifications are generally less important for the prototype (they will deserve greater attention in phase 4 - see section 7.3.3). In particular:
- functional specifications are largely based on the conceptual model developed in the previous task, which provides precise and detailed information about the desired coverage and scope (see section 9.3.2, Figure 9.1) of the prototype; they also deal with adequacy issues, including robustness, friendliness, transparency, usability, effectiveness, and efficiency (see section 9.3.2, Figure 9.1);
- technical specifications generally include preliminary indications for the selection of the hardware and software tools to be used for the development of the prototype;

• operational specifications mainly focus on integration issues and prescribe how communication and data exchange with the external world should be implemented or simulated in the prototype.

The product of task 3.6 is a document called *prototype specifications*, which provides a complete and definitive list of the functional, operational, and technical specifications of the prototype.

6.6   TECHNICAL DESIGN

6.6.1   Step execution

Figure 6.9 presents a detailed view of KLIC tasks and products of the 'technical design' step.

6.6.2   Task 3.7: Design of the logical model

The goal of this task is to design the logical model of the prototype. Task 3.7 takes in input the plausibility study report (from task 1.29), the conceptual model (from task 3.5), the prototype specifications (from task 3.6). The product of task 3.7 is a document called *logical model*.

The methodology to follow for logical modeling has already been illustrated in Figure 6.6. The many choices to be performed on the three dimensions KR, RE, and ARCH, are accomplished by matching available techniques (known by the designer) to the specific features of the conceptual model. Some authors [Kline and Dolins 89] have proposed specific guidelines to make this process easier and more systematic. Such techniques are based on the idea of first classifying the content of conceptual model in terms of general *technical features* and then proceeding through a matching of the identified technical features against the *properties* of the candidate techniques to adopt. This matching can be realized by means of design rules, which encode the know-how about what technique to use in front of a specific requirement. Once this first phase is terminated a draft logical model is produced, which is then further refined and tailored to the specific needs of the application domain at hand. During the process, evaluation check-points should be placed in order to monitor the quality of the design being developed. Such an approach is a good example of balance between discipline and exploration: the design is incrementally refined but each step is accurately monitored.

In some cases, during logical design shortcomings of the knowledge analysis and modeling performed in the previous step are identified. This calls for a backtracking to task 3.4.

An account of the issue of logical design from the point of view of standards may be found in [IEEE 1016 87], [ESA PSS-05-0 91], and [ESA PSS-05-04 91];

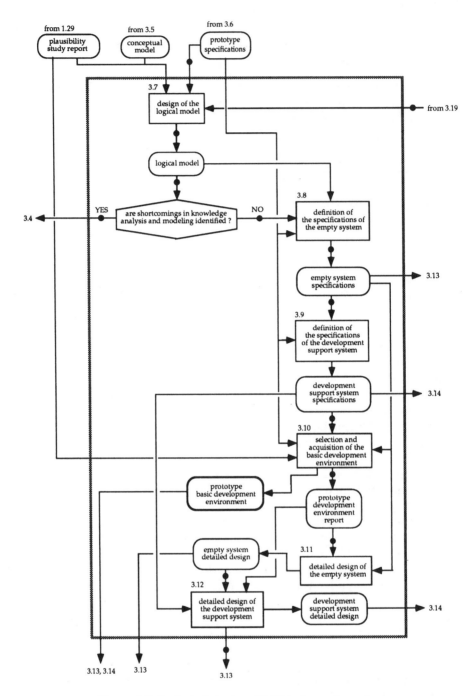

Figure 6.9 Technical design: KLIC tasks and products.

although they specifically concern the production of traditional software, some of the concepts presented in these documents may apply to KBSs as well.

The quality of the logical model is certainly one of the main issues for the success of a KBS project. As already mentioned in section 6.3.2, knowledge of the various components of knowledge-based technology is a prerequisite for a correct and effective design of the logical model. Therefore, in order to support the activity of the designer, we provide below a structured set of basic references to the main techniques that might be necessary for the design of the logical model (excluding the topic of software and external interfaces, which is mostly based on traditional software techniques).

Basic techniques
- knowledge representation techniques: [Ringland and Duce 84], [Sowa 84], [Brachman and Levesque 85], [Bench-Capon 90], [Davis 90-a], [Sowa 91], [Brachman et al. 92], [Davis et al 93], [Simmons and Davis 93];
- reasoning methods (including problem-solving, search, logic, and automated reasoning): [Chang and Lee 73], [Bledsoe 77], [Nilsson 80], [Pearl 84], [Schor et al. 86], [Genesereth and Nilsson 87], [Smets et al. 88], [Knight 89], [Allen et al. 90], [Bibel 93];
- knowledge organization, representation and use of meta-knowledge: [Davis 80-a], [Davis 80-b], [Georgeff 82], [Minton 88];
- architectures, distributed systems: [Hewitt 77], [Erman et al. 80], [Lesser and Erman 80], [Chandrasekaran 81], [Fox 81], [Kornfeld and Hewitt 81], [Lesser and Corkill 81], [Smith and Davis 81], [Davis and Smith 83], [Lesser and Corkill 83], [Hayes-Roth 85], [Minsky 85], [Yang et al. 85], [Agha 86], [Nii 86-a], [Nii 86-b], [Decker 87], [Huhns 87], [Bond and Gasser 88], [Engelmore and Morgan 89], [Gasser and Huhns 89], [Jagannathan et al. 89], [Craig 92].

Advanced techniques
- non-monotonic reasoning, constraint reasoning, and truth maintenance: [Doyle 79], [Doyle 79], [McDermott and Doyle 80], [Reiter 80], [McDermott 82-a], [de Kleer 86-a], [de Kleer 86-b], [de Kleer 86-c], [Ginsberg 87], [Poole 88], [Smith and Kellerher 88], [Geffner 90], [Shoham 90], [McDermott 91], [Dahl 93];
- case-based and analogical reasoning: [Carbonell 83], [Kolodner 84], [Carbonell 86], [Kolodner and Riesbeck 86], [Hall 89], [Riesbeck and Schank 89], [Stottler et al. 89], [Owen 90], [Slade 91];
- model-based reasoning: [Hart 82], [Michie 82], [Bobrow 84], [Davis 84-b], [de Kleer and Brown 84], [Forbus 84], [Chandrasekaran and Milne 85], [Kuipers 86], [Milne 87], [Chandrasekaran et al. 89], [Karp and Wilkins 89], [Weld and de Kleer 90], [Chandrasekaran 91], [Kuipers et al. 91], [Faltings and Struss 92], [Guida and Stefanini 92], [David et al. 93-b], [Kuipers 93];
- temporal reasoning: [Kahn and Gorry 77], [McDermott 82-b], [Vilain 82], [Allen 83], [Vere 83], [Allen 84], [Kowalsky and Sergot 86], [Rit 86], [Vilain and Kautz 86], [Dean and McDermott 87], [Dubois and Prade 89], [Maiocchi and Pernici 91] ;
- approximate and uncertain reasoning: [Zadeh 65], [Shafer 76], [Zadeh 79], [Dempster 68], [Zadeh 78], [Dubois and Prade 80], [Buchanan and Shortliffe 84],

[Cohen 85], [Driankov 86], [Farreny and Prade 86], [Kanal and Lemmer 86], [Bonissone 87], [Dubois and Prade 88], [Lemmer and Kanal 88], [Buxton 89], [Kanal et al. 89], [Bacchus 90], [Clark 90], [Henrion et al. 90], [Ng and Abramson 90], [Shachter et al. 90], [Shafer and Pearl 90], [Bonissone et al. 91], [Pearl 91], [Sheridan 91], [Ayyub et al. 92], [Zadeh and Kacprzyk 92], [Teramo et al. 92], [Yager et al. 93];

- machine learning: [Michalski et al. 83], [Michalski et al. 86], [Forsyth 89], [Carbonell 90], [Kodratoff and Michalski 90], [Shavlik and Dietterich 90], [Natarajan 91], [Morik et al. 93];
- planning: [Fikes and Nilsson 71], [Sacredoti 74], [Sacerdoti 77], [Nilsson 80], [Stefik 81-a], [Stefik 81-b], [Chapman 87], [Georgeff and Lansky 87], [Allen et al. 90], [Allen et al. 91];
- real-time systems and issues related to efficient reasoning: [Forgy 82], [O'Reilly and Cromarty 85], [Marsh and Greenwood 86], [Gupta 87], [Dean and Boddy 88], [Laffey et al. 88], [Lesser et al. 88], [Dodhiawala et al. 89], [Washington and Hayes-Roth 89], [Korf 90], [Brooks 91], [Ishida 91], [Padalkar et al. 91], [Russell and Zilberstein 91], [Ingrand et al. 92].

Human-computer interaction

The design of the user interface is a critical issue for the overall success of a KBS project. A poor user interface may lead to a negative judgement by the users with a consequent limited or ineffective exploitation of the system. The design of the user interface for a KBS is generally more demanding than for the case of traditional software, since the information exchanged between the user and the system is usually more complex and the processing performed by the system is more sophisticated. This calls for specific attention to be devoted to human-computer interaction factors. Basic references for this topic (excluding speech and vision) are:

- general: [Card et al. 83], [Hartson 85], [Kidd and Cooper 85], [Gains and Shaw 86], [Miyata and Norman 86], [Norman 86], [Norman and Draper 86], [Rasmussen 86], [Baecker and Buxton 87], [Hartson 88], [Helander 88], [Booth 89], [Weir and Alty 89], [Berry and Hart 90-a], [Dix et al. 93];
- user interface design and development: [Pfaff 85], [Gittins 86], [Anderson and Reitman 87], [Shneidermann 87], [Brown and Cunningham 89], [Hancock and Chignell 89], [Myers 89], [Wexelblat 89], [Laurel 90], [Sullivan and Tyler 91], [Vicente and Rasmussen 92], [Olsen 91], [Hix and Hartson 93], [McGraw 93];
- dialogue systems: [Bruce 75], [Levin and Moore 77], [Lehnert 78], [Cohen and Perrault 79], [Allen and Perrault 80], [Perrault and Allen 80], [Kaplan 82], [Lehnert and Ringle 82], [Brady and Berwick 83], [Reichman-Adar 84], [Reichman 85], [Brosz and Sidner 86], [Litman and Allen 87], [Polany 88];
- natural language processing: [Hendrix 82], [Winograd 83], [Simmons 84], [Harris 85], [McKeown 85], [Ferrari 86], [Allen 87], [Grishman 87], [Grosz et al. 86], [Kempen 87], [Patten 88], [Gazdar and Mellish 89-a], [Gazdar and Mellish 89-b], [Pereira and Grosz 93];

- intelligent help systems: [Miyata and Norman 86], [Norman 86], [O'Malley 86], [Owen 86], [Erlandsen and Holm 87], [Helander 88], [Weir and Alty 89], [Vicente and Rasmussen 92].

Explanation
The topic of explanation has a critical role in the design of a KBS. In fact, a KBS generally supports the user in the execution of knowledge-intensive tasks requiring complex reasoning capabilities. The behavior of the system may turn out to be not straightforward to understand for the user. The approach adopted to solve a problem, the alternatives examined, the strategic decisions made, the knowledge used and its validity, the questions asked to the user, the intermediate steps followed, the partial results obtained, and, eventually, the final solution proposed may have to be appropriately justified and explained to the user. An explanation facility is therefore essential for supporting the transparency of KBS behavior, thus improving understanding, enhancing interaction, and increasing confidence. Basic references for this topic are: [Weiner 80], [Clancey 83], [Swartout 83], [Wallis and Shortliffe 84], [McKeown et al. 85], [Neches et al. 85], [Scott et al. 86], [Swartout and Smoliar 87], [Chandrasekaran et al. 88], [Ellis 89], [Wick and Slagle 89], [Moore and Swartout 90], [Swartout et al. 91], [Cawsay 93], [Swartout and Moore 93], [Tanner et al. 93].

User modeling
User modeling [Kobsa and Wahlster 89], [Kay and Quilici 91] is the ability of a system to adapt its behaviour to the specific characteristics and nuances of an individual user, improving in such a way the usability of the system, the effectiveness and economy of the interaction, and the ability of the system to understand and process user requests beyond the pure content of utterances or commands. The application of user modeling techniques may be of primary importance in the design of both the user interface and the explanation system. Techniques for user modeling have been developed in many fields, such as dialog [Wahlster and Kobsa 89], intelligent tutoring [Self 88], and information retrieval [Belkin 88], [Daniels 86], [Brajnik et al. 87], [Brajnik et al. 90]. Basic references for this topic are: [Rich 79], [Rich 83], [Morik and Rollinger 85], [Daniels 86], [Brajnik et al. 87], [Carberry 88], [Kobsa and Wahlster 88], [Kass and Finnin 89], [Kobsa and Wahlster 89], [Rich 89], [Wahlster and Kobsa 89], [Kobsa 90], [Brajnik et al. 90].

6.6.3   Task 3.8: Definition of the specifications of the empty system

The goal of this task is to produce the detailed specifications of the empty system of the prototype. Task 3.8 takes in input the prototype specifications (from task 3.6) and the logical model (from task 3.7). The product of task 3.8 is a document called *empty system specifications*, which defines in detail the software modules of the empty system and how they implement the components of the logical model designed.

An account of the issue of specifications definition from the point of view of standards may be found in [ESA PSS-05-0 91] and [ESA PSS-05-03 91]; although they specifically concern the production of traditional software, some of the concepts presented in these documents may apply to KBSs as well.

6.6.4   Task 3.9: Definition of the specifications of the development support system

The goal of this task is to produce the detailed specifications for the development support system. Task 3.9 takes in input the prototype specifications (from task 3.6) and the empty system specifications (from task 3.8). The product of task 3.9 is a document called *development support system specifications*. It defines the main functions of the development support system of the prototype and how they should be provided through an appropriate and coherent set of development tools to be utilized in later tasks of the project.

Section 6.4.2 presents a list of possible tools to be included in the development support system.

6.6.5   Task 3.10: Selection and acquisition of the basic development environment

The goal of this task is to select and acquire the basic development environment to be used for the construction of the prototype. Task 3.10 takes in input the plausibility study report (from task 1.29), the prototype specifications (from task 3.6), the empty system specifications (from task 3.8), and the development support system specifications (from task 3.9). The products of task 3.10 are:
• a document called *prototype development environment report*, which illustrates the comparative analysis carried out to select the prototype basic development environment and the main reasons of the choice made;
• a set of software systems, namely the selected *prototype basic development environment*.

The methodology utilized for executing this task has been described in section 6.4.5. The tools utilized for prototype development are the most sophisticated of the whole KBS life cycle. The definition of the evaluation metrics to be used in tool selection should privilege features such as coverage, adequacy, flexibility, richness, usability, and productivity. Other factors, such as efficiency, robustness, reliability, and cost can be considered less important in this phase, pertaining to the target system. The specific characteristics of the application at hand may lead to different choices for the development tools:
• when the task to be performed by the KBS is well-defined, the problem complexity is limited, the project schedule requires fast development, and

training activities should be limited, then the choice can be oriented towards specific KBS development tools; if vertical tools are available for the specific application domain at hand, they should always be preferred to more generic horizontal tools or shells;
- in more complex situations, when an exploratory design is recommended and enough time can be devoted to training, then general-purpose programming languages might be preferred.

A final important point about the selection of the prototype basic development environment concerns the implications of this choice on the following phase 4. If it is possible to anticipate, at least to some degree, the specifications of the target system, one is often tempted to choose a development environment that can assure the most natural transition from the prototype to the target system, for example through incremental enhancement (see section 7.3.4). Balancing between the requirement of the prototype and those of the target system is however risky, and in general it should be avoided. Their requirements are often contrasting, and a satisfactory compromise can hardly be found. Unsuitable tools can make the development of the prototype more complex, longer, and more costly than expected. Moreover, the specifications of the target system are generally imprecise and uncertain at this stage of the KBS life cycle, and changes may occur before phase 4 is actually started.

6.6.6   Task 3.11: Detailed design of the empty system

The goal of this task is to produce the detailed design of the empty system of the prototype. Task 3.11 takes in input the empty system specifications (from task 3.8) and the prototype development environment report (from task 3.10). The product of task 3.11 is a document report called *empty system detailed design*, which describes how the empty system should be implemented by means of the prototype basic development environment selected.

The detailed design is the final step of the overall design activity and is aimed at providing a precise and fine-grained specification of all the technical characteristics of the software systems necessary for the implementation of the empty system. It takes into account both the logical model and the characteristics of the prototype basic development environment selected and produces a series of written documents and diagrams, focusing on the following issues:
- definition of the overall software architecture of the empty system, defined in terms of modules, interfaces, knowledge and data structures (both global and local), knowledge and data bases;
- precise and complete specifications of each system module (problem-solver or special-purpose module), defined in terms of inputs, outputs, and function;
- precise and complete specification of all knowledge and data structures, with details about representation, organization, and access methods;
- definition of the reasoning methods to exploit for the implementation of knowledge-based modules (problem-solvers or special-purpose modules);

- definition of the algorithms to exploit for the implementation of the modules which are not knowledge-based (heterogeneous problem-solvers or special-purpose modules);
- precise and complete specification of all knowledge and data bases, in terms of their structure and organization;
- description of the main control flow during system operation, in all different modes of operation.

The effort required to carry out this task may greatly vary depending on the prototype basic development environment selected. If this provides the knowledge representation techniques and reasoning mechanisms specified in the logical model ready-to-use, task 3.11 may focus on the design of heterogeneous problem-solvers and special-purpose modules. Instead, if it is necessary to design from scratch specific knowledge representation techniques and reasoning mechanisms, task 3.11 may become very demanding and require skilled and experienced designers and developers.

An account of the issue of detailed design from the point of view of standards may be found in [ESA PSS-05-0 91] and [ESA PSS-05-05 91]; although they specifically concern the production of traditional software, some of the concepts presented in these documents may apply to KBSs as well.

6.6.7   Task 3.12: Detailed design of the development support system

The goal of this task is to produce the detailed design of the development support system of the prototype. Task 3.12 takes in input the development support system specifications (from task 3.9), the prototype development environment report (from task 3.10), and the empty system detailed design (from task 3.11). The product of task 3.12 is a document called *development support system detailed design*, which describes how the development support system should be implemented by means of the prototype basic development environment selected.

Similarly to task 3.11, the effort for this task can greatly vary from case to case.

6.7   CONSTRUCTION OF THE EMPTY SYSTEM AND OF THE DEVELOPMENT SUPPORT SYSTEM

6.7.1   Step execution

Figure 6.10 presents a detailed view of KLIC tasks and products of the 'construction of the empty system and of the development support system' step.

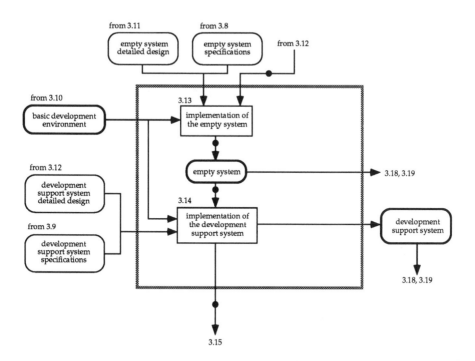

Figure 6.10 Construction of the empty system and of the development support system: KLIC tasks and products.

6.7.2   Task 3.13: Implementation of the empty system

The goal of this task is to produce the empty system of the prototype. Task 3.13 takes in input the empty system specifications (from task 3.8), the prototype basic development environment (from task 3.10), and the empty system detailed design (from task 3.11). The product of task 3.13 is a software system, namely the *empty system* of the prototype.

This task is constituted by a traditional software development activity; it starts from the specifications and the detailed design and proceeds along the traditional (waterfall) path of coding, debugging, testing, verification and validation. It does not involve any knowledge acquisition activity.

The final output obviously also includes the documentation for the technical choices and techniques adopted and the user manual.

6.7.3   Task 3.14: Implementation of the development support system

The goal of this task is to produce the development support system of the prototype. Task 3.14 takes in input the development support system specifications (from task 3.9), the prototype basic development environment (from task 3.10), and the development support system detailed design (from task 3.12). The product of task 3.14 is a software system, namely the *development support system* of the prototype.

This task is constituted by a traditional software development activity, and, from this perspective, it is largely similar to task 3.13.

6.8   DEVELOPMENT OF THE KNOWLEDGE BASE

6.8.1   Step execution

Figure 6.11 presents a detailed view of KLIC tasks and products of the 'development of the knowledge base' step.

This is one of the most important steps of the entire KBS life cycle. Its execution concerns the development of successive versions of the prototype until the stated specifications are fully met. The main activity to perform in this step is *extensive knowledge acquisition*, that is, the knowledge acquisition effort aimed at incrementally filling up the knowledge base of the KBS. This effort is usually a heavy challenge that requires a systematic approach to be successfully carried out. The step is organized around an "elicit - code - integrate - verify" cycle which allows an incremental construction of the knowledge base, by dividing the knowledge elicitation task in a sequence of small steps, each one followed by coding and checking.

Knowledge aquisition, the most characteristic activity of this step, has received great attention from the research community, and a huge amount of scientific and technical publications have been produced in the past years. A list of selected references concerning the methodological aspects of knowledge acquisition and modeling which can serve as a starting point for further investigations is proposed in the following: [LaFrance 86], [Boose 86], [Hart 86], [Waterman 86], [Hoffman 87], [Kidd 87], [LaFrance 87], [Olson and Reuter 87], [Wright and Ayton 87], [Gaines and Boose 88], [Greenwell 88], [Boose 89], [Boose and Gaines 88], [Cordingley 89], [Diaper 89], [Forsythe and Buchanan 89], [McGraw and Harbison-Briggs 89], [Roth and Woods 89], [Sanderson et al. 89], [Boose and Gaines 90], [Gaines and Boose 90], [Wielinga et al. 90], [Firley and Hellens 91], [Meyer and Booker 91], [Scott and Clayton 91], [Steels and Lepape 92], [Ford and Bradshaw 93], [Musen 93] .

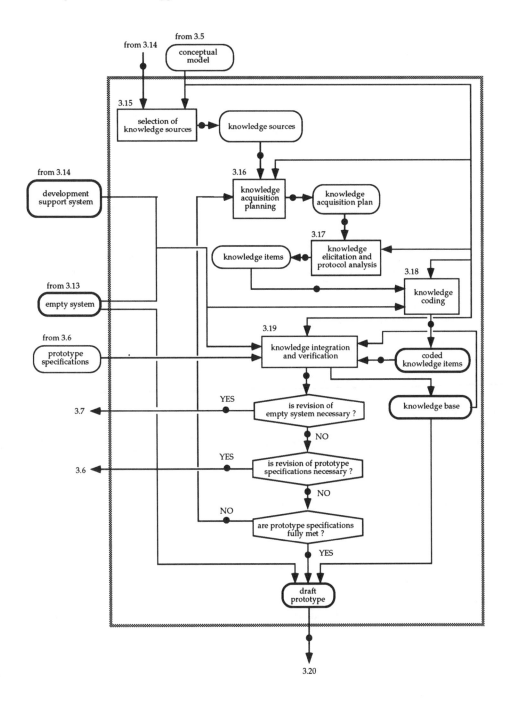

Figure 6.11 Development of the knowledge base: KLIC tasks and products.

6.8.2   Task 3.15: Selection of knowledge sources

The goal of this task is to select the knowledge sources to exploit for extensive knowledge acquisition. Task 3.15 takes in input the conceptual model (from task 3.5).

For each component of the conceptual model it is necessary to identify and analyze what sources are actually available for developing the corresponding part of the knowledge base. In general, three possible *types* of knowledge sources should be considered, namely: domain experts, written documents, and real-world contexts. These feature different characteristics, convey different types of knowledge, and have different roles.

The entire body of knowledge relevant to a given application can be viewed as including three *types* of knowledge:
- *factual knowledge*, concerning the entity layer of the conceptual model (entities, properties, relationships, constraints, procedures, operations);
- *inferential knwledge*, concerning the reasoning layer of the conceptual model (reasoning functions);
- *strategic knowledge*, concerning the problem-solving layer of the conceptual model (problem-solving strategies, strategic knowledge).

A knowledge source can generally play different *roles* in the knowledge acquisition process. The three main roles are:
- *knowledge collection*, i.e. contributing with an amount of substantially new knowledge;
- *knowledge refinement*, i.e. supporting the refinement of already acquired knowledge;
- *knowledge verification*, i.e. supporting the process of knowledge base verification (see section 9.3.2).

Domain experts

Domain experts are persons with a sound background and a broad experience in the application domain considered. Raw information extracted from domain experts by means of *interviews* is called *verbal data* and includes the sentences uttered by domain experts during interaction with the knowledge engineer. In general, two kinds of knowledge may be elicited from domain experts:
- *explicit knowledge*, that the domain expert is conscious to have, is able to access, and can express verbally by answering the questions asked by the knowledge engineer;
- *tacit knowledge*, that the domain expert is not conscious to have, is not able to access, and cannot express verbally; this type of knowledge is hardly mentioned in the answers the expert gives to the knowledge engineer (typically, the expert may say "I don't know"): its existence, however, is actually proved by the expert's capability of solving problems in the application domain considered.

Explicit knowledge is quite easy to elicit, but it is not sufficient to capture all the inferential and strategic knowledge used by the domain experts. Explicit knowledge is mostly factual in nature. Tacit knowledge, though much more difficult to obtain than explicit knowledge, is more information-rich, since it constitutes the knowledge actually exploited during expert problem solving. Being unconscious, tacit knowledge is hard to identify and to elicit, and the knowledge engineer for this purpose has to resort to sophisticated elicitation techniques.

Verbal data are often affected by several kinds of imperfections; quite often they are:

- incomplete: the expert forgets or does not want to report something, he believes that some knowledge is not necessary or has already been told;
- superficial: the expert cannot articulate knowledge in detail, he is not introspective enough or answers too quickly;
- imprecise: the expert does not know exactly;
- inconsistent: the expert falls into contradictions;
- incorrect: the expert is wrong;
- unstructured: the expert cannot articulate his knowledge in a well-organized way, proceeds in a scattered way, jumps freely from one topic to another, articulates knowledge in a fragmentary way.

However, verbal data are spontaneous, not controlled, not manipulated, and full of information. Domain experts constitute the primary knowledge source in the knowledge acquisition process: no KBS can be developed without domain experts. Domain experts are used for knowledge collection, refinement, and verification.

Written documents

Written documents are made up of texts written specifically in the considered application domain. Raw information extracted from written documents by means of *text analysis* is called *textual data* and includes the fragments of text that the knowledge engineer considers relevant to the knowledge acquisition task. Examples of written documents are text-books, hand-books, technical manuals, case reports, design documents, regulations, etc. Availability of written documents varies from case to case; in some domains there may be many documents, in others none at all. Written documents contain mostly factual knowledge.

Written documents are often complete, detailed, precise, consistent, correct, and well-structured. However, they are not spontaneous, strictly controlled, manipulated, and not full of information. Written documents are not always significant for the knowledge acquisition task nor are they always available. However, if significant written documents exist, their exploitation is often very economical, since it is time- and cost-effective. Written documents are mostly used for knowledge collection.

Real-world contexts

Real-world contexts are selected parts of the operative environment where phenomena relevant to the considered application domain occur. Raw information extracted from the real-word contexts by means of *naturalistic observation* is called *descriptive data* and includes the written notes taken by the knowledge engineer while observing, as objectively as possible, any phenomenon relevant to the application domain considered. For example, naturalistic observation may focus on the activity of a team of process operators during a shift, or on the job carried out by a diagnostic expert while dealing with a complex failure case, or on the tasks performed by a financial advisor while dealing with a client. The very point that characterizes naturalistic observation [Bell and Hardiman 89] is that observation should not affect or bias the context being observed nor interfere with it in any way (no interaction between the observer and the real-world context is allowed).

Naturalistic observation is generally very difficult and expensive to carry out. The specific observation sessions must be carefully organized and that the observer must be sufficiently acquainted with the application domain. Moreover, it is necessary that both the organization where observation takes place and all the involved persons give their explicit consent for this kind of activity and are available for cooperation. Sometimes, naturalistic observation is definitely impossible to carry out. When feasible, a way to make naturalistic observation easier and more effective is the use of video-recording. This allows the observation to be performed separately from the phenomena being observed. Moreover, this enables the knowledge engineer to perform observation in a comfortable and appropriate way.

Descriptive data produced by naturalistic observation are not easy to exploit. However, they are objective, and often convey essential knowledge that can not be acquired from other sources. Real world contexts are used mainly for knowledge verification.

Usually, several knowledge sources are available for the development of a KBS. In order to check whether they are sufficient for developing the knowledge base and to select the most appropriate ones to be used, a careful and detailed analysis is required. This task can be carried out taking into account the following list of attributes:

- *Quality*: the quality of the source. In particular, for the three types of knowledge source identified above, it is important to verify the following:
  - for domain experts: the adequacy of their expertise (see the item 'appropriateness of competence' in Figure 4.9 for a detailed check-list);
  - for written documents: the relevance of the content, the structure and organization, the level of formalization, the level of precision and detail, the reputation and the competence of authors;

- for real-world contexts: the appropriateness of the chosen contexts for demonstrating the various tasks and problem-solving activities carried out in the domain.
- *Coverage*: estimating what part of the conceptual model may be covered by the knowledge that might be elicited from the source considered.
- *Accessibility*: assessing the ease of eliciting the knowledge virtually provided by the source considered. In particular, for the three types of knowledge source identified above, it is important to verify the following:
  - for domain experts: level of articulation, ease of interaction, cooperativeness (see the item 'suitability for the knowledge acquisition process' in Figure 4.9 for a detailed check-list);
  - for written documents: the ease with reading the document, the transparency, the clarity, the conciseness;
  - for real-world contexts: the actual feasibility of observation sessions and the possibility of recording them.
- *Availability*: assessing how much a knowledge source is going to be actually available for exploitation when it will be needed during the construction of the knowledge base. This attribute is particularly important for domain experts (see the item availability in Figure 4.9 for a detailed check-list).
- *Acquisition cost*: estimating the expected effort needed for transforming the raw data provided by a source into usable knowledge. From this perspective, a knowledge source can be classified as:
  - *direct source*, that can provide knowledge which is directly usable, i.e. can be easily collected and immediately coded; this is the case, for example, of textual data: they usually do not require heavy processing in order to be exploited for knowledge acquisition;
  - *indirect source*, when the raw data provided by the source need to be analyzed and interpreted in order to elicit knowledge items that can be coded; verbal data are a typical example of this kind of source: they usually require a first low-level processing to transcribe hand-written notes and recorded knowledge acquisition sessions, and then a deep analysis of their content, carried out at linguistic, conceptual, and epistemological levels [Breuker and Wielinga 89]; if the domain expert is not adequate, verbal data may become almost a remote source, requiring much more complex and costly acquisition effort;
  - *remote source*, where knowledge can be collected neither directly nor indirectly, but must be obtained only through deep analysis and processing; descriptive data obtained through naturalistic observation are generally a remote source, since they require a lot of pre-processing to identify the relevant material and a deep transformation to identify the knowledge underlying the observed phenomena; examples of remote sources are also collections of cases or large files of experimental data, that may require heavy and sophisticated statistical processing in order to reveal the underlying knowledge.
- *Necessity*: assessing whether a knowledge source is the only one - or one of the few - available for a given type of knowledge.

The output of the evaluation is usually summarized in a table, where for each potential knowledge source, each attribute is analyzed and given a qualitative score.

Once all potential knowledge sources have been analyzed, one has to select those that will be actually exploited for extensive knowledge acquisition. The set of selected knowledge sources should guarantee that the following basic goals are met:

- covering all the components of the conceptual model;
- ensuring an adequate quality of the elicited knowledge;
- minimizing knowledge acquisition costs;
- ensuring a smooth and effective knowledge acquisition process through a sufficient level of availability of the selected knowledge sources and a limited degree of redundancy.

In the following, we mention some further remarks that may be profitably considered in the selection of knowledge sources.

First of all, special care is needed when considering a knowledge source which is unique and therefore strictly necessary, since its availability will directly influence the final result; the KBS cannot be developed if that source is not available or it is too costly.

Another important aspect to consider is the selection of domain experts [Dym and Mittal 85]. When several experts are available, a sound principle to follow is to select a single expert for each different competence area in the considered domain (*single expert approach*). This allows to interview each expert separately, thus avoiding the problem of dealing with multiple experts [Dym and Mittal 85], [McGraw and Harbison-Briggs 89], [Turban 91]. Utilizing just one expert for each competence area does not imply, however, that the other experts are excluded from the project. On the contrary, they should be kept involved in all the stages of the knowledge base construction process, avoiding, however, any direct interaction with the knowledge engineer. Their role is to serve as consultants for the selected expert, who may resort to them whenever he deems useful and appropriate, transferring the acquired knowledge to the knowledge engineer during regular knowledge acquisition sessions. In this way, the selected experts behave like spokesmen for the relevant competence areas.

This principle can help make the knowledge acquisition task simple and effective; more experts imply higher complexity and costs, but do not necessarily entail higher quality. The single expert approach is, however, not always applicable. If the exclusion of an expert in a specific competence area leads to problems with the desired coverage or quality, it is necessary to have more experts working together. Moreover, if domain experts in a given competence area disagree about some fundamental issues of the domain, they should be all involved in the knowledge acquisition process, taking into account their diverging opinions [Reboh 83], [Ling and Rudd 89]. Resorting to multiple experts may also be appropriate for verification and testing tasks. In all such cases, it is generally necessary to have several experts working together in small groups under the coordination of the knowledge engineer (*multiple expert approach*).

The selection of written documents can, in most cases, be based on the following principle: one good, recent, and accepted document for each competence area of the domain. It is usually not necessary nor useful to analyze more documents for a given competence area, since this could be ineffective and time consuming.

Finally, the selection of the real-world contexts to consider and the number of naturalistic observations to carry out largely depends on the specific application domain at hand. The number of contexts may vary from one or two to a few tenths. The number of observations should be neither too low nor too high. Too few observations may not provide sufficient material to consider, while too many may include details which could have been elicited more effectively from other sources.

The product of task 3.15 is a document, called *knowledge sources*. It contains, for each potential knowledge source considered, the following information:
- a name and a short description;
- the evaluation attributes considered, together with the scores assigned;
- the indication whether the knowledge source has been selected or not, with a justification of the reasons of the choice made;
- the expected coverage of the knowledge source with reference to the parts of the conceptual model it is expected to deal with;
- the expected types of knowledge the knowledge source is expected to provide (factual, inferential, strategic);
- the expected use in the knowledge acquisition process, with indication of when and how to use it.

6.8.3   Task 3.16: Knowledge acquisition planning

The goal of this task is to produce a detailed plan for the construction of the knowledge bases of the KBS. Task 3.16 takes in input the conceptual model (from task 3.5), and the knowledge sources (from task 3.15). The product of task 3.16 is a document called *knowledge acquisition plan*. It contains a precise specification of all activities relevant to the knowledge acquisition task, their logical organization, and their temporal scheduling. The knowledge acquisition plan is used to organize the subsequent tasks 3.17 through 3.19, and is possibly updated at each iteration of the KBS development loop, including tasks 3.16 through 3.19.

The knowledge acquisition plan is the backbone of the whole 'development of the knowledge base' step: it identifies clear objectives for the knowledge acquisition activities, allocates adequate resources, supports communication among project team members, and organizes the evaluation of the results achieved. More precisely, a typical knowledge acquisition plan can be organized like an agenda of the activities to perform. Each activity in the agenda specifies a single *knowledge acquisition act*, i.e. an elementary step in the knowledge acquisition process devoted to collect, refine, or verify a single piece of knowledge. A knowledge acquisition act consists of one iteration through tasks

3.17, 3.18, and 3.19. Each knowledge acquisition act is specified by means of the following information:
- goal to be attained: collection, refinement, verification;
- scope: topics to consider;
- involved knowledge source;
- knowledge elicitation technique to use;
- supporting materials to use during knowledge elicitation - if any;
- scheduled date and place of execution.

Generally, a knowledge acquisition act has one goal, it involves one knowledge source, and uses one elicitation technique. Composite knowledge acquisition acts should be avoided, since they are always more intricate but rarely more effective.

It is important that the knowledge acquisition plan be complete, even in its initial formulation, both in terms of time (it should cover the whole duration expected for knowledge base development) and in terms of coverage (it should consider all the parts of the knowledge base of the prototype). Obviously, the level of detail is usually finer-grained for the first stages but only coarse-grained and tentative for the later stages: as long as the execution of the plan proceeds, the knowledge engineer constantly refines and updates its content in order to provide precise and detailed directions for the knowledge acquisition activities to be performed.

An important preliminary decision for developing a knowledge acquisition plan is the definition of the most appropriate temporal strategy for developing the knowledge base. The selection of what parts of the knowledge base (or which knowledge bases) to develop first is a strategic decision influencing both the complexity of the 'development of knowledge base' step and the visibility on the intermediate results produced. Several strategies may be adopted for this purpose, depending on the specific goals of the KBS project, on the characteristics of the KBS being produced, on the features of the application domain at hand, and on the number and skills of the available knowledge engineers.

The selection of the most suitable knowledge elicitation technique to use in each knowledge acquisition act is a key issue in the definition of a correct and effective knowledge acquisition plan. In the literature a huge amount of specific elicitation techniques have been proposed. Mostly of them concern the interviews, i.e. the elicitation of verbal data. The approach proposed here focuses on a limited number of elicitation techniques (see section 6.8.4) that cover the large majority of the cases found in practice. Each technique has specific goals, can elicit some specific type of knowledge, and is appropriate only in a specific cases. The use of a single technique - or of a few ones - in all possible cases is therefore incorrect and should be discouraged.

General criteria to be taken into account in the design of a knowledge acquisition plan include:
- alternating knowledge acquisition acts with different goals (collection, refinement, verification);
- appropriately alternating the use of different knowledge acquisition techniques (see section 6.8.4);

- allocating enough time between knowledge acquisition acts so as to allow for protocol analysis, knowledge coding, integration, and verification.

As already mentioned above, at the end of each knowledge acquisition act it is necessary to verify whether the knowledge acquisition plan is still valid. If already planned knowledge acquisition acts need to be revised, re-scheduled or dropped, or if new knowledge acquisition acts not previously foreseen need to be added, the plan is updated accordingly. Moreover, as long as the development of the knowledge base proceeds, the following parts of the plan can be specified in greater detail and with more certainty. The result is a new version of the knowledge acquisition plan to be immediately considered in the next knowledge acquisition cycle.

6.8.4   Techniques for knowledge elicitation

Knowledge elicitation is the process of exploiting knowledge sources in order to extract raw information - namely verbal, textual, and descriptive data - to be later organized in knowledge items. *Knowledge elicitation techniques* are systematic procedures which support the knowledge engineer in performing knowledge elicitation. Of course, they differ according to the type of involved knowledge source. In the following, a selection of knowledge elicitation techniques for verbal, textual, and descriptive data are presented.

Eliciting verbal data: interview techniques

The elicitation of verbal data is the process of interacting with domain experts through appropriate *interview techniques* to stimulate the expression of knowledge and expertise [Chung 94]. Figure 6.12 (a, b, c, d, and e) presents a list of 11 interview techniques which, in the professional experience of the authors, have been identified as a basic set of techniques which covers the most frequent situations encountered. These techniques can be applied to interviewing single experts; they are not suitable for group work with multiple experts.

As far as the use of multiple experts is concerned, four suggested techniques are presented in Figure 6.13 (a and b). Most of these techniques are difficult and time-consuming. Some of them can, however, be facilitated by using computer technology to support group work [Turban 91]. Computer-facilitated collaborative work can enable conducting interviews with experts which are located in different places, they can support idea generation, and speed-up conflict resolution.

The interview techniques proposed in Figures 6.12 and 6.13 represent an effective compromise between complexity, efficiency, coverage, and specificity. Of course, several variations are possible. Knowledge engineers are encouraged to improve this first proposal through their personal experience. However, it is mostly important that one does not compromise discipline, efficiency, and ease of use in

TUTORIAL INTERVIEW	
goal	• knowledge collection • identifying the basic elements and the general structure of the application domain • collecting materials for preparing focused and structured interviews and forward scenario simulation
results	first elements of factual knowledge

procedure	informal conversation, open, not focused, not structured:
	    "What are the main features of the domain?"
	    "Describe a familiar task."
	    "Describe a typical problem."

suggested duration	1 to 2 hours
difficulty	medium: the knowledge engineer should stimulate the expert without however constraining or biasing him
applicability	sampling and extensive knowledge acquisition
suggested use	• the main technique for the first interviews • not to be applied in late stages of the knowledge acquisition plan • not to be applied in more than two or three subsequent sessions
support materials	survey papers, introductory reports
references	[Kidd and Cooper 85], [Gammak 87], [Cullen and Bryman 88], [Cordingley 89], [Firley and Hellens 91]

FOCUSED INTERVIEW	
goal	• knowledge collection • analyzing specific topics of the domain
results	factual knowledge
procedure	informal conversation on pre-defined topics (2 to 5), each one including a list of possible questions (5 to 15)
suggested duration	1 to 2 hours
difficulty	low: once the interview has been prepared, the knowledge engineer should only ask the questions and actively listen to the answers
applicability	sampling and extensive knowledge acquisition
suggested use	• the main technique for the initial knowledge acquisition sessions • especially suggested after a tutorial interview • can be profitably alternated with structured interviews
support materials	materials obtained through other interviews
references	[Breuker and Wielinga 87], [Greenwell 88], [Cordingley 89]

Figure 6.12 Interview techniques for single experts - a.

STRUCTURED INTERVIEW	
goal	• knowledge collection and refinement • analyzing in detail and in depth a list of issues related to a single topic
results	factual and inferential knowledge
procedure	dialogue on a single topic, aimed at exploring a list of issues (at most 10) through a sequence of logically inter-related questions (Socratic dialogue, maieutics)
suggested duration	1 to 2 hours
difficulty	medium: the interview must be carefully prepared, and the knowledge engineer must be able to follow the path of the dialogue and to dynamically adapt the questions to be asked to the answers provided by the expert
applicability	sampling and extensive knowledge acquisition
suggested use	• one of the main techniques for extensive knowledge acquisition • especially suggested after a focused interview • not to be repeated several times on the same topic
support materials	materials obtained through other interviews, text analysis, or naturalistic observation
references	[Freiling et al. 85], [Breuker and Wielinga 87], [Cullen and Bryman 88], [Greenwell 88], [Cordingley 89], [Firley and Hellens 91]

FORWARD SCENARIO SIMULATION	
goal	• knowledge collection, refinement, and verification • analyzing the reasoning functions and the problem- solving strategies of the expert
results	factual, inferential, and strategic knowledge
procedure	the expert describes how he performs a simple task assigned to him by the knowledge engineer
suggested duration	2 to 3 hours
difficulty	medium: the knowledge engineer should be familiar with the domain
applicability	sampling and extensive knowledge acquisition
suggested use	• one of the main techniques for collecting strategic knowledge • not to be repeated several times • can be profitably alternated with focused and structured interviews • the task assigned may be identified through other techniques
support materials	any material provided by the knowledge engineer
references	[Grover 83], [Greenwell 88], [Cordingley 89]

Figure 6.12 Interview techniques for single experts - b.

THINKING ALOUD	
goal	• knowledge collection, refinement, and verification • analyzing the reasoning and the problem-solving strategies of the expert
results	factual, inferential, and strategic knowledge
procedure	the expert freely describes how he performs a task he considers interesting and worth examination: the description can be at different levels of detail, i.e. the assignment for the expert can be: "Tell all." "Tell critical steps only." "Tell important steps only, discarding low-level details."
suggested duration	the time required to carry out the task completely
difficulty	high: the knowledge engineer should be familiar with the domain and should stimulate the expert, without however constraining or biasing him
applicability	extensive knowledge acquisition
suggested use	• one of the main techniques for knowledge verification • can be repeated on the same task at different levels of detail
support materials	any material provided by the expert
references	[Nisbett and Wilson 77], [Ericsson and Simon 80], [Ericsson and Simon 84], [Cordingley 89], [Firley and Hellens 91], [Meyer and Booker 91]

COMMENTARY	
goal	• knowledge refinement and verification • acquiring a critical perspective on the reasoning and the problem solving strategies of the expert
results	factual, inferential, and strategic knowledge
procedure	the expert freely comments on a task chosen by the knowledge engineer and performed by a third person (either directly or through video recording)
suggested duration	the time required to carry out the task completely
difficulty	high: the knowledge engineer should be familiar with the domain and should stimulate the expert, without however constraining or biasing him - moreover the setting for the interview may be complicated
applicability	extensive knowledge acquisition
suggested use	• one of the main techniques for knowledge refinement and verification • can be profitably alternated with forward scenario simulation and thinking aloud
support materials	any material provided by the expert
references	[Cullen and Bryman 88], [Greenwell 88], [McGraw and Harbison-Briggs 89]

Figure 6.12 Interview techniques for single experts - c.

INQUISITIVE OBSERVATION	
goal	• knowledge refinement and verification
	• verifying the reasoning and the problem-solving strategies of the expert
results	factual, inferential, and strategic knowledge
procedure	the expert is interviewed while actually performing a task assigned to him by the knowledge engineer
suggested duration	the time required to carry out the task completely
difficulty	high: the knowledge engineer should be familiar with the domain and with the problem-solving strategies used by the expert
applicability	extensive knowledge acquisition
suggested use	• one of the main techniques for knowledge refinement and verification
	• not to be repeated several times
	• can be profitably alternated with thinking aloud and commentary
support materials	any material provided by the expert
references	[Olson and Reuter 87], [Greenwell 88]

PAPER REVIEW	
goal	• knowledge refinement and verification
	• refining and verifying factual and inferential knowledge
results	factual and inferential knowledge
procedure	the knowledge engineer shows (intermediate) results of the knowledge analysis and modeling activity to the experts and users, and collects their feedback
suggested duration	1 to 2 hours
difficulty	medium: the knowledge engineer should prepare the materials to submit to the users and experts carefully
applicability	sampling and extensive knowledge acquisition
suggested use	• the main technique for refinement and verification of knowledge models
	• can be repeated several times with different users and experts
support materials	texts, diagrams, charts, etc.
references	[Greenwell 88], [Firley and Hellens 91]

Figure 6.12 Interview techniques for single experts - d.

TEACH BACK	
goal	• knowledge refinement and verification • refining and verifying inferential and strategic knowledge • improving the knowledge engineer's understanding of the domain
results	factual, inferential, and strategic knowledge
procedure	the knowledge engineer illustrates to the expert a topic or describes how he would perform a task, and the expert reacts with acknowledgements and corrections
suggested duration	1 to 2 hours
difficulty	high: the knowledge engineer should be very familiar with the domain and with the problem-solving strategies used by the expert
applicability	extensive knowledge acquisition
suggested use	• not to be repeated several times • can be profitably intermixed with thinking aloud and commentary
support materials	materials obtained through other interviews, text analysis, or naturalistic observation
references	[Johnson and Johnson 87], [Greenwell 88], [Cordingley 89]

REVIEW	
goal	• knowledge verification • collection of expert and user feedback
results	factual, inferential, and strategic knowledge
procedure	the knowledge engineer shows the running prototype to the experts and users, analyzes with them selected sample cases, and collects their feedback
suggested duration	2 to 3 hours
difficulty	medium: the knowledge engineer should prepare the sample cases to submit to the users and experts carefully
applicability	extensive knowledge acquisition
suggested use	• the main techniques for knowledge verification • can be repeated several times with different users and experts
support materials	any material provided by the knowledge engineer
references	[Breuker and Wielinga 87], [Greenwell 88]

Figure 6.12 Interview techniques for single experts - e.

BRAINSTORMING	
goal	knowledge collection, refinement, and validation
results	factual, inferential, and strategic knowledge
description	All involved experts may freely interact with each other, the knowledge engineer acting as a moderator.
suggested duration	1 to 3 hours
difficulty	low
applicability	sampling and extensive knowledge acquisition
efficiency	low elicitation rate
remarks	• a very effective technique since it encourages ideas generation, stimulates verbalization, and can bring to light a lot of hidden knowledge • it is often difficult for the knowledge engineer to come out with clear and well-organized data
references	[Osborne 53], [Rusk and Krone 84], [Moore 87], [Greenwell 88], [Van Gundy 88], [McGraw and Harbison-Briggs 89], [Turban 91]

BRAINSTORMING WITH DEBRIEFING	
goal	knowledge collection, refinement, and validation
results	factual, inferential, and strategic knowledge
description	after enough knowledge has been brought to light through brainstorming, the knowledge engineer attempts to formulate a conclusion which can be shared by several of the experts taking part in the group work.
suggested duration	2 to 3 hours
difficulty	medium
applicability	sampling and extensive knowledge acquisition
efficiency	medium elicitation rate
remarks	• an efficient technique, that enhances collection of clear and well-organized data • it is often difficult for the knowledge engineer to avoid bias
references	[Greenwell 88]

Figure 6.13 Interview techniques for multiple experts - a.

favour of higher sophistication, which does not necessarily ensure higher quality. Other references to interview techniques are: [Gordon 69], [Waterman and Newell 71], [Saaty 81], [Burley-Allen 82], [Kahn and Cannell 82], [Grover 83], [Ericsson and Simon 84], [Kahn et al. 85], [Stewart and Cash 85], [Waldron 86], [Wright and Ayton 87], [Davies and Hakiel 88].

The interview techniques mentioned above, called *direct interview techniques*, are all based on investigating the knowledge and expertise of domain experts through verbal interactions. In addition to these techniques, we mention a further class of techniques, called *indirect interview techniques*, which are based on requesting domain experts to perform specific tasks that enable the

BRAINSTORMING WITH CONSENSUS	
goal	knowledge collection, refinement, and validation
results	factual, inferential, and strategic knowledge
description	after enough knowledge has been brought to light through brainstorming, it goes through four steps: 1. the knowledge engineer formulates a conclusion, called the *consensus conclusion*, which represents the best compromise among the various opinions, and proposes it to the experts for approval 2. the consensus proposal is discussed and refined; advantages and disadvantages of alternative solutions are assessed systematically on the basis of agreed upon criteria. 3. then the experts vote on the proposal that seems to be acceptable by the majority of them. 4. finally, the conclusion approved be the majority is often proposed again to the experts in order to explore whether it can receive unanimous consensus.
suggested duration	2 to 4 hours
difficulty	high
applicability	extensive knowledge acquisition
efficiency	medium elicitation rate
remarks	• an effective technique, that can enhance a better mutual understanding among experts • it is necessary to assure that the decision process is enough democratic, that all experts are being treated equally and are really free of expressing their opinions, and that they are not pressured or biased by other experts or by the knowledge engineer
references	[McGraw and Harbison-Briggs 89], [Turban 91]

NOMINAL GROUP	
goal	knowledge collection, refinement, and validation
results	factual, inferential, and strategic knowledge
description	the experts do not interact face-to-face but only indirectly, and do not know each other: all interactions are managed by the knowledge engineer.
suggested duration	several days
difficulty	very high
applicability	extensive knowledge acquisition
efficiency	medium elicitation rate
remarks	• a useful technique that can avoid the negative effects of dominant behavior and stubbornness to change one's mind, that are often associated with brainstorming • especially appropriate when direct interaction among experts might lead to endless discussion and quarrelsome attitude
references	[Linstone and Turoff 75], [Greenwell 88], [Meyer and Booker 91], [Turban 91]

Figure 6.13 Interview techniques for multiple experts - b.

knowledge engineer to infer the knowledge and expertise they exploit while performing the tasks. Indirect techniques are generally grounded on psychological theories and include such well-known techniques as card sorting, multidimensional scaling, and repertory grids. All these techniques are generally difficult to apply and often require background statistical processing. Moreover, their are appropriate only in specific cases, not very frequent in practice. Therefore, they can not be recommended in general. The reader interested in this advanced topic can refer to: [Fransella and Banninster 77], [Kruskal and Wish 78], [Shepard 80], [Chi et al. 81], [Shaw 81], [Shiffman et al. 81], [Boose 85], [Gammak 87], [Shaw and Gaines 87-b], [Wright and Ayton 87].

Eliciting textual data: text analysis techniques

The elicitation of textual data is the process of extracting useful knowledge from written documents through appropriate *text analysis techniques* [Cordingley 89]. Figure 6.14 (a and b) presents a list of two text analysis techniques that can be applied to most of the cases of practical interest. Each technique is described through a set of attributes that help decide when it should be applied and how it should be carried out.

TEXT FRAGMENTATION	
goal	knowledge collection
results	factual and inferential knowledge
preconditions	the written document is well-structured, well-organized, and mostly formal
procedure	it goes through two steps: 1. first complete reading of the document 2. second reading, identification of significant text fragments, and classification according to the relevant domain elements
difficulty	medium
applicability	sampling and extensive knowledge acquisition
efficiency	very high elicitation rate
remarks	• the knowledge elicited must always be verified through appropriate techniques (at least through sample tests) • the obtained text fragments are supposed to be immediately ready to be coded

Figure 6.14 Text analysis techniques - a.

Eliciting descriptive data: naturalistic observation techniques

The elicitation of descriptive data is the process of extracting useful knowledge from real-world contexts through appropriate *naturalistic observation techniques* [Cordingley 89], [McGraw and Harbison-Briggs 89]. Figure 6.15 presents a list of two naturalistic observation techniques that can be applied to most of the cases of practical interest. Each technique is described through a set of attributes that help decide when it should be applied and how it should be carried out.

TEXT TRANSFORMATION	
goal	knowledge collection
results	factual and inferential knowledge
preconditions	the written document is enough structured, but not well organized, and mostly informal
procedure	in goes through three steps: 1. first complete reading of the document 2. second reading, identification of significant text fragments, and classification according to the relevant domain elements 3. re-organization of the document through cut and paste of the identified text fragments in such a way to facilitate knowledge coding
difficulty	high
applicability	extensive knowledge acquisition
efficiency	medium to high elicitation rate
remarks	• the knowledge elicited must always be verified through appropriate techniques (at least through sample tests) • the obtained text fragments - after document re-organization - are supposed to be ready to be coded

Figure 6.14 Text analysis techniques - b.

As a last remark, we mention that several of the elicitation techniques mentioned above can be supported by appropriate computer-based tools [Anjewierden 87], [Boose and Gaines 88], [Marcus 88], [Boose 89], [Gruber 89], [Wielinga et al. 90], [Runkel and Birmingham 93]. These address the following main tasks:

• supporting direct interview techniques (automated and mixed-initiative interviewing) and protocol analysis [Boose and Bradshaw 87], [Diederich et al. 87], [Eshelman et al. 87], [Kahn et al. 87], [Kitto and Boose 87], [Diederich and Linster 89], [Sanderson et al. 89];
• supporting psychology-based indirect interview techniques (card sorting, multidimensional scaling, repertory grids, etc.) [Boose and Bradshaw 87], [Shaw and Gaines 87-a], [Boose 90];
• interviewing multiple experts and supporting group work [Boose and Bradshaw 87];
• task analysis, knowledge analysis and modeling [Bennett 85], [Breuker and Wielinga 87], [Eshelman et al. 87], [Kahn et al. 87], [Klinker et al. 87], [Musen et al. 87], [Breuker and Wielinga 89], [Diederich and Linster 89], [Anjewerden et al. 90], [Wielinga et al. 92], [Linster 93], [Terpstra et al. 93];
• textual analysis and natural language analysis (extracting or generating knowledge directly by analyzing text) [Diederich et al. 87], [Motta et al. 89];

- learning-based techniques [Morik et al. 93]: decision tree and rule induction [Quinlan 79], [Michalski 83], [Quinlan 86], [Hart 87], [Quinlan 88], [Witten and MacDonald 88], explanation-based learning [Pazzani 87], [Wilkens et al. 87], analogy-based learning [Lenat et al. 86], apprenticeship learning [Smith et al. 85], [Musen et al. 87], [Wilkens et al. 87], [Bareiss et al. 88], and - more recently - neural networks and genetic algorithms.

DIRECT OBSERVATION	
goal	knowledge refinement, and verification
results	inferential and strategic knowledge
procedure	direct observation of the relevant real-world context and production of descriptive data
suggested duration	1 to 3 hours
difficulty	high
	• the knowledge engineer should understand what is happening and should know what to focus on
	• an appropriate setting is needed in order to minimize bias
applicability	extensive knowledge acquisition
efficiency	low elicitation rate
remarks	• often not applicable due to the difficulty of setting up an appropriate observation context
	• not to be repeated several times

INDIRECT OBSERVATION	
goal	knowledge refinement, and verification
results	inferential and strategic knowledge
procedure	it goes through two steps:
	1. recording of the real-world context
	2. analysis of the recorded materials and production of descriptive data
suggested duration	1 to 3 hours
difficulty	medium:
	• the knowledge engineer should understand what it is happening and should know what to focus on
	• an appropriate setting is needed to ensure a sufficient quality of recording
efficiency	low elicitation rate
applicability	extensive knowledge acquisition
remarks	• often not applicable since recording may hide important details
	• (possibly repeated) analysis of the recorded materials makes the task of the knowledge engineer easier and more effective

Figure 6.15 Naturalistic observation techniques.

Computer-based tools for knowledge elicitation are to a large extent still research prototypes. A broad survey of such tools is presented in [Boose 89]. Among the few systems available on the market we mention, as an example: InducPRL (by OXKO Corp., Annapolis, MD), Angoss Knowledge Seeker (by Angoss Software International Ltd., Toronto, Canada), and K-Vision (by Ginesys Corp., Greenville, SC). One may expect, however, that more commercial products will be available in the next future.

6.8.5   Task 3.17: Knowledge elicitation and protocol analysis

The goal of this task is to elicit raw knowledge from knowledge sources and to analyze it in order to derive knowledge fragments to be later inserted in the knowledge base. Raw knowledge extracted from a knowledge source is often called a *protocol* and, therefore, its analysis is called *protocol analysis*. Task 3.17 takes in input the conceptual model (from task 3.5) and the knowledge acquisition plan (from task 3.16). The product of task 3.17 is a set of documented fragments of domain knowledge, called *knowledge items*.

Given the primary role of interviews in knowledge elicitation and taking into account the objective difficulty of organizing and performing good interviews [Davies and Hakiel 88], we discuss in the following some fundamental issues concerning how to prepare an interview, how to perform it, and how to analyze the verbal data collected (i.e., the interview protocols). The illustration is independent from any specific interview technique utilized [Scott et al. 91]. As far as text analysis and naturalistic observation are concerned, far less experience is available and no specific suggestions of general validity can be proposed. The main practice is still to relay on common-sense and to design the most appropriate way to perform text analysis and naturalistic observation and to analyze the protocols elicited on a case-by-case basis.

Preparing an interview

A fundamental aspect for the final success of an interview is its preparation. The knowledge engineer should review or study the topics to deal with, formulate the specific questions to ask, and prepare the support materials to use during the interview. Then the expert should be adequately prepared: he should be given a meeting agenda and reminded of materials or documentation to bring. Moreover, the knowledge engineer should make sure that the domain expert actually has all the time needed to prepare himself for the interview, by thinking about the topics to be dealt with and by possibly retrieving, studying or reviewing specific materials. This effort on the part of domain experts is fundamental for the final success of the knowledge acquisition activity, and the concrete intention of the expert to provide this level of engagement has to be carefully checked in advance. Finally, time and location are to be appropriately arranged according to the knowledge acquisition plan, avoiding noise, interruptions, pressure, etc. All the necessary tools are to be identified and made timely available, including recording and display devices and specific systems possibly needed by the expert or by the knowledge engineer.

Performing an interview

Once the preparation of the interview has been completed, it is time to proceed with its execution. The general structure of an interview includes three stages:
1. *Introduction*. This is the opening stage of the interview. The knowledge engineer greets the expert, reminds him of the previous steps, describes the goal of the current session, and explains the adopted interview technique. Then the knowledge engineer defines the *assignment* of the interview, i.e. he provides the experts with detailed instructions about what he is expected to do during the interview and how he is expected to behave.
2. *Body*. This is the central stage of the interview, where a specific knowledge elicitation technique is used in order to collect from the expert the needed information. The knowledge engineer should try to keep as close as possible to the script of the selected interview technique; possible deviations - if needed - should be clearly explained to the expert.
3. *Closing*. This is the final stage of the interview. If the expert wishes to add something, he should be allowed to do it. The results obtained should then be reviewed and the next session scheduled: goals should be set, homework given, and scheduling made.

During the execution of the interview one fundamental task to be performed by the knowledge engineer is getting information, i.e. collecting the interview protocol. Several ways may be used:
• manual note taking by the knowledge engineer;
• use of (electronic) note-books or white-boards;
• audio recording (with previous permission of the expert);
• video recording (with previous permission of the expert).

It is important to stress that one form of recording should be used in any case. If this is absolutely not possible, an extra person helping the knowledge engineer should be engaged with the role of verbalizing the dialogue.

For each topic it is important to choose what to ask: some questions may have been already identified during the preparation of the interview, while others may follow from an analysis of the answers given to previous questions. Then the knowledge engineer has to select how to phrase the questions (vocabulary, structure, etc.) : this is very important since it directly affects the understandability and the clarity of the question and the attitude of the expert in the answering. Questions can be of two types: *open*, when the expert is requested to provide some information in generic terms or *closed*, when the expert's answer is constrained to belong to a pre-defined set of possible answers (for example, yes/no questions). Selecting the right type of a question is also an important issue for the success of an interview.

Then the questions have to be uttered appropriately (clearly, with the right tone of voice, etc.). At this point the knowledge engineer listens to the answer. However, sometimes it may happen that the expert does not answer. In these cases the knowledge engineer has to analyze the possible causes in order to intervene in different ways:
- if the question was too general (or to specific) it must be reformulated;
- if the expert did not understand the question it must be rephrased;
- if the expert did not capture the very meaning of the question, the knowledge engineer should try to explain it better and in more explicit terms - possibly using concrete examples or metaphors;
- if the expert is really not able to answer, the question should be delayed or dropped.

Once the expert answers, the knowledge engineer should listen actively in order to understand the meaning and not only to record the answers. In particular he should pay attention to those cases that require follow-up questions. These may be necessary to confirm understanding, to resolve ambiguities, to get further details, etc.

Making an interview is a craft: experience is fundamental for managing all the aspects that are to be considered to perform a good interview. The typical problems that the knowledge engineer should try to avoid in his behaviour are:
- being insensitiveness towards the expert;
- failing to use the right level of abstraction;
- formulating incorrect questions;
- phrasing the questions inappropriately;
- failing to listen to the expert;
- failing to verify understanding;
- deviating from the track;
- digressing;
- confusing the expert by providing too much information.

Several specific aspects deserve attention when performing an interview. A first fundamental aspect to take into account concerns the bias that the knowledge engineer can exert on the interviewed expert. *Bias* is defined as an altering of either the expert's knowledge, reasoning processes, and problem-solving strategies, or the reporting of these [Meyer et al. 89]. Bias can hinder knowledge elicitation and, in especially critical cases, definitely compromise the whole knowledge acquisition process. Several techniques have been proposed in the literature to avoid or minimize bias [Cleaves 88], [Meyer et al. 89], [Meyer and Booker 91]. Avoiding bias is an ability that the knowledge engineer should acquire through experience. The following points are especially important for this purpose:
- the knowledge engineer should be aware of the importance of avoiding bias and know about the negative effects of bias on the quality of his work;
- the knowledge engineer should keep his personal opinions clearly separated from those of the experts; any possible discrepancy must be solved by pursuing elicitation in greater depth;

- the knowledge engineer should phrase questions in an unbiased way as much as possible, avoiding to include in the question any reference to specific viewpoints, opinions, or expectations;
- the knowledge engineer should illustrate and discuss his personal viewpoints, opinions, or expectations only after the expert has freely and completely answered all submitted questions.

Another general issue to take into account concerns the communication that should be established between the knowledge engineer and the domain expert, or in some cases the user. Effective communication is essential for getting successful results and this is based on two main points: use of a common vocabulary and of verification and confirmation mechanisms. The former aspect should be dealt with by the knowledge engineer by learning the expert's vocabulary: one of the goals of the first interviews is establishing a common and agreed-upon terminology. The latter aspect concerns the continuous use of specific discourse structures that allow controlling comprehension; for example, the knowledge engineer may repeat a concept expressed by the expert and then ask for a confirmation (echoing), or he may ask the expert to repeat some idea (clarification).

A further point to take into consideration concerns the correct understanding of the mutual relationships between the knowledge engineer and the domain expert and their respective roles. Both participants in the interview should realize that the duration of their relation may be quite long (several weeks or even several months) and that they share a common goal (namely, having the knowledge base developed), even though they may not share the same motivations for being interested in the KBS project. The domain expert should also understand that the success of the whole knowledge acquisition activity depends on the quality of the information he provides, and this does not depend solely on the skills of the knowledge engineer, but - most importantly - on his capability of introspection. Mutual trust between the expert and the knowledge engineer should be as high as possible: the knowledge engineer should trust that the domain expert will provide accurate and correct information, while the domain expert should trust that the information he provides is appropriately utilized. If such mutual trust decreases, the effectiveness of their relation deteriorates, the cooperativeness decreases, and conflicts start to show up. In order to achieve the goal of mutual trust and cooperativeness stated above, the knowledge engineer should pay attention to interaction issues. He should be adequately sensitive to the expert's feelings. Therefore, the knowledge engineer should help the domain expert to feel as much as possible a part of the development process, he should respect the expert's knowledge, skills, opinions, and wishes, he should show a lot of patience. Sensitivity to non-verbal or indirect communication is very important as well; the knowledge engineer should identify, understand, and respond to the expert's non-verbal or indirect speech acts. He should determine the expert's normal communication style, learn to detect and interpret possible deviations, and behave accordingly. If the expert shows discrepancies between verbal and non-verbal speech acts, the knowledge engineer should detect them; usually non-verbal signs can be trusted more than verbal ones. And, of course, the knowledge engineer should control his own non-verbal and indirect messages towards the expert. Finally, the knowledge engineer should be sensitive to cultural differences. The level of formality in the communication, the way of dressing, the use of space, etc. can be important factors that make the expert feel comfortable during the interview.

Analyzing protocols

Protocol analysis [Waterman and Newell 71] is the process of analysing all the verbal data collected during the interviews in order to identify fragments of knowledge to be further utilized for the coding activity. The analysis may also highlight some specific problems (such as incompleteness, inconsistency, ambiguity, etc.) deserving further investigation in future interviews. Protocol analysis is a very important activity which usually takes substantial effort and time. For the specific techniques to be used for protocol analysis, the reader can referred to: [Ericsson and Simon 80], [Ericsson and Simon 84], [Belkin et al. 87], [Breuker and Wielinga 87], [Johnson et al. 87], [Littman 87], [Greenwell 88], [McGraw and Harbison-Briggs 89], [Meyer and Booker 91].

Protocol analysis is usually carried out manually and requires a huge amount of time; it may need from two to five times the actual time employed for collecting the protocol (i.e., the duration of the interview). The result is constituted by the documented fragments of knowledge, called *knowledge items*. These are usually represented by means of written natural language text or simple charts or diagrams. They also include the information needed to understand why a specific knowledge item has been identified, how it has been extracted from the protocol, and the assumptions eventually made. This material, that constitutes the documentation of the knowledge acquired, is expressed in abstract, implementation-independent terms. Often, knowledge items are later discussed with domain experts in subsequent interviews for solving specific problems encountered by the knowledge engineer. For this reason, the representation formalism utilized for knowledge items should be given adequate attention.

6.8.6   Task 3.18: Knowledge coding

The goal of this task is to code the newly acquired knowledge items. Task 3.18 takes in input the conceptual model (from task 3.5), the empty system (from task 3.13), the development support system (from task 3.14), and the knowledge items (from task 3.17). The product of task 3.18, called *coded knowledge items*, is a new piece of the knowledge base of the prototype containing the fragments of knowledge just elicited in the previous task, appropriately represented by means of the available knowledge representation language.

6.8.7   Task 3.19: Knowledge integration and verification

The goal of this task is to integrate the coded knowledge items produced in task 3.18 with the previous version of the demonstrator knowledge base, and to verify the knowledge base being developed (see section 9.3.2). More specifically, it is aimed at verifying that:
- examination of maintainability;
- checking of consistency and conciseness;
- probing of validity and completeness.

Task 3.19 takes in input the conceptual model (from task 3.5), the prototype specifications (from task 3.6), empty system (from task 3.13), the development support system (from task 3.14), the coded knowledge items (from task 3.18), and the knowledge base (from the previous execution of task 3.19). The product of task 3.19 is a new extended, improved, and verified version of the knowledge base of the prototype, called *knowledge base*.

After the knowledge base has been verified and before continuing with the next step of phase 3, it is necessary to evaluate problems possibly encountered during the execution of tasks 3.17, 3.18, and 3.19 that may indicate that a revision of the empty system or of the prototype specifications is necessary. This causes a backtracking to task 3.7 or 3.6, respectively.

Finally, it must be verified whether the prototype specifications are fully met. If this is the case, the loop started with task 3.16 is terminated, the *draft prototype* is produced, and the execution proceeds with the next step. Otherwise, the execution of the step continues with a new iteration of the loop (starting again from task 3.16).

6.9   TESTING AND EVALUATION

6.9.1   Step execution

Figure 6.16 presents a detailed view of KLIC tasks and products of the 'testing and evaluation' step.

6.9.2   Task 3.20: Prototype testing and refinement

The goal of this task is to test the prototype and, if needed, to refine it. Task 3.20 takes in input the prototype specifications (from task 3.6), the development support system (from task 3.14), and the draft prototype (from task 3.19). Testing may highlight minor problems which can be immediately corrected or deeper inadequacies that deserve major interventions. The product of task 3.20 is a software system, namely the *protoype*.

6.9.3   Task 3.21: Prototype evaluation

The goal of this task is to globally assess the KBS prototype developed and to produce its final evaluation. Task 3.21 takes in input the prototype specifications (from task 3.6) and the prototype (from task 3.20). The product of task 3.21 is a document called *prototype evaluation report*, which describes the results of the evaluation activities carried out. The criteria to adopt for prototype evaluation - and, accordingly, the evaluation activities to carry out - largely vary from case to case. No development activities are performed during this task.

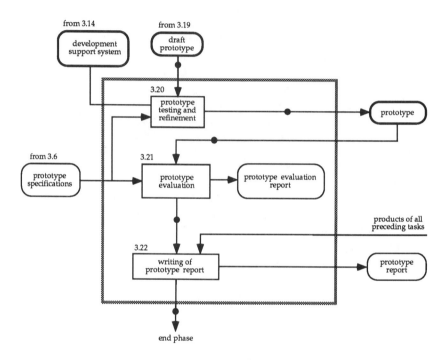

Figure 6.16 Testing and evaluation: KLIC tasks and products.

6.9.4   Task 3.22: Writing of prototype report

The goal of this task is to produce a document summarizing the activities carried out, the software systems developed, and the results obtained. Task 3.22 takes in input the products of all preceding tasks. The product of task 3.22 is a document called *prototype report*. A possible table of contents for the prototype report is shown in Figure 6.17.

The prototype report is directed to the management and to the project team in charge of phase 4.

1. **Introduction**
    - short introduction to the *development of the prototype* phase
    - specific management indications considered
    - difficulties encountered and solutions adopted
    - synthesis of the activities carried out and of the main results obtained

2. **Prototype specifications**
    - functional, operational, and technical specifications

3. **The conceptual model**
    - design principles, basic assumptions, representation language
    - description of the conceptual model

4. **The logical model**
    - design principles, basic assumptions, representation language
    - description of the logical model
    - alternatives considered and discussion

5. **Implementation of the empty system and of the development support system**
    - basic development environment adopted
    - detailed design
    - implementation notes

6. **Development of the knowledge base**
    - knowledge sources utilized
    - knowledge acquisition plan
    - notes on specific knowledge acquisition aspects

7. **Testing and evaluation**
    - test cases and testing techniques
    - prototype evaluation

8. **Main results and conclusion**
    - results obtained
    - functional, operational, and technical indications
      to be considered in the following phases of the life cycle
    - indications concerning project continuation

Figure 6.17 Prototype report: suggested table of contents.

7

IMPLEMENTATION, INSTALLATION, AND DELIVERY OF THE TARGET SYSTEM

7.1 PHASE OVERVIEW

7.1.1 Motivations and objectives

Generally, a KBS prototype is not appropriate to be installed in the target environment and released to the users. The purpose of the 'implementation, installation, and delivery of the target system' phase is to carry out the various activities needed to implement the target KBS, install it in the operational site, and eventually deliver it to the end-users.

The need for the 'implementation, installation, and delivery of the target system' phase is motivated by the following reasons. First of all, the target environment where the KBS is supposed to operate may impose hardware and software constraints which do not allow the prototype to run as it is. In the most simple cases, where the same operating system and programming environment of the prototype can be maintained, generating a run-time module through compilation may be sufficient, but in more complex cases complete re-implementation of the empty system may be necessary (see section 7.3.4). One might note that appropriate selection of the basic development environment for the prototype can greatly help in making implementation of the target system easier. But, the hardware and software requirements for the target system may not be clearly and definitely specified at the moment the selection of the basic development environment for the prototype takes place (task 3.10), or the requirements may change during the development of the prototype. The target environment where the KBS is supposed to operate may impose new functional and operational constraints on the KBS which where not considered at the moment of the plausibility study or of the development of the prototype. These may originate from a deeper understanding of the role of the KBS or from a more concrete analysis of the conditions for its effective insertion into the operational environment. In fact, both aspects, already faced at the moment of plausibility study, are generally considered from a different and more realistic perspective after the prototype has been developed when the time for installing it in the operational environment is approaching.

Moreover, one should remember that the basic development environment chosen for the development of the prototype should particularly support explorative programming and experimentation. Other issues, such as efficiency, reliability, security, and maintainability, generally receive only minor attention during the development of the prototype, but become important in the implementation of the target system.

Therefore, the problem of porting the prototype to the target environment can be concretely faced only after the prototype has been completed.

Quite often, installation may require not only porting the KBS to its target operational environment, but also - and more importantly - connecting it to the external environment (such as, for example, sensors, data acquisition systems, actuators, etc.) and with existing software systems (such as operating systems, data bases, utilities, application packages, etc.). Moreover, after installation, thorough field testing and validation must be performed.

Finally, before the target system is released, it is necessary to carry out all the needed organizational interventions for putting the KBS into routine use and for supporting its correct and effective exploitation. Appropriate user training must be provided as well, and the final and complete set of manuals must be delivered.

Delivering a KBS prototype for operational use without facing the issues mentioned above may cause critical situations which can turn a successful project into a failure [Liebowitz 91]. Delivery is often overlooked in KBS projects. It does not consist just in handing over the system to the users, but it involves all technical and organizational care needed to ensure that the KBS will be actually integrated in the organization and effectively used. Proper institutionalization of KBS is a key point for the success of an application and should be a central issue from the very beginning of the project [Liebowitz 91]. There is no way to turn a weak project into a success at the moment of delivery.

The goals of the 'implementation, installation, and delivery of the target system' phase are:
• building a KBS which:
  - ensures full achievement of specifications;
  - satisfies all operational and technical requirements imposed by the target environment;

- is equipped only with final interfaces, installed in the target environment, and connected to the external world
- is thoroughly field tested;
- training the users to work correctly and effectively;
- delivering the target system for operational use and supplying appropriate manuals.

An account of the issue of installation and delivery of software systems from the point of view of standards may be found in [ESA PSS-05-0 91] and [ESA PSS-05-06 91]; although they specifically concern the production of traditional software, some of the concepts presented in these documents may apply to KBSs as well.

Note that for complex and long projects where phase 3 has been organized stage-wise (see section 6.1.1), also phase 4 must be structured accordingly (staged development). Therefore, after a prototype version has been developed, the corresponding version of the target system is immediately implemented, installed, and delivered. In this way, the benefits of the KBS project are obtained earlier, and the return of investment is anticipated.

7.1.2   Inputs and products

The implementation, installation, and delivery of the target system is generally requested by the managers specifically interested in the KBS application considered. The 'implementation, installation, and delivery of the target system' phase takes in input:
- a document called *management indications*, which includes requirements, objectives, and constraints provided by the management, to be taken into account in the implementation, installation, and delivery of the target system;
- the plausibility study report produced in phase 1;
- the prototype, the development support system, and the prototype report produced in phase 3.

The products of the 'implementation, installation, and delivery of the target system' phase are:
- the *target system*;
- the *maintenance support system*;
- the *manuals*, including:
  - *user manuals*, devoted to supporting the end-users in the correct and effective exploitation of the delivered KBS;
  - *maintenance manuals*, which are used during the maintenance activity;
  - *technical manuals*, which provide a thorough technical description of the delivered system and will serve for future extension activities;
- the *target system report*, which contains a synthesis of the activities carried out, and a detailed illustration of the results achieved.

Finally, the 'implementation, installation, and delivery of the target system' phase may produce a specific *management report* in the case the prerequisites for its execution are not satisfied and the phase is stopped (see task 4.1). The products of the implementation, installation, and delivery of the target system are directed to the users and to the teams which will be in charge of maintenance and extension (phase 5).

7.1.3   Phase structure and task outline

Figure 7.1 presents an outline of the KLIC tasks of the 'implementation, installation, and delivery of the target system' phase.

The overall logical structure of the 'implementation, installation, and delivery of the target system' phase is organized into five steps:
- the 'start-up' step verifies that the prerequisites are satisfied and plans the whole phase;
- the 'preparation' step analyzes the target environment, refines KBS specifications, selects the most appropriate approach for target system production, and develops an organizational design;
- the 'production and installation' step is involved with the production of the target system and of the maintenance support system; it is in charge of carrying out the organizational interventions needed, of installing the target KBS in the operational environment, and of performing field testing and refinement;
- the 'first release and experimental use' step is concerned with the writing of draft manuals, the training of users, and the first release of the target KBS for experimental use;
- the 'final release' step includes the refinement of the target system, the writing of final manuals, the certification and acceptance, the final release of the KBS, and the writing of target system report.

As shown in Figure7.1, several tasks (or group of task) in the *preparation* and in the 'production and installation' step may be executed in parallel.

As we have already mentioned in section 2.1.3, the time it takes for the 'implementation, installation, and delivery of the target system' phase may greatly vary between 4 to 24 months (elapsed time). The actual duration of this phase basically depends on three points:
- the approach adopted for the implementation of the target system (task 4.6), which directly influences the duration of task 4.9 (production of the target system and of the maintenance support system); in particular, with reference to the approaches defined in section 7.3.4, in the case of incremental enhancement task 4.9 may take 2 to 6 months, while in the case of complete re-implementation 4 to 12 months may be needed;
- the duration of task 4.11 (installation) which may last from some days to a few months, depending on the complexity of the target environment and on the types of connections required with the external environment and with existing software systems;
- the duration of task 4.15 (first release and experimental use) which may last from two months up to one year and even more depending on the type of

application faced, the type of KBS developed, the characteristics of the target environment, the user and management requirements, etc.

START-UP		
	4.1	verification of prerequisites
IF		prerequisites are not satisfied
THEN	4.2	writing of management report
		stop phase
	4.3	planning of implementation, installation, and delivery of the target system
PREPARATION		
	4.4	analysis of target environment
	4.5	definition of specifications of the target system and of the maintenance support system
PARALLEL		
BEGIN		
	4.6	definition of the approach for target system implementation
	4.7	design of the target system and of the maintenance support system
END		
	4.8	organizational design
END-PARALLEL		
PRODUCTION AND INSTALLATION		
PARALLEL		
	4.9	production of the target system and of the maintenance support system
	4.10	organizational intervention
END-PARALLEL		
	4.11	installation
	4.12	field testing and refinement
FIRST RELEASE AND EXPERIMENTAL USE		
	4.13	writing of draft manuals
	4.14	training of users
	4.15	first release and experimental use
FINAL RELEASE		
	4.16	refinement of the target system and of the maintenance support system
	4.17	writing of final manuals
	4.18	certification and acceptance
	4.19	final release
	4.20	writing of target system report

Figure 7.1 Implementation, installation and delivery of the target system: KLIC tasks outline.

Splitting the complete duration of the entire phase into the individual durations of its component tasks is meaningless, due to the large variety of possible cases mentioned above and, in particular, to the fact that task 4.9 (production of the target system and of the maintenance support system), 4.11 (installation), and 4.15 (first release and experimental use) may take different periods of time to be performed. Instead, it may be useful to discard tasks 4.9, 4.11, and 4.15, and to focus only on the remaining part of phase 4. The table of Figure 7.2 show in percentages the duration of each task with respect to the duration of the whole phase - except tasks 4.9, 4.11, and 4.15. The data reported are, of course, only indicative; they refer to an average situation, and may vary from case to case. Percentages shown in parentheses refer to tasks which are carried out only subject to specific conditions, and, therefore, count over 100.

7.1.4   Project team composition

Implementation, installation, and delivery of the target system may be carried out by a project team internal to the user organization or they may be assigned to an external supplier. The former choice is common when the incremental enhancement approach to the implementation, installation, and delivery of the target system is chosen, while the latter is more appropriate when the complete re-implementation approach is adopted (see section 7.3.5). Quite often - especially when speeding up the execution of the phase is wanted - a mixed solution may be appropriate.

In particular, depending on the approach adopted (see section 7.3.5), for the implementation, installation, and delivery of the target system, the project team is typically made up of:

- 1 project manager, usually a senior manager, in charge of formally representing the target organization from the administrative point of view;
- 1 project leader, usually a senior professional, responsible for the results of the entire phase and in charge of the technical and organizational management of the project team; the project leader also provides specific support to all critical tasks of the phase;
- 0 to 2 designers (0 to 1 in the case of incremental enhancement, 1 to 2 in the case of complete re-implementation), in charge of the most technical tasks of implementation, installation, and delivery of the target system (tasks 4.6 and 4.7);
- 1 to 2 knowledge engineers, at least one of them being in a senior position, in charge of the development of the knowledge base (task 4.9, 4.12, and 4.16);
- 1 to 2 developers, in charge of developing the necessary software components of the target system and of the maintenance support system (task 4.9);
- 0 to 4 software designers and programmers (0 to 2 in the case of incremental enhancement, 3 to 4 in the case of complete re-implementation), in charge of developing the parts of the empty system and of the maintenance support system which are constituted by traditional software systems (task 4.9);
- 1 or more representatives of the top management;

TASKS	time %
START-UP	
4.1 verification of prerequisites	2
4.2 writing of management report	(5)
4.3 planning of implementation, installation, and delivery of the target system	3
PREPARATION	
4.4 analysis of target environment	3
4.5 definition of specifications of the target system and of the maintenance support system	2
4.6 definition of the approach for target system implementation	2
4.7 design of the target system and of the maintenance support system	5
4.8 organizational design	3
PRODUCTION AND INSTALLATION	
4.9 production of the target system and of the maintenance support system	-
4.10 organizational intervention	15
4.11 installation	-
4.12 field testing and refinement	15
FIRST RELEASE AND EXPERIMENTAL USE	
4.13 writing of draft manuals	18
4.14 training of users	15
4.15 first release and experimental use	-
FINAL RELEASE	
4.16 refinement of target system and of the maintenance support system	5
4.17 writing of final manuals	5
4.18 certification and acceptance	1
4.19 final release	1
4.20 writing of target system report	5

Figure 7.2 Implementation, installation and delivery of the target system: task duration in percentage.

- intermediate managers of all departments concerned with the application domain considered
- domain experts of the application domain considered;
- representatives of the potential users of the KBS.

In particular complex and large cases, the need may arise to support the project team with external consulting members. If some specific in-depth analyses are necessary in technical areas where the project team is not especially competent, specialists can be temporarily hired. In addition, an organization analyst is generally consulted to support the refinement of the organizational design and to supervise the performance of the organizational intervention (tasks 4.8 and 4.10). An advisor can also be consulted to support the project leader in the most important technical decisions and in the most critical steps of project management.

If possible, it is advisable - especially in the case where the incremental enhancement approach is adopted - that the project manager, the project leader, the designers, the knowledge engineers, and at least some of the domain experts be the same ones already involved in the previous phase 3 (development of the prototype).

The table shown in Figure 7.3 summarizes the composition of the project team for the development of the prototype.

	REGULAR MEMBERS	SUPPORTING MEMBERS	CONSULTING MEMBERS
project manager		1	
project leader	1		
designers	0-2		
knowledge engineers	1-2		
developers	1-2		
software designers and programmers	0-4		
top managers		1 or more	
intermediate managers		as appropriate	
domain experts		as appropriate	
potential users		as appropriate	
specialists			if needed
organization analyst			if needed
advisor			if needed

Figure 7.3 Implementation, installation, and delivery of the target system: project team composition.

As it can be noted, the composition of the project team can be tailored to the complexity and extent of the KBS application considered, by employing a higher or lower number of designers, knowledge engineers, developers, software designers, and programmers.

7.2   START-UP

7.2.1   Step execution

Figure 7.4 presents a detailed view of KLIC tasks and products of the 'start-up' step.

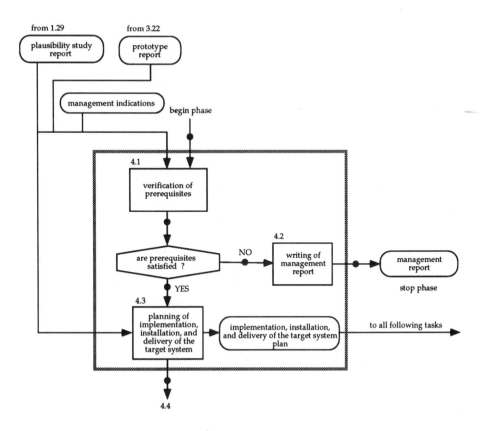

Figure 7.4 Star-up: KLIC tasks and products.

7.2.2   Task 4.1: Verification of prerequisites

Task 4.1 takes in input the management indications - if any, the plausibility study report (from task 1.29), and the prototype report (from task 3.22).

Specific prerequisites that should be satisfied before starting the implementation, installation, and delivery of the target system ai listed below:

- the top management must be fully aware of the objectives and consequences of implementation, installation, and delivery of the target system;
- the top management should make a firm decision about implementation, installation, and delivery of the target system;
- the intermediate managers, domain experts, and potential users should be available to cooperate with the project team in charge of the implementation, installation, and delivery of the target system;
- the requirements, objectives, and constraints proposed by the management - if any - must be consistent with the purpose and nature of the implementation, installation, and delivery of the target system;
- the needed resources for the execution of the phase must be available.

If prerequisites are not satisfied, the implementation, installation, and delivery of the target system should not continue. If such a case occurs, a report should be prepared for the management (task 4.2) and the implementation, installation, and delivery of the target system should be stopped. Otherwise, the execution of the phase continues with task 4.3.

7.2.3   Task 4.2: Writing of management report

In the case where prerequisites are not satisfied, the project leader in charge of implementation, installation, and delivery of the target system should prepare a report for the management and stop the execution of the phase. The product of task 4.2 is a document called *management report*. It should present a detailed account of why the implementation, installation, and delivery of the target system is unfeasible. If appropriate, the report can be personally discussed by the project leader with the management of the organization.

7.2.4   Task 4.3: Planning of implementation, installation, and delivery of the target system

Task 4.3 takes in input the management indications - if any, the plausibility study report (from task 1.29), and the prototype report (from task 3.22). The product of task 4.3 is a document called *implementation, installation, and delivery of the target system plan*.

The implementation, installation, and delivery of the target system plan should be discussed with all members of the project team, who should understand the importance of their role and of their involvement. It should also be formally approved by the management of the end-user organization. Note that, as shown in Figure 7.4, the implementation, installation, and delivery of the target system plan is not an input to any specific task. It will be used by the project leader for management and control issues throughout the whole phase (see section 9.3.2).

The implementation, installation, and delivery of the target system plan should be refined when, during the development of phase 4, new information is made available for a more precise and realistic definition and scheduling of the activities to carry out. Actually, a revision of the plan is probably appropriate after task 4.6 and before tasks 4.11, 4.15, and 4.19.

7.3   PREPARATION

7.3.1   Step execution

Figure 7.5 presents a detailed view of KLIC tasks and products of the 'preparation' step.

7.3.2   Task 4.4: Analysis of target environment

The goal of this task is to analyze the features of the target environment where the KBS is expected to be delivered, and to identify the main requirements it imposes on the target system in order to be appropriately installed and put into use. This task is of primary importance since the characteristics of target environment considered at the moment of plausibility study are often changed at the moment the prototype is completed and the target system has to be implemented. Therefore, a new analysis is needed. The analysis of the target environment should focus not only on operational and technical aspects, but also on organizational issues; the delivered KBS should fit into the human and organizational environments as neatly as it fits into its operational and technical environments [Jagodzinski and Holmes 89].

Task 4.4 takes in input the plausibility study report (from task 1.29) and the prototype report (from task 3.22). The specific issues dealt with by this task are:

analysis of user population
• definition of the intended user population;
• identification and characterization of user classes (typical traits, background, needs, goals, numerosity, etc.).

definition of the delivery environment
• delivery for internal use:
  - identification of installations and sites;
  - physical location of the various installations and sites;
  - distribution of the user population over the various installations and sites;

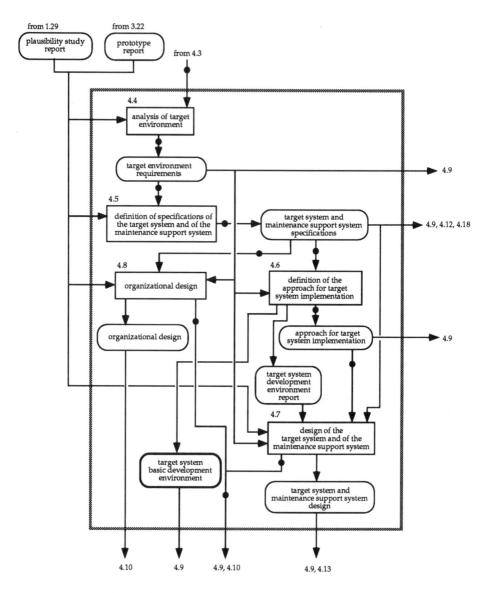

Figure 7.5 Preparation: KLIC tasks and products.

- legal aspects (liability issues);
• delivery for the market
  - identification of potential market (limited market or mass market);
  - expected number of sales;
  - contractual conditions;
  - legal aspects (property rights, liability issues, warranties, etc.).

user-system interaction requirements
- role of the KBS: support system, prescriptive system, autonomous system (see section 1.1.4);
- user interface requirements;
- explanation system requirements;
- maintenance support system requirements.

operational environment requirements
- identification of operational environment;
- characterization of operational environment: open-air, hostile environment (high temperature, dust, vibrations, etc.), factory environment, office environment, space, military, etc.

connection requirements
- connection to traditional software systems (software interface);
- connection with the external environment (external interface).

specific operational and technical requirements
- response time;
- real-time operation;
- continuous operation;
- reliability;
- fail-soft or fail-safe requirements;
- integrity, security, and privacy.

specific hardware and software requirements
- specifically suggested or requested hardware platform;
- specific hardware constraints;
- specifically suggested or requested system software or basic development environment;
- compliance with existing standards;
- compliance with corporate hardware and software policy;
- compliance with corporate commercial agreements and practices.

The product of task 4.4 is a document called *target environment requirements*, which presents a detailed account of the analysis carried out and of the requirements and constraints identified.

7.3.3   Task 4.5: Definition of specifications of the target system and of the maintenance support system

The goal of this task is to update and refine the KBS specifications stated at the moment of plausibility study. Task 4.5 takes in input the plausibility study report (from task 1.29), the prototype report (from task 3.22), and the target environment requirements (from task 4.4).

This task focuses on functional, operational, and technical specifications in turn. The starting point are the KBS specifications defined in tasks 1.13, 1.14, and 1.15, and acceptance criteria stated in task 1.16. As far as functional specifications are concerned, these are revised taking into account the results of prototype evaluation (task 3.21). Operational and technical specifications are revised according to the new requirements and constraints emerged in task 4.4. Moreover, this task should state precise specifications for the maintenance support system, a specific system taking into account both the experience gathered with the development support system during the development of the prototype (phase 3).

The product of task 4.5 is a document called *target system and maintenance support system specifications*, which provides a complete and definitive list of the functional, operational, and technical specifications of the target system.

7.3.4   Approaches to target system implementation

The implementation of the target system may be organized according to several approaches. The applicability of an approach and its appropriateness to a specific situation depend on a variety of conditions and should be analyzed in detail, as illustrated in section 7.3.5. Two main approaches can be identified, as illustrated below.

Incremental enhancement

This approach consists of an incremental enhancement of the prototype until the functional, operational, and technical specifications of the target system are fully met. Incremental enhancement is only possible if:
- the functional specifications reached by the prototype are close to those required from the target system;
- the tools adopted for the development of the prototype allow all the operational and technical specifications of the target system to be achieved.

In the incremental enhancement approach, the basic development environment of the prototype is used for the target system as well. Generally, after the target system is successfully completed, its code is compiled (*incremental enhancement with compilation*) or a run-time version is generated (*incremental enhancement with generation of run-time version*).

Clearly, a version of the target system with non-compiled code (source code) must be kept to be used for KBS extension (see section 8.5); extension interventions are first carried out on the non-compiled version of the system, and later compiled and ported to all KBS installations. Also the knowledge base can be compiled (for example, into a traditional procedural program like Fortran or C or into a decision tree (*incremental enhancement with knowledge base compilation*). Knowledge base compilation is, however, not very usual, since only some specific tools support knowledge compilation. Knowledge base compilation may enhance KBS efficiency, but it generally rises substantial problems for the maintenance activity. A version of the target system with non-compiled knowledge base must be kept for KBS maintenance (see section 8.6); maintenance interventions are first carried out on the non-compiled version of the knowledge base, and later compiled and ported to all KBS installations. This practice generally makes maintenance more complicated and more costly.

Sometimes the hardware platform of the target system is the same as the prototype; in other cases, however, the target system must be ported on a different hardware. For example, often the prototype is developed on a workstation and the target system is delivered on a personal computer. Many considerations justify the change of hardware: cost, performance, reliability, uniformity, maintainability, integrability, etc. In an ideal situation, porting should not require extensive effort. Most frequently, however, the KBS will not be completely portable and some parts will have to be modified or re-written - for example, the graphical user interface or the interface with the operating system [Prerau 90] (*incremental enhancement with partial re-implementation*).

Incremental enhancement is a very natural, easy, and effective approach. Although, it is not always possible to adopt. The possibility to adopt it basically depends on the features of the tools used for developing the prototype and on the requirements and constraints of the target environment. An important aspect to take into account is also the number of expected installations of the KBS. If several installations are foreseen and royalties for each (run-time) copy of the development tool are due, incremental enhancement may turn out to be very costly. Finally, as far as maintenance issues are concerned, this approach does not offer particular advantages, but, at the same time, does not raise specific additional problems. The same tools used during prototype development for creating, refining, and verifying the knowledge base may be released to the maintenance team, or, more appropriately, a specific maintenance support system may be developed. Particular attention should be paid to the case where the knowledge base has been compiled, as discussed above.

Complete re-implementation

If the above illustrated approach turns out to be impossible, the only solution is to resort to complete re-implementation of the prototype using a development environment which allows all the functional, operational, and technical specifications of the target system to be satisfied. Conceptual and logical design developed for the prototype are still valid, but a new detailed design and complete re-coding are required. The user interface is often completely re-designed and built from scratch. The knowledge base of the prototype is generally ported to the new empty system (eventually through re-coding) and then developed further; only very seldom the knowledge base needs to be completely re-built. After the target system has been completely developed, compilation of the system code and of the knowledge base may be undertaken.

Complete re-implementation is clearly a long and costly approach; it should be definitely avoided. It is adopted only if the target environment imposes very specific and strict requirements and constraints that make the incremental enhancement approach impossible. This may happen, for example, in some critical industrial applications, or in military equipment, or in space systems. Adopting the complete re-implementation approach may be very appropriate in the case the KBS is intended to be produced in large numbers to be mass-distributed. In this case a complete re-coding enables very high efficiency and low-cost to be reached.

7.3.5   Task 4.6: Definition of the approach for target system implementation

Once the specifications of the target system and of the maintenance support system have been defined, the most suitable approach to the implementation of the target system has to be identified. This is a critical and important task since the decision made may greatly influence the following steps of the work. Task 4.6 takes in input the target environment requirements (from task 4.4) and the target system and maintenance support system specifications (from task 4.5). This task (together with task 4.7) is executed in parallel to task 4.8.

Choosing among the available approaches for target system implementation is generally simple, but may sometimes require balancing between contrasting exigencies. Jeopardizing the final result by trying to get the maximum results with the minimum time and cost should clearly be avoided. It is generally impossible to seriously take into account many, complex, and specific requirements and specifications without accepting the fact that implementation time and costs are high.

If the complete re-implementation approach is chosen, the most appropriate development environment must also be chosen. In such a case, if the target environment does not impose a specific pre-defined choice, a general purpose programming language like C or C++ is nowadays very common (a general illustration of KBS development tools can be found in section 6.4).

The products of task 4.6 are:
- a document called *approach for target system implementation*, which provides a detailed definition of the approach chosen, appropriately tailored to the case at hand;
- a document called *target system development environment report*, which illustrates the comparative analysis carried out to select the target system basic development environment and the main reasons of the choice made;
- a set of software systems, namely the selected *target system basic development environment*.

7.3.6   Task 4.7: Design of the target system and of the maintenance support system

Task 4.7 develops a detailed design of the target system and of the maintenance support system. Task 4.7 takes in input the plausibility study report (from task 1.29), prototype report (from task 3.22), the target environment requirements (from task 4.4), the target system and maintenance support system specifications (from task 4.5), the approach for target system implementation (from task 4.6), and the target system development environment report (from task 4.6). This task (together with task 4.6) is executed in parallel to task 4.8.

If the incremental enhancement approach has been chosen, the design will focus on those features that were not considered in the development of the prototype. This includes both the refinement of the design of already developed KBS components and the design of new components, using either traditional software or knowledge-based technology (or both). If, instead, the complete re-implementation approach has been adopted, the design task will be much more substantial, concerning the whole system. The main concern of this activity is traditional software design. In fact, the basic technical choices relevant to the knowledge-based technology have already been made and experimented with during the development prototype. What is now needed is just a new implementation of an existing system, in addition to some refinements and extensions. This is typically a traditional software engineering task, which requires only a limited competence in knowledge-based technology.

The product of task 4.7 is a document called *target system and maintenance support system design*, which provides the detailed design of the software systems for implementing the target KBS.

7.3.7   Task 4.8: Organizational design

The goal of this task is to develop an organizational design for the an appropriate delivery and exploitation of the target system. It is mostly based on updating and refining the draft organizational design developed during opportunity analysis. Task 4.8 takes in input the plausibility study report (from task 1.29), the prototype report (from task 3.22), the target environment requirements (from task 4.4), and the target system and maintenance support system specifications (from task 4.5). This task is executed in parallel to the sequence of tasks 4.6 and 4.7.

This task is of crucial importance for the success of the project since the initial organizational design, developed several months before, may no longer be valid in the current situation. The target KBS may be different from what it was supposed to be, and the target environment may have changed. Updating and revising the organizational design is a necessary and delicate task which usually requires the intervention of an organization analyst. This task focuses on the following main points:

- providing a complete definition of the organizational interventions to be carried out before KBS delivery in order to guarantee an effective transition of the KBS into the operational environment and a smooth user acceptance [Muir 87], [Reason 87], [Mackie and Wylie 88];
- identifying the most critical aspects and of the main risks related to KBS delivery, and suggesting the most appropriate ways to handle them.

The product of task 4.8 is a document called *organizational design*, which contains a detailed definition of the organizational interventions to be carried out and a plan for their effective implementation.

7.4   PRODUCTION AND INSTALLATION

7.4.1   Step execution

Figure 7.6 presents a detailed view of KLIC tasks and products of the 'production and installation' step.

7.4.2   Task 4.9: Production of the target system and of the maintenance support system

The goal of this task is to produce the target system and the development support system, according to the approach defined in task 4.6. Task 4.9 takes in input the development support system (from task 3.14), the prototype (from task 3.21), the target environment requirements (from task 4.4), target system and maintenance support system specifications (from task 4.5), the approach for target system implementation (from task 4.6), the target system basic development environment (from task 4.6), and the target system and maintenance support system design (from task 4.7). This task is executed in parallel to task 4.10.

   The execution of this task is different depending on the approach taken. In the case of incremental enhancement, this task may exceptionally consist of just a few final activities carried out directly on the prototype, or in a considerable work including the development of new components, the re-implementation of some parts of the KBS, and a substantial revision and extension of the knowledge base. In the case of complete re-implementation, this task always entails a long and costly effort, including massive development of traditional software.

   The product of task 4.9 is a software system, namely the *draft target system and maintenance support system*.

7.4.3   Task 4.10: Organizational intervention

The goal of this task is to carry out the organizational intervention needed for a correct and effective exploitation of the KBS. Task 4.10 takes in input the organizational design (from task 4.8). The product of task 4.10 is a document called *organizational intervention report*, which illustrates the activities carried out and the results obtained. This task is executed in parallel to task 4.9.

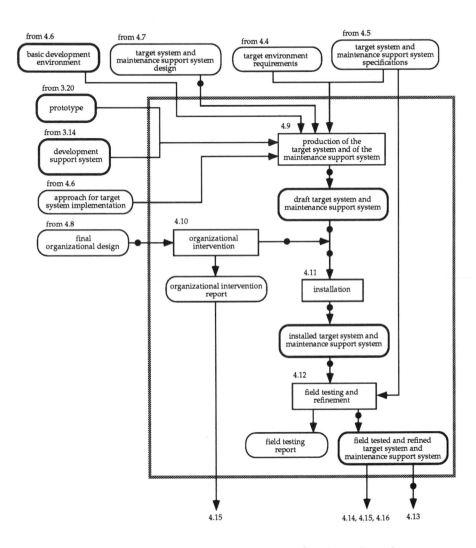

Figure 7.6 Production and installation: KLIC tasks and products.

Note that the organizational intervention can be appropriately carried out in parallel with the production of the target system and of the maintenance support system. This way, as soon as the target system is ready, the project team can proceed with KBS installation.

7.4.4   Task 4.11: Installation

Once the target system and the maintenance support system have been completed and the organizational intervention carried out, the KBS is installed in the target operational environment. If several installations are foreseen, the KBS is first installed only in one or two *pilot installations*. In this case, the following tasks 4.12, 4.14, and 4.15 are also carried out first on the pilot installations. Therefore, if the pilot installations approach is adopted, tasks 4.11, 4.12, and 4.15 (not 4.14, which must be resumed before task 4.19 and carried out for the user classes not considered here) are performed only on the pilot installations, thus saving time and money.

Task 4.11 takes in input the target system and the maintenance support system (from task 4.9). The product of task 4.11 is a software system, namely the *installed target system and maintenance support system*.

Installation includes:
- porting the KBS to the target hardware system;
- connecting the KBS to the external software systems with which it must interact, such as operating systems, data bases, utilities, application packages, etc.;
- connecting the KBS to the external environment in which it operates, such as sensors, data acquisition systems, actuators, etc.;
- performing all the operations necessary to tailor the KBS to the specific features of the operational environment.

Installation is a technical activity done without involving the users and the domain experts. The installed KBS is not made available for experimental use.

7.4.5   Task 4.12: Field testing and refinement

After installation has been successfully concluded, the KBS must undergo careful field testing and refinement. Field testing and refinement requires extensive involvement and availability of users and domain experts. If the pilot installations approach has been adopted in task 4.11, the field testing and refinement concerns only the pilot installations.

Task 4.12 takes in input the target system and maintenance support system specifications (from task 4.5) and the installed target system and maintenance support system (from task 4.11).

Field testing consists of an extensive experimentation with a series of real test cases, prepared by domain experts. This allows identification of possible errors or inadequacies and incremental KBS refinement. Depending on the type of KBS and on the application domain at hand, field testing and refinement may take from one or two weeks to a couple of months. If field testing tends to become exceedingly long, one should assume that the quality of the installed target system is not satisfactory. The KBS should be removed from the operational field and returned to the project team for a deep revision.

The product of task 4.12 includes a software system, namely the *field tested and refined target system and maintenance support system*, and a document, called *field testing report*, which contains a detailed account of the activities done.

7.5   FIRST RELEASE AND EXPERIMENTAL USE

7.5.1   Step execution

Figure 7.7 presents a detailed view of KLIC tasks and products of the 'first release and experimental use' step.

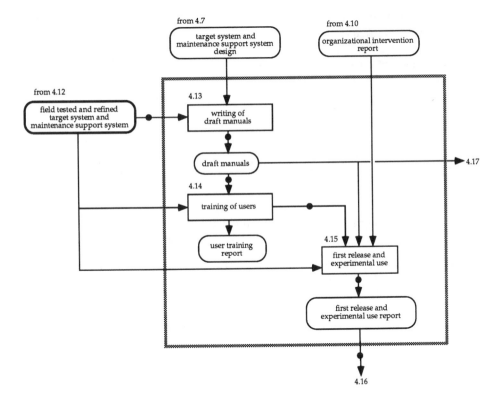

Figure 7.7 First release and experimental use: KLIC tasks and products.

7.5.2   Task 4.13: Writing of draft manuals

The goal of this task is to produce appropriate manuals that should accompany the target system. Task 4.13 takes in input the target system and maintenance support system design (from task 4.7) and the field-tested target system and maintenance support system (from task 4.12).

User manuals are an important point for effective delivery of a KBS. Inadequate manuals may cause several problems [Brockmann 86]:
- increased training costs;
- human errors (note that more that half of human errors in using a computer-based system are due to a lack of documentation [Bailey 83]);
- wasted time and ineffective exploitation of the potentials of the KBS;
- increased litigiousness and possible legal proceedings;
- lack of user acceptance and rejection of the KBS;
- difficulty and ineffective maintenance and extension.

Three types of manuals are generally appropriate for a KBS [Liebowitz 91]:
- *user manual* (or operative manual), directed to the users of the KBS; it illustrates the main system functions and the ways they may be obtained correctly and effectively; the user manual should also clearly emphasize the relations existing between the functions offered by the KBS and the user problems they are expected to solve;
- *maintenance manual*, directed to the maintenance team; it illustrates which maintenance interventions are possible and how they can be carried out correctly and effectively; the maintenance manual should be very specific and strictly goal-oriented, avoiding the provision of useless or redundant information, but, at the same time, being clear and complete about all issues relevant to the maintenance task;
- *technical manual* (or reference manual), directed to the project team in charge of KBS extension; it illustrates the main technical aspects of KBS design and implementation; in particular, the technical manual must contain at least the following: specifications, conceptual model, logical model, and detailed design.

Of the above manuals, the user manual is the most important one due to the great impact it may have on user acceptance. The following guidelines may be taken into account when designing the user manuals [McGraw 86], [McGraw 89], [Chinell 90]:
- analyze the intended users population and develop a user profile: general education, reading ability, background, experience, previous experience with computer-based systems and documentation, amount of specific training they are likely to receive, needs and goals in KBS use, expectations, etc.
- develop a task analysis focusing on the tasks the users are expected to execute with the support of the KBS;
- build an initial outline of the document: organize the user manual according to user tasks and human factors, not to KBS features; let the user manual be founded on a functional and conceptual view of the KBS, discarding any technical or internal details;
- develop a first draft of the user manual: use simple, familiar language; use short, active, positive sentences; be complete and specific when describing objects or actions; describe one thing at a time in a complete way; use lists,

tables, graphics, etc., rather than long prose passages; determine the most appropriate typographical style, exploit visual cues;
- write, edit and internally test the manual; use professional writers and an editor to coordinate work;
- test the first draft of the user manual with sample users and incorporate requested revisions; check level of detail, clarity, structure, easy and quick access to needed information, examples, etc.

An important issue is the problem of making manuals easily available to interested people without obliging them to consult heavy and impractical volumes. A common solution to this exigency is having electronic manuals on-line, equipped with an effective access and retrieval system (including, for example, on hypertext or hypermedia tools) [Horton 90]. This may also support an easy and timely updating of manuals as new versions of the KBS are released. Keeping manuals up-to-date with maintenance and extension is a crucial issue for the operational life of a KBS, since obsolete manuals are useless, if not even misleading.

The product of task 4.13 is a document called *draft manuals*, which contains the first version of user, maintenance, and technical manuals.

7.5.3   Task 4.14: Training of users

User training is a key issue for KBS acceptance and effective exploitation [Jagodzinski and Holmes 89], [Liebowwitz 91]. User training, although being the main concern of this task, is also the result of the whole set of user interactions accomplished during the entire project. Realistic expectation should be enforced among users. They should be instructed on the potentials and limits of the KBS developed and given information about critical situations. It is important that users understand why and how the KBS can help them. They should have a precise idea of the role the KBS plays in the organization. Unfounded fears have to be avoided or alleviated and possible political problems addressed and discussed openly [Prerau 90]. All these objectives cannot be achieved through this task only and must be carefully taken into account in any kind of interaction with the user, since the very beginning of a KBS project. Indirect training is perhaps more effective and more important than the specific training offered to the users before system delivery.

Task 4.14 takes in input the field tested and refined target system and the maintenance support system (from task 4.12) and the draft manuals (from task 4.13). If the pilot installations approach has been adopted in task 4.11, user training concerns only the pilot installations. User training should focus on the following:
- the analysis of user task;
- the illustration of the role of the KBS and of its main functions;
- the way the KBS can help users perform specific tasks or solve specific problems;

- the way the KBS can be used correctly and effectively;
- the illustration of the user manual and the analysis of how to use it appropriately;
- the illustration of possible problems in KBS use and the way to handle them.

User training is usually carried out through a specific course and utilizes the (draft) user manual as the main teaching material. The product of task 4.14 is a document called *user training report*, which provides an account of the training activities carried out.

7.5.4   Task 4.15: First release and experimental use

After user training is positively concluded, the KBS can be released for experimental use. First release and experimental use requires extensive involvement and availability of users and domain experts. If the pilot installations approach has been adopted in task 4.11, the first release and experimental use concerns only the pilot installations. Experimental use is a crucial aspect of a KBS delivery and should not be underestimated. It allows for an extended validation of the KBS, which is of primary importance for acceptance. During the experimental use the KBS is not modified or refined (apart from rare exception where immediate intervention is needed). This task stimulates and collects feedback, comments, suggestions, and requests; their analysis and processing is, however, postponed to the following task 4.16.

Task 4.15 takes in input the organizational intervention report (from task 4.10), the field tested and refined target system and maintenance support system (from task 4.12), the draft manuals (from task 4.13), and the user training report (from task 4.14). Experimental use may last from two months up to one year or even more depending on the type of application faced, the type of KBS developed, the characteristics of the target environment, the user and management requirements, etc. One should not try to compress this task; time spent for experimental use is well-spent and can help avoid a lot of future problems. Limiting the time dedicated to experimental use generally causes maintenance to become more difficult (especially in the first months after the final release), and extension needs to rise earlier.

The product of task 4.15 is a document called *first release and experimental use report*, which illustrates the main activities carried out and the feedback collected from users and domain experts.

7.6   FINAL RELEASE

7.6.1   Step execution

Figure 7.8 presents a detailed view of KLIC tasks and products of the 'final release' step.

7.6.2   Task 4.16: Refinement of the target system and of the maintenance support system

The goal of this task is to analyze and process the feedback, comments, suggestions, and requests collected during experimental use (task 4.15). The appropriate modifications and refinements of the target system and of the maintenance support system are carried out and the final version of the KBS is produced.

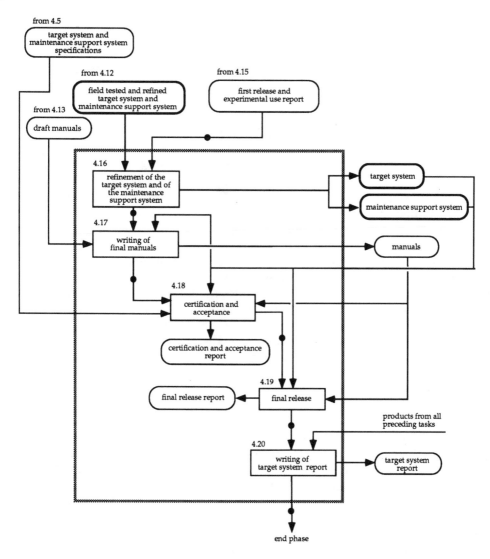

Figure 7.8 Final release: KLIC tasks and products.

Task 4.16 takes in input the field tested and refined target system and the maintenance support system (from task 4.12), and the first release and experimental use report (from task 4.15). The products of task 4.16 are two software systems, namely the *target system* and the *maintenance support system*.

7.6.3   Task 4.17: Writing of final manuals

After the needed revisions to the target system and the maintenance support system have been carried out, the final version of the manuals is prepared. Task 4.17 takes in input the draft manuals (from task 4.13), and the target system and maintenance support system (from task 4.16). The product of task 4.17 is a document called *manuals*, which contains the final version of user, maintenance, and technical manuals.

7.6.4   Task 4.18: Certification and acceptance

The goal of this task is to officially present the final result of the whole development effort to the management of the target organization - usually, the project manager - in order to certify that the work has been correctly executed as requested. Often the certification is just a formal activity, which does not go into functional, operational, or technical details. These have already been examined in the previous tasks and the project manager, having heard the opinions of all the involved people, formally declares the acceptance of the work done.

Task 4.18 takes in input the target system and maintenance support system specifications (from task 4.5), the target system and maintenance support system (from task 4.16), and the manuals (from task 4.17). The product of task 4.18 is a document called *certification and acceptance report*. It includes the formal certification of the work done, issued by the project leader, and the formal acceptance issued by the project manager.

7.6.5   Task 4.19: Final release

Once the KBS is completed, certified, and accepted it is eventually installed and released to the users. The target system and the maintenance support system must be ported to all installations and sites foreseen. Moreover, if the pilot installations approach has been adopted in task 4.11, task 4.14 (training of users) must be completed for the user classes not considered before. When dealing with a large number of users and several KBS installations are foreseen in different sites of the organization, then it may be appropriate to carry out installation, user training, and release separately for reasonably small groups of users (*incremental delivery*). Effective delivery cannot be managed with too many users, for too many installations, and in too many sites simultaneously.

Task 4.19 takes in input the target system and the maintenance support system (from task 4.16), and the manuals (from task 4.17). The product of task 4.19 is a document called *final release report*, which illustrates the main activities done and the obtained results.

7.6.6 Task 4.20: Writing of target system report

This task is meant to produce a document summarizing the activities carried out, the software systems developed, the organizational interventions carried out, and the delivery results. Task 4.20 takes in input the products of all preceding tasks. The product of task 4.20 is a document called *target system report*. A possible table of contents for the target system report is shown in Figure 7.9.

The target system report is directed to the management and to the project team in charge of the following phase 5.

7.7 LEGAL ASPECTS

7.7.1 Property rights

Copyright and patent

Property rights for KBSs are not such a critical aspect as they are for traditional software. In fact, KBSs are often built by the same organization who will use them; their property is not transferred from a producer to a customer and, therefore, property rights are generally not a controversial matter. Moreover, KBSs are not general-purpose, mass-distributed systems, like a word processor or a spreadsheet, but individually tailored applications. They are not distributed to a vast user population, but are destined to just one target organization. Protecting them from possible illegal use by people who do not pay for them is therefore not a major problem.

However, there are several aspects concerning property rights for KBSs which are worth attention. In order to analyze such issues we must distinguish between the software components of a KBS.

As far as the software components of a KBS are concerned, ownership rights are established through intellectual property [Ricketson 84]. Here, *copyright* may be used to protect the expression of ideas, i.e. the form rather than the content of the work, whereas *patent* may be adopted to protect ideas. Patents provide a much more substantial protection than copyright. They may require, however, a higher investment for the applicant and a longer time; moreover, tehy generally apply only for a relatively short period of time [Clarke 88], [Clarke 89]. Therefore, copyright has become the most common protection for software systems [Gray 88], [Zeide and Liebowotz 90]; only few items of software have qualified for patent protection [Hanneman 85]. Applicability of copyright to software systems has been explicitly stated in many countries; for example, in the United States since 1984, in the United Kingdom since 1985, and in the European Community since 1991. However, the conditions for applicability are not uniform and several open problems still exist [Sterling and Hart 87], [Clarke 88], [Clarke 89]. In fact, software is a utilitarian work showing a number of different features with respect to literary or other artistic works to which copyright has been traditionally applied. Moreover, the boundaries between ideas (not protected by copyright) and expression of ideas (protected by copyright) are not easy to determine, as well as the precise meaning of the clause "a substantial portion of a work" which is a core part of the concept of copyright. Finally, the various forms in which software may exist - source code, compiled code, executable code, etc. - make the issues related to copyright more intricate and less clear.

The general understanding of property rights for software systems and the definition of the most appropriate way for their protection is still an evolving matter. Software companies, courts, and governments have all an active role in the process of having clear and universal regulations for software protection.

---

1. Introduction
- short introduction to the *implementation, installation, and delivery of the target system* phase
- specific management indications considered
- possible difficulties encountered and solutions adopted
- synthesis of the activities carried out and of the main results obtained

2. Target system specifications
- analysis of the target environment
- functional, operational, and technical specifications

3. Production of the target system
- approach adopted for target system implementation
- design of the target system and of the maintenance support system
- implementation notes
- installation notes
- field testing and refinement

4. First release
- user training
- approach adopted for the first release
- experimental use

5. Final release
- refinement of the target system and of the maintenance support system
- certification and acceptance
- approach adopted for the final release

Figure 7.9 Target system report: suggested table of contents.

The software components of a KBS

Examining the case of the software components of a KBS closer, we must distinguish at least four situations, depending on the development tools adopted.

In the case where the software components are built from scratch using a programming language which can be compiled (such as, for example, C, C++, Lisp, Prolog, Smalltalk, etc.), their property rights belong to the producer. Buying just one license for a programming language package (generally including the language compiler, but also several other development support tools), the software producer can create as many new software systems as he wants and hold full property rights of them.

In other cases, more specific KBS development tools are used (such as, for example, advanced versions of Prolog or Lisp), which cannot be completely compiled into executable code but require that a substantial portion of the compiled code of the development tool - the so-called run-time module - be linked to the new software built using the development tool. In such cases, the developer does not hold all property rights on the software systems he created; in fact, these must include a part whose property is and remains with the producer of the development tool. Duplicating this portion of code to be included in the new software system developed cannot be done without explicit permission of the producer, who generally requires that an additional license is bought for each new copy generated. As one can easily imagine, this sharing of property rights may lead to complex and costly situations when the KBSs developed are mass-distributed. The end-users must pay royalties both for the portion of specific code written by the KBS producer and for the run-time module written by the producer of the development tool used for the construction of the software components of the KBS. Moreover, let us note that, apart from the aspects related to property rights, this situation may also bring about complex problems about legal liability concerning the KBS, since it is constituted - at least as far as its software components are concerned - by two linked parts produced by different subjects, each one responsible only for its own contribution.

In other cases still more specific KBS development tools are used (such as, for example, shells or toolkits), which are ready-made but can be tailored and extended by the KBS producer through appropriate programming. Such a case is quite similar to the one just examined above. The whole original development tool or at least a substantial compiled part of it - the so-called run-time module or delivery system - will constitute the core part of the software components of the KBS being developed, therefore configuring a situation where property rights are again shared between the producer of the development tool and the producer of the KBS. Clearly, if no tailoring or extension of the original development tool is required, all the property rights belong - at least as far as its software components are concerned - to the producer of the development tool.

Finally, in other cases ready-made specific KBS development tools are used, which cannot be tailored or extended by the KBS producer (these can call - or be called by - external programs). Once again, such a case is similar to the one examined above. The whole original development tool or at least a substantial compiled version of it - the so-called run-time module or delivery system - will constitute the software components of the KBS being developed. Therefore, property rights will entirely remain with the producer of the development tool, the producer of the KBS being only an intermediary between him and the end-user. Clearly, the property rights of external programs which will eventually be integrated in the complete application will remain with their original producer.

The knowledge base

As far as the knowledge base of a KBS is concerned, the key question concerning property rights and their protection is: Are knowledge bases software? Apparently the answer to this question cannot be positive. Knowledge bases are more like a collection of information items, than an information processing method coded into an executable program. And then, can they be treated as some other type of work to which copyright applies or are they are not subject to copyrigh? And in this case, how can the property rights be appropriately protected? The answer to these points is still unclear, and no generally accepted opinion exists. This lack of an established regulation does not however cause too many problems - at least for the time being - for KBS producers and users. In fact, knowledge bases are generally not products which are distributed and sold; they are typically dedicated systems, intended just for one specific user, who will hold all property rights over them. This situation could however greatly change in the near future, with the rapidly increasing interest in knowledge base interchange.

About property rights of knowledge bases, three more issues are worth mentioning which, although still controversial and without a sound legal foundation, may be of concrete concern even in present days.

A first point concerns property rights in knowledge. Consider, for example the case where a company wants to develop a KBS which will be based on the knowledge, competence and experience of some of its employees. What happens if the domain experts decline the invitation to express their knowledge in understandable terms and, therefore, to actively cooperate to the construction of the KBS? By what means can an employer seek to enforce their will? [Clarke 89]. Who is the real owner of the knowledge present in the mind of domain experts? The domain expert themselves, or the company which has offered them the concrete opportunity, the means and necessary background to develop such knowledge, or both? One might argue that such knowledge was produced under an employment contract during the execution of a specific job and it is only by chance that it is stored in the mind of an employee, but is sole property of the employer. But one might also argue that no employment contract provides an employer with anything approaching a property right in the knowledge of his employees; this has been produced and accumulated thanks to the personal efforts and capabilities of the employees and is their own property. And what about knowledge which was existent in the company before the domain experts were hired or which is of public domain? The situation is even more complicated in the case of persons which are not bound to the organization through an employment contract, such as contractors and consultants. If there are usually clear contractual obligations which forbid employees, contractors, and consultants to divulge knowledge they use or develop in the course of their job, generally there are no specific clauses which oblige them to articulate their knowledge and to transfer it explicitly to the organization they work for. Organizations should therefore establish clear contractual obligations if they want to be able to enforce employees, contractors and consultants to cede their knowledge.

A second case concerns the problem of shared authorship. Consider, for example, the case where the knowledge base of a KBS, after release for operational use, is modified, expanded and enhanced directly by the users and domain experts. After a period of time, how will property rights be shared between the end-user organization and team initially in charge of the development? One might argue that each one holds the property rights of the knowledge items he has created. But this claim could turn out to be simplistic. One could also claim that the value of a KBS derives from its performance which, in turn, depends on the content of the knowledge base as a whole. Each individual knowledge item contributes to the global performance of the KBS only through its interaction with all the others. A small piece of knowledge can be more important, from the point of view of performance, than a big one. Therefore property right on individual knowledge items belonging to the same knowledge base is meaningless.

A third and last case concerns meta-authorship, i.e. knowledge which is generated automatically by a program without human intervention. Consider, for example, the case of a learning program, such as rule-induction. Software and computers are not legal entities which can possess property, so, since the new knowledge has been generated thanks to a special-purpose program, one might argue that the property rights of such knowledge belong to the designers and developers of the program which has generated it. However, one might also argue that the program which has generated the new knowledge has exploited to this purpose specific data or cases that have been presented to it by the user. Without such inputs no knowledge had been generated, and the generated knowledge strictly depends on the inputs supplied. Therefore, property rights should at least be shared between the producer of the learning program and the user which has provided the inputs used for the synthesis of new knowledge.

7.7.2   Liability issues

Strict products liability and negligence

In traditional software systems *liability* issues are relatively well-understood [Scott 84], [Smedinghoff 86]; the matter becomes, however, less clear-cut with KBSs. The key question is: Are KBSs products or services - or hybrid? This question has no uniform answer. It depends on the nature of the application, on the intended behavior of the KBS and intended user community, on the type of interaction the KBS has with its users (support system, prescriptive system, autonomous system - see section 1.1.4). The answer to this question is therefore possible only on a case-by-case basis. In fact, depending on the nature of a KBS (a product or a service) two different liability schemes apply [Gemignani 90], [Tuthill 91]. Traditionally, manufacturers are held responsible under the theory of *strict products liability* when their products cause injury. When persons offering services cause harm in performing those services, they are charged with *negligence* [Zeide and Liebowitz 87]. Strict products liability is the liability of a manufacturer, seller, or supplier of goods to someone who suffers physical harm from those goods. Negligence is the failure to observe, for the protection of the interests of another person, that degree of care, precaution, and vigilance which the circumstances justly demand, whereby such other person suffers injury. Both negligence and strict liability fit under the heading of torts.

What happens when a user turns a KBS output into an action that has catastrophic results? What about the consequences of liability for the KBS producer and for the user?

Producer liability

As far as the KBS producer is concerned, both schemes of strict products liability and negligence may apply, depending on whether the KBS is considered a product or a service respectively.

Strict products liability applies to defective products. Products are usually viewed as tangible items, with set monetary values, that can be owned. KBSs have an intangible nature but are sold in tangible form. Only the software components and the knowledge embodied in a KBS have real value. Proving strict products liability requires that the plaintiff proves that the product had a defect in design or manufacture when sold or leased to the user, that the product was used in a normal, intended or reasonably foreseeable manner when it caused the injury, and that the defect was the proximate cause of the injury [Birnbaum 88]. Strict products liability does not apply to defective products incidental to the rendering of a service. KBS producers can attach disclaimers to products to lessen their liability and limit warranties (to be effective such disclaimers must generally meet formal requirements, such as to be in writing and be conspicuously placed) [Frank 88-a], [Frank 88-b]. For example, a KBS for tax advice might have a disclaimer stating that the conclusions reached and the suggestions supplied by the system are not final and the users should in any case consult a tax professional [Liebowitz 91]. Moreover, they might avoid overselling their products and be careful not to entice users into excessive reliance. On the contrary, users should be worned about the damages and injuries the KBS might cause and be advised to use the system appropriately and safely.

Negligence applies for design defects in a system specifically tailored for professional use. Negligence alone is insufficient, however, as a cause of action: there must be an obligation and consequences [Tuthill 91]. Proving negligence requires that the plaintiff specifies the very mistake in KBS behavior which has caused the injury, and then proves that such a mistake is due to negligence of the producer and that the injury was reasonably foreseeable [Zeide and Liebowitz 87]. This is usually very hard, if not impossible. Common arguments in defense of negligence are assumption of risk or contributory negligence. For example, if a KBS is a typical support system, designed to output options and suggestions as an advisor, users must determine their own course of actions and the KBS developer can hardly be claimed for negligence. Moreover, the plaintiff has the obligation to mitigate damages caused by negligence. If the plaintiff fails to do so, additional damages are not recoverable [Tuthill 91].

User liability

As far as KBS users are concerned, negligence may apply to a KBS user for use, misuse and non-use. Let us consider some paradigmatic situations.

A user applies the suggestions of a KBS which, being in error, causes an injury. If the user is an experienced professional and the KBS is a support system which only suggests possible decisions but does not prescribe any mandatory action leaving the user free to determine his own behavior, then he can be considered negligent and therefore liable for the occurred injury. He should have recognized the flaw in the KBS and not have followed its suggestions. If the user is a novice he should not have used the KBS in the first place [Mykytyn et al. 90], [Mykytyn and Mykytyn 91].

A user which is a novice in his field (for example, a newly hired person) relies in his routine job on a KBS of prescriptive type, validated by the organization he belongs to and released as a mandatory regulation. In the case that application of KBS prescriptions leads to an injury, he will not be liable for negligence. In fact, if his behavior followed the stated regulations, one might assume that he applied all his competence and knowledge in the best possible way to avoid the injury, which, however, being a novice, was insufficient to recognize the wrong prescription of the KBS. In this case, the responsibility for the injury might be attributed to the organization who has approved and adopted the KBS for improper or unreasonable reliance on the KBS, or to the KBS producers if strict product liability or negligence can be proved.

A novice utilizes a KBS for training purposes. In the case where he causes an injury during a training session, if misuse can be excluded, and if it can also be excluded that the injury was due to any not foreseeable event, most probably the KBS producer will be held responsible for the injury, if strict products liability or negligence can be proved. In fact, one might expect that the KBS was designed and constructed in such a way as to be totally safe both for the trainee and for other people and that any reasonably foreseeable cause of injury had been carefully excluded.

An experienced professional is expected to consult an accepted, established KBS as standard practice. In the case where he fails to utilize the KBS in his job and causes an injury, he might be liable for negligence for not having taken advantage of the best available technology [Zeide and Liebowitz 87]

Users of KBSs can limit their liability in several ways. If a user resorts to a KBS as a consequence of his own decision, he may give full disclosure of the use of the KBS to all interested people and get an explicit consent from them. For example, a physician using a KBS to treat a patient, might get a formal consent in writing from the patient [Liebowitz 91]. Or, if a user is obliged to employ a KBS as a consequence of a regulation or of an order, he may state in writing to all interested parties that the use of the KBS may cause damages for which he will, however, not be responsible. For example, a process operator who is obliged by the management to strictly keep to the suggestions of a KBS in his work, could state in writing that he will not be responsible for damage or injuries caused as a consequence of this obligation.

A final remark concerns specific application domains for which it may be reasonable that KBSs are subject to licensing requirements [Hayman et al. 88]. For example, a KBS for civil engineering design, or air traffic control, or medical diagnosis might be evaluated and licensed by an appropriate authority in the field (for example, an official regulation agency) before being put to use.

PART IV

THE PRIMARY PROCESSES: OPERATION

8

Maintenance and Extension

8.1   Phase overview

8.1.1   Motivations and objectives

By *maintenance* we mean any modification to a KBS which only involves the content of the knowledge base, while by *extension* we mean modifications which also concern the structure of the empty system or of the maintenance support system. Clearly, maintenance may only have a limited effect on KBS functions and performance, while extension can greatly change system behavior.

The need for the 'maintenance and extension' phase is motivated by two main reasons. The first one is to ensure a long operational life to a KBS. This is indeed a crucial point to improve the benefits/costs ratio of a project. Delivering a KBS for routine use without bothering with its operational life can only bring a scarce return of the investment made during the development phases, and the whole project may turn into a failure [Liebowitz 91]. Without appropriate maintenance a KBS may very quickly go out of use, and without appropriate extension it may become obsolete in a short time. Ensuring effective operation of a KBS is a must in order to keep the level of benefits and returns constantly high. Without appropriate maintenance and extension the functions and the performance of a KBS may rapidly fail, due to (i) the emergence of errors that have not been identified during KBS development, (ii) the changes in the environment where the KBS must operate, and (iii) the rise of new user needs and requirements.

Note that 'maintenance and extension' is an open phase of the life cycle; it starts with the release of the target KBS and lasts until the KBS is eventually dropped.

The goals of the 'maintenance and extension' phase are [Shatz et al. 87], [Newquist 88], [Prerau 90], [Liebowitz 91], [Cohen and Bench-Capon 93]:

- monitoring the operational life of the KBS and collecting feedback, remarks, and requests from the users;
- correcting errors in KBS behavior (i.e., discrepancies with respect to the stated specifications) which have survived the verification process and are detected only during the operational life of the KBS (*corrective interventions*);
- updating the delivered KBS in order to meet the changes in the hardware and software environment in which KBS must operate, for example a new version of the operating system, the adoption of a new graphical user interface, the porting to a new hardware/software platform, etc. (*adaptive interventions*);
- progressively updating the delivered KBS in order to meet the evolving or expanding needs of the users; this may range from minor parameter changes or limited interventions to the content of the knowledge base (*perfective interventions*) to major changes or even to the basic structure of the empty system or the maintenance support system (*evolutionary maintenance*);
- periodically assessing the global state of the KBS and to planning its future development.

An account of the issue of maintenance and extension of software systems from the point of view of standards may be found in [IEEE 1042 87], [IEEE 828 90], [ESA PSS-05-0 91], [ESA PSS-05-07 91], and [ESA PSS-05-09-91]; although they specifically concern the production of traditional software, some of the concepts presented in these documents may apply to KBSs as well.

8.1.2   Inputs and products

Maintenance and extension are generally requested by the managers of the departments where the KBS is installed. The 'maintenance and extension' phase takes in input:

- a document called *management indications*, which includes requirements, objectives, and constraints provided by the management, to be taken into account during maintenance and extension;
- the target system, the maintenance support system, the manuals (user, maintenance, and technical), and the target system report produced in phase 4.

The products of maintenance and extension are:

- a new version of the knowledge base of the target system and updated user manuals, concerning maintenance;
- new versions of the target system and of the maintenance support system, and updated manuals (user, maintenance, and technical), concerning extension;

- the *KBS history*, which includes the collection of *operation reports* collected form the users, containing their feedback, remarks, and requests, and a record of all activities carried out during maintenance and extension.

Finally, the 'maintenance and extension' phase may produce a specific *management report* in the case the prerequisites for the execution of a maintenance or extension intervention are not satisfied (see task 5.5). The products of maintenance and extension are directed to the users and to teams in charge of maintenance and extension (phase 5).

8.1.3   Phase structure and task outline

Figure 8.1 presents an outline of the KLIC tasks of the 'maintenance and extension' phase.
    The overall logical structure of the 'maintenance and extension' phase is organized into seven steps:
- the 'preparation' step defines the most appropriate approach for organizing the maintenance and extension activities and sets up and trains the maintenance team;
- the 'observation' step concerns the periodic collection of operation reports produced during KBS operational life;
- the 'intervention set-up' step analyzes the operation reports and the system history, verifies that the prerequisites are satisfied, defines new specifications for the KBS, identifies the appropriate intervention to undertake, and plans its performance;
- the 'maintenance' step carries out all the tasks required for the execution of a maintenance intervention;
- the 'extension' step carries out all the tasks required for the execution of an extension intervention;
- the 'release' step is concerned with the installation, field testing, and refinement and the new version of the KBS, the updating of manuals, the training of users and of the maintenance team, the certification and acceptance, and the release;
- finally, the 'intervention closing' step updates the KBS history, assesses the state of the KBS, and plans its future development.

As shown in Figure 8.1, phase 5 includes two loops. A major loop includes the entire phase, except the 'preparation' step and lasts until the KBS is in use. A small loop in the 'observation' step concerns the periodic collection of operation reports.
    As we have already mentioned in section 2.1.3, the 'maintenance and extension' phase lasts throughout the operational life of the KBS. Maintenance and extension interventions are carried out when needed and when appropriate.

PREPARATION		
	5.1	definition of the strategy for maintenance and extension
	5.2	training of the maintenance team

LOOP

OBSERVATION

LOOP		
	5.3	collection of operation reports
UNTIL		a meaningful number of operation reports has been collected

INTERVENTION SET-UP

	5.4	analysis of operation reports and verification of prerequisites
IF		prerequisites are not satisfied
THEN	BEGIN	
	5.5	writing of management report
		GO TO 5.17
	END	
	5.6	definition of new specifications
	5.7	identification of the appropriate intervention type and planning
CASE	maintenance:	GO TO 5.8
	extension:	GO TO 5.10
END-CASE		

MAINTENANCE

	5.8	revision of the knowledge base
IF		revision of target system is necessary
THEN		GO TO 5.10
	5.9	writing of maintenance report
		GO TO 5.12

EXTENSION

	5.10	revision of the target system and of the maintenance support system
	5.11	writing of extension report

RELEASE

	5.12	installation, field testing, and refinement
	5.13	updating of manuals
	5.14	training of users and of the maintenance team
	5.15	certification and acceptance
	5.16	release

INTERVENTION CLOSING

	5.17	updating of KBS history
	5.18	KBS development planning

UNTIL the KBS is in use

Figure 8.1 Maintenance and extension: KLIC tasks outline.

Maintenance usually requires 1 to 15 days (elapsed time) depending on the complexity and extent of the intervention; extension, being very similar to a limited and focused KBS development project, may require 1 to 8 months (elapsed time).

Splitting the complete duration of the entire phase into the individual durations of its component tasks is meaningless. The duration of each loop is hardy predictable, and also the duration of the 'observation', 'maintenance', and 'extension' steps is highly variable.

8.1.4   Project team composition

The main problem of the 'maintenance and extension' phase is the definition and organization of the project team who should be in charge of it.

As far as the first step ('preparation') is concerned, the project team is usually the one already in charge of the previous phase 4 ('implementation, installation, and delivery of the target system'). In fact, even if properly belonging to this phase, the preparation step is supposed to bridge the end of the KBS development process (the 'development' macro-phase) to the start of its operational life (the 'operation' macro-phase).

As far as the remaining six steps of maintenance and extension are concerned, it should first of all be noted that past experience has shown that assigning these tasks to the project team who was already in charge of phase 4 (and quite often also of phase 3) implies unacceptable drawbacks. In fact, this solution tends to create a permanent link between a project team and the released KBS applications, thus giving rise, in the long-run, to several problems. For example, when a maintenance or extension intervention becomes necessary, the original project team may not be available any more. Its members might be involved in other projects, or engaged in different project teams, or in the meantime some of them may have moved to another job or retired. In the hypothetical case where a project team could be kept indefinitely as it is at the time of KBS release, the load of maintenance and extension will interfere with the production of new applications in any case. The more applications are produced and delivered, the greater the need for maintenance and extension, and consequently the engagements of the project team for maintenance and extension will increase. Therefore, in the long-run, the team will be totally dedicated to maintenance and extension only, and will not be available for new projects any more.

This reasoning suggests that, after conclusion of phase 4 and of the first step of phase 5 (namely, 'preparation'), the link between a project team in charge of development and the delivered KBS should be definitely broken. The 'maintenance and extension' phase should be organized with different resources and carried out by different project teams.

As far as the 'extension' step is concerned, it is usually carried out by a regular KBS project team (either internal to the user organization or provided by an external supplier), much similar to the one in charge of phases 3 and 4 (see sections 6.1.4 and 7.1.4). As far as the 'maintenance' step is concerned, it is assigned to a specific maintenance team, usually internal to the user organization. In particular, depending on the approach adopted (see section 8.2.2), the maintenance team is typically made up of:

- 1 knowledge engineer, with the responsibility of project leader;
- 0 to 3 knowledge engineers (0 to 1 in the case of local maintenance team, 2 to 3 in the case of central maintenance team);
- intermediate managers of all departments concerned with the application domain considered
- domain experts of the application domain considered;
- representatives of the KBS users.

If possible, it is advisable that the knowledge engineer, with the responsibility of project leader and at least some of the domain experts be the same already involved in the previous phase 4 (implementation, installation, and delivery of the target system).

The table shown in Figure 8.2 summarizes the composition of the maintenance team for the development of the prototype.

	REGULAR MEMBERS	SUPPORTING MEMBERS	CONSULTING MEMBERS
project leader	1		
knowledge engineers	0-3		
intermediate managers		as appropriate	
domain experts		as appropriate	
users		as appropriate	

Figure 8.2 Maintenance team.

8.2   PREPARATION

8.2.1   Step execution

Figure 8.3 presents a detailed view of KLIC tasks and products of the 'preparation' step.

8.2.2   Approaches to maintenance and extension

Maintenance may be organized according to several approaches [Cohen and Bench-Capon 93]. The applicability of an approach and its appropriateness to a specific situation depend on a variety of conditions and should be analyzed in detail, as illustrated in section 8.2.3. Two main approaches can be identified, as illustrated below.

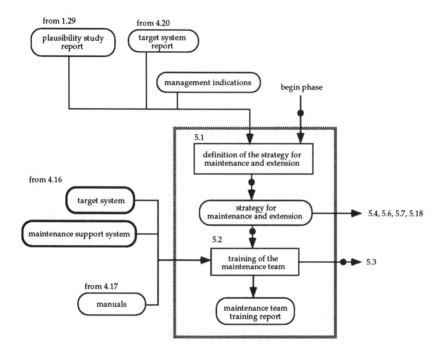

Figure 8.3 Preparation: KLIC tasks and products.

Local maintenance team

In this case, for each site where the KBS is installed (in one or more installations) a different *local maintenance team* is established. In the case where a site includes a great number of installations, it is divided into sub-sites and a maintenance team is set up for each sub-site. Each local maintenance team is in charge of carrying out all maintenance interventions concerning the KBS installations of the relevant site or sub-site. The local maintenance team will resort to the corporate KBS department or to an external supplier when an extension intervention seems appropriate. Usually, the local maintenance team members will not be involved full-time in the maintenance activity.

The establishment of a local maintenance team is subject to the following conditions:

- the KBS is delivered in several, different sites;
- in each site domain experts are available;
- it is possible to permanently assign a knowledge engineer to each site, or to train a technician from the site to become a knowledge engineer;

- the KBS is expected to have a sufficiently long operational life (at least four years).

Central maintenance team

In this case, a common *central maintenance team* is set up, in charge of carrying out all maintenance interventions. The central maintenance team will resort to the corporate KBS department or to an external supplier when an extension intervention seems appropriate. Of course, the central maintenance team will not be involved full-time in the maintenance activity.

The establishment of a central maintenance team is subject to the following conditions:
- it is possible to permanently assign an appropriate set of domain experts to the central maintenance team with part-time engagements;
- it is possible to set up an effective and efficient communication link between the various KBS installations and the central maintenance team.

Apart from the approach adopted, the assignment of the maintenance team includes not only the 'maintenance' step, but also the 'observation', 'intervention set-up' (possibly in cooperation with the team in charge of extension), 'release' (only after a maintenance intervention), and 'intervention closing steps.

Note also that maintenance includes the *user support service,* aimed at helping users exploit the KBS correctly and effectively in performing specific tasks or solving specific problems [Liebowitz 91]. The user support service is in a sense an extension of user training (see task 4.14) after KBS release. The user support service is usually guaranteed only for a limited period of time after delivery (for example, six months), and is provided by the maintenance team. There are various vehicles to provide KBS users with support; the most common ones include:
- a direct telephone line, usually toll-free, that users can call to obtain answers to questions regarding the KBS use;
- in-field support, providing service on call to interested users by experienced people;
- user groups, consisting of individuals who use the same KBS in several installations and sites and get together on a regular basis to discuss problems, analyze possible solutions, and propose new ideas.

Extension is generally organized as a limited-scope KBS project, with its own life cycle (from the plausibility study to the implementation, installation, and delivery of the target system), and carried out by a regular project team (see section 8.1.4). The need for an extension intervention is first identified by the maintenance team in the 'intervention set-up' step. After a careful evaluation, it defines the requirements and specifications of the potential extension intervention, it assesses its appropriateness from the applicative point of view, and then it requests the responsible project team to carry out a focused plausibility study. If this concludes with a positive evaluation, the extension intervention is started, otherwise it is postponed.

The assignment of the project team in charge of extension includes not only the 'extension' step, but also the 'intervention set-up' (as far as the assessment of the plausibility of the extension intervention is concerned) and 'release' (only after an extension intervention) steps.

8.2.3   Task 5.1: Definition of the strategy for maintenance and extension

The goal of this task is to define a global corporate strategy for maintenance and extension. This is of crucial importance to manage the operational life of the KBS rationally and effectively. A well-defined set of criteria can help make the main decisions of the 'maintenance and extension' phase in a uniform and objective way throughout the entire operational life of the KBS. Task 5.1 takes in input the plausibility study report (from task 1.29), the target system report (from task 4.20), and the management indications.

The definition of the strategy for maintenance and extension concerns the following main points:

- The management of KBS versions. The various installations of a KBS usually go through different operational lives and may undergo different maintenance and extension interventions. Therefore, they tend to progressively differentiate. A common strategy is needed to control their evolution over time. One may accept that they have totally independent lives or impose constraints on their development. For example, it might be decided that extensions are carried out on all running versions, or that any maintenance intervention carried out on any installation is proposed to all other installations.
- The criteria to initiate an extension intervention. Deciding whether an extension intervention is appropriate or not is usually important and critical. Extensions can substantially improve the capability of the KBS to satisfy the requirements, but they are generally complex and costly. Extensions in the first period of the operational life of a KBS should be avoided, but may be of crucial importance for extending the operational life of the KBS, when the final point of the operational life of the KBS is approaching.
- The criteria to initiate a maintenance intervention. Deciding whether a maintenance intervention should be initiated or not is usually not very critical but nevertheless important. Maintenance can help keep the behavior of the KBS up-to-date and its performance high. The need for maintenance recurs more in the first period of the operational life of a KBS and tends then to become less frequent. Maintenance interventions that are too many and too frequent should be avoided in order guarantee enough stability to the installed KBS. A defined set of criteria should therefore be established to guide the decision if and when to start-up a maintenance intervention in a uniform and

objective way throughout the entire operational life of the KBS, apart from the opinion of the persons in charge of maintenance and extension.
Moreover, an important issue to maintain a KBS is to use appropriate metrics to identify which elements of the knolwdge base require maintenance. For example, knowledge utilization (entirely unused knowledge may be redundant, knowledge employed excessively might need a more effective coding, etc.) [Madeo and Levary 90], knowledge stability and confidence (old knowledge which is intensively used without modification may be assumed to be more validated than more recent knowledge; old knowledge not used since a long time may be no longer valid, etc.).

- The selection between the central or local maintenance team approach. The main attributes that may help make the appropriate choice between central or local maintenance team include:
  - number of sites where the KBS is installed;
  - number of installations per site;
  - availability of domain experts and knowledge engineers;
  - requested maintenance time.
- The criteria for managing the last part of the operational life of the KBS, when the final point is approaching, i.e. the point where the requirements can no longer be satisfied and consequently the KBS is withdrawn from operational use. Two aspects are of primary importance in this respect:
  - when and how to decide that the KBS is approaching the final point and, therefore, should not be enhanced any more but only supported to carry out its tasks until a replacement is available;
  - how to plan the last part of the operational life of the KBS in such a way as to keep its performance above an acceptable limit, restricting, at the same time, maintenance and extension costs.

The product of task 5.1 is a document called *strategy for maintenance and extension*, which provides a structured illustration of the points mentioned above and constitutes a basic input to several subsequent tasks.

8.2.4   Task 5.2: Training of the maintenance team

The goal of this task is to train the central maintenance team or the various local maintenance teams in charge of KBS maintenance.
Task 5.2 takes in input the target system and maintenance support system (from task 4.16), the manuals (from task 4.17), and the strategy for maintenance and extension (from task 5.1). The training of the maintenance team focuses on:
- the analysis of the various tasks the maintenance team is in charge of;
- the illustration of the strategy adopted for maintenance and extension;
- the way the KBS can be maintained correctly and effectively;
- the illustration of the maintenance manual and the analysis of how to use it appropriately;

- the illustration of possible problems in KBS maintenance and of the way to handle them.

The training of the maintenance team is usually carried out through a specific course. In the case where the local maintenance team approach is adopted, the training course is generally repeated for each project team independently. The product of task 5.2 is a document called *maintenance team training report*, which provides an account of the training activities carried out.

8.3 OBSERVATION

8.3.1 Step execution

Figure 8.4 presents a detailed view of KLIC tasks and products of the 'observation' step.

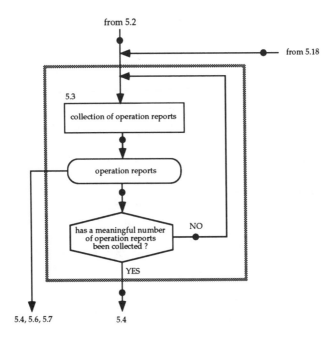

Figure 8.4 Observation: KLIC tasks and products.

8.3.2 Task 5.3: Collection of operation reports

This task is of primary importance for the whole phase. Operation reports are the sole source of information for assessing the capability of the KBS to satisfy the requirements for which it was built. *Operation reports* are formal documents that all persons concerned are invited to produce in order to point out malefactions, bugs, errors, problems, requests, suggestions, comments, about the KBS.

Users, domain experts, and managers should be appropriately stimulated to communicate to the maintenance team through operation reports. Any mean should be adopted for this purpose, for example:

- on-line clipboards, for easy note-taking during KBS use;
- on-line mailboxes, for sending messages to the maintenance team during KBS use;
- hotline, typically a toll-free telephone number that users can call to tell the maintenance team about any problem or need concerning the KBS;
- periodic reviews, organized by the leader of the maintenance team to stimulate feedback and critical discussion from the part of the users, domain experts, and managers;
- interviews, held by the leader of the maintenance team to collect comments and suggestions;
- user groups, consisting of individuals who use the same KBS in several installations and sites and get together on a regular basis to discuss problems, analyze possible solutions, and propose new ideas (see section 8.2.2).

The product of task 5.3 is the set of *operation reports*, collected in a given time period. The execution of this task is continued until a meaningful number of operation reports has been collected.

The production of operation reports is generally rather frequent in the first year after a KBS release, and several maintenance interventions are required. In some cases, monthly maintenance may be appropriate in the first year of operational use. In this period, however, only minor problems are generally reported. Later, operation reports tend to become less frequent and to focus on more substantial issues; maintenance interventions are consequently less frequent but more extensive. Extension interventions are not usual during the first two to three years of operational life of a KBS. After this period, some extensions may be appropriate, but sometimes no extension at all is required. Note that quite often in front of new, substantial requirements it may be more appropriate to develop a new KBS to be connected and integrated to the existing one, rather than extending the old system. A modular solution is always to be preferred to a substantial extension, and generally it leads to more effective and less costly results. It does not make sense to keep a KBS alive through costly - and sometimes not fully satisfactory - extensions if it is substantially obsolete and inappropriate for the current requirements. One should always be very careful in initiating a major extension intervention which actually hides a complete re-make of an old KBS.

8.4   INTERVENTION SET-UP

8.4.1   Step execution

Figure 8.5 presents a detailed view of KLIC tasks and products of the 'intervention set-up' step.

8.4.2   Task 5.4: Analysis of operation reports and verification of prerequisites

The goal of this task is to analyze the operation reports collected and to verify whether the prerequisites for a maintenance or extension intervention are satisfied. Task 5.4 takes in input the strategy for maintenance and extension (from task 5.1), the operation reports (from task 5.3), the KBS history (from the previous execution of task 5.17), and the KBS development plan (from the previous execution of task 5.18).

   If prerequisites are not satisfied, no maintenance or extension intervention is initiated, a report is prepared for the management (task 5.5), and the execution of the phase continues with task 5.17. Otherwise, the execution of the phase continues with task 5.6.

8.4.3   Task 5.5: Writing of management report

In the case where prerequisites are not satisfied, the leader of the maintenance team should prepare a report for the management and then continue the execution of the phase with task 5.17. The product of task 5.5 is a document called *management report*. It should present a detailed account of why no maintenance or extension intervention is appropriate.

8.4.4   Task 5.6: Definition of new specifications

The goal of this task is to update the KBS specifications taking into account the new requirements emerging from the operation reports collected. Task 5.6 takes in input the strategy for maintenance and extension (from task 5.1), the operation reports (from task 5.3), the KBS history (from the previous execution of task 5.17), and the KBS development plan (from task 5.18). The product of task 5.6 is a document called *new specifications*, which provides a complete list of the new functional, operational, and technical specifications of the target system.

   The execution of this task is very similar to tasks 1.11, 1.13; 1.14, 1.15, 3.6 and 4.5, even if more limited in scope and generally not as detailed. A thorough account can be found sections 4.5.2, 4.5.3, 4.5.4, 4.5.5, 4.5.6, 4.5.7, 6.5.4, and 7.3.3.

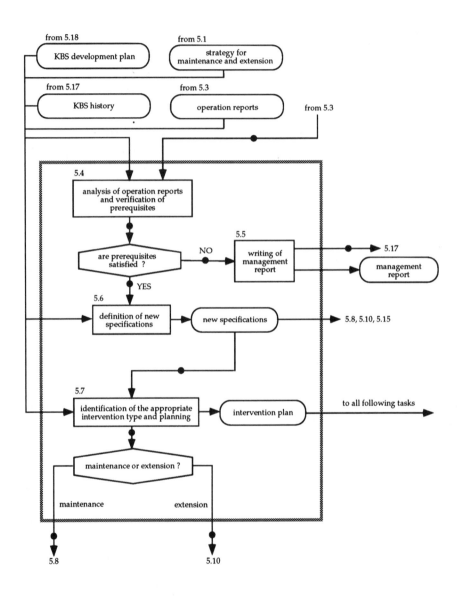

Figure 8.5 Intervention set-up: KLIC tasks and products.

8.4.5   Task 5.7: Identification of the appropriate intervention type and planning

This task identifies the appropriate type of intervention - namely , maintenance or extension - and plans it. Task 5.7 takes in input the strategy for maintenance and extension (from task 5.1), the operation reports (from task 5.3), the KBS history (from the previous execution of task 5.17), and the KBS development plan (from task 5.18). The product of task 5.7 is a document called *intervention plan*.

The intervention plan should be discussed with all members of the project team, who should understand the importance of their role and of their engagements. It should also be formally approved by the management of the end-user organization. Note that, as shown in Figure 8.5, the intervention plan is not an input to any specific task. It will be used by the project leader for management and control issues throughout the whole phase (see section 10.3.2).

The intervention plan should be refined when, during the development of phase 5, new information is made available for a more precise and realistic definition and scheduling of the activities to carry out. Actually, a revision of the plan is probably appropriate just after the beginning of tasks 5.8 and 5.10.

The execution of phase 5 continues with task 5.8 if a maintenance intervention has been identified or with task 5.10 if an extension intervention is necessary.

8.5   MAINTENANCE

8.5.1   Step execution

Figure 8.6 presents a detailed view of KLIC tasks and products of the 'maintenance' step.

This step is very similar to that dedicated to the development of the knowledge base for the KBS prototype (phase 3), even if carried out in a more focused and limited way. The tasks of this step are, therefore, only briefly illustrated; a more detailed analysis can be found in the description of the corresponding tasks of phase 3.

8.5.2   Task 5.8: Revision of the knowledge base

Task 5.8 takes in input the target sytem and the maintenance support system (from task 4.16 or 5.12) and new specifications (from task 5.6). The product of task 5.8 is a software system, namely the *new version of the knowledge base*.

The execution of this task is very similar to tasks 3.15, 3.16, 3.17, 3.18, and 3.19, even if more limited in scope and generally not as detailed. A thorough account can be found in sections 6.8.2, 6.8.3, 6.8.5, 6.8.6, 6.8.7.

If during the execution of this task the need for a revision of the target system arises, the phase continues with an extension intervention (task 5.10), otherwise task 5.9 is executed.

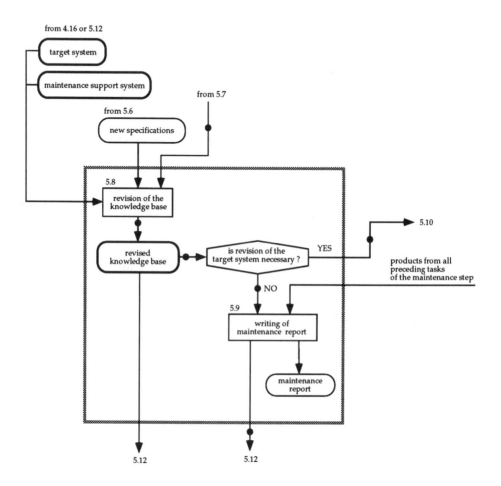

Figure 8.6 Maintenance: KLIC tasks and products.

8.5.3   Task 5.9: Writing of maintenance report

This task is meant to produce a document summarizing the maintenance activities carried out. Task 5.9 takes in input the products of all preceding tasks of the 'maintenance' step. The product of task 5.9 is a document called *maintenance report*, which is directed to the management and to the project team in charge of the following steps of phase 5. The execution of phase 5 continues with task 5.12.

8.6   EXTENSION

8.6.1   Step execution

Figure 8.7 presents a detailed view of KLIC tasks and products of the 'extension' step.

This step is very similar to those dedicated to the conceptual design, the technical design, the construction of the empty system and of the development support system, and the development of the knowledge base for the KBS prototype (phase 3), and the preparation and the production and installation for the target system (phase 4), even if carried out in a more focused and limited way. The tasks of this step are, therefore, only briefly illustrated; a more detailed analysis can be found in the description of corresponding tasks of phases 3 and 4.

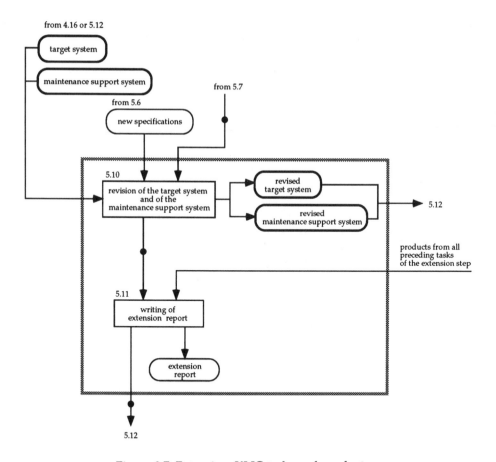

Figure 8.7 Extension: KLIC tasks and products.

8.6.2   Task 5.10: Revision of the target system and of the maintenance support system

Task 5.10 takes in input the new specifications (from task 5.6). The products of task 5.10 are two software systems, namely the *revised target system* and the *revised maintenance support system.*

The execution of this task is very similar to tasks 3.7, 3.11, 3.12, 3.13, 3.14, 3.15, 3.16, 3.17, 3.18, 3.19, 4.6, 4.7, 4.9 (if a major extension is carried out, also 4.8 and 4.10), even if more limited in scope and generally not as detailed. A thorough account can be found in sections 6.6.2, 6.6.6, 6.6.7, 6.7.2, 6.7.3, 6.8.2, 6.8.3, 6.8.4, 6.8.5, 6.8.6, 6.8.7, 7.3.5, 7.3.6, and 7.4.2 (7.3.7 and 7.4.3).

8.6.3   Task 5.11: Writing of extension report

This task is meant to produce a document summarizing the extension activities carried out. Task 5.11 takes in input the products of all preceding tasks of the 'extension' step.

The product of task 5.11 is a document called *extension report,* which is directed to the management and to the project team in charge of the following steps of phase 5.

8.7   RELEASE

8.7.1   Step execution

Figure 8.8 presents a detailed view of KLIC tasks and products of the 'release' step.

This step is very similar to those dedicated to the production and installation, the first release and experimental use, and the final release for the target system (phase 4), even if carried out in a more focused and limited way. The tasks of this step are, therefore, only briefly illustrated; a more detailed analysis can be found in the description of corresponding tasks of phase 4.

8.7.2   Task 5.12: Installation, field testing, and refinement

Task 5.12 takes in input the revised the knowledge base (from task 5.8), the revised target system and the revised maintenance support system (from task 5.10). The products of task 5.12 are two software system, namely the *new version of the target system* and the *new version of the maintenance support system.*

The execution of this task is very similar to tasks 4.11 and 4.12, even if more limited in scope and generally not as detailed. A thorough account can be found in sections 7.4.4 and 7.4.5.

8.7.3   Task 5.13: Updating of manuals

Task 5.13 takes in input the manuals (from task 4.7 or from the previous execution of task 5.13) and the new version of the target system and new version of the maintenance support system (from task 5.12). The product of task 5.13 is a document called *new version of manuals*, which contains the updated versions of user, maintenance, and technical manuals.

The execution of this task is very similar to tasks 4.13 and 4.17, even if more limited in scope and generally not as detailed. A thorough account can be found in sections 7.5.2 and 7.6.3.

8.7.4   Task 5.14: Training of users and of the maintenance team

Task 5.14 takes in input the new version of the target system and new version of the maintenance support system (from task 5.12) and the updated manuals (from task 5.13). The product of task 5.14 is a document called *user and maintenance team training report*, which provides an account of the training activities carried out.

The execution of this task is very similar to tasks 4.14 and 5.2, even if more limited in scope and generally not as detailed. A thorough account can be found in sections 7.5.3 and 8.2.4.

8.7.5   Task 5.15: Certification and acceptance

Task 5.15 takes in input the new specifications (from task 5.6), the final new version of the target system and new version of the maintenance support system (from task 5.12) and the updated manuals (from task 5.13). The product of task 5.15 is a document called *certification and acceptance report*.

The execution of this task is very similar to task 4.18, even if more limited in scope and generally not as detailed. A thorough account can be found in section 7.6.4.

8.7.6   Task 5.16: Release

Task 5.16 takes in input the new version of the target system and new version of the maintenance support system (from task 5.12), and the updated manuals (from task 5.13). The product of task 5.16 is a document called *release report*.

The execution of this task is very similar to task 4.19, even if more limited in scope and generally not as detailed. A thorough account can be found in section 7.6.5.

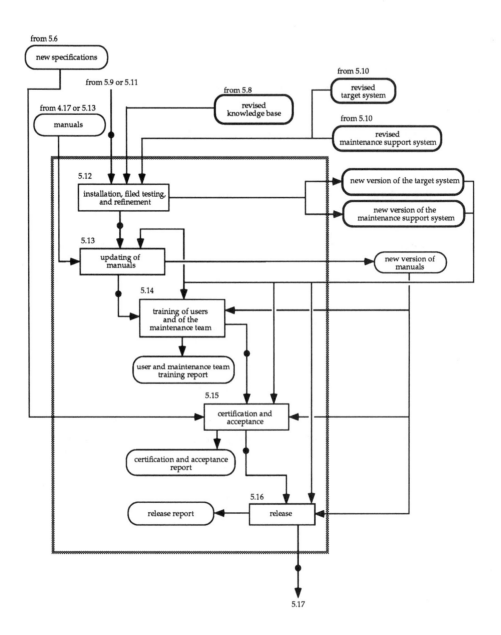

Figure 8.8 Release: KLIC tasks and products.

8.8 INTERVENTION CLOSING

8.8.1 Step execution

Figure 8.9 presents a detailed view of KLIC tasks and products of the 'intervention closing' step.

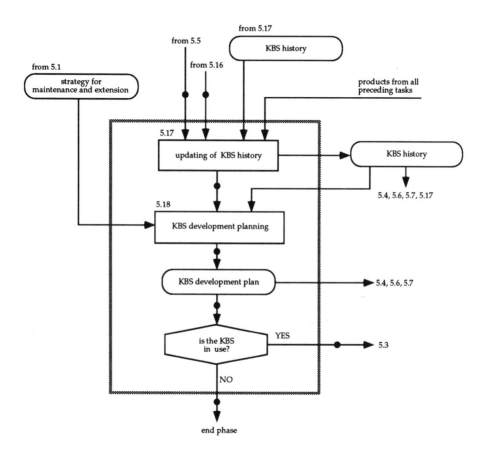

Figure 8.9 Intervention closing: KLIC tasks and products.

8.8.2 Task 5.17: Updating of KBS history

The *KBS history* is a log-book which contains a detailed and complete record of the main events which characterize the operational life of the KBS. In particular, it includes the following points:

- the strategy for maintenance and extension, defined at the beginning of the operational life (task 5.1);
- the operation reports collected (task 5.3);
- the management reports prepared in the case an inappropriate potential intervention is not carried out (task 5.5);
- the history of the evolution of KBS specifications (task 5.6);
- the maintenance reports (task 5.9);
- the extension reports (task 5.11);
- the main aspects concerning the release of the new versions of the KBS (tasks 5.12, 5.13, 5.14, 5.15, and 5.16).

It is important to keep track of the KBS history for a correct and effective management of the whole operational life of a KBS.

Task 5.17 takes in input the KBS history (from the previous execution of task 5.17) and the products of all preceding tasks. The product of task 5.17 is a document called *KBS history*.

8.8.3   Task 5.18: KBS development planning

The goal of this task is to periodically assess the global state of the KBS and to plan its future development.

The state of health of a KBS gradually changes during the operational life due to the maintenance and extensions interventions carried out and the modifications taken place in the target environment. A KBS can reasonably undergo several maintenance and some extension interventions, but cannot be arbitrarily modified to satisfy any new specification. The actual extent to which a KBS can be maintained and extended is initially determined by its design and by the way it has been developed (see section 6.3.4), and tends to rapidly decrease as more and more interventions are carried out. Trying to force maintenance or extension interventions beyond the limits permitted by the KBS in a given moment of its operational life may cause very serious problems to the global state of the system. Ultimately, this may cause an irreparable damage. Assessing the state of a KBS is therefore of primary importance for a correct management of its operational life and, in particular, for effectively planning the remaining part of its life.

Development planning concerns two issues:
- the identification of the goals and constraints that should be taken into account in managing future maintenance and extension interventions;
- the planning of the main stages of the future operational life of a KBS, with specific attention to the approach of the final point of the operational life of the KBS.

As far as the end-point of the KBS is concerned, at least three aspects should be taken into account:
- towards the end of the operational life of a KBS, maintenance and extension costs tend to increase, and - at the same time - the benefits obtainable tend to

decrease; one should not try to exploit a KBS beyond the point where costs exceed benefits;

- sometimes, the end of a KBS approaches very fast and unexpectedly, for example as a consequence of a change in the target environment; one should try to forecast the final point of a KBS very carefully so its substitution can be prepared in time;
- when a KBS is withdrawn from operational use, it is generally still a technically valid and well-performing tool; the reason that determines its withdrawal is a poor matching with the requirements of the users and of the target environment, not a loss of intrinsic technical value; if the final point of a KBS is carefully forecast and its substitution appropriately planned and managed, the KBS can often be resold or employed in other application contexts, thus providing some additional benefits (end benefits, see section 4.6.7) mostly monetary in nature and sometime actually interesting.

Task 5.18 takes in input the KBS history (from task 5.17) and the strategy for KBS maintenance and extension (from task 5.1). The product of task 5.18 is a document called *KBS development plan*.

If the KBS is still in use, the execution of phase 5 continues with task 5.3.

PART V

THE SUPPORTING PROCESSES

9

SUPPORTING PROCESSES

9.1   THE ROLE OF SUPPORTING PROCESSES

Supporting processes have a primary role for the success and the quality of a KBS project. These span the whole KBS project and concern general technical issues relevant to the production processes and to the product being developed. Supporting processes involve several tasks which are distributed over the entire KBS life cycle.

A supporting process is a continuous path through the life cycle, and its management requires constant attention by the project leader.

The three fundamental supporting processes deserving attention in a KBS project are:
* quality assurance;
* verification and validation;
* documentation.

These issues are dealt with in the next sections of this chapter.

9.2   QUALITY ASSURANCE

9.2.1   Basic concepts

Quality may be defined as the totality of features and characteristics of a KBS that relate to its ability to satisfy stated or implied needs [ISO 8402 86]. Quality may concern functional, operational, and technical features of a KBS pertaining its external behavior and overall performance, but also more substantial internal characteristics concerning the design and the construction. *Quality assurance* is a fundamental aspect of KBS project management and implements the quality policy

of the organization in charge of KBS development (generally the KBS department) [Meseguer and Plaza 92]. Quality assurance is a specific duty of the project leader. The issue of quality assurance involves four fundamental aspects, namely:
1. scope: What to control?
2. planning: When to control?
3. execution: How to perform quality control?
4. recording: How to structure and manage quality control records?

These issues are dealt with in some detail in the following sections.

When dealing with quality assurance it is necessary to mention the ISO 9000 standard which represents the basic general reference for quality management. This standard can cover any quality management system in any industry, so it needs to be carefully interpreted for the KBS industry [Ould 90]. For the interested readers, the relevant documents are: [ISO 8402 86], [ISO 9000 87], [ISO 9000-2 93], [ISO 9000-3 91], [ISO 9000-4 93], [ISO 9001 87], [ISO 9002 87], [ISO 9003 87], [ISO 9004 87], [ISO 9004-2 87], [ISO 9004-3 93], [ISO 9004-4 93], [ISO 10011-1 90], [ISO 10011-2 91], and [ISO 10011-3 91] (on several items work is in progress; old documents are being revised, multipart standards are being completed, and new documents are being produced). Specifically relevant to software products is [ISO/IEC 9126 91] (work is in progress to complete this multipart standard: [ISO/IEC CD 9126-1 93], [ISO/IEC CD 9126-6 93]).

An account of the issue of software quality assurance (also including reviews and audits) from the point of view of standards may be found in [IEEE 730 89], [IEEE 983 86], [IEEE 1028 88], [IEEE 610.12 90], [ESA PSS-05-0 91], [ESA PSS-05-11 91] (specific work is in progress also within ISO/IEC, in the frame of the multipart standard [ISO/IEC CD 12207.2 93]); although they specifically concern the production of traditional software, several of the concepts presented in these documents may apply to KBSs as well.

9.2.2   The scope of quality assurance

The objects to focus on in order to assure the quality of a KBS may be divided into four classes:
- the products developed during the KBS life cycle, including:
  - the demonstrator, prototype, and target system, which constitute the main outcome of the KBS life cycle;
  - the technical documents which are the outcome of analysis, modeling, and design activities;
- the primary processes;
- the supporting processes;
- the management process.

Of the items listed above, the first is clearly the most important one and, in a sense, the very object of quality assurance. The other three have a supporting role, and contribute to making quality assurance more effective and reliable [ISO/IEC CD 12207.2 93]. In particular, the assurance of the quality of the KBS is the specific goal of the verification and validation process (see section 9.3). Quality assurance of all other items listed above is, instead, the proper topic of this section. Note that the third item in the list above, namely supporting processes, includes verification and validation, and quality assurance as well.

9.2.3   Planning quality assurance

Quality assurance must be a structured, disciplined, and carefully planned activity. Quality control activities should be defined when project planning occurs (see section 10.3.2) and then it should be regularly executed. Clearly, quality control applies to any life-cycle phase, without exceptions. A *quality control plan* is a document setting out the specific quality control actions relevant to a particular product or process [ISO 8402 86]. A quality control action, called *quality control review*, should indicate in detail the specific item to focus on, the methods, techniques, procedures or practices to apply, the resources to employ, the schedule, and the responsibilities to assume.

Of course quality assurance can only be effective if regular quality control reviews are carried out during the whole life cycle of a KBS. In fact, assuring the quality of a KBS cannot be postponed until completion or delivery. In fact, at the end of the development process, quality control can only be partial, since several quality-relevant aspects concerning intermediate steps of the design and production process can no longer be inspected. In addition, it can only be a yes/no evaluation; if the quality does not conform to the expected standard there is only very little space - if any - to undertake corrective actions.

A quality control plan includes a number of quality control reviews that may vary from case to case. Considering the various objects of quality control, (namely: technical documents, primary processes, supporting processes, and management process) the following criteria may be taken into account in designing a quality control plan:
- technical documents: the final documents of each phase and at least one significant document for each step should always be examined; in complex cases, all main technical documents should be reviewed;
- primary processes: an average number of 1 to 2 reviews for each step is generally appropriate; in complex cases, 2 to 4 reviews may be necessary; of course, reviews are not uniformly distributed among the steps: for example in phase 3, the 'start-up' step may require no review at all, while the 'development of the knowledge base' step may require several periodic reviews;
- supporting processes: 1 to 3 checks for each phase are generally enough;
- management processes: 1 to 3 checks for each phase are generally enough.

Clearly, the above indications are only generic suggestions, that may be used as a starting point for quality assurance planning, but have to be carefully refined case by case and tailored to the specific context at hand. In particular, for specifically critical projects where a very high quality standard is required, the number of quality control reviews may be much higher (even two or three times greater). In any case, it is worth mentioning that whenever a quality control review concludes with a negative assessment, it should be repeated as soon as the corrective actions suggested have been undertaken.

A quality assurance plan must also define the specific quality standards to be adopted in implementing quality control reviews. These standards should express the global quality policy of an organization.

9.2.4   Quality checks and corrective actions

Implementing a quality control review includes two aspects:
- checking the quality of the object considered, to assess its correspondence to a defined quality standard, either chosen by the project leader or requested by the end-user or client organization
- suggesting appropriate corrective actions, in case the quality check identifies unacceptable deviations from the requested quality standard.

A typical quality control review may consist in an organized event at which a particular item (a design, a code module, a knowledge module, a written document, a plan, etc.) is scrutinized by an inspector who looks at it from different perspectives and tries to assess its compliance with a given quality standard. The inspector may be the project leader (except for the case where project management is the specific object of quality control), an external expert or a group of experts, for the most complex and critical cases. Resorting to an external expert for quality control is a very good practice which should be considered at least in all cases where the project leader is not yet fully acquainted with the issue of KBS quality assurance. It might also be very appropriate in the cases where quality assurance is specifically requested by the client or end-user organization. A quality control review should not be totally free and informal, but at best it should be guided by a check-list which states what to check and what to check it against (i.e. the expected quality standard). Clearly, depending on the specific item which is being examined, a different check-list should be considered.

Structured walk-throughs [Yourdon 89] and inspections [Fagan 76], [Fagan 86] are examples of quality control techniques often utilized in software projects. They may provide useful suggestions and ideas also for KBS projects.

9.2.5   Quality control records

All activities done to implement a quality assurance policy should be recorded in a careful and disciplined way. In particular, the documentation of the quality control plan and of the quality control review are the central part of a quality control record. This must be considered as an essential component of quality assurance, not as mere documentation. Generally, it is advisable to record the information relevant to a quality control review in a formal review report, which might specify, for example: the project reference, the item under review, the date, the participants, the problems identified and their severity, the corrective actions suggested, the next review eventually scheduled [Ould 90].

9.3   VERIFICATION AND VALIDATION

9.3.1   Basic concepts

As already discussed in section 9.2.2, the verification and validation process provides a concrete implementation of quality control for assuring the quality of a KBS (a demonstrator, a prototype, or a target system) [Ould 90].

Verification is the process of determining whether a KBS completely satisfies its specifications, while validation is the process of determining whether a KBS satisfactorily performs the real-world tasks for which it was created [Boehm 84], [Ould 90], [ISO/IEC CD 12207.2 93]. In other words, verification is checking that the system is built right, while validation is checking that the right system has been built [Boehm 84]. The former aspect concerns, for example, the quality of the KBS advice and decisions, the correctness of the reasoning techniques used, the quality of human-computer interface, and the KBS efficiency. The latter aspect includes such issues as benefit and utility analysis, cost effectiveness, user acceptance, organizational impact, etc. Therefore, while verification is aimed at measuring a set of technical properties of a KBS, independently of its actual use in a given organization, validation is concerned more with the investigation of the ultimate criterion of success for a KBS application.

Verification focuses on the intrinsic properties of a KBS and on the matching between the KBS and the stated specifications; verification means checking against specifications. Validation is concerned with relations between the KBS and the organization where it is applied. Clearly, this concept of validation is based on the implicit assumption that, despite the fact that detailed and accurate KBS specifications are provided, what the user or the organization actually want lies only in the heads of the people involved. This can hardly be clearly expressed in verbal or formal terms, so the ultimate check is only to put the KBS into practice [Ould 90]. Therefore, the difference between validation and verification originates from the fact that specifications are not a complete and correct interpretation of requirements. Moreover, in KBSs it is often impossible to fully specify the system before implementation begins. Although it is important to specify, as much as possible, the desired KBS behavior at the start of a project, it is often impossible to produce definitive specifications. As illustrated in section 1.2.2, iterative development typical of KBS technology allows changes to be made to specification during prototyping; so verification itself must be understood as an iterative process, which takes place, whenever appropriate, in the context of the current specifications [Berry and Hart 90-b].

Since KBSs are pieces of software, even if of a very particular type, several proposals for KBS verification and validation have been based on the attempt to extend known concepts and techniques of traditional software engineering to the new field of KBSs. However, approaches for verification and validation of traditional software [Adrion et al. 82], [Deutsch 82] (see also [Ramamoorthy and Bastani 82], [Goel 85] and [Musa et al. 87] on the specific issue of reliability) are not completely adequate for KBSs and require substantial modifications and extensions to be put to work [O'Leary et al. 90]. All such proposals have had, therefore, only little success.

Literature proposals for KBS verification and validation are very numerous [Ayel and Laurent 91], [Gupta 91], [Grogono et al. 91], [Guida and Mauri 93], [Preece and Suen 93]. Some of them are mostly informal and qualitative, while others - particularly in the field of verification - rely on more structured, formal, and quantitative methods. Quite often, the methods proposed are specifically designed for a particular KBS application and, therefore, of limited generality. Literature proposals to KBS verification and validation can be divided into three broad classes (se also [Bastani and Chen 93] on the specific issue of reliability):
- knowledge-base oriented approaches, focusing on possible logical problems of knowledge, such as consistency, completeness redundancy, etc.; most of these

approaches deal with production rules, some with propositional logic, and only few with frames and structured objects [Loveland and Valtorta 83], [Suwa et al. 84], [Marek 87], [Cragun and Steudel 87]; [Stachowitz et al. 87], [Ayel, 88], [Ginsberg 88], [Perkins et al. 89], [Preece 89], [Merlevede and Vanthienen 91], [Polat and Guvenir 91], [Jafar and Bahill 93];

- approaches based on evaluation criteria, focusing on the problem of what a KBS evaluation method should measure; these approaches propose long lists of evaluation criteria, which try to grasp the notion of verification and validation through enumeration of their components, including, among others: validity (correctness, quality, accuracy, and completeness of KBS solutions, decisions, advise, etc.), usability (quality of human-computer interaction, transparency, and explanation facilities), reliability (hardware and software reliability, robustness, and sensitivity), effectiveness (costs and benefits involved in solving a task), efficiency (response time, use of computer resources, development time and cost), maintainability and extensibility [Gaschnig et al. 83], [Buchanan and Shortliffe 84], [Yu et al. 84], [Liebowitz 86], [Marcot 87], [Hayes-Roth 89], [Hollnagel 89], [Berry and Hart 90-b], [O'Leary et al. 90], [Meseguer and Plaza 92], [Sharma and Conrath 92], [Guida and Mauri 93];

- approaches based on evaluation methods, focusing on the problems of how and when a KBS should be evaluated; most of these approaches are founded on a concept of KBS life cycle, the major part of them include qualitative empirical evaluations, and some consider also quantitative empirical evaluations [Chandrasekaran 83-a], [Gaschnig et al. 83], [Buchanan and Shortliffe 84], [Yu et al. 84], [Green and Keyes 87], [Marcot 87], [O'Keefe et al. 87], [Geissman and Schultz 88], [Parsaye and Chignell 88], [Levi 89], [O'Keefe and Lee 90], [O'Leary et al. 90], [Preece 90], [Suen et al. 90], [Meseguer and Plaza 92], [Agarwal et al. 93], [Guida and Mauri 93].

Verification and validation play a central role in the development of a KBS. An account of the issue of software verification and validation from the point of view of standards may be found in [IEEE 829 83], [IEEE 1012 86], [IEEE 1008 87], [IEEE 610.12 90], [ESA PSS-05-0 91], [ESA PSS-05-10 91], [ESA PSS-05-11 91] (specific work is in progress also within ISO/IEC, in the frame of the multipart standard [ISO/IEC CD 12207.2 93]) - see also [IEEE 610.12 90], [IEEE 982.1 88] and [IEEE 982.2 88] on the specific issue of reliability; although they specifically concern the production of traditional software, several of the concepts presented in these documents may apply to KBSs as well.

Our approach to verification and validation [Guida and Mauri 93] is illustrated in the following sections.

9.3.2   Verification

In order to implement KBS verification it is necessary to identify what specific features and characteristics of a KBS to verify. First of all, let us note that a KBS features two different aspects:

- the *behavior*, i.e. the external performance it is expected to provide when in operation;

- the *ontology*, i.e. the internal structure (organization and components) which produces the observable behavior.

Our approach to implementing KBS verification is to utilize a taxonomy of attributes, obtained through a top-down decomposition of the concepts of behavior and ontology into (independent) components. Figure 9.1 and 9.2 (a and b) show two taxonomies of possible behavioral and ontological attributes, respectively [McCall et al. 77], [Boehm et al. 78], [ISO/IEC 9126 91], [van Vliet 93], [Guida and Mauri 93].

According to the definition of verification, behavioral attributes can be assessed against the KBS specifications (functional, operational, and technical) explicitly stated during the life cycle. On the other hand, ontological attributes must be assessed against sound and widely recognized design and production principles. These principles are not explicitly stated in the KBS specifications, but their application must be always understood as a tacit requirements.

The evaluation of all behavioral attributes (and also of the correctness of the software components, which is indeed an ontological attribute) can be based on testing (or black–box) techniques, i.e., it relies on the analysis of a series of input/output pairs collected through appropriate experimentation with the KBS using sample test cases. Testing techniques, inspired by the classical Turing test [Turing 50], consist in observing the actual KBS behavior from outside the system, independently of how it is produced by its internal ontology, and in checking it against the desired behavior defined in KBS specifications. Instead, the evaluation of ontological attributes (except the correctness of the software components) can be based on inspection (or glass–box) techniques; i.e., it relies on the direct analysis of the internal structure and content of the KBS (clearly, included the source code). Inspection techniques consist in looking at the internal KBS ontology, and in checking KBS ontology against sound and accepted KBS design and construction principles. Let us now analyze testing and inspection in more detail [Guida and Mauri 93].

In order to clarify the concept of testing, let us first give a formal definition of the objects we are talking about. We assume that the inputs submitted to the KBS (e.g., queries, problems, requests for advice, etc.) and the outputs it provides (e.g., answers, solutions, advice, etc.) can be formalized as elements of an input domain IN and as elements of an output domain OUT, respectively. Thus, we can formalize the desired behavior of the KBS through a *specification function* SPEC: IN --> OUT, which can be derived from KBS specification. The actual behavior of the KBS can be represented by a behavior function BEHA: IN --> OUT. The task of checking a KBS with respect to a given behavioral attribute consists in measuring the value of a suitable distance between BEHA and SPEC, under the specific perspective of that attribute. Therefore, we are faced with the following three issues:

- Defining SPEC. The definition of SPEC is implicitly and informally contained in the KBS specifications; however, making SPEC explicit and formal is usually a complex task which requires a lot of intuition and subjective interpretation. Generally, we must resort to an ideal expert which is supposed to know, for each possible KBS input x, the desired output SPEC(x). Since such an ideal expert usually does not exist, it must be approximated; for example, consulting a number of real experts and combining their answers with some suitable procedure.
- Defining BEHA. This point is obvious, since, for each possible KBS input x, BEHA(x) can be computed by running the KBS itself.

APPROPRIATENESS - what a KBS can do
coverage
the property of a KBS to support a specified representation for a specified domain
scope
the property of a KBS to provide a specified set of functions for specified tasks

CORRECTNESS - how a KBS performs (within the actual coverage and scope)
the property of a KBS to generate results or effects according to specifications

ADEQUACY - how a KBS behaves (within the actual coverage and scope)
robustness
the property of a KBS to maintain a specified level of performance near or outside the borders of its coverage and scope
friendliness
the property of a KBS to support easy, natural and effective interaction and communication with the user
transparency
the property of a KBS to show, justify, and explain its internal mode of operation to the user
learnability
the properties of a KBS that determine the effort required to learn its application
operability
the properties of a KBS that determine the effort required to operate and control it
effectiveness
the property of a KBS to make disciplined, natural, focused, and economic use of the available knowledge in performing a function
time efficiency
the properties of a KBS that determine its response and processing times and its throughput rate in performing a function
resource efficiency
the properties of a KBS that determine the amount of resources used and the duration of such use in performing a function

RELIABILITY (within the actual coverage and scope)
the property of a KBS to avoid unaccounted variance in behavior for a specified time under specified conditions

Figure 9.1 A taxonomy of behavioral attributes.

- Measuring the distance between BEHA and SPEC. This issue involves two separate and complex sub-problems:
  - Firstly, we need to provide a point-to-point definition of distance, i.e. the distance (under the specific perspective of a given behavioral attribute) between SPEC(x) and BEHA(x), for each possible KBS input x. Clearly, this definition cannot be provided in general, depending on the specific features of the application domain dealt with by the KBS. For example, it might be based on a classification of the possible types of errors or deviations, or it might take into account some metrics defined on the output domain OUT.

STRUCTURE
the overall design of a KBS, including: architecture, knowledge representation structures, reasoning algorithms, special-purpose modules, development support system, and maintenance support system
   suitability
   the property of the overall design of a KBS (as defined in the logical model) to naturally and effectively match the features of the application domain
   soundness
   the property of the overall design of a KBS (as defined in the logical model) of being founded on sound, up-to-date, and accepted principles
   specificity
   the property of the detailed design of a KBS to implement the features of the logical model and to exploit the characteristics of the development environment
   extensibility
   the properties that determine the effort required to modify any part or aspect of the overall design of a KBS

SOFTWARE COMPONENTS
the software programs implementing the KBS (empty system, development support system, and maintenance support system)
   correctness
   the extent to which a program performs the intended functions
   testability
   the properties of a program that determine the effort required to ensure that it performs the intended functions
   maintainability
   the properties of a program that determine the effort required to locate and fix an error
   modifiability
   the properties of a program that determine the effort required to modify it
   portability
   the properties of a program that determine the effort required to transfer it from one hardware platform or software environment to another
   re-usability
   the extent to which a program (or parts thereof) can be re-used in other applications
   interoperability
   the properties of a program that determine the effort required to couple it to other systems

Figure 9.2 A taxonomy of ontological attributes - a.

- Secondly, we have to compute the global distance between the functions SPEC and BEHA from point-to-point distance values. Obviously, an exhaustive procedure, which computes the point-to-point distance for all x, is unfeasible, and, hence, we can only estimate it on the basis of a suitable (finite) sub-set of values, resorting to statistical techniques. This makes it possible to estimate, within a defined confidence interval, the probability that (for a given probability distribution of the inputs) the distance between BEHA(x) and SPEC(x) assumes specific values of interest (for example, in the simplest case, that BEHA(x) = SPEC(x)).

KNOWLEDGE-BASE CONTENT
the knowledge actually stored in the knowledge base of a KBS
    consistency
    the property of the knowledge base of being free from logical inconsistencies
    conciseness
    the property of the knowledge base of being free from useless objects
    validity
    the property of the knowledge base of representing faithfully the real knowledge in
    the specific application domain considered
    completeness
    the property of the knowledge base of containing sufficient knowledge to produce the
    intended behavior (within the actual coverage and scope)
    maintainability
    the properties of the knowledge base that determine the effort required to modify or
    extend it

Figure 9.2 A taxonomy of ontological attributes - b.

Turning now to inspection, we can note that it encompasses three types of substantially different activities which apply to different components of ontology:

- *examination* by an ideal designer and (subjective) assessment of the relevant attributes on the basis of sound and widely recognized design and production principles; examination applies to all the attributes concerning structure and software components (except correctness), and also to maintainability of knowledge-base content;
- *checking* through appropriate (computer-based) procedures and algorithmic (objective) assessment of the relevant attributes; checking applies to consistency and conciseness of knowledge-base content;
- *probing* by an ideal expert and (subjective) assessment of the relevant attributes by comparing represented knowledge against real domain knowledge and taking into account the desired coverage and scope of the KBS; probing applies to validity and completeness of knowledge-base content.

In our approach KBS verification is carried out in specific life-cycle tasks. More precisely, the tasks where verification takes place and the related verification activities are shown in Figure 9.3 (the labels TE, EX, CK, and PR denote the various types of verification activities, namely: testing, examination, checking, and probing).

9.3.3   Validation

In order to implement KBS validation it is necessary to identify what specific features and characteristics of a KBS to validate. Our approach includes two aspects, namely technical validation and social validation. These are illustrated in detail below [Sharma and Conrath 92].

Technical validation is concerned with the evaluation of the KBS considered as a technological product. It applies to the complete set of behavioral attributes defined in Figure 9.3 (clearly, it does not apply to the ontological attributes, that concern the internal structure and content of the KBS). However, while in the case of verification they are assessed against KBS specifications, now they must be evaluated taking into account the actual user requirements, as they are concretely perceived at the moment validation takes place.

Phase 2 - Construction of the demonstrator
2.10	implementation of the empty system	TE, EX
2.11	implementation of the development support system	TE, EX
2.15	knowledge integration and verification	TE, EX, CK, PR

Phase 3 - Development of the prototype
3.13	implementation of the empty system	TE, EX
3.14	implementation of the development support system	TE, EX
3.19	knowledge integration and verification	TE, EX, CK, PR
3.20	prototype testing and refinement	TE

Phase 4 - Implementation, installation, and delivery of the target system
4.9	production of the target system and of the maintenance support system	TE, EX
4.12	field testing and refinement	TE, EX, CK, PR
4.15	first release and experimental use	TE
4.16	refinement of the target system and of the maintenance support system	TE, EX, CK, PR

Phase 5 - Maintenance and extension
5.8	revision of the knowledge base	TE, EX, CK, PR
5.10	revision of the target system and of the maintenance support system	TE, EX, CK, PR
5.12	installation, field testing, and refinement	TE, EX, CK, PR

Figure 9.3 Verification activities.

Social validation is concerned with the validation of the KBS considered as a component of an organization, as a tool to perform a certain task and achieve precise goals [Emery and Trist 78], [Sharma et al. 91]. Therefore, it deals with the assessment of a KBS in relation to the global environment where it is applied, from a multiple-perspective point of view and involving the various types of people concerned (users, domain experts, and managers). A taxonomy of possible social attributes to take into account in social validation is shown in Figure 9.4 (a and b) [O'Leary and Turban 87], [Sharma and Conrath 92].

KBS validation generally involves informal qualitative methods. Technical validation can be based on testing techniques, while social validation relies on specific analysis techniques that strictly depend on the nature of the attributes considered (economical, organizational, physiological, sociological, etc.) [Berry and Hart 90-b], [Preece 90].

In our approach KBS validation is carried out in specific life- le tasks. More precisely, the tasks where verification takes place and the related val.   on activities are shown in Figure 9.5 (the labels TEC and SOC denote technical and social validation respectively).

TASK PERFORMANCE

the aspects concerning the matching between the KBS capabilities and the tasks it must perform

utility

the significance of the KBS with respect to the tasks for which it was developed

confidence

the level of confidence of the users in the problem-solving performance of the KBS

WORK REDISIGN

the aspects concerning the impact of the KBS on the resultant nature of work

novelty

the extent to which the KBS brings about new ideas, approaches, methods, and techniques

simplification

the level of reductions in the complexity of routine tasks brought about by the KBS

QUALITY OF WORK LIFE

the aspects concerning the impact of the KBS on the people (users, domain experts, and managers)

stimulation

the variety, challenge, autonomy, and recognition in the work content arising from using the KBS

relief

the extent to which the KBS brings about reductions to the workload and stress in the work lives of users

non-threatening

the extent to which the KBS is not detrimental to the people affected by it

rationalization

the extent to which the KBS makes it possible to organize, structure, and consolidate the individual experience of domain experts into a consistent body of knowledge

upgrade

the extent to which the KBS frees domain experts from routine tasks, giving them the opportunity to concentrate on areas of professional interest that they otherwise would not have had the time to pursue

informedness

the extent to which the KBS supports easy access and effective use of large bodies of knowledge for decision makers and managers

---

Figure 9.4 A taxonomy of social attributes - a.

ORGANIZATIONAL FIT
the aspects concerning the changes brought by the KBS to the organizational structure
  standardization
  the degree to which the problem-solving activity supported by the KBS is formalized
  and standardized
  education
  the level of training that results as a consequence of utilizing the KBS
  adaptiveness
  the extent to which the adoption of the KBS enables the organization to keep up with
  changes
  agreement
  the extent to which the use of the KBS brings about rationality and consensus in
  problem solving
  innovation
  the extent to which the KBS establishes an innovation corporate culture and public
  image of the organization

ECONOMIC BENEFITS
the aspects concerning the effects of the KBS on the main production processes of the target
organization
  performance
  improvements in the efficiency and effectiveness of the organization brought about by
  the KBS
  return
  the economic value of the totality of benefits obtained with respect to costs
  competitiveness
  the strategic benefit accrued to the organization due to the application of the KBS

Figure 9.4 A taxonomy of social attributes - b.

9.4   DOCUMENTATION

9.4.1   Basic concepts

Documentation records information produced during the KBS life cycle. Clearly, it is
possible to build a KBS without considering documentation at all. This has often
been the case in a number of projects in past years. However, since the life cycle of a
    KBS usually involves several people working over a long period of time, records
of activity are essential.
    Documentation concerns four different classes of objects:
• the life-cycle software products, including: the demonstrator, the prototype, the
  development support system, the target system, the maintenance support system,
  and the new versions of the target system and of the maintenance support system
  developed during KBS operational life;
• the intermediate software products acquired or developed during the life cycle,
  including: the demonstrator basic development environment, the prototype basic

development environment, the target system basic development environment, the demonstrator empty system, the empty system, the demonstrator development support system, the coded knowledge items, the demonstrator knowledge base, the knowledge base, the revised knowledge base, the draft prototype, the draft target system and maintenance support system, the installed target system and maintenance support system, the filed tested and refined target system and maintenance support system, the revised target system, and the revised maintenance support system;
- the primary processes;
- the supporting processes;
- the management process.

Phase 2 - Construction of the demonstrator
2.16	demonstration	TEC, SOC
2.17	evaluation	TEC, SOC

Phase 3 - Development of the prototype
3.21	prototype evaluation	TEC

Phase 4 - Implementation, installation, and delivery of the target system
4.12	field testing and refinement	TEC
4.15	first release and experimental use	TEC, SOC
4.18	certification and acceptance	TEC, SOC

Phase 5 - Maintenance and extension
5.3	collection of operation reports	TEC, SOC
5.4	analysis of operation reports and verification of prerequisites	TEC, SOC
5.12	installation, field testing, and refinement	TEC
5.15	certification and acceptance	TEC, SOC

Figure 9.5 Validation activities.

Let us stress that is very important that documentation is produced and delivered in time. Postponing preparation in order to speed-up other activities may cause serious problems to a project, since the documentation of a product or a process is generally an important input for subsequent tasks. Documentation concerning the target system and its operational use should be carefully updated after delivery whenever appropriate, in order to keep it up-to-date with the changing situation. Updates may consist in additions, deletions, and substitutions, or may require the preparation of entirely new versions. The complete history of documentation updates should be filed for future reference.

As a final remark, let us note that documentation produced should conform to some minimal quality standards, concerning:
- *correctness*, i.e. documentation should provide a faithful and up-to-date representation of the products or processes it describes;

- *consistency*, i.e. documentation should be free from logical conflicts;
- *completeness*, i.e. documentation should include, at the selected level of detail, all the elements of interest, represented in the appropriate way;
- *comprehensibility*, i.e. documentation should be easy to read, clearly organized, explicit, and easy to understand.

An account of the issue of software documentation from the point of view of standards may be found in [IEEE 1063 87]; although it specifically concerns the production of traditional software, some of the concepts presented in this document may apply to KBSs as well.

9.4.2   A pragmatic approach to documentation

Of the four components of documentation defined in section 9.4.1, the first, that is, the documentation of the life-cycle software products, is clearly the most important one and, in a sense, the very object of documentation. In our approach, appropriate documentation for each software system produced results from the collection of the products of the tasks which - directly or indirectly - contribute to its development. In particular,

- for the demonstrator (phase 2): tasks 2.6 , 2.7, 2.8, 2.9, 2.10 , 2.11, 2.12, 2.17;
- for the prototype (phase 3): tasks 3.5, 3.6 , 3.7, 3.8, 3.9, 3.10, 3.11, 3.12, 3.13 , 3.14, 3.16 , 3.20, 3.21;
- for the target system and the maintenance support system (phase 4): tasks 4.5, 4.6, 4.7, 4.9, 4.12, 4.16, 4.18;
- for the new versions of the target system and the maintenance support system (phase 5): tasks 5.6, 5.8, 5.10, 5.12, 5.15.

As far as the documentation of the intermediate software products acquired or developed during the life cycle is concerned, we assume that for each of them an appropriate documentation is produced. This is mostly intended for internal use within the project team or the KBS department.

As far as the documentation of the primary processes is concerned, in our approach, each life-cycle task generally concludes with a written working document. The structured collection of all such documents (apart from the management reports, that pertain to the documentation of the management process, as discussed below) constitute an appropriate documentation of the primary processes.

As far as the documentation of the supporting processes is concerned, we may note that:

- the documentation of the quality assurance process is an integral part of the quality management issue and must conform to the specific quality standards adopted (see section 9.2.5); it is produced during the quality control reviews (see section 9.2.3),
- the documentation of the verification and validation process results from the working documents produced in the specific life-cycle tasks where the verification and validation activities are carried out (see Figures 9.3 and 9.5);
- the documentation of the documentation development process consists of stating the specific standards for defining, producing, organizing, filing, and accessing documentation.

Finally, the documentation of the management process includes the various plans and management reports produced during the KBS life cycle and the specific reports prepared during specific management actions, including: internal and external check-points (see section 10.3.2), project reviews (see section 10.3.3), productivity reviews (see section 10.3.4), management reviews (see section 10.5.1), and auditing (see section 10.5.1).

PART VI

THE MANAGEMENT PROCESSES

10

MANAGING A KNOWLEDGE-BASED SYSTEM PROJECT

10.1   PROJECT MANAGEMENT: OBJECTIVES AND COMPONENTS

Management errors are widely recognized as the first cause of failure of KBS projects. To succeed in the management of a KBS project is not easy. First of all it requires a clear understanding of the practical objectives of the project, and of its long-term goals for the KBS department as well as for the whole organization. A KBS project cannot be managed using the traditional techniques appropriate for managing software development projects [van Vliet 93]. KBS project management must be based on a sound and specific technical background. A KBS project leader must have a wide experience in KBS design and construction, and, in addition, he must have specific management competence and skills.

Listed below are the main objectives of KBS project management, divided into three classes:

performance
- producing a KBS that can meet the stated specifications and quality standards, is correctly installed in the target operational environment, and is concretely and effectively used;

planning and control
- meeting the deadlines stated in the project plan and delivering the relevant products on schedule;
- not exceeding the budget allotted for the project;
- taking any action necessary to avoid waste of time and resources, in the unfortunate case the project runs into some major problem preventing a proper continuation;

human resources
- controlling and enhancing productivity of the project team;
- supporting a sound professional growth of all the members of the project team.

Meeting such objectives is a must for the project leader. Either a positive result is produced, or the project must be stopped as soon as a critical problem which might turn out to be fatal for the success of the project is identified. Clearly, an interrupted project may be restarted, after appropriate redefinition and re-planning, if new conditions for its successful continuation can be guaranteed.

Project management objectives may often compete with each other. A full achievement of some objectives may impose severe constraints on others, and vice versa. For example, the issue of continuing education may contrast the need to keep a low cost profile, or the objective of meeting the stated deadlines may interfere with the goal of quality assurance. Therefore, the project leader must generally find a compromise, which allows all objectives to be met at the most appropriate level for the specific project and context at hand.

An account of the issue of software project management from the point of view of standards may be found in [IEEE 1058.1 87], [IEEE 610.12 90], [ESA PSS-05-0 91], [ESA PSS-05-08 91] (work is in progress also within ISO/IEC, in the frame of the multipart standard [ISO/IEC CD 12207.2 93]). Although specifically concerning the production of traditional software, several of the concepts presented in these documents may apply to KBSs as well.

The management of a KBS project is a multifaceted competence domain, which includes several issues. Its main components are:
- the composition, structure, and organization of the project team;
- the methods for controlling and directing project development;
- the analysis of possible project failures and of their causes;
- the management rules and their successful application.

These issues are dealt with in the next sections of this chapter.

10.2   THE PROJECT TEAM

10.2.1   Professional roles

As already anticipated in the previous chapters, several specific *professional roles* are involved in the design and construction of a KBS over the various life-cycle phases. Moreover, persons taking part in the development of a KBS are not all involved in the activities of the project team in the same way. We may identify three classes of members of a KBS project team, namely:

- the *regular members*, who are specifically in charge of executing the tasks of the life cycle and delivering the relevant products;
- the *supporting members*, who have the basic function of supplying the project team with the information about the organization and the application domain necessary for the execution of the various tasks of the life cycle;
- the *consulting members*, who are expected to bring specific competencies needed in particular contexts.

The usual professional roles involved in KBS development are defined below. These are divided into the three classes introduced above [O'Neill and Morris 89], [Prerau 90].

Regular members include *project leader, knowledge engineers, designers,* and *developers*. Their profile is defined in Figure 10.1 (a, b, and c).

Quite often, a KBS project team also includes some more traditional professional roles, like *software designers* and *programmers*, which are in charge of the production of the traditional software components of the empty system, and system analysts which may support or substitute the knowledge engineers for some specific tasks not strictly bound to knowledge-based technology.

Some comments on the above professional roles may be appropriate. As far as the project leader is concerned, we stress that a specific technical background in knowledge-based technology is a necessary condition for proper management: a KBS project cannot be managed by generic, non-technical management personnel [Cupello and Mishelevich 88]. Technically trained and experienced personnel is needed, with additional proven management skill and appropriate training.

As far as the knowledge engineer is concerned, a key question is whether he should be knowledgeable in the specific problem domain considered or not. While the knowledge engineer should never try to substitute the expert, he should rapidly acquire a sufficient background in the application domain so as to interact with the experts in a competent and effective way. Particular attention should be paid to the selection and training of knowledge engineers, since this role is perhaps the most specific in knowledge-based technology and quite new with respect to software engineering [Clanon 85], [LaFrance 87].

Supporting members include *project manager, managers, domain experts,* and *users*. Their profile is defined in Figure 10.2 (a and b).

Note that even if no specific background is required for the supporting members, this does not mean that becoming a part of a project team is always easy and straightforward. Identifying appropriately the supporting members to involve in a project may often be critical, especially for domain experts and users. Moreover, a dedicated training for all supporting members, different for each class, is appropriate to ensure an effective contribution to the project. Section 11.5.6 deals with this topic.

PROJECT LEADER	
functions	• leads the project team during all life-cycle phases concerning KBS development, and is the sole responsible for the results of the project, both from the technical and the application perspectives • guides the project team through all technical aspects of the project • takes care of organization and general management of the project team • is responsible for the contacts with the project manager and the management in general
background	• computer science (graduate level) • specific, extensive education in knowledge-based technology
experience	• KBS designer (at least 2-3 years) • possibly, assistant to a senior project leader
skills	• has leading skill • is open-minded but aware of target goals • is sensitive to time scales and resources involved in the project • can explain technical topics to non-specialists • is a quick learner in new areas • is able to explain technical decisions and train the less experienced members of the project team • has the ability to foresee potential problems in the KBS development process, both organizational and technical, and is able to act promptly to avoid problems or to minimize their impact

Figure 10.1 Regular members - a.

Consulting members include *specialists, advisors,* and *organization analysts.* Their profile is defined in Figure 10.3.

Let us stress that in all cases where consulting members are utilized, the main point is to engage the most qualified and experienced people available. Note that the most expensive consultant will not always be the best, nor is the most expensive necessarily overpriced.

10.2.2   Project team structure and organization

The composition of a *project team* for each specific life-cycle phase has already been discussed in sections 3.14, 4.1.4, 5.1.4, 6.1.4, 7.1.4, and 8.1.4. Here, we focus on some general aspects concerning the internal structure and organization of a project team. Figure 10.4 illustrates the relationships between the various professional roles which may be present in a project team.

Regular members are denoted by normal rectangular boxes, supporting members by dashed rectangular boxes, and consulting members by rounded ones. Bold lines, from top to bottom, denote the hierarchical and functional dependencies between regular members of the project team, normal lines denote the interfaces between regular members and supporting members, and, finally, dashed lines denote interactions between consulting and regular members.

Several aspects of the schema proposed in Figure 10.4 are worth some attention. First of all, note that even if the project leader generally reports directly to the project manager, he does not depend on him from the functional point of view. In fact, the project leader should be free to organize and manage the project team and the project according to his own principles and methods, being the sole person responsible of the project's progress (due dates, delivered products, use of resources, costs, etc.) and of its final results.

As far as regular members are concerned, the internal structure of the project team is basically hierarchical, even though it also features some characteristics of a matrix organization [van Vliet 93]. The project leader is the center and the top-level of the team: designers and knowledge engineers depend him and report to him only. This allows a unitary and goal-oriented project management, which grants the necessary independence between designers and knowledge engineers. Developers depend on the designers and do not directly interact with the project leader or with the knowledge engineers. The purpose of this centralized structure is to avoid dispersion and free interaction between team members; in fact, t his

KNOWLEDGE ENGINEER	
functions	• is in charge of analyzing and modeling domain knowledge • performs sampling and extensive knowledge acquisition • develops the conceptual model of the application domain • acquires and formalizes knowledge necessary for the construction of the KBS knowledge base • develops the KBS knowledge bases and is the only one responsible for their content and quality • is responsible for contacts with domain experts and users
background	• computer science, or any technical field or some specific non-technical fields such as philosophy, psychology or linguistics (graduate level) • basic education in computer science • basic education in knowledge-based technology • specific education and training in knowledge engineering
skills	• has good communication skills, diplomacy, tact, and sensitivity • is a good listener • has professional maturity • is able to relate to specialists in other areas • has specific analysis, abstraction and synthesis capabilities, in addition to rationality and organization skills • can learn the important concepts of a new application domain quickly • has a good degree of imagination and creativity

Figure 10.1 Regular members - b.

DESIGNER

functions	• makes all fundamental technical choices concerning the design of a KBS • develops the logical model of the empty system • selects the basic development environment for the demonstrator, the prototype, and the target system • develops the detailed design of the empty system and of the support systems
background	• computer science (graduate level) • specific, extensive education in knowledge-based technology
experience	• KBS programmer (3-4 years) • possibly, assistant to a senior KBS designer • specific experience as a knowledge engineer can be a useful addition
skills	• has technical design skills • is fully acquainted and up-to-date with knowledge-based technology • is able to explain technical decisions and can train less experienced members of the project team • can understand the application domain of the project in depth

---

DEVELOPER

functions	• makes all specific technical choices concerning the implementation of a KBS • sets up the development environment and develops the empty system and the support systems • is in charge of installing and maintaining the current versions of the adopted development tools and of updating the development environment
background	• computer science (undergraduate or graduate level) and programming • specific education in knowledge-based technology, knowledge-based programming, and use of KBS development tools
skills	• has a solid understanding of KBS principles • can effectively use a variety of KBS development tools • is able to learn to use new languages and tools quickly • is able to understand technical specifications and design choices and to implement them correctly

Figure 10.1 Regular members - c.

PROJECT MANAGER	
definition	a manager of the organization where the KBS will be employed, officially in charge of representing the organization within the project
functions	• is in charge of monitoring the execution of the KBS project on behalf of the target organization • controls project development, focusing on deliverables, due dates, and costs

MANAGER	
definition	a (top or intermediate) manager of the organization where the KBS will be employed
functions	• is in charge of formally approving all critical decisions about the project, including project goals, project plan, KBS specifications, target system delivery plan, etc. • is responsible for the supporting members, especially domain experts and users, who will contribute to KBS development • is responsible for structuring and organizing the target environment where the KBS will be installed and used

Figure 10.2 Supporting members - a.

proved to be harmful both for productivity and for product quality. The expected cross learning advantage which has often been advocated as a major advantage of a more flexible interaction schema, has seldom been observed in practice. Training on the job and apprenticeship activities must always be carefully planned, and are not the result of random and naive interactions among team members.

According to the concept of a centralized structure proposed above, all consulting members refer only to the project leader. No direct contacts with other members of the project team are allowed. Similarly, domain experts and users directly interact only with the knowledge engineers.

The schema shown in Figure 10.4 may be used as an abstract and general reference to organize the various concrete project team structures appropriate for each specific KBS project, development environment, and application context considered. Quite often the above proposed project team structure is implemented very freely, depending on the availability of personnel, on organizational constraints, and - last but not least - on cost problems. Some of the variations most frequently found in practice are reported and commented below.

DOMAIN EXPERT	
definition	a specialist of the application domain considered, with specific background knowledge and practical experience
functions	• is the main knowledge source about the application domain during all life-cycle phases • takes active part in the definition of requirements and specifications, in sampling and extensive knowledge acquisition, and in verification and validation

USER	
definition	a member of the user community which currently utilizes (user) or is expected to utilize (potential user) the KBS
functions	• is one of the main sources of information about KBS requirements • takes active part in the definition of requirements and specifications, and in verification and validation

Figure 10.2 Supporting members - b.

It is quite usual that no specific professional roles are present in small KBS development groups (two to four technical people), still in a stage of experimentation with the new technology. The technical personnel employed is just divided into senior employees, often with no more than one to two years experience, with the function of project leaders, designer and knowledge engineers, and junior personnel, often novices, with the role of developers. Such a situation may be justified only in a very initial stage of informal familiarization with the knowledge-based technology. As soon as the KBS development group develops into a formal production unit, namely a KBS department, its structure should be upgraded to include at least the three professional roles of developer, knowledge engineer, and designer, with the additional responsibility of the project leader.

In medium-size (5 to 20 technical people) or large (more than 20 technical people) KBS departments, it is quite usual - and indeed good practice - to arrange a separate project team for each specific KBS project. In fact, it has been observed in several cases that the highest level of productivity and quality can be reached by allowing a project team to focus on just one project at a time, instead of carrying on several projects simultaneously. However, some critical problems may arise:

SPECIALIST	
function	• contributes to KBS design with specific competence in particular fields of the knowledge-based technology which are not adequately covered by the available designers and by the project leader
background	• an experienced KBS designer with specific competence in special fields of knowledge-based technology

ADVISOR	
function	• supports the project leader in the most critical steps of project management • supports the project leader in the fundamental aspects of KBS design, especially for complex projects involving applied research or innovative experimentation • contributes to increasing the productivity of the project team and the quality of products • provides technical credibility to the KBS project
background	• an experienced KBS project leader, often with specific competence in basic and applied research • has a good reputation in KBS development, having completed important research related to knowledge-based technology and having been involved in several and important KBS projects

ORGANIZATION ANALYST	
function	• supports the project leader in specific activities requiring particular competence in the science of organization
background	• organization science (graduate level), with specific education in information technology • concrete experience in company organization with specific attention for computer-supported processes • has a good reputation in solving complex organizational problems, especially those related to innovation and technology transfer issues

Figure 10.3 Consulting members.

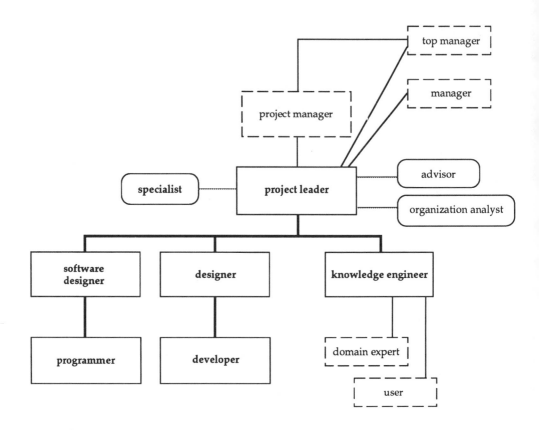

Figure 10.4 Relationships between professional roles.

- people with the necessary professional roles are not always easy to hire, especially knowledge engineers and designers;
- in-house training is long and requires a dedicated investment;
- people already on the job must have the opportunity to gradually progress in their professional career;
- usually, the number of projects a medium-size group is requested to run is larger than the number of complete project teams that it is possible to organize using the available human resources, and, therefore, some form of personnel sharing among the various projects is necessary.

Therefore, it turns out to be quite difficult if not almost impossible to organize a KBS department in separate and complete project teams, each one in charge of one specific phase of a project at a time. An interesting compromise between all the above mentioned needs is sometimes found - with good results - in a hybrid organization, where project teams assigned to a specific project are not complete

and some people with specific professional roles are shared among projects. Three frequent and successfully experimented solutions are:
- Project teams are composed by a project leader, having also the competence of a designer, by a knowledge engineer, and by one or two developers. Additional knowledge engineers and developers are available and can join a project team on request for a limited time period. Designers are shared among all project teams and operate as consultants to the project leader for the relevant tasks of the KBS life cycle.
- Project teams are composed by a project leader, having also the competence of a designer and of a knowledge engineer, and by one or two developers. Additional developers are available and can join a project team on request for a limited time period. Designers and knowledge engineers are shared among all project teams and operate as consultants to the project leader for the relevant tasks of the KBS life cycle.
- Each project leader is in charge of two projects and also has the competence of a designer. In this way, project leaders and designers, which are often the most critical resource in a KBS department, are shared between project teams. Knowledge engineers and developers are assigned to each project team according to actual needs and are not shared.

As a last remark it is worth noting that large KBS project teams are generally very difficult to manage. Expanding a project team may turn out to bring more difficulties than advantages; the increased personnel availability does not necessarily imply an improved productivity or a better quality. Minimal project teams should be preferred. Large project teams can be set up only if there are concrete and specific reasons (time constraints, project complexity or dimension, etc.), and provided that a really competent and skilled project leader is available.

Finally, let us note that regular members, supporting members, and consulting members generally do not belong to the same organization. In fact:
- supporting members are always internal to the end-user organization where the KBS is expected to be used;
- consulting members are external to the organization in charge of a KBS project, and are hired to support specific tasks of the KBS life cycle;
- regular members are internal to the end-user organization if this includes a KBS development group or a more formal KBS department; otherwise, if the execution of a KBS project is assigned to an external supplier, the regular members of the project team belong to the organization in charge of KBS development.

Quite often, however, regular members do not all belong to the organization which develops the KBS, but some of them are hired externally for a specific project. This may be motivated by two different purposes:
- to complete a weak project team, which lacks some specific technical role;
- to provide a quantitative support to an overloaded project team.

In the former case, the talents and experience of individuals are bought externally. External members should stay with a project team for the whole development cycle of a KBS, and should be able and willing to effectively transfer their knowledge and experience to the other members of the team. In the latter case, the personnel hired from outside is made part of the project team and is expected to work together with the regular members. This may help overcome a temporary lack of regular members of the needed professional roles. A good integration and a strict cooperation is however needed in order to achieve concrete results.

10.3   CONTROLLING AND DIRECTING PROJECT DEVELOPMENT

10.3.1   Why, when, and what to control

A KBS project needs appropriate control to progress correctly and effectively. Controlling and directing project development is a fundamental component of success. Of course, control must concern both the primary production processes (life-cycle phases and tasks) and the cross-processes.

To run a KBS project effectively it is necessary that control actions are carried out on a regular basis and that corrective interventions are fulfilled whenever needed. In particular, a constant supervision of the project leader and a frequent assessment of the project status are necessary, in order to identify and tackle problems as early as possible, before they become serious and difficult to recover. Moreover, whenever any problem is identified, a timely intervention is necessary so that the progress of the project is not affected.

The three fundamental issues of project control are:
- controlling that the project follows the plans initially stated, undertaking appropriate re-planning in case major deviations are identified;
- monitoring that the project is kept constantly oriented towards the stated objectives, making sure that unwanted, resource-consuming deviations bring it off the track;
- monitoring the productivity of the project team, so as to ensure that good products with a high quality standard are produced within reasonable time limits and costs;
- controlling that user and management expectations are kept within realistic and concrete limits and are met by the released products.

These topics will be dealt with in the following sections.

10.3.2   Project planning and re-planning

Planning is a crucial issue in the management and control of any project. As far as the primary production processes are concerned, the most appropriate points for planning are naturally at the start-up of a life-cycle phase. In addition, the outcome of the plausibility study leads to a global project plan. Moreover, specific plans may be useful for those phases which include major steps that should be planned separately. According to these criteria, the specific plans considered in the KLIC life cycle are:

- phase 0: opportunity analysis plan;
- phase 1: plausibility study plan, global project plan;
- phase 2: demonstrator plan;
- phase 3: prototype plan, knowledge acquisition plan;
- phase 4: implementation, installation, and delivery of the target system plan,
- phase 5: intervention plan, KBS development plan.

As far as the cross-processes are concerned, they should be planned individually for the entire duration of the KBS project. Especially important is the planning of quality assurance, since it does not rely on specific life-cycle tasks and, therefore, it requires greater care and attention (see section 9.2.3). Planning verification and validation and documentation development may be easily obtained by appropriately considering the life-cycle tasks that implement them (see sections 9.3.2, 9.3.3, and 9.4.2).

A typical plan for a KBS life-cycle phase should include the following:

- definition of the main activities to be carried out;
- detailed agenda of the phase and scheduling of activities (start and finish points);
- prerequisites and inputs needed to start the scheduled activities;
- engagement of the human resources necessary for the execution of the scheduled activities;
- definition of the necessary tools (computer hardware and software, bibliographic materials, background documents, etc.);
- products expected and delivery dates;
- internal and external check-points (see later, this section);
- project reviews (see section 10.3.3);
- productivity reviews (see section 10.3.4);
- quality control reviews (see section 9.2.3);
- management reviews (see section 10.5.1);
- auditing, if appropriate (see section 10.5.1);
- definition of phase budget.

Other types of plans - both for the primary production processes and for the cross-processes) may feature a more flexible structure and should be designed case by case according the exigencies of the specific project at hand.

Planning should always carefully take into account the specific requirements and features of the organization in question.

Generally, a plan may be appropriately organized in a graphical representation, for example using Gantt, PERT (Program Evaluation and Review Technique), or CMP (Critical Path Method) charts [van Vliet 93], or other similar tools tailored to the specific exigencies of the case at hand. This way the relationships between the four main variables of a plan - namely: activities, time, resources, and products - can be easily appreciated.

Finally, let us outline that a KBS plan must also foresee for an appropriate number of *check-points* to ascertain whether the plan is being executed correctly or whether there are unexpected deviations. Check-points may be organized in several ways according to their purpose. *Internal check-points* are aimed at allowing the project leader to assess how the project progresses and usually consist in an informal meeting of the project leader with the members of the project team, possibly including the analysis of written documents and the demonstration of the systems developed. *External check-points* are supposed to show the progress of the project to the project manager, to the management, or to the users. These are of primary importance to achieve management and user involvement and help gain their confidence. The most common forms of external check-points are:
• formal meetings of the project manager with the project leader;
• formal meetings of the management with the project leader, possibly including a presentation and a demonstration;
• illustration of the status of the project in a workshop to which the management, the experts, the users, and the whole project team take part.

Plans must be designed accurately and seriously, and applied with a certain degree of flexibility. Minor deviations should not be overestimated and should not cause a revision of the plan. However, whenever a major deviation of the project development from the plan is identified, the project leader must analyze the situation very carefully and try to identify its causes. Planning may have been inaccurate at the beginning, or unforeseen events may have affected the project. However, major deviations may be symptoms of real problems in the development of the project. With reference to the temporal indications concerning the various phases of the KLIC life cycle given in sections 3.1.3, 4.1.3, 5.1.3, 6.1.3, 7.1.3, and 8.1.3, we can note that, while the data reported are only indicative and should not be regarded as strict constraints, large violations to the values shown should be considered as symptoms of possible problems. For example:
• more than 3 times for percentages less than 10;
• more than 2 times for percentages between 10 and 20;
• more than 1.5 times for percentages larger than 20.

In the case where a delay of time suggests that problems might actually exist, these have to be identified, their causes diagnosed, and appropriate remedies planned and executed. For this purpose, auditing may sometimes be useful - see section 10.5.1. In any case, re-planning may be necessary in front of a major deviation. KBS plans must develop as a project progresses [Greenwell 88]: re-planning must, however, occur only after the causes of a deviation have been identified, and they must always be justified. Of course, re-planning must be strictly limited: only the parts of a plan directly influenced by the identified deviation should be changed, leaving the rest unaltered. Too frequent or too free re-planning is a common project management error; in this way, the effectiveness of planning - and re-planning - is completely lost, and project control becomes a useless overhead.

An account of the issue of software project management plans from the point of view of standards may be found in [IEEE 1058.1 87], [IEEE 610.12 90]. Although specifically concerning the production of traditional software, several of the concepts presented in these documents may apply to KBSs as well.

10.3.3   Goal orientation

A specific and important point in the management of a KBS project concerns the ability of the project leader to constantly control that the activities of the project team are coherent with the defined production goals and that they are closely oriented towards the achievement of the desired results. In fact, it is common experience that, without strict control from the project leader, KBS project teams naturally tend to disperse their efforts in a variety of directions, losing track of the main objectives of the project. The issue of goal orientation mostly concerns the primary production processes, being only marginally related to the cross-processes.

One possible critical aspect related to the issue of goal orientation is the control of experimentation and applied research activities, which may constitute an important component of a KBS project. In fact, quite often the development of a KBS requires that open problems be faced at the frontier of available technology. There is a direct link between research and application in the field of knowledge-based technology; the technology is relatively young and still rapidly expanding, and the application needs are growing fast in search of more and more powerful and sophisticated solutions. This situation may constitute a potential risk for the project, since intermixing KBS development and research may rapidly bring a project out of the planned track. Doing research may be quite appealing for some components of a project team, especially for those without previous experience in the field, who generally see scientific research as highly rewarding job.

In order to keep a KBS project firmly oriented towards its goals, it is generally not appropriate to allow a project team to freely face challenging research issues while developing a real application. The most conservative - and possibly the safest and most recommended - strategy is to strictly keep to the following procedure:
1.   as soon as a frontier problem is identified in a KBS project, the project leader should immediately and personally take care of it;
2.   the designers should be invited to temporarily freeze the critical issue found and wait for an appropriate solution to be offered to them by the project leader;
3.   the project leader should first resort to the assistance of an expert advisor in order to quickly assess the complexity of the problem encountered and realize the possible availability of advanced techniques or research results which might be used for its solution;
4.   in the case some appropriate technique is found, it may be transferred to the designers, who will tailor them to the case at hand, experiment with the

new approach developed, and, finally, apply it to the solution of the problem identified;

5.   otherwise, if a substantial amount of new research is deemed necessary, the project leader should first try to revise KBS specifications in order to eliminate the problem encountered.

This procedure tends to eliminate, as far as possible, research activities from the main track of a KBS life cycle. This strategy does not imply that applied research and innovative experimentation are excluded from the tasks of a KBS department. Simply, applied research and innovative experimentation must be kept separate from production, since they have different objectives and are developed according to different methods.

Regular *project reviews* can keep the project team firmly oriented towards sound productivity goals. These can assess the progress of a project with respect to its goals, identify possible deviations, analyze their causes, and prescribe appropriate remedies. Note that while check-points (see section 10.3.2) are concerned with comparing the execution of a project with its schedule, i.e. determining whether the plan is correctly executed, project reviews are concerned with comparing the execution of a project with its goals, i.e. determining whether the plan was right. Clearly, a project review may lead to revise the project plan.

Project reviews should be defined at the planning stage and then regularly executed. Resorting to an external advisor for a project review is very good practice and should be considered at least in all cases where the project leader does not have the needed experience and seniority.

10.3.4   Productivity

An important point in the development of a KBS project is having constant control over the *productivity* of the project team, intended as the capability of producing good products with a high quality standard, within reasonable time limits and costs.

In practice, productivity entails the ability of a project team to accomplish the various tasks it is in charge of in the shortest possible time, ensuring, however, that the products satisfy all stated specifications and conform to the requested quality standards. The issue of productivity, therefore, concerns both the primary production processes and the cross-processes.

Assessing and improving productivity is an important aspect of project management. This task is a specific duty of the project leader and turns out to be of utmost importance in the long-term. A very usual way to monitor productivity is to use *performance control forms*. For each specific job - usually a task or a limited group of interrelated tasks, a performance control form is designed so that all data relevant to productivity can be recorded; for example, description of the specific piece of work done (in terms of goals, inputs, expected results, outputs, etc.), total time spent, type of engagement on the job (full time, part time, etc.), critical technical points faced, time-critical events possibly occurred, organizational aspects, etc. During *productivity reviews* held regularly (monthly or bi-monthly), the project leader discusses with the relevant personnel the performance control forms.

Let us stress that productivity is sometimes perceived as potentially detrimental to the quality of the products developed. A strong emphasis on the productivity issue might push the personnel to work faster but worse. This risk can easily be avoided if productivity checks are appropriately intermixed with quality control reviews, thus ensuring that the project team has a correct and balanced perception of what is expected. Productivity and quality are clearly strictly interrelated. In practice, it is generally observed that either both of them are satisfactory or neither is. In particular, low productivity often means low quality; this may be a symptom of some serious problem in project management or a scarce mastery of the technology.

10.3.5   User and management satisfaction

One last important point which falls within the main duties of the project leader is the handling of user and management expectations. Especially during the execution of a long project, the management and the users should be kept constantly informed about the progress of the project and the obtained results. One cannot leave them outside the project for months and then expect the final result to be understood, accepted, and appreciated.

Generally, the management should be regularly informed on a periodic basis (for example, every three months for a two-year project) through specific *management reports* where the main results obtained are shown and the most important outcomes of the project illustrated. In addition to the management reports explicitly foreseen in the life-cycle tasks, several others should be planned. For example, monthly or bi-monthly reports or step-reports at the conclusion of each life-cycle step might be appropriate. Moreover, at least one or two times during the development of the central life-cycle phases (namely: phases 3, 4, and 5), the management should be invited to attend specific demonstrations or presentations about the KBS being developed, so as to be aware of what is happening. Management information has the following goals:
- getting management approval for the work done;
- collecting management reactions, requests, and suggestions;
- favoring a personal involvement of the managers in the project;
- assuring a continuous support of management to the project;
- keeping management expectations concretely bound to the real performance the KBS will be capable of providing.

The users should be concretely involved in a KBS project. They play an important role in several tasks of KBS life cycle and have an active part in the project team. Therefore, their correct and effective involvement should be a natural outcome of the adoption of a sound development methodology.

However, user involvement is quite often an underestimated point. In some projects, after the first contacts with the users for the definition of functional specifications during plausibility study, they are left completely outside the project until the time of KBS installation and release approaches. The project leader who is aware of this risk should make sure that users are concretely and appropriately involved in the life cycle tasks; that information on the project's progress is given; that the organizational and structural modifications to be applied to the target environment before KBS release have user involvement; that comments, suggestions and, reactions of the users are considered.

10.4   FAILURE TYPES AND CAUSES

10.4.1   How knowledge-based system projects fail

Experience in KBS project management shows that some projects succeed while others fail. While the causes of some failures are evident to everybody, others are more subtle and can be recognized only by an expert. Five main types of failures of a KBS project can be identified:

- a *basic failure*, when the project ends up in a dead-end path and is eventually stopped; in this case, in front of resources and time spent for the project, no concrete result is obtained and, more frequently, also a global negative evaluation of the knowledge-based technology follows;
- a *primary failure*, when the project comes to an end, but the KBS, while succeeding to some degree, fails to meet some substantial specifications leaving some important goals unachieved; in this case, there is generally no viable possibility to refine and complete the system according to specifications and the result obtained turns out to be definitely useless; like basic failures, primary failures may often be a real disaster;
- a *secondary failure*, when the KBS can meet almost all specifications, but nevertheless important user requirements are not satisfied; in this case, which is often due to insufficient user involvement, it is sometimes possible to identify, design, and implement the appropriate modifications necessary to ensure a better matching with user requirements;
- a *quality failure*, when a project succeeds in producing the expected KBS, but its quality is below the expected level; quality failures can never be recovered, they may have dramatic effects on the possibility to maintain and extend a KBS during its operational life, whose extent is often greatly reduced;
- a *cost and time failure*, when a project succeeds in producing the expected KBS, but its costs or its duration do not conform to those that one might expect from a well-managed project.

Basic and primary failures are immediately visible to everybody. Secondary failures are less explicit; they usually become apparent after some period of operational use of the KBS, when the users refuse to adopt the new system as a routine working tool. Quality failures are not apparent at all at the moment a

KBS is released; they need a specific and generally difficult investigation to be identified or may become apparent later, at the moment of maintenance or extension. Cost and time failures are also often not clearly visible in a KBS project; they need careful examination to be identified.

Experience shows that for every failure there is always a management error. The responsibility of the failure is always of the project leader. Finding out management rules to be followed to ensure success can only be based on a diagnosis of past cases, tracing the failures to their causes, and attempting to derive rules of general validity from a collection of cases. Generally, rules for managing a KBS project are relatively simple to state and understand, but not easily applicable in the specific context where one is working. Management rules - and not only for the case of knowledge-based technology - seem obvious and straightforward at first glance, but are frequently and easily violated in practice. The effects of their violation become apparent only much later in the project, and quite often it is then too costly or too late to fix the problem.

There may be a variety of causes of failure for a KBS project: a serious failure, however, is always due to some fatal error. A *fatal error* is either a major error or a set of several minor ones. Violating management rules is much like a threshold problem. If violations are only a few and of marginal importance, the project will proceed well and safely. But, if several violations - or a few critical ones - occur, then their effect will result in a major problem for the project. Management rules can help avoid fatal errors, but cannot ensure success.

10.4.2   Why knowledge-based system projects fail

Investigating the causes of KBS project failures is not an easy task. While successful stories are often made of public domain and widely illustrated and commented in the literature, failures are not advertised. However, failures are much more frequent than success.

Before examining how to manage a project to be a success, it might be instructive to review some of the main causes of failure reported in the literature [Bell 85], [Keyes 89], [Prerau 90], [Hillmer et al.91] and observed in the professional practice. This may help avoid some fatal errors already experienced by others.

Below a list of the major causes of failure is reported:
- lacking management support; the management must see the benefits of the project and provide all the support necessary for the project to catch on, to grow, and to produce successful results;
- setting objectives too high; a KBS project should never face issues beyond the concrete needs of the users, or exceed the potentials of knowledge-based technology or the capabilities of the available project team;
- underestimating user involvement; a KBS must first of all serve concrete user needs, this cannot be achieved without the appropriate involvement of the users in all relevant steps of KBS life cycle;
- underestimating operational and organizational issues, thus failing to produce a usable application;

- lacking competent, available, and cooperative domain experts; domain experts are the main source of knowledge in any KBS project; without domain experts a KBS can simply not be constructed;
- lacking the proper technical personnel; KBS design and construction is a serious job which must be faced with competent and experienced human resources; a weak project team always leads to a failure;
- using inappropriate tools, thus making design more complex and development less effective, and also spoiling the quality of the final result;
- involving too many domain experts, not really necessary for the development of the KBS; this may make the knowledge acquisition process longer and more costly, and may hinder the quality of the knowledge base;
- being unable to guide the project towards a concrete and satisfactory goal; a KBS project must be concluded within the scheduled deadline and produce a system which can fulfill the major part of stated specifications;
- underestimating the maintenance and extension issues, thus failing to deliver an application which can be profitably exploited over time; a system which cannot be maintained easily and effectively is destined to go rapidly out of use, therefore jeopardizing the return of investment.

As a final remark, let us point out that most of the causes of failure mentioned above are rooted in a scarce sensibility to risk and, consequently, in an inappropriate risk management. Typical causes of failure should be considered as potential risk factors and deserve specific attention. They should be analyzed in detail and their evolution over time carefully monitored.

10.5   MANAGEMENT FOR SUCCESS

10.5.1   Management rules

Providing a coherent set of management rules has been an important issue for several years. In the literature various proposals can be found. For example we mention the *triple C rule* proposed by [Badiru 88], which states that the key to successful development of KBSs is Communication, Cooperation, and Coordination, or the *four C's rule* proposed by [Sacerdoti 91], as stated below:
1. Be Copernican: always remember the KBS is not in the center of the universe. It is subordinate to other software systems, to the existing work practices, and to the skills and interests of your users.
2. Be Conservative: KBSs are riskier than conventional systems. Organize your project to reduce risk as early as possible.
3. Be Conventional: at the end of the project your happy users will probably believe you succeeded despite the use of knowledge-based technology, not because of it. Use conventional techniques wherever there is not a good reason to use knowledge-based techniques.
4. Be Confident: thousands of people have managed KBS projects to success. If you follow their advice, you are likely to succeed, too.

Providing a coherent set of management rules of general validity is a difficult task. Individual experience in project management are varied. Difficulties perceived by a project leader are unobserved by others and, more importantly, solutions successfully experimented in a context may not work in others. Thus, the list of management rules tends to grow continuously, in order to cover all cases and all possible situations. Therefore, the more management rules become detailed and refined, the more their application becomes difficult. Having management rules may help, but it also creates the new problem of applying them. So, a primary requirement for useful management rules is that they be clear and simple. Moreover, the issue of having the right rules and applying them correctly should not be overestimated: management is not the goal of a project, but only a way to reach the project goals more effectively.

According to the basic principles inspiring all our approach to KBS life cycle and development methodology and taking into account that good managers are principally good risk managers [Boehm 91], correct and effective management can be based on just one rule "*Avoid fatal errors*". Possible fatal errors, defined in section 10.4.1, are reasonably easy to list; consider, for example, the errors behind the ten major causes of failure listed in section 10.4.2. The main point is the difficulty to identify them in concrete contexts. Effective application of the above rule requires to constantly keep attention focused on checking for possible fatal errors, recognizing their possible occurrence as early as possible, before their effects become harmful. In fact, it is a common experience of several KBS professionals that some common and well-known errors which are more frequent than others are nevertheless continuously repeated in different projects by different people.

Therefore, the application of the rule stated above should not be left to common sense and personal intuition [Drucker 66], [Drucker 74], [Kerzner and Thamhain 84], [Cleland and Kerzner 86], [Drucker 86], [Blanchard and Johnson 87], [Meyer and Curley 89], [Barsanti 90]. Two specific methods can be adopted. These are illustrated below.

First of all, *management reviews* intended to assess the correctness and effectiveness of the current management practice, may offer a very appropriate support for self checking, for keeping attention focused on potential risks, and for detecting possible management errors early. Management reviews should be planned at the beginning of each phase of the KBS life cycle and then regularly executed. For example, 4 to 5 check-points for phase 1, 2 to 3 for phase 2, 5 to 10 for phase 3, and 2 to 3 for phase 4, could be appropriate for a KBS project of medium complexity. Each review should be based on a formal check-list prepared by the project leader, and concerning, for example, the following issues:
- analysis of early symptoms of potential problems and identification of possible causes;
- assessment of risk factors;
- analysis of management problems;
- evaluation of involvement and motivation of project team personnel.

Management reviews may often be more effective by resorting to an external consultant in order to obtain an objective assessment of the current management practice and possibly a concrete support. In fact, it is common experience that most of the management errors are hard to identify from within a project, but may be easily detected by an external observer. The regular support of an external advisor for project review is a very useful practice for all critical projects and for all young project leaders. A crucial point here is to have reviews on a regular basis, during the whole KBS life cycle: only in this way external support is really helpful to the project leader. Note that resorting to external support for management reviews is usually a decision of the project leader, not a request of the top management.

Finally, a last way to cope with fatal errors is resorting to *auditing*. Auditing is a focused intervention of an external advisor with the aim of assessing the current state of a project, diagnosing possible errors, suggesting remedies, and monitoring their application. Generally, auditing is requested by the project manager or the top management in case they feel the project is not proceeding correctly, or as effectively as expected. Substantial temporal delays, costs exceeding the budget, failure to deliver a scheduled product, or failure of the delivered products to meet expectations are only some examples of the most common causes which can suggest resorting to external auditing. Auditing is generally not foreseen in project plans, since it is requested only when a specific need arises (apart from very specific cases where it is considered necessary or appropriate from the very beginning of a project or of a life-cycle phase and, therefore, it is planned in advance). Auditing is usually restricted to time. After the problems identified have been fixed, auditing terminates.

A detailed analysis of the issue of software project reviews and auditing may be found in [IEEE 1028 88]. Although specifically concerning the production of traditional software, most of the concepts presented in this document may apply to KBSs as well.

Let us point out that, although all possible attention is paid to avoid fatal errors, management errors may still occur. Whenever an error - or a failure - is recognized, one should always resort to the assistance of a more experienced person, with the purpose of diagnosing the situation and identifying an appropriate corrective action. One should never accept a failure without understanding why it occurred. One should never make decisions before an accurate diagnosis of the critical situation has been done. Actions to be undertaken upon a failure are very different depending on whether the failure is considered still recoverable or not. In the former case one should try to recover from the failure as soon as possible, in spite of the high cost. In the latter, the only possible strategy is controlling project termination so as to avoid waste of resources and to preserve the partial results obtained.

10.5.2   Twenty issues for knowledge-based system project management

In managing a KBS project it may be useful to know in advance where the main critical points are located and how they can be faced successfully. We have identified twenty major issues of successful project management, divided into general issues and technical issues. They are listed below and illustrated through a collection of specific *management rules* (both in positive and negative form). These rules stem from personal practical experience of the authors and from an analysis of cases found in literature [Smith 84], [Shri et al. 85], [McCullough 87], [Cupello and Mishelevich 88], [Smith 88], [Irgon et al. 90], [Prerau 90], [Arora and Cooke 91], [Edwards 91], [Liebowitz 91], [Sacerdoti 91], [Sloane 91], [Fenn and Veren 91].

General issues

1. Management involvement
- have a management champion, a member of the top management who can strongly support the KBS project and protect the project team during the entire life cycle; knowledge-based technology is too new, too costly, and perceived as too risky to be supported by lower levels of management without some sign of support by senior management;
- build a foundation of awareness; do not begin by trying to explain what knowledge-based technology is, you must first develop trust not understanding;
- instruct the management on the main characteristics of knowledge-based technology, its potentials, its limits, and the usual life cycle of a KBS;
- point out to management the advantages of KBSs and how the new technology can help them meet their strategic goals;
- obtain approval from top management for the project;
- gain support and backing of management for the whole duration of the project;
- keep management constantly informed about the progress - and difficulties - of the KBS project and keep them involved in all evaluation activities.

2. User involvement
- have a user champion, a member of the middle-management of the department or business unit to which the application being developed belongs, who believes in the project and is firmly committed to it;
- gain the confidence of the users; listen to their problems, consider their perspective, make sure trusted personnel whom the users know are included in the project team;
- make the users believe in the usefulness of the KBS, show them how the KBS will help them, and convince them that the project will succeed;
- inform users correctly and early about the KBS project goals;

- get users actively involved in the whole KBS life cycle; consider them as the main agents of change, solicit their comments and take them seriously into account during KBS design and development;
- avoid the possible psychological threats a new technology may have on its potential users;
- get the end-users to feel ownership of the new system.

3. *Involvement of domain experts*
- instruct domain experts on knowledge-based technology and on its potentials before the project starts; establish credibility in the technology and in the project team;
- create a professional interest for domain experts to participate in the KBS project;
- provide incentives for the domain experts for their work in the KBS project team;
- try to keep the motivation of domain experts on a high level during the whole duration of the project;
- obtain a firm commitment from domain experts and gain their cooperation;
- avoid using domain experts who are continuously pulled away from the KBS project for other engagements considered urgent or more important;
- avoid using uninterested domain experts, who do not see any personal advantage in the success of the KBS project;
- avoid using skeptical domain experts, who do not trust knowledge-based technology.

4. *Setting-up and managing the project team*
- determine project staffing correctly and realistically;
- avoid overstuffing the project team; more people do not necessarily imply more productivity or higher quality;
- pay attention to the person-to-project match;
- do not accept to start with an ineffective project team;
- assume as the leading criterion for personnel management the development of the professional level and skill of each individual member of the project team;
- separate training, apprenticeship, and production;
- control personnel turn-over; try to foresee possible resignations, diagnose their causes, and, if possible, remove them; however, do not allow the personnel to blackmail the management of the project; in front of a resignation that cannot be avoided, mainstream the new member carefully into the project team;
- centralize management.

5. *Managing the training of personnel*
- make use of a variety of techniques, including: study, seminars, lectures, courses, term projects, demonstrations, practice, hands-on experimentation, review sessions, apprenticeship, etc.;

- make appropriate training materials available early, but not before they are needed;
- make clear to the trainees the specific objectives of each initiative, that should always be related to concrete production issues;
- avoid using training as an incentive for worthy personnel; training is a substantial part of a job not a prize for a good job done;
- keep the trainees involved and active throughout training; do not leave them without specific assignments for long periods;
- do not intermix training with regular production engagements;
- always evaluate the results of training.

6. Managing project planning and start-up
- determine specific project objectives in a structured and measurable way;
- avoid simultaneously attempting to develop a real KBS for actual use and making major advances in the state of the art of knowledge-based technology;
- identify products and due dates realistically;
- do not allow yourself to be pressured into unrealistic timetables;
- set up detailed, concrete, and realistic plans for each phase of the KBS life cycle.

7. Managing project development
- do not assume that all will go well; it will not, unless things are managed to do so;
- manage time and resources systematically;
- control quality systematically;
- control productivity systematically; plan and control the work of any member of the project team individually and frequently (every 2-3 weeks);
- be realistic; do not expect from the project team what is beyond its competence and capability;
- resort to external review before a fatal error occurs, when help is still useful;
- do not be afraid to ask for help; many of the problems you will face while managing a KBS project have been encountered before;
- avoid too frequent technical meetings; plan them in advance and rarely deviate;
- be sure you stay on the right track; collect as much feedback as possible from user, expert, and management during the entire project development;
- be creative; imagination is more important than knowledge - do not give up in front of difficulties.

8. Managing expectations
- create awareness of the knowledge-based technology within the organization;
- be clear, transparent, and realistic about the functions of the KBS and its role within the organization; manage expectations so that KBS capabilities are neither oversold nor underestimated;
- do not leave expectations about the KBS to grow in a free and uncontrolled way;

- keep users and management informed about the progress of the project; show them intermediate steps, and give them results as they occur.
- make sure benefits of the project are clearly understood and appreciated by the management and the users;
- make sure that the KBS project returns more money than the company invested in it; financial success is the ultimate target.

9. Managing change
- analyze and understand the culture of the organization in which the KBS will be delivered;
- be aware of the problems connected with practical use of the KBS and its insertion in the target environment;
- prepare users and managers for change; changes should be started early and carried out incrementally so that the organization can adapt to the use of the new tools and technology;
- pay attention to the integration issue.

10. Managing acceptance
- manage KBS acceptance from the project start and take care of it throughout the whole KBS life cycle;
- convince management and users that the right system was built and that it works according to specifications;
- establish KBS credibility; illustrate to the users the functions, the use, and the limits of the KBS and make them convinced of its competence and reliability;
- pay attention to possible legal or regulation problems concerning the operational use of the KBS and handle them in due time;
- train users appropriately before system release; teach them exactly what they are to do and the best way to do it;
- make sure that extensive field testing has been carried out before the final release;
- do not deliver an unfinished system which is not yet functioning as expected; this might definitely spoil the confidence of the management and of the users, thus preventing the project to be completed effectively;
- anticipate the reactions of the users, and respond effectively to user dissatisfaction;
- define acceptance criteria early and try to reduce the acceptance barriers during KBS development;
- do not underestimate the issue of user interface; an effective, friendly, and cooperative interface cannot turn a bad system into a good one, but an inappropriate interface can make a good system simply unusable.

Technical issues

11. Identifying the application domain
- choose simple but significant applications;

- try to meet fundamental and concrete corporate needs;
- do not try to solve problems that do not exist;
- avoid supplying technology-driven solutions rather than business-driven ones; a KBS must solve a proven business need and produce a high return of investment;
- provide solutions that managers and users need;
- if it is the first KBS project in the organization, do not be afraid to start small; do not choose the project with the biggest return, but that with the highest probability of success.

12. Defining KBS specifications
- in defining the functional specifications of the KBS resist adding too many functions; added complexity may make the difference between success and failure; leave space for future extensions;
- avoid stating too early too many technical specifications which may be too detailed; they should be derived from sound technical principles and not imposed a priori;
- identify operational specifications as soon as the final target environment can be accurately identified.

13. Applying sound design principles
- use sound design methodologies and tools;
- pay the highest attention to the conceptual model of the domain; it is the root of any good - or bad - design choice;
- carefully verify the correctness, completeness, and consistency of the conceptual model;
- avoid developing a conceptual model which depends on technical choices pertaining to the logical model; the former should guide the design of the latter, not vice versa;
- never forget that logical design has three dimensions, namely: architecture, knowledge representation techniques, and reasoning methods; do not give up their joint exploitation;
- leave enough space for exploration while developing the logical model of the KBS; consider any design decision as provisional until it has been verified in practice through appropriate experimentation;
- be prepared to revise your technical choices as soon as they reveal to be weak or inappropriate when the construction of the KBS progresses;
- verify that the logical model features the best possible fit to the conceptual model;
- carefully verify the technical consistency and soundness of the logical model;
- do not try to adapt the current problem to a known solution or to an available KBS development tool; each new application requires - in principle - a new and specific design effort;
- follow the design of the user interface closely; it is often the most important and critical component of the KBS, the one which eventually determines success or failure;

- remember that solutions which work well in the research laboratory do not always work so well in practice; avoid transferring research experience directly into real applications;
- remember that the use of experimental, highly innovative technologies to solve real problems generally raises new issues which had not previously been considered; do not let the technique drive the process.

14. Selecting the appropriate tools
- choose development tools carefully on the basis of the logical model; avoid being influenced by commercial reasons;
- remember that a wrong tool always determines a failure, but the right tool cannot guarantee the success of a project;
- remember that development tools do not support system design, but only system development;
- identify the requirements of the development support environment carefully before selecting the specific tools to be used;
- develop a proprietary tool only after a long experience with the use of market tools and after clear and stable requirements have been identified;
- when developing a proprietary tool, try to be general in order to cover the exigencies of several KBS projects; avoid developing a tool for just one project;

15. Constructing the knowledge base
- plan extensive knowledge acquisition carefully and keep the plan updated as the development of the knowledge base proceeds;
- remember that knowledge acquisition cannot succeed without appropriate methods, techniques and tools; naive knowledge acquisition cannot help to build real-size systems;
- do not acquire too much knowledge too fast; quantity and speed are often against quality, which can hardly be recovered later;
- make sure that the knowledge engineer does not get lost through experts' knowledge or is not tempted to substitute the expert;
- do not underestimate the bias problem;
- use all available knowledge sources synergically;
- start a new knowledge acquisition session only after the materials gathered in the previous one have been completely analyzed;
- remember that knowledge acquisition is not only the task of making knowledge explicit and transferring it into the knowledge base, but it involves constructing new knowledge which did not exist before;
- avoid a merely expert-driven development of the knowledge base; if a new, better way of solving a problem is discovered, it should be presented and discussed with domain experts.

16. Verification and validation
- make sure that sufficient test cases or an appropriate simulation environment are available for verification of the prototype;

• field testing must be carried out accurately and as long as needed.

17. Releasing the target system
• carefully plan and organize system release from the plausibility study;
• determine early the intended user population and define an appropriate distribution strategy;
• consider the issue of protection of property rights carefully.

18. Managing maintenance
• plan appropriate and effective maintenance procedures before KBS release;
• design the KBS for maintainability; maintainability is obtained automatically, it requires specific attention and care during KBS design and development;
• do not postpone maintenance interventions; their utility is fully exploited only if they are carried out in time.

19. Managing extension
• plan appropriate and effective maintenance procedures before KBS release;
• design the KBS for extensibility; extensibility is obtained automatically, it requires specific attention and care during KBS design;
• monitor the health state of the KBS carefully and regularly during the operationl life; try to forecast the events that might influence the state of the system, and to devise its likely evolution in detail;
• do not force extension interventions; it is often far better to build a new system than to work on an old one.

20. Technology transfer and reserach and development
• do not confuse applied reserach with training;
• do not confuse training, applied research, and innovative experimentation with production;
• remember that technology transfer means to transfer knowledge and know-how from experienced and skilled people to novices; it requires availability of the appropriate technology providers;
• remember that re-training usually fails, success is an exception.

11

MANAGING A
KNOWLEDGE-BASED SYSTEM
INITIATIVE

11.1   INNOVATION MANAGEMENT: OBJECTIVES AND COMPONENTS

Managing a KBS initiative entails all the problems of a typical innovation action [Humphrey 87], [Peters 87], [Davenport 93]. The success of the first KBS project is only a step - and often not the most critical one - towards introducing, establishing, and exploiting knowledge-based technology within an organization. To reach this goal it is necessary to make different actions converge, including:
- a clear understanding of all the factors which might influence, both positively and negatively, the initiative, and a precise identification of their possible evolution over time;
- a strong support from the top and middle management, who have to be motivated and involved and must see the return of the initiative;
- a correct and positive connection with the strategic goals and plans of the organization;
- a correct and sound technical basis, and a clear view of the role, characteristics, potentials, present status and development trends of the technology;
- a continuous control for ensuring acceptance and progress.

The leader of a KBS initiative must have a sound understanding of knowledge-based technology, but must also have the background, the skill, and the authority to be an innovator. His actions deeply affect large parts of the organization. The application of KBSs can change the roles and responsibilities of the personnel, it can influence the structure of the organization, and it can interfere with the long-term strategies. The leader of a KBS initiative must be aware of these effects, and must have appropriate tools to monitor and direct the actions undertaken.

The main objectives of managing a KBS initiative are:

• correctly introducing knowledge-based technology into an organization within reasonable time and cost constraints: tackling the right problems, creating sound technical competence, involving and motivating the users and the management;

• encouraging and propagating acceptance and diffusion of knowledge-based technology throughout the organization as an innovative working tool;

• assuring the most appropriate exploitation of the knowledge-based technology both from the economic and organizational points of view.

The management of a KBS initiative is a multifaceted competence domain, which includes several issues. Its main components are:

• the effective exploitation of the innovative power of knowledge-based technology;

• the approaches, the strategies, and the key success factors for introducing knowledge-based technology into an organization;

• the assurance of development and the monitoring of progress;

• the management of human resources;

• the management of research and development.

These issues will be dealt with in the next sections of this chapter.

Let us note that the set of activities aimed at introducing a new technology into an organization are often called *technology transfer*. This concerns transferring methodologies, techniques, know-how, and experience from a specialized group to a whole organization or part of it. Technology transfer is indeed a very comprehensive concept, but also a rather vague one. It has different meanings for different technologies, it requires different strategies in different contexts, and it follows different management rules in different organizations. Therefore, technology transfer for knowledge-based technology is a very specific issue which can inherit only little from experience undergone in other fields, even in the closely related field of traditional software technology [Smith 84], [Polit 85], [Shri et al. 85], [Hazeltine 87], [Law et al. 89], [Scharf et al. 92]. Knowledge-based technology may have a wide-spectrum impact on end-users, technical staff, and management. Its application requires new skills and design techniques not mastered by traditional software engineers, such as knowledge analysis and modeling, knowledge acquisition, and explorative programming.

The goal of this chapter is to analyze the various issues related to technology transfer for knowledge-based technology.

11.2   KNOWLEDGE-BASED TECHNOLOGY AND INNOVATION

11.2.1   Knowledge-based technology: a powerful leverage for innovation

Competition is a very important point in the dynamics of an economic organization. In recent years the rules of competition have gradually changed; technological factors have become more and more important with respect to the classical factors of marketing and finance. Nowadays competition is driven by the ability to match research results and business opportunities, understanding the potentials of advanced technologies and exploiting them at the right moment and in the right way. Technology-based business is a new concept which systematically exploits technological factors as the main leverage for competition. In technology-based business, technological innovation is a key point.

Over the last decade KBSs have emerged as a crucial technology which is expected to offer very high potentials as an innovation factor [Beerel 87], [Weitz 90]. Knowledge-based technology has rapidly developed as a concrete and reliable innovation tool, and its exploitation has offered a new competitive advantage to sensitive managers [Porter 85], [Feigenbaum et al. 88]. The role of knowledge-based technology as an innovation factor is twofold:

- it supports the innovation of production processes and tools, both in the industrial world as well as in the world of services and public administration - consider, for example, successful KBS applications in the domains of supervision of continuous processes, industrial diagnosis, quality control, production scheduling, design, financial decision making, fiscal services, economic scenarios simulation, technology assessment, etc.
- it supplies high-value components for the innovation of products, both material (goods) and immaterial (services) currently offered on the market - consider, for example, successful KBS applications in the domains of self-diagnosis of complex consumer products, embedded diagnosis and repair aids for industrial or military equipment, advanced man-machine interfaces for supervision and control systems, etc.

Thus, knowledge-based technology can help maintain competitiveness to saturated product lines and open up new market opportunities by stimulating demand through a continuously new and appealing offer.

The exploitation of knowledge-based technology within an organization as a leverage for innovation and competition raises two issues:

- if the organization is not yet acquainted with knowledge-based technology, the core problem is how to introduce it effectively, making it become an accepted production tool or product component;
- if, on the other hand, the organization has already had some experience with KBS development, the main issue is how to manage the correct and effective exploitation of the technology on a large-scale and in the long-term.

While the former point was the only one of interest up to some years ago, presently most of the large- and middle-size organizations have already carried out some experiments with KBSs, therefore making the latter issue become more and more important.

The absorption of a new technology by an organization is a complex process. After initial investment and experimentation, attentive management and control are necessary for a widespread acceptance and exploitation of the technology [Gattiker 90]. If organizations and managers do not understand the role of the new technology, its potential impact, and the effort required to realize the benefits of that technology, then they may be setting themselves up for failure.

11.2.2   Starting up innovation: issues and problems

A KBS initiative will deeply affect the organization where it is applied. KBSs may change production tools and working procedures, modify existing relationships, create new dependencies, change the distribution of knowledge and competence, alter the sharing of responsibilities, open up new challenges, affect the individual careers of personnel. In the long-run, the adoption of knowledge-based technology as a tool for innovation and competition affects the strategic thinking of the organization. Therefore, KBSs deeply interfere with the structure and organization of the target user environment and they often raise the need for extensive restructuring.

Moreover, the first steps of a KBS initiative always raise problems with the more traditional electronic data processing (EDP), software engineering (SE), and management information system (MIS) departments. The lack of confidence in the new technology, the fear of its revolutionary impact on established technologies and procedures, the conservative mentality of the managers, all these factors may initially generate a non-cooperative attitude which must be gradually turned into understanding and cooperation. SE, EDP, and MIS departments may pose hard obstacles to innovators. Inertia, conservatism, and obstruction are often directed towards protecting and keeping internal power.

Some common reasons why individuals may have a negative attitude towards new technologies are [Liebowitz 91]:
- obsolescence: "The technology may replace me";
- exploitation: "The technology may be used to exploit me";
- property: "The technology may be used to deprive me of my knowledge and professional know-how";
- dependence: "The technology may become a crutch";
- power: "The technology may lessen my personal power".

Choosing to adopt knowledge-based technology is not simply a matter of buying a new software package. It is a decision that will definitely change the organization. Not only must the knowledge-based technology find its own space and role in the organization, but it must also find out the best way to integrate with pre-existing technologies, both within the field of information technology and outside it. Therefore, applying knowledge-based technology cannot be a casual event of a limited scope confined within a specific period of time. The people in charge of a KBS initiative must be aware that they are initiating an innovation process which will have effects on the whole organization. They should strive to master the change and lead it towards profitable goals, avoiding being overwhelmed by the process begun. They cannot start without a plan and without the resources needed to grant success. They must be prepared to convince people, and be determined to conquer their own vital space in the organization. When major changes are brought about in an established context, understanding and support are not always initially found; resistance to change is most likely to occur while the organization goes on as before [Glazer 90].

According to [Feigenbaum et al. 88] the introduction of a new technology like KBSs into an organization requires hard work, vision, and luck. A combination of circumstances must work together to bring success.

The following issues are especially important for the success of an innovation effort [Feigenbaum et al. 88], [Edwards 91]:
- to have a *champion* of the KBS initiative, an individual or a group who takes the first steps with unwavering vision, has willingness to take risks, and is able to carry on in the face of obstacles;
- to have clear and realistic objectives, both in the short- and long-term;
- to have a correct approach and a concrete plan;
- to have a clear understanding of expected benefits and return of investment;
- to have a clear understanding of the concrete application opportunities within the organization and explicit criteria for ranking them;
- to have a plan for establishing a formal KBS department within the organization;
- to have a clear understanding of the difficulties and obstacles, and be prepared to overcome them.

As far as the ways in which knowledge-based technology may first enter into an organization, three typical situations can be mentioned:
- the champion is at the top, a general director or a vice-president, whose job is to devise the strategic vision of the company and to push towards its practical implementation; he can easily work top-down being far from the operative level;
- the champion of a KBS initiative is an employee, low in the company hierarchy; he works hard bottom-up, but he has the advantage of being in the right place, the operative level;
- the champion is in middle management; this is certainly the most difficult position for a champion to be, since he must work both ways in the hierarchy, up and down, he generally has limited resources, he lacks the leverage of the people at the top and the concrete vision of the people at the operative level, he can ruin his career if the project fails.

Independently on how the first steps are accomplished, knowledge-based technology definitely enters into an organization from the top. Without the personal involvement of some members of the top management, an initiative for introducing knowledge-based technology cannot succeed. However, in most contexts, a substantial pioneering work is needed before the top management can be involved.

For the reasons discussed above, introducing knowledge-based technology into an organization is a difficult and risky venture. If not carefully planned and controlled it may easily turn into a failure.

11.2.3   Pushing innovation forth: issues and problems

Starting up a KBS initiative and having success with the first projects does not guarantee that knowledge-based technology has entered the main stream of innovation and is exploited correctly and effectively throughout the organization. Two points - well beyond the start-up phase - deserve close attention:

- the propagation of KBS culture among all components of the organization, by making the managers and potential users familiar with the new technology and sensitive to its impact on applications;
- the control of the development of the KBS department, and the monitoring of its productivity and quality.

A well-started initiative does not grow naturally: without appropriate management and control even a successful KBS initiative may run into serious development problems and may fail to produce the expected benefits and returns.

11.3   INTRODUCING KNOWLEDGE-BASED TECHNOLOGY INTO AN ORGANIZATION

11.3.1   Approaches to knowledge-based technology

The introduction of a new technology into an organization, must first of all be based on a very specific and clear concept of innovation. The application of the new technology must fit current needs and goals of the organization and must specifically contribute to solving concrete, important problems. From this perspective it is appropriate to distinguish between integrative innovation and creative innovation. *Integrative innovation* addresses well-known problems, which need a solution. It rests on the following standpoints [Liebowitz 91]:

- involving end-users and having them participate to the development;
- creating a network of supporters for the project;
- extensive prototyping as a way of focusing user needs and system specifications;
- integration of the new solution in the pre-existing organizational environment.

Integrative innovation starts from an important and recognized exigency, and proposes a way for its solution through a gradual evolution.

On the contrary, *creative innovation* is aimed at identifying and solving new problems, which were not evident before. It rests on the following standpoints:

- involving the management and making it the primary actor of change;
- having a strong top-level supporter for the project;
- extensive prototyping as a way of focusing the new problem to face and its possible solutions;
- careful revision of the pre-existing organizational environment in order to ensure effective exploitation of the new solution available.

Creative innovation starts from a latent, unrecognized problem, proceeds with a detailed identification, and then proposes a way for its solution. While integrative innovation is on principle more conservative, creative innovation is more revolutionary. The former is in general easier, while the latter is more difficult and risky, but may ensure higher benefits and returns. Each type of innovation applies to different organizations and contexts; both may bring, however, substantial benefits.

Launching a new technology, even in an organization that explicitly recognizes technology's important role, still requires careful planning and execution. The *approaches* adopted to start an initiative with knowledge-based technology are as diverse as the organization themselves. Thus, analyzing the history of successful cases does not help much in setting up a new initiative. However, we can try to classify the main approaches experimented in the past and to discuss their main features, focusing on the general criteria and principles on which they are grounded. The results are presented in below.

Naive approach

There are many variations of the *naive approach* - also called *AI soup approach* [Helton 90]. For example, buying significant hardware and software resources, putting together some volunteers and some newly hired young people with some university background in knowledge-based technology headed by an experienced project leader taken from a different field, and letting them work for a period of time on some selected problem, quite often - unfortunately - very badly chosen. Or getting funded by a public agency which supports development and applications in the KBS field, and starting up a KBS initiative which was not foreseen or planned before. Or being pushed by end-users to develop a KBS application, and starting a KBS project without any knowledge of the technology and its use.

The naive approach was adopted by many organizations in past years. It rarely worked. The few positive results reported seem to have been obtained despite the approach, rather than because of it. In most cases the naive approach is only a way of wasting money and time and, more importantly, a way of losing credibility.

Strategic approach

The *strategic approach* [Helton 90] is based on the choice of one very specific KBS application, to which all available resources and efforts should be assigned. The chosen application, if successful, will represent a major convincing breakthrough. The first KBS developed must be a big success. Clearly, this approach takes a great deal of money and involves risk. It does not solve all problems related to the effective introduction and exploitation of knowledge-based technology into an organization, but it is quite effective in overcoming skepticism and mistrust. After a first major application has been successfully developed, the gap between a promising new technology and something which can be actually and profitably used is definitely bridged. The rest will follow naturally; for example, a broad-spectrum opportunity analysis and a plan for systematic exploitation of the technology may be appropriate. This strategy is quite tempting for its easy management and potentially large payoff. However, if the first application is not successful, the chance of introducing knowledge-based technology in the organization is definitely lost.

The cases of Digital Equipment Corporation with the R1 system for configuring VAX computers [McDermot 81], [Bachant and McDermott 84], FMC Corporation with the furnace-monitoring system [Feigenbaum et al. 88], and American Express Company with authorization advisor [Feigenbaum et al. 88] are brilliant examples of this approach.

Top-down approach

The *top-down approach* - also called *grand plan approach* [Bonnet 89] - is characterized by four standpoints:
- top-down initiative; it is initiated and directed by the top management;
- centralization; it is based on establishing a core KBS group to serve as a skilled engineering-services pool for the entire organization;
- top-down opportunity analysis; it starts from understanding the organization's strategy and identifying obstacles preventing higher performance that can be overcome cost-effectively through knowledge-based technology;
- disciplined and widespread training; it includes a structured long-term program for training and awareness, comprising technical and application development courses as well as introductory seminars for management familiarization.

The top-down approach allows duplication of skills in multiple locations to be avoided, supports higher specialization, and enables possible re-use of technical solutions in different application domains. It shares some similarities with the strategic approach, and, in some contexts, it can be appropriately merged giving rise to several possible variations.

The top-down approach has been applied with success at FMC Corporation [Bonnett 89].

An interesting variation of the top-down approach is presented in [Cupello and Mishelevich 88]. The recommended procedure for bringing knowledge-based technology into an organization is to convince senior management to fund a one year project to develop a prototype system that will demonstrate the competence of the project team and the potentials of the technology. The selection of the application domain and the problem to consider should be very careful, possibly using the assistance of an extremely qualified and experienced consultant. The project must be headed by a user champion with close reporting ties to senior management and the ability to manage the technology if and when it is adopted by the organization. The user champion will need the support of an executive champion throughout the entire project, until the prototype can convincingly demonstrate the value of the technology. The project should be no longer than one year, and it should be staffed with at least two full-time people (a user champion and a programmer). It should also be carefully planned with 4 to 6 major mileposts during the second half of the project.

Step-by-step approach

The *step-by step approach* [Freiling et al. 85] follows the six steps listed below:
1. building a foundation of awareness in the organization;
2. understanding how the initiative for introducing knowledge-based technology fits with the strategy of the organization;
3. explaining to the management and to the potential users how knowledge-based technology can meet organization needs;
4. focusing on an important project;
5. granting continuous support to the initiative;
6. pushing the technology towards producing a clear and measurable return.

The step-by-step approach shares several similarities with the strategic approach, however it enforces the concept of graduality.

The step-by-step approach has been successfully adopted at 3M Corporation through its Software and Electronics Resource Center [McCullough 87].

An interesting variation of the step-by-step approach is known as the *infusion approach* [Helton 90]. It aims at getting knowledge-based technology accepted into an organization as a system-development tool that can and should be integrated with other tools already in place, recognizing that KBSs are especially appropriate for certain potential mechanization tasks. It is based on the idea of proceeding gradually through several small steps, developing small systems with little investment and controlled risk. The results are also obtained and consolidated gradually. It consists of four stages:
1. Awareness, primarily oriented towards the management. This stage includes:
   - technology briefings and seminars for the top management;
   - surveys (concerning the technology, the products, the applications, etc.);
   - compilation of bibliographies;

- middle-management education;
- participation to specialized conferences.

Awareness is possibly the most critical stage, because it is here that the direction for a KBS development strategy is likely to be set. In this stage the technology should not be funded too rapidly, and one should not focus on one single application. Attention should also be paid to other advanced software technologies (object-oriented design and programming, CASE, neural networks, human-computer interaction, graphical user interface, multimedia and hypermedia, virtual reality, etc.).

2. Early implementation, dedicated to develop the first small (mainly based on personal computers) but significant KBS applications and to apply them concretely in the organization. This stage also includes substantial activity in getting knowledge-based technology definitely accepted and used:
    - establishing connections with related initiatives in other companies;
    - having a unitary concept of knowledge-based innovation at organization level (concretely supported, for example, by an ad hoc steering committee);
    - organizing broad-spectrum presentations of knowledge-based technology inside the organization;
    - selecting standard tools to be adopted company-wide for KBS development.

    The successful conclusion of this stage should provide a number of concrete applications in various stages of development.

3. Acceptance, focused on having knowledge-based technology accepted as a leading edge in the strategic plans for information technology. This stage also includes the start-up of internal training activities, a first standardization of KBS design and construction tools and methods, and the establishment of a KBS group. The main issue of acceptance is that of seeing knowledge-based technology moving from being just another new technology to one of legitimate and proven value. Managers at all levels should have learned enough about KBSs to consider them just as new tools for their activities. This stage should be driven by successful stories which help give confidence and bring awareness throughout the organization. Knowledge-based technology is now rapidly moving into the mainstream thinking, or corporate culture, of the organization.

4. Intensification, meant to consolidate and strengthen the KBS group and to support a regular production of KBS applications for all organization needs. Intensification focuses on diffusion of knowledge-based technology and includes:
    - the design of a complete training curriculum in the KBS field;
    - the execution of an opportunity analysis;
    - the start-up of a formal KBS department;
    - the integration of KBSs with other more traditional - but not less advanced - information technologies;
    - the first research and development efforts at the frontier of knowledge-based technology;

- the first continuing education activities.

Intensification focuses on leverage: instead of helping KBS explorers with any apparently useful and feasible KBS application, application proposals are solicited from the field and only the projects with bigger payoffs are supported.

The infusion approach has been successfully applied at Southwestern Bell Telephone Company [Helton 90].

Yet another variation of the step-by-step approach is the *incremental approach*. It aims at lowering the entry barrier of knowledge-based technology and goes through experimentation to discover opportunities. It is based on a kind of pirate ship operation. The original task force is a group of old friends, which constitute the embryo of a future KBS department. It is based on the adoption of a suitable development tool - developed internally or bought from the market. This approach initially involves a small support group charged with the task of stimulating the application of knowledge-based technology broadly and effectively enough through the organization. It focuses on training people to use the new technology; KBS specialists give consultations on how to get a system or project started, they give support and transfer expertise. Technology is centralized in order to avoid wasting time and efforts, but development and operation of KBS applications are fully decentralized.

The incremental approach was successfully applied at Du Pont [Feigenbaum et al. 88].

Bottom-up approach

The *bottom-up approach* [Peters and Waterman 82] is based on a champion. A company begins its experiments with KBSs thanks to the insight of some mid-level employees who work independently to explore this technology, evaluate it, and bring it into the company. The approach starts with a kind of personal innovation that is not officially approved by the organization, it goes through acquisition of a local success, and finally comes to a structured KBS department.

The bottom-up approach was successfully adopted by Canon and Kajima [Feigenbaum et al. 88]. A sort of the bottom-up approach is also suggested in [Darroy 91] and was successfully used at MATRA ESPACE.

A variation of the bottom-up approach is the *grassroots approach* [Bonnet 89]. It starts with just one person developing the first small and simple application. The KBS group grows slowly through the introduction of one or two novices at a time, and also applications - small and simple, but strategic for some primary activity of the company - expand gradually. The approach must be supported by the top management, who is confident that peer pressure and individual success will turn middle managers and staff into ardent believers. When the initiative has reached a meaningful dimension and produced convincing results, a committee can be created to plan and supervise the development and exploitation of knowledge-based technology organization-wide.

The grassroots approach has been successfully applied at Johnson & Johnson [Bonnett 89].

The approaches illustrated above are meant just to give a concrete idea of the several, diverse ways knowledge-based technology can be introduced into an organization. Such approaches may represent a valuable starting point to think about when and how defining the strategy of a KBS initiative. They can hardly be adopted as they are. Each case requires the identification of a specific approach, which can inherit some features from known approaches but also requires new elements to be added and a specific tailoring to the context at hand to be made.

11.3.2   Defining a strategy

Before starting an initiative for bringing knowledge-based technology into an organization it is appropriate to define a strategy. A *strategy* encompasses two issues:
- defining an *approach* appropriate for the context at hand;
- developing a detailed *implementation plan* o carry out the approach.

As far as the definition of the approach is concerned, one may start with analyzing known approaches and focusing the possible consequences of their application in the organization. This is a very useful practice in order to focus specific problems and issues and to gradually bring to light the requirements for the most appropriate approach for the context dealt with. At this point, a specific approach is defined: quite often a variation of one or more known approaches, very seldom a brand new one. One should pay particular attention to resist the charm of a refined and sophisticated approach. What is needed is an approach that can work effectively in the real world, not one which can win the first prize in a competition.

As far as the development of the implementation plan is concerned, four aspects should be carefully taken into account:
- technical soundness: the implementation plan should be first of all sound from a technical point of view, being based on a clear understanding of knowledge-based technology and of the rules for its effective acquisition and exploitation;
- organizational coherence: the implementation plan should be coherent with the current organizational practice of the context where it is expected to be applied;
- temporal scheduling: the implementation plan should cover a period of time acceptable for the organization considered and should demonstrate intermediate results; this way visibility on the progress is assured and management and user support are encouraged;
- resource availability: all the resources necessary for carrying out the implementation plan should be available or concretely obtainable.

A crucial point in defining an approach and implementation plan is to precisely identify the role the organization is expected to assume in front of knowledge-based technology. In fact, different roles imply different strategies, and, therefore, it is of primary importance that the most appropriate role is defined at the beginning of a KBS initiative. Four typical roles may be considered:

- The *pure user* delegates the design and construction of all KBS applications necessary for his organization to external suppliers. He only contributes to the project with the domain experts and the users, who, of course, cannot be found outside the end-user organization. The role of the pure user is generally only appropriate in very particular cases, since it creates a strict dependency between the end-user organization, which has not acquired the capability to develop or maintain its KBS applications internally, and the external supplier. This role may be acceptable, for example, in a very initial phase of technology experimentation. The role of the pure user can be recommended in the case where a large company decides to support the start of an external organization acting as an exclusive supplier of advanced information technology products for the whole company. In this case, the company may have full control on the external supplier, and the choice of being a pure user may be definitely appropriate.

- The *active user* develops his KBS applications through a close cooperation with an external supplier. He contributes to the project team not only with domain experts and users, but also with knowledge engineers, developers, and even designers. The responsibility for the projects is left, however, to the external supplier, who provides the project leader and all additional human resources that might be necessary. This role is appropriate as a first step towards establishing a KBS group internal to the end-user organization which can autonomously design and construct the KBS applications of interest. In this context, the support offered by the external supplier is not only oriented towards the development of specific KBS applications, but it has also the important goal of offering an appropriate coaching environment for the first kernel of the future KBS group.

- The *direct producer* can develop autonomously his KBS applications. This is the case of an organization which has established a KBS department internally and resorts to external support only in front of specific needs and exigencies, as already illustrated in section 10.2. This is the most natural and appropriate role foreseen for an organization entering the field of knowledge-based technology. KBSs should be developed, as much as possible, inside the user organization, with full control of the technology and its use.

- The *producer* is a specialized company which can supply knowledge-based products and services to client organizations. Quite often a producer does not originate from scratch, but starts as a spin-off of a mature KBS department internal to some end-user organization. This role is concerned with the use of knowledge-based technology as a primary business component.

Finally, let us mention that before a strategy is definitely delivered, it is always appropriate to submit it to close examination and criticism in order to identify and correct possible flaws, faults, or weak points. In evaluating the appropriateness of a strategy to a given organization the check-list proposed in Figure 11.1 may be used.

---

strategic matching
Do the objectives of the proposed approach match the strategic goals of the organization? Are the results of the proposed approach, if successful, consistent with the development plans of the organization?

operative matching
Are the objectives of the implementation plan consistent with the development plans of the organization? Are the actions of the implementation plan feasible, given the needed authorization and the appropriate resources, in the operational context of the organization?

simplicity and clarity
Is the proposed approach reasonably simple and clear? Is the proposed approach transparent and easy to understand?

motivation and justification
Can the proposed approach be concretely motivated and justified? Can the proposed approach be proved to be preferable in comparison to possible alternatives?

level of detail and completeness
Is the implementation plan developed at the right level of detail? Is the implementation plan complete?

presentation
Are the approach and the implementation plan presented in a clear and convincing document? Can the approach and the implementation plan be illustrated to a well informed audience in a clear and convincing way?

Figure 11.1 A check-list for the evaluation of the appropriateness of strategy.

11.3.3   Getting started: key success factors

Once an approach has been defined and an implementation plan developed, it is time to begin the new KBS initiative. Having a strategy does not ensure, however, that the initiative will succeed. Several factors may influence the appropriate execution of the plan and, ultimately, the success of the initiative, both positively and negatively. While the rules introduced in sections 10.5.1 and 10.5.2 for the appropriate management of a generic KBS project also apply to the case of the first projects, other considerations which more specifically refer to the introduction of knowledge-based technology into an organization must be introduced.

The key success factors for a KBS initiative - mentioned in literature cases [Polit 85], [McCullough 87], [Darroy 91], [Liebowitz 91] as well as supported by practical experience - are:

- being aware of the current state-of-the-art of knowledge-based technology, of its limits, and of its potentials;
- having a clear view of the reasons why knowledge-based technology is strategic for the organization (for example: accumulating and preserving corporate knowledge, automating cognitive tasks, distributing knowledge, etc.);
- assessing level of commitment the top management is prepared to make to the KBS initiative;
- developing a realistic analysis of the opportunities and risks of the initiative;
- helping management, experts and users become familiar with the potentials of knowledge-based technology and develop realistic expectations;
- being inventive in stimulating management curiosity about KBSs (for example, illustrate concrete successful stories, show potential benefits, report on similar applications, etc.);
- having a constructive attitude towards the end-users; preferring an offer-strategy rather than a request-strategy, putting users in front of concrete solutions instead of simply asking them to analyze their problems;
- showing a concrete and realistic attitude by demonstrating a strong commitment to operational delivery and by moving quickly from the prototype to the target system;
- paying attention to the effective integration of the KBS in the target operational context;
- applying only available technologies (see section 11.6.1) - at least in the first projects - in order to minimize risks;
- being flexible during development; several successful innovative applications in the end were used in a different way from the one initially defined.

The start-up of an initiative in the KBS field is subject to a variety of risk factors and knowing them in advance may be helpful. The most frequently reported are listed below:

- adopting a strategy which proceeds through steps that are too small; limited engagement, insufficient resources, and restricted time inevitably bring to minimal results which cannot cumulate over time into a significant outcome;
- focusing the first projects on problems which are not interesting for the organization, or are at the frontier of the current capabilities of knowledge-based technology, or are simply not suitable for knowledge-based technology;
- accepting deadlines that are too strict or technological constraints that are not appropriate for the initiative;
- underestimating the more technical aspects of knowledge-based technology; wrong or inappropriate technical choices may imply higher costs, longer

development time, and lower quality, thus spoiling the results of the first projects.
*   using inadequate tools or methodologies;
*   underestimating the issues of training and apprenticeship in the establishment of a new project team;
*   neglecting to appropriately manage relationships with EDP, SE, or MIS departments;
*   underestimating the importance of availability, cooperation, and involvement of domain experts and users.

11.4   ENSURING DEVELOPMENT AND MONITORING PROGRESS

11.4.1   Establishing a knowledge-based systems department

The success of the first KBS project is certainly a milestone for introducing knowledge-based technology into an organization, but it is not the whole story. The success of the first project is not yet the success of the technology. Widespread acceptance, effective exploitation, and return of investment are the basic objectives of a KBS initiative and must be pursued with realism and determination. After the first projects have been concluded successfully, the attention of the leader of the KBS initiative must be focused on pushing the innovation process forth and supplying it with a sound and robust foundation.
    The key points for reaching this goal are:
*   the establishment of a formal KBS department;
*   the achievement of an autonomous KBS design and development capability;
*   the rise of a consistent and continuous demand for KBS applications throughout the organization;
*   the adoption of a sound development methodology in order to ensure a reasonable level of quality and productivity.

The first steps of a KBS initiative are generally accomplished with an informal working group - and often with much external support, but this style of managing the insertion of knowledge-based technology into an organization cannot be continued for a long time after the first projects have been concluded. Either the early results are institutionalized, or their innovation power gets rapidly lost and the initiative, even if initially successful, will gradually turn into a failure [Liebowitz 91]. Moreover, the acceptance and diffusion of knowledge-based technology throughout the organization and the progressive understanding of its potentials must support a rapidly increasing demand for KBS applications. Innovation cannot have success if it is not firmly oriented towards the satisfaction of concrete user needs and it is not able to get user commitment.
    Establishing a *KBS department* is the most urgent action to be undertaken after the positive conclusion of the first projects in order to institutionalize the initial results of technology transfer. Postponing the transition from an informal KBS

group, or pilot unit to a formally recognized, structured department may cause serious problems and may hamper the success of a whole KBS initiative. This requires a firm involvement, a formal decision of the top management, and a clear design of the initial composition, organization, and tasks of the new KBS department. The proposal for a KBS department should therefore be supported by a detailed design that takes into consideration the following:

- the selection of the manager of the KBS department; quite often the leader of the KBS initiative;
- the initial staffing of the KBS department, including at least enough people to run a couple of projects in parallel;
- the initial resources necessary for the effective set-up and operation of the KBS department, including: computer systems, network facilities, software tools, bibliographic materials, know-how, training, external support, etc.;
- the definition, over a period of three to four years, which is generally considered appropriate for establishing and consolidating a new KBS department, of the following:
  - an activity plan which clearly indicates the projects that will be carried out and the expected results, both from the technical and application points of view;
  - a marketing plan specifying the strategies to acquire the projects considered in the activity plan;
  - a technology plan defining the development methodologies to be adopted, the software tools to be acquired and used, the production standards suggested;
  - an acquisition plan which identifies the resources needed for the effective execution of the proposed activity plan, as well as their distribution over time, with particular attention to personnel, tools, training, and consultation;
  - a cost analysis including all major expense and investment items, as well as their distribution over time;
  - an analysis of the expected benefits and returns of the initiative and its assessment in relation to the general strategies of the organization.

An important aspect to take into account in establishing a KBS department is its position within the organization. In fact, this is a critical decision which may have a crucial impact on the development of the new department. The placement of a KBS department may speed up or hamper its development, it may favor or hinder the acceptance of the new technology by the end-user environment, it may support or contrast integration with more traditional EDP, SE, and MIS departments, it may make the internal management of the department easier or more difficult and problematic. Clearly, a universal solution for all possible contexts does not exist; the specific features, needs, and constraints of each individual organization should be carefully taken into account before making a final decision about this point. In identifying the most appropriate positioning of a KBS department into an organization, we should distinguish between the very first start-up period in which the new department may be temporarily hosted inside an existing department, and the target situation where the KBS department will eventually be an autonomous operational unit. As far as the start-up period is concerned, the following should be considered:

- the start-up period should not last more than one year;
- the best possible configuration for a new KBS department is that of a pilot, innovation-oriented department, directly dependent upon a top-management executive in charge of its start-up;
- an appropriate allocation for a new KBS department may also be inside one important user department;
- the allocation of a new KBS department inside a traditional information system or software production department may be critical for its growth and for a correct understanding and acceptance of the new technology;

As far as the target positioning is concerned, the following points are worth mentioning:

- the best position for a KBS department to be in is a central special service of an organization, directly dependent upon the top management and with full visibility on the entire organization;
- in some cases, after KBS technology has been fully accepted by the organization and has become a common working tool, a KBS department may be effectively established as an operational unit at the same level of the traditional information systems or software production departments, but fully independent of them; this may greatly favor cooperation and integration;
- the allocation of a KBS department inside an important user department may sometimes turn out to be acceptable, but is never to be considered as an optimal one since it does not allow an organization-wide visibility;
- the allocation of a KBS as a special unit inside a traditional information system or software production department tends to be unstable and does not guarantee the necessary degree of independence; in such a case the growth of the KBS department is generally hampered.

11.4.2   Going from external support towards autonomy

At the beginning of a KBS initiative, the leader of the newly established KBS group has to balance between producing concrete and convincing results in a short time and the availability of a still weak and understaffed project team. Therefore, it is sometimes usual to resort to external support. This fulfills three objectives:

- providing project management competence to the leader of the new KBS group, who may still have limited experience in the specific fields of KBS technology and KBS project management;
- bringing specific technical know-how to a weak and still growing KBS group;
- supplying specifically trained and experienced human resources to expand the production capacity of a KBS group of still limited dimensions.

Resorting to external support can hardly be avoided during the first or second year of operational life of a new KBS group. The suppliers should be chosen through a detailed and concrete selection procedure and their interaction with the KBS group carefully planned. Resorting to an external support, especially in a critical phase as the start-up of a new initiative, may be successful only if a high technical level is guaranteed and an effective integration with the KBS group is achieved. In particular, the leader of the KBS initiative should carefully take into consideration the following points:

- planning the development of the new KBS group independently of potential external suppliers;
- looking for the necessary external suppliers according to the plans defined;
- verifying the real competence and experience of the potential suppliers before establishing a cooperation contract with them;
- making sure that the human resources offered by the external supplier are cooperative enough to work effectively together with internal members of the KBS group;
- having several check-points in order to monitor the activity of the external suppliers, who should not be allowed to drive the initiative according to their own objectives;
- defining precisely the results to be achieved at each check-point with external suppliers;
- resorting to different suppliers, such as a specialized KBS firm and a professional consultant, in the case where both technical and project management support are needed;
- choosing the KBS development tools and methodologies in cooperation with the external supplier, but without following only his advice.

During the second or third year of operational life of a KBS group, the use of external support should be gradually reduced and eventually abandoned. After a KBS department has been formally established, it is of primary importance to achieve rapidly a reasonable degree of autonomy in carrying out all the technical and managerial activities needed to design, develop, and maintain a KBS. In fact, operative autonomy is important from two points of view. First of all, it is a prerequisite for both productivity and quality. Secondly, it is necessary to effectively exploit the strategic value of KBSs, which cannot be fully unfolded without complete control on the production technology. If a KBS department cannot have complete autonomy from external suppliers, this is usually a symptom of serious disorders concerning the structure, the organization, or the available human resources. In any case, timely actions should be taken in order to assure a correct and effective development of the KBS initiative.

11.4.3   Marketing knowledge-based technology throughout the organization

The diffusion of knowledge-based technology throughout an organization must be carefully planned and controlled in order to guarantee that:
- it is rapid enough to ensure a fast acceptance by the various components of the organization;
- it is widespread and well-balanced, involving the operative and technical levels as well as the management;
- it is supported by specific initiatives, such as seminars, presentations, demonstrations, and workshops, to ensure a correct understanding of its content, potentials, and limits.

The leader of a KBS initiative should not let the new technology grow in a natural and uncontrolled way. He should have a clear understanding of the strategic goals of the initiative, of their impact on the various components of the organization, and of their distribution over time. He should carefully plan the most appropriate steps to reach the desired objectives, and carefully control their execution. Some specific actions can be helpful in encouraging the use of knowledge-based technology and promoting its adoption as an innovative working tool throughout the organization. These actions can be progressively planed as follows:
- familiarization seminars for the top and middle management;
- demonstrations of the results obtained through the first KBS projects;
- technical seminars on knowledge-based technology, tailored for the various components of the organization (technical management, potential users, software systems designers, etc.);
- application seminars, including state-of-the-art surveys and presentations of real cases in domains related to the main activities of the organization;
- informal identification of potential application domains and formulation of project proposals;
- development of plausibility studies in different potential application domains;
- development of a global opportunity analysis.

An important point in the first phase of diffusion of knowledge-based technology is the risk of pushing too much and being then overwhelmed by the work load. It is of primary importance for the growth of a new KBS department that all possible requests from potential users are considered and carefully evaluated. However, only projects really appropriate for knowledge-based technology and, possibly, of limited technical and organizational complexity - should be accepted. The leader of a KBS initiative should balance between two contrasting issues:
- on the one hand, he should make sure that the project team is constantly working on concrete production activities; failure to do so is an evident waste of time and resources and should be avoided by stimulating new assignments;
- on the other hand, he should also avoid engaging the project team in useless, marginal, or risky activities; project proposals should never be accepted

without a careful preliminary evaluation, even if the project team is working below capacity.

Assuring a high throughput is clearly a key point for the growth of a new KBS department. The accumulation of successful projects is, however, even more important. One failure can compromise the positive effects of many concrete achievements.

11.4.4   Monitoring the progress of a knowledge-based system initiative

Any change within an organization should be monitored, so that success may be measured. Monitoring is a key element of management [Humble 73]. The main reason which motivates the need to measure the success of change is to enable an organization to learn from what happened and to make more appropriate and accurate decisions for future actions.

Monitoring and managing progress require two basic skills, namely: a positive attitude towards planning and carrying out concrete activities, and an analytical and critical attitude in the identification and management of possible risks and critical points. In particular, the manager of a KBS department is in charge of several complex tasks:
- supporting the professional growth of all the members of the KBS department;
- enhancing productivity and quality;
- controlling and measuring the benefits of the delivered KBS applications and the global return for the organization deriving from the adoption of knowledge-based technology;
- balancing short-term needs bound to the current engagements in ongoing projects, and long-term objectives concerning the development of the KBS department and the impact of its activity throughout the organization;
- managing user requests for new projects, realistically taking into account the available resources and the goals of the KBS department.

As far as productivity and quality is concerned, a particular management action directed to these kind of problems should be mentioned. In the case where the manager of KBS department is unsatisfied with the productivity of the personnel or the quality of the work done, a possible solution is a *technology check-up*. This is a sort of external audit carried out by an experienced KBS consultant and aimed at identifying the causes of the observed symptoms and at proposing appropriate corrective actions. A technology check-up focuses on the overall technological know-how of the KBS department. It analyzes the coverage and the level of technology actually exploited in design and development tasks. It develops an analytical assessment of how the technological know-how is distributed among the KBS members. It analyzes the work procedures followed, the methods and the techniques used, the development tools adopted. It focuses on the present technological state of the KBS department and tries to identify its development process, the causes of the present situation and the plausible evolution trends. It provides an objective evaluation of the situation observed, with reference to the technological and production goals of the KBS department and to the most usual standards in similar contexts. The result of the technology check-up is a comprehensive and detailed document directed to the leader of the KBS department. It contains a thorough assessment of the current situation and the proposal of a plan of action to achieve a set of goals considered important for the correct growth of the KBS department. In some cases, a technology check-up may concern several KBS departments or similar production units belonging to the same organization or group. Usually, a technology check-up is a very positive and useful intervention. Of course, its conclusions must be seriously considered and concrete actions taken. Having a technology check-up each 4 to 6 years is highly recommended for all KBS departments.

The impact that knowledge-based technology has on the core business of an organization should be specifically addressed. In some cases, although the KBS department of an organization seems to work correctly and effectively, the impact of knowledge-based technology is weak and the return of investment lower or slower than expected. For example, the number of KBS applications actually used in practice is low with respect to the number of KBSs delivered; or the number of KBSs delivered is low with respect to the number of KBS project initiated. The cost of individual KBS projects is high and, apparently, each new project requires a new investment in technology. Technology costs are duplicated in several sites, each one with its own production methods and tools, and without any sharing of know-how between groups or any corporate standard. The diffusion of knowledge-based technology and its exploitation is slow with respect to usual standards and limited to a small number of business units. In these cases it may be appropriate to perform a *business check-up*. This is a broad-spectrum investigation, concerning the assessment of the effects of the exploitation of knowledge-based technology throughout the organization, the identification of possible problems, the diagnosis of their causes, and the proposal of a corrective action plan. A business check-up, especially for a large organization or a large industrial group, is generally carried out by a team led by an experienced KBS consultant including specialists from several fields (knowledge-based and traditional software technologies, work organization, business management, strategic planning, etc.). The scope, organization, and specific content of a business check-up largely depend on the specific context where it is developed and on the particular goals considered. Business check-up does not originate from within a KBS department, but it is generally started by a top manager in front of unsatisfactory achievements or as a preparatory step in view of some strategic action, such as business restructuring. Quite often, a business check-up also includes a technology check-up, and in several cases, it is not limited to knowledge-based technology but may concern the entire area of information technology or a set of interconnected innovative technologies.

## 11.5	MANAGING HUMAN RESOURCES

### 11.5.1	Acquiring human resources

The availability of appropriate human resources is a key point for the success of a KBS project. Human resources can be made available to a project team in two ways: hiring already trained and experienced people, or hiring people with appropriate education and background and supplying them later with the necessary specific training and practical apprenticeship.

Hiring versus internal training should be evaluated very carefully, since advantages and drawbacks of the two strategies vary greatly. Clearly, hiring trained and experienced people is the fastest way to have new resources immediately available on the job. However, this is often difficult since the offer is generally poor, especially for the highest professional roles such as knowledge engineer, designer, and project leader. This entails two negative effects: higher requests in terms of salary and fringe benefits and higher expectations about professional growth and career advancement. Moreover, in front of the difficulty to find people with the right professional competence, one is often tempted to scale down his requirements; for example, a senior developer might be hired to cover the position of a designer. This is clearly harmful and may cause serious problems to the correct and balanced development of a project team or of a KBS department.

Internal training of inexperienced people, even with the appropriate education and background, is long and costly, but better results may always be expected. People trained internally are trained specifically for the professional role they are going to assume, they are naturally tuned to the current techniques and methods adopted inside the KBS department, they have no problems of integration, they are psychologically motivated and consider themselves as an active part of the group where they are working. Training people, however, is a specific, serious and very demanding job not to be taken lightly: it has to be planned and executed as a regular, additional task both for the tutor and for the trainee. Internal training may be very different, depending on the specific target professional role:

- Training graduates to become developers is rather usual and easy. If the trainees have a sufficiently good background in computer science, the acquisition of the necessary competence in the use of the programming environments and KBS development tools currently adopted within a KBS department does not pose, in the large majority of cases, any particular problem.
- Training developers or designers already belonging to the KBS department to become designers or project leaders, respectively, is a common task within medium-size KBS departments. Offering concrete possibilities of professional advancement to project team members is one of the most serious and effective strategies for avoiding a too frequent turn-over of technical staff.
- Training just hired people - or KBS developers or, less frequently, designers - to become knowledge engineers is a more difficult task. Their original education and background usually does not include any specific topics related

to knowledge engineering. They need to be trained from scratch; internal training may be difficult, long, and costly.

In several cases developers or designers are hired and immediately after internally trained to become designers or project leaders, respectively. This is indeed a common practice for two reasons:

- technical personnel who do not see any possibility of improving their professional role in the organization where they are currently employed, are generally attracted by the perspective of obtaining a better position in another organization;
- the availability of designers and project leaders on the job market is generally very limited and, therefore, the head of the KBS department is often compelled to hire technical personnel of a lower professional role to be immediately trained internally for a higher position.

With this practice, however, critical problems may sometimes arise. The insertion of newly hired people in the KBS department and, at the same time, their training for a higher professional role may turn out to be conflicting and, eventually, may fail. A far more effective and safe approach is to insert the newly hired people in the same professional role already covered in the previous job, and postpone training for a higher professional role after a reasonable period of time (for example, one year). Moreover, it should be carefully taken into account that in all cases where new people are hired for a high-level professional role, such as project leader, designer or knowledge engineer, their insertion could cause conflicts with the people already employed at a lower level, or even at the same level. Before hiring new staff for a high-level professional role the head of a KBS department should make sure that no one already employed in the department can be trained for the new position. If any such person exists, internal training should always be preferred, and new personnel should be hired for the lower-lever professional role.

The case where employees with a professional background not in the KBS field are considered for possible re-training and insertion into a KBS department is very critical and deserves further attention. This case is dealt with in section 11.5.4.

11.5.2 Training paths

Training novices or already experienced employees in the field of knowledge-based technology requires different approaches according to the background and previous experience of the trainee and to the objectives of the training activity. Considering the professional roles introduced in section 10.2.1, a variety of *training paths* may be defined. These are summarized in Figure 11.2. The table must be read left-to-right. The left-most column indicates the initial background and practical experience of the trainee, the right-most column indicates the target professional role, and the two central columns the suggest an appropriate training path.

initial background	FORMAL TRAINING	APPRENTICESHIP	target professional role
computer science programming	KBS basic KBS programming KBS intermediate	senior developer 4-6 months	developer
computer science or other field	KBS basic KBS design - I KBS knowledge engineering	senior knowledge engineer 1 year	knowledge engineer

initial role practical experience	APPRENTICESHIP	FORMAL TRAINING	target professional role
developer 2-3 years	senior designer 1 year	KBS design - I KBS design - II KBS advanced	designer
designer 2-3 years	senior project leader 1 year	KBS project management	project leader

Figure 11.2 Training paths in knowledge-based technology.

As it can be noted, a training path generally includes two components, namely: formal training and apprenticeship.

Formal training is based on traditional teaching, namely *courses*, which include the following basic components:

- lectures;
- study, individual or in small groups, if necessary supported by exercises and discussions;
- laboratory work, including programming practice and KBS development;
- workshops, aimed at practicing with specific topics, including KBS design, knowledge acquisition, and project management;
- seminars on advanced topics and project management.

Clearly, the content and organization of formal training is substantially different for each training path. The choice of the topics to be taught, the most appropriate variety of training components to adopt, and their logical and temporal organization should be carefully evaluated case by case by the person in charge of designing the training curriculum, usually a senior project leader or an external advisor. In particular, the specification and organization of the practical activity to be carried out during experimentation - a fundamental component of any training path - is generally demanding. A training curriculum should always be designed carefully taking into account the specific background and profile of the trainees and the context where training takes place. Note also that the organization and execution of a training curriculum may usually involve several people:

- an educational director, in charge of defining the content and organization of the curriculum, supervising its execution, and evaluating the results;
- one or more lecturers, in charge of the lectures and seminars;
- one or more teaching assistants in charge of preparing the materials necessary for study, exercises, discussions, laboratory, and workshops, and for supporting the trainees in their daily work.

In the table of Figure 11.2, under the heading FORMAL TRAINING the names of the relevant *courses* are indicated. Each course generally includes a set of coordinated *units*, as it is illustrated in section 11.5.3.

Apprenticeship is understood as on-the-job coaching for a period of time with the assistance of a senior professional in order to consolidate and reinforce newly acquired professional knowledge. More specifically, apprenticeship includes two types of practice:

- cooperating with and assisting a senior professional in doing a job and, at the same time, being trained by him about the practical aspects of what is being done and the conceptual background of the matter (*passive apprenticeship*);
- doing a job with the guidance and support of a senior professional (*active apprenticeship*).

The former type of apprenticeship applies in the early periods of apprenticeship, while the latter is more appropriate for the later ones, when the apprentice has already reached a sufficient degree of confidence and autonomy on the job. The main purpose of apprenticeship is the fast and effective accumulation of valuable experience, which, without the assistance of a senior professional, could only be acquired during a long working period and generally through trial and error. Note that the apprentice, although cooperating in a real job, cannot be expected to be a fully productive employee: he is still on a training path and his primary objective must be fast and effective learning, not production. In the table of Figure 11.2, under the heading APPRENTICESHIP the professional roles involved and the suggested duration of apprenticeship are indicated.

Let us stress that formal training can never be substituted by informal *training on the job*. Mixing apprenticeship and informal training - which is the very concept of training on the job - generally results in the failure to meet objectives. Apprenticeship and formal training should always be strictly interrelated but are distinct activities. Also *self-training* through autonomous study is generally an ineffective substitute of formal training: this was the path followed by the pioneers, but does not apply for a mature technology as knowledge-based technology. Self-training is very often bound to fail for the lower professional roles such as developer and knowledge engineer, and generally ineffective also for the higher professional roles such as designer and project leader.

As it is clear from the table of Figure 11.2, training cannot transform just anyone, with any background, to an experienced professional of any professional role. For each role, there exists only one suggested training path, which starts from an initial background and practical experience and goes through specific apprenticeship and formal training. Experience has shown that for the target professional roles of developer and knowledge engineer, formal training must precede apprenticeship, while for designer and project leader, apprenticeship must precede formal training. Starting from the appropriate initial background and practical experience, after appropriate apprenticeship and formal training, a trainee becomes a *junior professional* after which he will become a *senior professional* at the end of a two to three year activity. The training schema proposed in Figure 11.2 is very rigid and, of course, several variations and exceptions are possible in order to cope with the specific features of each individual case. It should, however, be clear that variations and exceptions must always be motivated and justified and, most importantly, must guarantee that the main issues of the training schema presented in Figure 11.2 is fully respected. No training path can transform a graduate into a designer, or a developer into a project leader. No knowledge engineer may become a designer if he did not go through the developer experience first.

Finally, let us outline that an essential component of any training program is the evaluation of results. The educational director of a training program should assess the following points:

- how well was the training program implemented with respect to its original design (implementation evaluation);
- how appropriate was the program for the trainees (training program evaluation);
- what have the trainees learned from the program (trainee evaluation).

The evaluation methods may include:

- direct comparison of the design of the training program with its actual execution, for implementation evaluation;
- trainee questionnaires, for training program evaluation;
- tests, practical exercises, term projects (implementation or report writing) and examinations, for trainee evaluation.

Evaluation paths may greatly vary from case to case; their design is one of the most critical duties of the educational director.

11.5.3   Implementing training courses

Training courses are generally difficult to organize: they require experienced lecturers and involve a substantial effort for preparing or tailoring teaching materials. The most effective approach is clearly a training program especially designed and carried out for a limited group of trainees. However, this is not always feasible. Quite often, budget or time constraints - or simply the lack of experienced people who can design the course and supervise its execution - require that other approaches be adopted. So, courses, seminars, and workshops offered on the educational market sometime replace regular training. While

these may be a useful addition to a serious training program, they can never replace it entirely. In particular, let us note that:
- short courses (2-5 days) and seminars (1-2 days) of an introductory nature are generally useful only for initial information, but do not offer a concrete contribution to a formal training program; such courses, moreover, are often of poor quality and fail to provide a fair illustration of the nowledge-based technology; in addition, they are generally rather costly;
- dedicated courses and workshops (2-10 days) focusing on specific programming languages or KBS development tools may often be a useful component of a training program, provided that they are held by experienced lecturers and tutors;
- specialized tutorials (1-2 days) like those offered in connection with the main international conferences which span from basic topics to advanced issues are often of a very high quality and may be a useful complement of a formal training program.

In designing a training program, the implementation of the courses mentioned in Figure 11.2 is generally a major problem. The articulation of the courses into units and the choice of the most appropriate topics to be taught are difficult issues which require both a broad competence in knowledge-based technology and a concrete experience in teaching and designing technical courses. In order to facilitate this task, we propose in Figures 11.3 to 11.10 a sample design of the relevant courses mentioned in Figure 11.2. The specification of the various units is detailed enough to give a precise idea of their content and organization. Of course, this proposal is generic and is based on several subjective choices. It does constitute, however, a reference schema which can be used as a starting point in designing specific curricula tailored to the particular characteristics of the trainees and of the context at hand. To understand the proposal illustrated in Figures 11.3 to 11.10 correctly it should be noted that:
- an adequate background in computer science [Tucker 91] is needed as a prerequisite for the following courses: KBS basic, KBS design - I , KBS knowledge engineering, KBS project management;
- a sound background in computer science [Tucker 91] is required for the following courses: KBS programming, KBS intermediate, KBS design - II, KBS advanced;
- group projects and tutorials held by selected groups of trainees should be encouraged as a useful way to look into and consolidate the concepts learned during each individual course [Bahill and Ferrell 86] [Warman and Modesitt 88];
- the development of a pilot project of limited size but of realistic complexity (a training-oriented KBS) at the end of a curriculum is highly recommended so as a to acquire knowledge and good mastery of the technology [Scharf et al. 92].

The proposal of Figures 11.3 to 11.10 takes into account the experience of the authors in teaching KBS courses as well as some significant cases reported in the literature [Taylor 85], [Bahill and Ferrell 86], [Brown 87], [Warman and Modesitt 88], [Warman and Modesitt 89], [Chorafas 90], [Durkin 90], [Scharf et al. 92].

KBS INTRODUCTION	
topics	• KBS concepts and basic mode of operation • KBSs and traditional software systems • application issues: appropriate application domains, integration with traditional software technology, expected benefits, exemplary applications • design and development issues: life cycle, project team, design principles, knowledge engineering, case studies
lectures	5 days
study	3 days

KNOWLEDGE REPRESENTATION AND REASONING - 1	
topics	• knowledge representation: basic concepts, rules, frames, semantic networks • reasoning: basic concepts, problem solving and search, breadth-first, depth-first, backtracking, heuristic searching
lectures	5 days
study	10 days, with exercises and discussions

KNOWLEDGE REPRESENTATION AND REASONING - 2	
topics	• basic concepts of building rule-based, frame-based, and hybrid systems • exemplary cases
lectures	5 days
study	5 days, with exercises and discussions

LOGIC AND AUTOMATED REASONING	
topics	• propositional calculus and predicate calculus • non-classical logical systems • automated reasoning: principles and methods
lectures	7 days
study	10 days, with exercises and discussions

KBS ORGANIZATION AND ARCHITECTURE	
topics	• representation and use of meta-knowledge: approaches and applications • representation and use of procedural knowledge: approaches and applications • the KBS architectures: approaches and applications, distributed systems paradigms, cooperation, communication and control issues • exemplary cases
lectures	5 days
study	5 days, with discussions

Figure 11.3 Formal training in knowledge-based technology: KBS basic.

KBS PROGRAMMING - 1	
topics	• functional programming concepts (Lisp) • logic programming concepts (Prolog) • rule-based programming concepts (OPS-5, CLIPS) • object-oriented programming concepts (Smalltalk, CLOS, C++, object-oriented Prolog)
lectures	20 days
study	20 days
laboratory	10 days: programming exercises, implementation of basic KBS structures

KBS PROGRAMMING - 2	
topics	• KBS development tools: issues and problems • KBS programming with a selected KBS development tool
lectures	10 days
study	10 days
laboratory	10 days: development of a simple KBS

Figure 11.4 Formal training in knowledge-based technology: KBS programming.

DEVELOPING RULE-BASED, FRAME-BASED, AND HYBRID SYSTEMS	
topics	• rule-based systems design: basic principles and practice, implementation issues with a specific basic development environment • frame-based and hybrid systems design: principles and practice, implementation issues with a specific basic development environment • analysis of exemplary cases • definition and discussion of laboratory work
lectures	10 days
laboratory	25 days: development of exemplary KBSs

DEVELOPING ADVANCED ARCHITECTURES	
topics	• the exploitation of meta-knowledge • the exploitation of procedural knowledge • system architecture design: principles and practice • analysis of exemplary cases • definition and discussion of laboratory work
lectures	5 days
laboratory	20 days: development of exemplary KBSs

Figure 11.5 Formal training in knowledge-based technology: KBS intermediate.

```
┌─────────────────────────────────────────────────────────────────────────┐
│ KBS DESIGN: PRINCIPLES AND METHODS                                        │
├──────────┬────────────────────────────────────────────────────────────── │
│ topics   │ • phases of design: conceptual design, logical design, detailed design
│          │ • design as modeling and transformation                        │
│          │ • the design space and the dimension of KBS design: knowledge  │
│          │   representation techniques, reasoning methods, and architecture│
│          │ • the quality of design                                        │
│          │ • paradigm-driven, task-driven, and model-driven design        │
│          │ • exploration and iterative refinement                         │
│          │ • design documentation                                         │
│ lectures │ 2 days                                                         │
│ study    │ 3 days, with discussions                                       │
└──────────┴────────────────────────────────────────────────────────────────┘
```

```
┌─────────────────────────────────────────────────────────────────────────┐
│ CONEPTUAL DESIGN                                                          │
├──────────┬────────────────────────────────────────────────────────────── │
│ topics   │ • the scope of conceptual design                               │
│          │ • the conceptual model: goals, structure, and components       │
│          │ • conceptual design: approaches, methods, and techniques       │
│          │ • examples and case studies                                    │
│ lectures │ 3 days                                                         │
│ study    │ 3 days, with discussions                                       │
└──────────┴────────────────────────────────────────────────────────────────┘
```

```
┌─────────────────────────────────────────────────────────────────────────┐
│ LOGICAL DESIGN                                                            │
├──────────┬────────────────────────────────────────────────────────────── │
│ topics   │ • the scope of logical design                                  │
│          │ • the logical model: goals, structure, and components          │
│          │ • logical design: approaches, methods, and techniques          │
│          │ • examples and case studies                                    │
│ lectures │ 3 days                                                         │
│ study    │ 3 days, with discussions                                       │
└──────────┴────────────────────────────────────────────────────────────────┘
```

```
┌─────────────────────────────────────────────────────────────────────────┐
│ KBS DESIGN WORKSHOP                                                       │
├──────────┬────────────────────────────────────────────────────────────── │
│ topics   │ • practical aspects of KBS design                              │
│          │ • practice with selected methods and techniques                │
│ workshop │ 5 days                                                         │
└──────────┴────────────────────────────────────────────────────────────────┘
```

Figure 11.6 Formal training in knowledge-based technology: KBS design - I - a.

11.5.4   Re-training

A very special type of training concerns *re-training*, where the trainee is not a novice or a specialist of a lower professional role in the KBS field, but an employee - often even a senior one - in a related field (a programmer, a software engineer, an information system designer, a system analyst, etc.). In this case, three different cases may be considered.

KBS DEVELOPMENT TOOLS	
topics	• tools for KBS development: classes and general features • the development support system • tool evaluation and selection • survey of commercial tools • the development of proprietary tools
lectures	3 days
study	5 days, with discussions

DETAILED DESIGN	
topics	• the scope of detailed design • detailed design: approaches, methods, and techniques • examples and case studies
lectures	3 days
study	3 days, with discussions

Figure 11.6 Formal training in knowledge-based technology: KBS design - I - b.

In some cases, the motivation which pushes an employee or a professional to move to the new field of knowledge-based technology derives from a personal interest towards professional advancement. These cases do not pose, in general, any specific problem, being based on an individual choice supported by serious motivations. People who desire to approach the KBS field are generally prepared to go through a hard training curriculum and to follow a gradual progress through the specific professional roles of the KBS field. In the few cases where individual motivations or skills are weak, after some unsuccessful attempts the initial decision to move to the KBS field is retracted by the trainee.

In other cases, the opportunity of moving to the field of knowledge-based technology is offered to all interested employees having the background specified by the company management. The aim of such initiatives is generally to support the establishment or the growth of the KBS department, by exploiting the potentials of currently under-employed personnel. These cases are much more critical, require a great effort, and - apart from rare exceptions - fail to produce the expected results. Quite often, the people involved in a re-training plan are inextricably bound to their original competence domain. After having been employed for several years in a specific job, they are unwilling to start from scratch with a new one. Moreover, they have often lost the flexibility essential in the approach towards a new technology, they lack the necessary background, they are very slow, or definitely incapable of learning. The most critical point for re-training is not teaching a lot of new and difficult things rapidly, but changing a rooted culture.

KNOWLEDGE ACQUISITION - 1	
topics	• knowledge sources: verbal data, written documents, naturalistic observation • analysis and selection of knowledge sources • the knowledge acquisition process: overall organization, planning, and management • examples and case studies
lectures	3 days
study	3 days, with discussions

KNOWLEDGE ACQUISITION - 2	
topics	• techniques for knowledge acquisition: definition and use • knowledge documentation: issues and problems • knowledge acquisition support tools: a survey • automatic knowledge acquisition: principles and tools
lectures	3 days
study	10 days, with discussions

KNOWLEDGE ACQUISITION WORKSHOP	
topics	• practical aspects of knowledge acquisition • practice with selected methods and techniques
workshop	5 days

KNOWLEDGE BASE CONSTRUCTION	
topics	• knowledge base construction: issues and problems • extensive knowledge acquisition • structuring of the knowledge base • the quality of the knowledge base • knowledge base documentation • examples and case studies
lectures	3 days
study	3 days, with discussions

Figure 11.7 Formal training in knowledge-based technology: KBS knowledge engineering.

In still other cases, personnel already employed in a traditional software development job are moved to a KBS department in order to fill in the gaps of a project team which cannot be completed with personnel having the needed background and competence. In these cases a rapid re-training plan - quite often supplemented with training on the job - is expected to do the trick; transforming a specialist from one field into a specialist of a different one. Obviously, almost all of these cases fail.

SYSTEM INTEGRATION ISSUES	
topics	• the software interface: goals, structure, and components • the external interface: goals, structure, and components • design and implementation issues
lectures	2 days
study	2 days, with discussions

HUMAN-COMPUTER INTERACTION	
topics	• the user interface: goals, structure, and components • human-computer interaction: concepts, approaches, and design principles • user modeling issues • user interface development tools • multimedia and hypermedia systems • examples and case studies
lectures	5 days
study	10 days, with discussions

EXPLANATION	
topics	• the explanation system: goals, structure, and components • generation of explanations: concepts, approaches, an design principles • user modeling issues • examples and case studies
lectures	5 days
study	10 days, with discussions

THE DEVELOPMENT SUPPORT SYSTEM	
topics	• the development support system: goals, structure, and components • design and implementation issues
lectures	3 days
study	2 days, with discussions

THE MAINTENANCE SUPPORT SYSTEM	
topics	• the maintenance support system: goals, structure, and components • design and implementation issues
lectures	3 days
study	2 days, with discussions

Figure 11.8 Formal training in knowledge-based technology: KBS design - II.

As previously shown, very often re-training efforts fail. The probability of success can be increased by making sure that the personnel involved in a re-training initiative has the following qualities:
• a sound and updated background in the field of computer science;
• high motivation and personal interest in moving to the new field of knowledge-based technology;
• the flexibility and capability essential for quick and thorough learning;

- freedom from any other job engagement for the whole duration of the re-training initiative.

In any case it should be recognized that a re-training initiative can only be aimed at preparing developers and knowledge engineers; designers or project leaders cannot be obtained directly through re-training. In particular, as far as the role of

---

NON-MONOTONIC REASONING, CONSTRAINT REASONING AND TRUTH MAINTENANCE
seminars   7 days

CASE-BASED AND ANALOGICAL REASONING
seminars   3 days

MODEL-BASED REASONING
seminars   5 days

TEMPORAL REASONING
seminars   3 days

APPROXIMATE AND UNCERTAIN REASONING
seminars   5 days

MACHINE LEARNING
seminars   5 days

PLANNING
seminars   3 days

REAL-TIME SYSTEMS
seminars   2 days

DIALOGUE SYSTEMS
seminars   3 days

NATURAL LANGUAGE PROCESSING
seminars   5 days

USER MODELING
seminars   3 days

Figure 11.9 Formal training in knowledge-based technology: KBS advanced.

KBS PROCESS MODEL, LIFE CYCLE, AND METHODOLOGY	
topics	• KBS process model • KBS life cycle: phases and tasks • KBS methodology: activities and methods • standardization issues • start-up and management of a methodological project • examples and case studies
seminars	4 days

SUPPORTING PROCESSES	
topics	• the supporting processes: concept and structure • quality assurance • verification and validation • documentation development • examples and case studies
seminars	3 days

PROJECT MANAGEMENT	
topics	• KBS project management: objectives and components • the project team • controlling and directing project development • failure types and causes • management for success: management rules • examples and case studies
seminars	2 days

PROJECT MANAGEMENT WORKSHOP	
topics	• practical aspects of KBS project management • case studies
workshop	3 days

OPPORTUNITY ANALYSIS AND PLAUSIBILITY STUDY	
topics	• opportunity analysis: goals and tasks • plausibility study: goals and tasks • examples and case studies
seminars	3 days

MANAGING A KBS INITIATIVE	
topics	• knowledge-based technology and innovation • introducing knowledge-based technology into an organization • ensuring development and monitoring progress • managing human resources • applied research and innovative experimentation • examples and case studies
seminars	2 days

Figure 11.10 Formal training in knowledge-based technology: KBS project management.

project leader is concerned, it is often said that it is easier for an experienced project leader in any technical field to learn about knowledge-based technology than for an experienced designer or knowledge engineer in the specific KBS field to learn about project management [Sacerdoti 91]. This is, however, hardly true in practice; a KBS project leader at the same time should be the best developer, designer, and knowledge engineer and, on top of this, he should have the specific competence and skill for managing the project and the project team. A specific technical background and experience are essential to be knowledgeable and authoritative.

Moreover, one should not forget that the type of training necessary for re-training cannot be very different from the one suggested in sections 11.5.2 and 11.5.3. Some adjustments and reductions may be reasonable, but all major topics must be covered in a systematic way. In some cases it might be appropriate to merge a re-training initiative with a normal training program; but in other cases this might be definitely inappropriate and detrimental. In any re-training initiative, several and serious intermediate evaluation tests should be planned in order to assess the progress of each individual participant. The passing of a test should be considered a mandatory condition for continuing the re-training program. People failing the test should be removed from the re-training initiative in due time, thus saving time and resources.

11.5.5   Continuing education

Knowledge-based technology is a very broad field and is still rapidly evolving. Therefore, one can hardly consider himself definitely and completely trained in this field: professionals must keep up-to-date with the most recent advances and continuously learn new emerging topics. This is the purpose of *continuing education*, an important issue which is often considered just a costly and unnecessary option.

The need for continuing education is straightforward. The only critical point is how to perform it effectively. The table of Figure 11.11 shows some possible approaches to continuing education, and demonstrates the main features involved.

Clearly, in each specific context, a different mix of the approaches proposed may be appropriate.

Regardless of the specific approach adopted to continuing education, a crucial point is that it cannot be done on an irregular basis. It should be carefully planned for a short-term period (for example, a year), taking into account several issues and constraints:

- current trends in knowledge-based technology;
- general goals and exigencies of the KBS department;
- specific goals of the continuing education action;
- individual professional needs, interests, and availability;
- approaches to continuing education actually available in the period considered;

- budget;
- project and productivity constraints.

It should be clear that continuing education is not a prize for a good job done, but a contribution offered to employees for professional advancement.

APPROACH	FEATURES
participation to scientific seminars and workshops	focused, effective, high quality, time-intensive, sometimes costly
participation to scientific conferences	broad spectrum, generally high quality, time-intensive, sometimes costly
participation to technical conferences	broad spectrum, often poor quality, information-oriented (products, suppliers, projects, etc.), time-intensive, sometimes costly
participation to technical courses	ranging from focused to broad-spectrum, sometimes effective, medium-quality, often very costly
regular reading of scientific journals	broad spectrum, very high quality, time consuming, very low cost
regular reading of technical journals	broad spectrum, often poor quality, information-oriented (products, suppliers, projects, etc.), time consuming, very low cost
irregular reading of scientific or technical journals	generally useless
internal seminars and workshops	very effective, suitable to cope with specific needs, good quality, generally costly

Figure 11.11 Approaches to continuing education.

11.5.6   Training non-technical members of the project team

In addition to the regular members of a project team, the supporting members should also be carefully trained before taking part in a KBS development effort [Winston and Prendergast 84], [Reitman 84], [Feigenbaum et al. 88]. Training supporting members, very often underestimated in practice, is a crucial point for the success of a KBS project. It is aimed at achieving two specific goals:

- providing a correct and sound background so that the supporting members play their role in the project team in a competent and effective way and be fully productive on their job;
- establishing a common basis of shared technical knowledge among all members of the project team, in order to support effective communication and cooperation.

Different training paths may be designed for each class of supporting members. In particular:
- all the supporting members (including the project manager, managers, domain experts, and users) should be made familiar with knowledge-based technology; a series of seminars (2 to 4) may be appropriate (including the topics of the unit "KBS introduction");
- the project manager and the domain experts should receive additional training about KBS life cycle, methodology, and project management (some topics from the units "KBS process model, life cycle, and methodology" and "Project management");
- domain experts should be specifically instructed in the field of knowledge analysis, modeling, and acquisition (some topics from the units "KBS process model, life cycle, and methodology", "Knowledge acquisition-1", "Knowledge acquisition-2", and "Knowledge base construction");
- users should be made aware of the problems related to KBS specification, verification and validation, delivery, maintenance and extension.

Not providing appropriate training to all supporting members who are expected to cooperate to a KBS project may cause serious technical and management problems leading to failure.

11.6   MANAGING RESEARCH AND DEVELOPMENT

11.6.1   Basic concepts

Knowledge-based technology is rapidly evolving. From the point of view of its development, it may be viewed as divided into three levels:
- *available technologies*, whose possible accomplishments have already been proven in several successful projects, being routinely applied in practical applications in industry and business;
- *frontier technologies*, whose practical use has not been proven yet, concerning newly emerging methods and techniques still needing substantial research and experimentation before being accepted for routine use in applications;
- *research technologies*, dealing with open issues, far beyond the level of currently available technology, strongly oriented towards the achievement of advances in basic knowledge.

The three levels defined above dynamically interact in two ways. On one hand, the new results developed at the research level are gradually transferred to the level of frontier technologies, and, eventually, to that of available technologies. On the other hand, the unsolved application needs which originate at the level of available technologies make up new issues for the level of frontier technologies and new challenges for the research level. The continuous progress of knowledge-based technology is the result of such a complex process, whose control is distributed among several agents: individual companies (both users and producers), research laboratories, and universities. National and international technological programs mediate among the many different forces responsible for this development process [Buchanan 86].

Independent of the levels defined above, knowledge-based technology is also a composite technology. As already discussed in section 1.1.1, it includes several components which have developed into well-organized topics over the last decades.

The two perspectives of levels and components introduced above are somehow independent. Each component of the technology includes topics which fall into anyone of the three levels, and, vice versa, each level encompasses several different components. Taking into account the two dimensions of levels and components, we may get a clear view of the complexity and vastness of knowledge-based technology.

In the design of KBS applications it may often happen to encounter difficult or unusual problems that cannot be solved using currently available techniques. These problems may be of two types:
- problems that can be currently solved using available technologies, which, however, are not known or not fully mastered by the team in charge of the project;
- problems that actually require frontier technologies - or even a basic research effort - and, therefore, are definitely beyond the potentials of currently available technology.

Thus, people in the field of knowledge-based technology are generally faced with two frontiers when they try to tackle problems outside or beyond their current capabilities:
- the *subjective frontier*, which separates the sub-set of knowledge-based technology mastered by an individual from the rest of the entire class of the available technologies;
- the *objective frontier*, which separates available technologies form frontier technologies and from research.

The two frontiers defined above deserve specific and different attention. The subjective frontier should be progressively pushed forward through continuing education and training - see section 11.5.5. Pushing the subjective frontier forward is the first goal for people willing to work using the most up-to-date and appropriate tools.

The objective frontier should be known very precisely, in order to avoid incurring the fatal error of using frontier or research technologies as if they were available technologies. The advancement of the objective frontier is the cumulated result of several, different efforts; it should be addressed only exceptionally in the frame of a production-oriented KBS group. In particular, the exploration of pure research issues, mainly oriented towards the advancement of basic scientific knowledge, should be generally excluded from the main tasks of a KBS department and left to academic or institutional research laboratories. The investigation of frontier topics, instead, can sometimes turn out to be a necessary task in the design of advanced KBS applications. Frontier issues can therefore be appropriately dealt with and profitably exploited by a robust and experienced KBS department, provided that this is done in a competent, well-structured, and disciplined way. *Research and development* covers the various activities a KBS department carries out in order to investigate and exploit frontier topics [Buchanan 86]. It includes two paradigms, namely: applied research and innovative experimentation. Both aim to experiment in putting available frontier techniques to work, not to develop new techniques. However, it sometimes happens that they also bring important contributions to the definition of new methods of general validity.

11.6.2   The paradigm of applied research

Applied research aims at exploiting frontier technologies to solve current problems of practical interest. Applied research originates therefore from a concrete problem and proceeds towards the exploration of new potential solutions.

The paradigm of applied research goes through the following main steps:

1. focus on a concrete problem and make sure that the problem at hand cannot be solved using available technologies;
2. develop a broad analysis of scientific and technical literature in the field of interest;
3. identify a frontier technique that seems promising for the solution of the problem at hand and study it in depth;
5. find out a method to apply the chosen technique to the problem at hand and develop pen-and-paper experiments; refine the method identified and, if necessary, develop modifications to the chosen technique as well;
6. experiment with the method proposed in practice on the problem at hand; develop a running prototype and experiment with it extensively (a research oriented KBS) - the most credible demonstration that ideas in the KBS field have power is with a prototype which shows that a new method is appropriate for solving a given class of problems;
7. analyze the following issues in detail; what are the design and implementation features that contribute to success? which are redundant? where are improvements needed?
8. refine the method proposed until it is fully appropriate for the problem considered;
9. generalize the method proposed - progress results from providing new knowledge that not only solves one specific problem but is generally applicable;

10.   describe the developed method in clear and general terms; study their main properties, establish their robustness and scope of applicability, investigate their weakness as well as its strengths; if appropriate, refine it again.
11.   apply the developed method to the problem at hand and test its validity in practice.

The above defined paradigm is only a schematic guideline for organizing an applied research initiative. Its practical implementation should carefully take into account the nature of the specific problem considered, the degree of experience and skill of the research team, the particular objectives and constraints of the initiative, the available resources, and the features of the general context where the research program is to be carried out.

Moreover, it should also be considered that often applied research is developed in the frame of international or government-run programs, which offer financial support but also impose their own rules to the management of an individual initiative. In such a case, particular attention should be paid to verify that the additional objectives and constraints set by the financing agency are not detrimental to the very goals of the specific research initiative of interest. One should not risk jeopardizing the results of a research effort with the sole purpose of getting financed.

Finally, it is important to remember that one should never set up an applied research initiative without having a concrete problem to solve. Applied research is not a way to get financial support or to promote the technical image of the company; with these objectives in mind, applied research is bound to fail and will only be a frustrating experience.

16.6.3   The paradigm of innovative experimentation

Innovative experimentation aims at experimenting with frontier technologies and at developing methods to exploit them for the solution of potential problems of practical interest. Innovative experimentation originates, therefore, from a technical interest and proceeds towards the exploration of its possible application to the solution of concrete problems. Both applied research and innovative experimentation have therefore the same goal, but pursue it through different paths. The former proceeds bottom-up from a specific problem towards the investigation of possible solutions, while the latter proceeds top-down from the study of possible solutions to their application to potential problems.

The paradigm of innovative experimentation is very similar to that of applied research presented in the previous section. The only difference is in the start-up; steps 1. and 3. should be modified as follows:
1.   focus on a promising frontier technique;
3.   find out a problem of potential interest to be used as a test-bed for practical experimentation.

Given the several similarities shared by applied research and innovative experimentation, one should not be tempted to apply one of the two paradigms indifferently. They have, in fact, different goals - namely: solving a problem or acquiring new technical knowledge, they require that different preconditions are satisfied, and they follow different paths. Moreover, they show different features as far as risk, costs, and time are concerned.

Finally, it is also worth stressing that all the steps which are stated the same way in the two paradigms, have, however, a slightly different implementation, due to the different paths followed. The differences between the two paradigms proposed are deeper than what might appear at first glance; they serve different purposes and should be exploited appropriately.

12

PRACTICE AND EXPERIENCE

12.1   EXEMPLARY CASES: CONCEPT AND OBJECTIVES

As illustrated in chapters 9 and 10, managing a KBS project or a KBS initiative requires a specific technical background and a variety of skills. Most importantly, it requires practice and experience which can only be accumulated over the years through individual work, exploration, and learning.

In order to help the readers gain at least a more concrete insight into the practical application of the principles illustrated in previous chapters, we propose here a collection of selected *exemplary cases*. These are inspired from real cases, derived from professional practice. The original cases have been simplified, elaborated in some important aspects, and made anonymous; their context and the specific situations presented have been freely elaborated by the authors. Any reference to real persons, companies, or facts is merely casual.

Each case is introduced by a presentation showing its main points, and has a discussion part, which proposes an assessment of the case and some conclusions of general validity. The cases selected for presentation include successful stories and failures, and concern several aspects of the KBS life cycle. The treatment of these cases does not focus on technical issues, but rather on management aspects.

The cases proposed aim at providing concrete material for the readers interested in the project leader perspective. In this sense, they may be considered as a complement to chapters 9 and 10, devoted to consolidating and reinforcing the general knowledge acquired.

The cases are primarily designed as reading material. However, they may also serve as the starting point for active training in KBS project management. With the support of an experienced tutor, the cases may be further elaborated and can provide the background for full case-studies. New problems may be identified, specific goals may be considered, hypothetical solutions may be proposed, and their likely consequences analyzed and discussed.

12.2   EXEMPLARY CASES

Case 1.   A failed KBS initiative: the critical role of the first project

Case presentation

In 1987, a medium-size company active in the field of mechanical manufacturing decided to start a KBS initiative in order to assess the potentials of the new technology for the development of some advanced applications in the area of factory automation. Driven by the desire to be concrete, the management rejected the proposal of an opportunity analysis, and preferred to begin first with an experimental project. In order to keep the costs of this explorative effort reasonably low, a simple application was chosen, which concerned a KBS for the scheduling of preventive maintenance for a class of newly installed tool machines. This application, although simple, was considered appropriate for a first evaluation of the potential benefits of knowledge-based technology.

The design and development of the KBS was assigned to an external supplier and successfully carried out. After 14 months from the start, the first release of the KBS was running in the operational environment. After a couple of months of experimental use, the head of the maintenance department was fully satisfied with the performance of the KBS, and appreciated it as a useful and effective working tool.

The application was, however, greatly criticized by the manager of the data processing department. The key question raised was the necessity to resort to the new, difficult, and costly knowledge-based technology. Apparently, a fully equivalent (if not even better) system could have been produced using traditional software techniques in less time and at a lower cost.

The top management was highly influenced by this technical evaluation, and knowledge-based technology was not considered worth further attention.

Discussion

The case shows that scarce consideration of the strategic goals of a project may result in serious failures, even if a technical success is achieved.

In the KBS project reported, the primary strategic goal was to show the potentials and the benefits of KBSs, especially in comparison to traditional software. This goal was underestimated and not taken into account in the choice of the application domain to be faced. This was in fact too simple and poorly appropriate for the specific features of knowledge-based technology. The critical observations of the manager of the data processing department were correct. The reasons supporting the adoption of knowledge-based technology and its potential advantages remained unclear: only its technical difficulty, long development time, and high cost were evident. So, knowledge-based technology was definitely rejected, being considered worthless for the company.

The case presented is a typical example of a failed project, and demonstrates that often the failure of the first project may entail the failure of the whole technology.

Case 2.   A failed KBS initiative: the effect of many wrong decisions

Case presentation

The case concerns a large manufacturing company producing complex electro-mechanical equipment with computer-based control. In 1988, in the mechanical design department of the company the opportunity of utilizing knowledge-based technology to develop an intelligent interface for a large library of mathematical and engineering packages was envisaged. Therefore, the manager of the design department asked an external professional for technical support.

The consultant provided the basic concepts of knowledge-based technology, and illustrated the conditions for its correct and effective use. He focused on its potential benefits, risks, and costs, as well as on the main steps required for carrying out a successful KBS initiative. After an analysis of the situation, the consultant realized that there were several potential KBS applications in the company, and that the proposed KBS was too complex from the technical point of view and apparently worthless for the intended users. Therefore, he advised the manager of the mechanical design department that the most appropriate action for the company was to carry out an opportunity analysis before starting a concrete KBS project.

However, the manager insisted on keeping the first experiment with knowledge-based technology inside his department; according to him, it would have been too long and difficult to involve other company departments, and, especially, the top management. He also confirmed his intention to focus on the application domain initially proposed, disregarding its technical complexity. Therefore, he asked the consultant to prepare a plan to re-train three to four people to the new field of knowledge-based technology and thus putting together an appropriate project team. Once again, he was advised that re-training of personnel was hard and risky, most often failing to reach the desired results. The manager argued that there was no possibility to hire new people and that the persons to be involved in the re-training program had an excellent background and the capability to learn quickly.

A six months re-training program was then prepared and carried out. However, it turned out to be a real disaster. The participants were requested to take part in this program while doing their normal job. Actually, they had no more than half a day per week for training. They did not have enough time to attend the scheduled courses, to study, and to do experimental activity. Upon request of the external consultant, the re-training program was stopped after 12 weeks. Only half of the scheduled courses had been taught, no individual study and no experimental activity had been carried out.

Discussion

The initiative failed because of a combination of errors. The manager of the design department misunderstood the conditions for introducing the knowledge-based technology into the organization. The only right step was to ask an external

consultant; but, unfortunately, his advice was not considered. Many wrong decisions were made:
- limiting the initiative to the design department and not involving the top management;
- focusing on a technically complex application domain;
- underestimating the difficulty of re-training;
- omitting to create strong motivation and commitment within the group involved in the re-training course;
- facing the re-training plan with little determination.

The failure caused no consequences either to the company or to the manager of the design department. The initiative had such little impact that nobody, inside and outside the design department, actually noticed it.

Case 3. Strong and concrete motivation is necessary to support a KBS initiative: otherwise, a failure is most likely to occurs

Case presentation

In 1991, a small engineering company active in the field of industrial automation started a research and development project in the area of the knowledge-based technology, financially supported by a public agency. Initially, an analysis aimed at identifying the goals of the project and the potential application domain was carried out. It was decided to focus on a topic considered potentially beneficial for an important client operating in the field of injection-moulded products. In particular, the project was assigned the goal to develop a knowledge-based component of a CAD/CAM system for the design of moulds and the optimization of injection parameters.

The project plan developed for this goal included a ten month training program, structured in two parts, one for the technical staff and the other for the managers. More specifically, the training program for the managers included two full-day seminars on the following topics:
- basic concepts of knowledge-based technology;
- KBS life cycle, development methodologies, and project management;
- potential application areas;
- benefits and costs.

The training program for the technical staff was structured in three stages:
1. basic concepts and techniques, including: knowledge representation, reasoning paradigms, artificial intelligence programming using Prolog, knowledge acquisition and knowledge base construction;
2. KBS project management techniques, with specific emphasis on opportunity analysis, plausibility study and development of the prototype;
3. advanced topics, including KBS architectures, user interface, justification and explanation.

These three stages were expected to include lectures, autonomous readings, study, and homework on artificial intelligence programming and Prolog.

The management of the company decided to start the training program for the technical staff while the trainees were still engaged in the projects where they were previously assigned. In this way, they were supposed to carry out their current job (which was not very demanding since their projects were coming to an end) and, at the same time, follow the training program, so as to be ready ten months later for the start of the KBS project.

By September 1991 the training initiative was started as scheduled. The first courses on basic concepts and techniques were enthusiastically accepted, and the technical personnel started to work on specific assignments on artificial intelligence programming. The execution of the assignments was proceeding well, when, after three months from the start, an unforeseen event occurred. One of the most important clients of the company requested a substantial revision of the specifications of a system currently being developed. As a result, additional man-power was urgently requested. The management was then forced to allocate more personnel on this project, including the one involved in the training program. Therefore, these could progressively devote less and less time to the study and experimentation activities. Eventually, they had no time to attend the courses nor to carry out the assignments. Courses were delayed and the fulfilling of assignments was postponed. This made the initial enthusiasm and interest of the trainees towards the initiative decrease rapidly. After five months from the start, the training program was definitely behind schedule, and the management decided to temporarily stop it. The training program for the managers was never started.

In the meantime, the management realized that the client operating in the field of injection-moulded products who had initially declared his interest to experiment the new knowledge-based technology, was actually not available to start a concrete KBS project.

A couple of months later, it was decided that the whole KBS initiative was not worthwhile and it was definitely stopped.

Discussion

The case reported above illustrates the failure not only of a training program, but, more importantly, of a KBS initiative. A substantial critical point affected the case considered since the very beginning. There was no concrete motivation to acquire and apply knowledge-based technology other than that of obtaining the financial support offered by the funding agency. To this purpose a possible client for the technology was identified, a potential application domain chosen, and a training program started.

In front of concrete difficulties, the training program failed. The assumption that it could be carried out concurrently with ongoing production engagements was revealed to be overly optimistic. For a new KBS initiative, training is a very critical issue, and a full-time commitment of the trainees is necessary. Moreover, managers should always be trained first, since they must make the most important decisions. They have to be aware of the main features of the technology, of its potentials, of its limits, and of the rules for its correct and profitable use.

The first possible client, interested in seeing an experiment with KBSs, was not willing to invest money in a concrete project. Without actual application goals, the whole initiative ended in a failure.

Case 4.   A missed KBS opportunity: a strategic decision cannot be based on a superficial analysis

Case presentation

In 1988 a medium-size company active in the field of computer-based training decided to explore the potentials of new computer technologies. One of the external consultants of the company, who was not an expert in the KBS field, proposed to focus on artificial intelligence. The top management of the company accepted the proposal and decided to organize a short introductory course on knowledge-based technology and its impact on computer-based training. To this purpose an experienced researcher in the field of intelligent tutoring systems was invited.

During the course, several informal discussions with the participants, coming from different areas of the company, pointed out the existence of several apparently promising opportunities for extending and improving traditional training products with knowledge-based components. The top management was informed of the results of this discussion by the technical director of the company, and decided to explore the possibility of starting a specific project concerning the improvement of one of the most important and strategic products of the company. The same consultant who initially proposed considering artificial intelligence as a promising technology, was asked to carry out a preliminary study in order to analyze the problem in detail, to provide a precise specification of the new knowledge-based product, and to assess the benefits and the costs of the project. The management asked the consultant to conclude the study as soon as possible, so as to insert the project in an application for financial support in the field of applied research currently under preparation.

The analysis of the problem was superficial, the definition of the specifications poorly detailed, the identification of potential benefits vague, and the cost estimate very rough. The management, on the basis of such preliminary indications, came to the decision of not undertaking the project, since the potential benefits did not justify the estimated costs. As a consequence, knowledge-based technology was not investigated further in the company.

Discussion

The withdrawal of the project - indeed a strategic one - was mainly due to a superficial preliminary study. The problem approached and the issue of integration of the knowledge-based component with the pre-existing product were not analyzed in detail. It was not possible to precisely characterize the new product, and, as a consequence, identify the specific benefits of the project. Moreover, the technical aspects were overlooked, no project plan was developed, the resources necessary for the development of the KBS were not appropriately identified, and the required investments were wrongly estimated. The consultant in charge of the preliminary study, unable to develop a correct analysis, took a precautionary stand; he pointed out only a few benefits, but foresaw high costs. As an outcome, a promising opportunity was missed.

Just one basic mistake can be recognized in this case: the preliminary study was assigned to a consultant who was not competent in knowledge-based technology. The rest was only a consequence of this initial error.

Case 5.   A KBS initiative failed after a good start: strong management commitment and continuous support are necessary for the growth of a KBS group

Case presentation

In 1986, a production department of a large industrial group operating in the manufacturing field, stimulated by several successful stories reported in the literature, saw the opportunity of experimenting with the new knowledge-based technology to tackle the problem of on-line quality control of a rather complex product considered of crucial importance for the whole group. Therefore, the information technology company of the group was appointed to this activity and was encouraged to start an initiative in the KBS field. Three people with a sound background and a concrete experience in knowledge-based technology were hired: two of them were good developers and the third a knowledge engineer with some additional competence in KBS design. A simple KBS development tool was acquired and a first prototype developed. In less than one year the results of the project were demonstrated to the management of the production department. The feedback was very positive and therefore the KBS unit was asked to complete the application and to transfer it to field testing. After 15 months from the start of the project the target system was completed, fully tested, and eventually delivered for routine use with full user satisfaction.

Having successfully completed the first project, the KBS unit prepared a plan for future development; this included:

- enlarging the group with three more people;
- improving the technical level of the group through an appropriate training and continuing education program;
- carrying out a full opportunity analysis throughout the whole group with the support of an external consultant;
- starting-up a regular production activity in the KBS field.

Unfortunately, this plan was not supported by the technical manager of the information technology company for several reasons:

- the available budget was limited; it did not allow hiring new people, carrying out a training and continuing education program, and getting the cooperation of a consultant;
- an opportunity analysis at group level, although correct and appropriate from an abstract point of view, was difficult and risky to propose;
- the potentials of the new knowledge-based technology, shown in just one successful application, was still far from being definitely proven; who could guarantee that the following projects would also be successful?

Besides these justifications, the real reason of the negative attitude of the technical manager was that he did not understand the strategic value and the potentials of the new technology. The opportunity to exploit KBSs as a new, powerful leverage for innovation was quite clear to the KBS unit, but it did not have enough credibility and authority to convince the manager. This, in turn, was closely bound to more traditional information technologies, and did not have the foresight necessary to recognize a new opportunity.

Later, several other departments requested the KBS unit to analyze potential KBS applications and develop new KBSs; these needs, however, could be only partially satisfied. So, in about one year, the common opinion among the group was that the KBS unit had been successful just in one simple case - perhaps more by chance rather than for its competence and skill - but it was unable to satisfy regular requests for KBS applications. Most of the departments interested in KBS applications resorted to external suppliers.

Discussion

The case reported shows very clearly that a good start is not enough. A strong commitment by the management and a continuous support is necessary to ensure development. An initiative that does not consolidate and grow is destined to fail.

Case 6.   A KBS initiative with a good start but a too slow and weak development: strategic vision, concrete goals, and careful planning are necessary to push innovation forth

Case presentation

Towards the end of 1980, the corporate research and development laboratory of a large telecommunication group started a broad-spectrum initiative in the KBS field. The top management was convinced that knowledge-based technology might be very promising for the laboratory and, therefore, granted all needed support to the KBS initiative. It was well-funded, well-staffed, and correctly managed. After appropriate training and technology transfer, a five person KBS group was fully operative by mid 1982. Its activity was initially oriented towards the development of demonstrators, aimed at showing the potentials of knowledge-based technology to the various departments of the company. This activity was carried out for about two years and turned out to be a real success. The preliminary evaluation of the demonstrators developed was positive, and, therefore, the initiative gained further support by the top management. Later, the laboratory got involved in a large international research and development program in the field of information technology. The KBS group joined this initiative and became involved in the development of advanced research prototypes for a four year period. This activity proved to be quite successful too; several experimental systems were developed, international connections established, and valuable know-how acquired. The group also grew from the quantitative point of view; to the initial five people six more were gradually added.

After about seven years from the start, the KBS group had produced a lot of scientific results and a number of running systems; however, no crucial problem for the company had been solved. The KBS group had a very high technological profile but no concrete productivity. No real application had been tackled and the concrete needs of the various companies of the group had never been considered. The quality of the prototypes developed testified for the competence and skill of the technical personnel employed, but this know-how had not been sufficiently exploited. There was no concrete return from the investment made in knowledge-based technology.

The top management was disappointed by this outcome, decided to stop supporting the KBS initiative, and called an external consultant to check the situation.

Early in 1988, a new general manager was appointed for the laboratory. He resumed the case of the KBS group and, after a careful analysis of the situation, decided to carry out the following actions:
- he fired the manager of the KBS group;
- he divided the group into two units: a research and development (R&D) unit (three people) which continued with the well-established research and development initiatives, and an applications and products (A&P) unit (eight people) in charge of developing concrete applications and products to be delivered to the various companies of the group;
- he had the former external consultant in charge of the check-up prepare a detailed four-year activity plan for each unit;
- he appointed a new manager for each new unit, namely: the senior researcher of the former KBS group became the manager of the R&D unit, while the manager of the A&P unit was hired.

The key point of this new operation was to establish a close connection between technology, applications, and users. A progressive technology infusion in some selected production environments was started and a few concrete exemplary applications developed. Their success helped raise the confidence and the interest in knowledge-based technology and as a result new application projects were launched. Eventually, knowledge-based technology was largely accepted in several company areas and used as a powerful tool for the development of advanced, innovative applications. In three years the A&P unit produced three prototypes and two target systems were delivered for field testing. In addition, the activity of the R&D unit was directed towards more concrete exigencies; two advanced research prototypes were transferred to the A&P unit to be integrated into future applications.

By the beginning of the fourth year, it was decided to enlarge and further support this successful initiative. The R&D and A&P units became the kernel of a new corporate center for knowledge-based technology and applications.

Discussion

The case reported shows some important facts:
- a good start-up does not alone ensure a strong development;
- a timely and firm management action can put a weak initiative on the right track and turn it into a real success, provided that a sound technical background is available.

The manager of the initial KBS group was a scientist, a skilled researcher, without, however, a concrete understanding of the role of knowledge-based technology as an innovation leverage and a business factor. He was able to create an active and high-level research group, but the activity of the KBS group remained totally disconnected from the practical exigencies of the organization it belonged to. He lacked a strategic foresight of the KBS initiative and was unable to identify concrete goals.

The newly appointed manager of the laboratory was very fast in making complex decisions and could turn a failure into a success. He did its job correctly and effectively; he took the opportunity to support innovation, and, finally, checked results.

Research and development cannot be carried out indefinitely without any link to real problems and without any feedback from the users. In the case examined, technological experimentation was performed over more than seven years, indeed a period too long even for a large and rich organization. Technology advancements must be exploited in real domains and delivered to the end-users. A strong connection with a concrete application context is an essential component of any technology transfer initiative.

Case 7. Two plans for the start-up of a KBS initiative: a top-down and a bottom-up approach

Case presentation

In 1990, a large company operating in the area of canned foods - from cultivation to production, and distribution - decided to start an organic and well-structured initiative in the KBS field. Therefore, the management asked a consulting firm to analyze the situation and to propose a concrete plan for introducing knowledge-based technology correctly end effectively into the organization. The only explicit requirements stated by the management were:
• the plan should enable the company to assume in the mid-term the role of direct producer of KBSs;
• the plan should not exceed four years;
• the plan should be ready within four months.

The consulting firm, after four-months work, produced two alternative plans to be submitted to the management, inspired by different approaches, namely top-down and bottom-up. The essential points of these plans are reported below.

Top-down plan

phase 1: Analysis and familiarization   [4 months]
1.   Identify the role of the organization in front of knowledge-based technology (direct producer)
2.   Identify the objectives of the initiative (develop concrete KBS applications, make knowledge-based technology accepted within the organization, establish a formal KBS department)
3.   Identify the constraints of the initiative (availability of the management, the potential users, and the experts, budget, time, visibility of results)
4.   Plan and execute specific training actions to familiarize the management, the potential users, and the experts with knowledge-based technology

phase 2: Opportunity analysis   [4 months]
5.   Execute an opportunity analysis with the support of an external consultant
6.   Identify the first project to be carried out (a medium-complexity project in a significant domain)

phase 3: The first project: plausibility study   [4 months]
7.   Perform a plausibility study for the first project with the support of an external
      consultant
8.   Obtain approval from the management

phase 4: Project team aggregation and training   [8 months]
9.   Define the composition of the project team for the first project (four people to be
      trained internally, plus an external consultant as project leader and designer)
10.   Hire the necessary personnel (four graduates with a good background in
      computer science)
11.   Train personnel with the support of an external consultant or consulting
      company

phase 5: The first project: development   [8 months]
12.   Execute the first project

phase 6: The first project: assessment of results   [2 months]
13.   Evaluate the obtained results
14.   Plan developments (two more projects)
15.   Obtain approval from the management

phase 7: Consolidation   [12 months]
16.   Expand the KBS group with new people (a designer and project leader and two
      graduates with a good background in computer science)
17.   Train the newly hired personnel
18.   Execute the two selected projects

phase 8: Establishment of a KBS department   [2 months]
19.   Evaluate the obtained results
20.   Establish a formal KBS department

Bottom-up plan

phase 1: Analysis   [2 months]
1.   Identify the role of the organization in front of knowledge-based technology
      (direct producer)
2.   Identify the objectives of the initiative (develop concrete KBS applications,
      make knowledge-based technology be accepted within the organization,
      establish a formal KBS department)
3   Identify the constraints of the initiative (availability of the management, the
      potential users, and the experts, budget, time, visibility of results)

phase 2: The first two projects: plausibility study   [6 months]
4.   Identify the first projects to be carried out with the support of an external
      consultant (two simple but significant projects in different areas of the
      organization)
5.   Perform a plausibility study for the two projects with the support of an external
      consultant

6.   Obtain approval from the management

phase 3: The first two projects: development   [12 months]
7.   Execute the first two projects resorting to the support of an external consulting
      company

phase 4: Diffusion and familiarization   [4 months]
8.   Evaluate the obtained results and spread them throughout the organization
9.   Plan and execute specific training actions to familiarize the management, the
      potential users, and the experts with knowledge-based technology
10.   Plan developments (establishment of a formal KBS department)
11.   Obtain approval from the management

phase 5: Establishment of a KBS department   [8 months]
12.   Define the composition of a KBS department (four people to be trained
      internally, plus an experienced designer)
13.   Hire the necessary personnel (four graduates with a good background in
      computer science and one experienced designer)
14.   Train personnel with the support of an external consultant or consulting
      company
15.   Establish a formal KBS department

Discussion

The top-down plan spans a period of 44 months. In fact, it is very long; this is,
however, typical of all top-down approaches. Proceeding top-down is generally
more disciplined and transparent and less risky than proceeding bottom-up, but is
longer and more costly. Note that the long duration of the plan has, however, the
positive effect of allowing a distribution of costs over several years, thus keeping
yearly budgets within more acceptable constraints. Some variations might be
interesting. For example, if one wants to facilitate and shorten the plan, the execution
of opportunity analysis (phase 2) could be postponed after the establishment of the
KBS department (phase 8), i.e. after the conclusion of the plan. Or, the establishment
of a KBS department (phase 8) could be anticipated after phase 6, discarding
consolidation (phase 7). These modifications can speed up the introduction of
knowledge-based technology into the organization and make it less expensive.
However, they might be detrimental to the soundness and the robustness of the
initiative, thus causing possible problems to future developments (for example,
impairing acceptance and the exploitation of the technology throughout the
organization).
      The bottom-up plan spans a period of 32 months. It is shorter and less costly than
the top-down plan. It is also quite effective, even if it concludes with a smaller and
less experienced KBS department and with only two KBS applications instead of
three. Moreover, it may be risky since the impact and level of acquisition of the new
technology is directly bound to the two applications initially chosen. If this choice
reveals to be inappropriate during the execution of the plan, the global innovation
effort may be heavily compromised.

The company for which the two plans were developed, after careful consideration, decided to adopt the top-down plan, anticipating however phase 4 before phase 3. After successful execution of phases 1, 2, and 4, the company was unable to focus a concrete application domain for starting phase 3. After several months unsuccessfully spent in trying to convince the managers of the departments potentially interested in KBS applications to start with concrete projects, the entire KBS initiative gradually lost its initial drive. The top management was highly disappointed, but it did not have enough authority to be convincing nor was it willing to impose a technical choice, even if considered of strategic importance. In less than one year after the conclusion of phase 4, of the six people who had attended the training program, four were hired by other companies for a job in the specific KBS field, and two were re-employed in the EDP department.

A good plan is clearly not enough to guarantee the success of a KBS initiative. In the case considered, opportunity analysis (phase 2) was not performed correctly. It was assigned to a consulting firm (different from the one in charge of phases 1 and 4) and carried out with only minor involvement of the interested departments. The project leader in charge of opportunity analysis never personally met the managers of the departments where the analysis was carried out. They felt excluded from the initiative. Moreover, the master plan developed focused o only four potential KBS applications, and failed to produce a detailed analysis and ranking; no specific suggestion about the first project to consider was provided. A good opportunity analysis carried out correctly and precisely would have helped establish a more effective cooperation with the interested departments; most probably, the difficulties encountered in the starting of phase 3 could have been overcome.

Case 8.   Applying traditional software development methods to KBS projects may be a cause of serious failures

Case presentation

In 1987, the manager of a technical department of a large company operating in the field of information systems, decided to start an explorative effort with KBSs. A group of 12 mostly newly hired people was seriously trained in knowledge-based technology for about nine months. Later, four pilot projects were started. However, since all the newly trained people were fairly young and with only little experience in the company, it was decided to give the responsibility of these projects to four expert project leaders with a vast experience in managing software projects, but without any background in knowledge-based technology. The projects were managed appropriately, but according to strictly traditional software engineering principles. All four project leaders could not follow in detail the technical activity of their project teams, and could only partially check the results obtained from a strictly functional point of view. All four KBS projects failed to produce meaningful and technically coherent results. In particular:
• Project No. 1 produced a full demonstrator of a decision-support tool for assessing technologies (especially, the environmental impact) in eight months. This turned out, however, to be far from the requirements and expectations of the users. Therefore, the project was abandoned.

- Project No. 2 was concerned with a KBS devoted to support legal experts in assessing the correct application of complex regulations in the compilation of a specific class of contracts. The project did not succeed in producing the first demonstrator because of knowledge acquisition problems. After acquiring a limited and initial amount of knowledge, the knowledge acquisition task revealed to be very hard and quite impossible to continue. The project was stopped after four months from the start. Apparently, this failure was due to scarce availability and lack of cooperation on the part of domain experts, however, the main reason was the lack of an experienced project leader, capable of successfully guiding the team through difficulties.
- Project No. 3 dealt with the problem of scheduling the daily activity of a large computing center, and project No. 4 focused on the querying of a very large data base containing both textual information and images about an extensive collection of works of art. In about six months, both of them produced small application systems of limited utility, very far from the original goals, and, in particular, not KBSs. The former was a very traditional scheduler, based on dispatching rules, developed, however, using a rule-based shell; the latter was a simple hypertext application, linked to an image data base on a video-disk.

After the conclusion of the four pilot projects, the manager of the technical department where the KBS initiative had been developed, disappointed by the results obtained, informally asked an external consultant to assess the situation, and identify the major causes of the failure occurred. The analysis turned out to be very simple; lack of specific competence in KBS project management. This was clearly explained to the manager who eventually agreed upon the cause identified and recognized that the projects failed not because of knowledge-based technology but only because of incompetent project management. The experimentation of knowledge-based technology was, however, not encouraged further.

Discussion

The case reported shows an example of a multiple failure. Technical staff and training were adequate, but project management was inappropriate. Project leaders were chosen - according to company-wide accepted rules - only for their seniority, regardless of their specific competence. They did their best in managing their projects, but, of course, they kept to the only management methodologies they knew, namely those of information system design and software engineering.

More precisely:
- Project No. 1 failed because the project leader had no knowledge about the concept, scope, and objectives of a demonstrator and, therefore, the KBS developed turned out to be functionally weak and practically useless. For the managers and the users who attended the demonstration and evaluated the project, the system failed to produce the desired results.
- Project No. 2 could have reached a successful result, if an appropriate knowledge acquisition strategy would have been adopted from the very beginning. This was, however, beyond the competence of the project leader and of the project team. Traditional system analysis techniques applied to knowledge analysis and acquisition resulted being definitely inappropriate and ineffective.
- Projects No. 3 and 4, run in a strictly traditional way, produced only small, poorly useful traditional systems.

Case 9.   Skipping the plausibility study can definitely spoil a project

Case presentation

In 1985 a large company operating in the field of steel production began an explorative initiative with knowledge-based technology. By 1987, a first KBS project was started in the area of process supervision and operator support for a continuous casting plant. Contrary to the suggestion of the scientific consultant in charge of the project, the plausibility study was skipped and the project started with the construction of a demonstrator. The reason for this decision was the need to have concrete and quick results, able to convince the top management of the appropriateness and the potentials of the new knowledge-based technology.

The demonstrator turned out to be very successful. The top management was enthusiastic about the new technology, and decided to immediately start a full project for a prototype and, later, a target system installed on the plant. A competent and robust project team was formed, and all the needed resources were granted to the project. Results were expected in an 18 months period due to the fact that an important vice-president position was going to become vacant, and the manager who was specifically supporting the KBS initiative, wanted to exploit the project's positive results as a leverage for his personal career.

Once again, the scientific consultant of the project advised the project managers to carry out a regular plausibility study before starting with the prototype phase. However, the suggestion was rejected with the following reasons:

• there was no need to estimate resources and costs, since all necessary investments and expenses had already been approved;
• there was no need for further studying and analyzing the problem, since the demonstrator was sufficiently convincing;
• there was a real need to shorten the development time as much as possible, in order to meet the scheduled deadline.

In ten months the project failed. A number of unforeseen difficulties came up immediately after the start of the project:

• the definition of the functional specifications of the complete KBS, not faced during the construction of the demonstrator, turned out to be difficult and controversial; the different viewpoints of the persons involved (process operators, head plant manager, and department manager) pushed the specifications to continuously expand beyond reasonable limits, thus dramatically increasing the complexity of the project;
• the application domain considered turned out to be more complex and larger than estimated during the construction of the demonstrator;
• advanced technical issues had to be faced in order to meet the stated specifications; these included in particular:
  - representation of temporal knowledge and temporal reasoning;
  - real-time problem solving based on incremental reasoning strategies;
  - advanced knowledge acquisition aids (including learning capabilities and automatic knowledge checking tools) to support end-users in directly updating the knowledge base;
• the development tools utilized for the demonstrator which were supposed to be appropriate also for the prototype, on the contrary, had to be changed, thus requiring a re-training of the project team;

- the cooperation of domain experts turned out to be difficult to obtain; they could not guarantee the needed availability which, of course, was greater than that given to the construction of the demonstrator (most of them were even convinced that their contribution was no longer necessary in this phase of the project);
- the project team included competent and skilled personnel, hired specifically for this project, but with very different backgrounds and experience; the project leader had enormous difficulties in trying to establish a common methodology and working practice.

The project leader, fully aware of how these difficulties could be solved, lacked, however, the necessary authority and management support to make the appropriate decisions and, more importantly, the ability to implement them. He realized that the resources allocated to the project were mostly wasted in useless efforts, and the time constraints imposed to the project could not be met, therefore resulting in a dead-end situation. Eventually, he decided to stop the project. The manager supporting the initiative was strongly disappointed; the project leader was fired and the technical staff was transferred to a research and development department.

Discussion

A regular plausibility study would certainly have helped avoid the failure illustrated. It is apparent that most of the problems encountered could have been foreseen and easily solved. Moreover, the demonstrator had most probably been oversold, thus creating exaggerated expectations. In addition, the management was not aware of the potentials and the limits of knowledge-based technology and of the rules for a correct and effective application.

Case 10. The lack of rigid goal orientation and control may cause a project to get lost in never-ending technical discussions and eventually fail

Case presentation

In 1989, a medium-size chemical company active in the field of dyes decided to develop a KBS application for on-line process supervision. The project was assigned to the internal KBS group who had been active for the past four years. After a plausibility study carried out by an external consulting firm, the development of the prototype was started. In the first design steps it turned out that the different knowledge types and reasoning mechanisms involved in the application domain were more varied than foreseen. Moreover, the draft technical design developed during the plausibility study turned out to be absolutely inappropriate, and the technical problems to face far more complex than expected. The designer, the knowledge engineer, and the developers involved in the project started a long series of technical meetings in order to get a deeper insight into the matter. The conclusion of this extensive analysis, carried out during a three months period, was that further investigation was needed. The project leader, informed by the designer of the unexpected difficulty, paid only minor attention to the problem; he was quite satisfied to see that people were working hard and took technical problems into appropriate consideration. The work of the project team continued for more than two months. Diverging opinions among the designer and the knowledge engineer and the developers emerged. These were strongly supported by their proponents, and the team could not reach any final result shared by everybody.

Worried about the delay, the project leader eventually took active part in the technical debate and in a couple of meetings he validated and approved the solution proposed by the designer. The implementation of the empty system was then carried out and the construction of the knowledge base begun. However, the prototype never arrived to a satisfactory development stage. Some functional specifications turned out to be definitely out of reach; the operation of the KBS was weak and its behavior not convincing; the knowledge base was hard to check and to expand. The prototype left the users quite unsatisfied; the management was disappointed and it decided not to carry the prototype over to the target application field. The project was then stopped and considered a failure.

Discussion

Several reasons might be mentioned to explain the failure occurred, but all of them point to a lack of project management. The technical solution adopted was proposed by the designer and then imposed by the project leader. The developers were obliged to implement a solution that they did not consider appropriate. The knowledge engineer did his job using an empty system that failed to respond to his requirements. In such a situation, the quality of the work of the developers and of the knowledge engineer was definitely spoiled. Difficulties and problems arising during KBS development were all attributed to the technical choices considered inappropriate, for which only the designer and the project leader were responsible. No attempt was made to solve problems and overcome difficulties; both the developers and the knowledge engineer were tacitly happy to find concrete support in their original opinion in system failures. The technical decision made was wrong, and their negative consequences were eventually visible.

The main errors incurred by the project leader were:

- not having checked the quality of plausibility study at the moment of its delivery by the external consulting firm in charge of it;
- having paid only minor attention to the control of the temporal development of the project, far slower than normal;
- having overlooked the problem initially raised by the designer, neglecting to face it in time and in person;
- having allowed the developers and the knowledge engineer to interfere with the designer, thus overlapping their professional roles and competence;
- having allowed a free style of working, based on the harmful principle of involving everyone in all matters concerned, with the result of amplifying problems through endless technical discussions, failing, at the same time, to produce any concrete solution;
- having eventually made an important decision too fast, without offering sufficient technical motivations to all people involved, and, therefore, without gaining their approval and cooperation.

The critical situation occurred could have been dealt with easily by the project leader at different stages of the project development:

- at the very beginning, by requesting the external consulting firm to revise the plausibility study;
- at the time the first delay in the temporal development of the project occurred (about two months after the start of the design activity), by personally checking the situation, restoring a correct working practice, and - if necessary - providing the designer with the appropriate technical support;
- later, at the time the problem was first detected by the designer, by personally taking care of it in time;
- finally, after more than five months delay, by first re-establishing a correct management style, and then solving the technical problem identified together only with the designer.

All these opportunities were unfortunately not taken by the project leader.

Case 11. The attitude of a knowledge engineer to replace domain experts, if not diagnosed in time, may bring a project to failure

Case presentation

In 1990, a management consulting firm was asked by an important client to develop a KBS application in the domain of strategic decision making. After a short plausibility study developed by an external consultant, the project was started. All the technical tasks necessary for the design and construction of the KBS were assigned to an external supplier. A specialist in strategic planning of the management consulting firm was specifically trained in the field of knowledge analysis and acquisition and became part of the project team with the role of knowledge engineer. The project team included, as usual, two domain experts and some users from the client company. The project plan was divided into three phases:
- phase 1 (one year) was assigned the goal of developing a full prototype of the KBS to be delivered for experimental use;
- phase 2 (one year) was dedicated to concrete experimentation by end-users;
- phase 3 (six months) was expected to produce the final version of the KBS through a progressive refinement of the prototype, taking into account the feedback of the users and the new requirements that would emerge during phase 2.

The development of the KBS was based on the adoption of a powerful KBS shell. In less than six months a first limited version of the prototype (actually an early prototype) was developed; its performance was evaluated by the client as being very positive and promising. The remaining part of phase 1 was mainly devoted to extensive knowledge acquisition and knowledge base refinement.

This task, however, turned out to be much more complex and controversial than expected. In fact, both the knowledge engineer and the domain experts had a substantial background and competence in strategic planning, but they had different standpoints and quite often diverging opinions. They did not agree about what knowledge should be considered important for decision making and what should be discarded, nor did they conform about the criteria to use in the evaluation of alternatives. The knowledge engineer always tended to impose his own point of view, but of course the experts tried to defend their position. Since the adopted development tool was sufficiently easy to learn and user-friendly, the domain experts started writing their own knowledge base independently, without the assistance of the knowledge engineer.

As a result the knowledge engineer and the experts developed separate knowledge bases. The one developed by the knowledge engineer was well-structured and consistent, but - unfortunately - the behavior of the KBS failed to meet the requirements of the users and was not considered correct by the domain experts. The one developed by the domain experts embodied a lot of useful and interesting knowledge but was poorly organized and not completely consistent; in conclusion, the resulting KBS could hardly run correctly through a complete working session. Therefore, at the end of phase 1 there was no version of the prototype that could be delivered for experimental use. The project was stopped and never resumed.

Discussion

The case reported shows an example of a failure due to a dramatic confusion between the roles of knowledge engineer and domain expert. The reasons for the failure can be clearly identified:
- the project lacked a project leader;
- the knowledge engineer, although specifically trained, had, however, no opportunity to acquire any concrete experience in his new job; he basically remained a consultant in strategic planning and, coherently, continued to think and work as a consultant;
- the attitude of the knowledge engineer caused the domain experts to feel excluded from the project, and, as a reaction, they tried to build their own system; of course, they did not succeed, lacking the necessary technical background.

A continuous and careful monitoring of the project would have been enough to transform a failure into a success. The new knowledge engineer, appropriately guided by a project leader, would have gradually understood his role and acquired enough practice to do his job correctly. The trend towards the dangerous splitting of the project into two separate development efforts could have been diagnosed early and easily remedied through appropriate corrective actions.

The lack of a project leader, which was the primary cause of the failure discussed, could have been solved by assigning this role to the external consultant already in charge of carrying out the plausibility study.

Case 12. Unresolved problems in knowledge base development may definitely spoil a project

Case presentation

In 1990, a medium-size company active in the field of lubricants, started the development of a KBS to support sales engineers in configuring offers for client needs. This job, requiring specific technical skills at expert level, was carried out by sales engineers through a series of meetings with the client and, separately, with the company experts. This practice was, however, a recognized bottleneck; it was time consuming and costly for the experts and often introduced unwanted delays in the offer. Moreover, in order to reduce time and cost of offer configuration, the consultation of technical experts was sometimes reduced to a fast check, quite often only a telephone call, thus dramatically reducing the technical quality and economical advantage of the offers. The KBS, designed to assist sales engineers in producing an appropriate offer in real time, at the client's premises, was expected to have high potentials for the company.

The project was initiated under a government-supported innovation plan. The execution of the project was assigned to an external consulting firm specializing in KBS design and construction, and was regularly carried out until the development of the knowledge base. This step, however, turned out to be full of problems:

- the knowledge engineer had a lot of difficulty in understanding the application domain which, although very specific, was articulated and multifaceted, including a variety knowledge (physical principles, engineering and chemical aspects, available technologies, product availability and costs, client preferences, profit-related issues, etc.);
- the five experts dedicated to the project were not always available and willing to cooperate;
- the experts often changed their mind; the knowledge engineer had the impression that domain knowledge was not stable and that different opinions could exist;
- the experts often disagreed on important points concerning, for example, which decisions to make first, which alternatives to consider, what criteria to use in decision making;
- the users, not fully convinced of the specifications stated initially, were however unable to articulate their actual needs and requirements.

The project leader was appointed to this project only part time, being in charge of two other KBS projects in other domains, for other clients. In this phase of the project, after a good start-up and a successful development of the empty system, the project leader met the project team only every two weeks. Thus, he did not realize soon enough that the development of the knowledge base was progressing more slowly than expected. Six months had been scheduled for the first release of an early prototype, but after eight months the knowledge engineer was still unable to demonstrate a well-performing system. The project leader could not see the reasons for this delay, being only partially informed of the most critical problems. After ten months, the project manager of the client organization, formally asked the consulting firm to conclude the early prototype within two months, with no additional costs. The knowledge engineer was forced to conclude the work, without having really understood the unresolved problems. The KBS was eventually released, but during testing and evaluation it dramatically failed to show a consistent and reliable behavior. The project was not continued.

Discussion

At a first glance, the main cause of the failure seems to be due to the scarce competence of the knowledge engineer. This is, however, only one cause, and possibly not the most important one. In fact, as is often the case, the project failed for a number of coexisting causes concerning:

- the experts, who were not available and cooperative as needed;

- the experts, whose unstable and often conflicting competence was a clear indication of a critical KBS project;
- the users, who were unable to express what they were actually expecting from the KBS;
- the knowledge engineer who was neither able to solve the knowledge problems encountered nor to report them appropriately to the project leader.

But, all these critical aspects - not so unusual in a KBS project - could have been dealt with appropriately by a competent and careful project management. The real cause of the failure was a project leader who was not competent enough in his job. He underestimated the symptoms, did not try to diagnose the situation, and, as a consequence, failed to undertake any appropriate corrective action. A more accurate supervision of the project during the development of the knowledge base would have helped identify problems early and, most probably, find appropriate technical and organizational solutions.

Case 13. Delivering a KBS prototype to the end-users may be a cause of failure even for a technically sound project

Case presentation

During 1987-1989 a research and development laboratory active in the field of continuous process control, developed a sophisticated KBS application for on-line supervision of a plant section of a large chemical group. The KBS was intended as a support system, capable of assisting the process operator in a variety of tasks, such as: state identification and tracking, disturbance analysis, alarm analysis, fault detection and diagnosis, and intervention planning. The finished prototype was evaluated to be positive, and the management of the client organization wanted it to be put into experimental use as soon as possible, without waiting for completion of the target system. The project leader firmly discouraged this decision, explaining it could hinder the success of the initiative. However, the request of the client organization eventually prevailed, and the prototype was taken to the target environment with minor modifications.

During the four months the KBS prototype was experimentally used, the users developed a negative idea little by little. In fact, they felt that the system was not appropriately connected to the field and not fully matching the operational requirements of the target environment. They found it to be slow and poorly reliable. Due to this negative feedback, the management gradually changed its assessment as well. As an outcome, the KBS was finally withdrawn from the operational field and eventually dropped.

Discussion

The case reported is a concrete example of a frequently occurring situation. It may be risky to bring a prototype to the target field and deliver it for experimental use. The various tasks needed for implementation, installation, and delivery of a target system cannot be skipped because they are a crucial part of a project; they cannot transform a weak KBS into a robust application, but can spoil even a technically sound prototype.

Note that sometimes - differently from the case reported above - the management only requests that the prototype is taken to the target environment for a first field testing before the implementation of the target system starts. The last KBS development phase is not skipped but only postponed. This decision is, however, not less critical. Users generally do not take into account that the system they are experimenting with is only a prototype and not a target system. They evaluate the system as it is and, generally, they are not willing or able to consider how the system will eventually turn out upon release in the final target version.

Case 14. Little attention to organizational impact and lack of training may dramatically hinder user acceptance

Case presentation

In the years 1990-1991 a medium-size bank developed a KBS for stock portfolio management for private investors. The main purpose of the KBS was to support the application of sound and uniform portfolio management criteria throughout the branch offices of the bank, independently of the individual competence and skill of the different financial advisors. The KBS was developed by the central KBS department of the bank, it was then tested by several domain experts and users, and eventually validated by the management. It was later installed on the computer network of the bank and made available on-line to all financial advisors (about 60). The intended users were promptly informed of the new package through appropriate written documentation, and, later, they were formally invited by the management to adopt the KBS in their daily routine job, like all other software packages already in use.

Only a limited part of the intended user community (less than 40%) did actually start using the KBS; the majority of the financial advisors strongly refused the KBS, which was wrongly perceived as a substitute for their professional competence and skill. They did not see any personal advantage in using the system; on the contrary, they clearly identified the several drawbacks the use of the KBS would have on their clients, who were used to relying on people rather than on computers. Moreover, they considered the formal request of the bank to adopt the KBS as implying a negative assessment of their professional role.

In front of this unforeseen reaction, the management of the bank asked an external consultant to assess the situation and to propose a solution. The analysis carried out by the consultant revealed that:

- 62% of the intended users rejected the KBS and never experimented it in their job;
- 21% tried to use the KBS but gave up in front of the difficulties encountered; besides technical and operative problems, the major obstacle was found in the organization and concerned how the KBS could actually and effectively be used between a financial advisor and a client;
- only 17% of the financial advisors could exploit the system correctly; these, however, were only using a very limited sub-set of the available functions (mainly the access to data bases) and never experimented with others.

The following main reasons for the failure were identified:
- only little attention had been devoted to the analysis of the organizational impact and to the definition of the operational specification of the KBS, especially in the phase of target system implementation;
- no specific training had been offered to the intended users before delivering the system; in fact, the KBS was supported by a sophisticated on-line help and considered highly user-friendly by the head of the KBS department who assured the management that no training was actually needed for people already familiar with computer use;
- the KBS had been formally imposed to the intended users, thus causing a negative attitude towards acceptance;
- no effort was put into explaining to the financial advisors why they should have adopted the KBS as a new support tool for their job, nor was any incentive foreseen.

The failure occurred was hard to recover. The consultant suggested an intervention plan based on the following main points:
1.   withdrawal of the KBS, accompanied by a letter from the management illustrating and explaining the situation occurred (1 month);
2.   freezing the project for at least 6 months;
3.   resuming the project and establishing a pilot user group involving a large number of senior financial advisors (1 month);
4.   defining project goals carefully and concretely, planning the project, and informing the user community (2 months);
5.   focusing on operational specifications and organizational aspects and developing an in-depth analysis with the support of external consultants (3 months);
6.   on the basis of the results obtained in the previous step 5, carrying out the following activities (2 months):
     - assessing the old KBS and defining the necessary modifications for a new version
     - developing a detailed organizational design
     - defining an appropriate training program
     - defining a delivery plan, including specific initiatives to improve awareness, explain motivations, support acceptance
     - defining appropriate incentives to promote the use of the KBS;
7.   developing the new version of the KBS (4 months);
8.   implementing the necessary organizational interventions (4 moths - in parallel with step 7);
9.   executing the planned training program (4 months - in parallel with step 8);
10. delivering the new version of the KBS for experimental use (4 months);
11. carrying out the planned initiatives to improve awareness, explain motivations, support acceptance (4 months - in parallel with step 10);
12. final delivery of the KBS for operational use, supported by appropriate incentives to promote its use.

This plan, however, was considered too long (17 months, elapsed time) and costly by the management, and, therefore, was rejected.
     After about one year from the delivery, the maintenance, which was essential for the life of the KBS, was interrupted, and then the system was abandoned.

Discussion

The KBS developed was a fairly good piece of work and could have been put into use effectively with minor efforts. However, the issue of user acceptance was not taken in due account. In particular, training was left to the individual initiative of the users, and the complex organizational problem of the transition from the old job practice to a new style was underestimated.

The project resulted in a failure. The effective exploitation of a KBS can only result from a correct matching between a good product and an interested and cooperative user.

Case 15. Legal issues may be a serious impediment for effective KBS delivery and use

Case presentation

In 1989, a medium-size private electric company, was about to successfully conclude the development of a KBS to be used as a support system for control room operators. The KBS was intended to help and advise the operators in the supervision and management of a critical sub-system of a thermal power plant. The objectives of the KBS were twofold. It would ensure a better performance of each individual operator, in terms of early and accurate detection and diagnosis of abnormal, faulty or critical states, and in terms of timely decision making and intervention. It would also ensure a more uniform plant management practice, of great importance for the life of the plant. The KBS was considered especially useful since control room operators usually work shifts; they have only a limited view on the life of the plant, and, generally, apply largely individual plant management criteria.

The KBS was carefully field tested and then put into experimental use for a period of six months. It received a very positive evaluation by control room operators, domain experts, maintenance team, and plant manager. Therefore, it was decided to release it for routine use. All steps appropriate to ensure a smooth and effective adoption of the new tool were undertaken and, eventually, on October 1st 1989 it was released to the operators.

During the first six months, using the KBS was a free choice. Some operators did not use the KBS at all, others were accepting its advice totally, and still others adopted a practical compromise between these two extreme cases. The expected benefits of the KBS were only partially visible; the individual performance of the operators was improved only in a few cases and the plant management practice was apparently not more uniform than before. Therefore, the plant manager decided to impose the use of KBS as a company policy. All operators would regularly rely on its assistance, consider its advice, and adopt its suggestions. However, they were also reminded that the KBS did not free them of their obligations to respect the norms written in the operative manuals, and to undertake all actions necessary for a safe, technically correct, and economic plant operation.

The action of the plant manager clarified to the operators a new aspect not considered previously. The existence of the KBS was not only changing their work, but it was also making their professional and legal responsibilities more complex and less clear. Moreover, since using a KBS requires, at least in principle, more skills, the operators also realized that their professional level, and consequently their salary, would have to be updated accordingly. Therefore, they formally requested the management through their trade unions to establish precise regulations about responsibility and determine their new professional level. This action started a long period of negotiations between trade unions and company management. In the mean time, under the advice of the legal office of the company, the use of the KBS was suspended. Since negotiations did not arrive to a point acceptable for all the parties concerned, the use of the KBS was never resumed again.

Discussion

The case reported points out a fairly critical problem raised by KBS applications in the field of operator support. Without specific regulations, there is an intrinsic ambiguity about the intended use of the KBS. Should the KBS be considered only a provider of information and advice, useful but not mandatory, or should it be considered capable of prescribing the right actions to take in any situation? Often, the most effective exploitation of the KBS is obtained through an appropriate sharing of competence and responsibility between the operator and the KBS itself. Failing to define the intended use of a KBS in detail, to provide appropriate regulations, and to take care of the point of view of the personnel as far as responsibility and professional level are concerned, may be a primary cause of failure of a KBS application.

Case 16. A technical success but a practical failure: user acceptance cannot be obtained without a serious involvement of the users during development

Case presentation

During 1989-1990 a large engineering group developed a KBS to assess the risk related with industrial investments in developing countries. The KBS could do the following: accept the description of a specific investment opportunity, access appropriate data banks and collect all available relevant information, take into account historical data extracted from company data bases, investigate the main features of the investment, formulate a global evaluation of the opportunity, simulate alternative scenarios, and answer specific user queries. It encapsulated knowledge of several domain experts, either employees of the engineering group where the KBS was developed or external consultants specifically hired for the KBS project. Its competence level was considered more than satisfactory by recognized specialists.

The KBS was meant to be used by the top management of the group who was personally involved with the evaluation of important investment opportunities and was responsible for the related decision-making process. The top management had, however, been only occasionally involved in the KBS project. In fact, the development of the KBS was assigned to an external consulting company, and, after project approval and start-up, the contacts between the project team and the intended users of the KBS were very rare. The top management was very busy; after some unsuccessful attempts to involve them concretely in the KBS development process, the project leader decided to develop the KBS autonomously, with the assistance of the domain experts only.

When the system was delivered, the KBS was presented to the top management who was enthusiastic about the results obtained. The system looked really very competent, and a copy of it was installed in the office of all the members of the top management. The KBS was immediately used. However, little by little, at a closer and more concrete examination, it turned out to be difficult to use, boring, and time consuming. It was too detailed and required too many inputs. The user interface was too rigid and poorly cooperative. The scope of the KBS did not match the needs of the users. It was very competent in sophisticated and difficult problems, but definitely inadequate and useless in facing more frequent and concrete situations. After a couple of months from the delivery it was practically abandoned.

In front of these unexpected reactions, the external consulting firm in charge of KBS development proposed a revision of the system. This proposal was, however, rejected by the top management, who concluded that the technology was too new, possibly appropriate in facing advanced research problems, but not powerful enough for real-size applications.

Discussion

The case presented is a typical example of a project headed by domain experts. The system built turned out to be technically appropriate and highly skilled in the application domain, but unable to satisfy the real needs of the users. One major error was to exclude the users from the project with the excuse that they were very busy and regular contacts with them would have been difficult. It was thought that using a robust group of domain expert would have guaranteed high-quality results. This was in fact the case; but, unfortunately, high-quality did not turn out to be useful for the intended users.

There are many lessons to be learned from this case:
- letting domain experts head a KBS project may entail risks;
- the project leader should be very careful is making assumptions about user needs;
- users generally do not like to accept the result of a project they have not really contributed to;
- users must always be concretely involved in the development of a KBS, and never be excluded.

Case 17. A successful technology transfer and training program: careful design, detailed planning, and a high-level training can ensure concrete success

Case presentation

In 1987, the research and development laboratory of a large company in the field of cement production was entrusted by the top management to put a project team together, intended to constitute the first kernel of a future KBS unit to operate in one of the most important company plants.

A technology transfer and training program was prepared by an external consultant. The program was organized in four modules:

module 1: Basic training   [4 months]
- courses on the following topics:
  artificial intelligence and knowledge-based technology: basic concepts
  knowledge representation and problem solving
  rule-based systems: concepts and design techniques
  frame-based systems: concepts and design techniques
  knowledge organization, use of meta-knowledge, system architecture
- individual reading of selected literature materials
- homework on selected topics
- group discussions with the tutor

module 2: Programming   [4 months, in parallel with module 1]
- courses on the following topics:
  programming paradigms: imperative, functional, logic, object-oriented
  Lisp concepts and examples
  Lisp programming
- hands-on activity with the tutor
- individual programming activity on advanced exercises, followed by discussions with the tutor

module 3: KBS development   [2 months]
- courses on the following topics:
  introduction to KEE
  Lisp programming: advanced concepts
  advanced KEE
- hands-on activity with the tutor
- individual programming activity, followed by discussions with the tutor

module 4: Methodologies   [2 months, in parallel with module 3]
- courses on the following topics:
  KBS life cycle
  knowledge acquisition: issues and methodologies
  knowledge acquisition: techniques
  KBS project management
- individual reading of selected literature materials
- group discussions with the tutor

module 5: Development of a small KBS demonstrator   [6 months]
- selection of an application domain of potential interest for the plant: continuous process supervision;
- identification of a specific problem to face: supervision and control of the thermal state of the furnace (in a cement plant);
- development of a draft system design (group activity);
- organization of individual work on the main issues of:
  development of the empty system
  development of system interfaces

knowledge acquisition and knowledge base construction

- development of first version of the demonstrator, evaluation and critique
- KBS refinement
- release of the final KBS demonstrator.

The training plan described above was regularly executed with a group of seven recently graduated students in engineering and computer science. Three individual evaluation sessions were held: at the end of module 2, at the end of module 4, and at the end of module 5. The training team was composed of:

- a supervisor of the whole program, namely the external consultant in charge of the design of technology transfer and training program, who also took an active part as a tutor for module 5;
- a lecturer for module 1 and 4;
- a lecturer and a tutor for module 2 and 3.

All the people involved in the training team were chosen from the university environment.

The results of the technology transfer and training program were quite satisfactory; all seven people received a substantial education in knowledge-based technology and were able to work on specific KBS projects. Two of them reached the level of developers, three of knowledge engineers, and two of junior designers.

Discussion

The technology transfer and training program presented above were based on several important choices and motivations briefly discussed below:

- alternation of formal training and experimental activity in order to avoid separation between theory and practice and keep student interest constantly high;
- broad theoretical, technical, and methodological background in knowledge-based technology, not only focused on a specific KBS development tool;
- focus on one specific programming paradigm and language, namely functional and object-oriented programming using Lisp;
- adoption of a powerful KBS development toolkit, namely KEE, appropriate for advanced training;
- substantial practical activity focused on a small but realistic case fully supported by an experienced tutor;
- formal evaluation of results, both at the end of the program and during its development.

The reasons for the success of this technology transfer and training program were twofold; the careful design and detailed planning of the initiative by an experienced professional and the adoption of a high-level training team.

Case 18. A re-training program: scarce motivation, lack of a solid background, and part-time involvement are enough to guarantee a failure

Case presentation

In 1987, a major company operating in the field of information systems and software development, decided to start an initiative in the field of knowledge-based technology, which was considered to be a useful complement to the company's know-how. Unwilling to hire new people, the management decided to try a re-training initiative.

A re-training plan was prepared with the support of an external consultant. The plan comprised basic training in knowledge-based technology with lectures and experimental activity. The lectures covered most of the fundamental topics of knowledge-based technology, namely: introduction to artificial intelligence, knowledge representation, problem solving and reasoning, rule-based and frame-based systems, knowledge acquisition. A total of 90 hours of lectures were planned. The experimental activity was focused on rule-based programming using OPS-83.

The training initiative took place over a period of six months. Twice a week the students attended lectures, studied, did homework, and performed experimental activities. The other three days were devoted to their regular work. The tutoring support was good; the courses were held by assistant professors from the university and experienced teaching assistants helped the students in the experimental activity.

The persons selected for the re-training action had two to six years seniority on the job. The group consisted of a total of 14 persons.

The re-training plan was carried out regularly, apart from minor changes to the scheduled activities due to professional engagements of the participants. All students - except three who dropped out at the very beginning - attended most of the lessons. However, only two persons could devote some time to study and homework. About half of the participants actually performed a concrete experimental activity, and only two persons went through most of the exercises.

At the end of the re-training initiative an evaluation took place. Only nine of the original 14 people attended the evaluation, consisting in a written test and a discussion. Only four, out of nine people turned out to have received sufficient training and had acquired a minimal background in knowledge-based technology. Two of them could be employed as skilled senior developers and the other two just as junior developers.

The re-training action was almost a failure, especially considering the resources spent and the cost. The four people who attained the highest level of preparation were later employed in two pilot KBS projects in different companies of the same group. The remaining people continued with their old job; the re-training action had only been a useless and frustrating experience.

Discussion

The main reasons for the failure illustrated above were as follows:
- all participants were more or less distracted from the re-training initiative by the commitments and deadlines of their regular job;

- most of them did not have the necessary background in computer science to effectively attend all the lectures;
- most of the participants remained too close to the concepts, the methods, and the practice of their current job;
- several trainees no longer had the flexibility necessary to approach a new subject matter;
- most of them were frustrated by their current job and did not see any opportunity for professional growth; they lacked motivation.

With better planning and some minor changes, the failure illustrated above might have been avoided or at least its seriousness could have been reduced. For instance:
- only candidates with less than three years seniority should have been accepted;
- to participate in the re-training program, a background in computer science should have been required;
- two to three evaluations should have been carried out;
- participants involved in the program should have been exempted from their usual job, for a full-time dedication to re-training;
- trainees should have been further involved by participating to pilot projects.

Moreover, re-training should have been initiated only after having obtained the first successful results of a concrete KBS initiative and, possibly, after having established a KBS group. The lack of a concrete context made the re-training initiative not credible enough, therefore lacking participant motivation. A re-training program cannot be the first step of a KBS initiative.

Case 19. Continuing education: a flexible, hybrid approach

Case presentation

The KBS department of a large manufacturing company has been active for seven years. It presently employs 14 people. The head of the KBS department considers continuing education an important issue for the gradual introduction of new technologies and for the support of an incremental growth of the professional skills of the personnel. Continuing education is planned yearly taking into account the technical needs of the group, the individual interests of the employees (acquired through a questionnaire), and the engagements of the KBS department. The 1993 plan for continuing education included:
- 15 internal seminars on six focal topics held by well-known specialists; each seminar was scheduled for half a day and included three hours presentation and one hour discussion; all seminars were expected to take place between February and May;
- two weeks free for individual reading of technical and scientific materials; sabbatical weeks were scheduled in such a way as not to interfere with the regular production engagements; reading materials were suggested individually by an external consultant purposely hired;
- participation of three people (knowledge engineers or designers) to three major conferences in the field of knowledge-based technology - one person to each conference;

- participation of four people (developers and knowledge engineers) to two external seminars of two days each - two people to each seminar.

Every year the continuing education plan is different, but its concept is always the same; a variety of different types of events and activities. This concept of continuing education was applied for four years. Its cost was rather high but not beyond the possibilities offered by the budget of a KBS department of 14 people. This type of continuing education program was considered fully satisfactory by the employees, and its effects were thought to be good by the head of the KBS department.

Discussion

The case reported shows how a well-planned and realistic continuing education program, in line with the real exigencies of a KBS department, may bring very positive results with reasonable costs. Without an accurate and structured choice of the various activities to be included in the yearly plan and without a careful consideration of the individual needs of the members of the KBS department, a continuing education effort may be useless, but, nevertheless, costly.

Case 20. Continuing education: an approach based on external cooperation

Case presentation

A large company active in the field of telecommunications, has established a KBS unit operating inside the corporate research and development division for the past five years. The KBS unit comprises eight people and is still growing. Since the head of the KBS unit was not in the position to organize a satisfactory continuing education program for the personnel, he preferred to resort to external support. After some unsuccessful experimentation with specialized companies offering education services in the more traditional fields of information systems and software engineering, two years ago he contacted a private research laboratory with a large and sound KBS group. The head of the KBS unit proposed that the personnel of his group join the continuing education program in the field of knowledge-based technology which the laboratory ran annually for its technical staff and share the cost. The laboratory agreed to organize a continuing education program for the following year to meet the needs of both groups. In 1991, the first joint program was carried out; it turned out to be a real success. Moreover, this solution offered the two KBS groups the opportunity to discuss their practical experiences. This non-scheduled activity turned out to be interesting and useful.

Discussion

The case reported above is an example of how it is possible to reduce the costs of a continuing education program through external cooperation. Sharing a continuing education program among several companies is a very rewarding approach which should be encouraged. This requires an open-minded and cooperative attitude. The advantages are many; in addition to cost reduction, this generally allows higher-level continuing education programs to be carried out. More advanced technical topics can be dealt with and more experienced and specialized lecturers can be involved.

Case 21. A failed attempt to build a KBS development methodology: a weak project without any concrete results

Case presentation

In 1987 a medium-size company active in the field of computer applications, software development, and training for a large industrial group, after three years of successful experience with knowledge-based technology, decided to start a specific project to build a KBS development methodology. The primary motivation was to improve productivity.

The first steps of the methodological project addressed the following issues:
- definition of a life cycle concept (phases);
- development of management methods (project planning and control);
- development of documentation methods;
- development of methods for fast feasibility study, focusing in particular on cost/benefit analysis;
- knowledge acquisition.

Much attention and appropriate resources were given to the methodological project. Of the four people constituting the KBS department, one was dedicated full-time to this goal. After about 15 months, good results - even if only partial - had been obtained. The project was a success. The management decided to deliver to the users the methodological products developed so far for practical application, and to wait for a feedback from the field before entering a new development phase.

In the beginning of 1990, in front of the continuously increasing need for new technical personnel in the KBS department, the top management requested an independent check-up of the situation, in order to assess the reasons of the apparently low productivity. On this occasion it was discovered that the methodological project carried out about two years earlier had no tangible effect on productivity, therefore being quite useless. The results achieved were scattered and could not be put into practice. They had been directly derived from existing company standards or from current KBS literature; their methodological content was poor, being nothing more than common sense rules or general and abstract principles.

Discussion

The case reported shows how a methodological effort is always a critical step in the development of a KBS department. It is difficult to start, to carry out, and to evaluate. Even its results may be controversial. At first, they may appear as a partial success, however, after a period of practical application and closer examination they may turn out to be a real failure.

The main reasons of the failure reported above are:

- the methodological project was started too early; there was only little experience in KBS development; in the past three years, activity had been devoted to the development of demonstrators, with only an initial activity in prototyping, and without any experience in the implementation, installation and delivery of real target applications;
- there were no specific indications for a methodological project and the main motivation considered, namely low productivity, was weak; an appropriate training program and the adoption of suitable development tools would have been the right solution to the productivity problem;
- the KBS department was too little (only four people) to justify such a long-term, costly, and technically complex engagement as a methodological project;
- the methodological project was developed without a precise plan and incurred several technical errors:
  - the definition of the life cycle concept was superficial, focusing only on the major phases, without facing the crucial issue of decomposition into finer grained stages (steps, tasks, and activities);
  - priorities in designing methods were placed on what was easier to find, rather than what was more useful for the project team; in particular, the design of management methods was given priority to technical methods;
  - management methods (indeed very specific and detailed) were not really designed to meet the specific needs of the KBS department, but rather simply imported from other company fields;
  - no real technical methods were developed for the knowledge acquisition task; generic knowledge extracted from literature was embedded in a collection of very general rules, check-lists, procedures, and principles, whose interpretation and practical application was left to the knowledge engineers.

Case 22. Design and construction of a KBS development methodology: a successful case

Case presentation

Towards the end of 1989, the manager of the KBS department of a large engineering company, decided to launch a specific project dedicated to the methodological aspects of KBS development. The KBS department, employing 13 technicians and with four years of practical experience in the design and construction of real KBS applications, had been growing very fast. Its activity was featured by a practical approach to knowledge-based technology; only minor attention had been devoted so far to methodological issues. The manager had the impression that a sound methodological background could greatly help establish a better work practice, thus improving quality and productivity. Therefore, with the assistance of an external consultant, he carried out an in-depth analysis of the situation and prepared a detailed project plan. The plan was divided into three stages:

stage 1: Start-up and basic methods   [2 years]
- definition of the general concepts of the methodology

- definition of a reference life cycle (phases and tasks)
- development of technical methods for four priority areas:
  - conceptual design
  - logical design
  - knowledge elicitation, coding, integration, checking, and validation
  - KBS verification and validation

stage 2: Completion of the main body of the methodology   [2 years]
- development of technical methods for other important areas:
  - fast plausibility study
  - documentation
  - user training
  - delivery and maintenance
- delivery of the complete set of methodology manuals

stage 3: Advanced issues   [1 year]
- development of technical methods for specific areas:
  - opportunity analysis
  - cost/benefit analysis
  - user interface design
  - advanced design techniques
  - quality control and assurance
- development of main management methods
  - project planing
  - project budget
  - involvement of domain experts
  - productivity control
- updating of methodology manuals.

Towards the end of 1990, after the final approval of the top management, a dedicated project team was put together, including: a full-time project leader with a background in knowledge engineering, two part-time senior designers, a part-time knowledge engineer, and an external scientific advisor. Early 1991 stage 1 of the project was started. For each priority area, the relevant tasks were first identified and appropriately decomposed into activities. Then, for each activity appropriate methods were developed. The main issues faced in this stage, namely identification of activities and design of technical methods, are briefly illustrated below.

Identifying activities

In order to appropriately decompose tasks into activities, a bottom-up approach was initially taken. Attention was focused on the current practice for task execution, in order to identify possible problems and bottlenecks. Later, a thorough analysis of the possible ways of removing the identified critical points through the adoption of suitable methods was carried out. This included a literature survey in the relevant fields and a specific analysis of other available sources of methodological knowledge.

This analysis provided the background to start activity identification. To this purpose, it was decided to define as a candidate activity an elementary work process inside a task satisfying the following three conditions:
• the candidate activity had a crucial role in determining the effectiveness and the efficiency with which the task was executed;
• the execution of the candidate activity could be concretely enhanced by adopting an appropriate method;
• the design of an appropriate method for the candidate activity could be carried out with reasonable effort.

In this way, for the four priority areas focused which included eight tasks, a list of 25 candidate activities was compiled. Later, it was revised and refined top-down in order to ensure that each task was correctly decomposed, i.e. that the activities identified covered all the work processes needed to fully carry out the relevant task and that, as far as possible, they had a uniform grain-size. Thus, a final list of 34 activities was obtained.

Designing technical methods

The design of technical methods was organized in five steps:
1.   detailed specifications of the methods to be designed;
2.   targeted bibliographic research;
3.   method design and production;
4.   delivery to pilot project team for experimental use
5.   refinement and final delivery.

Whenever possible and appropriate, method design was based on formalization and generalization of informal working procedures already in use in the KBS department. More precisely, 19 technical methods out of 34 were produced in this way. The remaining 15 methods were designed starting from literature proposals and practical experience of the scientific advisor in charge of the methodological project.

At the end of the stage 1, all scheduled products had been completed and delivered. The methods developed were regularly being applied by all project teams of the KBS department. User acceptance was enthusiastic and feedback was very positive. Early in 1993, stage 2 of the methodological project was then undertaken.

Discussion

The above case is an example of a sound and successful methodological project. It is featured by a correct start-up, a realistic allocation of resources, and a reasonable scheduling.
    The development of the project is rather slow. In a methodological project, however, the key point is not being fast, but assuring a sure and constant progress. Since these two issues are generally in competition, effectiveness should always be preferred over speed.

The success of this initiative was due to the ability of the manager of the KBS department to identify the need for a methodological project in time and to plan its execution in a well-organized and concrete way. This was not an easy goal to reach due to the several practical engagements of the project teams and to the constant pressures from users and management for the delivery of new applications. The success of the project was also due to the gradual and concrete involvement of the users (i.e., the various components of the project teams) in the methodological effort, obtained through presentations, open discussions, and extended experimentation. The support of the top management was also an essential component of success; basic methodological actions with only indirect and long-term return must have a strong commitment to be carried out effectively.

Case 23. Technology check-up is not enough if concrete interventions are not undertaken

Case presentation

In 1986, the information technology company of a large industrial group started a new initiative in the area of knowledge-based technology. A KBS group was established and, during the period 1986-1989, three successful applications were delivered. The applications developed were very simple, being based on a low-level rule-based shell. The design and construction were, however, slow and costly.

At the beginning of 1990, the head of the KBS group, not satisfied with the technological level and the productivity achieved, decided to resort to a technology check-up. His intention was to utilize the results of the check-up to convince the management to establish a formal KBS department and to grant to it all the resources necessary for a significant step forward in quality and productivity.

Therefore, early in 1990 an external consultant was asked for a technology check-up. This was regularly carried out during three months time. The technology check-up identified the major bottlenecks of the current situation and analyzed their causes, namely:

- limited technical competence of most of the members of the KBS group, due to insufficient training in the specific field of knowledge-based technology;
- lack of any methodological background in knowledge-based technology, especially about life cycle, knowledge analysis and modeling, design principles, and knowledge acquisition;
- scarce experience of the head of the group about the specific issues of KBS project management;
- little awareness on the part of the management of knowledge-based technology and lack of a clear understanding of its potentials.

In front of this analysis, a detailed intervention program was developed, with the purpose of solving the problems identified and establishing a more robust KBS group in two years time.

The results of the technology check-up were first discussed with the head of the KBS group. He was disappointed in front of the sharp but precise diagnosis developed. He recognized that the analysis had been developed correctly and carefully by the consultant, but he claimed that the results were presented too realistically and dramatically. In reality, he feared being personally involved in the negative assessment reported, and having his career ruined.

Therefore, he asked the consultant to prepare a presentation of the results in more positive terms, less shocking and more convincing for the management. The consultant refused. Therefore, the head of the KBS department prepared an executive summary to present to the management. However, this report was so neutral that the management did not understand why, in front of an apparently positive situation, a long and costly intervention program was necessary. The proposal was not approved and the KBS group did not obtain any specific support from the company management. Thus, it continued working as before, being involved only in small projects of little importance.

When, towards the end of 1991 one of the major companies of the group launched an important KBS project, it was decided to resort to an external supplier, since the information technology company of the group was not considered competent enough for such a complex and demanding assignment.

Discussion

The case reported shows that no remedy, even if appropriate, can solve a critical situation if it is not correctly applied. The technology check-up had been correctly and carefully carried out, but the head of the KBS group was unable to understand and exploit its results appropriately. He felt threatened, and looked after more to his own career than to the development of the production group he was in charge of. The company management was not given a clear and transparent presentation of the situation, and missed out on an important opportunity.

Case 24. Business check-up in a large industrial group: issues and problems

Case presentation

In 1989, the central innovation department of a large international group operating in several interrelated fields including: telecommunications, information technology, computers, electronic components, and electro-mechanical devices, decided to analyze the level of diffusion and exploitation of knowledge-based technology throughout the whole group. The top management was under the impression that knowledge-based technology was not sufficiently exploited for innovation and wanted to assess the situation from the technological and business point of view.

To this purpose, a specific project was started headed by an external consultant and carried out by a working group including four specialists of various disciplines and four people from the central innovation department. In a period of one year and a half all KBS initiatives running in the group were analyzed. The resulting situation, described in an extensive two-volume report, featured the following main characteristics:

- the diffusion of knowledge-based technology was very low: out of 153 companies in the group, only 34 were actually interested in knowledge-based technology as an innovation factor; of these:
  - 10 were in a very preliminary information stage,
  - 4 were developing technology transfer programs,
  - 6 were in the stage of pre-competitive experimentation and prototyping,
  - 14 were actually applying knowledge-based technology in production-oriented projects;
- the level of expenses and investments in the area of knowledge-based technology was high in all the 34 companies considered;
- the global potential production power was, in average, very low, due to a moderate technological level and an unstable and poorly determined commitment of the management;
- apparently, the level of exploitation of knowledge-based technology for production and innovation in the 14 companies in the highest stage of assimilation was low and the return of investment too;
- the ongoing KBS initiatives were scattered and no cooperation between the companies of the group was evident:
  - there were no connections between companies able to produce KBS applications and companies that might be interested in their practical exploitation;
  - the achievements and the experience of the companies already active in the KBS field were not made available to other companies in earlier development stages;
  - the seven research and development laboratories active in the group in the KBS field worked separately, often duplicating research efforts;
  - the selection of production tools and external suppliers was managed locally so as the greatest variety of choices and specific situations were observable.

In view of such results a detailed diagnosis was developed and, then, a four-year intervention plan was prepared. The main points are reported below:
- establishing a central office at group level for planning, coordination, and monitoring of the various KBS initiatives in the different companies;
- establishing a central KBS laboratory at group level with the following goals:
  - carrying out of research and development programs of potential interest for the entire group;
  - developing generic application prototypes to be distributed to all interested companies which should then provide for their tailoring, targeting, delivery and exploitation;
  - defining standards for KBS design and development (including the use of tools) to be adopted by all interested companies;
  - taking care of all training, re-training, and continuing education initiatives;
  - establishing external cooperation programs at scientific and technological level;
- closing the seven research and development laboratories currently active in the group and collecting their know-how and ongoing activities in the central KBS laboratory;
- discouraging the direct exploitation of knowledge-based technology in all those companies still in a very preliminary technology transfer stage;
- supporting the establishment of effective KBS production units in all those companies where a sufficient technological level had already been achieved and concrete exploitation programs had already been devised;

- promoting a widespread awareness of the potentials and the limits of knowledge-based technology as a tool for process and product innovation.

The intervention plan was first presented to the top management of the group and then illustrated to the management of all interested companies. It was seriously considered and received the consent of all involved parties. However, it was not applied.

Discussion

At first, the case reported could be considered as a real success. It was large, technically difficult, complex from the organizational point of view, and politically delicate. It was carried out correctly and effectively. In its final analysis, the check-up was well-detailed; it proved to be reliable and able to come up with a concrete intervention plan.

From another point of view, however, it might look like a failure. It did not produce concrete effects within the group. Culturally speaking, it provided an interesting contribution as far as management and exploitation of innovative information technologies, but it missed the real objective of bringing change in the current situation.

One should not expect that a business check-up can always produce concrete effects in a short term, especially in large organizations.

REFERENCES

[Abelson and Sussman 85] H. Abelson and G.J. Sussman, *Structure and Interpretation of Computer Programs*, MIT Press, Cambridge, MA, 1985.

[Aben 93] M. Aben, Formally specifying reusable knowledge model components, *Knowledge Acquisition* 5, 1993, 119- 141.

[Abrett and Burstein 87] G. Abrett and M.H. Burstein, The KREME knowledge editing environment, *International Journal of Man-Machine Studies* 27, 1987, 103-127.

[Addis 85] T.R. Addis, *Designing Knowledge-Based Systems*, Kogan Page, London, UK, 1985.

[Adrion et al. 82] W.R. Adrion, M.A. Branstad, and J.C. Chernavsky. Validation, verification and testing of computer software, *ACM Computing Surveys* 14(2), 1982, 159–192.

[Agarwal and Tanniru 90] R. Agarwal and M. Tanniru, Systems development life-cycle for expert systems, *Knowledge-Based Systems* 3(3), 1990, 170-180.

[Agarwal et al. 93] R. Agarwal, R. Kannan, and M. Tanniru, Formal validation of a knowledge-based system using a variation of the Turing test, *Expert Systems with Applications* 6, 1993, 181-192.

[Agha 86] G. Agha, *Actors, A Model of concurrent computation in distributed systems*, MIT Press, Cambridge, MA, 1986.

[Agresti 86] W.W. Agresti, *New Paradigms for Software Development*, IEEE Computer Society Press, Washington, DC, 1986.

[Alavi 84] M. Alavi, An assessment of the prototyping approach to information systems development, *Communications of the ACM* 27(6), 1984, 556-563.

[Allard 93] F. Allard, *Knowledge-Based Systems: Recommendations for the Development Life-Cycle*, Report WGS/FA/92.055, ESA/ESTEC/WGS, 1.0/1.0, Noordwijk, The Netherlands, 1993.

[Allen 83] J.F. Allen, Maintaining knowledge about temporal intervals, *Communications of the ACM* 26(11), 1983, 832-843.

[Allen 84] J.F. Allen, Towards a general theory of action and time, *Artificial Intelligence* 23, 1984, 123-154.

[Allen 87] J. Allen, *Natural Language Understanding*, Benjamin/Cummings, Menlo Park, CA, 1987.

[Allen and Perrault 80] J.F. Allen and C.R. Perrault, Analyzing intention in utterances, *Artificial Intelligence* 15, 1980, 143-178.

[Allen et al. 90] J. Allen, J. Hendler, and A. Tate (editors), *Readings in Planning*, Morgan Kaufmann, San Mateo, CA, 1990.

[Allen et al. 91] J. Allen, H. Kautz, R. Pelavin, and J. Tenenberg, *Reasoning about Plans*, Morgan Kaufmann, San Mateo, CA, 1990.

[Alonso et al. 90] F. Alonso, J. Maté, and J. Pazos, Knowledge engineering versus software engineering, *Data & Knowledge Engineering* 5, 1990, 79-91.

[Alty 89] J.L. Alty, Expert system building tools, in G. Guida and C. Tasso (editors), *Topics in Expert System Design - Methodologies and Tools*, North-Holland, Amsterdam, The Netherlands, 1989, 181-204.

[Ambler et al. 92] A.L. Ambler, M.M. Burnett, and B.A. Zimmerman, Operational versus definitional: A perspective on programming paradigms, *Computer* 25(9), 1992, 28-43.

[Anderson and Reitman 87] N. Anderson and O.J. Reitman, Methods for designing software to fit human needs and capabilities, in R.M. Baecker and W.A.S. Buxton (editors), *Readings in Human-Computer Interaction: A Multidisciplinary Approach*, Morgan Kaufmann, Los Altos, CA, 1987, 540-554.

[Anjewerden et al. 90] A. Anjewerden, J. Wielemaker, and C. Toussaint, Shelley - Computer Aided Knowledge Engineering, in B. Wielinga, J. Boose, B. Gaines, G. Schreiber, and M. van Someren (editors), *Current Trends in Knowledge Acquisition*, IOS Press, Amsterdam, The Netherlands, 1990, 41-59.

[Anjewierden 87] A. Anjewierden, Knowledge acquisition tools, *AI Communications* 0(1), 1987, 29-38.

[Apt et al. 93] K.R. Apt, J.W. de Bakker, and J.J.M.M. Rutten, *Logic Programming Languages - Constraints, Functions, and Objects*, MIT Press, Cambridge, MA, 1993.

[Arora and Cooke 91] V. Arora and J.E. Cooke, Towards effective management of expert system projects, *Proceedings IEEE/ACM International Conference on Developing and Managing Expert System Programs*, Washington, DC, 1991, 339-345.

[Ayel 88] M. Ayel, A conceptual model for consistency of knowledge bases, in T. O'Shea and V. Sgurev (editors), *Artificial Intelligence III: Methodology, Systems, Applications*, North-Holland, Amsterdam, The Netherlands, 1988, 75-82.

[Ayel and Laurent 91] M. Ayel and J.-P. Laurent (editors), *Validation, Verification and Test of Knowledge-Based Systems*, John Wiley & Sons, Chichester, UK, 1991.

[Ayyub et al. 92] B.M. Ayyub, M.M. Gupta, and L. Kanal (editors), *Analysis and Management of Uncertainty - Theory and Applications*, Elsevier, Amsterdam, The Netherlands, 1992.

[Bacchus 90] F. Bacchus, *Representing and Reasoning with Probabilistic Knowledge*, MIT Press, Cambridge, MA, 1990.

[Bachant and McDermott 84] J. Bachant and J. McDermott, R1 revisited: Four years in the trenches, *AI Magazine* 5(3), 1984, 21-32.

[Bader et al. 88] J. Bader, J. Edwards, C. Harris-Jones, and D. Hannaford, Practical engineering of knowledge-based systems, *Information and Software Technology* 30(5), 1988, 266-277.

[Badiru 88] A.B. Badiru, Successful initiation of expert systems projects, *IEEE Transaction on Engineering Management* EM-35(3), 1988.

[Baecker and Buxton 87] R.M Baecker and W.A.S. Buxton (editors), *Readings in Human-Computer Interaction*, Morgan Kaufmann, Los Altos, CA, 1987.

[Bahill and Ferrell 86] A. Terry Bahill and William R. Ferrell, Teaching an introductory course in expert systems, *IEEE Expert* 1(4), 1986, 59-63.

[Bailey 83] R.W. Bailey, *Human Errors in Computer Systems*, Prentice-Hall, Englewood Cliffs, NJ, 1983.

[Banerji 90] R.B. Banerji (editor), *Formal Techniques in Artificial Intelligence - A sourcebook*, Elsevier, Amsterdam, The Netherlands, 1990.

[Baroff et al. 88] J. Baroff, R. Simon, F. Gilman, and B. Shneiderman, Direct manipulation user interfaces for expert systems, in J.A. Hendler (editor), *Expert Systems: The User Interface*, Ablex, Norwood, NJ, 1988, 99-125.

[Baron-Vartian and Baron-Vartian 91] E. Baron-Vartian and G. Baron-Vartian, Automating the application selection process, *Proceedings IEEE/ACM International Conference on Developing and Managing Expert System Programs*, Washington, DC, 1991, 356-359.

[Bareiss et al. 87] E.R. Bareiss, B.W. Porter, and C.C. Weir, Protos: An exemplar-based learning apprentice, *International Journal of Man-Machine Studies* 29, 1988, 549-562.

[Barr et al. 81-89] A. Barr, P.R. Cohen, and E.A. Feigenbaum (editors), *The Handbook of Artificial Intelligence*, Vol. I-IV, Addison-Wesley, Reading, MA, 1981-1989.

[Barsanti 90] J.B. Barsanti, Expert systems: Critical success factors for their implementation, *Information Executive - The Journal Information Systems Management* 3(1), 1990, 30-34.

[Bastani and Chen 93] F.B. Bastani and I-R. Chen, The reliability of embedded AI systems, *IEEE Expert* 8(2), 1993, 72-78.

[Beckman 91] T.J. Beckman, Selecting expert-system applications, *AI Expert* 6(2), 1991, 42-48.

[Beerel 87] A.C. Beerel, *Expert Systems: Strategic Implications and Applications*, Ellis Horwood, Chichester, UK, 1987.

[Belkin 88] N.J. Belkin, On the nature and function of explanation in intelligent information retrieval, *Proceeding 11th ACM SIGIR International Conference on Research and Development in Information Retrieval*, Presses Universitaires de Grenoble, Grenoble, France, 1988, 135-145.

[Belkin et al. 87] N.J. Belkin, H.M. Brooks, and P.J. Daniels, Knowledge elicitation using discourse analysis, *International Journal of Man-Machine Studies* 27, 1987, 127-144.

[Bell 85] M.Z. Bell, Why expert systems fail, *Journal of Operational Research Society* 36(7), 1985, 613-619.

[Bell and Hardiman 89] J. Bell and R.J. Hardiman, The third role - The naturalistic knowledge engineer, in D. Diaper (editor) *Knowledge Elicitation - Principles, Techniques and Applications*, Ellis Horwood, Chichester, UK, 1989, 49-85.

[Bench-Capon 90] T.J.M. Bench-Capon, *Knowledge Representation - An Approach to Artificial Intelligence*, Academic Press, London, UK, 1990.

[Benhamou and Colmerauer 93] F. Benhamou and A. Colmerauer (editors), *Constraint Logic Programming*, MIT Press, Cambridge, MA, 1993.

[Bennett 85] J.S. Bennett, ROGET: A knowledge-based system for acquiring the conceptual structure of a diagnostic expert system, *Journal of Automated Reasoning* 1(1), 1985, 49-74.

[Berry and Hart 90-a] D. Berry and A. Hart (editors), *Expert Systems - Human Issues*, Chapman and Hall, London, UK, 1990.

[Berry and Hart 90-b] D.C. Berry and A.E. Hart, Evaluating expert systems, *Expert Systems* 7(4), 1990, 199-208.

[Bibel 93] W. Bibel, *Deduction: Automated Logic*, Academic Press, London, UK, 1993.

[Bielawski and Lewand 91] L. Bielawski and R. Lewand, *Intelligent Systems Design: Integrating Expert Systems, Hypermedia, and Data Base Technologies*, John Wiley & Sons, Chichester, UK, 1991.

[Birnbaum 88] N.L. Birnbaum, Strict products liability and computer software, *Computer Law Journal* 8(2), 1988.

[Blanchard and Johnson 87] K. Blanchard and S. Johnson, *The One Minute Manager*, William Morrow, New York, NY, 1987.

[Bledsoe 77] W.W. Bledsoe, Non-resolution theorem proving, *Artificial Intelligence* 9, 1977, 1-35.

[Boar 84] B. Boar, *Application Prototyping*, Addison-Wesley, Reading, MA, 1984.

[Bobrow 84] D. G. Bobrow (editor), Special Volume on Qualitative Reasoning about Physical Systems, *Artificial Intelligence* 24, 1984.

[Bobrow et al. 86] D.G. Bobrow, S. Mittal, and M.J. Stefik, Expert systems: Perils and promise, *Communications of the ACM* 29(9), 1986, 880-894.

[Boden 87] M.A. Boden, *Artificial Intelligence and the Natural Man* (2nd edition), MIT Press, Cambridge, MA, 1987.

[Bodin 92] D.L. Bodin, Evolution and adaptation of a knowledge based shell for use in new products as embedded technology, in G. Guida and A. Stefanini (editors), *Industrial Applications of Knowledge-Based Diagnosis*, Elsevier, Amsterdam, The Netherlands, 1992, 145-167.

[Boehm 76] B.W. Boehm, Software engineering, *IEEE Transactions on Computers* C-25(12), 1976, 1226-1241.

[Boehm 81] B.W. Boehm, *Software Engineering Economics*. Prentice-Hall, 1981.

[Boehm 84] B.W. Boehm, Verifying and validating software requirements and design specifications, *IEEE Software* 1(1), 1984, 75-89.

[Boehm 88] B.W. Boehm, A spiral model of software development and enhancement, *Computer* 21(5), 1988, 61-72.

[Boehm 89] B.W. Boehm, *Software Risk Management*, IEEE Computer Society Press, Washington, DC, 1989.

[Boehm 91] B.W. Boehm, Software risk management - Principles and practices, *IEEE Software* 8(1), 1991, 32-41.

[Boehm et al. 78] B.W. Boehm, J.R. Brown, H. Kaspar, M. Lipow, G.J. MacLeod, and M.J. Merrit, *Characteristics of Software Quality*, North-Holland, Amsterdam, The Netherlands, 1978.

[Bond and Gasser 88] A.H. Bond and L. Gasser (editors), *Readings in Distributed Artificial Intelligence*, Morgan Kaufmann, San Mateo, CA, 1988.

[Bonissone 87] P.P. Bonissone, Summarizing and propagating uncertain information with triangular norms, *International Journal of Approximate Reasoning* 1, 1987, 71-101.

[Bonissone et al. 91] P.P. Bonissone, M. Henrion, L. Kanal, and J.F. Lemmer (editors), *Uncertainty in Artificial Intelligence 6*, Elsevier, Amsterdam, The Netherlands, 1991.

[Bonnett 89] K.R. Bonnett, From grassroots to grand plan, *AI Expert* 4(8), 1989, 54-59.

[Boose 85] J. Boose, A knowledge acquisition program for expert systems based on personal construct psychology, *International Journal of Man-Machine Studies* 23, 1985, 495-525.

[Boose 86] J. Boose, *Expertise Transfer for Expert System Design*, Elsevier, New York, NY, 1986.

[Boose 89] J. Boose, A survey of knowledge acquisition techniques and tools, *Knowledge Acquisition* 1, 1989, 3-37.

[Boose 90] J. Boose, Uses of repertory grid-centered knowledge acquisition tools for knowledge-based systems, in J. Boose and B. Gaines (editors), *The Foundations of Knowledge Acquisition*, Academic Press, London, UK, 1990, 61-84.

[Boose and Bradshaw 87] J. Boose and J.M. Bradshaw, Expertise transfer and complex problems: Using AQUINAS as a knowledge-acquisition workbench for knowledge-based systems, *International Journal of Man-Machine Studies* 26, 1987, 3-28.

[Boose and Gaines 88] J.H Boose and B.R Gaines (editors), *Knowledge Acquisition Tools for Expert Systems - Knowledge-Based Systems, Vol. 2*, Academic Press, London, UK, 1988.

[Boose and Gaines 90] J.H. Boose and B.R. Gaines (editors), *The Foundations of Knowledge Acquisition - Knowledge-Based Systems, Vol. 4*, Academic Press, London, UK, 1990.

[Booth 89] P.A. Booth, *An Introduction to Human-Computer Interaction*, Lawrence Erlbaum, Hillsdale, NJ, 1989.

[Brachman and Levesque 85] R.J. Brachman and H.J. Levesque (editors), *Readings in Knowledge Representation*, Morgan Kaufmann, Los Altos, CA, 1985.

[Brachman and Schmolze 85] R.J. Brachman and J. Schmolze, An overview of the KL-ONE knowledge representation system, *Cognitive Science* 9, 1985, 171-216.

[Brachman et al. 92] R.J. Brachman, H.J. Levesque, and R. Reiter (editors), *Knowledge Representation*, MIT Press, Cambridge, MA, 1990.

[Brady and Berwick 83] M. Brady and R.C. Berwick (editors), *Computational Models of Discourse*, MIT Press, Cambridge, MA, 1983.

[Brajnik et al. 87] G. Brajnik, G. Guida, and C. Tasso, User modeling in intelligent information retrieval, *Information Processing & Management* 23(4), 1987, 305-320.

[Brajnik et al. 90] G. Brajnik, G. Guida, and C. Tasso, User Modeling in expert man-machine interfaces: A case study in intelligent information retrieval, *IEEE Transactions on Systems, Man, and Cybernetics* SMC-20(1), 1990, 166-185.

[Bratko 90] I. Bratko, *PROLOG Programming for Artificial Intelligence* (2nd edition), Addison-Wesley, Reading, MA, 1990.

[Brayant 88] N. Brayant, *Managing Expert Systems*, John Wiley & Sons, New York, NY, 1988.

[Breuker and Wielinga 87] J. Breuker and B. Wielinga. Use of models in the interpretation of verbal data, in A.L. Kidd (editor), *Knowledge Acquisition for Expert Systems. A Practical Handbook*, Plenum Press, New York, NY, 1987, 17-44.

[Breuker and Wielinga 89] J. Breuker and B. Wielinga, Models of expertise in knowledge acquisition, in G. Guida and C. Tasso (editors), *Topics in Expert System Design - Methodologies and Tools*, North-Holland, Amsterdam, The Netherlands, 1989, 265-295.

[Breuker et al. 86] J.A Breuker, B.J. Wielinga, and S.A. Hayward, Structuring of knowledge based systems development, in The Commission of the European Communities (editor), *ESPRIT '85: Status Report of Continuing Work*, North-Holland, Amsterdam, The Netherlands, 1986, 771-784.

[Brockmann 86] R.J. Brockmann, *Writing Better Computer User Documentation: Form Paper to Online*, John Wiley & Sons, New York, NY, 1986.

[Brooks 91] R.A. Brooks, Intelligence without reason, *Proceedings 12th International Joint Conference on Artificial Intelligence,* St Paul, MN, 1991, 569- 595.

[Brown 87] D.C. Brown, A graduate-level expert system course, *AI Magazine* 8(3), 1987, 33-39.

[Brown and Cunningham 89] J.R. Brown and S. Cunningham, *Programming the User Interface - Principles and Examples,* John Wiley & Sons, New York, NY, 1989.

[Brownston et al. 85] L. Brownston, R. Farrel, E. Kant, and N. Martin, *Programming Expert Systems in OPS5. An Introduction to Rule-Based Programming.* Addison-Wesley, Reading, MA, 1985.

[Bruce 75] B.C. Bruce, Discourse models and language comprehension, *Computational Linguistics* 35, 1975, 19-35.

[Buchanan 86] B.G. Buchanan, Expert systems: Working systems and the research literature, *Expert Systems* 3(1), 1986, 32-51.

[Buchanan and Shortliffe 84] B.G. Buchanan and E.H. Shortliffe (editors), *Rule-Based Expert Systems - The MYCIN Experiments of the Stanford Heuristic Programming Project,* Addison-Wesley, Reading, MA, 1984.

[Burley-Allen 82] M. Burley-Allen, *Listening: The Forgotten Skill,* John Wiley & Sons, New York, NY, 1982.

[Buxton 89] R. Buxton, Modeling uncertainty in expert systems, *International Journal of Man-Machine Studies* 31, 1989, 415-476.

[Bylander and Chandrasekaran 87] T. Bylander and B. Chandrasekaran, Generic tasks for knowledge-based reasoning: The "right" level of abstraction for knowledge acquisition, *International Journal of Man-Machine Studies* 26, 1987, 231-243.

[Carberry 88] S. Carberry, Modeling the user's plans and goals, *Computational Linguistics* 14, 1988, 23-37.

[Carbonell 83] J.G. Carbonell, Learning by analogy: Formulating and generalizing plans from past experience, in R.S. Michalski, J.G. Carbonell, and T.M. Mitchell (editors), *Machine Learning - An Artificial Intelligence Approach,* Tioga, Palo Alto, CA, 1986, 137-162.

[Carbonell 86] J.G. Carbonell, Derivational analogy: A theory of reconstructive problem solving and expertise acquisition, in R.S. Michalski, J.G. Carbonell, and T.M. Mitchell (editors), *Machine Learning - An Artificial Intelligence Approach,* Vol. 2, Morgan Kaufmann, Los Altos, CA, 1986, 371-392.

[Carbonell 90] J. Carbonell (editor), *Machine Learning - Paradigms and Methods,* MIT Press, Cambridge, MA, 1990.

[Card et al. 83] S.K. Card, T.P. Moran, and A. Newell, *The Psychology of Human-Computer Interaction,* Lawrence Erlbaum, Hillsdale, NJ, 1983.

[Carey and Mason 83] T.T. Carey and R.E.A. Mason, Information system prototyping: Techniques, tools, and methodologies, *INFOR - The Canadian Journal of Operational Research and Information Processing* 21(3), 1983, 177-191.

[Carlsen and Stokke 87] S. Carlsen and G. Stokke, Conceptual modeling + prototyping = functional specification. *Proceedings 3th International Expert Systems Conference,* London, UK, 1987, 49-60.

[Casey 89] J. Casey, Picking the right expert system application, *AI Expert* 4(9), 1989, 44-47.

[Cawsay 93] A. Cawsay, *Explanation and Interaction - The Computer Generation of Explanatory Dialogues*, MIT Press, Cambridge, MA, 1993.

[Chandrasekaran 81] B. Chandrasekaran, Natural and social system metaphors for distributed problem solving: Introduction to the issue, *IEEE Transactions on Systems, Man, and Cybernetics* SMC-11(1), 1981, 1-5.

[Chandrasekaran 83-a] B. Chandrasekaran, On evaluating AI systems for medical diagnosis, *AI Magazine* 4(2), 1983, 34–37, 48.

[Chandrasekaran 83-b] B. Chandrasekaran, Towards a taxonomy of problem solving types, *AI Magazine* 4(1), 1983, 9-17

[Chandrasekaran 86] B. Chandrasekaran, Generic tasks in knowledge based reasoning: High-level building blocks for expert system design, *IEEE Expert* 1(3), 1986, 23-30.

[Chandrasekaran 88] B. Chandrasekaran, Generic tasks as building blocks for knowledge-based systems: The diagnosis and routine design examples, *The Knowledge Engineering Review* 3(3), 1988, 183-219.

[Chandrasekaran 90] B. Design problem-solving: A task analysis, *AI Magazine* 11(4), 1990, 59-71.

[Chandrasekaran 91] B. Chandrasekaran, Models versus rules, deep versus compiled, content versus form, *IEEE Expert* 6(2), 1991, 75-79.

[Chandrasekaran and Johnson 93] B. Chandrasekaran and T. Johson, Generic tasks and task structures: History, critique and new directions, in J-M. David, J-P. Krivine, and R. Simmons (editors), *Second Generation Expert Systems*, Springer-Verlag, Berlin, Germany, 1993, 232-272.

[Chandrasekaran and Milne 85] B. Chandrasekaran and R. Milne (editors), Special Section on Reasoning about Structure, Behavior and Function, *ACM SIGART Newsletter* 93, 1985.

[Chandrasekaran et al. 88] B. Chandrasekaran, M.C. Tanner, and J.R. Josephson, Explanation: The Role of Control Strategies and Deep Models, in J. Hendler (editor), *Expert System: The User Interface*, Ablex, Norwood, NJ, 1988, 219-248.

[Chandrasekaran et al. 89] B. Chandrasekaran, J. W. Smith, and J. Sticklen, Deep models and their relation to diagnosis, *Artificial Intelligence in Medicine* 1, 1989, 29-40.

[Chang an Lee 73] C.L. Chang and R.C. Lee, *Symbolic Logic and Mechanical Theorem Proving*, Academic Press, New York, NY, 1973.

[Chapman 87] D. Chapman, Planning for conjunctive goals, *Artificial Intelligence* 32, 1987, 333-378.

[Charette 89] R.N. Charette, *Software Engineering Risk Analysis and Management*, McGraw-Hill, New York, NY, 1989.

[Charniak and McDermott 85] E. Charniak and D. McDermott, *Introduction to Artificial Intelligence*, Addison-Wesley, Reading, MA, 1985.

[Charniak et al. 87] E. Charniak, C.K. Riesbeck, and J.R. Meehan, *Artificial Intelligence Programming* (2nd ed.), Lawrence Erlbaum, Hillsdale, NJ, 1987.

[Chen 76] P.P. Chen, The entity-relationships model - toward a unifying view of data, *ACM Transactions on Data Base Systems* 1(1), 1976, 9-36.

[Chi et al. 81] M.T.H. Chi, P.J. Feltovich, and R. Glaser, Categorisation and representation of physics problems by experts and novices, *Cognitive Science* 5, 1981, 121-152.

[Chinell 90] D.F. Chinell, *System Documentation - The In-Line Approach*, John Wiley & Sons, New York, NY, 1990.

[Chorafas 90] D.N. Chorafas, *Knowledge Engineering*, Van Nostrand Reinhold, New York, NY, 1990.

[Chung 94] P.W.H. Chung. Effective knowledge elicitation, in C. Tasso and E. de Arantes e Oliveira (editors), *Development of Knowledge-Based Systems for Engineering*, Springer-Verlag, Wien, Austria, 1994.

[Citrenbaum et al. 87] R. Citrenbaum, J.R. Geissman, and R. Schultz, Selecting a shell, *AI Expert* 2(9), 1987, 30-39.

[Clancey 83] W.J. Clancey, The epistemology of a rule-based expert system: A framework for explanation, *Artificial Intelligence* 20, 1983, 215-251.

[Clancey 85] W.J. Clancey, Heuristic classification, *Artificial Intelligence* 27, 1985, 289-350.

[Clanon 85] J. Clanon, *Guide to Knowledge Engineer Selection*, Artificial Intelligence Guide Series, Intelligent Systems Technologies Group, Digital Equipment Corporation, Merrimack, NH, 1985.

[Clark 90] D.A. Clark, Numerical and symbolic approaches to uncertainty management in AI, *Artificial Intelligence Review* 4, 1990, 109-146.

[Clarke 88] R. Clarke, Legal aspects of knowledge based technology, *Journal of Information Technology* 3(1), 1988.

[Clarke 89] R. Clarke, Property rights in knowledge-based products and applications, *Expert Systems* 6(3), 1989, 158-165.

[Cleaves 88] D.A. Cleaves, Cognitive biases and corrective techniques: Proposals for improving elicitation procedures for knowledge-based systems, in J.H Boose and B.R Gaines (editors), *Knowledge Acquisition Tools for Expert Systems - Knowledge-Based Systems, Vol. 2*, Academic Press, New York, NY, 1988, 23-34.

[Cleland and Kerzner 86] D.I. Cleland and H. Kerzner, *Engineering Team Management*, Van Nostrand Reinhold, New York, NY, 1986.

[Clocksin and Mellish 87] W.F. Clocksin and C.S. Mellish. *Programming in PROLOG* (3rd edition), Springer-Verlag, Heidelberg, Germany, 1987.

[Cohen 85] P.R. Cohen, *Heuristic Reasoning about Uncertainty: An Artificial Intelligence Approach*, Pitman, Boston, MA, 1985.

[Cohen and Bench-Capon 93] F. Cohen and T. Bench-Capon, *Maintenance of Knowledge-Based Systems - Theory, Techniques, and Tools*, Academic Press, London, UK, 1993.

[Cohen and Perrault 79] P.R. Cohen and C.R. Perrault, Elements of a plan-based theory of speech acts, *Cognitive Science* 3, 1979, 177-212.

[Cohen et al. 86] B. Cohen, W.T. Harwood, and M.I. Jackson, *The Specification of Complex Systems*, Addison-Wesley, Reading, MA, 1986.

[Cooper and Wogrin 88] T. Cooper and N. Wogrin, *Rule-based Programming with OPS5*, Morgan Kaufman, Los Altos, CA, 1988.

[Cordingley 89] E.S. Cordingley, Knowledge elicitation techniques for knowledge-bases systems, in D. Diaper (editor), *Knowledge Elicitation - Principles, Techniques and Applications*, Ellis Horwood, Chichester, UK, 1989, 87-176.

[Cragun and Steudel 87] B.J. Cragun and H.J. Steudel, A decision-table-based processor for checking completeness and consistency in rule-based expert systems, *International Journal of Man–Machine Studies* 26, 1987, 633–648.

[Craig 92] I.D. Craig, *Blackboard Systems*, Ablex, Norwood, NJ, 1992.

[Cullen and Bryman 88] J. Cullen and A. Bryman, The knowledge acquisition bottleneck: Time for reassessment?, *Expert Systems* 5(3), 1988, 216-225.

[Cupello and Mishelevich 88] J. Cupello and D. Mishelevich, Managing prototype knowledge/expert system projects, *Communications of the ACM* 31(5), 534-541, 550.

[Cutland 80] N.J. Cutland, *Computabilty: An Introduction to Recursive Functions Theory*, Cambridge University Press, Cambridge, UK, 1980.

[Dahl 93] Special Issue on Constraint Reasoning for Expert Systems, *International Journal of Expert Systems - Research and Applications* 6(4), 1993.

[Daniels 86] P.J. Daniels, The user modelling function of an intelligent interface for document retrieval systems. *Proceedings IRFIS 6: Intelligent Information Systems for the Information Society*, North-Holland, Amsterdam, The Netherlands, 1986, 162-176.

[Darroy 91] J.-M. Darroy, A.I. for space: A strategic approach for more than just a new technology, in *Proceedings Artificial Intelligence and Knowledge-Based Systems for Space*, Workshop, May 22-24 1991, ESTEC, Noordwijk, The Netherlands, ESA WPP-025, 1991, Vol. 1.

[Davenport 93] T.H. Davenport, *Process Innovation - Reengineering Work through Information Technology*, Harward Business School Press, Boston, MA, 1993.

[David et al. 93-a] J.-M. David, J.-P. Krivine, and B. Richard, Building and maintaining a large knowledge-based system from a 'knowledge level' perspective: The DIVA experiment, in J.-M. David, J.-P. Krivine, and R. Simmons (editors), *Second Generation Expert Systems*, Springer-Verlag, Berlin, Germany, 1993, 376-401.

[David et al. 93-b] J.-M. David, J.P. Krivine, and R. Simmons, Second generation expert systems: A step forward in knowledge engineering, in J.-M. David, J.-P. Krivine, and R. Simmons (editors), *Second Generation Expert Systems*, Springer-Verlag, Berlin, Germany, 1993, 3-23.

[Davies and Hakiel 88] M. Davies and S. Hakiel, Knowledge harvesting: A practical guide to interviewing, *Expert Systems* 5(1), 1988, 42-50.

[Davis 80-a] R. Davis, Meta-rules: Reasoning about control, *Artificial Intelligence* 15, 1980, 179-222.

[Davis 80-b] R. Davis, Content reference: Reasoning about rules, *Artificial Intelligence* 15, 1980, 223-239.

[Davis 84-a] G.B. Davis, *Management Information Systems: Conceptual Foundations, Structure, and Development*, McGraw-Hill, New York, NY, 1984.

[Davis 84-b] R. Davis, Diagnostic reasoning based on structure and behavior, *Artificial Intelligence* 24, 1984, 347-410.

[Davis 90-a] E. Davis, *Representations of Commonsense Knowledge*, Morgan Kaufmann, San Mateo, CA, 1990.

[Davis 90-b] J.S. Davis, Effect of modularity on maintainability of rule-based systems, *International Journal of Man-Machine Studies* 32, 1990, 439-447.

[Davis and Smith 83] R. Davis and R. G. Smith, Negotiation as a metaphor for distributed problem solving, *Artificial Intelligence* 20, 1983, 63-109.

[Davis et al. 93] R. Davis, H. Shrobe, and P. Szolovits, What is knowledge representation? *AI Magazine* 14(1), 1993, 17-33.

[Davison 92] S.J. Davison, Real-time knowledge-based supervision for continuous and batch processing applications using COGSYS, in G. Guida and A. Stefanini (editors), *Industrial Applications of Knowledge-Based Diagnosis*, Elsevier, Amsterdam, The Netherlands, 1992, 169-190.

[De Marco 79] T. De Marco, *Structured Analysis and System Specification*, Prentice-Hall, Englewood Cliffs, NJ, 1979.

[De Salvo et al. 87] D.A. De Salvo, A.E. Glamm, and J. Liebowitz, Structured design of an expert system prototype at the National Archives, in B.G. Silverman (editor), *Expert Systems for Business*, Addison-Wesley, Reading, MA, 1987, 41-77.

[de Kleer 86-a] J. de Kleer, An assumption-based TMS. *Artificial Intelligence* 28, 1986, 127-162.

[de Kleer 86-b] J. de Kleer, Extending the ATMS. *Artificial Intelligence* 28, 1986, 163-196.

[de Kleer 86-c] J. de Kleer, Problem solving with the ATMS. *Artificial Intelligence* 28, 1986, 197-224.

[de Kleer and Brown 84] J. de Kleer and J.S. Brown, A qualitative physics based on confluences, *Artificial Intelligence* 24, 1984, 7-83.

[Dean and Boddy 88] T. Dean and M. Boddy, An analysis of time-dependent planning, *Proceedings 7th National Conference on Artificial Intelligence*, Saint Paul, MN, 1988, 49-54.

[Dean and McDermott 87] T.L. Dean and D.V. Mc Dermott, Temporal data base management, *Artificial Intelligence* 32, 1987, 1-55.

[Decker 87] K.S. Decker, Distributed problem-solving techniques: A survey, *IEEE Transactions on Systems, Man, and Cybernetics* SMC-17(5), 1987, 729-740.

[Dempster 68] A.P. Dempster, A generalization of Bayesian inference, *Journal of the Royal Statistical Society* B 30, 1968, 205-247.

[Deutsch 82] M.S. Deutsch, *Software Verification and Validation - Realistic Project Approaches*, Prentice-Hall, Englewood Cliffs, NJ, 1982.

[Diaper 89] D. Diaper (editor), *Knowledge Elicitation - Principles, Techniques and Applications*, Ellis Horwood, Chichester, UK, 1989.

[Dickover et al. 77] M.E. Dickover, C.L. McGowan, and D.T. Ross, Software design using SADT, *Proceedings 1977 Annual Conference of the Association for Computing Machinery (ACM)*, Seattle, WA, 1977, 125-133.

[Diederich and Linster 89] J. Diederich and M. Linster, Knowledge-based knowledge elicitation, in G. Guida and C. Tasso (editors), *Topics in Expert System Design - Methodologies and Tools*, North-Holland, Amsterdam, The Netherlands, 1989, 323-350.

[Diederich et al. 87] J. Diederich, I. Ruhmann, and M. May, KRITON: A knowledge-acquisition tool for expert systems, *International Journal of Man-Machine Studies* 26, 1987, 29-40.

[Dijkstra 76] E.W. Dijkstra, *A Discipline of Programming*, Prentice-Hall, Englewood Cliffs, NJ, 1976.

[Dix et al. 93] A.J. Dix, J.E. Finlay, G.D. Abowd, and R. Beale, *Human-Computer Interaction*, Prentice-Hall, London, UK, 1993.

[DOD 88] DOD, United States Department of Defense, Defense System Software Development, *Military Standard DOD-STD-2167A*, Washington, DC, 1988.

[Dodhiawala et al. 89] R. Dodhiawala, N.S. Sridharan, P. Raulefs, and C. Pickering, Real-time AI systems: A definition and an architecture, *Proceedings 11th International Joint Conference on Artificial Intelligence*, Detroit, MI, 1989, 256-261.

[Downs et al. 88] E. Downs, P. Clare, and I. Coe, *SSADM: Structured Systems Analysis and Design Method*, Prentice-Hall, Englewood Cliffs, NJ, 1988.

[Doyle 79] J. Doyle, A truth maintenance system, *Artificial Intelligence* 12, 1979, 231-272.

[Driankov 86] D. Driankov, Uncertainty calculus with verbally defined belief-intervals, *International Journal of Intelligent Systems* 1, 1986, 219-246.

[Drucker 66] P.F. Drucker, *The Effective Executive*, Harper & Row, New York, NY, 1966.

[Drucker 74] P.F. Drucker, *Management: Tasks, Responsibility, Practices*, Harper & Row, New York, NY, 1974.

[Drucker 86] P.F. Drucker, *The Frontiers of Management*, Dutton, New York, NY, 1986.

[Dubois and Prade 80] D. Dubois and H. Prade, *Fuzzy Sets and Systems: Theory and Applications*, Academic Press, New York, NY, 1980.

[Dubois and Prade 88] D. Dubois and H. Prade, *Possibility Theory - An Approach to Computerized Processing of Uncertainty*, Plenum Press, New York, NY, 1988.

[Dubois and Prade 89] D. Dubois and H. Prade, Processing fuzzy temporal knowledge, *IEEE Transactions on Systems, Man, and Cybernetics* SMC-19(4), 1989, 729-744.

[Durkin 90] J. Durkin, Introducing students to expert systems, *Expert Systems* 7(2), 1990, 70-80.

[Dym and Mittal 85] C.L. Dym and S. Mittal, Knowledge acquisition from multiple experts, *AI Magazine* 7(2), 1985, 32-36.

[Ebrahimi 87] M. Ebrahimi, A structured approach to expert system design, *Proceedings WESTEX-87 Conference on Expert Systems*, Anaheim, CA, 1987, 18-24.

[Edwards 91] J.S. Edwards, *Building Knowledge-Based Systems - Towards a Methodology*, Pitman, London, UK, 1991.

[Eisenberg 90] M. Eisenberg, *Programming in Scheme*, MIT Press, Cambridge, MA, 1990.

[Ellis 89] C. Ellis (editor), *Expert Knowledge and Explanation*, Ellis Horwood, Chichester, UK, 1989.

[Emery and Trist 78] F.E. Emery and E.L. Trist, Analytical model of sociotechnical systems, in W.A. Pasmore and J.J. Sherwood (editors), *Sociotechnical systems: A Sourcebook*, University Associates, La Jolla, CA, 1978.

[Engelmore and Morgan 89] R. Engelmore and T. Morgan (editors), *Blackboard Systems*, Addison-Wesley, Reading, MA, 1989.

[Ericsson and Simon 80] K.A. Ericsson and H.A. Simon, Verbal Reports as Data, *Psychological Review* 87, 1980, 215-251.

[Ericsson and Simon 84] K.A. Ericsson and H.A. Simon, *Protocol Analysis: Verbal Reports as Data*, MIT Press, Cambridge, MA, 1984.

[Erlandsen and Holm 87] J. Erlandsen and J. Holm, Intelligent help systems, *Information and Software Technology* 29(3), 1987, 115-121.

[Erman et al. 80] L.D. Erman, F. Hayes-Roth, V.R. Lesser, and D.R. Reddy, The Hearsay-II speech-understanding system: Integrating knowledge to resolve uncertainty, *ACM Computing Surveys* 12(2), 1980, 213-253.

[ESA PSS-05-0 91] ESA, European Space Agency, *ESA Software Engineering Standards*, ESA PSS-05-0 Issue 2, Paris, 1991.

[ESA PSS-05-02 91] ESA, European Space Agency, *Guide to the User Requirements Definition Phase*, ESA PSS-O5-02, Paris, 1991.

[ESA PSS-05-03 91] ESA, European Space Agency, *Guide to the Software Requirements Definition Phase*, ESA PSS-O5-03, Paris, 1991.

[ESA PSS-05-04 91] ESA, European Space Agency, *Guide to the Architectural Design Phase*, ESA PSS-O5-04, Paris, 1991.

[ESA PSS-05-05 91] ESA, European Space Agency, *Guide to the Detailed Design and Production Phase*, ESA PSS-O5-05, Paris, 1991.

[ESA PSS-05-06 91] ESA, European Space Agency, *Guide to the Transfer Phase*, ESA PSS-05-06, Paris, 1991.

[ESA PSS-05-07 91] ESA, European Space Agency, *Guide to the Operations and Maintenance Phase*, ESA PSS-05-07, Paris, 1991.

[ESA PSS-05-08 91] ESA, European Space Agency, *Guide to Software Project Management*, ESA PSS-05-08, Paris, 1991.

[ESA PSS-05-09 91] ESA, European Space Agency, *Guide to Software Configuration Management*, ESA PSS-05-09, Paris, 1991.

[ESA PSS-05-10 91] ESA, European Space Agency, *Guide to Software Verification and Validation*, ESA PSS-05-10, Paris, 1991.

[ESA PSS-05-11 91] ESA, European Space Agency, *Guide to Software Quality Assurance*, ESA PSS-05-11, Paris, 1991.

[Eshelman et al. 87] L. Eshelman, D. Ehret, J. McDermott, and M. Tan, MOLE: A tenacious knowledge-acquisition tool, *International Journal of Man-Machine Studies* 26, 1987, 41-54.

[Fagan 76] M.E. Fagan, Design and code inspections to reduce errors in program development, *IBM Systems Journal* 15(3), 1976, 182-211.

[Fagan 86] M.E. Fagan, Advances on inspections, *IEEE Transactions on Software Engineering* SE-12(7), 1986, 744-751.

[Fairley 85] R.E. Fairley, *Software Engineering Concepts*, McGraw-Hill, New York, NY, 1985.

[Faltings and Struss 92] B. Faltings and P. Struss (editors), *Recent Advances in Qualitative Physics*, MIT Press, Cambridge, MA, 1992.

[Farreny and Prade 86] H. Farreny and H. Prade, Default and inexact reasoning with possibility degrees, *IEEE Transactions on Systems, Man and Cybernetics* SMC-16, 1986, 270-276.

[Feigenbaum et al. 88] E. Feigenbaum, P. McCorduck, and H.P. Nii, *The Rise of the Expert Company*, Macmillan, London, UK, 1988.

[Fenn and Veren 91] J.A. Fenn and L.C. Veren, Expert system development methodologies in theory and practice, *Proceedings IEEE/ACM International Conference on Developing and Managing Expert System Programs*, Washington, DC, 1991, 262-266.

[Ferrari 86] G. Ferrari (editor), Special Issue on Natural Language Processing, *Proceedings of the IEEE* 74(7), 1986, 899-1039.

[Fikes and Nilsson 71] R.E. Fikes and N.J. Nilsson, STRIPS: A new approach to the application of theorem proving to problem solving, *Artificial Intelligence* 2, 1971, 189-208.

[Finch et al. 92] F.E. Finch, G.M. Stanley, and S.P. Fraleigh, Using the G2 diagnostic assistant for real-time fault diagnosis, in G. Guida and A. Stefanini (editors), *Industrial Applications of Knowledge-Based Diagnosis*, Elsevier, Amsterdam, The Netherlands, 1992, 191-216.

[Firley and Hellens 91] M. Firley and D. Hellens, *Knowledge Elicitation - A Practical Handbook*, Prentice-Hall, Englewood Cliffs, NJ, 1991.

[Floyd 84] C. Floyd, A systematic look at prototyping, in R. Budde (editor), *Approaches to Prototyping*, Springer-Verlag, Berlin, Germany, 1983.

[Forbus 84] K. D. Forbus, Qualitative process theory, *Artificial Intelligence* 24, 1984, 85-168.

[Ford 87-a] L. Ford, Artificial Intelligence and software engineering: A tutorial introduction to their relationship, *Artificial Intelligence Review* 1, 1987, 255-273.

[Ford 87-b] N. Ford, *How Machines Think*, John Wiley & Sons, Chichester, UK, 1987.

[Ford and Bradshaw 93] K. Ford and J.M. Bradshaw (editors), *Knowledge Acquisition as Modeling*, John Wiley & Sons, Chichester, UK, 1993.

[Forgy 82] C.L. Forgy, Rete: A fast algorithm for the many pattern/many object pattern match problem, *Artificial Intelligence* 19, 1982, 17-37.

[Forman and Nagy 87] E.H. Forman and T.J. Nagy, EXSYS vs. TOPSI/OPS5 vs. MICRO-PS: A multicriteria model to select an expert system generator, *Telematics and Informatics* 4(1), 1987, 37-54.

[Forsyth 89] R. Forsyth, *Machine Learning: Principles and Techniques*, Chapman and Hall, London, UK, 1989.

[Forsythe and Buchanan 89] D.E. Forsythe and B.G. Buchanan, Knowledge acquisition for expert systems: Some pitfalls and suggestions, *IEEE Transactions on Systems, Man, and Cybernetics* 19(3), 1989, 435-443.

[Fox 81] M.S. Fox, An organizational view of distributed systems, *IEEE Transactions on System, Man, and Cybernetics* SMC-11(1), 1981, 70-80.

[Frank 88-a] S.J. Frank, What AI practitioners should know about the low: Part one, *AI Magazine* 9(1), 1988, 63-75.

[Frank 88-b] S.J. Frank, What AI practitioners should know about the low: Part two, *AI Magazine* 9(2), 1988, 109-114.

[Fransella and Banninster 77] F. Fransella and D. Banninster, *A Manual for Repertory Grid Technique*, Academic Press, London, UK, 1977.

[Freeman 87] M.S. Freeman, *HSTDEK: Developing a methodology for construction of large-scale, multi-use knowledge bases*, NASA Conference Publications 2492, NASA, Marshall Space Flight Center, 1987, 89-94.

[Freeman and Wasserman 77] P. Freeman and A.I. Wasserman, *Tutorial on Software Design Techniques*, IEEE Computer Society, Silver Spring, MD, 1977.

[Freiling et al. 85] M. Freiling, J.H. Alexander, S.L. Messick, S. Rehfuss, and S.J. Shulman, Starting a knowledge engineering project: A step-by-step approach, *AI Magazine* 6(3), 1985, 150-164.

[Gaines and Boose 88] B. Gaines and J.H Boose (editors), *Knowledge Acquisition for Knowledge-Based Systems - Knowledge-Based Systems, Vol. 1*, Academic Press, New York, NY, 1988.

[Gaines and Boose 90] B.R. Gaines and J. Boose (editors), *Machine Learning and Uncertain Reasoning - Knowledge-Based Systems, Vol. 3*, Academic Press, New York, NY, 1990.

[Gaines and Shaw 86] B.R. Gaines and M.L.G. Shaw, From timesharing to the sixth generation: The development of human-computer interaction, *International Journal of Man-Machine Studies* 24, 1986, Part 1: 1-27, Part 2: 519-543.

[Gammak 87] J. G. Gammack, Different techniques and different aspects on declarative knowledge, in A.L. Kidd (editor), *Knowledge Acquisition for Expert Systems. A Practical Handbook*, Plenum Press, New York, NY, 1987, 137-163.

[Gane and Sarson 79] C. Gane and T. Sarson, *Structured Analysis and Systems Analysis: Tools and Techniques.* Prentice-Hall, Englewood Cliffs, NJ, 1979.

[Gaschnig et al. 83] J. Gaschnig, P. Klahr, P. Pople, H. Shortliffe, and A. Terry, Evaluation of expert systems: Issues and case studies, in D.A. Waterman, R. Hayes–Roth, and D. Lenat (editors), *Building Expert Systems*, Addison–Wesley, Reading, MA, 1983, 241–280.

[Gasser and Huhns 89] L. Gasser and N.M. Huhns (editors), *Distributed Artificial Intelligence, Volume II*, Pitman, London, UK, 1989.

[Gattiker 90] U.E. Gattiker, *Technology Management in Organizations*, Sage Publications, Newburt Park, CA, 1990.

[Gazdar and Mellish 89-a] G. Gazdar and C. Mellish, *Natural Language Processing in Lisp*, Addison-Wesley, Wokingham, UK, 1989.

[Gazdar and Mellish 89-b] G. Gazdar and C. Mellish, *Natural Language Processing in Prolog*, Addison-Wesley, Wokingham, UK, 1989.

[Geffner 90] H. Geffner, *Default Reasoning - Causal and Conditional Theories*, MIT Press, Cambridge, MA, 1990.

[Geissman and Schultz 88] J.R. Geissman and R.D. Schultz, Verification and validation of expert systems, *AI Expert* 3(2), 1988, 26–33.

[Gemignani 90] M.C. Gemignani, Liability for the malfunction of an expert system, *Proceedings IEEE Conference on Managing Expert System Programs and Projects*, 1990, 8-15.

[Genesereth and Nilsson 87] M.R. Genesereth and N.J. Nilsson, *Logical Foundations of Artificial Intelligence*, Morgan Kaufmann, Los Altos, CA, 1987.

[Georgeff 82] M.P. Georgeff, Procedural control in production systems, *Artificial Intelligence* 18, 1982, 175-201.

[Georgeff and Lansky 87] M. Georgeff and A.L. Lansky (editors), *Reasoning about Actions and Plans*, Morgan Kaufmann, Palo Alto, CA, 1987.

[Gevarter 87] W.B. Gevarter, The nature and evaluation of commercial expert system building tools, *IEEE Computer* 20(5), 1987, 24-41.

[Ginsberg 87] M.L. Ginsberg (editor), *Readings in Nonmonotonic Reasoning*, Morgan Kaufmann, San Mateo, CA, 1987.

[Ginsberg 88] A. Ginsberg, Knowledge-base reduction: A new approach to checking knowledge bases for inconsistency & redundancy, *Proceedings 7th National Conference on Artificial Intelligence*, Saint Paul, MN, 1988, Vol. 2, 585-589.

[Gittins 86] D. Gittins, Icon-Based Human-Computer Interaction, *International Journal of Man-Machine Studies* 24, 1986, 519-543.

[Gladden 82] G.R. Gladden, Stop the life cycle, I want to get off, *ACM Sigsoft* 7(2), 1982, 35-39.

[Glazer 90] D.A. Glazer, Strategies for managers to reduce employee fear when introducing a new technology, in D.A. De Salvo and J. Liebowitz (editors), *Managing Artificial Intelligence and Expert Systems*, Prentice-Hall, Englewood Cliffs, NJ, 1990.

[Goddard 89-a] Goddard Space Flight Center, *Expert System Development Methodology User Guide*, DSTL-90-004, Revision 1, National Aeronautics and Space Administration, Goddard Space Flight Center, Greenbelt, MD, 1989.

[Goddard 89-b] Goddard Space Flight Center, *Expert System Development Methodology Standard*, DSTL-90-005, Revision 1, National Aeronautics and Space Administration, Goddard Space Flight Center, Greenbelt, MD, 1989.

[Goddard 89-c] Goddard Space Flight Center, *Expert System Development Methodology Reference Manual*, DSTL-90-006, Revision 1, National Aeronautics and Space Administration, Goddard Space Flight Center, Greenbelt, MD, 1989.

[Goel 85] A.L. Goel, Software reliability models: Assumptions, limitations, and applicability, *IEEE Transactions on Software Engineering* SE-11(12), 1985, 1411-1423.

[Goldberg and Robson 89] A. Goldberg and D. Robson, *SMALLTALK-80 - The Language*, Addison-Wesley, Reading, MA, 1989.

[Gordon 69] R. Gordon, *Interviewing Strategies, Techniques, and Tactics*, The Dorsey Press, Homewood, IL, 1969.

[Gray 88] B.W. Gray, Copyright in computer software, *Computer, Law & Security Report* 4(2), 1988, 11-15.

[Green and Keyes 87] C.J.R. Green and M.M. Keyes, Verification and validation of expert systems, *Proceedings IEEE Knowledge–Based Engineering & Expert System Conference (WESTEX–87)*, Anaheim, CA, 1987, 38–43.

[Greenwell 88] M. Greenwell, *Knowledge Engineering for Expert Systems*, Ellis Horwood, Chichester, UK, 1988.

[Grigoriou and Willey 87] M.M. Grigoriou and P.C.T. Willey, Multi-criteria method for selecting an expert system shell, *Proceeding 3th International Expert Systems Conference*, London, UK, 1987, 277-289.

[Grishman 87] R. Grishman, *Computational Linguistics - An Introduction*, Cambridge University Press, Cambridge, MA, 1987.

[Grogono et al. 91] P. Grogono, A. Batarekh, A. Preece, R. Shinghal, and C. Suen, Expert systems evaluation techniques: A selected bibliography, *Expert Systems* 8(4), 1991, 227-238.

[Grosz and Sidner 86] B.J. Grosz and C.L. Sidner, Attentions, intention, and the structure of discourse, *Computational Linguistics* 12, 1986, 175-204.

[Grosz et al. 86] B. Grosz, K. Spark Jones, and B.L. Webber (editors), *Readings in Natural Language Processing*, Morgan Kaufmann, Los Altos, CA, 1986.

[Grover 83] M. D. Grover, A pragmatic knowledge acquisition methodology, *Proceedings 8th International Joint Conference on Artificial Intelligence*, Karlsruhe, Germany, 1983, 436-438.

[Gruber 89] T. Gruber, *The Acquisition of Strategic Knowledge*, Academic Press, San Diego, CA, 1989.

[Gudes et al. 86] E. Gudes, S. Shafrir, and S. Gerlitz, Software and knowledge engineering methods in building expert systems, *Proceedings 2nd International Expert Systems Conference*, London, UK, 1986, 237-245.

[Guida and Mauri 93] G. Guida and G. Mauri, Evaluating performance and quality of knowledge-based systems: Foundation and methodology, *IEEE Transactions on Knowledge and Data Engineering* KDE-5(2), 1993, 204-224.

[Guida and Stefanini 92] G. Guida and A. Stefanini (editors), *Industrial Applications of Knowledge-Based Diagnosis*, Elsevier, Amsterdam, The Netherlands, 1992.

[Guida and Tasso 89-a] G. Guida and C. Tasso (editors), *Topics in Expert System Design, Methodologies and Tools*, North-Holland, Amsterdam, The Netherlands, 1989.

[Guida and Tasso 89-b] G. Guida and C. Tasso, Building expert systems: From life cycle to development methodology, in G. Guida and C. Tasso (editors), *Topics in Expert System Design, Methodologies and Tools*, North-Holland, Amsterdam, The Netherlands, 1989, 3-24.

[Gupta 87] A. Gupta, *Parallelism in Production Systems*, Morgan Kaufman, Los Altos, CA, 1987.

[Gupta 91] U.G. Gupta (editor), *Validating and Verifying Knowledge-Based Systems*, IEEE Computer Society Press, Los Alamitos, CA, 1991.

[Hall 89] R. Hall, Computational approaches to analogical reasoning: A comparative analysis, *Artificial Intelligence* 39, 1989, 39-120

[Hancock and Chignell 89] P.A. Hancock and M.H. Chignell (editors), *Intelligent Interfaces: Theory, Research and Design*, North-Holland, Amsterdam, The Netherlands, 1989.

[Hanneman 85] H.W.A.M. Hanneman, *The Patentability of Computer Software*, Kluwer, Dordrecht, The Netherlands, 1985.

[Harel 88] D. Harel, On visual formalisms, *Communications of the ACM* 31(5), 1988, 514-530.

[Harmon and King 85] P. Harmon and D. King, *Expert Systems: Artificial Intelligence in Business*, John Wiley, New York, NY, 1985.

[Harmon and Sawyer 90] P. Harmon and B. Sawyer, *Creating Expert Systems for Business and Industry*, John Wiley & Sons, New York, 1990.

[Harmon et al. 88] P. Harmon, R. Maus, and W. Morrissey, *Expert Systems: Tools and Applications*, John Wiley & Sons, New York, NY, 1988.

[Harris 85] M.D. Harris, *Introduction to Natural Language Processing*, Reston, Reston, VA, 1985.

[Harris and Davis 86] L.R. Harris and D.B. Davis, *Artificial Intelligence Enters the Marketplace*, Bantam Books, New York, NY, 1986.

[Hart 82] P.E. Hart, Directions for AI in the eighties, *ACM SIGART Newsletter* 79, 1982, 11-16.

[Hart 86] A. Hart, *Knowledge Acquisition for Expert Systems*, Kogan Page, London, UK, 1986.

[Hart 87] A. Hart, Role of induction in knowledge elicitation, in A.L. Kidd (editor), *Knowledge Acquisition for Expert Systems. A Practical Handbook*, Plenum Press, New York, NY, 1987, 165-189.

[Hartson 85] H.R. Hartson (editor), *Advances in Human-Computer Interaction - Vol. 1*, Ablex, Norwood, NJ, 1985.

[Hartson 88] H.R. Hartson (editor), *Advances in Human-Computer Interaction - Vol. 2*, Ablex, Norwood, NJ, 1988.

[Hayball and Barlow 90] C. Hayball and D. Barlow, Skills support in the ICL (Kidsgrove) bonding shop - A case study in the application of the KADS methodology, in D. Berry and A. Hart (editors), *Expert Systems: Human Issues*, Chapman and Hall, London, UK, 1990, 85-97.

[Hayes 81] J.R. Hayes, *The Complete Problem Solver*, The Franklin Institute Press, Philadelphia, PA, 1981.

[Hayes-Roth 85] B. Hayes-Roth, A blackboard architecture for control, *Artificial Intelligence* 26, 1985, 251-321.

[Hayes-Roth 89] F. Hayes-Roth, Towards benchmarks for knowledge systems and their implications for data engineering, *IEEE Transactions on Knowledge and Data Engineering* 1(1), 1989, 101-110.

[Hayes-Roth et al. 83] F. Hayes-Roth, D.A. Waterman, and D.B. Lenat (editors), *Building Expert Systems*, Addison-Wesley, Reading, MA, 1983.

[Hayman et al. 88] W.A. Hayman, W.L. Johnston, and S. Spar, Knowledge based expert systems: System safety and legal issues in AI, *Computers & Industrial Engineering* 15(1-4), 1988.

[Hayward et al. 88] S.A. Hayward, B.J. Wielinga, and J.A. Breuker, Structured analysis of knowledge, in J.H. Boose and B.R. Gaines (editors), *Knowledge Acquisition Tools for Expert Systems - Knowledge-Based Systems, Vol. 2*, , Academic Press, London, UK, 1988, 149-160.

[Hazeltine 87] N. Hazeltine, Knowledge systems technology transfer, *Proceedings Annual Artificial Intelligence and Advanced Computing Technology Conference*, Long Beach, CA, 1987, 271-272.

[Heath 94] J. Heath, Expert systems resource guide, *AI Expert* 9(4), 1994, 40-49.

[Helander 88] M. Helander (editor), *Handbook of Human-Computer Interaction*, North-Holland, Amsterdam, The Netherlands, 1988.

[Held and Carlis 89] J.P. Held and J.V. Carlis, Conceptual data modeling of expert systems, *IEEE Expert* 4(1), 1989, 50-61.

[Helton 90] T. Helton, AI infusion: Getting your company involved, *AI Expert* 5(3), 1990, 54-59.

[Henderson 80]] P. Henderson, *Functional Programming. Application and Implementation*, Prentice-Hall, Englewood Cliffs, NJ, 1980.

[Hendler 88] J.A. Hendler, *Expert Systems: The User Interfaces*, Ablex, Norwood, NJ, 1988.

[Hendrix 82] G.G. Hendrix, Natural language interface, *Computational Linguistics* 8, 1982, 56-61.

[Heng 87] M.S.H. Heng, Why evolutionary development of expert systems appears to work, *Future Generation Computer Systems* 3(2), 1987, 103-109.

[Henrion et al. 90] M. Henrion, R.D. Shachter, L. Kanal, and J.F. Lemmer (editors), *Uncertainty in Artificial Intelligence 5*, Elsevier, Amsterdam, The Netherlands, 1990.

[Hewitt 77] C. Hewitt, Viewing control structures as patterns of passing messages, *Artificial Intelligence* 8, 1977, 323-364.

[Hickman et al. 89] F.R. Hickman, J.L. Killin, L. Land, T. Mulhall, D. Porter, and R.M. Taylor, *Analysis for Knowledge-Based Systems: A practical Guide to the KADS Methodology*, Ellis Horwood, Chichester, UK, 1989.

[Highland and Iwaskiw 89] F.D. Highland and C.T. Iwaskiw, Knowledge base compilation, *Proceedings 11th International Joint Conference on Artificial Intelligence*, Detroit, MI, 1989, 227-232.

[Hilal and Soltan 91] D.K. Hilal and H. Soltan, A suggested descriptive framework for the comparison of knowledge-based systems methodologies, *Expert Systems* 8(2), 1991, 107-114.

[Hilal and Soltan 93] D.K. Hilal and H. Soltan, Towards a comprehensive methodology for KBS development, *Expert Systems* 10(2), 1993, 75-91.

[Hillman 90] D.H. Hillman, Integrating neural nets and expert systems, *AI Expert* 5(6), 1990, 54-59.

[Hillmer et al.91] D. Hillmer, A.J. La Salle, L. Medsker, and G. Welsh, Identifying risks in expert system projects, *Proceedings IEEE/ACM International Conference on Developing and Managing Expert System Programs*, Washington, DC, 1991, 45-52.

[Hix and Hartson 93] D. Hix and R. Hartson, *Developing User Interfaces - Ensuring Usability through Product and Process*, John Wiley & Sons, Chichester, UK, 1993.

[Hoffman 87] R.R. Hoffman, The problem of extracting the knowledge of experts from the perspective of experimental psychology, *AI Magazine* 8(2), 1987, 53-67.

[Hogger 84] C.J. Hogger, *Introduction to Logic Programming*, Academic Press, Orlando, FL, 1984.

[Hollnagel 89] E. Hollnagel, Evaluation of expert systems, in G. Guida and C. Tasso (editors), *Topics in Expert System Design – Methodologies and Tools*, North–Holland, Amsterdam, The Netherlands, 1989, 377–416.

[Hopkins and Horan 93] T. Hopkins and B. Horan, *Smalltalk-80*, Prentice-Hall, London, UK, 1993.

[Horton 90] W.K. Horton, *Designing and Writing Online Documentation - Help Files to Hypertext*, John Wiley & Sons, New York, NY, 1990.

[Huhns 87] N.M. Huhns (editor), *Distributed Artificial Intelligence*, Pitman, London, UK, 1987.

[Hull and Kay 91] L.G. Hull and P. Kay, Expert system development methodology and management, *Proceedings IEEE/ACM International Conference on Developing and Managing Expert System Programs*, Washington, DC, 1991, 38-44.

[Humble 73] J.W. Humble, *Management by Objectives*, British Institute of Management, London, UK, 1973.

[Humphrey 87] W.S. Humphrey, *Managing for Innovation: Leading Technical People*, Prentice-Hall, Englewood Cliffs, NJ, 1987.

[Humphrey 90] W.S. Humphrey, *Managing the Software Process*, Addison-Wesley, Reading, MA, 1990.

[IBM 75] *HIPO - A design aid and documentation technique*, GC20-1851-1, IBM Corporation, White Plains, NY, 1975.

[IEEE 91] IEEE, Institute of Electrical and Electronic Engineers, *IEEE Software Engineering Standards Collection*, The Institute of Electrical and Electronic Engineers, New York, NY, 1991.

[IEEE 610.12 90] IEEE, Institute of Electrical and Electronic Engineers, *Glossary of Software Engineering Terminology*, IEEE Std 610.12 1990 (ANSI), The Institute of Electrical and Electronic Engineers, New York, NY, 1989.

[IEEE 730 89] IEEE, Institute of Electrical and Electronic Engineers, *Software Quality Assurance Plans*, IEEE Std 730-1989 (ANSI), The Institute of Electrical and Electronic Engineers, New York, NY, 1989.

[IEEE 828 90] IEEE, Institute of Electrical and Electronic Engineers, *Standard for Software Configuration Management Plans*, IEEE Std 828-1990, The Institute of Electrical and Electronic Engineers, New York, NY, 1990.

[IEEE 829 83] IEEE, Institute of Electrical and Electronic Engineers, *Standard for Software Test Documentation*, IEEE Std 829-1983 (ANSI), The Institute of Electrical and Electronic Engineers, New York, NY, 1983.

[IEEE 830 84] IEEE, Institute of Electrical and Electronic Engineers, *Guide for Software Requirements Specifications*, IEEE Std 830-1984, The Institute of Electrical and Electronic Engineers, New York, NY, 1984.

[IEEE 982.1 88] IEEE, Institute of Electrical and Electronic Engineers, *Standard Dictionary of Measures to Produce Reliable Software*, IEEE Std 982.1-1988 (ANSI), The Institute of Electrical and Electronic Engineers, New York, NY, 1988.

[IEEE 982.2 88] IEEE, Institute of Electrical and Electronic Engineers, *Guide for Software Quality Assurance Planning*, IEEE Std 982.2-1988 (ANSI), The Institute of Electrical and Electronic Engineers, New York, NY, 1988.

[IEEE 983 86] IEEE, Institute of Electrical and Electronic Engineers, *Standard Dictionary of Measures to Produce Reliable Software*, IEEE Std 983-1986 (ANSI), The Institute of Electrical and Electronic Engineers, New York, NY, 1986.

[IEEE 1008 87] IEEE, Institute of Electrical and Electronic Engineers, *Standard Software Unit Testing*, IEEE Std 1008-1987 (ANSI), The Institute of Electrical and Electronic Engineers, New York, NY, 1987.

[IEEE 1012 86] IEEE, Institute of Electrical and Electronic Engineers, *Standard Software Verification and Validation Plans*, IEEE Std 1012-1986 (ANSI), The Institute of Electrical and Electronic Engineers, New York, NY, 1986.

[IEEE 1016 87] IEEE, Institute of Electrical and Electronic Engineers, *Recommended Practice for Software Design Descriptions*, IEEE Std 1016-1987, The Institute of Electrical and Electronic Engineers, New York, NY, 1987.

[IEEE 1028 88] IEEE, Institute of Electrical and Electronic Engineers, *Standard for Software Reviews and Audit*, IEEE Std 1028-1988 (ANSI), The Institute of Electrical and Electronic Engineers, New York, NY, 1988.

[IEEE 1042 87] IEEE, Institute of Electrical and Electronic Engineers, *Guide to Software Configuration Management*, IEEE Std 1042-1987, The Institute of Electrical and Electronic Engineers, New York, NY, 1987.

[IEEE 1058.1 87] IEEE, Institute of Electrical and Electronic Engineers, *Standard for Software Project Management Plans*, IEEE Std 1058.1-1987 (ANSI), The Institute of Electrical and Electronic Engineers, New York, NY, 1987.

[IEEE 1063 87] IEEE, Institute of Electrical and Electronic Engineers, *Standard for Software User Documentation*, IEEE Std 1063-1987 (ANSI), The Institute of Electrical and Electronic Engineers, New York, NY, 1987.

[Ingrand et al. 92] F.F. Ingrand, M.P. Georgeff, and A.S. Rao, An architecture for real-time reasoning and system control, *IEEE Expert* 7(6), 1992, 34-44.

[Ingwersen 92] P. Ingwersen, *Intelligent Interaction for Information Retrieval*, Taylor Graham, Los Angeles, CA, 1992.

[Irgon et al. 90] A. Irgon, J. Zolnowski, K.J. Murray, and M. Gersho, Expert system development: A retrospective view of five systems, *IEEE Expert* 5(3), 1990, 25-40.

[Ishida 91] T. Ishida, Parallel rule firing in production systems, *IEEE Transactions on Knowledge and Data Engineering* KDE-3(1), 1991, 11-17.

[ISO 8402 86] ISO, International Organization for Standardization, *Quality - Vocabulary*, ISO 8402, Geneva, Switzerland, 1993.

[ISO 9000 87] ISO, International Organization for Standardization, *Quality Management and Quality Assurance Standards - Guidelines for Selection and Use*, ISO 9000, Geneva, Switzerland, 1987.

[ISO 9000-2 93] ISO, International Organization for Standardization, *Quality Management and Quality Assurance Standards - Part 2: Generic Guidelines for the Application of ISO 9001, ISO 9002 and ISO 9003*, ISO 9000-2, Geneva, Switzerland, 1993.

[ISO 9000-3 91] ISO, International Organization for Standardization, *Quality Management and Quality Assurance Standards - Part 3: Guidelines for the Application of ISO 9001 to the Development, Supply and Maintenance of Software*, ISO 9000-3, Geneva, Switzerland, 1991.

[ISO 9000-4 93] ISO, International Organization for Standardization, *Quality Management and Quality Assurance Standards - Part 3: Guide to Dependability Programme Management*, ISO 9000-4, Geneva, Switzerland, 1993.

[ISO 9001 87] ISO, International Organization for Standardization, *Quality Systems - Model for Quality Assurance in Design/Development, Production, Installation and Servicing*, ISO 9001, Geneva, Switzerland, 1987.

[ISO 9002 87] ISO, International Organization for Standardization, *Quality Systems - Model for Quality Assurance in Production and Installation*, ISO 9002, Geneva, Switzerland, 1987.

[ISO 9003 87] ISO, International Organization for Standardization, *Quality Systems - Model for Quality Assurance in Final Inspection and Test*, ISO 9003, Geneva, Switzerland, 1987.

[ISO 9004 87] ISO, International Organization for Standardization, *Quality Management and Quality System Elements - Guidelines*, ISO 9004, Geneva, Switzerland, 1987.

[ISO 9004-2 87] ISO, International Organization for Standardization, *Quality Management and Quality System Elements - Part 2: Guidelines for Services*, ISO 9004-2, Geneva, Switzerland, 1987.

[ISO 9004-3 93] ISO, International Organization for Standardization, *Quality Management and Quality System Elements - Part 2: Guidelines for Processed Materials*, ISO 9004-3, Geneva, Switzerland, 1993.

[ISO 9004-4 93] ISO, International Organization for Standardization, *Quality Management and Quality System Elements - Part 2: Guidelines for Quality Improvement*, ISO 9004-2, Geneva, Switzerland, 1993.

[ISO 10011-1 90] ISO, International Organization for Standardization, *Guidelines for Auditing Quality Systems - Part 1: Auditing*, ISO 10011-1, Geneva, Switzerland, 1990.

[ISO 10011-2 91] ISO, International Organization for Standardization, *Guidelines for Auditing Quality Systems - Part 2: Qualification Criteria for Quality Systems Auditors*, ISO 10011-2, Geneva, Switzerland, 1991.

[ISO 10011-3 91] ISO, International Organization for Standardization, *Guidelines for Auditing Quality Systems - Part 3: Management of Audit Programmes*, ISO 10011-3, Geneva, Switzerland, 1991.

[ISO/IEC 9126 91] ISO, International Organization for Standardization, International Electrotechnical Commission, *Information Technology - Software Product Evaluation - Quality Characteristics and Guideline for their Use*, ISO/IEC 9126, Geneva, Switzerland, 1991.

[ISO/IEC CD 9126-1 93] ISO, International Organization for Standardization, International Electrotechnical Commission, *Software Product Evaluation - General Guide*, ISO/IEC JTC1 - SC7 - WG6 CD 9126-1, Geneva, Switzerland, 1993.

[ISO/IEC CD 9126-6 93] ISO, International Organization for Standardization, International Electrotechnical Commission, *Guide to Software Product Evaluation - The Evaluator's Guide*, ISO/IEC JTC1 - SC7 - WG6 CD 9126-6, Geneva, Switzerland, 1993.

[ISO/IEC CD 12207.2 93] ISO/IEC, International Organization for Standardization, International Electrotechnical Commission, *Software Life Cycle Process*, ISO/IEC JTC1 - SC7 - WG7 CD 12207.2, Geneva, Switzerland, 1993.

[Jackson 90] P. Jackson, *Introduction to Expert Systems* (2nd edition), Addison-Wesley, Reading, MA, 1990.

[Jacob and Froscher 85] R.J.K. Jacob and J.N. Froscher, Designing expert systems for ease of change, *Proceedings IEEE Symposium on Expert Systems in Government*, IEEE Computer Society Press, Los Alamitos, CA, 1985, 246-251.

[Jacob and Froscher 90] R.J.K. Jacob and J.N. Froscher, A software engineering methodology for rule-based systems, *IEEE Transactions of Knowledge and Data Engineering* KDE-2(2), 1990, 173-189.

[Jafar and Bahill 93] M. Jafar and A.T. Bahill, Interactive verification of knowledge-based systems, *IEEE Expert* 8(1), 1993, 25-32.

[Jagannathan et al. 89] V. Jagannathan, R. Dodhiawala, and L.S. Baum (editors), *Blackboard Architectures and Applications*, Academic Press, Boston, MA, 1989.

[Jagodzinski and Holmes 89] A.P. Jagodzinsky and S.E. Holmes, Expert systems acceptability: Human and organizational contexts for expert systems, in C. Ellis (editor), *Expert Knowledge and Explanation - The Knowledge-Language Interface*, Ellis-Horwood, Chichester, UK, 1989.

[Johnson 89] N. Johnson, Mediating representations in knowledge elicitation, in D. Diaper (editor), *Knowledge Elicitation: Principles, Techniques and Applications*, Ellis Horwood, Chichester, UK, 1989, 179-194.

[Johnson and Johnson 87] L. Johnson and N.E. Johnson, Knowledge elicitation involving teachback interviewing, in A.L. Kidd (editor), *Knowledge Acquisition for Expert Systems. A Practical Handbook*, Plenum Press, New York, NY, 1987, 91-108.

[Johnson et al. 87] P.E. Johnson, I. Zualkernan, and S. Garber, Specification of expertise: Knowledge acquisition for expert systems, *International Journal of Man-Machine Studies* 26, 1987, 161-182.

[Kahn 89] G.S. Kahn, Prototyping: Tools and motivations, in G. Guida and C. Tasso (editors), *Topics in Expert System Design - Methodologies and Tools*, North-Holland, Amsterdam, The Netherlands, 1989, 47-68.

[Kahn and Cannell 82] R. Kahn and C. Cannell, *The Dynamics of Interviewing*, John Wiley & Sons, New York, NY, 1982.

[Kahn and Gorry 77] K. Kahn and G.A. Gorry, Mechanizing temporal knowledge, *Artificial Intelligence* 9, 1977, 87-108.

[Kahn et al. 85] G. Kahn, S. Nowlan, and J. McDermott, Strategies for knowledge acquisition, *IEEE Transactions on Pattern Analysis and Machine Intelligence* PAMI-7(5), 1985, 511-522.

[Kahn et al. 87] G.S. Kahn, E.H. Breaux, P. De Klerk, and R.L. Joseph, A mixed-initiative workbench for knowledge acquisition, *International Journal of Man-Machine Studies* 27, 1987, 167-179.

[Kanal and Lemmer 86] L. Kanal and J.F. Lemmer (editors), *Uncertainty in Artificial Intelligence*, Elsevier, Amsterdam, The Netherlands, 1986.

[Kanal et al. 89] L. Kanal, T.S. Levitt, and J.F. Lemmer (editors), *Uncertainty in Artificial Intelligence 3*, Elsevier, Amsterdam, The Netherlands, 1989.

[Kaplan 82] S.J. Kaplan, Cooperative responses from a portable natural language query system, *Artificial Intelligence* 19, 1982, 165-187.

[Karp and Wilkins 89] P.D. Karp and D.W. Wilkins, An analysis of the distinction between deep and shallow expert systems, *International Journal of Expert Systems* 2(1), 1989, 1-32.

[Kass and Finnin 89] R. Kass and T. Finnin, The role of user models in cooperative interactive systems, *International Journal of Intelligent Systems* 4, 1989, 81-112.

[Kay and Quilici 91] J. Kay and A. Quilici (editors), *Proceedings 12th International Joint Conference on Artificial Intelligence, Workshop on Agent Modelling for Intelligent Interaction,* Sydney, Australia, 1991.

[Keene 89] S. Keene, *Object-Oriented Programming in Common Lisp,* Addison-Wesley, Reading, MA, 1989.

[Kelly 88] B. Kelly, Knowledge management: The organizational perspective, *Proceedings 2nd International Expert Systems Conference,* London, UK, 1988, 77-84.

[Kempen 87] G. Kempen (editor), *Natural Language Generation,* Nijhoff, Dordrecht, The Netherlands, 1987.

[Kerzner and Thamhain 84] H. Kerzner and Thamhain, *Project Management for Small and Medium Size Business,* Van Nostrand Reinhold, New York, NY, 1984.

[Ketonen 89] J.A. Ketonen, Toward reasoning about data, *AI Expert* 4(2), 1989, 44-49.

[Keyes 89] J. Keyes, Why expert systems fail, *AI Expert* 4(11), 1989, 50-53.

[Kidd 87] A.L. Kidd, *Knowledge Acquisition for Expert Systems. A Practical Handbook,* Plenum, New York, NY, 1987.

[Kidd and Cooper 85] A.L. Kidd and M.B. Cooper, Man-machine interface issues in the construction and use of an expert system, *International Journal of Man-Machine Studies* 22, 1985, 91-102.

[Kingston 92] J. Kingston, Pragmatic KADS: A methodological approach to a small knowledge-based system project, *Expert Systems* 9(4), 1992, 171-180.

[Kitto and Boose 87] C.M. Kitto and J. Boose, Heuristics for expertise transfer: An implementation of a dialog manager for knowledge acquisition, *International Journal of Man-Machine Studies* 26, 1987, 183-202.

[Klein and Beck 87] G. Klein and P.O. Beck, A decision aid for selecting among information systems alternatives, *MIS Quarterly* 11(2), 1987, 177-185.

[Kline and Dolins 89] P.J. Kline and S.B. Dolins, *Designing Expert Systems,* John Wiley & Sons, Chichester, UK, 1989.

[Klinker et al. 87] G. Klinker, J. Bentolila, S. Genetet, M. Grimes, and J. McDermott, KNACK - Report-driven knowledge acquisition, *International Journal of Man-Machine Studies* 26, 1987, 65-79.

[Knight 89] K. Knight, Unification: A multidisciplinary survey, *ACM Computing Surveys* 21(1), 1989, 93-128.

[Kobsa 90] A. Kobsa, Modeling the user's conceptual knowledge in BGP-MS, a user modeling shell system, *Computational Intelligence* 6(4), 1990, 193-208.

[Kobsa and Wahlster 88] A. Kobsa and W. Wahlster (editors), Special Issue on User Modeling, *Computational Linguistics* 14, 1988.

[Kobsa and Wahlster 89] A. Kobsa and W. Wahlster (editors), *User Modeling in Dialog Systems,* Springer-Verlag, Berlin, Germany, 1989.

[Kodratoff and Michalski 90] Y. Kodratoff and R.S. Michalski (editors), *Machine Learning: An Artificial Intelligence Approach*, Vol. III, Morgan Kaufmann, Los Altos, CA, 1990.

[Kolodner 84] J.L. Kolodner, *Retrieval and Organization Strategies in a Conceptual Memory: A Computer Model*, Lawrence Erlbaum, Hillsdale, NJ, 1984.

[Kolodner and Riesbeck 86] J.L. Kolodner and C.K. Riesbeck, *Experience, Memory, and Reasoning*, Lawrence Erlbaum, Hillsdale, NJ, 1986.

[Korf 90] R.E. Korf, Real-time heuristic search, *Artificial Intelligence* 42, 1990, 189-211.

[Kornfeld and Hewitt 81] W.A. Kornfeld and C.E. Hewitt, The scientific community metaphor, *IEEE Transactions on Systems, Man, and Cybernetics* SMC-11(1), 1981, 24-33.

[Kowalsky and Sergot 86] R. Kowalsky and M.J. Sergot, A logic-based calculus of events, *New Generation Computing* 4, 1986, 67-95.

[Kruskal and Wish 78] J.B. Kruskal and M. Wish, *Multidimensional Scaling*, Sage, Beverly Hills, CA, 1978.

[Kuipers 86] B. Kuipers, Qualitative simulation, *Artificial Intelligence* 29, 1986, 289-338.

[Kuipers 93] B. Kuipers, Reasoning with qualitative models, *Artificial Intelligence* 59, 1993, 125-132.

[Kuipers et al. 91] B. Kuipers, C. Chiu, D. Dalle Molle, and D. Throop, Higher-order derivative constraints in qualitative simulation, *Artificial Intelligence* 51, 1991, 343-379.

[Laffey et al. 88] T.J. Laffey, P.A. Cox, J.L. Schmidt, S.M. Kao, and J.Y. Read, Real-time knowledge-based systems, *AI Magazine* 9(1), 1988, 27-45.

[LaFrance 86] M. LaFrance, *Guide to Knowledge Acquisition for Expert Systems*, Artificial Intelligence Guide Series, Intelligent Systems Technologies Group, Digital Equipment Corporation, Merrimack, NH, 1986.

[LaFrance 87] M. LaFrance, The knowledge acquisition grid: A method for training knowledge engineers, *International Journal of Man-Machine Studies* 26, 1987, 245-256.

[Laubsch 84] J. Laubsch, Advanced LISP programming, in T. O'Shea and M. Eisenstadt (editors), *Artificial Intelligence - Tools, Techniques, and Applications*, Harper & Row, New York, NY, 1984, 63-109.

[Laufmann et al. 90] S.C. Laufmann, D.M. DeVaney, and M.A. Whiting, A methodology for evaluating potential KBS applications, *IEEE Expert* 5(6), 1990, 43-62.

[Laurel 90] B. Laurel, *The Art of Human Computer Interface Design*, Addison-Wesley, Reading, MA, 1990.

[Law et al. 89] P.-L. Law, M.T. Tseng, and P. Ow, Managing AI technology transfer for manufacturing applications, *Proceedings 2nd International Workshop on Artificial Intelligence in Economics and Management*, Singapore, 1989, Elsevier, Amsterdam, The Netherlands, 1989.

[Lawler and Yazdani 87] R.W. Lawler and M. Yazdani (editors), *Artificial Intelligence and Education, Volume 1 - Learning Environments and Tutoring Systems*, Ablex, Norwood, NJ, 1987.

[Lawless and Miller 91] J.A. Lawless and M.M. Miller, *Understanding CLOS*, Digital Press, Digital Press, Burlington, MA, 1991.

[Le Blanc and Tawfik Jelassi 91] L.A. Le Blanc and M. Tawfik Jelassi, An evaluation and selection methodology for expert system shells, *Expert Systems with Applications* 2, 1991, 201-209.

[Lehnert 78] W.G. Lehnert, *The Process of Question Answering*, Lawrence Erlbaum, Hillsdale, NJ, 1978.

[Lehnert and Ringle 82] W.G. Lehnert and M.H. Ringle (editors), *Strategies for Natural Language Processing*, Lawrence Erlbaum, Hillsdale, NJ, 1982.

[Lemmer and Kanal 88] J.F. Lemmer and L. Kanal (editors), *Uncertainty in Artificial Intelligence 2*, Elsevier, Amsterdam, The Netherlands, 1988.

[Lenat et al. 86] D. Lenat, M. Prakish, and M. Shepard, CYC: Using common sense knowledge to overcome brittleness and knowledge acquisition bottlenecks, *AI Magazine* 6(4), 1986, 65-85.

[Lesser and Corkill 81] V.R. Lesser and D.D. Corkill, Functionally accurate, cooperative distributed systems, *IEEE Transactions on Systems, Man, and Cybernetics* SMC-11(1), 1981, 81-96.

[Lesser and Corkill 83] V.R. Lesser and D.D. Corkill, The distributed vehicle motoring testbed: A tool for investigating distributed problem-solving networks, *AI Magazine* 4(3), 1983, 15-33.

[Lesser and Erman 80] V.R. Lesser and L.D. Erman, Distributed interpretation: A model and experiment, *IEEE Transactions on Computers* C-29(12), 1980, 1144-1163.

[Lesser at al. 88] V.R. Lesser, J. Pavlin, and E. Durfee, Approximate processing in real-time problem solving, *AI Magazine* 9(1), 1988, 49-61.

[Levi 89] K. Levi, Expert systems should be more accurate than human experts: Evaluation procedures for human judgment and decision making, *IEEE Transactions on Systems, Man, and Cybernetics* SMC-19(3), 1989, 647-657.

[Levin and Moore 77] J.A. Levin and J.A. Moore, Dialogue games: Metacommunication structures for natural language interaction, *Cognitive Science* 1, 1977, 395-420.

[Liebowitz 86] J. Liebowitz, Useful approach for evaluating expert systems, *Expert Systems* 3(2), 1986, 86–96.

[Liebowitz 91] J. Liebowitz, *Institutionalizing Expert Systems - A Handbook for Managers*, Prentice-Hall, Englewood Cliff, NJ, 1991.

[Liebowitz and De Salvo 89] J. Liebowitz and D.A. De Salvo (editors), *Structuring Expert Systems: Domain, Design, and Development*, Prentice-Hall, Englewood Cliffs, NJ, 1989.

[Ling and Rudd 89] X. Ling and W.G. Rudd, Combining opinions from several experts, *Applied Artificial Intelligence* 3, 1989, 439-459.

[Linster 93] M. Linster, Explicit and operational models as a basis for second generation knowledge acquisition tools, in J-M. David, J-P. Krivine, and R. Simmons (editors), *Second Generation Expert Systems*, Springer-Verlag, Berlin, Germany, 1993, 456-494.

[Linstone and Turoff 75] H. Linstone and M. Turoff, *The Delphi Method: Techniques and Applications*, Addison-Wesley, Reading, MA, 1975.

[Littman 87] D.C. Littman, Modeling human expertise in knowledge engineering: Some preliminary observations, *International Journal of Man-Machine Studies* 26, 1987, 81-92.

[Litman and Allen 87] D.J. Litman and J.F. Allen, A plan recognition model for subdialogues in conversations *Cognitive Science* 11, 1987, 163-200.

[Loveland and Valtorta 83] D.W. Loveland and M. Valtorta, Detecting ambiguity: An example in knowledge evaluation, *Proceedings 8th International Joint Conference on Artificial Intelligence*, Karlsruhe, Germany, 1983, 182–184.

[Lowry 92] M.R. Lowry, Software engineering in the twenty-first century, *AI Magazine* 14(3), 1992, 71-87.

[Mackie and Wylie 88] R.R. Mackie and C.D. Wylie, Factors influencing acceptance of computer based innovations, in M. Helander (editor), *Handbook of Human-Computer Interaction*, North-Holland, Amsterdam, The Netherlands, 1988, 1081-1106.

[Madeo and Levary 90] L.A. Madeo and R.R. Levary, On maintaining and updating expert systems, *Expert Systems* 7(2), 1990, 121-123.

[Maguire 88] B. Maguire, An incremental approach to expert systems development, *Proceedings 8th International Workshop on Expert Systems and their Applications*, Avignon, France, 1988, Vol. 1, 249-259.

[Maiocchi and Pernici 91] R. Maiocchi and B. Pernici, Temporal data management systems: A comparative view, *IEEE Transactions on Knowledge and Data Engineering* KDE-3(4), 1991, 504-524.

[Marcot 87] B. Marcot, Testing your knowledge base, *AI Expert* 2(8), 1987, 42–47.

[Marcus 88] S. Marcus (editor), *Automating Knowledge Acquisition for Expert Systems*, Kluwer, Boston, MA, 1988.

[Marek 87] W. Marek, Completeness and consistency in knowledge base systems, in L. Kerschberg (editor), *Expert Database Systems*, Benjamin/Cummings, Menlo Park, CA, 1987, 119–126.

[Marsh and Greenwood 86] J. Marsh and J. Greenwood, Real-time AI: Software architecture issues, *Proceedings IEEE 1986 National Aerospace and Electronics Conference*, Washington, DC, 1986, 67-77.

[Maude and Willis 91] T. Maude and G. Willis. *Rapid Prototyping - The Management of Software Risk*, Pitman, London, UK, 1991.

[McBurney 83] D.H. McBurney, *Experimental Psychology*, Wadsworth, Belmont, CA, 1983.

[McCall et al. 77] J.A. McCall, P.K. Richards, and G.F. Walters, *Factors in Software Quality*, RADC-TR-77-369, US Department of Commerce, Washington, DC, 1977.

[McCarthy 60] J. McCarthy, Recursive functions of symbolic expressions and their computation by machine - Part 1, *Communications of ACM* 3(4), 1960, 184-195.

[McCullough 87] T. McCullough, Six steps to selling AI, *AI Expert* 2(12), 1987, 55-60.

[McDermott 81] J. McDermott, R1 - The formative years, *AI Magazine* 2(2), 1981, 21-29.

[McDermott 82-a] D. McDermott, Non monotonic logic II, *Journal of the ACM* 29, 1982, 33-57.

[McDermott 82-b] D.A. McDermott, A temporal logic for reasoning about processes and plans, *Cognitive Science* 6, 1982, 101-155.

[McDermott 88] J. McDermott, A taxonomy of problem-solving methods, in S. Marcus (editor), *Automating Knowledge Acquisition for Expert Systems*, Kluwer, Boston, MA, 1988, 225-256.

[McDermott 91] D. McDermott, A general framework for reason maintenance, *Artificial Intelligence* 50, 1991, 289-329.

[McDermott and Doyle 80] D. McDermott and J. Doyle, Non monotonic logic I, *Artificial Intelligence* 13, 1980, 41-72.

[McGraw 86] K.L. McGraw, Guidelines for producing documentation for expert systems, *IEEE Transactions on Professional Communications* PC-29(4), 1986, 42- 47.

[McGraw 89] K.L. McGraw, Guidelines for developing expert systems documentation, in J. Liebowitz and D.A. De Salvo (editors), *Structuring Expert Systems: Domain, Design, and Development*, Prentice Hall, Englewood Cliffs, NJ, 1989.

[McGraw 93] K.L. McGraw, *User Interfaces for Knowledge-Based Systems - Design and Evaluation*, Ellis Horwood, Chichester, UK, 1993.

[McGraw and Harbison-Briggs 89] K.L. McGraw and K. Harbison-Briggs, *Knowledge Acquisition - Principles and Guidelines*, Prentice-Hall, Englewood Cliffs, NJ, 1989.

[McKeown 85] K.R. McKeown, *Text Generation*, Cambridge University Press, Cambridge, MA, 1985.

[McKeown et al. 85] K.R. McKeown, M. Wish, and K. Matthews, Tailoring explanations for the user, *Proceedings 9th International Joint Conference on Artificial Intelligence*, Los Angeles, CA, 1985, 794-798.

[Merlevede and Vanthienen 91] P. Merlevede and J. Vanthienen, A structured approach to formalization and validation of knowledge, *Proceedings IEEE/ACM International Conference on Developing and Managing Expert System Programs*, Washington, DC, 1991, 149-158.

[Meseguer and Plaza 92] P. Meseguer and E. Plaza, Validation of KBS: The VALID project, in L. Steels and B. Lepape (editors), *Enhancing the Knowledge Engineering Process*, Elsevier Science, Amsterdam, The Netherlands, 1992.

[Mettrey 87] W. Mettrey, An assessment of tools for building large knowledge-based systems, *AI Magazine* 4(4), 1987, 81-89.

[Metzger 73] P.W. Metzger, *Managing a Programming Project*, Prentice-Hall, Englewood Cliffs, NJ, 1973.

[Meyer 88] B. Meyer, *Object-Oriented Software Construction*, Prentice-Hall, Englewood Cliffs, NJ, 1988.

[Meyer and Booker 91] M.A. Meyer and J.M. Booker, *Eliciting and Analyzing Expert Judgment - A Practical Guide - Knowledge-Based Systems, Vol. 5*, Academic Press, London, UK, 1988.

[Meyer and Curley 89] M.H. Meyer and K.F. Curley, Expert system success models, *Datamation* 35(17), 1989, 35-38.

[Meyer et al. 89] M.A. Meyer, S.M. Mniszewski, and A.T. Peaslee Jr., Using three minimally biasing elicitation techniques for knowledge acquisition, *Knowledge Acquisition* 1, 1989, 59-71.

[Michalski 83] R.S. Michalski, Theory and methodology of inductive learning, in R.S. Michalski, J.G. Carbonell, and T.M. Mitchell (editors), *Machine Learning: An Artificial Intelligence Approach*, Morgan Kaufmann, Los Altos, CA, 1983.

[Michalski et al. 83] R.S. Michalski, J.G. Carbonell, and T.M. Mitchell (editors), *Machine Learning: An Artificial Intelligence Approach*, Morgan Kaufmann, Los Altos, CA, 1983.

[Michalski et al. 86] R.S. Michalski, J.G. Carbonell, and T.M. Mitchell (editors), *Machine Learning: An Artificial Intelligence Approach, Vol. II*, Morgan Kaufmann, Los Altos, CA, 1986.

[Michie 82] D. Michie, High-road and low-road programs, *AI Magazine* 3(1), 1982, 21-22.

[Milne 87] R. Milne, Strategies for diagnosis, *IEEE Transactions on Systems, Man, and Cybernetics* SMC-17(3), 1987, 333-339.

[Minsky 85] M. Minsky, *The Society of Mind*, Simon & Schuster, New York, NY, 1985.

[Minton 88] S. Minton, *Learning Search Control Knowledge: An Explanation-based Approach*, Kluwer, Boston, MA, 1988.

[Miyata and Norman 86] Y. Miyata and D.A. Norman, Psychological issues in support of multiple activities, in D.A. Norman and S.W. Draper (editors), *User Centered System Design*, Erlbaum, Hillsdale, NJ, 1986, 265-284.

[Moll 86] R.G. Moll, A method for analysing requirements for possible expert system implementations, *Proceedings 2nd International Expert Systems Conference*, London, UK, 1986, 339-349.

[Montgomery 89] A. Montgomery, GEMINI: Government expert systems methodology initiative, *Proceedings 5th International Expert Systems Conference*, London, UK, 1989, 45-54.

[Moore 87] C.M. Moore, *Group Techniques for Idea Building*, Sage Publications, Newburt Park, CA, 1987.

[Moore 91] R.L. Moore, Expert systems in real-time applications experience and opportunities, in E.J. Kompass, S.K. Whitlock, and T.J. Williams (editors), *Expert Systems Applications in Advanced Control, Proceedings 17th Annual Advanced Control Conference*, West Lafayette, IN, 1991, 15-33.

[Moore and Swartout 90] J.D. Moore and W.R. Swartout, Pointing: A way toward explanation dialogue, *Proceedings 8th National Conference on Artificial Intelligence*, Boston, MA, 1990, 457-464.

[Morik and Rollinger 85] C. Morik and C. Rollinger, The real estate agent - Modeling users by uncertain reasoning, *AI Magazine* 6(2), 1985, 44-52.

[Morik et al. 93] K. Morik, W. Emde, J.-E. Kietz, and S. Wrobel, *Knowledge Acquisition and Machine Learning - Theory, Methods and Applications*, Academic Press, London, UK, 1993.

[Morris 90] A. Morris, The expert system life cycle, *Expert Systems* 7(2) 1990, 115-116.

[Motta et al. 89] E. Motta, T. Rajan, and M. Eisenstadt, A methodology and tool for knowledge acquisition in KEATS-2, in G. Guida and C. Tasso (editors), *Topics in Expert System Design - Methodologies and Tools*, North-Holland, Amsterdam, The Netherlands, 1989, 297-322.

[Muir 87] B.M. Muir, Trust between humans and machines, and the design of decision aids, *International Journal of Man-Machine Studies* 27, 1987, 527-539.

[Musa et al. 87] J.D. Musa, A. Iannino, and K. Okumoto, *Software Reliability - Measurement, Prediction, Application*, McGraw-Hill, New York, NY, 1987.

[Musen 93] M. Musen, An overview of knowledge acquisition, in J-M. David, J-P. Krivine, and R. Simmons (editors), *Second Generation Expert Systems*, Springer-Verlag, Berlin, Germany, 1993, 405-427.

[Musen et al. 87] M.A. Musen, L.A. Fagan, D.M. Combs, and E.H. Shortliffe, Use of a domain model to drive an interactive knowledge-editing tool, *International Journal of Man-Machine Studies* 26, 1987, 105-121.

[Myers 89] B. Myers, User-interface tools: Introduction and survey, *IEEE Software* 6(1), 1989, 15-23.

[Mykytyn and Mykytyn 91] P.P. Mykytyn Jr. and K. Mykytyn, Legal perspectives on expert systems, *AI Expert* 6(12), 1991, 40-45.

[Mykytyn et al. 90] P.P. Mykytyn Jr., K. Mykytyn, and C. Slinkman, Expert systems: A question of liability, *MIS Quarterly* 14(1), 1990, 27-42.

[Narayannan and Bennun 91] A. Narayanan and M. Bennun (editors), *Law, Computer Science and Artificial Intelligence*, Ablex, Norwood, NJ, 1991.

[Natarajan 91] B.K. Natarajan, *Machine Learning, A Theoretical Approach*, Morgan Kaufmann, Los Altos, CA, 1991.

[Nauman and Palvia 82] J.D. Nauman and S. Palvia, A selection model for systems development tools, *MIS Quarterly* 6(1), 1982, 39-48.

[Neches et al. 85] R. Neches, W.R. Swartout, and J.D. Moore, Enhanced maintenance and explanation of expert systems through explicit models of their development, *IEEE Transactions on Software Engineering* SE-11(11), 1985, 1337-1351.

[Newell 81] A. Newell, The knowledge level, *Artificial Intelligence* 19, 1982, 89-127.

[Newquist 88] H.P. Newquist III, Struggling to maintain, *AI Expert* 3(8), 1988, 69-71.

[Ng and Abramson 90] K.-C. Ng and B. Abramson, Uncertainty management in expert systems, *IEEE Expert* 5(2), 1990, 2948.

[Nii 86-a] H.P. Nii, Blackboard systems: The blackboard model of problem solving and the evolution of blackboard architectures, *AI Magazine* 7(2), 1986, 38-53.

[Nii 86-b] H.P. Nii, Blackboard systems: Blackboard application systems, blackboard systems from a knowledge engineering perspective, *AI Magazine* 7(3), 198, 82-106.

[Nilsson 80] N.J. Nilsson, *Principles of Artificial Intelligence*, Tioga, Palo Alto, CA, 1980.

[Nisbett and Wilson, 1977] R.E. Nisbett and T.D. Wilson, Telling more than we can know: Verbal reports on mental processes, *Psychological Review* 84, 1977, 231-259.

[Nomura and Lunn 87] T. Nomura and S. Lunn, Integration of knowledge-based systems with data processing, *Knowledge-Based Systems* 1(1), 1987, 24-31.

[Norman 86] D.A. Norman, Cognitive engineering, in D.A. Norman and S.W. Draper (editors), *User Centered System Design*, Erlbaum, Hillsdale, NJ, 1986, 31-61.

[Norman and Draper 86] D.A. Norman and S.W. Draper (editors), *User Centered System Design*, Erlbaum, Hillsdale, NJ, 1986.

[O'Keefe and Lee 90] R.M. O'Keefe and S. Lee, An integrative model of expert system verification and validation, *Expert Systems with Applications* 1, 1990, 231-236.

[O'Keefe et al. 87] R.M. O'Keefe, O. Balci, and E.P. Smith, Validating expert system performance, *IEEE Expert* 2(4), 1987, 81–89.

[O'Leary and Turban 87] D.E. O'Leary and E. Turban, The organizational impact of expert systems, *Human Sciences Management* 7(1), 1987, 11-19.

[O'Leary et al. 90] T. O'Leary, M. Goul, K.E. Moffitt, and A.E. Radwan, Validating expert systems, *IEEE Expert* 5(3), 1990, 51-58.

[Olsen 91] D. Olsen, *User Interface Management Systems: Models and Algorithms*, Morgan Kaufmann, San Mateo, CA, 1991.

[O'Malley 86] C.E. O'Malley, Helping users help themselves, in D.A. Norman and S.W. Draper (editors), *User Centered System Design*, Erlbaum, Hillsdale, NJ, 1986, 377-398.

[O'Neill and Morris 89] M. O'Neill and A. Morris, Expert systems in the United Kingdom: An evaluation of development methodologies, *Expert Systems* 6(2), 1989, 90-99.

[O'Reilly and Cromarty 85] C.A. O'Reilly and A.S. Cromarty, "Fast" is not "Real- Time" in designing effective real-time AI systems, *Proceedings Applications of Artificial Intelligence II*, Bellingham, WA, 1985, 249-257.

[Oliver 86] A.E.M. Oliver, Control of rapid prototyping in expert systems development, *Proceedings 2nd International Expert Systems Conference*, London, UK, 1986, 247-252

[Oliver 87] A.E.M. Oliver, How to make rapid prototyping effective when developing expert systems, *Proceedings 3rd International Expert Systems Conference*, London, UK, 1987, 45-48.

[Olson and Reuter 87] J.S. Olson and H.H. Reuter, Extracting expertise from experts: Methods for knowledge acquisition, *Expert Systems* 4(3), 1987, 152-168.

[Osborn 53] A. Osborn, *Applied Imagination: Principles and Procedures of Creative Thinking*, Scriber's, New York, NY, 1953.

[Ould 90] M.A. Ould, *Strategies for Software Engineering - The Management of Risk and Quality*, John Wiley & Sons, Chichester, UK, 1990.

[Owen 86] D. Owen, Answers first, then questions, in D.A. Norman and S.W. Draper (editors), *User Centered System Design*, Erlbaum, Hillsdale, NJ, 1986, 361-375.

[Owen 90] S. Owen, *Analogy for Automated Reasoning*, Academic Press, New York, NY, 1990.

[Padalkar et al. 91] S. Padalkar, G. Karsai, C. Biegl, J. Sztipanovits, K. Okuda, and N. Miyasaka, Real-time fault diagnostics, *IEEE Expert* 6(3), 1991, 75-85.

[Paepcke 93] A. Paepcke (editor), *Object-Oriented Programming - The CLOS Perspective*, MIT Press, Cambridge, MA, 1993.

[Park et al. 91] E.K. Park, K. Chae, and C.S. Kang, The structured prototyping life cycle model for systems development management, *Proceedings IEEE/ACM International Conference on Developing and Managing Expert System Programs*, Washington, DC, 1991, 267-272.

[Parnas 72] D.L. Parnas, On the criteria to be used in decomposing systems into modules, *Communications of the ACM* 15(12), 1972, 1053-1058.

[Parsaye and Chignell 88] K. Parsaye and M. Chignell, *Expert Systems for Experts*, John Wiley & Sons, New York, NY, 1988.

[Partridge 86] D. Partridge, Engineering artificial intelligence software, *Artificial Intelligence Review* 1, 1986, 27-41.

[Partridge 91] D. Partridge (editor), *Artificial Intelligence and Software Engineering*, Ablex, Norwood, NJ, 1991.

[Partridge 92-a] D. Partridge, *AI and Business Management*, Ablex, Norwood, NJ, 1992.

[Partridge 92-b] D. Partridge, *Engineering Artificial Intelligence Software*, Ablex, Norwood, NJ, 1992.

[Partridge and Wilks 87] D. Partridge and Y. Wilks, Does AI have a methodology which is different from software engineering?, *Artificial Intelligence Review* 1, 1987, 111-120.

[Patten 88] T. Patten, *Systemic Text Generation as Problem Solving*, Cambridge University Press, Cambridge, MA, 1988.

[Pazzani 87] M.J. Pazzani, Explanation-based learning for knowledge-based systems, *International Journal of Man-Machine Studies* 26, 1987, 413-434.

[Pearl 84] J. Pearl, *Heuristics*, Addison-Wesley, Reading, MA, 1984.

[Pearl 91] J. Pearl, *Probabilistic Reasoning in Intelligent Systems* (2nd edition), Morgan Kaufmann, Los Altos, CA, 1991.

[Pereira and Grosz 93] F.C.N. Pereira and B.J. Grosz (editors), Special Volume on Natural Language Processing, *Artificial Intelligence* 63, 1993, 1-532.

[Perkins et al. 89] W.A. Perkins, T.J. Laffey, D. Pecora, and T.A. Nguyen, Knowledge base verification, in G. Guida and C. Tasso (editors), *Topics in Expert System Design - Methodologies and Tools*, North–Holland, Amsterdam, The Netherlands, 1989, 353–376.

[Perot 91] F.C. Perot, A crystal model of knowledge based application design, *Proceedings IEEE/ACM International Conference on Developing and Managing Expert System Programs*, Washington, DC, 1991, 279-285.

[Perrault and Allen 80] C.R. Perrault and J.F. Allen, A plan-based analysis of indirect speech acts, *Computational Linguistics* 6, 1980, 167-182.

[Peters 87] T. Peters, *Thriving on Chaos: Handbook for Management Revolution*, Knopf, New York, NY, 1987.

[Peters and Waterman 82] T. Peters and R. Waterman, *In Search of Excellence*, Harper and Row, New York, NY, 1982.

[Peterson 81] J.L. Peterson, *Petri Net Theory and Modelling of Systems*, Prentice-Hall, Englewood Cliffs, NJ, 1981.

[Pfaff 85] G. Pfaff (editor), *User Interface Management Systems*, Springer-Verlag, Berlin, Germany, 1985.

[Philip 93] G.C. Philip, Guidelins on improving the maintainability and consultation of rule-based expert systems, *Expert Systems with Applications* 6, 1993, 169-179.

[Philip and Schultz 90] G.C. Philip and H.K. Schultz, What's happening with expert systems?, *AI Expert* 5(11), 1990, 57-59.

[Polany 88] L. Polanyi (Ed.), *The Structure of Discourse*, Ablex, Norwood, NJ, 1988.

[Polat and Guvenir 91] F. Polat and H.A. Guvenir, A unification-based approach for knowledge base verification, *Expert Systems* 8(4), 1991, 251-259.

[Polit 85] S. Polit, R1 and beyond: AI technology transfer at DEC, *AI Magazine* 5(4), 1985, 76-78.

[Poole 88] D. Poole, A logical framework for default reasoning, *Artificial Intelligence* 36, 1988, 27-47.

[Porter 85] M.E. Porter, *Competitive Advantage: Creating and Sustaining Superior Performance*, Free Press, New York, NY, 1985.

[Preece 89] D. Preece, Verification of rule-based expert systems in wide domains, in N. Shadbolt (editor), *Research and Development in Expert Systems VI: Proceedings Expert Systems 89*, Cambridge University Press, Cambridge, UK, 1989, 66-77.

[Preece 90] A.D. Preece, Towards a methodology for evaluating expert systems, *Expert Systems* 7(4), 1990, 215-223.

[Preece and Suen 93] A.D.Preece and C.Y. Suen (editors), Special Issue on Verification and Validation, *International Journal of Expert Systems - Research and Applications* 6(2) and 6(3), 1993.

[Prerau 85] D.S. Prerau, Selection of an appropriate domain for an expert system, *AI Magazine* 6(2), 1985, 26-30.

[Prerau 89] D.S. Prerau, Choosing an expert system domain, in G. Guida and C. Tasso (editors), *Topics in Expert System Design - Methodologies and Tools*, North-Holland, Amsterdam, The Netherlands, 1989, 27-43.

[Prerau 90] D.S. Prerau, *Developing and Managing Expert Systems - Proven Techniques for Business and Industry*, Addison-Wesley, Reading, MA, 1990.

[Prerau et al. 90] D.S Prerau, A.S. Gunderson, R.E. Reinke, and M.R. Adler, Maintainability techniques in developing large expert systems, *IEEE Expert* 5(3), 1990, 71-80.

[Pressman 92] R.S. Pressman, *Software Engineering: A Practitioner's Approach* (3rd edition), McGraw-Hill, New York, 1992.

[Price 91] C. Price, *Knowledge Engineering Toolkits*, Ellis Horwood, Chichester, UK, 1991.

[Quinlan 79] J.R. Quinlan. Discovering rules from large collections of examples: A case study, in D. Michie (editor), *Expert Systems in the Microelectronics Age*, Edinburgh University Press, Edinburgh, UK, 1979, 168-201.

[Quinlan 86] J.R. Quinlan. Induction in decision trees, *Machine Learning* 1(1), 1986, 81-106.

[Quinlan 88] J.R. Quinlan. Simplifying decision trees, in B.R. Gaines and J.H. Boose (editors), *Knowledge Acquisition for Knowledge-Based Systems - Knowledge-Based Systems, Vol. 1, ,* Academic Press, London, UK, 241-254.

[Ramamoorthy and Bastani 82] C.V. Ramamoorthy and F.B. Bastani, Software reliability: Status and perspectives, *IEEE Transactions on Software Engineering* SE-8(4), 1982, 354-371.

[Rasmussen 86] J. Rasmussen, *Information Processing and Human-Machine Interaction: An Approach to Cognitive Engineering*, North Holland, New York, NY, 1986.

[Reade 89] C. Reade, *Elements of Functional Programming*, Addison-Wesley, Reading, MA, 1989

[Reason 87] J. Reason, Cognitive aids in process environments: Prostheses or tools?, *International Journal of Man-Machine Studies* 27, 1987, 463-470.

[Reboh 83] R. Reboh, Extracting useful advice from conflicting expertise, *Proceedings 8th International Joint Conference on Artificial Intelligence*, Karlsruhe, Germany, 1983, 145-150.

[Reichman 85] R. Reichman, *Getting Computers to Talk like You and Me*, MIT Press, Cambridge MA, 1985.

[Reichman-Adar 84] R. Reichman-Adar, Extended person-machine interface, *Artificial Intelligence* 22, 1984, 157-218.

[Reiter 80] R. Reiter, A logic for default reasoning, *Artificial Intelligence* 13, 1980, 81-132.

[Reitman 84] W. Reitman (editor), *Artificial Intelligence Applications for Business*, Ablex, Norwood, NJ, 1984.

[Rich 79] E. Rich, User modeling via stereotypes, *Cognitive Science* 3, 1979, 329-354.

[Rich 83] E. Rich, Users are individuals: Individualizing user models, *International Journal of Man-Machine Studies* 18, 1983, 199-214.

[Rich 89] E. Rich, Stereotypes and user modeling, in A. Kobsa and W. Wahlster (editors), *User Models in Dialog Systems.* Springer-Verlag, Berlin, Germany, 1989, 35-51.

[Rich and Knight 91] E. Rich and K. Knight, *Artificial Intelligence* (2nd edition), McGraw-Hill, New York, NY, 1991.

[Richardson and DeFries 90] J.J. Richardson and M.J. DeFries (editors), *Intelligent Systems in Business - Integrating the Technology*, Ablex, Norwood, NJ, 1990.

[Richer 86] M.H. Richer, An evaluation of expert system development tools, *Expert Systems* 3(3), 1986, 166-183.

[Ricketson 84] S. Ricketson, *The Law of Intellectual Property*, Butterworths, London, UK, 1984.

[Riesbeck and Schank 89] C.K. Riesbeck and R.C. Schank, *Inside Case-Based Reasoning*, Lawrence Erlbaum, Hillsdale, NJ, 1989.

[Ringland and Duce 84] G.A. Ringland and D.A. Duce, *Approaches to Knowledge Representation: An Introduction*, John Wiley & Sons, New York, NY, 1984.

[Rit 96] J.-F. Rit, Propagating temporal constraints fro scheduling, *Proceedings 5th National Conference on Artificial Intelligence*, Philadelphia, PA, 1986, 383-388.

[Rock et al. 90] D. Rock, J. Azarewicz, R. Klobuchar, and J. Oshin, AI and the Military: Time for a standard, *AI Expert* 5(8), 1990, 56-64.

[Rolston 88] D.W. Rolston, *Principles of Artificial Intelligence and Expert Systems Development*, McGraw-Hill, New York, NY, 1988.

[Ross 77] D.T. Ross, Structured analysis (SA): A language for communicating ideas, *IEEE Transactions on Software Engineering* SE-3(1), 1977, 16-34.

[Ross and Schoman 77] D.T. Ross and K.E. Schoman Jr., Structured analysis for requirement definition, *IEEE Transactions on Software Engineering* SE-3(1), 1977, 6-15.

[Roth and Woods 89] E.M. Roth and D.D. Woods, Cognitive task analysis: An approach to knowledge acquisition for intelligent system design, in G. Guida and C. Tasso (editors.), *Topics in Expert System Design - Methodologies and Tools*, North-Holland, Amsterdam, The Netherlands, 1989, 233-264.

[Rothenberg 89] J. Rothenberg, Expert system tool evaluation, in G. Guida and C. Tasso (editors), *Topics in Expert System Design - Methodologies and Tools*, North-Holland, Amsterdam, The Netherlands, 1989, 205-229.

[Royce 70] W.W. Royce, Managing the development of large software systems: Concepts and Techniques, *Proceedings IEEE WESCON*, 1970.

[Runkel and Birmingham 93] J.T. Runkel and W.P. Birmingham, Knowledge acquisition in the small: Building knowledge-acquisition tools from pieces, *Knowledge Acquisition* 5, 1993, 117-243.

[Rusk and Krone 84] R.A. Rusk and R.M. Krone, The Crawford Slip Method (CSM) as a tool for extraction of expert knowledge, in G. Salvendy (editor), *Human-Computer Interaction*, Elsevier, New York, NY, 1984, 279-282.

[Russell and Zilberstein 91] S.J. Russell and S. Zilberstein, Composing real-time systems, *Proceedings 12th International Joint Conference on Artificial Intelligence*, Sydney, Australia, 1991, 212-217.

[Saaty 80] T.L. Saaty, *The Analytical Hierarchy Process*, McGraw-Hill, New York, NY, 1980.

[Sacerdoti 74] E.D. Sacerdoti, Planning in a hierarchy of abstraction spaces, *Artificial Intelligence* 5, 1974, 115-135.

[Sacerdoti 77] E.D. Sacerdoti, *A Structure of Plans and Behavior*, Elsevier, New York, NY, 1977.

[Sacerdoti 91] E.D. Sacerdoti, Managing expert-system development, *AI Expert* 6(5), 1991, 26-33.

[Sagalowicz 84] D. Sagalowicz, Development of an expert system, *Expert Systems* 1(2), 1984, 137-141.

[Sanderson et al. 89] P.M. Sanderson, J.M. James, and K.S. Seidler, SHAPA: An interactive software environment for protocol analysis, *Ergonomics* 32(11), 1989, 1271-1302.

[Schalkoff 90] R.J. Schalkoff, *Artificial Intelligence: An Engineering Approach*, McGraw-Hill, New York, NY.

[Scharf et al. 92] P.B. Scharf, V.S. Sanger, and R. Elio, Corporate perspectives on technology transfer: The expert-systems apprenticeship program, *IEEE Expert* 7(3), 1992, 6-14.

[Schor et al. 86] M. Schor, T. Delay, H.S. Lee, and B.R. Tibbitts, Advances in Rete pattern matching, *Proceedings 5th National Conference on Artificial Intelligence*, Philadelphia, PA, 1986, 226-232.

[Schreiber et al. 93] G. Schreiber, B. Wielinga, and J. Breuker (editors), *KADS: A Principled Approach to Knowledge-Based System Development*, Academic Press, London, UK, 1993.

[Schur 88] S. Schur, The intelligent database, *AI Expert* 3(1), 1988, 26-34.

[Scott 84] M.D. Scott, *Computer Law*, John Wiley & Sons, New York, NY, 1984.

[Scott and Clayton 91] A.C. Scott and J.E. Clayton, *A Practical Guide to Knowledge Acquisition*, Addison-Wesley, Reading, MA, 1991.

[Scott et al. 86] A.C. Scott, W.J. Clancey, R. Davis, and E.H. Shortliffe, Methods for generating explanations, in B.G. Buchanan and E.H. Shortliffe (editors), *Rule-based expert systems - The MYCIN experiments of the Stanford Heuristic Programming Project*, Addison-Wesley, Reading, MA, 1986, 338-362.

[SEAI 90] SEAI, *Expert Systems 1991*, SEAI Technical Publications, Atlanta, GA, 1990.

[Self 88] J. Self, Student models: What use are they?, in P. Ercoli and R. Lewis (editors), *Artificial Intelligence Tools in Education*, North Holland, Amsterdam, The Netherlands, 1988, 73-86.

[Shachter et al. 90] R.D. Shachter, T.S. Levitt, L. Kanal, and J.F. Lemmer (editors), *Uncertainty in Artificial Intelligence 4*, Elsevier, Amsterdam, The Netherlands, 1990.

[Shafer 76] G. Shafer, *A Mathematical Theory of Evidence*, Princeton University Press, Princeton, NJ, 1976.

[Shafer and Pearl 90] G. Shafer and J. Pearl (editors), *Readings in Uncertain Reasoning*, Morgan Kaufmann, San Mateo, CA, 1990.

[Shapiro 87] S.C. Shapiro (editor), *The Encyclopedia of Artificial Intelligence*, Johw Wiley, New York, NY, 1987.

[Sharma and Conrath 92] R.S. Sharma and D.W. Conrath, Evaluating expert systems: The socio-technical dimension of quality, *Expert systems* 9(3), 1992, 125-138.

[Sharma et al. 91] R.S. Sharma, D.W. Conrath, and D.M. Dilts, A socio-technical model for developing expert systems. Part I: The general theory, *IEEE Transactions on Engineering Management* EM-38(1), 1991, 14-23.

[Shatz et al. 87] H. Shatz, R. Strahs, and L. Campbell, Expertax: The issue of long-term maintenance, *Proceedings 3rd International Expert Systems Conference,*, London, UK, Learned Information, Oxford, UK, 1987, 291-300.

[Shavlik and Dietterich 90] J. Shavlik and T. Dietterich (editors), *Readings in Machine Learning*, Morgan Kaufmann, Los Altos, CA, 1990.

[Shaw 81] M.L.G. Shaw (editor), *Recent Advances in Personal Construct Technology*, Academic Press, New York, NY, 1981

[Shaw 93] J. Shaw, AI language resource guide, *AI Expert* 8(4), 1993, 44-51.

[Shaw and Gaines 87-a] M.L. Shaw and B.R. Gaines, KITTEN: Knowledge initiation and transfer tools for experts and novices. *International Journal of Man-Machine Studies 27*, 1987, 251-280.

[Shaw and Gaines 87-b] M.L. Shaw and B.R. Gaines, An interactive knowledge-elicitation technique using personal construct technology, in A.L. Kidd (editor), *Knowledge Acquisition for Expert Systems. A Practical Handbook*, Plenum Press, New York, NY, 1987, 109-136.

[Shaw and Zeichick 92] J. Shaw and A. Zeichick, Expert system resource guide, *AI Expert* 7(12), 1992, 42-49.

[Shepard 80] R. N. Shepard, Multidimensional scaling, tree-fitting, and clustering, *Science* 210, 1980, 390-398.

[Sheridan 91] A survey of techniques for inference under uncertainty, *Artificial Intelligence Review* 5, 1991, 89-119.

[Shiffman et al. 81] S. Shiffman, M.L. Reynolds, and F.W. Young, *Introduction to Multidimensional Scaling*, Academic Press, London, UK, 1981.

[Shneidermann 87] B. Shneidermann, *Designing the User-Interface: Strategies for Effective Human Computer Interaction*, Addison-Wesley, Reading, MA, 1987.

[Shoham 90] Y. Shoham, Nonmonotonic reasoning and causation, *Cognitive Science* 14, 1990, 213-252.

[Shooman 83] M.L. Shooman, *Software Engineering*, McGraw–Hill, New York, NY, 1983.

[Shri et al. 85] K. Shri, D.S. Prerau, A.V. Lemmon, A.S. Gunderson, and R.E. Reinke, COMPASS: An expert system for telephone switch maintenance, *Expert Systems* 2(3), 1985, 112-126.

[Simmons 84] R. Simmons, *Computation from the English*, Prentice-Hall, Englewood Cliffs, NJ, 1984.

[Simmons and Davis 93] R. Simmons and R. Davis, The role of knowledge and representation in problem solving, in J-M. David, J-P. Krivine, and R. Simmons (editors), *Second Generation Expert Systems*, Springer-Verlag, Berlin, Germany, 1993, 27-45.

[Simon 86] H.A. Simon, Whether software engineering needs to be artificially intelligent, *IEEE Transactions on Software Engineering* 12(7), 1986, 726-742.

[Slade 91] S. Slade, Case-based reasoning: A research paradigm, *AI Magazine* 12(1), 42-55.

[Slagle and Wick 88] R. Slagle and M.R. Wick, A method for evaluating candidate expert system applications, *AI Magazine* 9(4), 1988, 44-53.

[Slagle et al. 90] J.R. Slagle, D.A. Gardiner, and K. Han, Knowledge specification of an expert system, *IEEE Expert* 5(4), 1990, 29-38.

[Sloane 91] S.B. Sloane, The use of artificial intelligence by the United States Navy: Case study of a failure, *AI Magazine* 12(1), 1991, 80-92.

[Slow et al. 86] R. Slow, S. Lunn, and P. Slatter, How to identify business applications of expert systems, *Proceedings 2nd International Expert Systems Conference*, London, UK, 1986, 327-338.

[Smedinghoff 86] T.J. Smedinghoff, *The Legal Guide to Developing, Protecting and Marketing Software*, MacMillan, London, UK, 1986.

[Smets et al. 88] P. Smets, E.H. Mamdani, D. Dubois, and H. Prade (editors), *Non-Standard Logics for Automated Reasoning*, Academic Press, New York, NY, 1988.

[Smith 84] R.G. Smith, On the development of commercial expert systems, *AI Magazine* 5(3), 1984, 61-73.

[Smith 88] D.L. Smith, Implementing real world expert systems, *AI Expert* 3(12), 1988, 51-57.

[Smith and Davis 81] R.G. Smith and R. Davis, Frameworks for cooperation in distributed problem solving, *IEEE Transactions on Systems, Man, and Cybernetics* SCM-11(1), 1981, 61-70.

[Smith and Kellerher 88] B. Smith and G. Kellerher, *Reason Maintenance Systems and their Application*, Ellis Horwood, Chichester, UK, 1988.

[Smith et al. 85] R.G. Smith, H.A. Winston, T.M. Mitchell, and B.G. Buchanan, Representation and use of explicit justifications for knowledge base refinements, *Proceedings 9th International Joint Conference on Artificial Intelligence*, Los Angeles, CA, 1985, 673-680.

[Sol 83] H.G. Sol, A feature analysis of information systems design methodologies: Methodological considerations, in T.W. Olle, H.G. Sol, and C.J. Tully (editors), *Information Systems Design Methodologies: A Feature Analysis*, North-Holland, Amsterdam, The Netherlands, 1983.

[Sommerville 89] J. Sommerville, *Software Engineering* (3rd edition), Addison-Wesley, Reading, MA, 1989.

[Sowa 84] J.F. Sowa, *Conceptual Structures - Information Processing in Mind and Machine*, Addison-Wesley, Reading, MA, 1984.

[Sowa 91] J.F. Sowa (editor), *Principles of Semantic Networks - Explorations in the Representation of Knowledge*, Morgan Kaufamann, San Mateo, CA, 1991.

[Stachowitz et al. 87] R.A. Stachowitz, C.L. Chang, T. Stock, and J.B. Combs, Building validation tools for knowledge–based systems, *Proceedings 1st Annual Workshop on Space Operations*, Automation and Robotics, Houston, TX, 1987, 209-216.

[Steele 84] G.L. Steele, *Common LISP* , Digital Press, Burlington, MA, 1984.

[Steels 90] L. Steels, Components of expertise, *AI Magazine* 11(2), 1990, 28-49.

[Steels 93] L. Steels, The compositional framework and its role in reusability, in J-M. David, J-P. Krivine, and R. Simmons (editors), *Second Generation Expert Systems*, Springer-Verlag, Berlin, Germany, 1993, 273-298.

[Steels and Lepape 92] L. Steels and B. Lepape (editors), *Enhancing the Knowledge Engineering Process*, Elsevier, Amsterdam, The Netherlands, 1992.

[Stefik 81-a] M. Stefik, Planning with constrains (MOLGEN: Part 1), *Artificial Intelligence* 16, 1981, 111-139.

[Stefik 81-b] M. Stefik, Planning and meta-planning (MOLGEN: Part 2), *Artificial Intelligence* 16, 1981, 141-169.

[Stefik and Bobrow 86] M. Stefik and D. Bobrow, Object oriented programming: Themes and variations, *AI Magazine* 6(4), 1986, 40-62.

[Stefik et al. 83-a] M. Stefik, J. Aikins, R. Balzer, J. Benoit, L. Birnbaum, F. Hayes-Roth, and E. Sacerdoti, Basic concepts for building expert systems, in F. Hayes-Roth, D.A. Waterman, and D.B. Lenat (editors), *Building Expert Systems*, Addison-Wesley, Reading, MA, 1983, 59-86.

[Stefik et al. 83-b] M. Stefik, J. Aikins, R. Balzer, J. Benoit, L. Birnbaum, F. Hayes–Roth, and E. Sacerdoti. The architecture of expert systems, in F. Hayes-Roth, D.A. Waterman, and D.B. Lenat (editors), *Building Expert Systems*, Addison Wesley, Reading, MA, 1983, 89-126.

[Sterling and Hart 87] J.A.L. Sterling and G.E. Hart, Reproducing and adapting computer programs, *Computer, Law & Security Report* 3(3), 1987, 21-23.

[Sterling and Shapiro 86] L. Sterling and E. Shapiro, *The Art of PROLOG*, MIT Press, Cambridge, MA, 1986.

[Stewart and Cash 85] C. Stewart and W. Cash, *Interviewing Principles and Practices*, William Brown, Dubuque, IA, 1985.

[Stottler et al. 89] R.H. Stottler, A.L. Henke, and J.A. King, Rapid retrieval algorithms for case-based reasoning, *Proceedings 11th International Joint Conference on Artificial Intelligence*, Detroit, MI, 1989, 233-237.

[Stroustrup 86] B. Stroustrup, *The C++ Programming Language*, Addison-Wesley, Reading, MA, 1986.

[Stroustrup and Ellis 90] B. Stroustrup and M.A. Ellis, *The annotated C++ Reference Manual*, Addison-Wesley, Reading, MA, 1990.

[Suen et al. 90] C.Y Suen, P.D. Grogono, R. Shinghal, and F. Coallier, Verifying, validating, and measuring performance of expert systems, *Expert System with Applications* 1(2), 1990, 93-102.

[Sullivan and Tyler 91] J.W. Sullivan and S.W Tyler (editors), *Architectures for Intelligent Interfaces - Elements and Protoypes*, Addison-Wesley, Reading, MA, 1991.

[Suwa et al. 84] M. Suwa, A.C. Scott, and E.H. Shortliffe, Completeness and consistency in a rule–based system, in B.G. Buchanan and E.H. Shortliffe (editors), *Rule–based expert systems – The MYCIN Experiments at the Stanford Heuristic Programming Project*, Addison–Wesley, Reading, MA, 1984, 159–170.

[Swafield and Knight 90] G. Swafield and B. Knight, applying systems analysis techniques to knowledge engineering, *Expert Systems* 7(2), 1990, 82-92.

[Swartout 83] W.R. Swartout, XPLAIN: A system for creating and explaining expert consulting programs, *Artificial Intelligence* 21, 1983, 285-325.

[Swartout and Moore 93] W. Swartout and J. Moore, Explanation in second generation expert systems, in J-M. David, J-P. Krivine, and R. Simmons (editors), *Second Generation Expert Systems*, Springer-Verlag, Berlin, Germany, 1993, 543-585.

[Swartout and Smoliar 87] W.R. Swartout and S.W. Smoliar, On making expert systems more like experts, *Expert Systems* 4(3), 1987, 196-207.

[Swartout et al. 91] W. Swartout, J. Moore, and C. Paris, Design for explainable expert systems, *IEEE Expert* 6(3), 1991, 58-64.

[Tanimoto 87] S. L. Tanimoto, *The Elements of Artificial Intelligence - An Introduction Using LISP*, Computer Science Press, Rockville, MD, 1987.

[Tanner et al. 93] M. Tanner, A. Keuneke, and B. Chandrasekaran, Explanation using task structure and domain functional models, in J-M. David, J-P. Krivine, and R. Simmons (editors), *Second Generation Expert Systems*, Springer-Verlag, Berlin, Germany, 1993, 586-613.

[Tansley and Hayball 93] D.S.W. Tanslay and C.C. Hayball, *Knowledge Based Systems Analysis and Design - A KADS Developers Handbook*, Prentice-Hall, Englewood Cliffs, NJ, 1993.

[Taylor 85] E.C. Taylor, Developing a knowledge engineering capability in the TRW Defense Systems Group, *AI Magazine* 6(2), 58-63.

[Teichroew and Herschey 77] D. Teichroew and E.A. Herschey III, PSL-PSA: A computer-aided technique for structured documentation and analysis of information processing systems, *IEEE Transactions on Software Engineering* SE-3(1), 1977, 41-48.

[Teramo et al. 92] T. Teramo, K. Asai, and M. Sugeno, *Fuzzy Systems Theory and its Applications*, Academic Press, New York, NY, 1992.

[Terpstra et al. 93] P. Terpstra, G. van Heijst, N. Shadbolt, and B. Wielinga, Knowledge acquisition process support through generalized directive models, in J-M. David, J-P. Krivine, and R. Simmons (editors), *Second Generation Expert Systems*, Springer-Verlag, Berlin, Germany, 1993, 428-455.

[Tripp 88] L.L. Tripp, A survey of graphical notations for program design - An update, *ACM SigSoft Software Engineering Notes* 13(4), 1988, 39-44.

[Tucker 91] A.B. Tucker, Computing curricula 1991, *Communications of the ACM* 34(6), 1991, 68-84.

[Turban 91] E. Turban, Managing knowledge acquisition from multiple experts, *Proceedings IEEE/ACM International Conference on Developing and Managing Expert System Programs*, Washington, DC, 1991, 129-138.

[Turing 50] A.M. Turing, Computing machinery and intelligence, *Mind*, 1950, 433–460.

[Tuthill 91] G.S. Tuthill, Legal liabilities and expert systems, *AI Expert* 6(3), 1991, 44-51.

[Van de Velde 93] W. Van de Velde, Issues in knowledge level modelling, in J-M. David, J-P. Krivine, and R. Simmons (editors), *Second Generation Expert Systems*, Springer-Verlag, Berlin, Germany, 1993, 211-231.

[Van Gundy 88] A.B. Van Gundy, *Techniques for Structured Problem Solving* (2nd edition), Van Nostrand Reinhold, New York, NY, 1988.

[van Koppen 86] J. van Koppen, A survey of expert system development tools. *Proceedings 2nd International Expert Systems Conference*, London, UK, 1986, 157-173.

[van Vliet 93] H. van Vliet, *Software Engineering - Principles and Practice*, John Wiley & Sons, Chichester, UK, 1993.

[Vargas and Raj 93] J.E. Vargas and S. Raj, Developing maintainable expert systems using case-based reasoning, *Expert Systems* 10(4), 1993, 219-226.

[Vedder 89] R.G. Vedder, PC-based expert system shells: Some desirable and less desirable characteristics, *Expert Systems* 6(1), 1989, 28-42.

[Vere 83] S.A. Vere, Planning in time: Windows of duration for activities and goals, *IEEE Transactions on Pattern Analysis and Machine Intelligence* PAMI-5(3), 1983, 246-267.

[Vesoul 88] P. Vesoul, A specification and documentation approach to expert systems. *Proceedings 8th International Workshop Expert Systems and their Applications*, Avignon, France, Vol. 1, 1988, 297-316.

[Vicente and Rasmussen 92] K.J. Vicente and J. Rasmussen, Ecological interface design: Theoretical foundations, *IEEE Transactions on Systems, Man, and Cybernetics* SMC-22(4), 1992, 589-606.

[Vilain 82] M.B. Vilain, A system for reasoning about time, *Proceedings 1st National Conference on Artificial Intelligence*, Pittsburgh, PA, 1982, 197-201.

[Vilain and Kautz 86] M. Vilain and H. Kautz, Constraint propagation algorithms for temporal reasoning, *Proceedings 5th National Conference on Artificial Intelligence*, Philadelphia, PA, 1986, 377-382.

[Wahlster and Kobsa 89] W. Wahlster and A. Kobsa, User models in dialog systems, in A. Kobsa and W. Wahlster (editors),*User Models in Dialog Systems*. Springer-Verlag, Berlin, Germany, 1989, 4-34.

[Waldron 86] V. Waldron, Interviewing for knowledge, *IEEE Transaction on Professional Documentation* PD-29(2), 1986, 31-35.

[Wallis and Shortliffe 84] J.W. Wallis and E.H. Shortliffe, Customized explanations using causal knowledge, in B.G. Buchanan and E.H. Shortliffe (editors), *Rule-Based Expert Systems - The MYCIN Experiments of the Stanford Heuristic Programming Project*, Addison-Wesley, Reading, MA, 1984, 371-388.

[Walters and Nielsen 88] J. Walters and N.R. Nielsen, *Crafting Knowledge-Based Systems - Expert Systems Made Easy Realistic*, John Wiley & Sons, New York, NY, 1988.

[Warman and Modesitt 88] D. Warman and K.L. Modesitt, A student's view: Learning in an introductory expert system course, *Expert Systems* 5(1), 1988, 30-39.

[Warman and Modesitt 89] D. Warman and K.L. Modesitt, Learning in an introductory expert system course, *IEEE Expert* 4(1), 1989, 45-49.

[Washington and Hayes-Roth 89] R. Washington and B. Hayes-Roth, Input data management in real-time AI systems, *Proceedings 11th International Joint Conference on Artificial Intelligence*, Detroit, MI, 1989, 250-255.

[Wasserman et al. 83] A.L. Wasserman, P. Freeman, and P. Pacella, Characteristics of software development methodologies, in T.W. Olle, H.G. Sol, and C.J. Tully (editors), *Information Systems Design Methodologies: A Feature Analysis*, North-Holland, Amsterdam, The Netherlands, 1983,

[Waterman 86] D.A. Waterman, *A Guide to Expert Systems*, Addison-Wesley, Reading, MA, 1986.

[Waterman and Hayes-Roth 78] D.A. Waterman and F. Hayes-Roth (editors), *Pattern-Directed Inference Systems*, Academic Press, New York, NY, 1978.

[Waterman and Newell 71] D.A. Waterman and A. Newell, Protocol analysis as a task for artificial intelligence, *Artificial Intelligence* 2, 1971, 285-318.

[Watkins and Elliot 93] P. Watkins and L.B. Elliot (editors), *Expert Systems in Business and Finance - Issues and Applications*, John Wiley & Sons, Chichester, UK, 1993.

[Watson et al. 92-a] I. Watson, A. Basden, and P. Brandon, The client-centered approach: Expert system development, *Expert Systems* 9(4), 1992, 181-188.

[Watson et al. 92-b] I. Watson, A. Basden, and P. Brandon, The client-centered approach: Expert system maintenance, *Expert Systems* 9(4), 1992, 189-196.

[Weiner 80] J.L. Weiner, BLAH, a system which explains its reasoning, *Artificial Intelligence* 15, 1980, 19-48.

[Weir and Alty 89] G. Weir and J.L. Alty (editors), *Human-Computer Interaction and Complex Systems*, Academic Press, London, UK, 1989.

[Weitz 90] R.R. Weitz, Technology, work, and the organization: The impact of expert systems, *AI Magazine* 11(2), 1990, 50-60.

[Weitzel and Kershberg 89] J. Weitzel and L. Kershberg, Developing knowledge-based systems: Reorganizing the system development life cycle, *Communications of the ACM* 32(4), 482-487.

[Weld and de Kleer 90] D.S. Weld and J. de Kleer (editors), *Readings in Qualitative Reasoning about Physical Systems*, Morgan Kaufmann, San Mateo, CA, 1990.

[Wexelblat 89] R.L. Wexelblat, On interface requirements for expert systems, *AI Magazine* 10(3), 1989, 66-78.

[Wick and Slagle 89] M.R. Wick and J.R. Slagle, An explanation facility for today's expert systems, *IEEE Expert* 4(1), 1989, 26-36.

[Wielinga et al. 90] B. Wielinga, J. Boose, B. Gaines, G. Schreiber, and M. van Someren (editors), *Current Trends in Knowledge Acquisition*, IOS Press, Amsterdam, The Netherlands, 1990.

[Wielinga et al. 92] B. Wielinga, G. Schreiber, and J. Breuker, KBS development through knowledge modeling, in L. Steels and B. Lepape (editors), *Enhancing the Knowledge Engineering Process*, Elsevier Science, Amsterdam, The Netherlands, 1992.

[Wielinga et al. 93] B. Wielinga, W. Van de Velde, G. Schreiber, and H. Akkermans, Towards an unification of knowledge modeling approaches, in J-M. David, J-P. Krivine, and R. Simmons (editors), *Second Generation Expert Systems*, Springer-Verlag, Berlin, Germany, 1993, 299-335.

[Wilkens et al. 87] D.C. Wilkens, W.J. Clancey, and G.G. Buchanan. Knowledge base refinement by editing abstract control knowledge, *International Journal of Man-Machine Studies* 27, 1987, 281-294.

[Wilkerson 85] W.S. Wilkerson, *Guide to Expert Systems Program Management*, Artificial Intelligence Guide Series, Intelligent Systems Technologies Group, Digital Equipment Corporation, Merrimack, NH, 1985.

[Winograd 83] T. Winograd, *Language as a Cognitive Process - Volume 1: Syntax*, Addison-Wesley, Reading, MA, 1983.

[Winston 92] P.H. Winston, *Artificial Intelligence* (3rd edition), Addison-Wesley, Reading, MA, 1992.

[Winston and Horn 89] P.H. Winston and B.K.P. Horn, *LISP* (3rd edition), Addison-Wesley, Reading, MA, 1989.

[Winston and Prendergast 84] P.H. Winston and K.A. Prendergast (editors), *The AI Business: The Commercial Uses of Artificial Intelligence*, MIT Press, Cambridge, MA, 1984.

[Wirth 71] N. Wirth, Program development by stepwise refinement, *Communications of the ACM* 14(4), 1971.

[Witten and MacDonald 88] I.H. Witten and B. MacDonald, Using concept learning for knowledge acquisition, *International Journal of Man-Machine Studies* 29, 1988, 171-196.

[Wright and Ayton 87] G. Wright and P. Ayton, Eliciting and modelling expert knowledge, *Decision Support Systems* 3(1), 1987, 13-26.

[Yager et al. 93] R. Yager, M. Fedrizzi, and J. Kacprzyk (editors), *Advances in Dempster-Shafer Theory of Evidence*, John Wiley & Sons, New York, NY, 1993.

[Yang et al. 85] J-Y.D. Yang, M.N. Huhns, and L.M. Stephens, An architecture for control and communication in distributed artificial intelligence systems, *IEEE Transactions on Systems, Man, and Cybernetics* SMC-15(3), 1985, 316-327.

[Yazdani and Lawler 91] M. Yazdani and R.W. Lawler (editors), *Artificial Intelligence and Education, Volume 2- Principles and Case Studies*, Ablex, Norwood, NJ, 1991.

[Yen and Lee 93] J. Yen and J. Lee, A task-based methodology for specifying expert systems, *IEEE Expert* 8(1), 1993, 8-15.

[Yost and Newell 89] G. Yost and A. Newell, A problem space approach to expert system specification, *Proceedings 11th International Joint Conference on Artificial Intelligence*, Detroit, MI, 1989, 621-627.

[Young 87] R.M. Young, The role of intermediate representations in knowledge elicitation, in D.S. Moralee (editor), *Research and Development in Expert Systems IV*, Cambridge University Press, Cambridge, MA, 1987, 287-288.

[Yourdon 75] E. Yourdon, *Techniques of Program Structure and Design*, Prentice-Hall, Englewood Cliffs, NJ, 1975.

[Yourdon 89] E. Yourdon, *Modern Structured Analysis*, Yourdon Press/Prentice-Hall, Englewood Cliffs, NJ, 1989

[Yourdon and Constantine 75] E. Yourdon and L.L. Constantine, *Structured Design*, Yourdon Press, New York, NY, 1975.

[Yu et al. 84] L. Yu, L.M. Fagan, S.W. Bennet, W.J. Clancey, A.C. Scott, J.F. Hannigan, B.G. Buchanan, and S.N. Cohen, An evaluation of MYCIN's advice, in B.G. Buchanan and E.H. Shortliffe (editors), *Rule–based expert systems – The MYCIN Experiments at the Stanford Heuristic Programming Project*, Addison–Wesley, Reading, MA, 1984, 589–596.

[Zack 87] B.A. Zack, Selecting an application for knowledge-based system development, *Proceedings 3rd International Expert Systems Conference*, London, UK, 1987, 257-269.

[Zadeh 65] L.A. Zadeh, Fuzzy sets, *Information and Control* 8, 1965, 338-353.

[Zadeh 78] L.A. Zadeh, Fuzzy sets as a basis for a theory of possibility, *Fuzzy Sets and Systems* 1, 1978, 3-28.

[Zadeh 79] L.A. Zadeh, A theory of approximate reasoning, in J.E. Hayes, D. Michie, and L.I. Mikulich (editors), *Machine Intelligence 9*, Ellis Horwood, Chichester, UK, 1979, 149-194.

[Zadeh and Kacprzyk 92] L. Zadeh and J. Kacprzyk (editors), *Fuzzy Logic for the Management of Uncertainty*, John Wiley & Sons, New York, NY, 1992.

[Zeide and Liebowitz 87] J.S. Zeide and J. Liebowitz, Using expert systems: The legal perspective, *IEEE Expert* 2(1), 1987, 19-22.

[Zeide and Liebowitz 90] J.S. Zeide and J. Liebowitz, A critical review of legal issues in artificial intelligence, in D.A. De Salvo and J. Liebowitz (editors), *Managing AI and Expert Systems*, Prentice-Hall, Englewood Cliffs, NJ, 1990.

[Zualkernan et al. 86] I. Zualkernan, W.T. Tsai, and D. Volovik, Expert systems and software engineering: Ready for marriage? *IEEE Expert* 1(4), 1986, 24-31.

Subject Index